ISIDOREAN PERCEPTIONS OF ORDER

MEDIEVAL EUROPEAN STUDIES XVII
Patrick W. Conner, Series Editor

OTHER TITLES IN THE SERIES:

Beowulf and the Grendel-kin: Politics and Poetry in Eleventh-Century England
Helen Damico

The Book of Emperors: A Translation of the Middle High German Kaiserchronik
Edited and translated by Henry A. Myers

The Old English Poem Seasons for Fasting: *A Critical Edition*
Edited by Mary P. Richards with the assistance of Chadwick B. Hilton Jr.

Sir Gawain and the Green Knight
Translated by Larry Benson
with a foreword and Middle English text edited by Daniel Donoghue

Perspectives on the Old Saxon Hêliand:
Introductory and Critical Essays, with an Edition of the Leipzig Fragment
Edited by Valentine A. Pakis

Cross and Cruciform in the Anglo-Saxon World:
Studies to Honor the Memory of Timothy Reuter
Edited by Sarah Larratt Keefer, Karen Louise Jolly, and Catherine E. Karkov

The Cross and Culture in Anglo-Saxon England
Edited by Karen Jolly, Catherine E. Karkov, and Sarah Larratt Keefer

Cædmon's Hymn and Material Culture in the World of Bede
Edited by Allen J. Frantzen and John Hines

The Power of Words: Anglo-Saxon Studies Presented
to Donald G. Scragg on his Seventieth Birthday
Edited by Jonathan Wilcox and Hugh Magennis

Innovation and Tradition in the Writings of the Venerable Bede
Edited by Scott DeGregorio

Ancient Privileges: Beowulf, Law, and the Making of Germanic Antiquity
Stefan Jurasinski

Old English Literature in its Manuscript Context
Edited by Joyce Tally Lionarons

Theorizing Anglo-Saxon Stone Sculpture
Edited by Catherine E. Karkov and Fred Orton

Naked Before God: Uncovering the Body in Anglo-Saxon England
Edited by Benjamin C. Withers and Jonathan Wilcox

Hêliand: Text and Commentary
Edited by James E. Cathey

Via Crucis: Essays on Early Medieval Sources and Ideas
Thomas N. Hall, Editor, with assistance from Thomas D. Hill and Charles D. Wright

Isidorean Perceptions of Order

THE EXETER BOOK RIDDLES
AND MEDIEVAL LATIN ENIGMATA

MERCEDES SALVADOR-BELLO

WEST VIRGINIA UNIVERSITY PRESS
MORGANTOWN 2015

Copyright 2015 West Virginia University Press
All rights reserved
First edition published 2015 by West Virginia University Press
Printed in the United States of America
22 21 20 19 18 17 16 15   1 2 3 4 5 6 7 8 9

ISBN:
PB: 978-1-935978-51-0
EPUB: 978-1-935978-52-7
PDF: 978-1-940425-43-6

Library of Congress Cataloging-in-Publication Data:
Salvador-Bello, Mercedes.
Isidorean perceptions of order : the Exeter book riddles and medieval Latin enigmata / Mercedes Salvador-Bello. -- First edition.
   pages   cm.
(Medieval European studies ; xvii)
Includes index.
ISBN 978-1-935978-51-0 (paper back) -- ISBN 978-1-935978-52-7 (epub) -- ISBN 978-1-940425-43-6 (pdf)
1. Riddles, English (Old)--History and criticism. 2. English poetry--Old English, ca. 450-1100--History and criticism. 3. Riddles, Latin--History and criticism. I. Title.
PR1764.S35 2015.
829'.1009--dc23
                              2015007968
Book and cover design by Than Saffel
Cover image: Detail of Noah's Ark illustrating Isidorean zoological categorization. From Beatus's *Super Apocalypsim* in Manchester, John Rylands University Library, Latin MS 8 (fol. 15r). Copyright of The University of Manchester.

Contents

Abbreviations ix

Acknowledgments xi

1. Introduction 1
   1.1 The Exeter Book Riddles, Latin *Enigmata*, and Isidorean Encyclopedic Tradition
   1.2 An Outline of This Book

2. Early Medieval Riddling and Isidore's *Etymologiae* 12
   2.1 A General Overview of the Riddling Genre in the Early Middle Ages
      2.1.1 From the Seventh to the Ninth Century
      2.1.2 From the Tenth to the Eleventh Century
      2.1.3 Early Medieval Riddling: Some Conclusions
   2.2 Isidore and His Work in the Context of Visigothic Spain
   2.3 The Success and Influence of Isidore's *Etymologiae*
   2.4 The Impact of Isidore's *Etymologiae* on Early Medieval Riddling: How Grammar and Encyclopedia Merged with *Enigmata*

3. Isidore's *Etymologiae* and the Compilation
   of Early Medieval Latin Riddle Collections   88
   3.1 An Insight into the Scheme
       of Isidore's *Etymologiae*
       3.1.1 The First Decade (Books I–X)
       3.1.2 The Second Decade (Books XI–XX)
             3.1.2.1 Books XI–XII
             3.1.2.2 Books XIII–XVI
             3.1.2.3 Books XVII–XX
             3.1.2.4 Some Final Considerations
                     on the Second Decade
       3.1.3 Analogy, Contrast,
             and Structural Irregularities
   3.2 The Foundations of Early Medieval Riddling:
       Symphosius's *Enigmata*
       3.2.1 Introduction to Symphosius's *Enigmata*
       3.2.2 The Organization of Symphosius's *Enigmata*
             3.2.2.1 Section 1 (*Enigmata* 1–6)
             3.2.2.2 Section 2 (*Enigmata* 7–11)
             3.2.2.3 Section 3 (*Enigmata* 12–39)
             3.2.2.4 Section 4 (*Enigmata* 40–49)
             3.2.2.5 Section 5 (Enigmata 50–92)
             3.2.2.6 Section 6 (Enigmata 93–99)
             3.2.2.7 Final Considerations
                     on Symphosius's *Enigmata*
   3.3 Aldhelm's Pioneering *Enigmata*
       3.3.1 Introduction to Aldhelm and His Works
       3.3.2 Introduction to Aldhelm's *Enigmata*
       3.3.3 The Organization of Aldhelm's *Enigmata*
             3.3.3.1 Section 1 (*Enigmata* 1–8)
             3.3.3.2 Section 2 (*Enigmata* 9–39)
             3.3.3.3 Section 3 (*Enigmata* 40–80)
             3.3.3.4 Section 4 (*Enigmata* 81–99)
             3.3.3.5 Final Considerations on the
                     Organization of Aldhelm's *Enigmata*

3.4 The Continuation of the Riddling Tradition
in England: Tatwine and Eusebius
   3.4.1 Tatwine's *Enigmata*
   3.4.2 Eusebius's *Enigmata*
3.5 Medieval Riddle Collections by Other Authors
   3.5.1 The Bern Riddles
   3.5.2 The Lorsch Riddles
   3.5.3 The Vatican Collection

4. The Compilation of the Exeter Book Riddles   284
   4.1 An Introduction to the Exeter Book Riddles
   4.2 An Encyclopedic Source Collection:
   Group 1 (Riddles 1–40)
      4.2.1 Section 1 (Riddles 1–6)
         4.2.1.1 Riddle 1-2-3: An Encyclopedic Test
         4.2.1.2 Riddles 4–6
      4.2.2 Section 2 (Riddles 7–15)
         4.2.2.1 Subgroup A (Riddles 7–11): Birds
         4.2.2.2 Subgroup B (Riddles 12–15): Quadrupeds
         4.2.2.3 A Final Reflection on Section 2
      4.2.3 Section 3 (Riddles 16–39)
         4.2.3.1 Thematic Exceptions: Riddles 22, 24, 29, 33, 38, and 39
      4.2.4 Riddle 40: A Misplaced Coda?
      4.2.5 Some Final Thoughts on Group 1
   4.3 An Addition Based on Analogy:
   Group 2 (Riddles 41–59)
      4.3.1 Section 4 (Riddles 42–46)
      4.3.2 Section 5 (Riddles 47–66)
         4.3.2.1 Subgroup A (Riddles 47–51)
         4.3.2.2 Subgroup B (Riddles 52–59)
   4.4 Striving for the Canonical Century:
   Group 3 (Riddles 61–95)
      4.4.1 Section 5 (A Continuation)

      4.4.1.1 Subgroup C (Riddles 61–66)
      4.4.1.2 A Final Word on Section 5
  4.4.2 Section 6 (Riddles 67–94)
      4.4.2.1 Fragmentariness and Manuscript Loss: Riddles 67, 70a, and 70b
      4.4.2.2 A Careless Compilation: Riddles 68–69, 79–80, and 75–76
      4.4.2.3 Riddles 77 and 78: An Aquatic Duo
      4.4.2.4 Riddle 81: A Contemporary Touch
      4.4.2.5 Thematic Duplications and Textual Variants: Riddles 84, 87, 88, 93, and 94
      4.4.2.6 Riddle 95: A Final Coda?
  4.4.3 Some Final Thoughts on Group 3

5. Conclusions   438
  5.1 The Compilation of the Exeter Book Riddles and Latin *Enigmata*
  5.2 Some Final Thoughts on Early Medieval Riddling

Appendices   453
  Appendix I: Chronology
  Appendix II: Isidore's *Etymologiae*
  Appendix III: Symphosius's Collection
  Appendix IV: Aldhelm's Collection
  Appendix V: Tatwine's Collection
  Appendix VI: Eusebius's Collection
  Appendix VII: The Bern Collection
  Appendix VIII: The Lorsch Collection
  Appendix IX: The Vatican Collection
  Appendix X: The Exeter Book Riddles

Bibliography   475

Index   513

About the Author   531

Abbreviations

ANQ: *American Notes and Queries*
ASE: *Anglo-Saxon England*
ASPR: *The Anglo-Saxon Poetic Records*, ed. George Philip Krapp and Elliott Van Kirk Dobbie, 6 vols. (New York: Columbia University Press, 1931–42)
ASSAH: *Anglo-Saxon Studies in Archaeology and History*
BT: James Bosworth and T. Northcote Toller, *An Anglo-Saxon Dictionary* (Oxford, 1898), with Supplement by T. Northcote Toller (Oxford, 1921) and Revised and Enlarged Addenda by Alistair Campbell (Oxford, 1972)
CCSL: *Corpus Christianorum Series Latina*, ed. Fr. Glorie (Turnhout: Brepols)
DOE: *Dictionary of Old English*, ed. Angus Cameron, Ashley Crandell Amos, Antonette diPaolo Healey, et al. (Toronto: University of Toronto, 1986–)
Du Cange: Charles Du Fresne Du Cange, *Glossarium mediae et infimae latinitatis*, 7 vols. (Paris, 1840–50)
EETS: Early English Text Society. o.s., original series; s.s., supplementary series
ELN: *English Language Notes*
ES: *English Studies*
JEGP: *Journal of English and Germanic Philology*
L&S: Charlton Thomas Lewis, *A Latin Dictionary Founded on Andrews' Edition of Freund's Latin Dictionary. Revised, Enlarged and in Great Part Rewritten by Charlton T. Lewis and Charles Short* (Oxford: Clarendon Press, 1998)

MGH: *Monumenta Germaniae Historica*
MLR: *Modern Language Review*
MLN: *Modern Language Notes*
MP: *Modern Philology*
NM: *Neuphilologische Mitteilungen*
N&Q: *Notes and Queries*
ODNB: *Oxford Dictionary of National Biography*, online edition, ed. Lawrence Goldman (Oxford: Oxford University Press)
OED: *The Oxford English Dictionary* (online access, Oxford University Press, 2009)
PL: J. P. Migne, ed. *Patrologia latina*, 221 vols. (Paris, 1844–64)
PLAC: *Poeta latini aevi carolini (Monumenta Germaniae Historica)*
PQ: *Philological Quarterly*
PMLA: *Publications of the Modern Language Association of America*
RES: *Review of English Studies*
SN: *Studia Neophilologica*
The Exeter DVD: *The Exeter DVD: The Exeter Anthology of Old English Poetry*, ed. Bernard J. Muir (Exeter: Exeter University Press, 2006)
ZfdA: *Zeitschrift für deutsches Altertum und deutsche Literatur*

Acknowledgments

This book is the product of many years studying Latin *enigmata* and the Exeter Book Riddles. Fruits of this work have already appeared in "Allegorizing and Moralizing Zoology in Aldhelm's *Enigmata*," *Revista canaria de estudios ingleses* 68 (2014): 209–18; "Patterns of Compilation in Anglo-Latin *Enigmata* and the Evidence of a Source-Collection in Riddles 1-40 of the Exeter Book," *Viator* 43 (2012): 339–74; "Clean and Unclean Animals: Isidore's Book XII from the *Etymologiae* and the Structure of Eusebius's Zoological Riddles," *English Studies* 93 (2012): 572-582; "The Oyster and the Crab: A Riddle Duo (Nos. 77 and 78) in the *Exeter Book*," *Modern Philology* 101 (2004), pp. 400-19 (© 2004 by The University of Chicago, all rights reserved); and "The Key to the Body: Unlocking Riddles 42-46," *Naked Before God: Uncovering the Body in Anglo-Saxon England*, ed. Benjamin C. Withers and Jonathan Wilcox (Morgantown: West Virginia University Press, 2003), pp. 60-96. The materials found in those essays, which have been thoroughly revised and for the most substantially enlarged, are reproduced in this book. I am therefore grateful to these journals, the Universidad de La Laguna, the UCLA Center for Medieval and Renaissance Studies, Taylor & Francis, the University of Chicago, and the University of West Virginia for granting permission to publish them in this book. I am particularly indebted to R. D. Fulk for his invaluable collaboration with the publication of "Patterns of Compilation."

Financial support for the writing of this volume came from a research project (P09-HUM-5186), granted by the Andalusian Government. Several stays at Cambridge University as an honorary research associate of the Department of Anglo-Saxon, Norse and Celtic in 2009 and as a visiting scholar of Wolfson College in 2009 and 2014 have decisively contributed to the research that I carried out for this book. Special thanks for this should therefore go to Simon D. Keynes and Rosalind C. Love from the University of Cambridge and Michelle Searle from Wolfson College.

The final stages of the process of writing have been affected by severe budget cuts that have dramatically affected the University of Seville. Thanks to the efficient work of the librarians, I have hardly felt these effects regarding the library facilities, electronic resources, and interlibrary loans. I here gladly acknowledge the endeavors of the library staff of the Biblioteca de Humanidades, especially Covadonga Lucio-Villegas and Carmen Sanzo, as well as those of the interns of the Biblioteca de Literatura Española, Lengua Inglesa, and Literatura Inglesa of the University of Seville, particularly Daniel García. For granting access to their collections as well as supplying information and digitized copies of manuscripts, I am grateful to the staffs of the Bodleian Library at Oxford, the British Library (especially Kathleen Doyle and James Freeman), the Cambridge University Library, the Exeter Cathedral Library, the Vatican Apostolic Library, e-codices, and Bibliotheca Laureshamensis-digital.

The biennial conferences of ISAS have enabled me to come into contact with many experts in the field of Anglo-Saxon studies whom I should thank for their collaboration: Anna Gannon, Marilina Cesario, Patrick W. Conner, Stephen J. Harris, Stacy S. Klein, Patrizia Lendinara, Hugh Magennis, Bernard J. Muir, Gale Owen-Crocker, Sara M. Pons-Sanz, Sharon Rowley, Donald Scragg, Thomas Shippey, and Loredana Teresi. I am deeply indebted to Michael D. C. Drout, John D. Niles, and Jonathan Wilcox for their support and generous feedback for this book. My research also greatly benefited from the conferences of the Spanish Society for Medieval English Language and Literature (SELIM) and from my long-standing friendship with some of its members: J. Camilo Conde-Silvestre, Julia Fernández-Cuesta, María F. García-Bermejo, Trinidad Guzmán, Beatriz Hernández, and Inmaculada Senra.

My research on Latin *enigmata* and the Exeter Book Riddles was directed by María José Mora, who guided me in an extremely generous way with her insightful feedback, criticism and collaboration throughout these years. It was thanks to her advice that I got a grant to study Old English literature at Cornell University with Thomas D. Hill and Andrew Galloway. My friends, Carlos Gamito, Fernando Lage, Nieves Rodríguez, Marta Simino, and Christie Snowdon have assisted me in innumerable ways. I should also mention my friends and colleagues of the research group "Estudios Medievales y Renacentistas Ingleses," who have frequently collaborated with me, especially: Leticia Álvarez, María José Gómez, Manuel J. Gómez-Lara, Josefa Fernández, Rafael Portillo, Juan Antonio Prieto-Pablos, Jordi Sánchez, and María José Sánchez de Nieva. The Head of my department, Ramón Espejo, has also been very sensitive to my research needs. He must be thanked for his kind help, together with Ana Luisa Martín and María Ángeles Toda. Francisco García Tortosa, who suggested me to start doing research on the Exeter Book Riddles, should be mentioned here. I am also grateful to my colleagues Emma Falque, Juan Gil, Leonor Molero, Ana Pérez, and José Solís of the Department of Filología Griega y Latina of the University of Seville. María del Mar Gutiérrez-Ortiz, Pablo Toribio, and Rafael J. Pascual have revised the Latin and Old English passages, offering many insightful comments on them. My warmest thanks go to them and to Francisco Alonso-Almeida for his support and wise advice on many occasions.

I want to express here my tribute to many of my students from whom I got the inspiration to continue doing research in the fascinating subject of medieval riddling. Without this stimulus and the support of the people I have mentioned, my dissertation would have ended unpublished, as is the case of much valuable research produced in Spanish universities. I must here recognize Jason Gosnell's good offices as editor of West Virginia University Press. I thank my parents, Estrella and Jesús, for their generosity in providing the best possible education for me. I should also mention my sister, Estrella, who has taught me much about life and literature. My in-laws Daniel and Pepita have always been there for me, as well as my sister-in-law Alicia. Finally, I thank my husband Daniel Rodríguez Fernández for his enduring patience, for his immense understanding, and for admirably taking care of our son Daniel along the process of writing. Without his help and collaboration, this book, which is dedicated to him and my family, would not have been possible.

CHAPTER ONE

Introduction

1.1. *The Exeter Book Riddles*, Latin Enigmata, *and Isidorean Encyclopedic Tradition*

In its current state, Exeter, Cathedral Library, MS. 3501—better known as the Exeter Book—contains ninety-odd riddles that are all in Old English with the exception of a single Latin piece. The importance of these riddles stems from the fact that they constitute the only English vernacular collection that has been preserved from the early Middle Ages. But, as part of a literary genre, the Exeter Riddles are not alone, for they are antedated by a solid tradition of Latin riddling. A collection of one hundred riddles by an obscure late-Roman author known as Symphosius is considered to have laid the foundations of European medieval riddling. In England, Aldhelm started to develop the genre, a task that would be followed by authors such as Tatwine, Eusebius, Boniface, Alcuin, and one Pseudo-Bede. Apart from this, we need to take into account other riddle assemblages that circulated anonymously in the Continent and have Anglo-Saxon affiliations of some kind: the so-called Bern and Lorsch Riddles.[1] All these riddle collections deserve to be studied here, for they can help us reconstruct the background necessary

---

1. Of uncertain date and authorship, these two riddle assemblages have been suspected to be of Insular provenance, even if that claim has not yet been susbtantiated with concrete proof. See further on pp. 250–74.

to grasp the peculiarities of the Exeter Riddles and view them as part of the literary niche in which they appeared.

As a matter of fact, a great deal of critical attention has been focused on the Exeter Riddles, particularly with regard to the solving of individual pieces. However, the principle behind the organization of these riddles has been studied less and remains unclear. For this reason, I intend to look at the Exeter Riddles in their entirety as the result of a process of compilation that involved the selection of riddle materials from different sources and their organization into pairs and clusters that were distributed according to ongoing encyclopedic principles of order. My chief claim in this book is that major Latin riddle collections and the Exeter Book Riddles were organized according to structural criteria deriving from encyclopedic tradition, more specifically from Isidore's *Etymologiae*, an unquestionable landmark of medieval encyclopedism.

The application of contemporary prejudices with respect to organizational aspects has prevented modern scholarship from recognizing that riddle compilations in general share structural parallelisms with medieval encyclopedias. To take a paradigmatic case, when commenting on the Exeter Riddles, Paull F. Baum considered thematic distribution as a concept naturally incompatible with a riddle collection: "Orderly arrangement is not to be expected in a collection of riddles ... to group them according to the answers would offer too much help. Even the Latin *Enigmata*, where the answers are provided as titles, are not placed in any definite order."[2] Baum's argument stems from current views on the riddling genre. In this sense, if we compare medieval compilations with modern collections, it is obvious that there are great divergences. First of all, riddles in general have long been associated with children's literature or folklore. Second, compared to medieval compilations, this different status informs contemporary collections in such a way that the teaching goal is subservient to the entertaining element. In this sense, the majority

---

2. Paull F. Baum, trans. *Anglo-Saxon Riddles of the Exeter Book* (Durham, NC: Duke University Press, 1963), xix. For a similar stand, see Frank H. Whitman, "Aenigmata Tatwini," *NM* 88 (1987): 16.

of the riddle collections that are edited nowadays are rarely organized thematically because this would prevent readers from rejoicing at the solving of the puzzle, as Baum notes. However, from the medieval perspective, it was reasonable to offer an arrangement of the riddling material in a similar way to that observed in encyclopedias, where the classification of information was essential. Furthermore, as I intend to show, when approaching a riddle collection, medieval readers would probably study the different components as if these were chapters of an encyclopedia. Before I take up the full analysis of the proposed riddle collections, I will advance some examples of thematic organization in order to show the viability of these arguments.

At first sight, most medieval riddle assemblages offer interesting thematic clusters that are worth examining in detail. A notable case is observed in Symphosius's *Enigmata*. Even if this collection theoretically predates Isidore's *Etymologiae*, it is worth comparing the layout of these topics in the two works:

Symphosius's Section 2	Isidore's *Etymologiae*
8. fog	XIII.x.10
9. rain	XIII.x.2
10. ice	XIII.x.6
11. snow	XIII.x.6

The four riddles describe weather phenomena in an encyclopedic-like layout that recalls the way in which Isidore displayed homologous topics in Book XIII, where meteorological subjects are handled. A further illustration of this is Aldhelm's section 1, Eusebius's section 2, and Bern section 6, which all provide subjects related to cosmology (see appendices).

Apart from cosmology, it is evident that riddle compilations, like encyclopedic works, had an interest in the description of the natural world. Thus, in the Bern Riddles a grouping of plants stands out:[3]

---

3. Note that bold letters are henceforth used for thematic exceptions, as well as in the appendices.

Bern Section 4	Isidore's *Etymologiae*
33. Violet	XVII.ix.19
34. Rose	XVII.ix.17
35. Lilies	XVII.ix.18
36. Saffron flower	XVII.ix.5
37. Pepper	XVII.viii.8
38. Ice	—
39. Ivy	XVII.ix.22

As can be drawn from the comparative chart, the first three topics of this series—notably, violet, rose, and lily—appear consecutively in Isidore's *Etymologiae* while ivy is also dealt with in a neighboring passage. Also in the Bern collection, section 2 offers agricultural subjects. Similarly, Symphosius's section 3 offers a subgroup of riddles which treat botanical topics.

This attention to biological topics is likewise observed in the final group of riddles from Eusebius's collection (section 5D). Again, an outline comparing the contents of this section with the location of Isidore's corresponding entries in chapter vii (*De avibus*, On birds) of Book XII (*De animalibus*, On animals) can shed light on the way in which medieval authors made use of encyclopedias as a source to compose riddle collections.

Eusebius's Section 5D	Isidore's *Etymologiae*
56. Stork	XII.vii.16–17
57. Ostrich	XII.vii.20
58. Night Owl	XII.vii.40–41
59. Parrot	XII.vii.24
60. Horned owl	XII.vii.39

Apart from deriving the contents of these riddles from Isidore's chapter on birds,[4] Eusebius also intended to imitate the consistent thematic

---

4. For the pervasive occurrence of Isidorean echoes in Eusebius's bird section, see the notes in the edition of these riddles in *CCSL*, vol. 133, 267–71.

organization observed in the encyclopedic source, as the description of those birds occurs in close-by passages of the *Etymologiae*. Notably, "night owl" and "horned owl" are adjacent motifs in vii.39–40 and the other birds included in Eusebius's section appear as neighboring motifs in vii.16–17 (stork), vii.20 (ostrich), and vii.24 (parrot). Most of the collections offer zoological clusters, an example being Symphosius's section 3, Aldhelm's section 2, and Eusebius's section 5.

It is also worth noting that Latin riddle collections show a logical interest in a further thematic category that I have called "instrumental,"[5] as it is mainly represented by tools and implements of different kinds even if the nature of these topics is often extremely varied. Tatwine's *Enigmata* can exemplify this third topic:

Tatwine's Section 5	Isidore's *Etymologiae*
27. Tongs	XIX.vii.3
28. Anvil	XIX.vii.1
29. Table	—
30. Sword and Sheath	XVIII.vi.1 (sword); XVIII.ix.2 (sheath)
31. Spark	XIX.vi.6 (spark from which the ashes result)
32. Arrow	XVIII.viii.1
33. Fire	XIX.vi.5
34. Quiver	XVIII.ix.1
35. Ember	XIX.vi.7
36. Winnowing fork	XX.xiv.10
37. Sower	—
38. Charcoal	XIX.vi.7
39. Whetstone	XVI.iii.6

---

5. The word *instrument* derives from Latin *instrumentum*, meaning "an implement, utensil, tool, instrument." But this term also designates a "store, provision, supply, means, assistance, furtherance, etc." Unless indicated otherwise, all definitions of Latin terms are from L&S. In this book, *instrument* or *instrumental* will therefore be used as generic words referring to house implements, agricultural tools, weapons, food, drinks, and musical instruments, thus effectively conveying the essence of the thematic categories offered by Isidore's Books XVII–XX.

Tatwine's section clearly dwells on the tools employed by the smith in the forge. Interestingly, Isidore also deals with most of these subjects in *Etymologiae* XIX.vi–vii, where he describes tools such as the anvil and the tongs and, like Tatwine, includes the different stages of fire. Apart from this, Tatwine's series effectively alternates these topics with the resulting products of the smithy—sword, sheath, arrow, and quiver—which are treated in *Etymologiae* XVIII.vi–ix. Apart from this sequence, Tatwine's section 2 also seems to comply with an instrumental series. Further illustrations of instrumental clusters in other collections are Symphosius's sections 1 and 5, Eusebius's section 4, and Bern sections 1 and 3.

All these examples therefore suggest that, when considering the influence of Isidore's *Etymologiae* in riddle collections, attention should be directed not only to the textual parallelisms shared by riddles and excerpts drawn from this work, as has been done so far, but also to the imitation of encyclopedic structural patterns. Besides, it seems that Latin riddle collections, like encyclopedias, are informed on the basis of three primary classification categories: cosmological, biological, and instrumental. There are of course further organizational criteria at work in riddle collections, which also stem from those observed in Isidore's *Etymologiae*, but I will deal with them later in this book.

At least in its first sequence (Riddles 1–40),[6] the Exeter collection displays some thematic segments that clearly accord with the three major categories that I have just discussed. Formerly thought to be three separate pieces known as the "Storm Riddles," Exeter Riddle 1-2-3, with its lavish description of meteorological phenomena, complies with the cosmological opening observed in both Symphosius's and Aldhelm's collections. On the other hand, the Exeter Riddles present a zoological group, which comprises birds and quadrupeds. Of these, the bird topics constitute a fairly consistent ornithological series that recalls the one found in Eusebius's *Enigmata*. But, unlike Eusebius's section 5D, the Exeter bird riddles are not subservient in

---

6. On the numbering of the Exeter Riddles, see further on p. 284 (n.1).

content to Isidore's work. Also, even though the first three motifs are dealt with in the *Etymologiae*, these are comparatively distant from one another in this encyclopedia, and the barnacle goose is simply absent, as observed in the following table:

Exeter Section 2A	Isidore's *Etymologiae*
7. Swan	XII.vii.18–19
8. Nightingale	XII.vii.37
9. Cuckoo	XII.vii.67
10. Barnacle Goose	—

These divergences notwithstanding, it is feasible that the Exeter compilers aimed to reproduce the thematic groupings observed in encyclopedic works through the imitation of Latin riddle collections such as Eusebius's *Enigmata*. Furthermore, if we consider the topics coming after the birds, it is noteworthy that the Exeter Riddles at this point offer a substantial sequence of tools that looks like a typical instrumental series. For these reasons, and given that further thematic clusters are discernible beyond Riddle 40 (see Appendix X), it will be worthwhile studying this phenomenon in detail.

As I will later expound with regard to Isidore's *Etymologiae*, the topic-centered compilation can also convey cases in which the associative patterns are offered by means of pairings that range from simple thematic connections as with Bern Riddles 4 and 5—whose subjects are "bench" and "table," respectively—to more subtle links such as Tatwine's nos. 24 (humility) and 25 (pride). As we will see later on, Aldhelm's collection abounds in pairings of this second kind. For instance, the couple formed by Riddles 63 (raven) and 64 (dove) would thus conjure up the first two birds released by Noah in the chronological order offered in the corresponding episode of Genesis (8.6–12).[7] In the Exeter Book, intricate correspondences of

---

7. This connection has already been pointed out by W. F. Bolton, *A History of Anglo-Latin Literature 597–1066*, vol. 1: 597–740 (Princeton, NJ: Princeton University Press, 1967), 84, and Michael Lapidge and James L. Rosier, eds.

this kind can also be detected. An example of this may be illustrated with Riddles 42 (rooster and hen) and 43 (soul and body), the juxtaposition of which seems to suggest that the two texts were read as a pair in an allegorical plane.[8]

It is also important to note that the occurrence of some thematic exceptions may occasionally clash with the overall encyclopedic principle ruling a section and give the impression of a faulty organization, as will later be illustrated with Isidore's *Etymologiae*. But at this point, Eusebius's *Enigmata* will help exemplify this issue in riddle collections. In Eusebius's section 2, cosmological themes clearly predominate (see Appendix VI); however, two exceptional motifs stand out: nos. 7 (letters) and 9 (alpha). The presence of these two riddles might simply point to an occasional disruption of thematic order. Yet it may be inferred that the author/compiler probably intended to raise letters to the rank of cosmological topics, since these were considered essential for the knowledge of God's Creation. The letter alpha conjures up the well-known iconographic function of this Greek letter, which, together with omega, often accompanies the figure of Christ in pictorial art, signifying the beginning and the end.[9] The occurrence of alpha alone also seems to allude to Creation, a notion that is supported by the following clue in Eusebius's *Enigma 9*: "Atque uocari primus per me coepit Adamus" (3) [and Adam was the first whose name started with me].[10] These thematic links may seem rather loose for

---

and trans., *Aldhelm: The Poetic Works* (Cambridge: Cambridge University Press, 1985), 63-64.

8. For a detailed analysis of the possible allegorical association of these two riddles, see my "The Key to the Body: Unlocking Riddles 42-46," in *Naked Before God: Uncovering the Body in Anglo-Saxon England*, ed. Benjamin C. Withers and Jonathan Wilcox (Morgantown: West Virginia University Press, 2003), 75–76.

9. The symbolic use of these letters stems from Revelation 1.8, 21.6, and 22.13.

10. The edition of this passage is from Glorie, *CCSL*, vol. 133. My translation.

our contemporary order standards but, far from being inconsistencies, nos. 7 (letters) and 9 (alpha) comply with the cosmological thread of the series.

In like manner, in the Exeter Book collection thematic digressions occasionally disrupt larger series. The case of Riddle 22 (Charles's Wain), which could potentially function as a cosmological topic but appears in an instrumental cluster, is worth considering here. This thematic exception reveals its meaningful role in the compilation only if its association with preceding Riddle 21 (plow) is taken into account. L. Blakeley already hinted at this possible relationship: "Is it by pure chance that this riddle [no. 22] occurs next to one with the solution 'Plough'?"[11] Indeed, the adjacency of these two texts acknowledges the connection between the name of the constellation and that of the agricultural tool, both of which could be referred to as Latin *plaustrum*. Far from being accidental, the pairing of Riddles 21 and 22 is suggestive of school practice. The possible occurrence of thematic irregularites of this kind is therefore a further aspect to consider in the study of both Latin collections and the Exeter Book Riddles, for it may provide us with valuable information about the ways in which medieval compilers applied orderly parameters with a didactic intent in mind. When analyzing riddle collections, attention must therefore be paid to the presence of both thematic digressions and pairings that can hinder our perception of the existence of a rationale underlying the compilation.

What I show in this book is that encyclopedic patterns, in the form of either thematic clusters or pairs, pervade all major Latin riddle collections and can also be detected in the Exeter Book Riddles. With these ideas in mind, much is to be gained from contemplating Latin riddle collections and the Old English Riddles from the point of view of the structuring principles governing them. As a result of this, relevant issues such as the different sources that might have been at play in the Exeter collection and the possible use of these riddles in the school context can be raised in order to achieve a broader perspective

---

11. L. Blakeley, "Riddles 22 and 58 of the Exeter Book," *RES* 9 (1958): 247.

on these texts and a better understanding of both the Latin and the Anglo-Saxon dimensions of the riddling genre.

1.2. An Outline of This Book

I have distributed the contents of this book into five chapters, the first of which provides an introduction to the Exeter Book Riddles and medieval Latin collections in light of the thematic structure observed in Isidore's *Etymologiae*. The second chapter opens with an overview of the early medieval riddling genre (2.1), which is followed by an introduction to Isidore and the *Etymologiae* (2.2). The last two sections of Chapter 2 (2.3 and 2.4) supply an appraisal of the ways in which this encyclopedia has exerted a considerable influence on various literary genres, with a special focus on grammatical works and riddle collections.

In the first part of Chapter 3, I offer a brief sketch of the overall scheme of Isidore's *Etymologiae* in order to compare the organizational criteria observed in this work with those discerned in riddle collections. In an attempt to handle the structural complexities of the medieval riddling genre in as accurate a way as possible, sections 3.2 and 3.3 provide a separate analysis of the encyclopedic patterns that can be detected in the collections of Symphosius and Aldhelm, since these are the foundational antecedents of medieval riddling. Subsequently, section 3.4 studies the continuity of the genre with the *enigmata* of Tatwine and Eusebius.

The analysis is then followed by the inspection of structural principles in the Bern and Lorsch Riddles (3.5). This survey is next complemented by the examination of the assemblage found in Vatican City, Biblioteca Apostolica Vaticana, Reg. Lat. 1553, which will allow us to explore the peculiarities of a hybrid compilation. As a whole, Chapter 3 argues that all these collections deploy thematic clusters revealing a deliberate imitation of the Isidorean encyclopedic compilation system. This inference in turn suggests that riddle assemblages, like encyclopedias, were designed for educational purposes.

The fourth chapter centers on the Exeter Book Riddles, which are introduced in section 4.1. The study then focuses on the examination of any traces of an organizational plan underlying the three major subdivisions that I have proposed on account of the thematic segments observed in the compilation and my assumption that they reflect three phases in the compilation process. Section 4.2 thus provides a study of Group 1, formed by Riddles 1–40. This introductory series seems to derive from a source collection that was probably enlarged by adding more riddles from other collections.[12] Similarly, section 4.3 carries out an analysis of internal thematic structures observed in Group 2, which comprises Riddles 41–59, while section 4.4 in turn examines Group 3 (Riddles 61–95), which constitutes the final textual sequence in the manuscript. A comparative study of the variable degree of cohesiveness, thematic irregularities, and the presence of frequent repetitions observed in these three main groups that have been delineated provides us with valuable information on the Exeter Riddles' compilation, suggesting that their assembling was guided, to a great extent, by the observance of structural patterns akin to those detected in the Latin collections and Isidore's *Etymologiae*.

Finally, in Chapter 5, the results drawn from the study carried out in the four main parts of this book are brought together, establishing that all major Latin collections and the Exeter Riddles exhibit a notable concern with the organization of their subjects on the basis of thematic criteria similar to those discernible in Isidore's *Etymologiae*. As with encyclopedias, the topic-centered arrangement of riddles would then be pursued by compilers as a strategy intended to optimize the didactic and instructional possibilities inherent in these texts and favor the readers' assimilation of their contents. This idea thus brings us to the conclusion that riddle collections were an important part of the early medieval school curriculum.

---

12. A summarized version of the comparative discussion of three Anglo-Latin collections—those of Aldhelm, Tatwine and Eusebius—and this first subdivision of the Exeter Riddles has been gathered in my "Patterns of Compilation in Anglo-Latin *Enigmata* and the Evidence of a Source-Collection in the *Exeter Book* Riddles (nos. 1–40)," *Viator* 43 (2012): 339–74.

CHAPTER TWO

Early Medieval Riddling and Isidore's *Etymologiae*

2.1. A General Overview of the Riddling Genre in the Early Middle Ages[1]

The riddling genre is well known from antiquity. The Bible, for example, famously offers Samson's riddle[2] and the account of how King Solomon's wisdom was tested by the Queen of Sheba by means of queries.[3] These riddles are not preserved in the Bible but are provided in the Talmud (Midrash Mishle) and the Second Targum to the Book of Esther. Among these pieces, the riddle of Lot and his daughters

---

1. The reading of this chapter can be accompanied by the use of Appendix I, which offers a chronological diagram of early medieval riddling.
2. Having seen the carcass of a lion with a swarm of bees and honey inside it, Samson proposed the following riddle to the Philistines: "Out of the eater came something to eat. Out of the strong came something sweet" (Judges 14.14). The answer to the riddles is given up later in the biblical account: "What is sweeter than honey? What is stronger than a lion" (Judges 14.18). All references to the Bible in this book are from Herbert G. May and Bruce M. Metzger, eds., *The New Oxford Annotated Bible with the Apocrypha* (New York: Oxford University Press, 1977). It is precisely this famous riddle that Isidore uses to illustrate the concept *enigma* in *Etymologiae* I.xxxvii.26.
3. "Now when the queen of Sheba heard of the fame of Solomon concerning the name of the Lord, she came to test him with hard questions" (I Kings 10.1).

has proved to be the most popular, with a continuity well beyond the Middle Ages.⁴ In Greek literature, two major collections have survived: Book X of the *Deipnosophistae* (The Philosophers' Dinner, c. 228 CE)⁵ by Athenaeus—offering a large representation of riddles by different authors—and Book XIV of the Greek Anthology,⁶ containing a section devoted to arithmetical puzzles, oracles, epigrams, and riddles,⁷ a famous example of which is the Sphinx's enigma on man.⁸

Riddles in Roman literature are comparatively scarce and appear only sporadically as part of other works. An example of this is the two riddles found at the end of Virgil's *Eclogue* 3 (104–7).⁹ A further illustration is Petronius's *Satyricon*, in which the guests at Trimalchio's dinner are expected to solve some riddles related to the food that they are offered (56, 58).¹⁰ Also set in the context of a ban-

---

4. For these riddles, see J. B. Friedreich, *Geschichte des Räthsels* (Dresden, 1860), 98–103.
5. This work in turn follows the model set by Plato's *Symposium*, dating from c. 385–380 BCE.
6. The Greek Anthology, also known as the Palatine Anthology, was found in a manuscript by French classicist Claude Saumaise in 1606 in the Palatine library at Heidelberg. It contains epigrams and other poetic materials, whose dates range from the seventh century BCE to 600 CE.
7. Editions of these two collections can be found in Charles Burton Gulick, ed. and trans., *Athenaeus: The Deipnosophists*, vol. 4 (Cambridge, MA: Harvard University Press, 1927–61), 530–83, and W. R. Paton, ed. and trans., *The Greek Anthology*, vol. 5 (Cambridge, MA: Harvard University Press, 1979), 26–107. For further information on the Greek riddling tradition, see Konrad Ohlert, *Rätsel und Rätselspiele der alten Griechen* (Berlin, 1886).
8. "There is on earth a two-footed, and four-footed, and three-footed, whose name is one, and it changes its nature alone of all creatures that move creeping on earth or in the air and sea. But when it moves supported on most feet, the swiftness of its legs is at its weakest." Cited from Paton, *The Greek Anthology*, vol. 5, XIV.64, 59.
9. See D. E. W. Wormell, "The Riddles in Virgil's Third *Eclogue*," *The Classical Quarterly* 10 (1960): 29–32.
10. For the presence of riddles in Roman literature, see Raymond Theodore Ohl, ed. and trans., "The Enigmas of Symphosius" (Unpublished PhD Dissertation, Philadelphia, 1928), 12–13, and Mary Jane McDonald Williams,

quet, Symphosius's *Enigmata* constitutes the only complete riddle collection of this period that has been preserved. Medieval riddle collections in general are all indebted to this unknown late Latin author who was perhaps active in the early sixth century.

2.1.1 From the Seventh to the Ninth Century

Contrasting the sparse representation of riddling in the literature of the Roman period, the numerous extant collections of early medieval riddles bear witness to the flourishing of this genre in the seventh and eighth centuries, when the composition of *enigmata* achieved a notable popularity in Europe. The anonymous Bern Riddles, probably dating from the seventh century, constitute an early illustration of Continental riddling that reveals the influence of Symphosius. But, as mentioned before, this literary phenomenon became extraordinarily prominent in the British Isles, where a substantial group of writers developed the genre. The first riddle collection produced in England that has survived to our days is that of Aldhelm (c. 639–709), who certainly knew about his predecessor Symphosius, as he expressly mentions his name in a passage of the *Epistola ad Acircium* (c. 686), the work in which the riddles were originally inserted.

Aldhelm's *Enigmata* soon made an impression on Anglo-Saxon culture, as two other writers—Tatwine (d. 734) and Eusebius (d. 747), both contemporary with Bede—each took up the composition of a riddle collection.[11] These subsequent collections are in Latin, but evidence of an early attempt to render Aldhelm's *Enigmata* to the vernacular is offered by the so-called Leiden Riddle, which is extant in

---

"The Riddles of Tatwine and Eusebius" (Unpublished PhD dissertation, University of Michigan, 1974), 1–9.

11. Actually two or more generations of writers fell under Aldhelm's great sphere of influence. Among others were Boniface and his circle of correspondents. For this, see Christine E. Fell, "Some Implications of the Boniface Correspondence," in *New Readings on Women in Old English Literature*, ed. Helen Damico and Alexandra Hennessey Olsen (Bloomington: Indiana University Press, 1990), 29–43, and Barbara Yorke, "The Bonifacian Mission and Female Religious in Wessex," *Early Medieval Europe 7* (1998): 145–72.

Leiden, Universiteitsbibliotheek, Voss. Lat. Q. 106.[12] This poem, a Northumbrian translation of Aldhelm's *Enigma* 33 (coat of mail) dating from the eighth century,[13] was later added by a tenth-century hand on folio 25v right after Aldhelm's *Enigmata*.[14] This Northumbrian version therefore offers an interesting counterpart to Exeter Riddle 35, in turn a West-Saxon rendering of Aldhelm's *Enigma* 33.[15] Apart from the Leiden Riddle, further activity related to this literary genre in the vernacular might be ascribed to this early phase. On linguistic grounds, R. D. Fulk contends that the Exeter Riddles "seem close in date to *Beowulf* and the early biblical narratives."[16] Considering that this scholar offers c. 685–825 as the most probable timespan for the composition of *Beowulf*,[17] it may be surmised that the Leiden Riddle and the majority of the Exeter Riddles were produced in the late seventh or the early eighth century, thus practically coinciding with the composition of Latin *enigmata* by Aldhelm and other authors.

The initial impulse to riddling was probably started by Aldhelm

---

12. For a full description of this manuscript and its contents, see Rolf H. Bremmer Jr. and Kees Dekker, *Manuscripts in the Low Countries* (Tempe: Arizona Center for Medieval and Renaissance Studies, 2006), 107–12.

13. For the dialectal features and the dating of this riddle, see Albert H., Smith, ed., *Three Northumbrian Poems: Cædmon's Hymn, Bede's Death Song, and the Leiden Riddle* (London: Methuen, 1933), 18, 23–25, and 37. The Leiden Riddle is edited and commented upon in Elliott Van Kirk Dobbie, ed., *ASPR*, vol. 6, *The Anglo-Saxon Minor Poems* (New York: Columbia University Press, 1942), cviii–cx, 109, and 199–200. Also see R. D. Fulk, *A History of Old English Meter* (Philadelphia: The University of Pennsylvania Press, 1992), 404–5.

14. See M. B. Parkes, "The Manuscript of the Leiden Riddle," *ASE* 1 (1972): 216–17.

15. On the relationship between Exeter Riddle 35 and the Leiden Riddle, see Smith, *Three Northumbrian Poems*, 17–19 and 45–47; Craig Williamson, *The Old English Riddles of the Exeter Book* (Chapel Hill: University of North Carolina Press, 1977), 243–45; and Thomas Klein, "The Old English Translation of Aldhelm's Riddle Lorica," *RES* 48 (1997): 345–49.

16. Fulk, *History*, 408.

17. Ibid., 381–92. An overwhelming battery of proofs supporting Fulk's inference is found in Leonard Neidorf, ed., *The Dating of Beowulf: A Reassessment* (Woodbridge: Boydell & Brewer, 2014).

in England, and from there the genre spread to the Continent.[18] The considerable number of manuscripts containing Aldhelm's *Enigmata* that have been preserved in different Continental repositories testifies to the significant role that this collection could have played in the medieval school curriculum.[19] As argued by Michael Lapidge and James L. Rosier, Aldhelm's *Enigmata*, together with other works, were probably brought to the Continent with Boniface's mission in 716.[20] When Boniface (c. 675–754) founded the monastery at Fulda in 744[21] and two years later became Archbishop of Mainz, he established a permanent focus of Anglo-Saxon culture in the region.[22] The geographical area of Anglo-Saxon influence was however much wider

---

18. As stated by McKitterick, "Aldhelm's Aenigmata were known in Neustria by the mid-eighth century. . . ." Rosamond McKitterick, "The Diffusion of Insular Culture in Neustria between 650 and 850: the Implications of the Manuscript Evidence," in *La Neustrie. Les pays au nord de la Loire de 650 à 850*, ed. Hartmut Atsma (Sigmaringen: Thorbecke, 1989), 403.
19. See the list of manuscripts offered in Glorie, *CCSL*, vol. 133, 360–64; and *Aldhelmi opera, MGH, Auctores Antiquissimi*, vol. 15, ed. Rudolph Ehwald (Berlin: Weidmann, 1919), 58.
20. Boniface traveled to Frisia in 716 and at some point came back to Nursling. In 718, he set off for the continent but never returned to England again. Lapidge and Rosier, *Aldhelm: The Poetic Works*, 2. These scholars (ibid., 220, n. 3) also mention a letter from Lull, Boniface's successor at the mission in Mainz, to some Dealwine (dated 745–46), asking for copies of Aldhelm's works to be brought from England to Germany. See Michael Tangl, ed., *S. Bonifatii et Lullii Epistolae, MGH, Epistolae selectae*, vol. 1 (Berlin: Weidmann, 1916), 144 (no. 71); and Ehwald, *Aldhelmi opera*, 520.
21. As Irvine notes, the monastery of Fulda "would become one of the leading centers of Carolingian textual culture throughout the ninth century." Martin Irvine, *The Making of Textual Culture: 'Grammatica' and Literary Theory, 350–1100* (Cambridge: Cambridge University Press, 1994; repr. 1996), 299.
22. In Stenton's words, "As a direct result of his [Boniface's] policy, English learning rapidly came to extend beyond the monasteries newly founded by English missionaries to older houses like St. Gall and Reichenau, where Irish traditions had always been strong. Books which had a special interest for Englishmen were multiplied in such houses and some of the oldest materials for English history have only been preserved in copies made there."

than the Fulda and Mainz dioceses.[23] As pointed out by David Ganz and Rosamond McKitterick, the relationship between Grimo, abbot of Corbie (d. 748), and Boniface was a close one.[24] Evidence of the interest in Aldhelm's Riddles in this area is provided by St Petersburg, Rossijskaja Nacionalnaja Biblioteka, F.v.XIV.1,[25] a late-eighth-century codex that was produced at Corbie.[26] The Anglo-Saxon connection with this monastery[27] is also shown by the presence of Aldhelm's *Enigmata* in St Petersburg, Rossijskaja Nacionalnaja Biblioteka, Q.v.I.15.[28] This manuscript originated in southwest England but was

---

Frank Stenton, *Anglo-Saxon England* (Oxford: Oxford University Press, 1943; repr. 1998), 172.
23. Note that Boniface had previously founded the monasteries of Fritzlar, Tauberbischofsheim, Kitzingen, and Ochsenfurt. See *ODNB*, s.v. "Boniface," by I. N. Wood.
24. See David Ganz's "The Merovingian Library of Corbie," in *Columbanus and Merovingian Monasticism*, ed. Howard B. Clarke and Mary Brennan (Oxford: B.A.R., 1981), 163, and *Corbie in the Carolingian Renaissance* (Sigmaringen: Jan Thorbecke, 1990), 20; McKitterick, "The Diffusion of Insular Culture," 413–14.
25. On this manuscript, see Bernhard Bischoff, *Katalog der festländischen Handschriften des neunten Jahrhunderts (mit Ausnahme der wisigotischen), Teil II: Laon-Paderborn* (Wiesbaden: Harrassowitz, 2004), 81 (no. 2317).
26. This manuscript also contains an extract from Aldhelm's verse *De virginitate* and the *Enigmata* of Symphosius and Boniface. Ganz, *Corbie in the Carolingian Renaissance*, 142.
27. As McKitterick states, "That there were insular links generally at Corbie, and men and women from the British Isles active in the Corbie area ... is absolutely clear from the number of books of Corbie provenance and Neustrian origin which betray their presence." McKitterick, "The Diffusion of Insular Culture," 416. The fact that Balthild (c. 626–80)— Clovis II's wife, of probable Anglo-Saxon origin—founded the monastery of Corbie between 657–61 may have contributed to this. See Ganz, *Corbie in the Carolingian Renaissance*, 15.
28. For the contents of this manuscript, see Helmut Gneuss and Michael Lapidge, *Anglo-Saxon Manuscripts: A Bibliographical Handlist of Manuscripts and Manuscript Fragments Written or Owned in England up to 1100* (Toronto: University of Toronto Press, 2014), 606–7 (no. 845). See also Bischoff, *Katalog, Teil II*, 82 (no. 2317g).

soon brought to Corbie, where it must have been from the mid-eighth century.[29] Furthermore, the hypothesis that one of the scribes of this codex might be Boniface himself[30] would support the contention that it was thanks to him and his fellow Anglo-Saxon missionaries that Aldhelm's *Enigmata* started to be disseminated in the Continent.

Probably from his own direct acquaintance with Aldhelm's Riddles, Boniface envisaged the possibilities of this literary genre and used it for his theological reflection on virtues and vices, which usually appears in manuscripts as "Aenigmata Bonifatii."[31] Interestingly, the fragmentary version of Boniface's *Enigmata* contained in the late eighth-century flyleaves binding Paris, Bibliothèque Nationale, Lat. 13046 was claimed by Ludwig Traube to be the work of three of

---

29. As Ganz explains, the manuscript is written in insular script, but on column 1 of folio 71v (line 25) the text continues in eN script, which is characteristic of Corbie. See his *Corbie in the Carolingian Renaissance*, 42. McKitterick points out that the eN script is normally dated to the mid-eighth century. McKitterick, "The Diffusion of Insular Culture," 413.

30. See M. B. Parkes, "The Handwriting of St Boniface: a Reassessment of the Evidence," *Beiträge zur Geschichte der deutschen Sprache und Literatur* 98 (1976): 161–79, and Michael Lapidge, "Autographs of Insular Latin Authors of the Early Middle Ages," in *Gli autografi medievali, Problemi paleografici e filologici, Atti del convegno di studio della Fondazione Ezio Franceschini*, ed. Paolo Chiesa and Lucia Pinelli (Spoleto: Centro italiano di studi sull'Alto Medioevo, 1994), 108–15.

31. Being a set of poems essentially describing abstractions, the collection however lacks the encyclopedic insight of other *enigmata*, as Lapidge and Rosier have already pointed out: "In casting his enigmata in a straightforward dogmatic, hortatory form, Boniface lost the potential for imaginative exploration of the external world which characterizes the Enigmata of Aldhelm." Lapidge and Rosier, *Aldhelm: The Poetic Works*, 67. For this reason, I have excluded the study of this collection from this monograph and will only occasionally refer to these poems when there is a significant aspect that deserves to be mentioned in relation to the corpus of riddles that I analyze. Boniface's *Enigmata* are edited as part of *Bonifatii carmina*, *MGH*, *PLAC*, vol. 1, ed. Ernst Dümmler (Berlin: Weidmann, 1881), 1–15, and in *CCSL*, vol. 133, with a German translation by K. J. Minst (Turnhout: Brepols, 1968), 273–343.

his students.[32] If Traube's assumption is correct, we may conclude with McKitterick that it then implies "that these three had some connection with Corbie, and may even have written the manuscript there."[33] Early medieval riddling is therefore a literary phenomenon that should be considered as tightly associated with pre-Carolingian scriptoria with marked Insular affiliations.

Formerly attributed to Bede, the *Collectanea Pseudo-Bedae* is a miscellaneous assemblage of materials and riddlic questions included among the complete works of Bede, printed in Basel in 1563.[34] No manuscript containing the *Collectanea* has been preserved. The comparison of these texts with other literary works led Lapidge to deduce that this florilegium probably originated "either in Ireland or England, or in an Irish foundation on the Continent."[35] The inclusion of five pieces from Symphosius's *Enigmata* and five from Aldhelm's leaves no room for doubt that the author of the *Collectanea* was acquainted with major riddle collections.[36] This compilation, which probably dates from the early ninth century,[37] shares numerous characteristics with other riddling dialogues. As with other early

---

32. Ludwig Traube, "Die älteste Handschrift der *Aenigmata Bonifatii*," *Vorlesungen und Abhandlungen* 3 (1920): 164–67. Ganz in turn observed that these flyleaves were "copied by several inept scribes, one of whom wrote in insular script, and one of whom was trying to write eN script." *Corbie in the Carolingian Renaissance*, 42.
33. McKitterick, "The Diffusion of Insular Culture," 413.
34. The full title of this collection is *Excerptiones patrum, collectanea, flores ex diversis, quaestiones et parabolae* and is present in Johann Herwagen [the Younger], *Opera Bedae Venerabilis presbyteri Anglo-Saxonis* (Basel, 1563), vol. 3, 647–74. A recent critical edition of this work is Martha Bayless and Michael Lapidge, eds. and trans., *Collectanea Pseudo-Bedae* (Dublin: Institute for Advanced Studies, 1998). See also Frederick Tupper Jr., "Riddles of the Bede Tradition. The 'Flores' of Pseudo-Bede," *MP* 2 (1904): 561–72, esp. 561–65.
35. Bayless and Lapidge, *Collectanea*, 12.
36. Ibid., 22.
37. Ibid., 42. Daniel Anlezark, ed. and trans., *The Old English Dialogues of Solomon and Saturn* (Cambridge: Brewer, 2009), 16.

medieval florilegia, the *Collectanea* might have been "written by clerics for the lay nobles they advised" in the Carolingian period, as Daniel Anlezark has pointed out.[38]

Of uncertain provenance and date, the *Versus cuiusdam Scoti de alphabeto* (Verses of some Scotus on the alphabet)[39] offers riddlic descriptions of the letters of the alphabet in Latin tristichs, the format employed by Symphosius in his *Enigmata*.[40] This collection is also known as *Versus de nominibus litterarum* (Verses on the names of the letters), a title given to it in Oxford, Bodleian Library, Rawlinson C.697, the earliest codex (third quarter of the ninth century) where this work has been preserved.[41] The *Versus* is inserted between Riddles 98 and 99 of Aldhelm's *Enigmata* in this manuscript (fols. 13v-14v), a fact suggesting that the compiler viewed the two collections as being tightly interconnected.[42] Also interestingly, the description of letter i in the *Versus* bears undeniable parallelisms with Eusebius's enigma on the same topic (no. 39).[43] Another early codex offering the *Versus* together with Aldhelm's and Symphosius's Riddles is Paris, Bibliothèque Nationale, Lat. 2773 (fols. 108v-10r), which was probably

---

38. Anlezark, *The Old English Dialogues*, 16.
39. Latin *Scotus* could also allude to its possible Irish authorship. See further on p. 21 (n. 46).
40. This collection is also edited in *CCSL*, vol. 133A, 729–41.
41. This date was proposed by Bernhard Bischoff in "Bannita: I. Syllaba, 2. Littera," in *Latin Script and Letters A. D. 400–900: Festschrift presented to Ludwig Bieler*, ed. J. J. O'Meara and B. Naumann (Leiden: Brill, 1976), 211.
42. Some echoes of Aldhelm's and Eusebius's Riddles are found in this work. The parallelisms of the *Versus* with some of Symphosius's Riddles also suggest that the author of this work was acquainted with this collection. See, for example, the notes ("Loci paralleli") accompanying the text of letter A in the edition of the *Versus* in *CCSL*, vol. 133, 729. See also Bischoff, "Bannita," 211, n. 17.
43. See further on p. 240 (n. 452). Bücheler believes that some of Eusebius's Riddles are clearly indebted to *Versus*. See Franz Bücheler, "Coniectanea," *Rheinisches Museum für Philologie* 36 (1881): 340. See also Bischoff, "Bannita," 211, nn. 18 and 19.

produced in Rheims in the second half of the ninth century.[44] The collection similarly accompanies the *Enigmata* of Symphosius and Aldhelm in both London, British Library, Royal 12.C.xxiii (fols. 137v-38v) and Cambridge, University Library, Gg.5.35 (fols. 381r-82r), two codices of English origin.[45] The Insular affiliation of the *Versus*, as argued by several scholars,[46] is therefore not to be dismissed.

A further collection of Latin verse riddles that might tentatively be associated with the work of Anglo-Saxon monks in the Continent is the so-called Lorsch Riddles, extant only in Vatican City, Biblioteca Apostolica Vaticana, Pal. Lat. 1753 (late eighth century).[47] The name alludes to their provenance from the Abbey of Lorsch, a reputed Carolingian center with demonstrable Anglo-Saxon links where this codex was produced. Not surprisingly, echoes from the riddles by Aldhelm, Tatwine, and Eusebius can be detected in this collection. The Lorsch *Enigmata* are accompanied in Vatican City, Pal. Lat. 1753 by the collections of Symphosius and Aldhelm. A composite assemblage that includes riddles by Symphosius and Aldhelm, as well as a good number of those from the Bern *Enigmata*, is found in Vatican City,

---

44. See Nancy Porter Stork, *Through a Gloss Darkly: Aldhelm's Riddles in the British Library MS Royal 12.C.xxiii* (Toronto: Pontifical Institute of Mediaeval Studies, 1990), 17. Also see a description of this manuscript's contents in Ehwald, *Aldhelmi opera*, 48–49.
45. For further information on these two codices, see further in this chapter pp. 35–37.
46. Omont, who edited the *Versus*, argued that the collection was "very probably" the work of an English author, "who lived at the time of the Carolingian Renaissance" (my translation). Henri Omont, "Poème anonyme sur les lettres de l'alphabet," *Bibliothèque de l'école des chartes* 42 (1881): 429. Manitius, by contrast, believed that the author was an Irishman, as Latin *Scotus* in the title may be suggesting, who composed the poem in the mid-seventh century. Max Manitius, *Geschichte der lateinischen Literatur des Mittelalters*, vol. 1 (Munich: Beck'sche, 1911), 190–92.
47. On this manuscript, see Élisabeth Pellegrin, et al., *Les manuscrits classiques latins de la Bibliothèque Vaticane*, vol. 2, Part 2 (Paris: Éditions du Centre national de la recherche scientifique, 1982), 400–404.

Biblioteca Apostolica Vaticana, Reg. Lat. 1553 (early ninth century)[48] from Lorraine, another area with Insular connections.[49] Vatican City, Pal. Lat. 1753 and Reg. Lat. 1553 therefore bear witness to the prominence that riddles achieved during the Carolingian Renaissance.

Apart from Aldhelm, another well-known English ecclesiastic who experimented with the riddling genre was Alcuin of York (c. 740–804).[50] Well-known as Charlemagne's advisor and paramount engine of the Carolingian educational program,[51] Alcuin was the author of the *Disputatio regalis et nobilissimi iuvenis Pippini cum Albino scholastico* (The debate of the royal and the very noble youth Pippin with Albinus the teacher).[52] Set in a dialogue format, this eminently didactic work, dated by Martha Bayless between 790 and 93,[53] features prose riddles that are posed by Alcuin to Pippin, son of Charlemagne, as a way to test Pippin's knowledge. Of the seventeen queries contained in the *Disputatio*, four follow closely riddles by Symphosius and three others have parallels in Pseudo-Bede's *Collectanea* and Aldhelm's *Enigmata*.[54] Also probably by Alcuin, the *Prop*

---

48. On the dating of this manuscript, see Chauncey Finch, "The Bern Riddles in Codex Vat. Reg. Lat. 1553," *Transactions and Proceedings of the American Philological Association* 92 (1961): 146.
49. See further on p. 27 and n. 77.
50. See *ODNB*, s.v. "Alcuin," by D. A. Bullough.
51. For Alcuin's decisive role in the context of the Carolingian cultural burgeoning, see Peter Godman, ed. and trans., *Poetry of the Carolingian Renaissance* (London: Duckworth, 1985), 17–22.
52. *Albinus* was one of the names that Alcuin received at Charlemagne's court. For the text of the *Disputatio*, see *PL*, vol. 101 (cols. For the exchange of riddles in l manifestations"ssential role as disseminator of riddle culture has already been discussed, s 978–80) and L. W. Daly and W. Suchier, eds., *Altercatio Hadriani Augusti et Epicteti Philosophi* (Urbana: University of Illinois Press, 1939), 137–43. The latter is reprinted with an introduction and notes in Martha Bayless, "Alcuin's *Disputatio Pippini* and the Early Medieval Riddle Tradition," in *Humour, History and Politics in Late Antiquity and the Early Middle Ages*, ed. Guy Halsall (Cambridge: Cambridge University Press, 2002), 157–78.
53. Bayless, "Alcuin's *Disputatio*," 166.
54. Ibid., 170 and 177–78. See also further on pp. 137–38 (n. 143).

ositiones ad acuendos iuvenes (Problems to sharpen the young) offers a collection of arithmetical puzzles that are similarly presented as a list of questions and answers.⁵⁵ Alongside these two prose assemblages, Alcuin composed some verse riddles that have come down to us as part of his *Carmina*, a couple of which bear an undeniable resemblance to two of Symphosius's *Enigmata*.⁵⁶

A further illustration of the enigmatic genre in the early Middle Ages is the riddling-dialogue subgenre, of which Alcuin's *Disputatio* and *Propositiones* are good examples. The question-and-answer format of Alcuin's two works in turn derives from a tradition of a group of dialogues known as the *Ioca monachorum* (The jokes, games of the monks).⁵⁷ Early copies of this dialogue are extant in eighth-

---

55. An edition of this text is found in *PL*, vol. 101 (cols. 1145–60) and in Menso Folkerts and Helmuth Gericke, "Die Alkuin zugeschriebenen Propositiones ad acuendos iuvenes (Aufgaben zur Schärfung des Geistes der Jugend)" in *Science in Western and Eastern Civilization in Carolingian Times*, eds. Paul Leo Butzer and Dietrich Lohrmann (Basel: Birkhäuser Verlag, 1993), 283–362.

56. One of these riddles deals with a comb and has two versions, one in verse and another in prose, the latter contained in one of Alcuin's letters. For an edition of the verse piece, see *Alcuini (Albini) carmina, MGH, PLAC*, vol. 1, ed. Ernst Dümmler (Berlin: Weidmann, 1881), 223 (no. 5); for the prose version, see *Alcuini sive Albini epistolae, MGH, Epistolae*, vol. 4, ed. Ernst Dümmler (Berlin: Weidmann, 1895), 67 (no. 26). See also Paul Sorrell, "Alcuin's 'Comb' Riddle," *Neophilologus* 80 (1996): 311–18. Apart from these two pieces, Alcuin composed three variant riddles on a furnace and one on a bath, the latter following the model set by Symphosius's *Enigma* 90 (bathhouse). For two of the oven riddles (nos. 64.1–2), see Dümmler, *PLAC*, vol. 1, 282–83; a third version of the oven riddle is no. 100.3, ibid., 328; for the bath riddle (no. 92.1), see ibid., 318. For five further verse logographs, see ibid., 281–82 (nos. 63.1–5). A discussion of some of these pieces is found in Dieter Bitterli, "Alkuin von York und die Angelsächsische Rätseldichtung," *Anglia* 128 (2010): 4–20.

57. Several versions of the *Ioca monachorum* are edited in Walther Suchier, *Das mittellateinische Gespräch Adrian und Epictitus und verwandten Texten (Joca Monachorum)* (Tübingen: Niemeyer, 1955). See 90–92, for the list of manuscripts containing this work.

century Continental manuscripts, some of them with verifiable Insular links.[58] Indeed, several queries offered in various codices containing the *Ioca monachorum* are found in Pseudo-Bede's *Collectanea*, as well as in the later Old English dialogues *Solomon and Saturn* and *Adrian and Ritheus*.[59] Interestingly, the *Ioca monachorum* follow Symphosius's Riddles in St Gall, Stiftsbibliothek, Cod. Sang. 196 (second third of the ninth century), where they occur under the heading "Enigmata interrogatiua" (p. 388). The first riddle offered by the *Collectanea*, whose answer is "sapientia" (wisdom), is, for example, found in the St Gall codex but not attested in any other manuscript version of the *Ioca monachorum*.[60]

2.1.2 From the Tenth to the Eleventh Century

In England, a revival of riddling took place in the late Anglo-Saxon period, coinciding with the Benedictine reform initiated in the 950s.[61] As with the preceding phase, this second stage should be analyzed in relation to the cultural exchange with the Continent that had been favored by the establishment of the Anglo-Saxon missions in the seventh and eighth centuries. The notable role played by rid-

---

58. For example, St Gall, Stiftsbibliothek, Cod. Sang. 193 and 903 are two codices, written on the Continent in the late seventh or early eighth century, with clear Insular ties. See Bayless and Lapidge, *Collectanea*, 14–15.
59. See ibid., 17–18.
60. For the text and translation of the wisdom riddle, see ibid., 122–23. Cf. *Ioca Monachorum* in the St Gall version in ibid., 199, and Suchier, *Das mittellateinische Gespräch*, 123 (no. 13).
61. Insightful accounts of the Benedictine reform period can be found in Barbara Yorke, ed., *Bishop Æthelwold: His Career and Influence* (Woodbridge: Boydell, 1988; repr. 1997), 1–12; Michael Lapidge and Michael Winterbottom, eds. and trans., *Wulfstan of Winchester: The Life of St Æthelwold* (Oxford: Clarendon, 1991), li–lx; Joyce Hill, "The Benedictine Reform and beyond," in *A Companion to Anglo-Saxon Literature*, ed. Phillip Pulsiano and Elaine Treharne (London: Blackwell, 2001), 151–69; and Michael D. C. Drout, *How Tradition Works: A Meme-Based Cultural Poetics of the Anglo-Saxon Tenth Century* (Tempe: Arizona Center for Medieval and Renaissance Studies, 2006), 61–73.

dling in the Carolingian Renaissance was no doubt a determining factor as regards the development of the genre.[62] As I will comment further in this book, Symphosius's and Aldhelm's *Enigmata* became part of the literary canon in the educational program favored by the Carolingian *renovatio*.[63] It is therefore in this context that the second flourishing of riddling in the medieval period must be assessed.

The tenth-century reform in England was deeply influenced by Carolingian Benedictinism as observed in Continental monasteries, some of which, as discussed above with regard to Corbie, had developed strong links with Anglo-Saxon culture. Indeed, two of the reform leaders had first-hand experience of Continental Benedictinism. Dunstan,[64] for example, spent some time at the monastery of St Peter at Ghent (Flanders) during his exile in 956.[65] Later on, Womar, the abbot of St Peter, stayed at the Old Minster (Winchester), probably after having been invited by Dunstan.[66] In turn, Oswald received part of his education at Fleury in the 950s. Back in England, he founded the monastery of Ramsey (969), which, as Lapidge states,

---

62. For the exchange of riddles in the letters of Paul the Diacon and Peter of Pisa, two prominent scholars of Charlemagne's court, between 782 and 786, see Mary Garrison, "The Emergence of Carolingian Latin Literature and the Court of Charlemagne (780–814)," in *Carolingian Culture: Emulation and Innovation*, ed. Rosamond McKitterick (Cambridge: Cambridge University Press, 1994), 121–22. See also further on pp. 254–55.
63. See further on pp. 135–37 and 171–72, and Irvine, *The Making*, 356–57.
64. For a detailed account of the ways in which the three main monastic leaders—Dunstan, Æthelwold, and Oswald—coordinated their efforts and collaborated with King Edgar to ensure the Benedictine reform, see Simon Keynes, "Edgar, rex admirabilis," in *Edgar, King of the English 959–975: New Interpretations*, ed. Donald Scragg (Woodbridge: Boydell & Brewer, 2008), 3–59, esp. 40–48.
65. See a reference to this event in Janet M. Bately, ed., *The Anglo-Saxon Chronicle: A Collaborative Edition*, vol. 3, *MS. A* (Cambridge: Brewer, 1986), 75.
66. Michael Lapidge, John Blair, Simon Keynes, and Donald Scragg, eds., *The Wiley Blackwell Encyclopedia of Anglo-Saxon England* (Oxford: Blackwell, 1999; repr. Wiley-Blackwell, 2014), s.v. "Dunstan," by Michael Lapidge, 150–51.

"was modelled on Fleury,"⁶⁷ a prototype of Benedictinism and a most prestigious center of learning at that time.⁶⁸ It was at Oswald's behest that Abbo, a renowned scholar from Fleury, was summoned to teach at Ramsey for two years (986–987).⁶⁹ After he returned to the Continent, Abbo maintained contact with Dunstan, as evinced from a surviving letter addressed to the English archbishop and three poems composed in his honor.⁷⁰

At some point in his career, Æthelwold was also determined to travel to the Continent, probably to Fleury as well, but King Eadred did not consent to his leaving the country. The monarch subsequently commissioned him the restoration of the monastery of Abingdon (c. 954), which would soon become one of the main strongholds of English Benedictinism.⁷¹ Committed to this task, Æthelwold invited some monks from Corbie⁷² to teach the Continental practice of

---

67. Michael Lapidge, ed. and trans., *Byrhtferth of Ramsey: The Lives of St Oswald and St Ecgwine* (Oxford: Clarendon, 2009), xxi–xxii.
68. The fame of the monastery of Fleury was due mainly to the possession of St Benedict's relics, which allegedly had been brought there from Monte Cassino in the eighth century. Since then, the monastery became an important focus of pilgrimage, favoring the continuous presence of a cosmopolitan community of monks, which contributed to the flourishing of culture, particularly after its reform according to the Cluniac model (c. 930). See L. Gougaud, "Les relations de l'abbaye de Fleury-sur-Loire avec la Bretagne Armoricaine et les Îles Britanniques (Xe et XIe siècles)," *Mémoires de la Société d'histoire et d'archéologie de Bretagne* 4 (1923): 4–30.
69. See Patrick Wormald, "Æthelwold and his Continental Counterparts," in Yorke, *Bishop Æthelwold*, 23. Also, Germanus (d. 1013), who would later become abbot of Ramsey himself, spent some time in Fleury at Oswald's request, as accounted by Byrhtferth in the *Vita sancti Oswaldi* (iii.7). See Lapidge, *Byrhtferth of Ramsey*, xxi–xxii and 66–67.
70. This letter is edited in W. Stubbs, *Memorials of St Dunstan* (London, 1874), 378–80. See also 410–12 for Abbo's poems dedicated to Dunstan.
71. Alan Thacker, "Æthelwold and Abingdon," in Yorke, *Bishop Æthelwold*, 43–64.
72. See above, pp. 17 and 19. Like Fleury, Corbie was a Benedictine abbey with a large library. See Ganz, "The Merovingian Library of Corbie," and *Corbie in the Carolingian Renaissance*, 36–67. This monastic house is also

plainchant at Abingdon.[73] In addition to this, Osgar, a monk of Abingdon, went to Fleury at Æthelwold's request to study the Benedictine discipline there. He was eventually summoned to come back and took over as abbot of Abingdon on Æthelwold's appointment as bishop of Winchester in 963.[74] The *Regularis concordia* (c. 973),[75] the chief document of the English reform, was probably drafted with the assistance of monks who had been expressly brought from Fleury and Ghent.[76] The connection with Continental centers defined a notably wide area of influence since, as Frank Stenton pointed out, "Æthelwold and his associates were acquainted, not only with the customs of Fleury and Ghent, but also with those of the reformed houses of upper Lorraine, and in particular with those of Einsiedeln."[77] Decades of contact and a fluent exchange of ideas brought about the development of more

---

renowned for the experimentation with different scripts and the development of the Caroline minuscule in the eighth century. Leslie Webber Jones, "The Scriptorium at Corbie: I. The Library," *Speculum* 22 (1947): 191–204.
73. See Joseph Stevenson, ed., *Chronicon Monasterii de Abingdon, Volume 1: From the Foundation of the Monastery until the Norman Conquest* (London, 1858; repr. Cambridge: Cambridge University Press, 2012), 129. See also Lapidge's and Winterbottom's comments on this excerpt in *Wulfstan of Winchester*, lxxxiii.
74. For the reference to Osgar in the *Vita sancti Æthelwoldi* (c. 996), see Lapidge and Winterbottom, *Wulfstan of Winchester*, 26–27 (c. 14). These events must have been viewed as relevant by the author of the twelfth-century *Historia ecclesie Abbendonensis*, as he devotes a full chapter to them. See John Hudson, ed. and trans., *Historia ecclesie Abbendonensis: The History of the Church of Abingdon*, vol. 1 (Oxford: Oxford University Press, 2007), 54–55 (c. 31).
75. See Thomas Symons, ed. and trans., *Regularis Concordia* (London: Nelson, 1953).
76. Stenton, *Anglo-Saxon England*, 448. The preface to the *Regularis concordia* alludes to the presence of these Continental monks. See Symons, *Regularis concordia*, 3. Womar, abbot of Ghent and an acquaintance of Dunstan's, might have been one of the ecclesiastics who were invited to Winchester on that occasion. See above, p. 25.
77. Stenton, *Anglo-Saxon England*, 453.

efficient techniques in handwriting[78] and the so-called Winchester style, which has its most outstanding representative in the *Benedictional of Æthelwold*.[79]

The fact that the Exeter Book Riddles appear in a manuscript that was produced when such an intense cultural exchange between monastic centers of both sides of the English Channel was at its height does not seem to be haphazard.[80] In my view, the Old English Riddles not only suggest a renewed interest in this literary format but also constitute an attempt to reach the standards of the earlier stage of this genre, for the didactic potential of riddling might have been much appreciated by the reformers who strongly admired Aldhelm, Boniface, Alcuin, and their literary successors. The production of a collection of riddles in English also dovetails with the great boost that vernacular culture experienced during the reform period.[81]

---

78. Strongly influenced by Continental models, Style I Anglo-Caroline script is first attested in the early 960s. T. A. M. Bishop, *English Caroline Minuscule* (Oxford: Clarendon, 1971), 9 and 12.

79. For a detailed account of the features of this work as an illustration of the Winchester style, see Robert Deshman, *The Benedictional of Æthelwold* (Princeton, NJ: Princeton University Press, 1995), 215–50.

80. The script of the Exeter Book suggests that it was copied between 950 and 990. On paleographical grounds, Flower points out that its script resembles that of London, Lambeth Palace, MS. 149, affirming that that both manuscripts were written "early in the period 970 and 990." R. W. Chambers, *The Exeter Book of Old English Poetry*, with introductory chapters by Max Förster and Robin Flower (London: Lund & Humphries, 1933), 90. In turn, Conner claims that the script suggests a date between 950 and 970. Patrick W. Conner, *Anglo-Saxon Exeter: A Tenth-Century Cultural History* (Woodbridge: Boydell, 1993), 76. Muir, the latest editor of the Exeter Book, proposes a timespan between 965 and 975. Bernard Muir, ed., *The Exeter Anthology of Old English Poetry: An Edition of Exeter Dean and Chapter MS 3501* (Exeter: University of Exeter Press, 1994), vol. 1, 1.

81. Gretsch, for example, affirms that "the literary culture nurtured by the Benedictine reform, even in its nascent stage, based itself decisively on the pivotal role of the vernacular . . . ." Mechthild Gretsch, *The Intellectual Foundations of the English Benedictine Reform* (Cambridge: Cambridge University Press, 1999), 5. Gretsch (4–5) offers conclusive proofs that the Old English

That these riddles were also probably much valued later in the post-reform context of the eleventh century is also proved by the fact that the Exeter Book was among the donations that Bishop Leofric (d. 1072) made to the newly founded episcopal see at Exeter (1050) in order to furnish the library there.[82] Also interestingly, Cambridge, Corpus Christi College 41, containing an incomplete version of *Solomon and Saturn I* (pp. 196–98), provides further evidence of the interest in the riddling genre at Exeter. As ascertained from the Old English and Latin inscription found in this manuscript (p. 488),[83] the book was donated by Leofric to the cathedral library there.[84] It

---

glosses found in the psalter contained in London, British Library, Royal 2.B.v, as well as those offered in Aldhelm's prose *De virginitate* in Brussels, Bibliothèque Royale, 1650 are by Æthelwold and his intellectual circle. As argued by Lapidge, the translation of St Benedict's Rule and the Old English tract known as "King Edgar's Establishment of Monasteries" are most likely the work of Æthelwold. See Lapidge et al., *The Wiley Blackwell Encyclopedia*, s.v. "Æthelwold," by Michael Lapidge, 21.

82. Under the auspices of Edward the Confessor, Leofric transferred the episcopal see from Crediton to Exeter in 1050. It is generally assumed that the reference found in a catalogue of books affixed to Exeter, Cathedral Library, MS. 3501 alludes to this codex as ".i. mycel Englisc boc be gehwilcum þingum on leoðwisan geworht" (one large English book on various subjects composed in verse). This list has usually been identified with Leofric's inventory of donations to Exeter Cathedral and, apart from books, it mentions relics, ecclesiastical vestments, furniture, and other implements possibly donated by Leofric himself. However, Conner has made a case to demonstrate that this text is actually a list of the property belonging to the Church of St Peter the Apostle at Exeter. This would suggest that the Exeter Book was already at Exeter before the inventory was produced. See Conner, *Anglo-Saxon Exeter*, 15–16. For an introduction, an edition, and a translation of Leofric's list, see ibid., 226–35.

83. See Mildred Budny, *Insular, Anglo-Saxon, and Early Anglo-Norman Manuscript Art at Corpus Christi College, Cambridge: An illustrated Catalogue*, vol. 1 (Kalamazoo, MI: Medieval Institute Publications, 1997), 508–9 (no. 41). See also Conner, *Anglo-Saxon Exeter*, 3 (no. 5). The manuscript is, however, not mentioned in Leofric's inventory.

84. Conner has convincingly demonstrated that the monastery at Exeter must have been a vibrant learning community prior to Leofric's invigorating

is worth noting that the monastery of Exeter had been previously refounded with monks from Glastonbury under Abbot Sidemann's leadership and King Edgar's auspices in 968.[85] With this contextual background in mind, the Old English Riddles should therefore be viewed as a product of the revival of the enigmatic genre that probably started in the middle decades of the tenth century and would last until approximately the mid-eleventh century.

But before the Exeter Book was produced, evidence of the conspicuous interest in this literary genre in the (pre-)reform period comes from the presence of Aldhelm's *Enigmata* in two ninth-century manuscripts of Frankish origin—London, British Library, Royal 15.A.xvi and Oxford, Bodleian Library, Rawlinson C.697.[86] In the second half of the tenth century, the London codex[87] was brought to St Augustine's, Canterbury,[88] "and probably used there as a mo-

---

endeavors with the cathedral library in the mid-eleventh century. Among the extensive evidence provided by this scholar, it is remarkable that Boniface, whose essential role as propagator of Aldhelm's *Enigmata* in the Continent has already been discussed, was instructed in Exeter. Conner, *Anglo-Saxon Exeter*, 22 and 48–49. For the prominence of the Exeter monastic house, also see ibid., 21–32 and, by the same author, "Exeter's Relics, Exeter's Books," in *Essays on Anglo-Saxon and Related Themes in Memory of Dr Lynne Grundy*, ed. J. Roberts and J. Nelson (London: King's College London Medieval Studies), 117–56.

85. Conner, *Anglo-Saxon Exeter*, 29. Sidemann became abbot of the monastery at Exeter and eventually bishop of Crediton, the post later occupied by Leofric before the see was relocated to Exeter.

86. On these two codices, see N. R. Ker, *Catalogue of Manuscripts containing Anglo-Saxon* (Oxford: Clarendon, 1977; repr. 1990), 334 (no. 267) and 427 (no. 349). See also Gneuss and Lapidge, *Anglo-Saxon Manuscripts*, 395 (no. 489) and 506 (no. 661).

87. Bishop states that this manuscript was copied "perhaps in the latter half of the ninth century." T. A. M. Bishop, "Notes on Cambridge Manuscripts, Part IV: Manuscripts connected with St Augustine's Canterbury," *Transactions of the Cambridge Bibliographical Society* 2 (1957): 329.

88. Bishop (ibid., 329) has associated this manuscript to St Augustine's (Canterbury) on the basis of its presenting a supply-leaf (fol. 7), whose handwriting is similar to that of scribe D of Oxford, Bodleian Library, Auct. D.

nastic schoolbook."[89] In turn, Oxford, Rawlinson C.697, which originated in northeastern France,[90] eventually reached England at some point in the tenth century. The exact date of the arrival of the Oxford manuscript is hard to ascertain with precision, but the presence of an eight-line acrostic poem offering the name "Adalstan," which Lapidge convincingly identified as King Æthelstan (924–939),[91] on its last page (fol. 78v) suggests the codex could have been in England before the mid-tenth century.[92]

As regards the English destination of Oxford, Rawlinson C.697, the manuscript possesses a thirteenth-century *ex libris* from Bury St Edmunds (fol. 1r). However, as pointed out by Katherine O'Brien O'Keeffe, "Bury could not have housed the manuscript in the early tenth century, since it was not founded until the reign of Cnut (1016–35)."[93] T. A. M. Bishop affirmed that some of the square-minuscule cor-

---

Inf. 2.9, Part I (fols. 17–23). Rella in turn explains that this codex could be at St Augustine's by the second half of the tenth century "when additions were made in English Caroline minuscule on fols. 7, 67, 74 to 83." F. A. Rella, "Continental Manuscripts Acquired for English Centers in the Tenth and Early Eleventh Centuries: A Preliminary Checklist," *Anglia* 98 (1980): 112 (no. 20).
89. Rella, "Continental Manuscripts," 112 (no. 20).
90. For the provenance of this manuscript, see Bischoff, "Bannita: I. Syllaba, 2. Littera," 211.
91. On the possible identity of "Adalstan" as King Æthelstan and the author of the acrostic poem as John the Old Saxon, see Michael Lapidge, "Some Latin Poems as Evidence for the Reign of Athelstan," in his *Anglo-Latin Literature, 900–1066* (London: Hambledon, 1993), 60–71. In the same book, in "Schools, Learning and Literature in Tenth-Century England," 9, Lapidge also hypothesizes that Oxford, Rawlinson C. 697 "may have been brought to England by John himself."
92. For this, see Katherine O'Brien O'Keeffe, "The Text of Aldhelm's *Enigma* no. C in Oxford, Bodleian Library, Rawlinson C. 697 and Exeter Riddle 40," *ASE* 14 (1985): 67. Lapidge is similarly of the opinion that this manuscript "was in England by the mid-tenth century at the latest (perhaps somewhat earlier), as is revealed by some annotations in an Anglo-Caroline hand of s. X^{med} as well as by some Old English glosses to the Aldhelm's texts." See his "Some Latin Poems," 60.
93. O'Brien O'Keeffe, "The Text of Aldhelm's *Enigma* no. C," 67.

rections found in Oxford, Rawlinson C.697 resemble those produced by the second scribe of mid-tenth century London, British Library, Cotton Cleopatra A.iii, a codex containing three glossaries that have been ascribed to the scriptorium at St Augustine's, Canterbury.[94] O'Brien O'Keeffe corroborated Bishop's inference and added that many of the annotations in the Oxford manuscript are also similar to those found in London, Royal 12.C.xxiii and Cambridge, Gg.5.35, concluding that the Rawlinson codex "came into contact with the exemplar of the two eleventh-century English manuscripts."[95] Furthermore, the fact that some of the black-ink corrections offered by the Bodleian book have been done by a scribe, usually referred to as Hand D and generally identified as Dunstan,[96] is further proof of the connection of this manuscript with the Canterbury milieu.

In addition to London, Royal 15.A.xvi and Oxford, Rawlinson C.697, a third Frankish book containing an incomplete version of the *Enigmata* of Symphosius is present in London, British Library, Royal 15.B.xix.[97] This composite manuscript contains two codices

---

94. T. A. M. Bishop, "Notes on Cambridge Manuscripts, Part V: Manuscripts connected with St Augustine's Canterbury, Continued," *Transactions of the Cambridge Bibliographical Society* 3 (1959): 93. For further information on London, Cotton Cleopatra A.iii, see Ker, *Catalogue*, 180–82 (no. 143). Apart from sharing a scribe with the latter manuscript, Rawlinson, C.697 "contains numerous Canterbury hands," as pointed out by Philip G. Rusche, "Isidore's *Etymologiae* and the Canterbury Aldhelm Scholia," *JEGP* 104 (2005): 445.
95. O'Brien O'Keeffe, "The Text of Aldhelm's *Enigma* no. C," 67.
96. See T. A. M. Bishop, "An Early Example of Insular Caroline," *Transactions of the Cambridge Bibliographical Society* 4 (1968): 399, and *English Caroline Minuscule*, 2 (no. 3). Also, see O'Brien O'Keeffe, "The Text of Aldhelm's *Enigma* no. C," 66–67, and Gretsch, *The Intellectual Foundations*, 350–51. For the list of manuscripts that may arguably contain annotations and corrections by Dunstan, see Lapidge, "Schools, Learning and Literature," 27 (n. 82).
97. On this manuscript, see Gneuss and Lapidge, *Anglo-Saxon Manuscripts*, 396–98 (nos. 491–93). See also G. F. Warner and J. P. Gilson, *Catalogue of Western Manuscripts in the Old Royal and King's Collection*, vol. 2 (London:

which were copied at the Abbey of St Remi at Rheims, a place with well-known Anglo-Saxon connections.[98] Like the first (fols. 36–78), the second codex from London, Royal 15.B.xix (fols. 79–199) might have been brought to England by the mid-tenth century although evidence of this has not yet been provided.[99] Apart from Symphosius's fragmentary collection (fols. 79r-82r), this second Rheims manuscript offers a version of the *Liber monstrorum* (fols. 103v-105v),[100] a catalogue of wondrous creatures, which enjoyed a wide circulation in the Middle Ages. Suspected to be of Anglo-Saxon authorship,[101] the work shows remarkable parallels with Aldhelm's and Eusebius's riddles.[102] As convincingly demonstrated by Patrizia

---

British Museum, 1921), 159. For the presence of Symphosius's collection in this codex, see further on pp. 135–36.

98. The Anglo-Saxon ties with Rheims are already attested in King Alfred's period. See M. B. Parkes, "The Palaeography of the Parker Manuscript of the Chronicle, Laws and Sedulius, and Historiography at Winchester in the late ninth and tenth Centuries," *ASE* 5 (1976): 149–71, esp. 164–66. The relations with Rheims continued in the reform period. For example, Radbod of Rheims was a tutor of Edith, King Edgar's daughter. See Douglas Dales, *Dunstan: Saint and Statesman* (Cambridge: Lutterworth Press, 1988), 80 and 143.

99. Codoñer Merino provides a detailed description of these two Frankish codices, which she designates as B1 and B2. See Carmen Codoñer Merino, "Un manuscrito escolar del siglo IX: Royal 15. B.XIX," *Segno e testo: International Journal on Manuscripts and Text Transmission* 1 (2003): 232 and 240. As stated by Rella, the first manuscript (Codoñer Merino's B1) may have reached England "by s. X med. when it acquired added matter in early Insular-Caroline minuscule . . . ." Rella, "Continental Manuscripts," 113 (no. 21).

100. For an edition of the *Liber monstrorum*, see Andy Orchard, ed., *Pride and Prodigies. Studies in the Monsters of the Beowulf-Manuscript* (Cambridge: Brewer, 1995), 254–317.

101. Lapidge hypothesized that the *Liber monstrorum* may be the work of a student, or a colleague from Aldhelm's Malmesbury intellectual circle. For this, see Michael Lapidge, "*Beowulf*, Aldhelm, the *Liber monstrorum* and Wessex," in his *Anglo-Latin Literature, 600–899*, (London: Hambledon, 1996) 271–312.

102. Patrizia Lendinara, *Anglo-Saxon Glosses and Glossaries* (Aldershot: Ashgate, 1999), 120–23.

Lendinara, the *Liber monstrorum* served as a source for the *Corpus Glossary*, which is preserved in Cambridge, Corpus Christi College 144 (c. 800), containing additions which were possibly produced at St Augustine's, Canterbury.[103] Like the *Liber monstrorum*, Symphosius's collection also denotes an interest in teratological subjects,[104] a fact that may explain the joint occurrence of these two works in London, Royal 15.B.xix.

All in all, these three codices were imported from Francia, coinciding either with the pre-reform period,[105] when the arrival of Oxford, Rawlinson C.697 took place, or with the early stages of the Benedictine revival of learning, when London, Royal 15.A.xvi and, arguably, Royal 15.B.xix (fols. 79–199) were brought. The incorporation of these three Frankish manuscripts into English libraries, in particular Canterbury, no doubt paved the way for the production of the Exeter Book in some southwest scriptorium[106]

---

103. On this codex and its contents, see Rudny, *Insular*, 95–108 (no. 4). The manuscript actually preserves two glossaries, the second of which contains some glosses, which, as explained by Lendinara, "show an extremely close verbal correspondence with the *Liber monstrorum*, unparalleled in other works." See Lendinara, *Anglo-Saxon Glosses*, 137. The second glossary (fols. 4r–64v), in which the glosses discussed by Lendinara are found, is edited in W. M. Lindsay, *The Corpus Glossary* (Cambridge: Cambridge University Press, 1921).

104. Note, for example, that the gouty soldier of Symphosius's *Enigma* 94 is described as a six-footed creature (2), and in the *Liber monstrorum* (i.4) there is a reference to exceedingly bellicose men ("bellicosissimos") who have six fingers in their hands and six toes in their feet. Orchard, *Pride and Prodigies*, 260–61. See Lendinara's comments on this passage in her *Anglo-Saxon Glosses*, 125–26.

105. It is well known that King Æthelstan imported several books from the Continent, three of which are known to have been donated to the two main monastic houses at Canterbury. Notably, London, British Library, Cotton Tiberius A.ii and London, Lambeth Palace 1370 were given to Christ Church; in turn, London, British Library, Royal I.A.XVIII was donated to St Augustine's. See Simon D. Keynes "King Æthelstan's Books," in Lapidge and Gneuss, *Learning and Literature in Anglo-Saxon England*, 147–59 and 165–70.

106. On this manuscript, see Ker, *Catalogue*, 153 (no. 116); Gneuss and Lapidge,

with links to the metropolitan see[107] in the second half of the tenth century.

The two main compendia of riddle collections have been associated by scholars with two well-known Canterbury centers that were remarkably productive during the reform period. Notably, London, Royal 12.C.xxiii (either from the late tenth or the beginning of the eleventh century)[108] displays paleographical caracteristics that connect it to the handwriting observed in three other manuscripts from Christ Church.[109] As for Cambridge, Gg.5.35 (mid-eleventh century),[110] this manuscript was produced at the scriptorium of St

---

Anglo-Saxon Manuscripts, 201-03 (no. 257). The exact provenance of the Exeter Book is unknown. Different hypotheses have been provided, and most of them agree that the manuscript originated in a monastic house in southwest England. In *Anglo-Saxon Exeter*, Conner proposed Exeter, an idea that has been recently supported by Michael D. C. Drout, *Tradition and Influence in Anglo-Saxon Literature: An Evolutionary, Cognitivist Approach* (New York: Palgrave, 2013), 136. Gameson, by contrast, considered that the origin of the Exeter Book should be Glastonbury or, alternatively, Crediton. Richard Gameson, "The Origin of the Exeter Book of Old English Poetry," *ASE* 25 (1996): 179. Butler similarly conjectured that the manuscript could be from Glastonbury. Robert M. Butler, "Glastonbury and the Early History of the Exeter Book," in *Old English Literature in its Manuscript Context*, ed. Joyce Tally Lionarons (Morgantown: West Virginia University Press, 2004), 173–215. The Exeter provenance has however been strongly backed up by the finding of two fragments of the West-Saxon Gospels in two manuscript strips (c. 960–80), which probably originated in Exeter and whose text was copied by the same scribe who wrote the Exeter Book, as inferred paleographically by Peter Stokes.

107. As Gameson concludes in "The Origin of the Exeter Book," 179, the Exeter Book must have been produced in a monastic house "which had connections with Canterbury."

108. On this manuscript, see Ker, *Catalogue*, 331–32 (no. 263); Gneuss and Lapidge, *Anglo-Saxon Manuscripts*, 388–89 (no. 478).

109. Notably, with Cambridge, University Library, Ff.4.43, London, British Library, Cotton Otho E.i, and Harley 1117, Part I. See T. A. M. Bishop, "Notes on Cambridge Manuscripts, Part VII: The Early Minuscule of Christ Church Canterbury," *Transactions of the Cambridge Bibliographical Society* 3 (1963): 421–22.

110. Cambridge, Gg.5.35 constitutes a compendium of riddle collections, comprising those of Symphosius, Aldhelm, Eusebius, Tatwine,

Augustine.[111] On the other hand, the last part of London, Royal 15.B.XIX (fols. 200–05),[112] containing the *Enigmata* of Symphosius and Boniface, is a further codex of English origin. It was produced at Salisbury Cathedral in the last quarter of the eleventh century.[113]

In light of this discussion, the three Frankish codices—Oxford, Rawlinson C.697, London, Royal 15.A.xvi and 15.B.xix (fols. 79–199)— together with the other four English manuscripts—the Exeter Book, Cambridge, Gg.5.35, London, Royal 12.C.xxiii and 15.B.xix (fols. 200–05)—all provide a substantial corpus of riddles that were housed in Anglo-Saxon libraries from the early tenth to the late eleventh century. Importantly, four of these codices have Canterbury links,[114] a fact that

---

and Boniface, among others. In turn, London, Royal 12.C.xxiii supplies all these collections with only the exception of Boniface's *Enigmata*. The Cambridge codex, which has convincingly been identified as a schoolbook, can afford an interesting insight into the possible pedagogic uses of medieval riddle collections. See A. G. Rigg and G. R. Wieland, "A Canterbury Classbook of the Mid-Eleventh Century (the 'Cambridge Songs' manuscript)," *ASE* 4 (1975): 113–30. Also, see Ker, *Catalogue*, 21–22 (no. 16); and Gneuss and Lapidge, *Anglo-Saxon Manuscripts*, 25–28 (no. 12).

111. Rigg and Wieland, "A Canterbury Classbook," 118–19. For the relations between the two Canterbury monastic houses, see Bishop, *English Caroline Minuscule*, xx, and Nicholas Brooks, *The Early History of the Church of Canterbury: Christ Church from 597 to 1066* (Leicester: Leicester University Press, 1984), 261–64. On the Cambridge codex, see Rigg and Wieland, "A Canterbury Classbook," and Jan M. Ziolkowski, ed. and trans., *The Cambridge Songs (Carmina Cantabrigensia)* (New York: Garland, 1994), xvii–xxxix. For further information on Cambridge, Gg.5.35 and London, Royal 12.C.xxiii, see Ehwald, *Aldhelmi opera*, 50–52, and O'Brien O'Keeffe, "The Text of Aldhelm's *Enigma* no. C," esp. 64–66.

112. Codoñer Merino conveniently refers to this last part of London, Royal 15.B.xix as C in "Un manuscrito escolar del siglo IX."

113. Ker considers this part of the manuscript as a continuation of Salisbury, Cathedral Library, MS. 115, since "A pattern of wormholes is common to the Royal and the last leaf of 115." See N. R. Ker, "The Beginnings of Salisbury Cathedral Library," in *Medieval Learning and Literature: Essays presented to R. W. Hunt*, ed. J. J. G. Alexander and M. T. Gibson (Oxford: Oxford University Press, 1976), 25.

114. O'Brien O'Keeffe, "The Text of Aldhelm's *Enigma* no. C," 68.

confidently suggests that the riddling genre was highly regarded there, particularly at St Augustine's. This assumption is of particular significance, since it reveals that riddle collections had the endorsement of the highest ecclesiastical authority in Anglo-Saxon England. In this sense, we must not forget that the two major English anthologies of riddles—London, Royal 12.C.xxiii and Cambridge, Gg.5.35—uniquely provide the *Enigmata* of Tatwine, who was Archbishop of Canterbury from 731 to 734. It comes as no surprise to us that the collection produced by a "local" author might have received special attention there.[115]

The tradition of Canterbury as a prestigious learning center from the time of St Augustine's mission (597) is unquestionable. Theodore (602–690) and Hadrian (d. 710) established their reputed school there.[116] As reported by Bede, this institution attracted a large number of students,[117] most famously Aldhelm.[118] The Canterbury school continued to thrive under Tatwine's direction in the early 730s. The long archiepiscopate of Oda (941–958), an enthusiastic promoter of learning with connections with Fleury,[119] contributed to the high intellectual standards of the school in the middle decades of the tenth century.[120] It was probably in Oda's days that the arrival in Canterbury of Frankish manuscripts might have started to take place.[121]

---

115. Tatwine was actually a native of Breedon on the Hill (Leicestershire). See further on p. 221.
116. See Michael Lapidge, "The School of Theodore and Hadrian," in his *Anglo-Latin Literature, 600–899*, 141–68.
117. Bede, *Historia ecclesiastica* (IV.2). For this passage, see Bertram Colgrave and R. A. B. Mynors, *Bede's Ecclesiastical History of the English People* (Oxford: Clarendon Press, 1969), 332–33.
118. See further on pp. 164–65.
119. As recorded by William of Malmesbury, Oda became a monk at Fleury. See *William of Malmesbury, Gesta pontificum anglorum, Vol. 1: Text and Translation*, Michael Winterbottom and Rodney M. Thomson (Oxford: Clarendon Press, 2007), 27 (I.14.6).
120. On Oda, see Lapidge, "Schools, Learning and Literature," 29.
121. The intellectual flourishing of the Canterbury community during Oda's time was also probably due to the presence of the Frankish scholar Frithegod (fl. c. 950–c. 958), the author of the *Breviloquium vitae Wilfridi*

Dunstan's archiepiscopate covered the time between 959 and 988, an even more extensive and fruitful period than that of Oda's, when the reform reached its high point.[122] An outstanding leader of the Benedictine movement, Dunstan brought to Canterbury the cultural baggage that he had hoarded, together with Æthelwold, in an intense period of learning during the 940s and 950s at Glastonbury, while he served as abbot there.[123] Thanks to Mechthild Gretsch's valuable investigations, we know that Aldhelm's works were a top priority during this seminal period of study.[124] The influence of Dunstan was perceived in Canterbury well after his death. With the exception of Ælfric (d. 1005)—who had been instructed at Abingdon under Æthelwold and Osgar—three successors of Dunstan at the episcopal see had previously been monks at Glastonbury— notably Æthelgar (d. 990), Sigeric (d. 994), and Ælfheah (d. 1012).[125] In this light, it is not surprising to see that the production of London, Royal 12.C.xxiii at Christ Church, Canterbury, falls pre-

---

and the tutor of Oda's nephew Oswald. See *ODNB*, s.v. "Frithegod," by Michael Lapidge. Also by the same author, see "A Frankish Scholar in Tenth-Century England: Frithegod of Canterbury/Fredegaud of Brioude," in his *Anglo-Latin Literature, 900–1066*, 157–81.

122. As pointed out by Dales, "From the two Canterbury houses of Christ Church and St Augustine's there issued a stream of books which has its beginning in the closing years of Dunstan's archiepiscopate." Dales, *Dunstan*, 140. See ibid., 58–61, for an account of Dunstan's activities in the cathedral of Christ Church and the monastery of St Augustine.

123. This is reported in the *Vita sancti Æthelwoldi*; see Lapidge and Winterbottom, *Wulfstan of Winchester*, 14–17 (c. 9). Also, see Gretsch, *The Intellectual Foundations*, 5.

124. As concluded by Gretsch, "it was Æthelwold and Dunstan who were responsible for placing the study of Aldhelm in a central position in the late Anglo-Saxon curriculum . . . ." *The Intellectual Foundations*, 426.

125. See the list of archbishops in Lapidge et al., *The Wiley Blackwell Encyclopedia*, 544. A former student of Æthelwold, Æthelgar had also been a monk at Abingdon and later abbot of the New Minster (964–88). See *ODNB*, s.v. "Æthelgar," by William Hunt (rev. Mary Frances Smith). As noted by Yorke, *Bishop Æthelwold*, 10, Glastonbury is the monastic house that produced "the greatest number of post-reformation bishops."

cisely in the late tenth or early eleventh century, when the continuity of Dunstan's reformist endeavors were maintained by a succession of Glastonbury-educated archbishops. By the same token, the production of Cambridge, Gg.5.35, the other major compendium of riddles, was probably coeval with the issuing of the copies of the *Regularis concordia* at Christ Church in the mid-eleventh century.[126] In addition to this, we must not forget that it was also around 1050 that Leofric donated the Exeter Book to the monastic house at Exeter, a community that had been refounded in 968 with a colony of Glastonbury monks.

The relevance of riddling at Canterbury must therefore be assessed in relation to the school curriculum at Glastonbury, in which riddles probably figured prominently. Evidence of this is provided by an entry in a medieval catalogue from the Glastonbury library—now Cambridge, Trinity College, R.5.33 (724), fols. 102r–3v[127]—dating from 1247–48. Among three *vitae* of St Guthlac and other hagiographic materials, the reading "enigmata multor*um*" (fol. 103v) occurs.[128] As pointed out by James P. Carley, the description "remains too vague for an obvious identification,"[129] but its closeness to the Guthlac hagiographies, two Old English versions of which jointly appear with the collection of riddles in the Exeter Book, is at best significant. Furthermore, the adjacency of the "enigmata multor*um*" entry to a certain "lib*er* p*r*onosticor*um* et de *a*nim*a*b*us* defunctor*um* *et* de ultima resurrexione"

---

126. See Lapidge et al., *The Wiley Blackwell Encyclopedia*, s.v. "Regularis Concordia," by Lucia Kornexl, 399–400. This document is extant in London, British Library, Cotton Tiberius A.iii and Cotton Faustina B.iii. On these manuscripts, see Ker, *Catalogue*, 248 (no. 187) and 196–97 (no. 155). See also Joyce Hill, "The 'Regularis Concordia' and its Latin and Old English Reflexes," *Revue Bénédictine* 101 (1991): 299–315.
127. For the edition of the catalogue, see T. W. Williams, *Somerset Medieval Libraries* (Bristol, 1877), 55–76.
128. Cited from James P. Carley, "Two Pre-Conquest Manuscripts from Glastonbury Abbey," *ASE* 16 (1987): 201. Butler also comments on this catalogue entry, which he provides as proof of the connection of riddling with the cultural context of the reform. Butler, "Glastonbury," 198–99.
129. Carley, "Two Pre-Conquest Manuscripts," 202.

(A book on prognostications, the souls of the dead and the last resurrection)¹³⁰ made Carley suspect that the reference could imply London, Royal 12.C.xxiii, which contains both Aldhelm's Riddles and Julian of Toledo's *Prognosticum futuri saeculi* (A prognostication of the future centuries). Interestingly, Julian's work co-occurs in a further entry in the same inventory (fol. 103v) as "Libri pronosticorum duo. in altero sunt enigmata sancti aldelmi. uetusti" (two books on prognostications; the riddles of old Saint Aldhelm are in the second).¹³¹ If Carley's contention is correct, the London codex could have traveled to Glastonbury some time after its production at Christ Church. With four generations of archbishops coming from Glastonbury (starting with Dunstan), the exchange of manuscripts between this monastery and the libraries of the metropolitan see seems quite natural.¹³²

The existence of at least an important compendium of riddle collections—which scholars have attempted to associate with both London, Royal 12.C.xxiii and Cambridge, Gg.5.35—is mentioned by John Leland (c. 1503–52) in the account of his visit to Glastonbury library about 1536:

> inveni librum *Ænigmaton*, quem *Tatvinus* hexametris versibus scripserat. Neque hic lectorem celabo, quod ibidem repererim libellos *Symposii, Aldhelmi & Eusebii*, qui de eadem materia scripserunt carmine non omnino improbando.¹³³

---

130. Cited from ibid., 201.
131. Ibid., 202.
132. Bishop provides a study of a group of manuscripts that present interesting interconnections and were copied by either "Glastonbury (or monks trained at Glastonbury) or St Augustine's." "Notes on Cambridge Manuscripts, Part IV," 323. Moreover, as Bishop explains (324), "In one of the chain of revivals and new foundations, promoted by the post-Cluniac movement in tenth-century England, St Augustine's was closely linked to Glastonbury, to which it may have owed part of its library."
133. Citation from A. Hall, ed., *Commentarii de scriptoribus Britannicis, auctore Joanne Lelando Londinate* (Oxford, 1709), vol. 1, 131 (c. 96). Italics are from this edition. My translation. This passage is discussed in James P. Carley's "Two Pre-Conquest Manuscripts," 202–3 and "John Leland and

[I came across a book of riddles which Tatwine had written in hexameters. Nor will I hide here from the reader that I discovered in the same place (this manuscript) the little works of Symphosius, Aldhelm, and Eusebius, who wrote on the same matter poems which are not at all to be rejected].

The manuscript alluded to in Leland's report has been identified by Carley as the book that was described in the 1247–48 Glastonbury inventory as containing both Aldhelm's Riddles and Julian's *Prognosticum*—in other words, London, Royal 12.C.xxiii.[134] Whether the Royal manuscript was that meant by Leland or simply a different anthology containing riddles, what becomes clear from his valuable testimony is that, before the monastery was dissolved in 1539, the Glastonbury library possessed a codex with the four major riddle collections. Being the cradle of the Benedictine movement and a possible original place for the Exeter Book,[135] the strong association of Glastonbury with riddling is no doubt enlightening and dovetails with the contemporary resonances that I have detected in some of the Old English Riddles.[136] In this train of thought, it is not rash to assume that the Glastonbury monks that repopulated the monastery at Exeter maintained their penchant for riddling and transferred it to their new monastic milieu.

---

the Contents of English Pre-Dissolution Libraries: Glastonbury Abbey," *Scriptorium* 40 (1986): 116–17 (no. 24).

134. Carley, "John Leland," 116–17, and "Two Pre-Conquest Manuscripts," 201–4. Additionally, see Williams, "The Riddles of Tatwine and Eusebius," 93–96, for further comments on the two Glastonbury catalogue references.

135. Butler, for example, claims that the Exeter Book could have been compiled at "the monastery of St. Mary at Glastonbury during or shortly after the abbacy of Dunstan." "Glastonbury," 215.

136. With this I do not mean to concur with Butler that Glastonbury is the original place of the Riddles or the Exeter Book. Conner has provided an overwhelming battery of proof to show that from the mid-tenth century Exeter already possessed a well-endowed scriptorium in which a poetic miscellany like the Exeter Book could well have been compiled. On this, see his *Anglo-Saxon Exeter*, esp. 33–47, and "Exeter's Relics, Exeter's Books."

The second flourishing of riddling is also manifest in the survival of riddle collections in tenth- and eleventh-century Continental manuscripts that betray in some way or another a connection with Anglo-Saxon England. A good illustration of this is Leiden, Voss. Lat. Q. 106, which contains the riddle collections of both Symphosius and Aldhelm, along with the Leiden Riddle, and was copied at St Benedict at Fleury (c. 900), a monastery with well-known traditional Anglo-Saxon ties.[137] On the other hand, Maddalena Spallone has also pointed out the occurrence of Symphosius's *Enigmata* in Rome, Biblioteca Angelica, MS. 1515, which was produced in Francia toward the end of the tenth century.[138] Interestingly, Spallone has noted that the accompanying works in this manuscript show features that are typical of the hermeneutic style[139] that characterized Anglo-Saxon literary works at that time.[140]

The presence of isolated riddles and smaller riddling groups in various manuscripts is also worth looking at in the context of this revival of riddling and in relation to the cultural background of the

---

137. Parkes, "The Manuscript of the Leiden Riddle," esp. 212–15. Apart from the presence of the Leiden Riddle, further evidence of the relationship of this manuscript with Anglo-Saxon culture is the occurrence of six glosses offering types of elves in Old English. See Bremmer and Dekker, *Manuscripts in the Low Countries*, 110, and Herbert D. Meritt, *Old English Glosses: A Collection* (New York: Modern Language Association of America, 1945), 61.
138. Maddalena Spallone, "Tradizioni insulari e letteratura scolastica: il ms. Angelicanus 1515 e gli *Aenigmata* di Simposio," *Studi Classici e Orientali* 35 (1985): 185.
139. Campbell describes hermeneutic composition as indulging in "recondite vocabulary derived from glossaries." Alistair Campbell, *The Chronicle of Æthelweard* (London: Nelson, 1962), xiv. Lapidge later defines it as "a style whose most striking feature is the ostentatious parade of unusual, often very arcane and apparently learned vocabulary." Michael Lapidge, "The Hermeneutic Style in Tenth-Century Anglo-Latin Literature," *ASE* 4 (1975): 67. For a thoroughgoing analysis of hermeneutic vocabulary in Anglo-Saxon texts, see Gretsch, *The Intellectual Foundations*, and Drout, *How Tradition Works*, esp. 187–92.
140. Spallone, "Tradizioni insulari," 196.

Benedictine reform. An Old English prose piece, which Max Förster has associated with the Lot-riddle type,[141] is found on folio 16v of London, British Library, Cotton Vitellius E.xviii (mid-eleventh century), a manuscript from Winchester.[142] The codex also contains the Vitellius Psalter, a Gallican version as was preferred in Benedictine circles with a strong Continental influence.[143] Frederick Tupper pointed out the presence of a Latin analogue to Eusebius's *Enigma* 37 (calf) and Exeter Riddle 38 (bullock) in London, British Library, Burney 59 (fol. 11v).[144] This early-eleventh-century manuscript from the Benedictine Abbey of St Benigne at Dijon also contains Alcuin's *Propositiones*.[145] Tony Perrello in turn discovered a macaronic riddle, which seems to be based on Ælfric's *Grammar* and is found in Brussels, Bibliothèque Royale, MS 1828–30 (early eleventh century), from the

---

141. For the text of this riddle, see Max Förster's "Ein altenglisches Prosa-Rätsel," *Archiv* 115 (1905): 392–93. See also Förster's discussion of its possible solution (Eva) in "Die Lösung des ae. Prosarätsels," *Archiv* 116 (1906): 367–71. A recent analysis is provided by Dieter Bitterli, "Two Old English Prose Riddles of the Eleventh Century," *Words, Words, Words: Philology and Beyond: Festschrift for Andreas Fischer on the Occasion of his 65th Birthday*, ed. Sarah Chevalier and Thomas Honegger (Tübingen: Francke, 2012), 1–11. Following Dietrich, Bitterli reads the text as two riddles. See F. Dietrich, "Die Räthsel des Exeterbuchs: Würdigung, Lösung und Herstellung," *ZfdA* 11 (1859): 489–90.
142. For the manuscript, see James L. Rosier, ed., *The Vitellius Psalter* (Ithaca, NY: Cornell University Press, 1962), esp. xv–xxv; and Ker, *Catalogue*, 298–301 (no. 224).
143. As Gretsch explains, the Gallican version of the psalter became "established only gradually in the wake of the Benedictine reform with its close contacts with Continental reformed monasteries." *The Intellectual Foundations*, 23.
144. For the text of this riddle, see Frederick Tupper, "Originals and Analogues of the Exeter Book Riddles," *MLN* 18 (1903): 99. A further parallel to this Latin piece is no. 194 of the *Collectanea*. See Bayless and Lapidge, *Collectanea*, 144–45 and 243.
145. For the contents of this codex, see *Catalogue of Manuscripts in the British Museum*, vol. 1, part II: *The Burney Manuscripts* (London: 1840), 21 (no.59).

Abbey of Anchin (near Douai).¹⁴⁶ As Perrello points out, the riddle shares with the accompanying Latin-Greek glossaries and other materials found in this codex an interest in arcane vocabulary and wordplay as typical of the hermeneutic style.¹⁴⁷

A verse Latin riddle, for which David W. Porter coined the title "Æthelwold's Bowl," occurs in a flyleaf (fol. 1r) of Antwerp, Plantin-Moretus Museum M.16.2 (formerly 47, first half of the eleventh century).¹⁴⁸ The manuscript originally formed part of London, British Library, Add. 32246.¹⁴⁹ By means of wordplay, the riddle provides the following clue: "Bis bine fiale caritatis nos uocitamur" (1) [We are called twice two cups of *caritas*].¹⁵⁰ The term *caritas* has confidently been interpreted by Porter as a playful reference to the generous allowance of beer, known as "St Æthelwold's bowl," as we learn from a reference to this in the *Chronicle of Abingdon* (thirteenth century).¹⁵¹ The key to solving the riddle, as Porter explains, thus lies in the read-

---

146. Tony Perrello, "An Undiscovered Riddle in Brussels, Bibliothèque Royale MS 1828–1830," *ELN* 43 (2005): 8–14.
147. For further information on the contents of this manuscript, see Scott Gwara, "Ælfric Bata's Manuscripts," *Revue d'histoire des textes* 27 (1997): 249 (n. 40). Also, see Ker, *Catalogue*, 7–8 (no. 9) and Gneuss and Lapidge, *Anglo-Saxon Manuscripts*, 574–75 (no. 807).
148. See David W. Porter, "Æthelwold's Bowl and *The Chronicle of Abingdon*," *NM* 97 (1996): 163–67, and "A Double Solution to the Latin Riddle in MS. Antwerp, Plantin-Moretus Museum M16.2," *ANQ* 9 (1996): 3–9. The riddle is also edited in Max Förster, "Die altenglische Glossenhandschrift Plantinus 32 (Antwerpen) und Additional 32246 (London)," *Anglia* 41 (1917): 155.
149. See Ker, *Catalogue*, 1–3 (no. 2).
150. The translation is by Porter, "A Double Solution," 3.
151. The exact phrase is "bollam sancti Athelwoldi," as found in Joseph Stevenson, ed., *Chronicon monasterii de Abindon, Volume 2: From the Norman Conquest until the Accession of Richard the First* (London, 1858; repr. Cambridge: Cambridge University Press, 2012), 279. For Porter's comments on this passage, see "Æthelwold's Bowl," 163–64. Also alluding to a special gratification of drink, the term is attested in the *Regularis concordia*. As Symons explains, in this text *caritas* "was a special Saturday indulgence." *Regularis concordia*, 23, n.2.

ing of *fiala* as a synonym of *scala*, also meaning "cup" but suggesting the idea of the scales as well. The solution is therefore *scalae* in its double semantic dimension: a pair of scales to measure food or drink and the equivalent to two full cups of alchoholic beverage that were generously permitted at the monastery, probably in an attempt to attract members of the nobility to monastic life.[152] The term *scala* appears in the Latin/English glossary contained in the Antwerp manuscript as "Fiala . [ue]l Scale . bledu"[153] and, interestingly, denotes the use of Isidore's *Etymologiae* XX.v.5, where this word occurs among other drinking vessels (*De vasis potatoriis*).[154]

In the same flyleaf in which "Æthelwold's Bowl" occurs, there are four hexameters dedicated to Edith, Ælfgifu,[155] and Æthelthryth,[156] three female saints who formed part of the newly created Benedictine pantheon. In addition, six further hexameters praising three male saints—Edward, Eustace, and Kenelm—complement the preced-

---

152. Thacker, "Æthelwold and Abingdon," in Yorke, *Bishop Æthelwold*, 56.
153. Cited from David W. Porter, *The Antwerp-London Glossaries, Volume 1: Texts and Indexes* (Toronto: Pontifical Institute of Mediaeval Studies, 2011), 62. See also Porter, "A Double Solution," 3.
154. Also, note that Isidore provides "phiale" as a glass goblet in *Etymologiae* XX.v.1.
155. Ælgifu was the mother of King Edgar (959–75), a major champion of the reform. This fact and her role as patroness of the nunnery at Shaftesbury probably contributed to her promotion to sainthood after her death (944). By the same token, Edith, a daughter of Edgar, became the patron saint of Wilton Abbey after she died (984).
156. As the daughter of King Anna of East Anglia, Æthelthryth was first married to Tondberht, ealdorman of the South Gyrwas. On the ealdorman's death, she married Ecgfrith, King of Northumbria (670–685). Despite these two marriages, she always claimed to have remained a virgin. As narrated by Bede in his *Historia ecclesiastica* (IV.20), and later by Ælfric in an Old English version of the *vita*, Æthelthryth managed to convince the king that she should be released from the marital bonds in order to take the veil. She eventually founded the monastery at Ely, becoming the first abbess. See *ODNB*, s.v. "Æthelthryth," by Alan Thacker. For the prominence of Æthelthryth in the cultural context of the reform, see Deshman, *The Benedictional of Æthelwold*, 206–7.

ing part.[157] Finally, an eight-line obituary poem dedicated to Archbishop Ælfric of Canterbury (d. 1005) precedes the Latin riddle.[158] As pointed out by N. R. Ker, "part of the body of St. Edward and a relic of St. Eustace were at Abingdon and Ælfric had been a monk there."[159] On this basis, Ker concludes that the texts contained in the Antwerp flyleaf are most likely from Abingdon.[160]

This comes as no surprise to us if we consider that before his appointment as Archbishop of Canterbury in 995, Ælfric had been a monk at Abingdon in the period of Æthelwold's and Osgar's abbacies[161] and thus formed part of the second generation of reformers.[162] In this light, the inclusion of the poems commemorating saints con-

---

157. This poem is edited in Michael Lapidge, "Æthelwold and the *Vita S. Eustachii*," in his *Anglo-Latin Literature, 900–1066*, 218. As Lapidge points out (218), "The poem is a *titulus* commemorating an altar dedicated to SS. Edward, Eustace and Kenelm." For the remainder of the materials contained in the Antwerp flyleaf, see Förster, "Die altengsliche Glossenhandschrift," 154–55. Note also the interest in royal or royally related saints in these poems, the only exception being Eustace.

158. A detailed description of the contents of the Antwerp flyleaf is found in Ker, *Catalogue*, 2–3 (no. 2).

159. Ker, *Catalogue*, 3. For the cult of St Eustace in this period, see Michael Lapidge's "Litanies of the Saints in Anglo-Saxon Manuscripts: A Preliminary List," *Scriptorium* 40 (1986): 264–77, at 66 and 120, and "Æthelwold and the *Vita S. Eustachii*," 213–23. Also interestingly, Æthelwold donated 21 books to the monastery at Peterborough. Among these books, a *Vita Eustachii* was included. On this, see ibid., 213, and Michael Lapidge, "Surviving Booklists from Anglo-Saxon England," in Lapidge and Gneuss, *Learning and Literature in Anglo-Saxon England*, 52–55.

160. See Ker, *Catalogue*, 2–3 (no. 2). For a similar opinion, see Porter, "Æthelwold's Bowl," 164.

161. Æthelwold was abbot of Abingdon c. 954–63. Osgar succeeded him in 963 and remained in that post until 984.

162. Ælfric must have been actively involved in the process of the reform. As pointed out by Simon Keynes, he endeavored to make the community at Christ Church "fully monastic." Lapidge et al., *The Wiley Blackwell Encyclopedia*, s.v. "Ælfric," 9. His prominence during this period is also suggested from the fact that B.'s *Vita sancti Dunstani* is dedicated to him. See Lapidge's "B. and the *Vita S. Dunstani*," in his *Anglo-Latin Literature, 900–1066*, 290.

nected either to Abingdon or to the reform seems to be quite logical. The elegiac poem dedicated to Archbishop Ælfric and the Latin riddle alluding to a particular monastic custom at Abingdon could have similarly been placed in the Antwerp flyleaf as a way to honor the deceased prelate. The special attention that riddling received in the Canterbury milieu has already been pointed out above.[163] In addition to this, Ælfric would have had first-hand experience at Abingdon so that he could know about the drinking prescription known there as "Æthelwold's bowl." The suggestive local references prompted by the riddle,[164] its connection to the hermeneutic style—as revealed from its use of etymological wordplay and arcane vocabulary deriving from glossaries—, and the evidence provided by the accompanying texts found in the flyleaf all add further weight to my contention that riddle composition was particularly encouraged in Benedictine monastic circles.

Apart from these isolated pieces, we should take into account a sequence of three Latin verse riddles that are found in Edinburgh, National Library of Scotland, Adv. 18.6.12 (late eleventh or early twelfth century).[165] The manuscript was produced at Thorney Abbey, which had been reformed by Æthelwold and had doubtless played an important role during the Benedictine revival.[166] The first

---

163. No texts authored by Ælfric have been preserved. However, his efforts to boost the intellectual level of the community at Christ Church have been noted by Keynes, who states that "impetus was given there to the production of manuscripts." *The Wiley Blackwell Encylopaedia*, s.v. "Ælfric," 9.
164. Ælfric was buried at Abingdon and later translated to Canterbury (c. 1023). Ibid.
165. On this manuscript, see Gneuss and Lapidge, *Anglo-Saxon Manuscripts*, 199 (no. 252). See also André Vernet, "Notice et extraits d'un manuscrit d'Edimbourg (Adv. Mss. 18.6.12, 18.7.8, 18.7.7)," *Bibliothèque de l'école de chartes* 107.1 (1948): 33–51. For a detailed account of the contents of this manuscript, see ibid., 39–47, and Michael Baldzuhn, *Schulbücher im Trivium des Mittelalters und der frühen Neuzeit*, vol. 2 (Berlin: De Gruyter, 2009), 511–14. For the three riddles, see Vernet, "Notice," 46.
166. Note, for example, that Godemann, the scribe of the *Benedictional of Æthelwold* and the author of its introductory poem, was appointed abbot of

riddle of the series, whose solution is "turtle-dove" (Latin *turtur*),[167] also occurs in London, British Library, Harley 3020, an English composite codex dating from the end of the tenth century or the beginning of the eleventh. The *turtur* distich is the first text that is extant in this manuscript's third booklet (fol. 95r), where it precedes the anonymous *Passio sanctae Iulianae*.[168] Although Canterbury and Winchester have also been proposed, it is very probable that the Harley manuscript is of Glastonbury provenance.[169]

A couple of Latin riddles on medical subjects, which are discussed by Lapidge as representative of the hermeneutic style, are extant in Cambridge, Gg.5.35 (fols. 422v-23r).[170] Also in the Cambridge miscellany (fols. 423v-25r), the *Bibliotheca magnifica* presents a dozen Latin verse riddles that deal with subjects related to the Seven Liberal Arts.[171] Interestingly, the first riddle of this sequence ("De sapientia") has some parallels with *Collectanea* no. 1 and one of the queries of the *Ioca monachorum* version found in St Gall, Cod. Sang.

Thorney by Æthelwold, although the exact date is not known. For the reference to Thorney Abbey and Godemann's abbacy in the *Vita sancti Æthelwoldi*, see Lapidge and Winterbottom, *Wulfstan of Winchester*, 40–43 (xxiv). Also see Deshman, *The Benedictional of Æthelwold*, 260 (n. 10); Keynes, "Edgar, rex admirabilis," 43, and Yorke, ed., *Bishop Æthelwold*, 3.

167. The text of this riddle is as follows: "Prima sonat quartae, respondet quinta secundae, / tertia cum sexta: nomen habebit avis" (The first sounds like the fourth and the fifth echoes the second, just as the third [echoes] the sixth: a bird has that name [my translation]). The clues therefore play on the repetition of the letters offered by Latin *turtur*. The edition is from Franz Buecheler and Alexander Riese, eds., *Anthologia latina: sive poesis latinae supplementum* (Leipzig, 1894), vol. 1.2, 220 (no. 738a).

168. Gneuss and Lapidge, *Anglo-Saxon Manuscripts*, 356 (no. 433.3). See also James P. Carley, "More Pre-Conquest Manuscripts from Glastonbury Abbey," *ASE* 23 (1994): 277.

169. Carley, "More Pre-Conquest Manuscripts," 271.

170. These are edited and discussed by Lapidge, "The Hermeneutic Style," 84–85 and 103–4.

171. These riddles are edited in Rev. Dr. [J. A.] Giles, *Anecdota Bedae, Lanfranci, et aliorum* (London, 1851), 50–53.

196.[172] Resonances of Aldhelm's and Tatwine's *Enigmata* can also be detected in this collection. A group of riddles with a spurious Bedan ascription is the so-called *Joco-seria*. These are nineteen prose queries, most of them logogriphs, whose solutions appear in the form of glosses in Cambridge, Gg.5.35 (fols. 418v-19r), the only manuscript where they have survived.[173]

An interesting triad of prose Latin riddles is found after the *Ioca monachorum* in late-ninth century St Gall, Cod. Sang. 196, which originated in the monastery of St Gall.[174] These three pieces occur under the heading "Item enigmata vulgaria" (p. 389) and offer remarkable parallels with Pseudo-Bede's *Collectanea* (nos. 18, 197 and 198) and Lorsch *Enigma* 8.[175] A product from the same scriptorium is St Gall, Stiftsbibliothek, Cod. Sang. 446 (dated between 845 and 870), a manuscript containing three prose Latin riddles (p. 1),[176] whose affinities with Lorsch *Enigmata* 5 and 7 have been pointed out.[177] Six Latin *enigmata*, which have their origin at Reichenau Abbey, are found in Karlsruhe, Badische Landesbibliothek, Aug. 205 (fol.

---

172. See ibid., 50–51, and Bayless and Lapidge, *Collectanea*, 122–23 (no. 1). See also above, p. 24 and n. 60.
173. For an edition of these texts with a brief introduction, see Tupper, "Riddles of the Bede Tradition," 565–71. As Tupper points out (566), the spurious attribution of these riddles can be explained by "the immediate precedence of the enigmas by Bede's well-known 'Versus de Die Judicii'" (fol. 416a)."
174. For these riddles, see Daly and Suchier, *Altercatio Hadriani*, 144, n. 91. For information about the manuscript, see Rolf Bergmann and Stefanie Stricker, *Katalog der althochdeutschen und altsächsischen Glossenhandschriften*, vol. 3 (Berlin: De Gruyter, 2005), 500 (no. 200).
175. For the similarities shared between the *Collectanea* queries and the St Gall Riddles, see Bayless and Lapidge, *Collectanea*, 245. On the parallel with the Lorsch *enigma* see ibid., 206, and below in this book, p. 266.
176. These riddles are edited in Ernst Dümmler, "Lateinische Rätsel," *ZfdA* 22 (1878): 421–22. As noted by Dümmler, the text of the three riddles seems to have been glued to the first page of this codex, complicating their reading (421).
177. See below, pp. 266–67.

70r/v, late tenth century). The Reichenau Riddles or *Enigmata risibilia*,[178] as they are also known, offer their solutions in an encrypted form and occur after Alcuin's *Propositiones* in the manuscript.[179]

In light of this discussion, it is not rash to assume that the two St Gall triads and the Reichenau Riddles might have an Anglo-Saxon affiliation of some kind. The connection of Insular culture with the two monastic centers in which the manuscripts containing these riddles originated is well known. St Gall was an Irish foundation as well as a typical route of passage for pilgrims coming from the British Isles.[180] Stenton has pointed out that the Anglo-Saxon links with St Gall and Reichenau reach as early as 929, when Bishop Cenwald of Worcester traveled to these centers.[181] As a result of this contact, the liturgical service of the churches of St Gall, Reichenau, and Pfäfers included prayers for King Æthelstan,[182] whose name is

---

178. An edition of these riddles is found in K. Müllenhoff and W. Scherer, *Denkmäler deutscher Poesie und Prosa aus dem VIII-XII Jahrhundert* (Berlin, 1873), 13–14. See also Robert Petsch, "Rätselstudien I. Zu den Reichenauer Rätseln," *Beiträge zur Geschichte der deutschen Sprache und Literatur* 41 (1916): 332–44.

179. They are entitled "Enigmata rkskbklkb" in the codex, that is, "Enigmata risibilia" or funny riddles. As Bitterli observes, this code of vowel substitution is also similarly used in one of the solutions of the *Propositiones*. Dieter Bitterli, *Say What I Am Called: The Old English Riddles of the Exeter Book and the Anglo-Latin Riddle Tradition* (Toronto: University of Toronto Press, 2009), 73.

180. Bernhard Bischoff, *Manuscripts and Libraries in the Age of Charlemagne*, trans. Michael Gorman (Cambridge: Cambridge University Press, 1994), 13.

181. As Stenton explains, "It is clearly significant for the history of English culture that an eminent ecclesiastic of this period should have come acquainted with a region where ... the tradition of Carolingian scholarship was strong." Stenton, *Anglo-Saxon England*, 444. For the political ties established between Anglo-Saxon England and the Carolingian empire, see Joanna Story, *Carolingian Connections: Anglo-Saxon England and Carolingian Francia, c. 750–870* (Aldershot: Ashgate, 2003).

182. Stenton, *Anglo-Saxon England*, 444. More information about Cenwald's German sojourn is found in Keynes, "King Æthelstan's Books," 198–201.

also present in the *libri vitae* produced in these places.[183] But the Anglo-Saxon influence may actually antedate Cenwald's visit, since in the case of Reichenau, grammatical treatises by Bede and Alcuin are listed in the oldest library catalogue dating from 821–822.[184] Also importantly, Nancy Porter Stork affirms that "as early as the ninth century, there were copies of Aldhelm's works at both St. Gall and Reichenau."[185] Given that riddling was particularly relevant in medieval Insular culture, it is not surprising that both the St Gall and Reichenau riddlic pieces originated in this geographical area.

The presence of riddling dialogues in manuscripts from the tenth and eleventh centuries similarly bears witness to the resurgence of the genre in Anglo-Saxon England and the Continent. Related to the *Ioca monachorum*, a work known as *Adrianus et Epictitus* is extant in multiple copies, the earliest one being Arras, Bibliothèque Municipale, 636 (tenth century).[186] The riddling-dialogue subgenre is well represented in the vernacular, with versions of *Adrianus et Epictitus* in Welsh, French, and Provençal, as well as with the Old English *Adrian* and *Ritheus*[187] and *Solomon and Saturn*, the latter in both verse and prose. To these we should add the brief piece known

---

183. See Lapidge et al., *The Wiley Blackwell Encyclopedia*, s.v. "liturgical commemoration," by Simon Keynes, 297.
184. Bischoff, *Manuscripts and Libraries*, 96–97.
185. Stork, *Through a Gloss Darkly*, 16. For example, Aldhelm's *Epistola ad Acircium* and the Riddles are extant in Karlsruhe, Badische Landesbibliothek, Aug. 85, an early-ninth-century manuscript from Reichenau. A further illustration is St Gall, Stiftsbibliothek, Cod. Sang. 242 from the late ninth or the early tenth century. A product of the St Gall scriptorium, this manuscript also contains Aldhelm's *Enigmata*.
186. An edition of this riddling dialogue is found in Suchier, *Das mittellateinische Gespräch*, 11–16, 16–19, and 30–17. Also see Stephanie Hollis and Michael Wright, *Annotated Bibliographies of Old and Middle English Literature: Old English Prose of Secular Learning*, with the assistance of Gwynneth M. D. Mills and Adrienne Pedder (Cambridge: Brewer, 1992), 54–56.
187. *Adrian and Ritheus* is preserved in London, British Library, Cotton Julius A.ii from the mid-twelfth century. Ker, *Catalogue*, 202 (no. 159). An edition of this dialogue is found in James E. Cross and Thomas D. Hill,

as *Pharaoh* in the Exeter Book, which has also been convincingly associated with riddling dialogues of this type.[188]

The verse *Solomon and Saturn I* appears in mid-tenth-century Cambridge, Corpus Christi College 422 (Part A), where it is separated from the other poetic work known as *Solomon and Saturn II* by a further fragmentary dialogue of the same name in prose. In turn, Cambridge, Corpus Christi College 41 from the mid-eleventh century provides the first 95 lines of *Solomon and Saturn I*.[189] As mentioned above,[190] this manuscript bears Leofric's donation inscription, thus implying that the book was owned by the Cathedral Library at Exeter, a monastery with Glastonbury roots. Anlezark has recently studied these Old English dialogues and has pointed out their possible association with the cultural background of Glastonbury.[191] As Anlezark explains, two passages from *Solomon and Saturn I* agree with a phrasing provided in the alphabetic *Versus* and a reading found in the final acrostic poem on King Æthelstan, the latter attributed to John the Old Saxon and uniquely preserved in Oxford, Rawlinson C.697.[192] These parallels suggest that these two works could have been used by the author of *Solomon and Saturn I* as a source for the two passages in question. As pointed out above, Oxford, Rawlinson C.697 displays some of the annotations carried out by Hand D, generally assumed to be that of Dunstan, a notion that led Anlezark to conclude

---

The Prose Solomon and Saturn and Adrian and Ritheus (Toronto: University of Toronto Press, 1982), 35–40.

188. See Joseph B. Trahern, "The 'Ioca monachorum' and the Old English 'Pharaoh,'" *ELN* 7 (1970): 165–68.

189. All these texts are edited by Anlezark, *The Old English Dialogues*, 61–95.

190. See p. 29.

191. The mid-twelfth-century Southwick Codex of the *Beowulf* manuscript—London, British Library, Cotton Vitellius A.XV—offers a prose version of this dialogue (fols. 86v–93v). This text is edited in Cross and Hill, *The Prose Solomon and Saturn*, 25–34. Anlezark, however, states that this dialogue "does not appear to have emerged from the same close circle that produced the other three texts." Anlezark, *The Old English Dialogues*, vii.

192. Anlezark, *The Old English Dialogues*, 51–55. On this poem, see above, p. 31.

that the manuscript probably "passed through the hands of the poet, as well as Dunstan's."[193] Interestingly, Anlezark has also pointed out the co-occurrence of a gloss with the lemma *Tantalus .i. diues auarus* in the *Collectanea* (no. 72)[194] and Antwerp, M.16.2,[195] the manuscript containing the riddle known as "Æthelwold's Bowl." This coincidence suggests the availability of the *Collectanea* either at Abingdon, where the Antwerp texts were copied, or maybe at Glastonbury, where Dunstan might have had the work at hand.[196] In any case, the connection of *Solomon and Saturn I* with some of the contents of Rawlinson C.697 and the co-occurrence of the same gloss in both the *Collectanea* and the Antwerp manuscript all support the assumption that riddling was particularly prominent in monastic centers that were under the sphere of influence of the Benedictine reform.

2.1.3 Early Medieval Riddling: Some Conclusions

From this comprehensive review of the riddling genre in the early Middle Ages, it is possible to draw some relevant conclusions that are worth having in mind when reading the upcoming chapters in which I analyze the structure of major verse collections in detail. To begin with, it is quite evident that the golden age of riddling approximately covered the period from the late seventh to the mid-eighth century. The collections of Aldhelm, Tatwine, and Eusebius, the anonymous Bern Riddles, the *Collectanea*, and the *Ioca monachorum* dialogues all pertain to this initial phase. To these we could add the Leiden Riddle as the only surviving vernacular piece of this period, although, as explained above, the language of the greater bulk of the Exeter Riddles

---

193. Ibid., 51. Anlezark even takes a step further from this and offers the provocative hypothesis that Dunstan may be the author of *Solomon and Saturn I* (52).
194. Bayless and Lapidge, *Collectanea*, 130–31.
195. Anlezark, *The Old English Dialogues*, 55.
196. As the *Collectanea* displays contents of Irish origin, Anlezark conjectures that it might have been in one of the books left by a pilgrim, as Glastonbury was well known as a "destination for Irish pilgrims and scholars." Ibid. 54.

suggests that these texts also derive from this early stage. It is also at this time that thanks to the Bonifacian mission, Aldhelm's *Enigmata* and, we may tentatively infer, other Insular riddle assemblages such as the *Collectanea*[197] started to circulate in the Continent, where the study of these collections and the composition of new riddles were probably encouraged in Anglo-Saxon monastic foundations.

After its heyday in the seventh and eighth centuries, riddling declined in England, just as cultural life did in general during the period of the Scandinavian invasions. However, proof of the continuing interest in this literary genre in the ninth century is Alcuin's *Disputatio, Propositiones*, and the other riddles contained in his *Carmina*, even if all these works were most likely composed abroad. In addition to this, the production of new *enigmata*, though far from the quality standards of the Symphosian and Aldhelmian models, still carried on, as illustrated with the Lorsch Riddles and the two St Gall triads. The anthologizing of the older collections of Symphosius, Aldhelm, and the Bern author in a substantial number of late-eighth and early-ninth-century compilations from the Continent similarly denotes the attention that this literary genre received during the Carolingian Renaissance. Also importantly, most of these codices containing riddles are from scriptoria such as Corbie, Fleury, Rheims, Lorsch, St Gall, and other well-known houses that were akin to Insular tradition.[198]

In the mid-tenth century, a renewed impulse toward riddling,

---

197. Note, for example, the significant resemblance of some queries from the *Collectanea*, the St Gall Riddles, and the Lorsch *Enigmata* (see above, p. 49).
198. As pointed out by Bischoff, "Carolingian humanism began with the reforms of Charlemagne and matured in the monasteries founded by Anglo-Saxons and those under their influence, centres like Fulda, Lorsch, St Gall, Reichenau, and the great French monasteries of the Carolingian era, like Corbie, Tours, Fleury and many others." Bischoff, *Manuscripts and Libraries*, 19. It is thus no coincidence that several codices containing riddles come from several monastic centers listed by Bischoff. See also Stork's survey of Continental manuscripts containing Aldhelm's *Enigmata* in *Through a Gloss Darkly*, 12–19.

which coincides with the heyday of the Benedictine movement, can be detected in England. It was probably around this time that the three Frankish manuscripts containing riddle collections—Oxford, Rawlinson C.697, London, Royal 15.A.xvi, and Royal 15.B.xix (fols. 79–199)—arrived in England to meet the scholarly demands of the ecclesiastical elite of the moment. This second phase, which extends from the middle decades of the tenth century to the late eleventh century, is also characterized by the copying of vernacular riddles, the Exeter Book collection and the *Solomon and Saturn* dialogues being the only surviving examples, however. The isolated Old English piece found in a codex from Winchester—London, Cotton Vitellius E.xviii—is similarly illustrative of vernacular riddling in this period.

The production of Latin *enigmata* continued in this second phase and was associated mainly with English Benedictine circles, as the piece known as "Æthelwold's Bowl" found in an Abingdon codex evinces. As illustrated by the bullock *enigma* found in Continental London, Burney 59 and the turtle-dove pieces offered in Edinburgh, Adv. 18.6.12 and London, Harley 3020 (both of English provenance), the renovation of older specimens also bears witness to the continuity of the genre. The Reichenau Riddles, too, suggest a revival of the genre which is mainly observed in Continental houses with Anglo-Saxon ties. However, as inferred from the scattered occurrence of these pieces and the scanty number of riddles that have come down to us from the tenth and the eleventh centuries, riddle composition was comparatively not as intense as in the preceding period. Still, the copying of the Exeter Riddles, the only vernacular collection that has come down to us, is a remarkable fact to take into account.

On the other hand, the classic collections from the golden period continued to be included in English manuscripts, as illustrated with London, Royal 12.C.xxiii, Cambridge, Gg.5.35, and London, Royal 15.B.xix (fols. 200–05). Considered as a whole, the Latin collections, the Exeter Riddles, and the sporadic pieces and small riddlic series that have survived to our days all constitute a significant corpus of riddles that can confidently be ascribed either to Continental monasteries with Anglo-Saxon affiliation or to prominent Benedictine scriptoria such as Canterbury, Glastonbury, Abingdon, Winchester, Exeter, and Thorney. In England, therefore, it is quite clear that riddling was recuperated as a literary genre in reform-oriented schools of the tenth and eleventh centuries.

2.2. Isidore and His Work in the Context of Visigothic Spain

In the following pages, I will provide a sketch of the biography and literary production of Isidore of Seville (c. 560–636), which may help us grasp the political and religious circumstances underlying the composition of his *Etymologiae*.[199] As it is generally assumed, Isidore's family migrated from Cartagena to Seville in the aftermath of the Byzantine invasion of the southeastern coast of Spain in 554. Once established in Seville, Isidore's parents died while he was still young, so his elder brother Leander probably undertook his raising, for it is known that there was a significant age difference between them. Leander himself was an extremely learned man who was in contact with the higher intellectual circles of the period. His friendship with Gregory the Great, whom he met during his stay at Constantinople before the latter became pope, is well attested through the surviving correspondence.[200]

Leander might have thus been responsible for his younger brother's education. It is usually conjectured that Isidore first studied at a

---

199. A comprehensive introduction to Isidore's life and his work in its historical context by Manuel C. Díaz y Díaz is found in José Oroz Reta and Manuel-A. Marcos Casquero, *San Isidoro de Sevilla: Etimologías*, vol. 1 (Madrid: Biblioteca de Autores Cristianos, 1993), 7–257. Also see Stephen A. Barney, et al., trans., *The Etymologies of Isidore of Seville* (Cambridge: Cambridge University Press, 2006), 3–28, and Claudia di Sciacca, *Finding the Right Words: Isidore's Synonyma in Anglo-Saxon England* (Toronto: University of Toronto Press, 2008), 3–11.

200. A thorough account of Leander's career, supported by an edition of major documentary excerpts, is found in J. Madoz, "San Leandro de Sevilla," *Estudios eclesiásticos* 56 (1981): 415–53.

monastery over which Leander held the abbacy and later at the episcopal school once his brother became bishop of Seville (c. 579). As Manuel C. Díaz y Díaz explains, Spanish episcopal schools of this period had taken over the old local Roman teaching institutions.[201] These circumstances would most likely have contributed to affording Isidore a thorough intellectual training in the Scriptures, patristic literature, and classical works by pagan writers.[202] In this sense, it is noteworthy that Gregory the Great's *Regula pastoralis* (composed c. 590), which promoted demanding standards of education among the clergy, soon reached the peninsula, probably at Leander's own instigation.[203] Leander himself had been the dedicatee of both the *Regula pastoralis* and another of Gregory's key works, the *Moralia in Job* (Morals on the Book of Job), which would later be of great influence for Isidore's *Sententiae* and *Synonyma*. These facts suggest that it is probably thanks to Leander's efforts and intellectual connections that Seville became a flourishing cultural center under his bishopric, and no doubt Isidore benefited from this.

With Leovigild's accession to the throne in 571, Arianism had gained ground.[204] Leander, who was actively engaged in the politics of the Visigothic period, played an important part in the conversion

---

201. Oroz Reta and Marcos Casquero, *San Isidoro*, vol. 1, 105.
202. For the wide-ranging bibliographical resources that Isidore might have had at hand at the Cathedral Library of Seville, see Sciacca, *Finding the Right Words*, 7–9.
203. As pointed out by Díaz y Díaz, a copy of Gregory's major work was probably at the Seville episcopal library, since Isidore effectively summarizes its contents in his *De viris illustribus* (On illustrious men, c. 27). Oroz Reta and Marcos Casquero, *San Isidoro*, vol. 1, 42 (n. 106).
204. This variant of the Christian doctrine originated in the teachings of Arius (c. 250–336?), an Alexandrian presbyter who had developed a theory that denied the equal and co-eternal condition of the three persons of the Trinity. This belief had been declared heretic at the First Council of Nicaea in 325 and was later more energetically censured in the First Council of Constantinople in 381. For further information on this, see Maurice Wiles, *Archetypal Heresy: Arianism through the Centuries* (Oxford: Clarendon Press, 1996), esp. 45–51.

from Arianism to Catholicism of the monarch's sons Hermenigild and Reccared. After having claimed rulership over the southern part of the realm, Hermenigild was exiled in Valencia and eventually murdered in Tarragona in 585. On Leovigild's death, Reccared acceded to the throne in 586. In the context of the Third Council of Toledo (589), the king and his wife publicly embraced the Catholic faith, thus starting a period of fruitful cooperation between the monarchy and the Church.[205] Reccared then undertook the dismantling of the Arian Church by applying political measures directed at producing a peaceful and effective transition to the Catholic system. He thus allowed Arian bishops to maintain their posts on condition that they converted to Catholicism. The king also ordered the burning of Arian books, but no violent enforcement of dissidents during this period has been recorded.

This was the political and religious atmosphere in which Isidore took over as bishop of Seville on Leander's death (c. 600).[206] Like his brother and predecessor, Isidore equally became deeply involved in contemporary politics. After Reccared's death in 601, Isidore continued his close relationship to the monarchy, as evinced by his frequent collaboration with the kings reigning during this period. He had an especially tight connection with King Sisebut (612–621), who had a remarkable interest in learning. Isidore dedicated *De natura*

---

205. A contemporary account of major events connected to this period appears in John of Biclaro's *Chronicle* (finished c. 590). For an edition of this work, see J. Campos Ruiz, *Juan de Bíclaro, Obispo de Gerona: su Vida y su Obra* (Madrid: CSIC, 1960). A passage from this *Chronicle* recording King Reccared's conversion is cited and commented upon by Díaz y Díaz in Oroz Reta and Marcos Casquero, *San Isidoro*, vol. 1, 25–26.

206. As Díaz y Díaz explains, Isidore's accession to the episcopal see right after his brother's death may have been due to the fact that they belonged to what is known as an "episcopal family." This term is commonly used to refer to families, frequently wealthy and of noble stock, who could provide various members for different ecclesiastical positions. This might well have been the case, for Isidore's brother Fulgentius was made Bishop of Écija and his sister Florentina joined a nunnery. For this, see Oroz Reta and Marcos Casquero, *San Isidoro*, vol. 1, 102.

rerum to this king, who in turn composed a poem on lunar eclipses as a token of gratitude for the bishop. More importantly for the purpose of this study, Sisebut was later the dedicatee of a first version of the *Etymologiae*.

Isidore exerted a great influence not only in the political arena but also in the religious field. Holding a high position in the ecclesiastical hierarchy for years, his authority was crucial as regards his participation in two important Church assemblies of this period, notably the Second Council of Seville (619) and the Fourth Council of Toledo (633), over which he presided.[207] In the council at Seville, significant political measures were adopted to control the Arian heresy. Later, at Toledo, the basic guidelines for the government of the Catholic Church in Spain were established. Among the accomplishments of this synod stands out a decree dictating the bishops' duty to create schools and maintain them at the sees of which they were in charge.

Isidore's prolific production is in line with his continuous concern with improving the educational system in Visigothic Spain. As a reflection of his own profession, *De ecclesiasticis officiis* (On the ecclesiastic professions, composed c. 610–615) gave Isidore the opportunity to offer his own view on the situation of the clergy in Spain.[208] In consonance with his pastoral duties, Isidore designed a rule for the monks of a community close to Seville (c. 615–618), thus contributing to the development of monasticism in Spain.[209] He also undertook the composition of a number of treatises intended to fight heresy or any other deflection from the orthodoxy of the Catholic faith. An illustration of this endeavor is *De fide*

---

207. For information about the Church councils held during this period, see José Vives, *Concilios visigóticos e hispanorromanos* (Barcelona: CSIC, 1963).
208. For an edition of this work with an introduction in English, see Christopher M. Lawson, *Sancti Isidori Episcopi Hispalensis: De Ecclesiasticis Officiis, CCSL*, vol. 113 (Turnhout: Brepols, 1989).
209. An edition with a Spanish translation of this Rule is found in J. Campos Ruiz, *Reglas monásticas de la España visigoda. Santos padres españoles* (Madrid: Biblioteca de Autores Cristianos, 1971), vol. 2, 90–125.

catholica contra Iudaeos (On the Catholic faith against the Jews).[210] It is assumed that Isidore's own discrepancies with King Sisebut's harsh policy against the Jews may have motivated the writing of this work. In it the bishop takes a different stand by opposing force measures and appealing instead to logical reasoning based on a thorough knowledge of the Scriptures as a key method of achieving conversions.

Probably grounded on his own vital experience, Isidore's personal desire to improve the education of his fellow countrymen was no doubt the driving force behind several of his works. This may be the case for the *Institutionum disciplinae* (On the disciplines of instruction) a treatise for the education of a nobleman,[211] and *De viris illustribus*, the latter providing the biographies of illustrious men, including that of his brother Leander, as models of Christian conduct and virtue.[212] Isidore also composed historical works such as the *Chronicon*, which records the whole period from Creation to Sisebut's time, and scientific treatises such as his *De natura rerum* (On the nature of things), which was possibly issued at the beginning of 613.[213] In the latter, Isidore shows a concern with establishing, so to speak, the "scientific" causes of natural phenomena in an attempt to rule out ongoing popular and superstitious beliefs related to this subject.

One of the greatest preoccupations in Isidore's works was grammar, in particular the mastery of language. As noted by Claudia di

---

210. A recent study of this work is found in Eva Castro Caridad and Francisco Peña Fernández, *Isidoro de Sevilla: sobre la fe católica contra los judíos* (Sevilla: Universidad de Sevilla, 2012).

211. This work is edited by Paul Pascal, "'The Institutionum Disciplinae' of Isidore of Seville," *Traditio* 13 (1957): 425–31.

212. A critical edition of this work is Carmen Codoñer Merino, ed., *El "De viris illustribus" de Isidoro de Sevilla* (Salamanca: Universidad de Salamanca, 1964). A reprint is found in Valeriano Yarza Urquiola and Carmen Codoñer Merino, eds., *Ildefonsi Toletani episcopi De virginitate Sanctae Mariae, De cognitione baptismi, De itinere deserti, De viris illustribus, CCSL*, vol. 114A (Turnhout: Brepols, 2007).

213. An edition of this work is Jacques Fontaine, *Isidore de Séville: Traité de la nature* (Bordeaux: Féret et Fils, 1960).

Sciacca, "Even in a highly romanized area such as Spain, by the late sixth century proficiency in Latin had noticeably deteriorated, a fact which would later become a matter of concern for Isidore himself."[214] Probably as a consequence of Isidore's awareness of this situation, he composed the *De differentiis* (c. 598)[215] and the *Synonyma* (c. 595–631),[216] two treatises that basically aim at endowing readers with advanced linguistic competence by having them pay attention to the exact meaning of a word. As explained by Sciacca, with these works Isidore inaugurated a successful pedagogic formula by applying the concepts of *differentia, analogia, glossa*, and *etymologia*[217] from classical grammar and combining them with exegetical interpretation, philosophy, and pagan lore.[218]

Isidore's great concern with raising the standards of education in Spain is no doubt best reflected in the *Etymologiae* (c. 615),[219] a

---

214. Sciacca, *Finding the Right Words*, 7.
215. As explained by Sciacca, there are actually two works with that title: *De differentiis uerborum* (On differences in words) and *De differentiis rerum* (On differences in things). An edition of the first is Carmen Codoñer Merino, *Differentiae de Isidoro de Sevilla, Libro I* (Paris: Belles Lettres, 1992) and the second is edited by María Adelaida Andrés Sanz, *Isidori episcopi Hispalensis Liber differentiarum (II), CCSL*, vol. 111A (Turnhout: Brepols, 2006). See also Sciacca, *Finding the Right Words*, 193 (n. 140).
216. For this text, see Jacques Elfassi, ed., *Isidori Hispalensis Episcopi, Synonyma, CCSL*, vol. 111B (Turnhout: Brepols, 2009). For its dating, see ibid., xvi. Also see Sciacca, *Finding the Right Words*, 16–20.
217. Sciacca, *Finding the Right Words*, 12–13. For further information on these grammatical categories, see Irvine, *The Making*, 221–22.
218. Lendinara affirms that "Isidore's *Etymologiae* were not only a source of vocabulary: they also exerted a more subtle influence, helping to fashion a mode of thought or confidence in a set of equivalents, and to connect inseparably some names and their interpretations, and couples or even strings of words." Lendinara, *Anglo-Saxon Glosses*, 40.
219. As Sisebut is the dedicatee of the *Etymologiae*, his death (621) has generally been considered a *terminus ante quem* for the compilation of the encyclopedia. According to Díaz y Díaz, Isidore took up the composition of the *Etymologiae* around the year 615. Oroz Reta and Marcos Casquero, *San Isidoro*, vol. 1, 163 and 172–74. Also, see Barney et al., *The Etymologies*, 9 and 10.

massive treatise that evidently shares with the *De differentiis* and the *Synonyma* the notable linguistic focus and the use of the same effective methodology.[220] The *Etymologiae*, which were surely subject to several revisions carried out by Isidore himself, is however unfinished in its current state, since the author died in 636 before its full accomplishment. A milestone of European medieval encyclopedism,[221] the *Etymologiae* were surely designed as a vehicle for transmitting the contemporary official stand of the Catholic Church. In an attempt to achieve this goal, Isidore sought to produce a compendium of the knowledge available at that time by means of the etymological method that he consistently applied throughout his treatise.[222]

---

220. Actually, the *De differentiis* and the *Synonyma* have been traditionally considered to be the precursors of the *Etymologiae*. Also, the three works are thought to form a sort of "linguistic trio." For this, see Sciacca, *Finding the Right Words*, 14.

221. The origins of the medieval encyclopedic genre can be traced back to the Roman period, when the first treatises were produced. Of the vast production taking place in this period, a lost treatise entitled *Disciplinarum* (On the Disciplines) by Marcus Terentius Varro (116–27 BCE) and the *Naturalis historia* by Pliny the Elder (23–79 CE) are known to have exerted a powerful influence on later medieval encyclopedias. For the pre-Isidorean encyclopedic tradition, see Barney et al., *The Etymologies*, 10–13. For Isidore's contribution to the development of the encyclopedic genre from the Roman models, see Jacques Fontaine, "Isidore de Séville et la mutation de l'encyclopédisme antique," *Cahiers d'histoire mondiale* 9 (1966): 519–38. For the influence of Christianity on the development of encyclopedias in the early Middle Ages, see F. H. Whitman, *Old English Riddles* (Ottawa: Canadian Federation for the Humanities, 1982), 62. Also see Michael W. Twomey's "Medieval Encyclopedias," in R. E. Kaske, *Medieval Christian Literary Imagery: A Guide to Interpretation* (Toronto: University of Toronto Press, 1988), 182–215.

222. As pointed out by Fontaine and Sciacca, Isidore's didactic method was not new, as it was in fact grounded on the classical teaching of grammar, most notably on Varro's *De lingua latina*, which strongly influenced Isidore's perception. Sciacca, *Finding the Right Words*, 12–13, and Jacques Fontaine, "Isidorus Varro Christianus?," in *Bivium, Homenaje a M.C. Díaz y Díaz*, ed. S. Álvarez (Madrid: Gredos, 1983), 89–106.

2.3. The Success and Influence of Isidore's Etymologiae

Isidore describes his own pedagogic practice in his definition of etymology, the key idea on which it was based: "Etymologia est origo vocabulorum,[223] cum vis verbi vel nominis per interpretationem colligitur" (I.xxix.1) [Etymology is the origin of words, for the meaning (literally, the strength, the power) of a term or a noun is deduced through its interpretation].[224] He then exemplifies this concept with the term *flumen* as deriving from Latin *fluendo*, flowing. Isidore further expounds on the benefits of his own pedagogic method, while acknowledging its limitations:

> Omnis enim rei inspectio etymologia cognita planior est. Non autem omnia nomina a veteribus secundum naturam inposita sunt, sed quaedam et secundum placitum, sicut et nos servis et possessionibus interdum secundum quod placet nostrae voluntati nomina damus. Hinc est quod omnium nominum etymologiae non reperiuntur, quia quaedam non secundum qualitatem, qua genita sunt, sed iuxta arbitrium humanae voluntatis vocabula acceperunt. (I.xxix.2–3)

---

223. The Greek term ἔτυμον, meaning "true sense," is thus roughly equivalent to Latin *origo*; hence, the alternative title of the *Etymologiae as Origines*. For the debate on the appropriateness of the title of the *Etymologiae*, see Carmen Codoñer Merino, "*Origines o Etymologiae*," in *Thesauramata philologica Iosepho oblata. II. Graeca-latina*, eds. M. R. Herrera, S. García Jalón, and Manuel A. Marcos Casquero (Salamanca: Universidad Pontificia de Salamanca, 1994), 511–27; and Jacques Fontaine, *Isidore de Séville: genèse et originalité de la culture hispanique au temps des Wisigoths* (Turnhout: Brepols, 2000), 175 and 285.
224. The edition for the passages from Isidore's *Etymologiae* is Oroz Reta and Marcos Casquero, *San Isidoro*, vols. 1 and 2, which improves and revises W. M. Lindsay, *Isidori Hispalensis Episcopi Etymologiarum sive Originum Libri XX* (Oxford: Clarendon Press, 1911). Unless indicated otherwise, the translation of all passages of the *Etymologiae* and other Latin excerpts from other works cited in this book is mine.

[In fact, the analysis of anything is more evident when its etymology is known. However, not all the names were assigned by our forefathers according to their nature but some of them were produced on a whim, just as we give names to our servants and our belongings as it pleases our will. Hence it is not possible to ascertain the etymologies of all the words, for some things received their names not from the quality with which they were born but from human free will.]

For Isidore, the chief issue was to provide an explanation of a given concept in the most accurate way possible in order not to deflect from its essential meaning. As pointed out by the editors of *The Etymologies*, "In an era when the gravest dangers to Christianity were thought to be intellectual errors, errors in understanding what one read—that is, heresies like Arianism—mastery of the language arts was the Church's best defense."[225] Accordingly, the *Etymologiae* reveal the author's desire to fight heresy and spread the Catholic dogma by promoting verbal exactness.

Isidore's interest in curbing the misinterpretation of the Scriptures, or of texts in general, is thus one of the reasons why his *Etymologiae* became a crucial work for the Anglo-Saxon Continental missions and, later, in the scenario of the reform of learning carried out in the Carolingian period. The large number of manuscripts containing Isidore's *Etymologiae* that were copied in Carolingian scriptoria attests to the great popularity that this work achieved in the context of Charlemagne's cultural *renovatio*.[226] The encyclopedia would later similarly gain prominence with the advent of the Benedictine reform in England, when the cultural revival favored an intense lexicographical scrutiny.[227]

Isidore's *Etymologiae* similarly owe their remarkable success to the

---

225. Barney et al., *The Etymologies*, 19.
226. Note, for example, the frequent occurrence of Book I of the *Etymologiae* in Irvine's list of manuscripts with grammatical materials in *The Making*, 395–404.
227. Helmut Gneuss, "The Origin of Standard Old English and Æthelwold's School at Winchester," *ASE* 1 (1972): 63–83.

fact that this work could make a great deal of information readily accessible to the public in a relatively synthesized format. This practical character of Isidore's *Etymologiae* is reflected, for example, in the following comment preceding Book XIII (*De mundo et partibus*, On the world and its parts): "In hoc vero libello quasi in quadam brevi tabella quasdam caeli causas situsque terrarum et maris spatia adnotavimus, ut in modico lector ea percurrat, et conpendiosa brevitate etymologias eorum causasque cognoscat" [In this little book (i.e., Book XIII) we have recorded as if in a brief notebook the origins of the sky, the location of the lands and the areas occupied by the ocean, so that the reader may go through them in a short while, and thanks to this compendious brevity he may learn about their etymologies and sources]. From this excerpt, we can perceive that Isidore, who was clearly aware of the utilitarian character of his encyclopedia, aimed at making an efficient reference work which could grant readers a rapid access to all sorts of information. Besides, Isidore's remark about its "condensed brevity" ("conpendiosa brevitate") suggests that Book XIII was also initially meant to function as a separate unit. Actually, this might have been the case with most of the books of the *Etymologiae*. A comprehensive grammatical handbook in itself, Book I soon circulated independently from the rest of the work. Also, Book XII very rapidly achieved an authoritative status as a treatise on zoology.

Alongside this outstanding practicality, a plethora of citations and allusions from classical and medieval canonical works are everywhere interspersed in the *Etymologiae*.[228] It is therefore quite logical that this encyclopedia would thrive in the cultural environment of the last quarter of the seventh century and the beginning of the eighth, when a great interest in classical tradition has been detected as a result of the firm impulse given by the school of Theodore and Hadrian at Canterbury.[229] Seen in this light, it may be assumed that

---

228. For this, see Barney et al., *The Etymologies*, 14–16.
229. Michael W. Herren, "The Transmission and Reception of Graeco-Roman Mythology in Anglo-Saxon England, 670-800," *ASE* 27 (1998): 87–103, esp. 102–3.

both Anglo-Saxon and Continental libraries that were not so well furnished might have found in Isidore's *Etymologiae* a worthy investment that could compensate for an originally deficient endowment. This may explain the extraordinarily early and rapid transmission of the work, since, as Díaz y Díaz points out, at the beginning of the ninth century at least one copy of the *Etymologiae* could be found in most libraries in Europe.[230]

It is possible that the *Etymologiae* had arrived in Ireland by the mid-seventh century.[231] An early testimony of the use of the *Etymologiae* is the so-called *Hisperica Famina* (The Hisperic or western utterances) dated by Herren to c. 650–660.[232] A great deal of vocabulary found in this group of poems doubtless comes from Isidore's encyclopedia or glossaries deriving from this work.[233] Isidore's *Etymologiae* eventually reached England, where Aldhelm may have been a pioneering author using it as a source for his *Enigmata*[234] in the

---

230. Oroz Reta and Marcos Casquero, *San Isidoro*, vol. 1, 210.
231. For the dissemination of the work in Ireland, see Michael W. Herren, "On the Earliest Irish Acquaintance with Isidore of Seville," in *Visigothic Spain: New Approaches*, ed. E. James (Oxford: Oxford University Press, 1980), 243–50; J. P. Carley and A. Dooley, "An Early Irish Fragment of Isidore of Seville's *Etymologiae*," *The Archaeology and History of Glastonbury Abbey, Essays in Honour of the Ninetieth Birthday of C. A. Raleigh Radford*, ed. L. Abrams and J. P. Carley (Woodbridge: Boydell, 1991), 135–61; and J. N. Hillgarth, "Ireland and Spain in the Seventh Century," *Peritia* 3 (1984): 1–16. See also Sciacca, *Finding the Right Words*, 38–39.
232. See Michael Herren, ed., *Hisperica Famina I: The A-Text* (Toronto: Pontifical Institute of Mediaeval Studies, 1974), 32–35.
233. For the notable influence of the *Etymologiae* on the peculiar vocabulary that is characteristic of the Hisperic style, see ibid., 19–22.
234. As pointed out by Herren, "Aldhelm was probably the first English writer to consult the *Etymologiae* for his own compositions, especially his *Enigmata* or 'Riddles.'" Herren, "The Transmission," 90. For the exact passages used by Aldhelm as a source for his *Enigmata*, see the notes (*Fontes*) of the *CCSL*, vol. 133, 359–540; Michael Lapidge, *The Anglo-Saxon Library* (Oxford: Oxford University Press, 2006), 181; and Nicholas Howe, "Aldhelm's *Enigmata* and Isidorean Etymology," *ASE* 14 (1985): 37–59.

late seventh century.²³⁵ Apart from this, Lapidge mentions the *Etymologiae* as one of the sources used by Aldhelm for his *Carmen rhythmicum* and also detects echoes from this encyclopedia in the *Epistola ad Acircium*.²³⁶ After Aldhelm, the other prominent Anglo-Saxon scholar who turned to the *Etymologiae* for the composition of his works was Bede.²³⁷ Notably, he used this encyclopedia in his educational works—*De ortographia* (On orthography), *De schematibus et tropis* (On the figures of speech and tropes), and *De arte metrica* (On the art of meter)—as well as in his *Historia ecclesiastica*.

There is evidence that the *Etymologiae* were known in both Anglo-Saxon England and the Continent at an early stage of its transmission history. In this sense, Lapidge draws attention to the presence of an epitome of the *Etymologiae*, in Paris, Bibliothèque Nationale, Lat. 1750 (fols. 146v-52r), a manuscript that was copied in northern France around the year 800. This epitome, for which Lapidge proposes the title *De diuersis rebus* (On diverse things),²³⁸ contains

---

235. It is feasible that Aldhelm might have learned about the *Etymologiae* through his Irish acquaintances. See Barbara Yorke, "Aldhelm's Irish and British Connections," in *Aldhelm and the See of Sherborne: Essays to celebrate the Founding of the Bishopric*, ed. Katherine Barker and Nicholas P. Brooks (Oxford: Oxbow Books, 2009), 164–80. It has also been argued that Isidore's works were available at the Canterbury school of Theodore and Hadrian, which Aldhelm attended for about two years. For this, see Claudia di Sciacca, "Isidorian Scholarship at the School of Theodore and Hadrian: the Case of the *Synonyma*," *Quaestio* 3 (2002): 76–106, esp. 76–91. In particular, two large passages from the *Etymologiae* are cited verbatim in the Biblical Commentaries from this school. See Sciacca, *Finding the Right Words*, 47; for these texts, see Bernhard Bischoff and Michael Lapidge, eds. and trans., *Biblical Commentaries from the Canterbury School of Theodore and Hadrian* (Cambridge: Cambridge University Press, 1995), 204–05.
236. Lapidge, *The Anglo-Saxon Library*, 181. See also the notes to the *Epistola* in Michael Herren and Michael Lapidge, *Aldhelm: The Prose Works* (Cambridge: Brewer, 1979), 188–90.
237. On this, see Sciacca, *Finding the Right Words*, 51. For a thoroughgoing survey of the impact of Isidore's works on Anglo-Saxon literature, see ibid., 47–55.
238. Michael Lapidge, "An Isidorian Epitome from Anglo-Saxon

eight glosses with Mercian characteristics (c. 700). In addition to this, paleographical proofs suggest that the epitome derives from an exemplar that was written in Anglo-Saxon minuscule.[239] As Lapidge points out, *De diuersis rebus* "provides valuable evidence that in Anglo-Saxon England the *Etymologiae* were excerpted, studied and glossed in the vernacular from as early as c. 700."[240]

With this early wide reception and uninterrupted success in the medieval period,[241] it goes without saying that the *Etymologiae* would be instrumental in the development of the medieval encyclopedic genre. Its trace can, for instance, be perceived in Hrabanus Maurus's *De universo* or *De rerum naturis*,[242] a Carolingian adaptation of Isidore's encyclopedia that emerged in the context of the educational reforms that were carried out at that time.[243] Compiled between 842 and 846, *De rerum naturis* is a reworking of Isidore's *Etymologiae*, which was held in high regard in Carolingian monastic

---

England," in his *Anglo-Latin Literature, 600–899*, 183–223; for an edition of this text, see ibid., 199–223.

239. As Lapidge argues, "An Isidorian Epitome," 187, the scribe who copied *De diuersis rebus* "reproduced faithfully but incomprehendingly a number of Insular abbreviations and compendia which he found in his exemplar but could not decipher, inasmuch as they were not in use in Francia at that time."

240. Ibid., 185.

241. For a study of the manuscripts containing Isidore's *Etymologiae* in medieval European libraries, see José María Fernández Catón, *Las etimologías en la tradición manuscrita medieval medieval estudiada por el prof. Dr Anspach* (León: Consejo superior de investigaciones científicas, Centro de Estudios e Investigación "San Isidoro," 1966).

242. This work is edited in *PL*, vol. 111 (cols. 9–614). A new edition that is currently in preparation is William Schipper, ed., *Hrabani Mauri: De rerum naturis* (Turnhout: Brepols, forthcoming). I will henceforth refer to it as *De rerum naturis*, as preferred by this editor.

243. For further encyclopedias using Isidore's *Etymologiae* as a source, see Robert Collison, *Encyclopedias: Their History throughout the Ages* (New York: Hafner, 1964; repr., 1966), 44–81. For the influence of Isidore's *Etymologiae* on later encyclopedias and other literary texts, see Barney et al., *The Etymologies*, 24–26.

circles. As Isidore did not offer explanations in the manner of figurative or allegorical tradition, Hrabanus—a distinguished disciple of Alcuin—took the initiative to furnish the *Etymologiae* with interpretative passages that would be much appreciated by ecclesiastical audiences. In England, Byrhtferth of Ramsey also drew largely from Isidore's *Etymologiae* to compose his *Manual* or *Enchiridion*, written between 1011 and 1012 in Latin and English.[244] This work, which was meant to address the didactic needs of the secular clergy, offers a compilation of typically encyclopedic subjects ranging from computus and arithmetics to metrics and grammar.

But the impact of Isidore's work on medieval culture goes beyond the bounds of encyclopedism, since the development of bestiaries, glossaries, and grammars, as well as riddle collections (as I later intend to show), was significantly affected by the influence of the *Etymologiae*. In the case of bestiaries, for example, Ron Baxter notes that these works have their origin in the Latin versions of the *Physiologus*,[245] to which textual modifications—notably, the incorporation of excerpts from the *Etymologiae*—were made.[246] Isidore's work therefore made an important contribution to the rise of the bestiary genre. In turn, the author of the *Liber monstrorum* made use of both the *Physiologus* and Isidore's *Etymologiae*.[247]

---

244. For Byrhtferth's heavy indebtedness to the *Etymologiae*, see Peter S. Baker and Michael Lapidge, eds. and trans., *Byrhtferth's Enchiridion*, EETS, s.s. 15 (Oxford: Oxford University Press, 1995), esp. lxxxi–lxxxii.

245. Originally in Greek, the *Physiologus* was probably produced in Alexandria in the second century. It was translated into Latin in the late fourth century. See the introduction to this work in Michael J. Curley, trans., *Physiologus* (Austin: University of Texas Press, 1979), ix–xxxiii.

246. See Ron Baxter's entry for "bestiaries" in Paul E. Szarmach, M. Teresa Tavormina, and Joel T. Rosenthal, eds., *Medieval England: An Encyclopedia* (New York: Garland, 1998). In England, the earliest Latin bestiary that has come down to us is found in Oxford, Bodleian Library, Laud misc. 247, which was probably compiled in the early twelfth century. See Ron Baxter's comments on this text in *Bestiaries and their Users in the Middle Ages* (Phoenix Mill: Sutton, 1998), 83–85.

247. For the use of Isidore's *Etymologiae* as a source for this work, see

This encyclopedia would also be instrumental in the development of medieval glossaries and grammars. The general concern with verbal accuracy and correction of the medieval period encouraged the production of these works, which in most cases reused material from the *Etymologiae*. As regards glossaries, the decisive part played by the *Etymologiae* in the development of European medieval lexicography has been fully acknowledged by scholarship. The so-called *Liber glossarum*, probably compiled at Corbie during the Carolingian revival of learning in the late eighth or early ninth century, is a good example of the powerful influence of this encyclopedia on the shaping of glossaries.[248] In Anglo-Saxon England, an early illustration of the uses of the *Etymologiae* as a source is the "Épinal-Erfurt Glossary," whose compilation has been dated to c. 700.[249] Apart from this, Loredana Lazzari has also proved that the impact of the *Etymologiae* on further Anglo-Saxon glossaries—Leiden, Corpus, Cleopatra, and Harley, among others—has generally been underestimated by scholarship.[250] Also, as she has pointed out, the influence of this encyclopedia "increased in the tenth century, as demonstrated by the Cleopatra and Harley Glossaries, owing to the fact that the *Etymologiae* offered a wide choice of rare words and Graecisms."[251] Indeed,

---

Orchard, *Pride and Prodigies*, esp. 318–20.
248. An abridged edition of the *Liber glossarum*, also known as *Glossarium Ansileubi*, is W. M. Lindsay, *Glossaria Latina*, vol. 1 (Paris: Les Belles Lettres, 1926). For further information, see David Ganz, "The 'Liber Glossarum': A Carolingian Encyclopedia," in *Science in Western and Eastern Civilization in Carolingian Times*, ed. Paul Leo Butzer and Dietrich Lohrmann (Basel: Birkhäuser Verlag, 1993), 127–35.
249. For the presence of some glosses from Isidore's *Etymologiae* in the "Épinal-Erfurt Glossary," see J. D. Pheifer, ed., *Old English Glosses in the Épinal-Erfurt Glossary* (Oxford: Oxford University Press, 1974; repr. 1988), liii–liv. See also Lapidge, "An Isidorean Epitome," 190–93.
250. Loredana Lazzari, "Isidore's *Etymologiae* in Anglo-Saxon Glossaries," in *Foundations of Learning: The Transfer of Encyclopaedic Knowledge in the Early Middle Ages*, ed. Rolf H. Bremmer Jr. and Kees Dekker (Leuven: Peeters, 2007), 93.
251. Ibid.

the revival of the hermeneutic style, of which Aldhelm is its greatest exponent, is a major characteristic of the school of Æthelwold during the period of the Benedictine reform.[252] It is therefore quite logical that the *Etymologiae*, with its colossal display of Latin lexicon, could have attracted the reformers. Isidorean influence is also perceptible in the methodological approach and the contents of later glossaries. In this sense, Ælfric's *Glossary*, composed between 997 and 999, testifies to the significant role played by Isidore's *Etymologiae* in the evolution of these works.[253]

As regards grammatical treatises, the influence of the *Etymologiae* on these works is equally pervasive in medieval culture. Frequently circulating as a separate unit or in an excerpted format, Book I from the *Etymologiae* was one of the few grammars that were "widely available in Anglo-Saxon England during the earlier period."[254] As revealed from Irvine's study of Carolingian library catalogues, Isidore's Book I occupied a prominent position in major scriptoria from the ninth century and continued to be so well beyond the eleventh.[255] Viewed as an effective means to deter heresy and promote grammatical correctness,[256] Isidore's Book I no doubt exerted

---

252. See above, p. 42 (n. 139); also see further in this book on p. 170.
253. For an edition, see Julius Zupitza, *Ælfrics Grammatik und Glossar* (Berlin, 1880; repr. Max Niehans, 2003, with preface by Helmut Gneuss). As noted by Lendinara, class glossaries like Ælfric's usually employed Isidore's *Etymologiae* as a source. See her *Anglo-Saxon Glosses*, 14. Also, see Lazzari's analysis of the Isidorean borrowings in this glossary. "Isidore's *Etymologiae* in Anglo-Saxon Glossaries," 80–87.
254. Frederick M. Biggs, Thomas D. Hill, and Paul E. Szarmach, *Sources of Anglo-Saxon Literary Culture: A Trial Version* (Binghamton, NY: Center for Medieval and Early Renaissance studies, 1990), 85. There is also an *Ars grammatica*, often attributed to Isidore, which borrows extensively from this first book. As pointed out by Díaz y Díaz, when acknowledging their debt to Isidore, later grammarians actually alluded to this work. Oroz Reta and Marcos Casquero, *San Isidoro*, vol. 1, 211.
255. Irvine, *The Making*, 334–44.
256. Ibid., 223.

an enormous influence on later grammatical treatises.[257] Bede's *De ortographia*,[258] for instance, drew freely on the *Liber glossarum*, in turn deriving from Isidore's work—as noted above.[259] More importantly, both Tatwine and Boniface, each of them being the author of a riddle collection, used the first book of Isidore's *Etymologiae* as a source to compose their grammatical treatises—known as *Ars Tatuini* and *Ars Bonifatii*, respectively.[260] A further treatise on meter known as *Ars metrica* or *Caesurae Versuum*,[261] which is attributed to Boniface, also borrowed extensively from Isidore's *Etymologiae*. This encyclopedia is also recognized to be one of the sources used by Alcuin among the materials he compiled for his *De ortographia*.[262]

In light of this discussion, it is evident that the impact of Isidore's *Etymologiae* on medieval culture was intense and long-standing. This encyclopedia was no doubt thoroughly studied in Irish monastic centers and, once it arrived in England, the school of Canterbury

---

257. For the effective blending of classical and medieval sources as the key to the great popularity of Book I throughout the Middle Ages and well beyond, see ibid., 211–43.
258. An edition of this work is found in *Bedae Venerabilis Opera, Pars I, Opera Didascalica, CCSL*, vol. 123A, ed. Charles W. Jones (Turnhout: Brepols, 1975), 7–57.
259. See p. 70 in this book.
260. For the two treatises, see Vivien Law, "The study of Latin Grammar in eighth-century Southumbria," *ASE* 14 (1983): 61–64, and *The Insular Latin Grammarians* (Woodbridge: Boydell, 1982; repr. 1987), 64–67 and 77–80. For further information on the *Ars Tatuini*, see Williams, "The Riddles of Tatwine and Eusebius," 26–36. For an edition of the *Ars Bonifatii*, see *Bonifatius (Vynfreth), Ars grammatica, Ars metrica, CCSL*, vol. 133B, eds. George John Gebauer and Bengt Löfstedt (Turnhout: Brepols, 1980), 15–99. An edition of the *Ars Tatuini* is found in Maria de Marco, *CCLS*, vol. 133 (Turnhout: Brepols, 1968), 1–141. For more information on this work, see Law, "The study of Latin Grammar," 64–66.
261. An edition of Boniface's metrical tract is found in Gebauer and Löfstedt, *CCSL*, vol. 133B, 109–13.
262. As noted by Irvine, "Boniface and Alcuin both regarded heresy as a defect in textual tradition or textual-grammatical competence." *The Making*, 303.

adopted it as an essential work. The *Etymologiae* were equally valued as a reference work and a pedagogic tool by the subsequent generation of Anglo-Saxon missionaries[263] who eventually transferred their intellectual and didactic endeavors to the context of the Carolingian *renovatio*.[264] The encyclopedia was also held in high regard in the scenario of the Benedictine revival, which, as explained above, in turn drew from the Carolingian cultural heritage.[265] On the other hand, the influence of the *Etymologiae* was also far-reaching, since this work not only firmly established the foundations of medieval encyclopedism, but also had significant implications on the evolution of other literary genres such as bestiaries, catalogues of wonders, glossaries, and grammars, all of them equally thriving in this period.[266] It is therefore in this wide-ranging cultural context and in association with the boom of didactic works of this kind that we must approach the study of riddle collections, since, as I am trying to show, they are but a further manifestation of this penchant for knowledge classification that pervaded the early Middle Ages.

---

263. As Sciacca points out, "In the eighth century, the group of Anglo-Saxon missionaries working with Boniface (c. 675–754) appear to have created a distinctive intellectual environment that held Isidorian scholarship in high esteem and contributed to its diffusion." *Finding the Right Words*, 51.
264. Bremmer concludes that encyclopedic texts, notably those by Isidore, cover about 25 per cent of the corpus he has analyzed, thus revealing "the importance of such works in the libraries that were being built up by the first generations of missionaries in Germany." Rolf H. Bremmer Jr., "The Anglo-Saxon Continental Mission and the Transfer of Encyclopaedic Knowledge," in Bremmer and Dekker, *Foundations of Learning*, 37.
265. See above, pp. 24–25.
266. I have centered this discussion primarily on the influence of Isidore's *Etymologiae* on works that are essentially related to teaching and learning. But, as pointed out by other scholars, the impact of this encyclopedia also extended to Anglo-Saxon hagiography, history, exegetical works, and so forth. See Sciacca, *Finding the Right Words*, 51–53.

2.4. The Impact of Isidore's Etymologiae on Early Medieval Riddling: How Grammar and Encyclopedia Merged with Enigmata

As can be drawn from the last part of the preceding discussion, there is no room for doubt that the authors of riddle collections had a good knowledge of grammar, since at least four of them produced a grammatical treatise of some kind. Also, it just takes a quick look at the "Index scriptorum" of the *CCLS* edition of the Latin collections to see how extensive the list of echoes and parallels from Isidore's *Etymologiae* is, suggesting that this encyclopedia was particularly well known to Aldhelm, Eusebius, and the Bern author.[267] In fact, riddle collections allowed their authors to display an interesting blend of both grammar and encyclopedism, simultaneously offering a great range of possibilities as regards didactic strategies, as will be later studied in depth. This is probably one of the main reasons why *enigmata* became so popular, especially from the late eighth century to the end of the first half of the ninth century, when the composition, dissemination, and study of grammar and encyclopedic treatises were strongly promoted by the Carolingian Renaissance. Indeed, the emergence of riddle collections coincides with the proliferation of grammars, handbooks, glossaries, and encyclopedic works. Accordingly, much is to be gained from the study of the interaction that existed between *enigmata* and these other works.

The ostensible relationship between *enigmata* and grammar is, for example, discerned in the *Bibliotheca magnifica*. As pointed out above, this riddle collection exhibits a concern with the Seven Liberal Arts, thus starting with "Wisdom" (*De sapientia*) as an introductory subject and ending with three riddles on grammar, rhetoric, and dialectic.[268] Interestingly, Isidore's Books I–III, as will be explained below, deal with the Seven Liberal Arts and thus serve as an introduction to the remainder of the *Etymologiae*. The alphabetic *Versus* in

---

267. *CCSL*, vol. 133A, 857–60 and 867–68.
268. For these riddles, see Giles, *Anecdota Bedae*, 53 (nos. 10, 11, and 12).

turn illustrates a collection that was designed entirely for grammatical purposes. Thus, each riddle describes a letter of the alphabet and, interestingly, influence from Isidore's *Etymologiae*, especially from Book I, is pervasive in this work.[269] In addition to this, some of the topics found in other riddle collections are clearly connected to the training of this cardinal discipline of the medieval curriculum. This is for instance observed in Eusebius's Riddles 7 (letters), 9 (alpha), 19 (the letter u), and 39 (the letter i)—the latter three with evident echoes from Isidore's Book I[270]—and Tatwine's Riddles 4 (letters) and 16 (prepositions with two cases).

By the same token, riddles could be conceived to illustrate or practise a particular aspect of grammar. In this sense, some of Aldhelm's riddles are basically exercises intended to secure mastery of Latin vocabulary. A representative case is *Enigma* 86, in which the intended solution "aries" and the clues of the riddle playfully indulge in the polysemic character of the Latin word, which can refer to the ram, the star constellation, and the artifact used for the besieging of a town. In the like manner, the clues of Aldhelm's *Enigma* 91 play on the multiple meanings of Latin *palma*, thus alluding to the palm of the hand, the tree, and the branch as a sign of victory in typically Isidorean fashion.[271]

Manuscripts containing riddle collections usually abound in scholia that supply additional information about grammatical cases, Old English equivalents, as well as other lexical, metrical, and syntactic details. A good illustration of this is London, Royal 12.C.xxiii, whose varied and profuse glossing apparatus leaves no room for doubt that the version of Aldhelm's Riddles contained in this manuscript was used to teach Latin grammar and metrics.[272] For instance, in this codex there are numerous glosses indicating the grammatical case of many words. Gernot R. Wieland affirms that the glosses found

---

269. See the notes (*Fontes*) found in *CCSL*, vol. 133A, 729–41.
270. See notes (*Fontes*) in *CCSL*, vol. 133, 219, 229, and 249.
271. See Howe, "Aldhelm's *Enigmata*," 44–45. See further on p. 218 (n. 390).
272. Stork, *Through a Gloss Darkly*, 31–40.

in the London manuscript, as well as those in Cambridge, Gg.5.35, denote a particular interest in the ablative case, which offered special learning difficulties for native Anglo-Saxons.[273] Another interesting example is given by the presence of numeral glosses in the London codex for Aldhelm's Riddles 84 (pregnant sow) and 90 (woman giving birth to twins), which, as Stork points out, could suggest that these texts might have been designed to practice Latin numerals.[274] Riddle collections in general abound in examples of this kind, confirming the idea that *enigmata* were used as exercises for the teaching of grammar.[275]

The riddling phenomenon was probably also associated with the teaching tasks carried out by the authors of *enigmata* who might have been aware of the pedagogic benefits of using this literary genre in the classroom. As mentioned above, it is therefore no surprise to see that writers who produced grammatical treatises—notably, Boniface, Alcuin,[276] and Tatwine—or studies on metrics—as with Aldhelm and Boniface—also composed riddles. Bede might be a further name to add to this list, as he wrote *De orthographia, De arte metrica, De schematibus et tropis*,[277] and tentatively, we could assume, some riddles that

---

273. For this, see Gernot R. Wieland, *The Latin Glosses on Arator and Prudentius in Cambridge University Library, MS Gg.5.35* (Toronto: Pontifical Institute of Mediaeval Studies, 1983), 53–58, and Stork, *Through a Gloss Darkly*, 32–33.
274. Stork, *Through a Gloss Darkly*, 33.
275. See the list of manuscripts containing Aldhelm's Riddles, indicating the number of glosses found in them in ibid., 11–13. Note, for example, that St Gall, Stiftsbibliothek, Cod. Sang. 242 contains 1,249 glosses and London, Royal 12.C.xxiii offers 1,286. As Stork affirms, both manuscripts were designed to be glossed texts, ibid. 5 and 18.
276. For Alcuin's *De grammatica*, see *PL*, vol. 101 (cols. 849–902); for *De dialectica*, *PL*, vol. 101 (cols. 949–76); on *De ortographia*, see *De Orthographia, Grammatici latini*, vol. 7, ed. Heinrich Keil (Leipzig: Teubner, 1880), 295–312. On Alcuin's *De rhetorica*, see W. S. Howell, ed., *The Rhetoric of Alcuin and Charlemagne* (Princeton, NJ: Princeton University Press, 1941; repr. New York: Russell & Russell, 1965). For Alcuin's contribution to the development of grammatical culture in the Carolingian period, see Irvine, *The Making*, 313–33.
277. For an edition of these works, see Jones, *CCSL*, vol. 123A, 7–57 for *De*

have not been preserved, as those contained in the *Collectanea* and the *Joco-seria* are only spuriously attributed to him.[278] Interestingly, Lapidge draws attention to the reference to some "Enigmata Bedae" in a lost book owned by Milred, Bishop of Worcester from 745 to 775. Milred's codex (c. 750) recorded epigrams and other poems by prominent eighth-century writers;[279] its contents were partially reproduced in John Leland's *Collectanea, containing an account of some of the manuscripts inspected by this antiquarian between 1533 and 1543*.[280] The veracity of Leland's transcription led Lapidge to conclude that "Bede did in fact compose 'riddles' or *enigmata* in some form or other."[281] On this basis, Bede would thus constitute a further example of an Anglo-Saxon author with demonstrable teaching experience who would have devoted himself to riddle composition, presumably for pedagogic uses.

In Rome, MS. 1515, the close connection between *enigmata* and the teaching of grammar is further illustrated by the designation of Symphosius as *physicus*—in other words, as a person well-versed in the natural sciences and, hence, clearly attaching his *enigmata* to the teaching of encyclopedic lore.[282] By the same token, in Paris, Bibliothèque Nationale, Lat. 10318 (the so-called Salmasian codex), Symphosius is styled *scholasticus*, that is, someone trained in rhetoric or a teacher of rhetoric, thus supporting the notion that riddles were used to teach disciplines typically related to the learning of Latin.[283] On the other hand, the full title of one of Alcuin's riddling dialogues,

---

ortographia, 81–141 for *De arte metrica*, and 142–71 for *De schematibus et tropis*.
278. See Tupper, "Riddles of the Bede Tradition," 566. For these riddle collections, see above, pp. 19 and 49.
279. For example, an epitaph on Tatwine's death that is not attested elsewhere is cited there. See Michael Lapidge, "Some Remnants of Bede's Lost Liber epigrammatum," *English Historical Review* 90 (1975): 811–12 (no. 19).
280. See ibid., 798.
281. Ibid., 803, (no. 4).
282. The exact reading is "Enigmata Siphusii phisici" (fol. 23v). See Spallone, "Tradizioni insulari," 188.
283. The phrasing as found in this manuscript is "Enigmata Symfosi scolastici" (p. 142).

Disputatio regalis et nobilissimi iuvenis Pippini cum Albino scholastico (The debate of the royal and the very noble youth Pippin with Albinus the teacher), expressly attributes to this author a role as master of rhetoric. As regards the Bern Riddles, this collection is ascribed to a certain Tullius in Berlin, Staatsbibliothek, Phillipps 1825 (fol. 37v). This name was probably intended to bring to mind Roman author Marcus Tullius Cicero, thus indicating the riddles' connection to rhetoric, which, together with grammar and logic, formed part of the trivium. Furthermore, it must be appreciated that the Bern collection is introduced in seven manuscripts as follows: "Incipiunt enigmata quaestionum artis rhetoricae" [Here begin the *enigmata* on various issues related to the art of rhetoric].[284] Finally, a similar teaching role is assigned to Aldhelm, who is referred to as "grammaticus" in London, Royal 15.A.xvi (fol. 60r).[285] All this therefore supports the idea that in the Middle Ages the riddling genre was intimately linked to the study of grammar and rhetoric.[286]

It is also worth remarking that riddle collections often accompany grammatical works in the compilations in which they are extant, as illustrated with St Petersburg, Q.v.I.15, a codex in which Isidore's *Synonyma* and *De differentiis* appear together with Aldhelm's *Enigmata*.[287] This manuscript was initially compiled in southwest England (c.

---

284. With minor variations, this introductory phrase is present in Vatican City, Reg. Lat. 1553 (fol. 8v); Leipzig, Stadtbibliothek, Rep. I. 74 (fol. 15v); Zwettl, Zisterzienserstift, Cod. 53 (fol. 153r); Chicago, Newberry Library, MS f.11 (formerly, Admont, Benediktinerstift, Cod. 277, fol. 1r,); Graz, Universitätsbibliothek, Cod. 85 (fol. 266v); and Vienna, Österreichische Nationalbibliothek, Cod. 67 (fol. 168r) and 2285 (fol. 206r). See *CCLS*, vol. 133A, 544–45, although the list of codices is incomplete.

285. Interestingly, this riddle collection is followed by some excerpts from Bede's *De arte metrica* and *Scolica Grecarum glossarum*, a glossary of Greek words.

286. On the connection between riddling and rhetoric, see Andrew Galloway, "The Rhetoric of Riddling in Late-Medieval England: The 'Oxford' Riddles, the *Secretum philosophorum*, and the Riddles in *Piers Plowman*," *Speculum* 70 (1995): 68–105.

287. For information on the role of this manuscript in the history of the

718)²⁸⁸ but, as commented above, by the mid-eighth century was sent to Corbie,²⁸⁹ where the process of copying continued with the addition of further works.²⁹⁰ The St Petersburg codex is also noteworthy because it contains Boniface's autograph,²⁹¹ thus suggesting that this author might have used Aldhelm's *Enigmata* as part his own teaching activities. The history of this manuscript therefore indicates that the combination of riddles and grammatical works such as Isidore's *Synonyma* and *De differentiis* was probably being experimented with for didactic purposes both in England—before Boniface's departure (718)—and in Anglo-Saxon Continental foundations in the pre-Carolingian period.²⁹²

A further noteworthy illustration of how riddle collections converge with grammatical works is Cambridge, Gg.5.35, which, as pointed out by Irvine, offers a representative synthesis of the medieval

---

dissemination of Isidore's *Synonyma* in the Continent, see Matthew T. Hussey, "*Transmarinis litteris*: Southumbria and the Transmission of Isidore's *Synonyma*," *JEGP* 107 (2008): 158–61.

288. On the basis of the probable presence of the missionary's handwriting in the St Petersburg codex, Lapidge states that this manuscript could date to "some time before 718, when Boniface left England for ever." See his "The Archetype of *Beowulf*," *ASE* 29 (2000): 18.

289. See pp. 17–18. For this codex in the context of the Corbie scriptorium, see Ganz, *Corbie in the Carolingian Renaissance*, 42; McKitterick, "The Diffusion of Insular Culture," 413–14; and Sciacca, *Finding the Right Words*, 73–75.

290. As Sciacca points out, "at least some of the contents—such as the poems on the zodiac and the winds—were added at Corbie, and parts of the *Synonyma* were continued there as well." *Finding the Right Words*, 72. See also Parkes, "The Handwriting of St Boniface," 127.

291. See above, p. 18 (no. 30). Boniface's handwriting in principle appears on folios 57r-63r, and may also occur on 15v, 17v and 37v. On this, see Parkes, "The Handwriting of St Boniface"; Lapidge, "Autographs," 108–15; and Hussey, "*Transmarinis litteris*," 160.

292. As Irvine states, Latin riddles "formed the basis for exercises in reading and interpreting, especially in schools within the Anglo-Saxon sphere of influence." *The Making*, 357.

school canon.[293] As explained by A. G. Rigg and G. R. Wieland, this manuscript consists of four parts,[294] of which three are clearly schoolbooks, whose contents were graded "according to difficulty and educational value."[295] In their current sequence of display in the manuscript, the first part or schoolbook thus offers "a fundamental literary programme in Christian Latin poetry"[296] with works by Juvencus, Sedulius, Arator, Tiro Prosper, Prudentius, Lactantius, and Boethius, as well as some pieces by Hrabanus Maurus that were later appended.[297] The second part provides poems by Aldhelm, Milo of St Amand, Abbo of St Germain, and Hugbald, as well as some other anonymous poetic texts of considerable difficulty. Among other works, the third part offers the *enigmata* of Eusebius, Tatwine, the *Versus*, Boniface, Symphosius, and Aldhelm, alongside the other anonymous riddle assemblages such as the *Joco-seria*, the medical riddles, and the *Bibliotheca magnifica*. The care with which the compilers planned the compilation is also discernible in the distinction between collections with a recognizable author—including Scotus in the case of the *Versus*—which come before the anonymous assemblages. Interestingly, Aldhelm's Riddles appear in the last place of this first sequence, probably on account of their greater degree of complexity. The riddle collections of this third part co-occur with works with an undeniable grammatical character, such as the *Disticha Catonis*, a classic for the training of Latin, or a Greek alphabet with the equivalent Roman characters.

---

293. See Irvine's discussion of the works found in this manuscript in *The Making*, 358–64. Also, for a detailed breakdown of the contents of this manuscript, see Rigg and Wieland, "A Canterbury Classbook," 120–29.
294. The fourth part, containing the "Cambridge Songs," was incorporated later in the initial three-schoolbook plan but was not probably meant for didactic purposes. Rigg and Wieland, "A Canterbury Classbook," 119.
295. Ibid., 129.
296. Ibid., 130.
297. As explained by Rigg and Wieland, ibid., 113–14, the order of composition of the three parts was as follows: Ia (fols. 1–209), III (fols. 370–431), and II (fols. 280–369). Part Ib (fols. 210–76) thus corresponds to some extra quires including Hrabanus Maurus's materials, which were also meant to be part of the first schoolbook.

As noted by F. H. Whitman, Vatican City, Pal. Lat. 1753 (late eighth century) is a further example of a compilation that jointly offers riddles—notably the collections of Aldhelm and Symphosius as well as the anonymous Lorsch Riddles—and works such as Marius Victorinus's *Ars Grammatica*.[298] Another manuscript from the Vatican Library, Biblioteca Apostolica Vaticana, Reg. Lat. 2078 (tenth century) from Rheims, combines the riddle collections of Symphosius and Aldhelm with Agroecius's treatise on orthography.[299] In addition to this, in some manuscripts with a conspicuous focus on grammar, riddle collections frequently co-occur with Isidore's *Etymologiae* and other grammatical sources, usually in an excerpted form.[300] Containing Boniface's *Enigmata* and the hybrid assemblage made of pieces from the Bern collection and the riddles of Symphosius and Aldhelm, Vatican City, Reg. Lat. 1553 displays extracts from Donatus's *Ars maior* and Isidore's Book I from the *Etymologiae*. Furthermore, five other manuscripts offer the Bern Riddles either in combination with excerpts from Isidore's *Etymologiae* or the whole encyclopedia.[301] It is therefore quite clear that riddle collections were frequently assembled with grammatical works, among which Isidore's Book I stands out, in medieval manuscript compilations intended for teaching purposes.

There is evidence that riddle collections were studied side by side with encyclopedias, particularly with Isidore's *Etymologiae*. The

---

298. Whitman, *Old English Riddles*, 58. For a description of this manuscript's contents, see E. Dümmler, "Lörscher Rätsel," *ZfdA* 22 (1878): 262.
299. For this manuscript, see Irvine, *The Making*, 404 (no. 106) and Chauncey E. Finch, "Symphosius in Codices Pal. Lat. 1719, 1753 and Reg. Lat. 329, 2078," *Manuscripta* 13 (1969): 8-11.
300. For a review of the affinities shared by grammars, encyclopedias, and other medieval literary genres, see Whitman, *Old English Riddles*, 57-60, and Patrizia Lendinara, "The World of Anglo-Saxon Learning," in *The Cambridge Companion to Old English Literature*, ed. Malcolm Godden and Michael Lapidge (Cambridge: Cambridge University Press, 1991), 278.
301. These codices are Bern, Cod. 611; Vienna, Cod. 67; Zwettl, Cod. 53; Graz, Universitätsbibliothek, Cod. 85; and Chicago, MS f.11 (formerly, Admont, Cod. 277). See further on pp. 256-57.

profuse presence of glosses from this work in manuscripts containing *enigmata* makes clear that this was so. London, Royal 12.C.xxiii, for example, offers three large excerpts from Isidore's *Etymologiae* on folio 83r.[302] A further substantial passage from *Etymologiae* XIV.i.1–2 accompanies Aldhelm's *Enigma* 1 (earth) in the upper margin of folio 84r of this manuscript.[303] As explained by Stork, the glossator of the London codex made a thorough use of this encyclopedia to the extent that in the case of commentary and encyclopedic glosses he "quotes more often from Isidore's *Etymologiae* than any other text."[304] In Stork's view, the presence of such large glosses from this encyclopedia suggests that the London manuscript was planned for the use of advanced students.[305] A manuscript presenting scholia similar to those found in Royal 12.C.xxiii is Vatican City, Reg. Lat. 2078, mentioned above. Some of these glosses are also made of large excerpts from Isidore's *Etymologiae*.[306]

Accordingly, it seems that grammatical treatises and encyclopedias, either in a complete or in an excerpted format, frequently circulated in combination with riddle collections, forming part of the medieval school canon that was shaped during the pre-Carolingian period and would eventually set the model for later school-centered compilations such as Cambridge, Gg.5.35 and London, Royal 12.C.xxiii. In addition to this, the remarkable presence of glosses from the *Etymologiae* as found in manuscripts such as the latter codex evinces the combined study of riddles and Isidore's major work. In this sense,

---

302. Two of the glosses are from *Etymologiae* VIII.xi.27 and a third one is from XIV.viii.11. This folio also includes a passage from Donatus's *Ars grammatica*. For the text of these glosses, see Stork, *Through a Gloss Darkly*, 96–97.
303. See Stork, *Through a Gloss Darkly*, 100, and Lapidge and Rosier, *Adhelm: The Poetic Works*, 68. A shorter gloss from *Etymologiae* V.xxxv.6 also occurs on the right margin of this folio. For this, see Stork, ibid., 101.
304. Stork, *Through a Gloss Darkly*, 68. For further information on the Isidorean glosses found in this this manuscript, see 56–59 and 66–68. See also Lapidge and Rosier, *Adhelm: The Poetic Works*, 247 (n. 42).
305. Stork, *Through a Gloss Darkly*, 75.
306. Ibid., 19.

Isidore's *Etymologiae* seem to have served as a bridge linking riddles, encyclopedic knowledge and grammatical lore in didactic compilations such as the Cambridge and London codices.

In light of this discussion, it is therefore reasonable to assume that in the Middle Ages *enigmata* were studied alongside grammars and encyclopedias. In this sense, riddles were used "first as texts for analysis . . . and secondly as a medium for the practical application of theory."[307] But this also extended to further grammatical works such as metrical treatises. This is evident in the case of Aldhelm's *Enigmata*, which were initially inserted in the *Epistola ad Acircium*, between the treatises *De metris* (On meters) and *De pedum regulis* (On the rules of feet). This is precisely the layout of Aldhelm's triad as offered in Vatican City, Pal. Lat. 1753, which suggests the presence of these riddles as exercises to practise Latin metrics. Interestingly, this combined pattern of a metrical treatise plus riddles further occurs in the same manuscript. Thus Boniface's *Caesurae versuum* is split into two parts, and four of the Lorsch Riddles (fol. 115r/v) are placed in the middle of these two sections. Also importantly, right after these four riddles, Isidore's definition of *vates* (poet) from *Etymologiae* VIII.vii.3 (fol. 116r) precedes the second part of the metrical tract.

There are further compelling examples of the interplay between riddles and works of the grammatical field. This is the case of the two isolated riddles found in Antwerp, M.16.2 and Brussels, 1828–30, both of which were mentioned above.[308] The two riddles, which co-occur in these two manuscripts with glossaries, evince a strong interest in wordplay and etymology, which set them in the orbit of the hermeneutic style. In their analyses of these riddles, both Porter and Perrello separately conclude that the two pieces are clearly the work of a teacher who was aiming at providing a vocabulary lesson.[309] As discussed above, Porter demonstrates that the double solution of

---

307. Whitman, *Old English Riddles*, 58.
308. See pp. 43–45.
309. Porter, "A Double Solution," 6, and Perrello, "An Undiscovered Riddle," 13.

the riddle found in the Antwerp codex—*scalae*, meaning both cups or a pair of scales—derives from an entry in the glossary found in the same manuscript, which in turn stems from Book XX of Isidore's *Etymologiae*.[310] In like manner, the macaronic riddle of the Brussels codex denotes a tight connection with the glossaries co-occurring in the same manuscript, as well as with Ælfric's *Grammar*. Both the Brussels and the Antwerp pieces therefore illustrate the interaction of riddles with grammar, glossaries, and encyclopedias.

The relationship between riddles and Isidore's *Etymologiae* thus reaches beyond their sharing a similar status in the medieval school curriculum,[311] as the contents of *enigmata* seem to have been informed by this encyclopedia in many cases. Just as Isidorean encyclopedic design made its way through the structure and contents of bestiaries, glossaries, grammars, and other literary genres, riddle collections were similarly deeply affected by this compelling influence. As with all these texts, the composition of *enigmata* necessarily involved the selection and assemblage of a large amount of information. It is therefore quite natural that authors would turn to encyclopedias to compose riddle collections. Compared to the vast size of encyclopedic compilations, it is obvious that the riddle-collection format is comparatively much more limited. Yet the marked comprehensiveness of medieval riddle assemblages leaves no room for doubt that the compilers sought a similar storage effect to that discerned in encyclopedias.[312] Accordingly, a medieval riddle collection was probably viewed as a synthesized version of an encyclopedia.

---

310. As Porter points out, the Antwerp glossaries exhibit a "generous representation of words from Isidore's *Etymologiae*." See his "A Double Solution," 6 (n. 3).
311. As Whitman states by, "There is no reason to think that the material in the riddle would have had any lesser status than that in the encyclopedias generally." *Old English Riddles*, 62.
312. When discussing the concept *encyclopedia* with regard to Pliny's *Naturalis historia*, Murphy defines it as "a self-contained book that encapsulates a total or universal body of knowledge, organizing it in order to preserve it and make it accessible to a large audience." Trevor Murphy, *Pliny the Elder's*

The influence of Isidore's *Etymologiae* is clearly perceived in the contents of riddles from different collections. The most evident case is perhaps that of Eusebius's collection, which directly borrowed a great deal of information from Isidore's Book XII (*De animalibus*) for his zoological riddles.[313] But Eusebius was of course not alone at this, since as observed throughout the critical apparatus of the *CCSL* editions, the contents of many riddles by Aldhelm, Tatwine, and the Bern and Lorsch authors disclose a thorough acquaintance with Isidore's *Etymologiae*. For example, the clues of Aldhelm's *Enigma* 15 are clearly derivative of *Etymologiae* XII.iv.36, which describes how the salamander is unharmed by fire. As pointed out by Stork, the glossator in London, Royal 12.C.xxiii included this piece of information from the *Etymologiae* on folio 85v so that "both riddle and gloss tell the reader, in different words, that the salamander lives in fire."[314] The Exeter Book Riddles also reflect a concern with etymological interpretation, as pointed out by several scholars. As regards Exeter Riddle 7, Roberta Frank, for example, discusses the etymological connection between the solution OE *swan/swon* and the clues alluding to the bird's musical abilities, which are described by means of an alliterative cluster of verbs: "swogað," "swinsiað," and "singað" (7–8a). She explains that this association evidently recalls Isidore's linking "cycnus" (swan) and "canendo" (from *cano*, to sing) in his *Etymologiae* (XII.vii.18).[315] In the case of Exeter Riddle 8, the phrase "eald æfensceop" (literally, an old evening singer) describing the bird

---

Natural History: The Empire in the Encyclopedia (Oxford: Oxford University Press, 2004), 11.
313. See, for example, Manitius, *Geschichte der lateinischen Literatur*, vol. 1, 206–7; Bücheler, "Coniectanea," 341–42; Lapidge and Rosier, *Aldhelm: The Poetic Works*, 67. Also, see my "Clean and Unclean Animals: Isidorean Compilation Criteria in Eusebius's Zoological Riddles," *ES* 93 (2012): 572–82, and further on pp. 240–250.
314. See Stork, *Through a Gloss Darkly*, 67; also, see ibid., 116, for the text of this gloss in the London codex.
315. Roberta Frank, "The Unbearable Lightness of Being a Philologist," *JEGP* 96 (1997): 493–94.

in line 5a has been identified by several scholars as referring to the solution *nihtegale*, the "singer of the night."[316] The frequent use of etymological clues is therefore attested to in both Latin and vernacular riddling.

Apart from the frequent use of Isidore's *Etymologiae* as a source for the composition of riddles, the imitation of the methodology and techniques displayed in this encyclopedia is also remarkable and has been duly noted by several scholars. Nicholas Howe, for example, demonstrates that Aldhelm's *Enigmata* not only incorporated information from Isidore's *Etymologiae*, but also imitated this treatise's didactic approach.[317] Thus, for example, in the case of Aldhelm's *Enigma* 43, the clues of this riddle revolve around the term *sanguisuga* (leech) as deriving from Latin *sanguis* (blood). As Howe states, "This type of linguistic riddle is solved by first locating the etymon and then using it to derive the etymology of the title word."[318] By the same token, Stork states that, since many of Aldhelm's riddles rely on the correct appreciation of the etymological meaning of their solutions, these texts usually dwell on etymological clues. She thus illustrates this with Aldhelm's *Enigma* 18 (ant-lion), which is entirely devoted to suggest the composite term *myrmicoleon*, containing the key to solve the riddle.[319] Again, in the case of London, Royal 12.C.xxiii, the glossator recognizes the relevance of the Isidorean source of this riddle by adding an excerpt from the corresponding passage of the *Etymologiae* (XII.iii.10) at the bottom of folio 85v.[320]

---

316. See A. J. Wyatt, ed., *Old English Riddles* (Boston: D. C. Heath, 1912), 69. Following Wyatt, Williamson, *The Old English Riddles*, 154, affirms that "the *eald æfensceop* (line 5) could be none other than the sweet-singing nightingale, O.E. *nihtegale*, 'singer of the night.'" For a recent reassessment of the etymological clues in Exeter Riddles 7 and 8, see Bitterli, *Say What I Am Called*, 44 and 55.
317. Howe, "Aldhelm's *Enigmata* and Isidorean Etymology." See also M. I. Cameron, "Aldhelm as Naturalist: A Re-examination of some of his *Enigmata*," *Peritia* 4 (1985): 117–33.
318. Howe, "Aldhelm's *Enigmata* and Isidorean Etymology," 45.
319. Stork, *Through a Gloss Darkly*, 57.
320. Ibid., 119.

By way of concluding this section, it is quite evident that the development of riddle collections in general went hand in hand with the flourishing of grammatical works of diverse kind and encyclopedias, most importantly Isidore's *Etymologiae*, which no doubt played a decisive role in the evolution of this genre from the beginning.[321] But the influence of this work on riddle collections, as I intend to show, reaches beyond the latter's notable grammatical scope, the presence of accompanying glosses from this encyclopedia, the riddles' occasional textual dependence on the former as a source, and the emulation of the etymological technique, as has been argued by other scholars so far. As anticipated in the introduction to this book, my aim is to provide evidence that the relationship beween riddles and the *Etymologiae* extends to internal organizational patterns as well. In order to achieve this main goal, in the following section I will consider the overall plan of Isidore's *Etymologiae* so that it can be taken into account when I approach the study of Latin riddle collections.

---

321. As Whitman points out "the riddles belong to a period steeped in the tradition of the encyclopedists, Varro and Flaccus, Suetonius and Pliny, Isidore and Cassiodorus, when encylopedic learning had taken hold and had even been strengthened by the activities of Bede and Alcuin." *Old English Riddles*, 61.

CHAPTER THREE

Isidore's *Etymologiae* and the Compilation of Early Medieval Latin Riddle Collections

3.1. An Insight into the Scheme of Isidore's Etymologiae

3.1.1 The First Decade (Books I–X)

On the basis of traditional manuscript layout,[1] the *Etymologiae* seem to be divided into two main groups or "decades" made up of ten books each (see Appendix II).[2] The resulting structure thus displays

---

1. For the analysis of the work's structure and its changes with respect to the early stages of its transmission history, prior to Braulio's possible manipulation of the book's distribution, see Díaz y Díaz's introduction in Oroz Reta and Marcos Casquero, *San Isidoro*, vol. 1, 174–77. See also María Adelaida Andrés Sanz, et al., "Isidorus Hispalensis Ep.," in *La trasmissione dei testi latini del Medioevo, Mediaeval Latin Texts and their Transmission, TE.TRA.* 2, ed. P. Chiesa and L. Castaldi (Florence: SISMEL-Edizioni del Galluzzo, 2005), 274–417.
2. As authors of riddle collections only occasionally deal with topics included in the first decade, I will provide a more succint overview of this part of the *Etymologiae* than the one I will present for the second decade. With the exception of Boniface's *Enigmata*, whose description of the virtues and the vices would entirely correspond to topics that Isidore treats in the first decade, the other riddle collections usually display subjects that comply

a diptych format, whose two parts offer complementary subjects. The first decade offers a complex organization, as Isidore combined at least four different classification methods,[3] but a principle of internal organization is clearly discerned throughout.[4] To start with, two parts can be distinguished, as observed in the following outline:

First Section	Second Section
I. De grammatica	VII. De Deo, angelis et sanctis
II. De rhetorica et dialectica	VIII. De ecclesia et sectis
III. De mathematica	IX. De linguis, gentibus, regnis,
IV. De medicina	militia, civibus, affinitatibus
V. De legibus et temporibus	X. De vocabulis
VI. De libris et officiis ecclesiasticis	

In the first section, Book I (*De grammatica*, On grammar) offers an introduction to the primary concepts *disciplina* and *ars*, which is followed by the definition of the Seven Liberal Arts. The remainder of Book I is devoted to explaining the basics of grammar. Book II in turn covers the other two disciplines of the trivium by dealing with rhetoric and dialectic. Book III then introduces the quadrivium with subjects connected to arithmetic, geometry, music, and astronomy, thus completing the whole of the Seven Liberal Arts.

---

with the thematic categories observed in the second decade. Still, a few exceptions are found in Eusebius's first section, whose reflection on the Chain of Being would parallel the topics and the organization offered in Isidore's Book VII (*De Deo, angelis et sanctis*, On God, the angels and the saints). A further exceptional case is, for example, found in Tatwine's *Enigma* 1 (Philosophy), which would correspond with *Etymologiae* II.xxiv.3.
3. These are propaedutic, encyclopedic, alphabetical, and chronological. See Barney et al., *The Etymologies*, 20.
4. For a description of the contents and the general arrangement of the *Etymologiae*, see Díaz y Díaz's introduction to Oroz Reta and Marcos Casquero, *San Isidoro*, vol. 1, 174–77. See also Barney et al., *The Etymologies*, 19–20; Fontaine, *Isidore de Séville: genèse*, 176–78; and Andrés Sanz, "Isidorus Hispalensis Ep.," 278.

Books IV and V supplement this first part with topics related to medicine, law, and the measuring of time, the latter part with an account of the six ages in a chronological order, starting with Adam as the forefather of all human beings and ending with the conversion of the Jews during King Sisebut's reign. The encyclopedia subsequently centers on the Scriptures, libraries, writing materials and tools, and other aspects concerning the ecclesiastical profession in Book VI. This first section of the *Etymologiae* therefore covers education, with a description of all the disciplines and professional activities associated with it.

The second part of the first decade starts with Book VII, which broadens the scope of the preceding section by focusing on basic religious concepts such as God, Christ, the Holy Spirit, the Trinity, the angels, and so forth. Book VIII next concentrates on heresy and gives an account of heretical sects in both the Jewish and Christian religions, as well as witchcraft, sorcery, divination, and pagan practices of diverse kinds. An underlying thread is clearly discerned in this part, in which Book VII represents the official Christian doctrine whereas Book VIII deals mainly with heresy, schismatic phenomena, and deviations from orthodoxy.[5] Isidore's *Etymologiae* then turn to human subjects with Book IX, which concentrates on the varieties of languages, races, and nationalities, as well as a study of institutions, starting with large administrative structures and professions associated with these (such as *regnum* and *rex*), military hierarchies, and finally aspects related to the smallest social cell, the family. Closing the first decade, Book X (*De vocabulis*, On words) is concerned with providing a lexicon that is mainly intended to describe human beings. This part thus begins with the definition of *homo* (human being), followed by a list of words that are alphabetically organized.

---

5. Also, as the editors of *The Etymologies*, 20, have pointed out, a movement from "the essentially pagan character of the liberal disciplines of the first books . . . to the religious matter of the following books" is also detected in this part, thus confirming the twofold structure of the first decade.

3.1.2 The Second Decade (Books XI–XX)

The structure of the second decade is comparatively simpler than that observed in the first, since it consistently adheres to an encyclopedic principle of organization; in other words, the information is arranged by topics.[6] As summarized by the editors of *The Etymologies*, in the second decade two major subdivisions are discerned, the first of which (XI–XVI) "ranges (below celestial matters) from higher to lower things—from intelligent animals (humans; Book XI) through other animals (XII), cosmic and non-earthly phenomena (XII), the earth (XIV), and earthy materials (XVI)."[7] The second subdivision (Books XVII–XX) deals roughly with agriculture, war, entertainment, ships, metalwork, construction, clothing, and accessories. The resulting scheme offers two parts with six and four books, respectively, thus conveying a structure that parallels the underlying subdivision observed in the first decade:

First Section	Second Section
XI. De homine et portentis	XVII. De rebus rusticis
XII. De animalibus	XVIII. De bello et ludis
XIII. De mundo et partibus	XIX. De navibus, aedificiis et vestibus
XIV. De terra et partibus	
XV. De aedificiis et agris	XX. De penu et instrumentis domesticis et rusticis
XVI. De lapidibus et metallis	

I will therefore start by examining the arrangement of the first part, comprising Books XI–XVI. Within this first block, a separate analysis will concern Books XI and XII, exemplifying the cases that are most relevant to the subsequent investigation of the structure of

---

6. For this reason, as anticipated above, I will focus on the scheme discerned in the second decade in a detailed way, as this part of the *Etymologiae* can best help elucidate the encyclopedic criteria observed in riddle collections.
7. Barney et al., *The Etymologies*, 20.

riddle collections. I will later carry out the study of the second section, formed by Books XVII–XX.

3.1.2.1 Books XI–XII

Apart from an evident attempt at prioritization, as observed in the distinction between creatures endowed with intelligence in Book XI and those lacking it in Book XII, an internal order can also be detected in the contents of this part of the *Etymologiae*. A detailed outline providing the titles of the four chapters found in Book XI (*De homine et portentis*, On the human being and prodigies), together with some examples of the topics offered in them, may be helpful to clarify this point:

i. *De homine et partibus eius* (on the human being and his/her parts):[8] nature, birth, life, man, soul, spirit, mind, body, flesh, five senses, head.
ii. *De aetatibus hominum* (On the ages of human beings): infancy, childhood, adolescence, youth, maturity, and old age.
iii. *De portentis* (On prodigies): minotaur, cynocephali, cyclops, blemmyans, satyrs, hydra, chimaera, centaur, onocentaur.[9]
iv. *De transformatis* (On metamorphosed creatures): cases of humans turning into animals (e.g., Circe transformed Ulysses and his companions into swine).

As observed in this outline, Book XI first offers two chapters that deal with aspects related to human beings, the foremost part of God's Creation. After an introduction to some basic ideas, chapter i describes terms such as soul and spirit, and then focuses on ideas such as body, flesh, and the five senses. It then continues with

---

8. Here and elsewhere in this chapter, Roman numerals as found in outlines of this kind correspond to internal units or chapters, which are usually entitled in the *Etymologiae*, as offered in the edition provided in Oroz Reta and Marcos Casquero, *San Isidoro*, vol. 2.
9. I am here providing a breakdown of some of the contents of this chapter because they will be relevant to compare with some of the topics appearing in riddle collections.

human anatomy, in other words, with the tangible constituents of human beings, thus clearly distinguishing the spiritual and fleshly sides of man in a rather coherent way. Also, this chapter provides a quite orderly account that ranges from the description of the upper parts of the body to the lower, as well as from the outer organs to the viscera. Chapter ii in turn follows this organizational pattern by handling concepts related to the six stages of man's life, which in turn parallel the six ages of mankind as presented in the chronology found in the first decade (V.xxxix).

By contrast, chapters iii and iv cover, so to speak, the "anomalous" dimension of Creation with a representation of hybrid creatures that partake of human and animal characteristics—such as the minotaur and the cynocephalus—and human beings who have undergone some kind of transformation, as in the case of Ulysses and his mates. Just as issues related to Christian dogma in Book VII preceded the account of topics related to heresy in Book VIII in the first decade, a priority principle from "normal" (chapters i and ii) to "anomalous" (chapters ii and iv) therefore similarly applies in Book XI.

A notable illustration of the consistent arrangement of Isidore's second decade is perceived in Book XII (*De animalibus*, On animals), for which I am offering the following simplified breakdown of contents:[10]

i. *De pecoribus et iumentis* (On cattle and beasts of burden): sheep, wether, ram, lamb, kid, goat, deer, tragelaphus, stag, hare, pig, bullock, bull, ox, cow, calf, buffalo, aurochs, camel, ass, horse, mule.

ii. *De bestiis* (On beasts): lion, tiger, panther, pard, rhinoceros, elephant, giraffe, lynx, beaver, bear, wolf, dog, fox.

---

10. For the sake of space restrictions, this selection of animals is obviously not comprehensive; it is intended mainly to illustrate some of the zoological categories that will later be studied with regard to medieval riddle collections.

iii. *De minutis animantibus* (On small animals): mouse, weasel, mole, hedgehog, cricket, ant.
iv. *De serpentibus* (On snakes): dragon, basilisk, viper, scytale, amphisbaena, hydra, chelydros, lizard, salamander.
v. *De vermibus* (On worms): spider, leech, scorpion, slug, silkworm.
vi. *De piscibus* (On fish): whale, sea-horse, dolphin, tuna fish, crocodile, hippopotamus, echenais, eel, octopus, electric ray, squid, crab, oyster, turtle, frog, sponge.
vii. *De avibus* (On birds): eagle, vulture, crane, stork, swan, ostrich, heron, phoenix, parrot, bat, horned owl, night owl, jackdaw, peacock, rooster, duck.
viii. *De minutis volatilibus* (On small flying animals): bee, wasp, glow-worm, butterfly, locust, fly, gnat, horse-fly, weevil.

Book XII thus presents eight chapters for eight fundamental zoological categories: cattle and beasts of burden, wild beasts, small animals, snakes, vermin, fish, birds, and small flying animals (insects). Book XII similarly suggests a hierarchy based on the degree of usefulness of the animals and their size. Priority of place is thus given to larger four-footed animals that are of use to human beings in chapter i, which is then followed by wild beasts (ii) and smaller animals (iii). A similar size criterion applies to crawling creatures, with a distinction between snakes (iv) and vermin (v),[11] as well as birds (vii) and insects (viii). On the basis of size and physiognomical features, three oppositional pairs arise:

Big quadrupeds (i and ii)	Small quadrupeds (iii)[12]
Big crawling creatures (iv)	Small crawling creatures (v)
Big flying animals (vii)	Small flying animals (viii)

---

11. In medieval zoology, worms were understood to be animals sharing some characteristics with the snake type, as were lizards.
12. With the exception of the cricket and the ant, which also form part of Chapter iii.

These contrastive structures are by no means haphazard, as Isidore probably had them in mind when compiling the zoological information for the *Etymologiae*.

Isidore's Book XII also evinces a threefold distribution of the zoological material: land (chapters i–v), water (vi) and air (vii–viii). This subclassification is based on the author's belief that the four elements pervade Creation, as explained by Isidore in *Etymologiae* XIII.iii.3: "Sunt [omnia elementa] autem divina providentia propriis animantibus distributa: nam caelum angelis, aerem volucribus, mare piscibus, terram hominibus caterisque animantibus Creator ipse inplevit" [(All the elements) are distributed to the corresponding animated beings by the Divine Providence, for the Creator himself has filled up heaven with angels, the air with birds, the sea with fish, and the earth with people and the other creatures]. According to this, three of the elements (air, water, and earth)[13] have been expressly designed by God to be the physical medium where each of these three major types of animals lives and moves.

The tripartite structure and the size criterion in Isidore's Book XII follow closely the organizing principles found in Pliny's *Naturalis historia*.[14] Pliny's Book VIII features land animals; Book IX offers water creatures, while X and XI are devoted to the description of

---

13. Fire, the fourth element, would in turn correspond to angels and other heavenly creatures.

14. Pliny's work in turn owes much to Aristotle's *Historia animalium* (History of the animals), which distributed the zoological material into two main categories: blooded and bloodless creatures, roughly equivalent to our modern vertrebrates and invertebrates. See P. Pellegrin, *La classification des animaux chez Aristote. Statut de la biologie et unité de l'aristotelisme* (Paris: Les Belles Lettres, 1982), 20–21. For a comparative outline of Aristotle's and Pliny's zoological classification methods, see Rosalía García Cornejo, "A propósito de los ictiónimos en 'De piscibus,' *Etymologías* 12.6 de Isidoro de Sevilla," *Habis* 32 (2001): 555. Also interestingly, Aristotle applied a hierarchical principle, later known as the *scala naturae* (the ladder of nature), which ranked living creatures at different levels, with human beings at the top.

birds and insects, respectively.¹⁵ As regards size, Pliny, like Isidore, applies this criterion in a roughly decreasing way. Thus, for instance, Book VIII starts with the elephant, which is followed by the lion, the panther, the tiger, the camel, and the like. The same decreasing principle applies to water animals in Book IX, which describes the whale, the shark, along with aquatic creatures such as tritons and nereids, dolphins, and so forth.

Nevertheless, there are notable divergences between the two encyclopedias that need to be pointed out. Even if Isidore's zoological categories have a precedent in Pliny's classification, the *Etymologiae* offer clear-cut subdivisions of eight major zoological classes, which, by contrast, are offered in a rather disjointed way in the *Naturalis historia*. To take an example, Pliny's Book X is devoted to birds but a substantial part of it focuses on animal reproduction and the five senses as observed in different species, thus including animals of all kinds. Also, the majority of the zoological topics described in Books VIII–XI are retaken in Books XXVIII XXXII on account of the medicinal uses of the animals. For instance, Pliny makes only passing reference to the viper in chapter lix of Book VIII, which deals with land animals, in relation to the snail's capacity to hibernate. Later in X.lxxxii, this snake is mentioned again on account of its peculiar reproduction method. In chapters xxi–xxii and xxxviii of Book XXIX the viper is alluded to once more in order to explain various medicinal remedies issuing from this animal. By contrast, in Isidore's Book XII the viper is dealt with in a passage in the chapter on snakes (iv.10–11), in which the main characteristics of this animal, including its reproductive peculiarities and a brief reference to its medicinal uses, are fully described. The information about a particular animal in Pliny's *Naturalis historia* is therefore interspersed in various sections of the work, whereas in Isidore's *Etymologiae* the description of the different animals is normally condensed in a specific chapter of Book XII.

---

15. See *Pliny: Natural History*, ed. and trans. H. Rackham (London: Heinemann, 1940; repr. 1967), vol. 3 (libri VIII–XI).

Compared to Pliny's disperse method,[16] Isidore's practice generally results in a well-defined categorization, which is supported by the *tituli* of the different chapters of Book XII. Isidore's concern with systematization has to do with the Christian scope of the *Etymologiae*. When explaining how encyclopedic knowledge was of service to Christianity in the Middle Ages, Whitman states that "In the divine scheme of things everything was thought to have a place, and although knowledge of this complex design was beyond comprehension, something of its wonder could be felt in the magnificence of its parts, even in the intricacies of the simplest of things."[17] It is therefore quite logical that Isidore endeavored, even if not always successfully, to convey the image of a harmoniously well-structured Creation in the *Etymologiae*, a work that denotes the author's preoccupation with achieving as coherent a systematization as possible. By contrast, Pliny's *Naturalis historia* rather shows a concern with extreme inclusiveness, even at the price of resulting in a rather chaotic assemblage of information.

A further important discrepancy that should be noted is the distinctive way in which Isidore's Book XII deals with domestic animals. Even though Pliny, like Isidore, differentiates between wild and domestic animals in Book VIII of the *Naturalis historia*, it is worth noting that wild animals—elephant, lion, and the like—precede domestic beasts such as horses or oxen. Conversely, livestock and beasts of burden lead the zoological chapters in Isidore's Book XII.[18] The reasons

---

16. As affirmed by Murphy, "The *Natural History* is so diffuse and miscellaneous that there is hardly a single long description of any subject that is not at some point interrupted by a digression, and even short discussions of simple subjects meander or trail away into other topics without marked transitions." *Pliny*, 32.
17. Whitman, *Old English Riddles*, 62. See this source also for patristic excerpts illustrating this view.
18. Even though Isidore also included wild animals in this part, these were probably viewed as game or beasts of burden—as is the case of the deer (i.18) or the camel (i.35), in other words, useful to human beings as opposite to, say, felines such as the lion, the tiger or the panther occuring in section ii.

for this departure from the Plinian model stem from the Christian scope of the *Etymologiae*, where cattle and other domestic animals are prioritized because of their tight connection to man, thus once more acknowledging human pre-eminence in the order of nature.

It may therefore be confidently inferred that when compiling zoological material in the *Etymologiae*, Isidore was following some structural plan found in a Christian-oriented work. Although Ambrose's *Hexameron* stands out as the major Christian source for Book XII,[19] it is remarkable that Isidore did not adhere to the structure of this work, in which, paralleling the account of Genesis, water animals and birds appear in Book V and land animals are the subject of Book VI, illustrating God's Creation on the fifth and sixth days, respectively. It is therefore quite clear that the basis of Isidore's structural plan is to be sought in a Christian source other than Ambrose's *Hexameron* or the biblical Genesis (1.20–25).

Interestingly, Manuela Bergamin has drawn attention to the fact that the encyclopedic mood of Symphosius's *Enigmata* may have something to do with Eucherius of Lyons's *Formulae spiritalis intellegentiae* (Formulas of spiritual intelligence), a tract from the first half of the fifth century, which may give us an interesting insight into Christian pre-Isidorean zoological classification.[20] In his *Formulae*, Eucherius provides a didactic approach to a good number of symbols

---

19. On Isidore's thorough use of Ambrose's *Hexameron* as a source for Book XII, see Jacques André, ed. and trans., *Isidore de Séville: Étymologies, Livre XII* (Paris: Les Belles Lettres, 1986), 16. A further source used by Isidore is Solinus's *De mirabilibus mundi* (The wonders of the world), also known as *Collectanea rerum memorabilium* (Collection of remarkable things) and *Polyhistor* (Multi-descriptive). In this work, the contents, which are much indebted to Pliny's *Naturalis historia*, are organized on a geographical basis. An edition of this text is Theodor Mommsen, ed., *C. Iulii Solini Collectanea rerum memorabilium* (Berlin: 1895; repr. Weidmann, 1958).

20. Manuela Bergamin, "Eucherio di Lione e la poesia epigrammatica. Materiali per un'indagine," *Incontri triestini di filologia classica* 6 (2006–7): 313–31. The work is edited in C. Mandolfo, *Eucherii Lugdunensis: Formulae spiritalis intelligentiae, Instructionum libri duo, CCSL*, vol. 66 (Turnhout: Brepols, 2004).

occurring in the Scriptures in order to allow readers to have access to the allegorical interpretation of the different concepts and ideas appearing in the Bible. In each entry, the author expounds on the allegorical significance of a particular concept and accompanies it with at least an illustrative quotation from the Bible. In this work, Book IV offers an allegorical description of several animals, which are distributed into three main groups—birds, quadrupeds, and "worms"—although no distinction of these zoological categories is made by means of headings. An analysis of the three zoological sequences also reveals an internal subclassification. Thus, a series of birds (eagle, ostrich, pelican, crow, partridge, dove, and so on) is followed by a cluster of small flying creatures (bat, beetle, locust, bee and fly). The quadrupeds section coming next offers a first subgroup on wild animals (lion, leopard, elephant, bear, etc.), a second on beasts of burden (horse, mule, ass, and so forth), and a third on cattle (cow, calf, pig, etc.). Finally, a sequence of "vermin," which includes the mole, the frog, the ant, the spider, the snake, and the like, closes Book IV.[21] Notwithstanding obvious significant discrepancies, it is worth comparing the structures observed in the *Etymologiae* and Eucherius's *Formulae*:

Isidore's Book XII	Eucherius's Book IV
1. Big quadrupeds (i and ii)	1. Birds (402–54)[22]
2. Small quadrupeds (iii)	2. Small flying creatures (455–64)
3. Big crawling creatures (iv)	3. Big (wild) quadrupeds (465–98)
4. Small crawling creatures (v)	4. Small quadrupeds (499–504)
5. Fish (vi)	5. Beasts of burden (505–24)
6. Big flying animals (vii)	6. Cattle (525–53)
7. Small flying animals (viii)	7. Vermin (554–74)

---

21. Books III and V would also be worth studying in detail, but this study would reach far beyond the scope of this book.
22. The lines correspond to those offered by the edition found in Mandolfo, *Eucherii Lugdunensis*, CCSL, vol. 66.

Eucherius's Book IV thus shares with Isidore's Book XII the use of the size criterion and the distinction of the three elements, although the category of fish as representing water is absent in the former.[23] The parallels are no doubt outstanding, but, still, Isidore's Book XII constitutes a further step in the method of classification.

In his study of medieval bestiaries, Ron Baxter explains that Isidore's Book XII "directly follows, not the chronological order of Creation described in the Genesis myth, which in any event is not detailed enough to provide an organizing principle, but the hierarchy of the food laws given in Leviticus and Deuteronomy."[24] Indeed, just as Isidore starts this series with an account of cattle and beasts of burden, Leviticus (11.3) initiates the list with this type of animals that are regarded as "clean": "Whatever parts the hoof and is cloven-footed and chews the cud, among the animals, you may eat." Deuteronomy (14.3–6) endorses these major characteristics but, unlike Leviticus, enumerates some clean domestic and wild animals as way of example. The following outline offers a simplified version of the reference to clean and unclean animal categories as found in Leviticus 11 and Deuteronomy 14, so that the arrangement they offer can be compared to the internal structure of Isidore's Book XII:[25]

Leviticus 11	Deuteronomy 14
3. Clean animals (parted hoof and chews cud): cattle.	3–6. Clean animals (parted hoof and chews cud). Cattle: ox, sheep, and goat. Wild animals: hart, gazelle, roebuck, wild goat, ibex, antelope, and mountain-sheep.

---

23. A terse reference to fish in general is included in Eucherius's Book III (389–90).
24. Baxter, *Bestiaries and their Users*, 84.
25. Again, note that the outline is not comprehensive and that I have focused for the most part on animals that are later included in riddle collections. The figures on the left correspond to current verse numbering as found in May and Metzger, *The New Oxford Annotated Bible*.

Leviticus 11	Deuteronomy 14
4. Unclean quadrupeds: camel.	7–8. Unclean quadrupeds/small animals: camel, hare, rock badger, swine.
5–8. Unclean small animals: rock badger, hare, and swine.	
9–12. Clean fish (fins and scales). Unclean fish: the rest.	9–10. Clean fish (fins and scales). Unclean fish (no fins and no scales).
13–19. Unclean birds: e.g., eagle, vulture, night-hawk, ostrich, owl, stork.	11–18. Unclean birds: eagle, vulture, ostrich, nighthawk, little owl, great owl, stork, etc.
20–23. Clean insects: locust, cricket, and grasshopper. Unclean insects: the rest.	19–21. Clean insects (certain kinds of winged insects). Unclean insects: the rest.
29–30. Unclean small animals: e.g., weasel, mouse, lizard, chameleon.	

Leviticus and Deuteronomy thus evince a systematization based on the three elements: land (cattle and big wild quadrupeds), water (fish), and air (including birds and insects). Besides, a differentiation is made between cattle, which is given priority of place, and wild four-footed animals.

A further subdivision is discerned in terms of size, with large quadrupeds and small animals, as well as in the distinction between birds and insects. All in all, there are five basic criteria:

1. habitat (terrestrial, aquatic or aerial)
2. distinction between domestic and wild
3. size (large vs. small)
4. physiognomy (e.g., all winged creatures are grouped together)[26]

---

26. These first four criteria have also been noted by André in *Isidore de Séville*, 8–9.

5. the position they occupy in the order of Creation (e.g., clean domestic quadrupeds come first)

Interestingly, these five criteria meet the taxonomic principles of Isidore's Book XII discussed above. It therefore seems that Isidore combined the Plinian model, from which the first four criteria derive, with further encyclopedic-oriented works such as Eucherius's *Formulae* and the structural design of Leviticus and Deuteronomy, thereby offering a fifth governing principle, the rank in God's Creation,[27] obviously absent from the *Naturalis historia*.[28] In an attempt to adapt classical encyclopedic knowledge to the Christian context of his time, Isidore thus managed to offer a fairly consistent systematization that would make Book XII the zoological authority *par excellence* during the Middle Ages.

3.1.2.2 Books XIII–XVI

The internal cohesion of the second decade is also perceived in the block formed by Books XIII to XVI. Book XIII deals with cosmological concepts such as the world, the atoms, the elements, the sky, the clouds, the wind, the sea, and so forth. As with the zoological topics of Book XII, the different sections are here distributed on the basis of the distinction of the three elements: earth, air, and water. Book XIV in turn focuses on geography. After explaining basic concepts such as *terra* and *orbis*, Book XIV clearly applies a size criterion, starting with the larger parts of the by-then-known world (Asia, Europe and Libya). Here, the conspicuous Christian character of

---

27. The distinction between clean and unclean categories is not, however, always fully consistent in Isidore's *Etymologiae*. For example, Chapter vii on birds offers a series of clean specimens: pheasant, rooster, hen, duck, and goose (vii.49–52). But the coot is next (53) alluded to with the remark that its flesh tastes like that of hare. The distinction is thus not regularly maintained throughout Book XII.
28. Still, the idea is no doubt in consonance with Aristotle's hierarchical classification, later known as the *scala naturae* (the ladder of nature), which ranked living creatures at different levels, with human beings at the top. See Pellegrin, *La classification des animaux chez Aristote*, 20–21.

the work again has an impact on the internal order. Accordingly, it is quite natural that Isidore would consider Asia as a starting point, with "Paradisus" (XIV.iii.2) as the first entry after the introductory explanation of the term "Asia." From this eastern remote place, the different geographical subjects advance westward, implying an order from less civilized to more civilized. In the case of Europe, the account starts with lower Scythia (XIV.iv.3), equivalent to central Eurasia and reputedly inhabited by barbarians, and logically ends in Hispania (XIV.iv.28). The geographical sequence closes with chapter v—Libya (roughly, the northern part of Africa), allegedly inhabited by uncivilized races and wondrous creatures.[29] Once more, as done before with the last chapters of Book XI, Isidore's Christian perspective relegates the "anomalous" (i.e., the "other") to the end of this series. Book XIV then continues with smaller geographical concepts such as islands and mountains, and ends with the inner lower regions. In a way that recalls the description of human anatomy from the external parts to the internal in *Etymologiae* XI.i, a progression from the surface to the entrails of the earth is also discerned in Book XIV, culminating in the description of terms related to the underworld (*De inferioribus*, On the lower regions, ix).

Book XV (*De aedificiis et agris*, On buildings and fields) concentrates, among other subjects, on cities, different kinds of buildings, defensive constructions, tents, sepulchers, and the distribution of rural land. As reflected in the title of this book, the chapters reveal a twofold structure that hinges on the contrast between urban and rural spaces. Also, the contents roughly define a sequence from large to small and a movement from civilization to the countryside, thus conjuring up the size criterion observed in the contents of Book XIV, which proceed from the description of the continents to the smaller geographical features, as well as the distinction between domestic and wild animals in Book XII.

The Christian drive of the *Etymologiae* can also be perceived in

---

29. See, for example, *Etymologiae* XIV.v.4 for a reference to the barbarian peoples and the abundance of basilisks living in those regions.

Book XVI. Chapter i in this book (*De pulveribus et glebis terrae*, On dirt and lumps of earth) opens with the explanation of the term *pulvis* (dirt) and continues with a description of related concepts such as mud, mire, clay, sulfur, and the like. It then continues with a succession of common stones and earthy materials, which leads up to gems. The chapters on precious stones establish an internal classification on the basis of color. Also interestingly, chapter xvi on glass (*De vitro*) comes right after the sequence of gems, as if comparing the perfection of Creation with the modest product of human skill, which always attempts to imitate the former. The subsequent chapters on metals introduce gold (xviii) as the first and finest of a series of natural materials and continue in a decreasing order based on their worth.[30] The sequence thus logically ends with tin (xxiii, *De stagno*). There follows a description of the electrum (xxiv), which deals with the alloy of gold and silver that can be found naturally or made artificially. As with the contrastive pattern observed in the juxtaposition of gems and glass, Isidore once more deliberately places a product of divine creation next to one that is manufactured by humans, in an attempt to emulate nature.

Up to this point, it seems quite clear that Books XIII to XVI as a whole offer a rather systematic arrangement that extends from larger concepts such as the world, the sky, the ocean, the earth, continents, islands, cities, buildings, and fields to the smallest components of Creation (stones and metals). The three major organizing criteria in these four books are therefore the distinction of the elements, size, and the worth that each item may comparatively have, usually in a downward gradation. Also, these books typically reveal the presence of subtler organizational principles, such as the contrastive juxtaposition of elements that aims at enhancing the perfection of God's Creation in comparison to human craftsmanship.

---

30. This has also been pointed out by the editors of *The Etymologies* (20): "the treatment of metals from the most to the least valuable, of gems by color, or the division of the world's objects into those composed of each of the four elements."

3.1.2.3 Books XVII–XX

The second major subdivision of the second decade of the *Etymologiae* (XVII–XX) also evinces an attempt to achieve overall coherence, although the resulting organization is more miscellaneous than that found in the preceding sequence.[31] The first two books of this part are devoted to human activities and professions, thus complementing those presented in the first decade, which were related mainly to the Seven Liberal Arts, the church, medicine, and law. Books XVII (*De rebus rusticis*, On rural things) and XVIII (*De bello et ludis*, On war and games) include topics related to agriculture, war, and entertainment. Books XIX (*De navibus, aedificiis et vestibus*, On ships, buildings and clothes) and XX (*De penu et instrumentis domesticis et rusticis*, On provisions and domestic and rural utensils)[32] in turn convey descriptions of any sort of artifact that is created by humans. Notably, Book XIX centers on subjects having to do with ships, work in the forge, the construction of buildings, the carpenter's profession, as well as anything related to clothing and accessories, while Book XX concentrates mainly on home utensils, food, drinks, and agricultural implements.

As a whole, the second subdivision of the second decade may not seem as coherent as that of the preceding part, but the study of some of the sections shows a similar concern with keeping the organizational practice observed in the first subdivision. For example, after two introductory chapters, a priority criterion seems to apply in Book XVII, which focuses first on cereal (chapter iii), legumes (iv), and vines (v), probably on the basis that these are all cultivated by

---

31. As these books comprise a great number of chapters, an inclusion of these either in the main text or the appendices is not possible because it would take the discussion far beyond the reasonable limits of this monograph. A complete outline of the books and their corresponding chapters as found in the second decade is offered in Oroz Reta and Marcos Casquero, *San Isidoro*, vol. 2, 2–11.

32. Note that Book XX lacked a title in the early manuscript versions of the *Etymologiae*. See Barney et al., *The Etymologies*, 395 (n. 1).

human beings and essential to their lives. Book XVII then moves to topics concerning trees (chapters vi-viii), herbs (ix), and vegetables (x–xi), thus basically complying with a criterion based on size. Also noteworthy is the differentiation made between aromatic trees (*De aromaticis arboribus*, viii) and vegetables (*De odoratis oleribus*, xii). This distinction is not maintained, however, in the case of herbs, since the aromatic and common types are treated jointly in chapter ix (*De herbis aromaticis sive communibus*).

3.1.2.4 Some Final Considerations on the Second Decade

The overall plan of Isidore's second decade in the *Etymologiae* therefore suggests an implicit twofold structure: on the one hand, the first subdivision (Books XI–XVI) would correspond to the "Opera Dei," including any creature or object created by God; on the other, the second subdivision (XVII–XX) entails the "Opera hominis," that is, anything that has been made by human beings.[33] An outline supplying the titles of the books in the second decade may conveniently illustrate this twofold subdivision:

Opera Dei	Opera hominis
XI. De homine et portentis	XVII. De rebus rusticis
XII. De animalibus	XVIII. De bello et ludis
XIII. De mundo et partibus	XIX. De navibus, aedificiis et vestibus
XIV. De terra et partibus	
XV. De aedificiis et agris	XX. De penu et instrumentis domesticis et rusticis
XVI. De lapidibus et metallis	

By arranging this second half of the *Etymologiae* into two, Isidore probably aimed at contrasting God's macrocosm with human microcosm.

---

33. "Opera Dei" and "Opera hominis" are my own coinages in an attempt to supply typical encyclopedic titles for these implicit subdivisions. The editors of *The Etymologies* (20) similarly recognize this twofold structure and name the first subdivision "On the Nature of Things" after Lucretius's *De rerum natura*, which Isidore himself appropriated for his homonymous work.

However, the thematic arrangement of these two major subdivisions is not fully coherent. An evident exception to the general consistency of the first subdivision (the "Opera-Dei" motifs) is Book XV (*De aedificiis et agris*, On buildings and fields), which, as explained above, deals broadly with cities, buildings, and rural land. These topics obviously do not match the general "Opera-Dei" plan of this part. Also, there is a thematic overlap here, as Book XIX partly handles topics connected to the construction of buildings. As mentioned above, the second subdivision is even more heterogeneous, and the internal structure of the different chapters lacks the cohesion observed in the first. For example, in the case of Book XVII, the sections dealing with trees and herbs might have been more suitable as part of the first subdivision (the "Opera-Dei" motifs).[34] In addition to this, Books XIX and XX result in a miscellany whose only common factor seems to be objects made and activities performed by human beings.

If we now consider the subjects handled in the books comprising the second decade from a thematic point of view, we may draw some interesting conclusions:

Second Decade	Thematic Categories
XI. De homine et portentis	Biological topics
XII. De animalibus	
XIII. De mundo et partibus	
XIV. De terra et partibus	Cosmological concepts
XV. De aedificiis et agris	
XVI. De lapidibus et metallis	

---

34. In *The Etymologies*, 20, the editors have similarly noted this inconsistency: "Book XVII begins in this way, at least, with agriculture, though the bulk of the book treats flora in detail—our (ultimately Aristotelian) sense of order would prefer to place this material among the books on animals and minerals."

Second Decade	Thematic Categories
XVII. De rebus rusticis	
XVIII. De bello et ludis	Instrumental subjects
XIX. De navibus, aedificiis et vestibus	
XX. De penu et instrumentis domesticis et rusticis	

The second decade thus reveals a clear concern with offering a wide-ranging representation of living creatures in a sort of *ordo creaturarum*, with *homo* logically leading it. Cosmological concepts follow so as to define the physical dimension in which humans and animals reside and move. Finally, the third category entails all kinds of objects, tools, and artifacts created and used by human beings—as well as trees, herbs and vegetables at the service of mankind. These three fundamental categories constitute a skeleton which, as I show below, resembles the basic structure observed in Symphosius's *Enigmata*, much imitated by subsequent authors. I can thus propose that most riddle collections show a concern with offering a variety of subjects that concern the three major categories discerned in Isidore's second decade.[35] Accordingly, the *Etymologiae* not only served as a source for the contents of the riddles but also as a model of organization for their assembling. It is therefore quite evident that the classification method observed in the second decade of the *Etymologiae* must be taken into account when analyzing the structure of medieval riddle collections.

3.1.3 Analogy, Contrast, and Structural Irregularities

From the analysis of the structure of the two decades, we can appreciate that there is continually an attempt at providing the material in an orderly way. This was probably part of Isidore's initial plan, since this no doubt complies with the ubiquitous pedagogic character of the encyclopedia. Apart from major organizing principles that

---

35. The processing of information is an encyclopedia's main goal, which is appropriately described by Murphy as follows: "to circumscribe and parcel it [knowledge] into useful categories and subcategories." *Pliny*, 13.

have already been dealt with, the *Etymologiae* seem to dwell on the basic principles of analogy and contrast, which are frequently combined and parallel the notions of *analogia* and *differentia* mentioned above.[36] An example of the way in which the *Etymologiae* builds on these two structural criteria is observed in the juxtaposition of the crab and the oyster (XII.vi.51–52). The pairing of these two animals is obviously first based on analogy or simple association of ideas, for the two are mollusks. In fact, Isidore explains that Latin *cancer* is connected to Latin *concha*, shellfish. The term *ostrea* in turn shares a similar etymology, for the corresponding Greek ὄστρεον also alludes to the oyster's shell.[37] But apart from the philological relationship, the two animals also convey an antithetical pair on the grounds of traditional lore, which accounts for the crab's hostility to the oyster. As explained by Isidore (XII.vi.51), the crab is said to throw a pebble in the oyster's interior so that it cannot close the protective shell:

Cancros vocari, quia conchae sunt crura habentes: inimica ostreis animalia. Eorum enim carnibus vivunt miro ingenio; nam quia valida testa eius aperiri non potest, explorat quando ostrea claustra testarum aperiat, tunc cancer latenter lapillum inicit atque inpedita conclusione ostreae carnes erodit.

[Crabs are named so because they are shellfish which have legs; these animals are hostile to the oysters. They live on their flesh by means of a wondrously clever device; as its strong shell cannot be opened, the crab waits for the oyster to open its valves, and then, without being noticed, casts a pebble inside so that this prevents its closing and devours the oyster's flesh].

---

36. These principles are also observed in Pliny's *Naturalis historia*. On this see, Murphy, *Pliny*, 41–48. On this classification criteria as used by Aristotle, see Roger French, *Ancient Natural History* (London: Routledge, 1994), 44–45 and 56–58.

37. "Ostrea dicta est a testa, quibus mollities interior carnis munitur; Graeci enim testam ὄστρα vocant" (XII.vi.52) [The oyster (*ostrea*) is so called because of the shell with which the inner tenderness of its flesh is protected; in fact, Greeks call a shell ὄστρα].

Thanks to this cunning stratagem, the crab manages to eat the oyster. It may therefore be inferred that the pairing of these two animals in Isidore's *Etymologiae* could have been intended to underscore this well-known association.

But the juxtaposition of the crab and the oyster in Book XII also suggests the acknowledgement of the two animals as an allegorical pair, an inferrence that can be supported by a passage from Ambrose's *Hexameron*, in which the antithetical roles of the crab and the oyster as sly predator and innocent victim, respectively, are further elaborated: "Sunt ergo homines, qui cancri usu in alienae usum circumscriptionis irrepant, et infirmitatem propriae virtutis astu quodam suffulciant, fratri dolum nectant, et alterius pascantur aerumna" (V.viii.23)[38] [Then, there are men who, like the crab, creep into the use of other people's property and sustain the weakness of their own virtues by means of their cunning; they plot against their brother and feed on their neighbor's misery]. This passage allegorically associates the greedy crab with ambitious human beings who deceive weak naïve people by means of their artfulness.[39] Though not overtly expressed by Isidore in Book XII, the connection of the two animals was therefore implicit in the pairing of the two encyclopedic entries so that it could be easily recognized by learned readers.

A further interesting example is conveyed by the unexpected juxtaposition of the bat and the nightingale (XII.vii.36–37). Here analogy once more builds on the recognition of the etymological meaning of the two names, which is explained on the basis of the different ways in which the two animals react to light. In the case of the bat, Latin *vespertilio* alludes to this animal's preference for darkness: "Vespertilio pro tempore nomen accepit, eo quod lucem fugiens crepusculo vespertino circumvolet praecipiti motu acta, et tenuissimis brachiorum membris suspensa" (XII.vii.36) [The bat receives its name from

---

38. Text from *PL*, vol. 14 (cols. 216A–216B).
39. For the discussion of Ambrose's full passage from the *Hexameron* and my comments, see "The Oyster and the Crab: A Riddle Duo (Nos. 77 and 78) in the *Exeter Book*," *MP* 101 (2004): 400–19, specially, 417–18.

the time (when it appears); by fleeing light, it starts to flutter around at dusk (i.e., "crepusculo vespertino") with hasty movements, sustaining itself thanks to the thin membranes of its arms].[40] As regards the nightingale, Isidore explains this bird's name on account of its etymological connection to Latin *lux* (light): "Luscinia avis inde nomen sumpsit, quia cantu suo significare solet diei surgentis exortum, quasi lucinia" (XII.vii.37) [The nightingale obtained its name because its song usually indicates the coming of the rising day, as if (we said) *lucinia* (the one endowed with light)]. From our modern perspective, the two animals have very little in common but what interests Isidore is the analogical relationship of the two terms (*vespertilio* and *luscinia*) which are both associated with the time of the day when the animal appears for the first time, dusk and dawn, respectively. Besides, the two entries constitute an antithetical pair, since *vespertilio* suggests darkness whereas *luscinia* evokes light.

As with the pair formed by the oyster and the crab, the bat and the nightingale would also be allegorically suggestive but, as is typical, Isidore does not offer any further explanation of this. Hrabanus Maurus, however, adds the following remark to Isidore's description of the bat in his *De rerum naturis*: "Vespertiliones sunt idolorum monstra tenebris dedita; ut in Esaia legitur: Vt adoretis talpas et uespertiliones" (VIII.vi.950–51) [Bats are monsters (portents) devoted to the darkness of idols (i.e., pagan gods), for in Isaiah (2.20) we read: as you worship moles and bats].[41] Similarly, he appends the following comment in the entry for the nightingale: "Haec forsan sanctos predicatores typice significare potest, qui futurae lucis exortum praenuntiant, et ad eius aduentum animo uigilanti intendere fideles quosque exhortantur" (VIII.vi.966–67) [This can perhaps fig-

---

40. In spite of the meaning of textual *membris* (limbs), I have preferred the alternative reading *membranis* (membranes) as proposed by Oroz Reta and Marcos Casquero in *San Isidoro*, vol. 2, 112, n. 79. Also, see Barney et al., *The Etymologies*, 266 (n. 28).
41. This and the following excerpt from *De rerum naturis* are from Schipper, *Hrabani Mauri*. I thank William Schipper for kindly allowing me to have a pre-publication copy of this edition.

uratively signify the holy preachers who foretell the rising of future light and urge all the believers to strain themselves to be on the alert for his (Christ's) coming]. The contrastive pattern could thus reach as far as the allegorical significance of darkness as associated with the bat, representing the ignorance of pagan idolatry, and light as symbolizing the good news that is announced in advance by priests.

Analogical and contrastive relationships of this kind are pervasive in the *Etymologiae* and serve to define an intricate mesh of semantic interconnections and latent allegorical layers that make this encyclopedia such an attractive literary product. However, even in parts whose structure seems to have been carefully planned, thematic ruptures and digressions abound. To take an example, the marked cohesion of Book XII, which has been studied in detail earlier in this chapter—is occasionally disrupted. For example, chapter ii—dealing mainly with large wild quadrupeds such as lion, tiger, panther, and the like—also offers a small animal like the chameleon (ii.18). In all likelihood, the reason for this is Isidore's concern with presenting the etymological connection between the Latin term *camelopardus* (giraffe), which occurs in the following entry (ii.19), and *cameleon*. Isidore, we may infer, associated the first term with the camel and the pard, in the case of the giraffe, and the camel and the lion as regards the chameleon. The two names would thus prompt the image of big wild quadrupeds and, in turn, offer an interesting philological connection, as they both share the first compound.

The *Etymologiae* also contain numerous repetitions. In fact, when there is an aspect that requires further elaboration, this often results in cases of repetition or overlap.[42] As to be expected, the hydra features as part of the sequence of snakes in *Etymologiae* XII.iv.23. But it also appears as a portent in Book XI, where it is said to represent heresy (iii.34–35), thus providing one of the few cases in which Isidore

---

42. As Díaz y Díaz affirms, Isidore subordinated the rational structuring of his material to its didactic potential. Oroz Reta and Marcos Casquero, *San Isidoro*, vol. 1, 184. In Barney et al., *The Etymologies*, 21, the editors note that "on the whole Isidore does not explain the order of things beyond what is implicit in their sequence in the text."

takes the opportunity to openly comment on the allegorical meaning of a term by quoting a passage from Ambrose's *De fide* (On faith).[43] Being a snake with multiple heads, the hydra was traditionally considered to be practically indestructible. If any of the heads was cut off, three more would rapidly spring up in the same place. The hydra thus constituted a powerful image of how heresy could spread and how difficult it was to eradicate. Isidore's strong concern with heresy, we may infer, probably motivated the duplication of this topic.

Another illustration of repetition is found in the idea that *homo* (man) derives from *humus* (earth), which is first used to illustrate the key concept *etymologia* (I.xxix.3). This notion is obviously based on the reference found in Genesis (2.7) that man was made from dust. Later (VII.vi.4), Isidore recalls this association when expounding on the traditional meaning of the name Adam, as alluding to his being terrestrial ("terrenus") or made of red earth ("terra rubra"). The paronomastic pair *homo/humus* occurs once more[44] as part of the introduction to the catalogue of terms that are used to describe human beings (X.1). Finally, Isidore alludes to the connection between the two words in relation to the Genesis reference offered in Book XI (i.4). In all these cases the idea is coherently inserted, apparently disregarding the fact that the same explanation appears four times in the *Etymologiae*.

An even more striking case of repetition is observed in Book III (*De mathematica*, On mathematics), in which a substantial section on astronomy (chapters xxiv–lxxi) is supplied. The organization seems to be perfectly coherent, since this forms part of the overview of the Seven Liberal Arts that Isidore offers in Books I–III. Yet, further in the *Etymologiae*, notably in chapter v (*De partibus caeli*, On the parts of heaven) of Book XIII (*De mundo et partibus*, On the world and its parts), Isidore incorporates virtually the same materials found in chapters xxxiii, xxxvii, xxxix, and xlvi of Book III

---

43. For this excerpt, see *PL*, vol. 16 (cols. 538B–39A).
44. The contents of Book X are organized alphabetically, as pointed out above; hence, the lack of indication of the chapter number.

(*De mathematica*).⁴⁵ The resulting repetition and overlap of information might have been perfectly acceptable from a medieval perspective, since these topics should be dealt with in Book XIII, which could function as an independent cosmological tract in the encyclopedia.

Isidore's encyclopedia is clearly replete with thematic digressions, repetitions, and overlaps. All these examples seem to be reasonably understandable if we take into account that Isidore's *Etymologiae* constitute a huge compilation that was carried out over the course of many years. In this light, the keeping of systematic order must have been hard to accomplish in the medieval context, with the logical limitations imposed by parchment technology.⁴⁶ As several editors have pointed out, it is hard to ascertain whether this final layout, which is far from being perfect from our modern standards, was Isidore's own work. Like Pliny and preceding encyclopedists, Isidore only occasionally offers cursory comments on his organizational method. For example, he briefly discusses the arrangement of a couple of sections at the end of the part devoted to the construction materials and the beginning of the discussion of decoration, probably because its organization might have been viewed as potentially hard to understand: "Hucusque partes constructionis: sequitur de venustate aedificiorum" (XIX.xi) [So far, the parts of construction (have been dealt with); the decoration of buildings follows next]. But this comment rather seems like a minimal reminder of an obvious coherence, which is generally expected to be grasped by readers.

---

45. Oroz Reta and Marcos Casquero, *San Isidoro*, vol. 2, 129 (n. 10). Barney et al., *The Etymologies*, 271 (n. 1).
46. In Pliny's *Natural History*, digression is extremely frequent. For example, as Murphy notes, the sequence of land animals in Book VIII starts with the elephant but is soon interrupted by the description of the snake (VIII.xiv), which is traditionally considered the elephant's worst adversary, thus offering an antithetical pair. By the same token, a digression in the part devoted to water animals takes place when Pliny starts to describe tritons and nereids (IX.iv). On Pliny's fondness for digression, see Murphy's comments in *Pliny*, 30–36.

Also, as mentioned above, it must be borne in mind that in its current state the *Etymologiae* are unfinished. The so-called *Renotatio Isidori*[47]—a list of Isidore's works produced by Braulio,[48] Bishop of Saragossa—as well as two letters by Isidore addressed to the former, seem to corroborate this.[49] A passage of the *Renotatio* in which Braulio alludes to the *Etymologiae* has been frequently quoted in an attempt to cast light on the partially imperfect arrangement of this work: "Etymologiarum codicem nimiae magnitudinis distinctum ab eo titulis, non libris, quem, quia rogatu meo fecit, quamuis inperfectum ipse reliquerit, ego in uiginti libros diuisi" [The *Etymologies*, a codex of massive proportions, divided by him (Isidore) into titles (i.e., into subjects), not books. (The work) was however left incomplete but I (Braulio) divided it into twenty books because it was made at my bidding].[50] If we trust this assertion, the current layout of the *Etymologiae* might actually be the work of Braulio.[51] However, it is hard to prove if this is so because the distribution in books is attested to even in the earliest manuscripts containing the work.[52]

---

47. The full title is *Renotatio librorum domini Isidori* (Notes on the works of Dom Isidore).
48. Isidore became acquainted with Braulio in Seville. After the latter's accession to the Saragossa episcopal see, their friendship continued, as attested to in the surviving letters. An English version of their correspondence is found in Barney et al., *The Etymologies*, 409–13.
49. See Letters IV and V in ibid., 410–13.
50. This passage is from José Carlos Martín Iglesias, *Scripta de vita Isidori Hispalensis episcopi*, *CCSL*, vol. 113B (Turnhout: Brepols Publishers, 2006), 203–4. For a full English version of the *Renotatio*, see Barney et al., *The Etymologies*, 7–9. As Díaz y Díaz points out, various manuscripts containing Braulio's *Renotatio* allude to a distribution into fifteen books instead of twenty, but no evidence of such version of the *Etymologiae* has been preserved. Oroz Reta and Marcos Casquero, *San Isidoro*, vol. 1, 177.
51. According to Martín Iglesias, it was Braulio's own initiative that triggered the division of the *Etymologiae* in twenty books and not Isidore's decision. See his *Scripta de vita Isidori*, 261–62.
52. As affirmed by Díaz y Díaz, "so far no manuscript of the *Etymologiae* presenting the old division in titles, and not in books, has been found" (my translation). Oroz Reta and Marcos Casquero, *San Isidoro*, vol. 1, 179.

Moreover, Díaz y Díaz called into question the relevance of Braulio's intervention in this sense.[53] Still, the fact that the *Etymologiae* could have been manipulated to a large extent by other people after—and even before[54]—Isidore's death is a plausible explanation for the occasional irregularities observed in some parts of the encyclopedia.

The last part of this chapter has showed that, despite occasional breaches and overlaps, the overall structure of Isidore's *Etymologiae* evinces a conscious organization of its contents. If we consider that this is a colossal project, in which Isidore, and probably several collaborators, were working for about fifteen or twenty years, errors in the final layout are quite understandable. Given the natural limitations faced by authors of the parchment era, it seems quite reasonable that they would frequently have to sacrifice coherence for the sake of elaborating a specific concept or idea at a particular point. Cases like the inclusion of the chameleon among quadrupeds of great size and the fourfold reference to the *homo/humus* association seem to corroborate this. Also, miscellanies such as Books XIX and XX would be unavoidable, even if planning had been done before the copying process took place.

Finally, the design of Isidore's encyclopedic treatise responds to medieval perceptions of order that are not as strict or demanding as they should be according to our contemporary standards. All this is to be borne in mind when approaching *enigmata*, since structural inconsistencies of the kind observed in the *Etymologiae* are also to be found in riddle collections, which, like Isidore's work, indulge in "unexpected juxtapositions" and inconsistencies,[55] as illustrated at the beginning of this book with Eusebius's Riddles 7 (letters) and 9

---

53. Ibid., 177–80.
54. Isidore had asked Braulio to help him with the revision of the *Etymologiae* to prevent spelling and grammatical errors, as his bad health did not allow him to do it himself. For this, see letter V in Barney et al., *The Etymologies*, 412–13. Also, see ibid., letter IV, where Braulio complains that the *Etymologiae* are already in the hands of many people and have thus been "mutilated and corrupted" (412).
55. I am borrowing this expression from Murphy, *Pliny*, 36.

(alpha) as well as Exeter Riddles 21 (plow) and 22 (Charles's Wain).[56] Indeed, though significantly smaller in size compared to Isidore's *Etymologiae*, riddle collections did not escape organizational flaws and orderly anomalies.

3.2. The Foundations of Early Medieval Riddling: Symphosius's Enigmata

3.2.1 Introduction to Symphosius's Enigmata

Although Symphosius is the author of the most influential collection in the history of European riddling, nothing is known about his identity. Even his name and the exact spelling of it have been a matter of debate.[57] August Heumann understood the term *symposium* as referring to a lost work by Lactantius.[58] This idea was accepted

---

56. See pp. 8–9.
57. See Reinold Merkelbach, "Zwei Gespensternamen: Aelafius und Symphosius," *Zeitschrift für Papyrologie und Epigraphik* 51 (1983): 228–29, where it is argued that the correct spelling of the name should be *Symposius*. Of the same opinion is Maddalena Spallone, "Symphosius o Symposius? Un problema di fonetica nell'Anthologia Latina," *Quaderni dell'Istituto di Lingua e Letterature Latina. Università 'La Sapienza.' Facoltà di Magistero* 4 (1982): 41–48. Bergamin similarly prefers this spelling throughout her *Aenigmata Symposii: la fondazione dell'enigmistica come genere poetico* (Florence: SISMEL-Edizioni del Galluzzo, 2005). I am however retaining the traditional form *Symphosius* because it is by far the most most common spelling, with slight variations, observed in the *incipits* of the manuscripts in which the collection is extant (see *CCSL*, vol. 133A, 621). It is therefore clear that Symphosius was known as such in the Middle Ages. Also, the form *Symphosius* has been preferred by most scholars since Alexander Riese's edition of this collection in *Anthologia Latina sive poesis latinae supplementum* (Leipzig, 1869). A second edition, to which I have already referred and will be using henceforth, is Buecheler and Riese, eds., *Anthologia latina* (Leipzig, 1894), vol. 1.1, 221–46 (no. 286).
58. August Heumann, *Caelii Firminiani Lactantii Symphosium* (Hannover, 1722). The work is mentioned by Jerome in his *De viris illustribus* (On illustrious men, c. 80): "Habemus ejus Symposium, quod adolescentulus scripsit"

by scholarship for some time,⁵⁹ but it was eventually altogether discarded. Nowadays critics agree on the existence of a certain Symphosius as the author of a collection of one hundred riddles written in three-line hexameters.⁶⁰

It is worth noting, however, that Reinold Merkelbach has argued that this name might be no more than a pseudonym that playfully evokes the entertaining function of riddles at banquets (Greek συμπόσιον, literally, a drinking party).⁶¹ In fact, Symphosius's preface to the *Enigmata* explicitly alludes to the riddles as originating in the festive context of the Roman Saturnalia,⁶² when banquets and liberal drinking took place:

Annua Saturni dum tempora festa redirent
perpetuo semper nobis sollemnia ludo,
post epulas laetas, post dulcia pocula mensae,
deliras inter uetulas puerosque loquaces,
cum streperet late madidae facundia linguae,
tum uerbosa cohors studio sermonis inepti
nescio quas passim magno de nomine nugas
est meditata diu; sed friuola multa locuta est. (1–8)⁶³

[From him (Lactantius) we have the *Symposium* which he wrote when he was quite young]. *PL*, vol. 23 (col. 687B). For further conjectures concerning Symphosius's name and identity, see Ohl, "The Enigmas," 13–14, and 31–32, and Bergamin, *Aenigmata Symposii*, xi–xiv.
59. Symphosius's Riddles also appear as part of Lactantius's works in *PL*, vol. 7 (cols. 288–98), and O. F. Fritzsche, ed., *Lactantius*, vol. 2 (Leipzig, 1845).
60. Ohl, "The Enigmas," 14.
61. Merkelbach, "Zwei Gespensternamen," 229. Lapidge and Rosier similarly consider the possibility that the name may be a pseudonym fitting the convivial character of the work. See *Aldhelm: The Poetic Works*, 243–44, n. 16.
62. The Roman Saturnalia is conveniently described in T. J. Leary, ed. and trans., *Martial: Book XIII, The Xenia* (Duckworth: London, 2001), 4–8.
63. Citations from the Latin riddle collections are all from Glorie, ed., *CCSL*, vols. 133 and 133A. Unless indicated otherwise, translations of the Latin texts provided in this book are mine. In the case of Symphosius's *Enigmata*, I have also consulted the following editions, which have been extremely useful: Buecheler and Riese, *Anthologia Latina* (1894);

[While Saturn's yearly holiday had returned, always for us a festival of continuous entertainment, after lavish courses and the sweet drinks of the meal, when among raving elderly women and loquatious children, the eloquence of the tipsy tongues shouts far and wide, then the talkative band, eager for idle conversation, for a long while considered I do not know what trifles with great titles; but lots of silly things were said].

It is in this lighthearted and relaxed atmosphere that Symphosius sets his *Enigmata*, which emerge as "nugas" (7)[64] in an attempt to entertain the guests after a dinner with a great riddling contest ("magni certaminis," 9). Not having prepared anything for the occasion, Symphosius says he felt compelled to compose these riddles on the spot.[65] The preface thus concludes in a humorous tone: "Da ueniam, lector, quod non sapit ebria Musa" (15) [Pardon, reader, the bad taste of a drunken Muse].[66] This final line functions as a *captatio benevolentiae* by means of which the author asks for the readers'

D. R. Shackleton Bailey, *Anthologia Latina I: Carmina in codicibus scripta 1, Libri Salmasiani aliorumque carmina* (Stuttgart: Teubner, 1982); and Bergamin, *Aenigmata Symposii*. The translations of the passages from Symphosius's preface and riddles are my own. A new edition is T. J. Leary, *Symphosius: The Aenigmata. An Introduction, Text and Commentary* (London: Bloomsbury Academic, 2014) but was published too late to be taken account of here.

64. As pointed out by Leary, *Martial: Book XIII*, 43, the term *nugae* usually "applied to poetic trifles or the lighter forms of verse." Catullus, for example, uses the term "nugas" to refer to minor poetic compositions in his *Carmina* (I.4). Peter Green, ed. and trans., *The Poems of Catullus: A Bilingual Edition* (Berkeley: University of California Press, 2005), 44.

65. The group of riddles appearing in Book X of the *Deipnosophists* of Athenaeus are similarly set in the context of a banquet. See above, p. 13.

66. This final line of the preface offers a punning on *sapio*, which can mean either "to have a taste, savor" or "to know," also implying the idea of knowing how to behave. This translation would thus maintain the intended wordplay, alluding to the fact that drinking has provoked not only the author's bad breath but also his bad manners, nasty jokes, and, consequently, bad taste—i.e., bad poetry or, at least, not as good as Symphosius presumably composes. I owe this idea to David Moreno Olalla. Also, see my comments

forgiveness if the quality of his verse does not live up to their expectations, as these poems are the product of Saturnalian revelry.

Not surprisingly, some scholars have associated Symphosius's collection with the contents found in Martial's Books XIII and XIV of the *Epigrams*, known as *Xenia* (83–84 CE) and *Apophoreta* (85 CE), respectively.[67] The titles of these two works allude to the gifts that were exchanged by guests at banquets celebrated during the Saturnalia. Martial's *Xenia* thus center on the different courses of a typical Saturnalian dinner, whereas the *Apophoreta* describe a variety of objects brought by the guests as gifts.[68] It is noteworthy that these two works offer some topics that are also the subject of some of Symphosius's Riddles, such as frankincense, pepper, ham, beet, crane, whip, broom, sponge, and bell, among others.[69] In addition to this, the contents of both the *Xenia* and the *Apophoreta* are organized into different thematic groups, although Symphosius's encyclopedic method of classification, as we will see later on, significantly broadens the epigrams' scope with a greater variety of topics. Still, it is worth mentioning that in the *Xenia*, for example, the epigrams are subdivided into appetizers, fowl, and a further group combining fish, seafood, and game. In the *Apophoreta* several subdivisions can be distinguished: writing tools, housewares, toiletries, and so forth.[70]

---

in "The Sexual Riddle Type in Aldhelm's *Enigmata*, the Exeter Book, and Early Medieval Latin," *PQ* 90 (2011): 362.

67. On the dating of these two works, see Leary, *Martial: Book XIII*, 13, and R. A. Pitcher, "The Dating of Martial Books XIII and XIV," *Hermes* 113 (1985): 330–39. For the association of Martial's works with Symphosius's Riddles, see María José Muñoz Jiménez, "Enigma y epigrama: de los *Xenia y Apophoreta* de Marcial a los *Aenigmata Symposii*," *Cuadernos de filología clásica* 19 (1985): 187–95, and Bergamin, *Aenigmata Symposii*, xxxiii–xxxv.

68. For the meaning of the *Xenia* as the "guest gifts" and the *Apophoreta* as "left-over food . . . 'to be carried away,'" see Leary, *Martial: Book XIII*, 1.

69. Muñoz Jiménez, "Enigma y epigrama," 192; Bergamin, *Aenigmata Symposii*, xxxiv–xxxv.

70. On the arrangement of the different topics of the epigrams, see J. P. Sullivan, *Martial: The Unexpected Classic* (Cambridge: Cambridge University Press, 1991), 12–13; and María José Muñoz Jiménez, "Rasgos comunes y

Apart from the thematic arrangement of the topics, Martial's epigrams make use of stylistic and rhetorical devices that are also present in riddles, a typical example of this being personification.[71] Besides, the *Xenia* and the *Apophoreta* have in common with Symphosius's *Enigmata* their mood and conciseness, since the epigrams are riddle-like distichs describing food, drinks, and tokens of diverse kind. Further parallels in Symphosius's Riddles naturally arise from the Saturnalian setting they share with Martial's two books. For example, the *Xenia* begin by stating that the poems are produced in the context of the "ebria bruma" (I.4, drunken winter) and the epigrams, like Symphosius's riddles, are referred to as "nugas" (II.4).[72] There is therefore no doubt that Symphosius knew Martial's *Xenia* and *Apophoreta* and drew some inspiration from them.

Apart from Symphosius's obscure identity, a further problematic aspect of his *Enigmata* is their dating, for which scholars have proposed from the second to the sixth century. Without going into much detail, proponents of an early dating of the riddles argue that these texts present excellent Latinity and prosody. Raymond Theodore Ohl, for example, contends that the only few features that could be regarded as late do not offer sufficient evidence.[73] It has also been pointed out that the riddles lack Christian allusions, but this cannot be considered as a conclusive proof of their pagan origins. Besides, as Ohl points out, Symphosius's *Enigmata* have much in common with the work of several late Roman authors, concluding that his

---

estructura particular de *Xenia y Apophoreta, Cuadernos de filología clásica, Estudios latinos* 10 (1996): 136–46, esp. 140–43.

71. Actually, the thin line between epigrams and riddles has usually been pointed out by scholars. See, for example, Lapidge and Rosier, *Aldhelm: The Poetic Works*, 243 (n. 15); and Muñoz Jiménez, "Enigma y Epigrama," 193–95. Also, Bergamin, *Aenigmata Symposii*, xxxiii, has affirmed that the enigma is a sub-type of the epigram. She further illustrates this idea with some examples from Martial's epigrams (xxxv).

72. Cf. "nugas" (7) and "ebria musa" (15) in Symphosius's preface above. For further echoes from Martial's Books XIII and XIV of the *Epigrams* in Symphosius's *Enigmata*, see the list offered in *CCSL*, vol. 133A, 862.

73. Ohl, "The Enigmas," 16.

riddle collection should date from the late fourth or the early fifth century.[74]

However, Alexander Riese conjectures that Symphosius's *Enigmata* could be contemporary with the works included in the so-called African or Latin Anthology, in which the riddles also occur.[75] Probably compiled at Carthage at the beginning of the sixth century, this poetic miscellany is extant in the Salmasian codex—Paris, Lat. 10318—which was copied in Central Italy (c. 800).[76] Accordingly, Symphosius might have formed part of a flourishing group of poets[77]

---

74. Ibid., 15.
75. Riese, for example, points out that Symphosius is styled *scholasticus*, which is equivalent to typical titles such as "uir clarissimus" or "uir inlustris" that are given to other poets in the Latin Anthology. For this see, Buecheler and Riese, *Anthologia latina*, vol. 1.1, xxvi.
76. The name of the manuscript stems from Claude de Saumaise, its owner between 1609 and 1620. An exhaustive introduction to the codex and its contents is found in Francisco Socas Gavilán, *Antología Latina, Repertorio de poemas extraído de códices y libros impresos* (Madrid: Gredos, 2011), 9–17. See also E. A. Lowe, *Codices latini antiquiores: A Palaeographical Guide to Latin Manuscripts Prior to the Ninth Century*, vol. 9 (Oxford: Clarendon, 1959), 593 (no. 5). For the dating of this manuscript, see Bernhard Bischoff, "Centri scrittori e manoscritti mediatori di civiltà dal VI secolo all'età di Carlo Magno," in *Libri e lettori nel medioevo*, ed. G. Cavallo (Bari: Laterza, 1977), 92, n. 133. On paleographical grounds, Spallone concludes that the Salmasian codex was copied from a late exemplar from one of the main cultural centers of Italy in the second half of the sixth century such as Rome, Ravenna, Capua or Naples. Maddalena Spallone, "Il Par. Lat. 10318 (Salmasiano): dal manoscritto alto-medievale ad una raccolta enciclopedica tardo-antica," *Italia Medioevale e Umanistica* 25 (1982): 69.
77. Interestingly, the leading figure of this group was Luxorius, whose epigrams follow Symphosius's *Enigmata* in the Salmasian codex (p. 156). See Judith W. George, "Vandal Poets in their Context," in *Vandals, Romans and Berbers: New Perspectives on Late Antique North Africa*, ed. Andrew H. Merrills (Aldershot: Ashgate, 2004), 133–45. On Symphosius as an African poet, see B. Baldwin, "Some Pleasures of Later Roman Literature: the African Contribution," *Acta classica* 32 (1989): 51; and Erin Sebo, "Was Symphosius an African? A Contextualizing Note on Two Textual Clues in the *Aenigmata Symphosii*," *N&Q* 56 (2009): 323–24.

who thrived under the rule of Vandal kings.[78] Riese's hypothesis may be supported by the fact that the *Enigmata* are preceded in the Salmasian codex by an epigram known as "De conviviis barbaris" (On foreign guests),[79] which famously contains some Germanic words that have been identified by some scholars as Vandalic.[80] This poem, like Symphosius's preface, expresses the impossibility of composing good poetry on such an occasion. The subsequent epigram,[81] which is understood by some scholars as a continuation of the preceding one,[82] adds that Calliope, the druken muse ("ebria Musa," 2), must run away from Bacchus so that she can avoid the shame of not being able to stand on her feet. Apart from this, the presence of similar topics and verbal parallelisms in Symphosius's Riddles and various poems contained in the Latin Anthology suggests that Symphosius was acquainted with the literary production of this African intellectual circle, which probably influenced his *Enigmata*.[83]

---

78. The vandals' occupation of Roman Africa started with Geiseric's invasion in 429 and concluded with the wars against the Byzantines in 533–534. See Andreas Schwarcz, "The Settlement of the Vandals in North Africa," in Merrills, ed., *Vandals, Romans and Berbers*, 49–58.
79. An edition of the epigram is found in Buecheler and Riese, *Anthologia latina*, vol. 1.1, 221 (nos. 285–285a), and Shackleton Bailey, *Anthologia Latina I*, 201–2 (nos. 279–80). For further information on the epigram, see W. van Helten, "Zu Anthologia Latina Ed. Riese No. 285 und 285A (*De conviviis barbaris*)," *Beiträge zur Geschichte der deutschen Sprache und Literatur* 29 (1904): 339–43.
80. See, for example, Hermann Reichert, "Sprache und Namen der Wandalen in Afrika," in *Namen des Frühmittelalters als sprachliche Zeugnisse und als Geschichtsquellen*, ed. Albrecht Greule and Matthias Springer (Berlin: De Gruyter, 2009), 49–50.
81. The two epigrams occur on p. 141 of the Salmasian codex before Symphosius's Riddles.
82. For this appreciation, see Magnús Snædal, "The 'Vandal' Epigram," *Filologia Germanica* 1 (2009): 181–215.
83. For example, Lapidge and Rosier, *Aldhelm: The Poetic Works*, 244, n. 16, comment on the closeness between line 3 of Symphosius's preface and the beginning of poem 382 (Shackleton Bailey 377 as offered by these scholars) of the Latin Anthology. Also, see Lapidge and Rosier, ibid.,

A further idea in favor of Riese's late dating is given by the presence of some of Symphosius's Riddles in the *Historia Apollonii Regis Tyri*. This work has come down to us in two textual forms, known as Recension A and Recension B, which, according to G. A. A. Kortekaas, may have been produced in the late-fifth and early sixth centuries, respectively.[84] For Kortekaas, these riddles constitute an addition to the romance that derives from the work of "a probably contemporary author."[85] Finally, Bergamin has provided substantial evidence of the presence of late features in Symphosius's *Enigmata*, as well as an analysis of numerous passages suggesting the author's acquaintance with the Latin Anthology and other texts ranging from the fifth to the sixth century.[86]

As regards the allegedly pagan background of the riddles, it is notable that Symphosius's *Enigmata* lack explicit Christian references. By contrast, the riddles indulge in classical mythological allusion. For example, Symphosius has the stone say in the first line of Riddle 74: "Deucalion ego sum" [I am Deucalion]. This line thus acts the riddle in the mythological dimension by alluding to the way the earth was repopulated after a destructive deluge thanks

---

243, n. 15. Furthermore, some of the topics of the poems of the Anthology are also found in the *Enigmata*. This is, for example, the case for poems 119–24 and 210–13, all of them dealing with baths. Here and elsewhere in this book, the numbering of the poems contained in the Latin Anthology corresponds to that found in Buecheler and Riese, *Athologia latina*. For a list itemizing thematic correspondences found in Symphosius's Riddles and the Latin Anthology, see Bergamin, *Aenigmata Symposii*, xlvi–xlvii.

84. G. A. A. Kortekaas, *The Story of Apollonius, King of Tyre: a Study of its Greek Origin and an Edition of the two oldest Latin Recensions* (Leiden: Brill, 2004), 3. For the edition of the two versions of the *Historia Apollonii*, see 104–249.

85. Ibid., 94. María José Muñoz Jiménez has even conjectured that both the romance and the riddles may be the work of the same author. See her "Algunos aspectos de los *Aenigmata Symphosii*: título, autor y relación con la *Historia Apollonii regis Tyri*," *Emerita* 55.2 (1987): 307–12.

86. See Bergamin, *Aenigmata Symposii*, xl–xli and xlvi–l.

to the stones that Deucalion and his wife Pyrrha threw over their shoulders. By the same token, Riddle 82 introduces the jar in line 1 as the daughter of Tellus (the earth) and Prometheus: "Mater erat Tellus, genitor est ipse Prometheus." Presented in a typically succint way imposed by the tristich format, this riddle would remind learned readers that Prometheus created man from clay and stole fire from the gods in order to offer it to humans for different purposes. This clue thus effectively refers to the two elements involved in the clay-firing process.

With their frequent allusions to classical myth, Symphosius's Riddles comply with the distinctive pagan flavor of many of the poems offered in the Latin Anthology. As Stephan Busch affirms, by the time the Latin Anthology was compiled, Christianity had long been established as the norm in Carthage. He thus explains that this "anachronistically mythological setting" of the contents of the Anthology "is the expression of a need for continuity, of participation in the discourse of classical ancient poetry."[87] The presence of classical allusions did not constitute a hindrance to the uses of Symphosius's *Enigmata* in the Christian milieu. The case may be compared to Lactantius's *De ave phoenice*, in which explicit references to pagan gods and other mythological figures are similarly found.[88] However, these elements did not prevent the work from becoming a favorite of the medieval curriculum, as the story of the phoenix lent itself particularly well to allegorical interpretation. On the other hand, mythological elements are equally abundant in Aldhelm's *Enigmata*, whose

---

87. Stephan Busch, "*Versus ex variis locis deducti*. On Ancient Collections of Epigrams," in *The Neo-Latin Epigram: A Learned and Witty Genre*, ed. Susanna de Beer, Karl A. E. Enenkel, and David Rijser (Leuven: Leuven University Press, 2009), 36.
88. The poem, for example, mentions Phaeton (11), Deucalion (14), Phoebus (33, 58, 140) and Venus (165). For an edition of this poem, see Mary Cletus Fitzpatrick, ed. and trans., *Lactanti de Ave Phoenice* (Philadelphia: University of Pennsylvania Press, 1933). For her comments on these passages, see 62–63, 67, and 90.

Christian character is unquestionable.[89] The collections of Tatwine, Eusebius, and Boniface are likewise not devoid of references to pagan gods and classical myth.[90] In this light, it is therefore not surprising that Symphosius's Riddles co-occur with Christian classics such as Juvencus's *Evangelia*, Sedulius's *Carmen paschale*, Arator's *De actibus apostolorum*, Prudentius's *Psychomachia*, Lactantius's *De ave phoenice*, and Boethius's *De consolatione philosophiae*, among others, in the school anthology contained in Cambridge, Gg.5.35.[91]

Despite their apparent pagan stance, Symphosius's *Enigmata* were doubtlessly considered acceptable from a Christian point of view.[92] Indeed, some of the subjects contained in Symphosius's *Enigmata* would at least be suggestive for a Christian audience. This is, for example, the case of frankincense (no. 47), myrrh (48), sponge (63), whip (66), and die (91), all of which could easily illustrate objects traditionally associated with episodes of the Gospels. With its solution being *malum*, Riddle 85 would prompt the double meaning apple/evil and thus conjure up the episode of Genesis in the same way that Aldhelm's *Enigma* 76 (apple-tree) does.[93] In the Salmasian codex (p. 154), the addition of the following explanatory

---

89. Aldhelm's Riddles 5, 8, 28, 45, 57, 95, and 97 contain mythological allusions, which are conveniently explained in Herren, "The Transmission," 94–96. See also Zoja Pavlovskis, "The Riddler's Microcosm: From Symphosius to St. Boniface," *Classica et mediaevalia* 39 (1988): 235–36.
90. By way of example, references to Mars can be found in Tatwine's Riddles 17 (5) and 32 (1). Allusions to Phoebus occur in Tatwine's *Enigma* 1 (5) and Eusebius's Riddles 11 (1) and 53 (5). Bellerophon is alluded to in Eusebius's *Enigma* 52: (7).
91. For a discussion of this manuscript, see above, pp. 79–80. For a list of the contents in Cambridge, Gg.5.35, see Rigg and Wieland, "A Canterbury Classbook," 120–29, and Irvine, *The Making*, 360–62.
92. Still, in London, Royal 12.C.xxiii (fol. 104r), the name "Simphosius" is preceded in the upper margin by the phrase "i. uir gentilis," which might have been added as an acknowledgement of the pagan origin of the author.
93. Also, see further on p. 210 for the use of punning *malum* in Aldhelm's Riddle 76. For an analysis of the multiple semantic layers observed in the clues of this riddle, see Bergamin, *Aenigmata Symposii*, xxix and 182–83.

line alluding to the vowel length differentiating *mālum* (apple) from *mălum* (evil) leaves no room for doubt that this wordplay was meant: "Hoc uolo ne breuiter mihi syllaba prima legatur" [I want this: that the first syllable is not read as short].[94] In turn, the clues offered by *Enigma* 83 allude to the three basic ingredients (pepper, honey, and wine) to produce *conditum* (spiced wine): "Tres olim fuimus qui nomine iungimur uno; / ex tribus est unus, et tres miscentur in uno" (1–2) [We were formerly three who are now united by one name; from three comes one, and in one three are mixed]. As Bergamin explains, the phrasing used in this riddle evokes the three substances of the Trinity as united in one concept.[95] In the context in which the Latin Anthology was compiled, the riddle may have been particularly meaningful, as it could have been representative of the tension between concurring Trinitarian theology and the Arianism of Vandal rulers. On the other hand, Bergamin has also argued that some of the subjects of Symphosius's Riddles are close in terms of content and style to early medieval hagiographies. For example, she contends that *Riddle* 45 (rose) displays some metaphorical resonances

---

94. This line, which is here directly transcribed from the Salmasian codex (p. 154), is not used in the *CCSL* edition, vol. 133A, 706. However, it is employed by Buecheler and Riese, *Anthologia Latina*, vol. 1.1, 242, Shackleton Bailey, *Anthologia Latina I*, 229, and Bergamin, *Aenigmata Symposii*, 60. As the latter affirms (183), this line may have originally been a gloss that was at some point inserted as part of the riddle, as observed in the version found in the Salmasian codex. A further manuscript containing this line, as well as the unusal four-line format of the Salmasian version, is reported by Chauncey E. Finch in "Codex Vat. Barb. Lat. 721 as a Source for the Riddles of Symphosius," *Transactions and Proceedings of the American Philological Association* 98 (1967): 178. Interestingly, Aldhelm knew this version of Symphosius's Riddle 85, since he quotes this line in *De metris*. See Ehwald, *Aldhelmi opera*, 96.
95. Bergamin brings up a passage from Aponius's *Expositio in Canticum Canticorum*, in which the dogma of the Trinity is explained by means of the symbolic parallelism of the "uinum conditum." Aponius was an author active in the Roman area in the early fifth century. See Bergamin, *Aenigmata Symposii*, liii–liv and 180–81.

that connect this composition with the hagiographies of St Agnes from the area of central Italy.[96]

Further evidence of the fact that Symphosius's *Enigmata* could have been used in a Christian context is the presence of numerous evocative pairs in the collection. As regards Symphosius's Riddles 47 (frankincense) and 48 (myrrh), these texts convey a typical analogical pair with Christian resonances, since in Matthew 2.11 these two aromatic resins are mentioned among the gifts brought by the Magi to the child Jesus.[97] The juxtaposition of Riddles 7 (smoke) and 8 (fog) is also noteworthy, as it invites comparison between an artificially made phenomenon and another one that is naturally produced, a contrastive pattern that was discussed in Isidore's *Etymologiae*. As we will see below, Aldhelm's *Enigmata* illustrate this kind of pairing in which man's craftmanship is frequently contrasted with God's Creation. Besides, a similar juxtaposition of topics occurs with Symphosius's Riddle 7 (smoke) and Aldhelm's *Enigma* 3 (cloud), corresponding to queries 102 and 103 of Pseudo-Bede's *Collectanea*.[98] A further interesting duo is observed in Symphosius's Riddles 22 (ant) and 23 (fly), where the two creatures are set as positive and negative examples, respectively, thus recalling oppositional patterns such as that of the oyster and the crab in Isidore's *Etymologiae*.[99] The clues of these riddles do not leave room for doubt that

---

96. See ibid., xiv–xv and 139–40, and Manuela Bergamin, "Il riccio e la rosa. Vicende di immagini e parole dall'antico al tardoantico (a proposito di Simposio, aenig. 29 e 45)," *Incontri triestini di filologia classica* 3 (2003–2004): 199–214. Interestingly, Bergamin has also pointed out the presence of verbal parallelisms with the works of Christian authors, particularly with Paulinus of Nola's *Carmina* 19 and 23, which were devoted to the cult of St Felix. See *Aenigmata Symposii*, xiv.

97. Bergamin has detected further interesting allegorical connotations, since in Riddle 48 myrrh could also be seen as an ointment for the deceased. The phrase "imago doloris" (3) would thus be suggestive of the idea of Christ's sepulchre. *Aenigmata Symposii*, xxii and 146.

98. See Bayless and Lapidge, *Collectanea*, 134–35.

99. As noted by several critics, the moral roles are probably based on the tradition of fables such as that of the ant and the fly from *Phaedrus*

the two were conceived as an antithetical pair. In Riddle 22 the ant is described as "prouida" (1, prudent, foresighted), whereas Riddle 23 characterizes the fly as "improba" (1, wicked).[100] The usual juxtaposition of these two riddles in the manuscripts containing Symphosius's collection thus acknowledges this veiled interconnection, offering suggestive deontological implications that would be much welcomed by Christian readers.

As the ant/fly pair illustrates, the choices of zoological subjects in Symphosius's *Enigmata* do not seem to be haphazard, since most of them are potentially meaningful from a Christian point of view. The clues of the riddle on the phoenix (no. 31), for instance, could no doubt be interpreted allegorically: "Vita mihi mors est; morior si coepero nasci. / Sed prius est fatum leti quam lucis origo" (1–2) [My death is life. I die if my birth begins; / but the fate of death is before the beginning of light].[101] This passage could well dovetail with the Christian idea that real life starts when death occurs. Furthermore, the bird was a traditional symbol of Christ, so that the paradox contained in these two lines could easily be interpreted as referring to the resurrection as well. Apart from the phoenix, Symphosius's collection offers other zoological subjects that seem to bear Christian resonances. As Bergamin notes, the mole (21), the bat (28), and the wolf (33) frequently illustrate the figure of the heretic

---

(4.25). For an edition of this fable, see Ben Edwin Perry, ed., *Babrius and Phaedrus* (Cambridge, MA: Harvard University Press, 1965), 340–43. See Ziolkowski's comments on the relationship of Symphosius's riddle pair and this fable. Jan M. Ziolkowski, *Talking Animals: Medieval Latin Beast Poetry, 750–1150* (Philadelphia: University of Pennsylvania Press, 1993), 41–42.

100. For a similar appreciation of these two riddles as an antithetical pair, see Ziolkowski, *Talking Animals*, 41–42, and Javier Pizarro Sánchez, "Estructura y tipología de los Aenigmata Symphosii," *Cuadernos de Filología clásica. Estudios latinos* 16 (1999): 242.

101. Some echoes from Lactantius's *De ave phoenice* have been detected. See the notes to this riddle in *CCSL*, vol. 133A, 652. However, Ohl, "The Enigmas," 65, has downplayed the significance of these parallels. By contrast, Bergamin, *Aenigmata Symposii*, 123, attaches more importance to these common features.

in exegetical literature.[102] This is also the case of the viper (15), the frog (19), and the moth (16), the latter often used as an allegory for the way in which heretics tampered with the interpretation of the Scriptures in their writings.[103] Peter Scott Dale in turn has detected the presence of subtle allegorical connotations in Symphosius's Riddle 29 (hedgehog).[104] Bergamin confirms this inference by pointing out the closeness of some of the expressions describing the hedgehog in Riddle 29 and typical references describing St Sebastian in hagiographic works.[105]

Evidence of the medieval compilers' awareness of the allegorical potential of some of Symphosius's subjects is also attested to in the deliberate placement of the riddle on the anchor at the close of the collection in some codices.[106] As Chauncey E. Finch states, three manuscripts, all of them belonging to family D, place the anchor riddle at the end:[107] Vatican City, Biblioteca Apostolica Vaticana, Barb. Lat. 721; Leiden, Voss. Lat. Q. 106;[108] and St Gall, Stiftsbibliothek 273.[109] To these three codices we should add Vatican City, Pal. Lat. 1753, in which *Enigma* 61 figures at the close of the collection (fol. 113r). Moreover, in Cambridge, Gg.5.35 (fol. 394r) and London,

---

102. Bergamin, *Aenigmata Symposii*, lii–liii.
103. For the viper, the frog, and the moth as representative of heretics, see, for example, Hrabanus Maurus, *De rerum naturis*, VIII.iii.495–96, VIII.ii.351–52, and VIII.iv.634-635 (from Schipper's forthcoming edition). See also Bergamin, *Aenigmata Symposii*, 103.
104. Peter Scott Dale, "Rhetorical and Symbolic Ambiguity: Symphosius and Aldhelm," in *Saints, Scholars and Heroes: Studies in Medieval Culture in Honor of Charles W. Jones*, ed. Margot H. King and Wesley M. Stevens (Collegeville, MN: Saint John's Abbey and University Press, 1979), 120.
105. Bergamin, *Aenigmata Symposii*, xxv–xxvi and 120–21, and "Il riccio e la rosa," 207–10.
106. As Finch explains, manuscripts belonging to what Riese and Ohl defined as family D transfer the anchor riddle "to a position after 100." "Symphosius" 5.
107. Finch, "Codex Vat. Barb. Lat. 721," 176.
108. See Bremmer and Dekker, *Manuscripts in the Low Countries*, 109.
109. See Finch "Codex Vat. Barb. Lat. 721," 176.

Royal 12.C.xxiii (fol. 113v) the anchor riddle occurs at the end, right after the one entitled "monumentum." An early Christian symbol representing hope of salvation,[110] the anchor would no doubt be an evocative topic, so we might infer that it was at some point considered appropriate as a conclusion to the *Enigmata*. It is therefore reasonable to assume that the acknowledgment of the anchor's symbology might have motivated this notable structural change in these manuscripts.[111]

The fact that Symphosius's *Enigmata* could well adjust to the literary tastes of a Christian audience is also illustrated by a peculiar scribal reading that can be observed in the Salmasian codex. In the *CCSL* edition, the second line of Riddle 14 (chicken in the egg) reads "Nondum natus fueram matris iam natus in aluo" (2) [I was not yet born, but already born in my mother's womb]. In the Salmasian manuscript (p. 144), this line is interestingly rendered as "nondum natus eram matris damnatus in aluo" (Not yet born, I was damned in my mother's womb), as if suggesting that the chicken in the egg would already be affected by the original sin.[112] Whether this was an intentional alteration or a misreading we cannot know. But this example reveals that efforts to read Symphosius's Riddles from a Christian point of view were no doubt made even at the earliest stages of the history of the manuscript transmission of this work.[113]

There is a further compelling addition to Riddle 47 (frankincense)

---

110. The idea is based on Paul's comparison of hope of salvation as "a sure and steadfast anchor of the soul" (Hebrews 6.19). For exegetical passages in which the anchor figures as an emblem of hope for Christians, see Bergamin, *Aenigmata Symposii*, 160. Furthermore, the proximity of Latin *ancora* (anchor) to *anachoreta*, as used for a religious person who has withdrawn from the world, seems to have strengthened the allegorical association of the two concepts. See *DOE*, s.v. "ancor, ancra."

111. For the order of Symphosius's Riddles, see further on p. 141 (n. 157).

112. As Ohl comments, "One wonders what subtlety of theology was in the mind of the monk who wrote *damnatus*." "The Enigmas," 47.

113. Bergamin provides parallels from exegetical literature in which the symbol of the chicken in the egg is used to discuss the concept of Christian hope and the origin of the human soul. *Aenigmata Symposii*, 100.

in the Salmasian codex which may have to do with the manipulation of Symphosius's *Enigmata* to make them accord with Christian ideology. Without this addition and in a typical tristich format, the riddle, as offered by Fr. Glorie's edition, reads as follows:

Dulcis odor nemoris flamma fumoque fatigor,
et placet hoc superis, medios quod mittor in ignes,
cum mihi peccandi meritum natura negauit.

[Sweet odor of the forest, I am fatigued by flame and fume,[114] as it pleases the gods that I should be thrown in the middle of fire although nature denied me the rewards of the sinner (i.e., hell).]

The allusion to burning as a way of punishment was probably capitalized upon by some compiler who, in an attempt to adjust the riddle to Christian doctrine, supplied a further line to this riddle in the Salmasian codex (p. 149): "nec in pena datur sed habetuir (i.e., habetur) gratia dandi" [I am not given (to fire) as a punishment but (I am) spent for the grace of giving (i.e., as a votive offering)].[115] With this addition,[116] the clues more strongly insist on the paradox that frankincense, unlike human beings, cannot sin but is nevertheless cast into fire. The modification, which is present in other manuscripts,[117] was probably meant to make readers reflect on the punishment that awaits sinners.[118]

---

114. Like Ohl, I maintain the original alliterating sounds. See *CCSL*, vol. 133A, 668.
115. This is a direct transcription from the Salmasian codex, which is rendered by some editors as "Nec mihi poena datur, sed habetur gratia dandi." See Riese, *Anthologia Latina*, vol. 1.1, 233; Shackleton Bailey, *Anthologia Latina I*, 217); and Bergamin, *Aenigmata Symposii*, 34, the latter with the variant spelling "danti." In these editions, this reading replaces the third line of *Enigma* 47 ("Cum mihi peccandi meritum natura negauit") of Glorie, *CCSL*, vol. 133A, 668.
116. For a similar four-line presentation of this riddle with slight variant readings, see Finch, "Codex Vat. Barb. Lat. 721," 178.
117. See ibid.
118. Symphosius's Riddle 75 (lime) offers a similar veiled reference to

A further scribal intervention has been noted by some editors in the case of Symphosius's Riddle 80 (broom). The first line of this riddle offers the clue "Mundi magna parens" (great mother of cleanliness), which plays on the double meaning of the term *mundus*, meaning both "clean" and "world." This phrase is however substituted by "in siluis genita" (born in the forests) in manuscripts belonging to Recension B. As "Mundi magna parens" (great mother of the world) recalls the typical epithets alluding to the Virgin Mary in medieval hymns, it has been argued that the alteration responds to an attempt to avoid an offensive comparison of Christ's mother with the broom.[119] This case therefore illustrates how Symphosius's *Enigmata* were accommodated to Christian ideology in the Middle Ages.

The ability of the riddles to adjust so promptly and malleably to Christian culture was probably one of the reasons why Symphosius's collection achieved such a high degree of popularity. As part of the Latin Anthology, Symphosius's *Enigmata* might have arrived in Europe via Visigothic Spain, where African Christians, fleeing from continuing instability in their homeland, sought refuge there in the mid-sixth century.[120] Bernhard Bischoff alludes to a passage from Ildefonsus of Toledo's *De viris illustribus*, which narrates how Abbot Donatus disembarked on the coast near Valencia (c. 560) with seventy monks ("cum septuaginta monachis") and many books ("copiosisque librorum codicibus"), escaping from the violence of the Barbarian peoples ("uiolentias barbararum gentium").[121] A further reference to

---

the fiery torments of hell ("ignis tormenta," 1). See Bergamin, *Aenigmata Symposii*, xxvi and 173.

119. Johann Christian Wernsdorf, ed., *Poetae latini minores*, vol. 6 (Helmstadt, 1794), 554; N. E. Lemaire, ed., *Poetae latini minores: De re hortensi et villatica carmina*, vol. 6 (Paris, 1826), 409; Ohl, "The Enigmas," 111; Bergamin, *Aenigmata Symposii*, 177–78.

120. Bischoff affirms that "Some Latin literature from Africa was preserved by being transmitted through Spain, like the *Anthologia Latina* in the Codex Salmasianus. . . ." *Manuscripts and Libraries*, 3. For a similar opinion, see Ludwig Traube, "Zur lateinischen Anthologie. I. Über Gedichte des Codex Salmasianus," *Philologus* 54 (1895): 124–34.

121. This citation is from Yarza Urquiola and Codoñer Merino, *CCSL*, vol.

the arrival of a group of African monks led by Abbot Nanctus in 570 or 580 is recorded in Paul the Deacon of Mérida's *Vitae sanctorum patrum Emeretensium* (The lives of the holy fathers of Mérida).[122] Being a select compendium of the work of African authors, the Latin Anthology might have been among the books brought to Spain by those refugees. The fact that Symphosius's Riddles were known and appreciated in Spanish monastic circles is also proved by the survival of a fragmentary version of the collection in a mid-tenth-century codex from the Monastery of St Millán de la Cogolla, which forms part of Madrid, Academia de la Historia, Aemilian. 39.[123]

There is no doubt that Symphosius's *Enigmata* were a literary success in the Middle Ages. The collection appears in about thirty codices from different repositories in Europe, although in some of them the text has been only partially preserved.[124] Symphosius's *Enigmata* must have been known in England, as they occur in a complete form in the two main English riddle compendia: Cambridge, Gg.5.35 (fols. 389r-94r) and London, Royal 12.C.xxiii (104r 13v).[125] They are

---

114A, 605 (c. 3). See also Bischoff, *Manuscripts and Libraries*, 3, and Socas Gavilán, *Antología latina*, 10.
122. Codoñer Merino, *El 'De Viris Illustribus,'* 51; Yarza Urquiola and Codoñer Merino, *CCSL*, vol. 114A, 531. For the specific passage from Paul the Deacon of Mérida's work, see *PL*, vol. 80 (col. 126), and A. T. Fear, *Lives of the Visigothic Fathers* (Liverpool: Liverpool University Press, 1997), 55.
123. Díaz y Díaz brought attention to this manuscript, which is actually made of two codices, designated by him as A and B. In codex B, from the mid-tenth century, 33 riddles of Symphosius's collection are extant (fols. 260rb-61r). Manuel C. Díaz y Díaz, "Para la crítica de los Aenigmata de Sinfosio," *Helmantica* 28 (1977): 121-36. For further information about this manuscript, see Dámaso Alonso, "La primitiva épica francesa a la luz de una nota Emilianense," *Revista de filología española* 37 (1953): 1-94, esp. 1-3 and 8-9. Also, see Bergamin, *Aenigmata Symposii*, lxxii.
124. For information on manuscripts containing the collection, see Ohl, "The Enigmas," 25-29; Finch, "Symphosius"; and *CCSL*, vol. 133A, 612-14. Bergamin, *Aenigmata Symposii*, cxiii-cxv, offers the most complete, accurate, and updated list of the manuscripts in which Symphosius's Riddles are extant. For a detailed account of them, see ibid., lxxiv-lxxxvii.
125. On these two codices, see above, pp. 35-36.

also extant in London, Royal 15.B.xix (fols. 202r-03v), which, as mentioned above, is a Salisbury codex from the late eleventh century.[126] In this case, the sequence of riddles starts with *Enigma* 18 (snail) and ends with Pseudo-Symphosius's Riddle 2 (snow).[127] A further composite manuscript containing Symphosius's *Enigmata*, which has passed unnoticed to editors, is Edinburgh, Adv. 18.6.12 (late eleventh or early twelfth century), a codex from the monastery of Thorney which has already been discussed.[128] In the third part of this manuscript, designated by Vernet as C, there is an addition of two folios that were torn from a thirteenth-century codex.[129] It is in these two folios (36v-37v) that an incomplete version of Symphosius's collection reaching up to Riddle 52 (flour) occurs.[130]

Together with Aldhelm's Riddles, Symphosius's *Enigmata* were included in the Carolingian school curriculum, thus becoming part

---

126. See above, p. 36. I thank Kathleen Doyle from the British Library for helping me discern that the actual foliation of this part of the manuscript is that of the pencil that supercedes the ink foliation.
127. Interestingly, Pseudo-Symphosius's Riddle 2 also occurs in a final position in St Gall, Stiftsbibliothek, Cod. Sang. 273 (p. 37), after the anchor riddle (no. 61). See Bergamin, *Aenigmata Symposii*, lxxx. For the text of the snow riddle, see *CCSL*, vol. 133A, 722.
128. See above, pp. 47–48. For the reference to Symphosius's poems as an item no. 7 in Sir Henry Savile's catalogue (1609–17), see Vernet, "Notice et extraits," 38.
129. Ibid., 37. The continuing success of Symphosius's Riddles is also attested by the survival of a late-medieval English codex containing Symphosius's *Enigmata* in London, British Library, Cotton Vespasian B.xxiii, a fourteenth-century manuscript from York. On this manuscript, see J. Planta, *A Catalogue of the Manuscripts in the Cottonian Library deposited in the British Museum* (London: 1802), 442; Spallone, "Tradizioni insulari," 213–14; and Bergamin, *Aenigmata Symposii*, lxxxiii.
130. Only the first line of this riddle has been preserved. See Vernet, "Notice et extraits," 47. Interestingly, part B of this manuscript also contains the *turtur*-enigma and two further Latin riddles (fol. 35v), which were mentioned above (see p. 48). See Vernet, ibid., 46–47, and Baldzuhn, *Schulbücher im Trivium*, 512.

of the "medieval literary canon."[131] As riddling was a particularly relevant phenomenon in Anglo-Saxon England, it is no surprise to find Symphosius's Riddles in manuscripts that were produced in monastic centers with well-known Insular ties such as St Gall, Lorsch, Corbie, and Rheims. An example of this kind of compilation is Vatican Pal. Lat. 1753, a codex from Lorsch, which contains Symphosius's *Enigmata* (fols. 110r-13r).[132] A further product of the Lorsch scriptorium is the first part of Vatican City, Pal. Lat. 1719, which offers Symphosius's *Enigmata* on folios 15r-20r. Bergamin has also brought attention to the presence of a fragmentary version of the collection starting with Riddle 40 (poppy) in a tenth-century codex from Rheims contained in London, Royal 15.B.xix (fols. 79r-82r), which was mentioned above.[133] Though with a somewhat disjointed appearance,[134] Symphosius's Riddles are present in Rome, MS. 1515, a Frankish manuscript containing works that are akin to the hermeneutic style which was cultivated in England in the second half of the tenth century, as discussed earlier in this book.[135]

---

131. Irvine, *The Making*, 356.
132. On this manuscript, see pp. 21–22.
133. Bergamin, *Aenigmata Symposii*, lxxxv. Spallone and Codoñer Merino had previously observed the presence of Symphosius's Riddles in this part of London, Royal 15.B.xix. See Spallone, "Tradizioni insulari," 199–200, and Carmen Codoñer Merino, "Un manuscrito escolar," 232 and 240. As pointed out above, p. 33, this is one of the three Frankish codices containing riddle collections that might have been brought to England in the second half of the tenth century.
134. As explained by Bergamin in her *Aenigmata Symposii* (lxxix–lxxx), Riddles 23–100 were copied by one scribe in the upper and lower margins of fols. 1r-20r of this manuscript; a second scribe later corrected the text and added the preface as well as Riddles 81 and 51 on the margins of fols. 20r–22r. For further details, see Maddalena Spallone, "Storia del libro, storia del texto: una interazione possibile," in Jacqueline Hamesse, ed., *Les problèmes posés par l'édition critique des textes anciens et médiévaux* (Louvain-la-Neuve: Publications de l'Institut d'études médiévales de Louvain-la-Neuve, 1992), 73-93.
135. See above, p. 42.

The influence of Symphosius's *Enigmata* on the work of Carolingian authors also proves how relevant this collection was in this period. Evidence of this is the presence of Symphosian parallels observed in Alcuin's *Disputatio*[136] and *Carmina*.[137] In addition to Alcuin's works, the imprint of Symphosius's *Enigmata* can be traced in the anonymous poem known as "Karolus Magnus et Leo Papa" from the late eighth century.[138] As Bergamin notes,[139] numerous echoes from Symphosius's preface can be detected in the *Carmina centulensia*, a collection of poems composed by three monks from the Abbey of Saint-Riquier in the ninth century.[140] It is noteworthy that these poems accompany Symphosius's *Enigmata* in St Petersburg, F.v.XIV.1.[141]

Symphosius soon developed a status as a canonical enigmatist.[142] The continuing success of his *Enigmata* throughout the Middle Ages is attested to by the fact that five of these riddles are fully cited in Pseudo-Bede's *Collectanea*.[143] Apart from being the model for subse-

---

136. Notably, Symphosius's Riddles 76 (flint), 30 (louse), 14 (chicken in egg), 12 (river and fish), and 99 (sleep). See corresponding nos. 93, 95, 96, 98, and 99 in Alcuin's work. Bayless, "Alcuin's *Disputatio*," 177.
137. Especially in the poem describing a bath, which parallels Symphosius's *Enigma* 90 (bath-house). Cf. Alcuin's poem in Dümmler *MGH, PLAC*, vol. 1 (no. 92.1), p. 318.
138. This poem, which was composed a few years after Charlemagne's coronation as emperor, incorporates line 3 of Symphosius's preface almost verbatim. See ibid., 379 ("Post laetas epulas et dulcia pocula Bachi," 531). On this poem, see Irvine, *The Making*, 311–12.
139. Bergamin, *Aenigmata Symposii*, lix.
140. For an edition of these poems, see Ludwig Traube, *MGH, PLAC*, vol. 3 (1896). Cf. "post dulces epulas" (11) and "da ueniam, lector" (24) in poem no. 160 (362) of this collection and lines 3 and 15 of Symphosius's preface. For further echoes from Symphosius's Riddles in the *Carmina centulensia*, see Bergamin, *Aenigmata Symposii*, lix.
141. On this manuscript, see above, p. 17. For a list of its contents, see Ganz, *Corbie in the Carolingian Renaissance*, 142.
142. Apart from the 100-riddle collection, at least four other compositions have been traditionally attributed to him. For an edition of Pseudo-Symphosius's Riddles, see *CCSL*, vol. 133A, 722–23.
143. Notably, Riddles 1 (stylus), 7 (smoke), 4 (key), 12 (river and fish), and

quent Latin *enigmata*—like those of Aldhelm,[144] Tatwine, and Eusebius—the influence of the Symphosian model is similarly discernible in vernacular tradition. For example, in the Exeter collection three pieces (nos. 47, 85, and 86) were probably inspired by Symphosius's corresponding Riddles 16 (bookworm), 12 (fish in river), and 95 (one-eyed man selling garlic). The impact of Symphosius's *Enigmata* on medieval culture extends beyond the field of riddling, too, as ten of these pieces were incorporated into the popular *Historia Apollonii Regis Tyri*,[145] which was later rendered from Latin into diverse European vernacular versions.[146] A further early citation occurs in the anonymous *De dubiis nominibus* (On doubtful nouns),

---

10 (ice) correspond to poems 101, 102, 239, 240, and 241 in the *Collectanea* (the numbering is from the edition of Bayless and Lapidge). See also Tupper, "Riddles of the Bede Tradition," and Bayless and Lapidge, *Collectanea*, 22.
144. For Aldhelm's citations from these riddles in his *Epistola* ad *Acircium*, see further on pp. 174-75 (n. 273).
145. In Recension B of the *Historia Apollonii*, which constitutes a shortened and revised version of A, the number of riddles was reduced from ten to seven. In Recension A (cc. xlii–xliii) these riddles correspond to nos. 12 (fish and river), 2 (reed), 13 (ship), 90 (bath-house), 61 (anchor), 63 (sponge), 59 (ball), 69 (mirror), 79 (wheels), and 78 (stairs) of Symphosius's *Enigmata* and thus do not appear in the same order as they are found in the collection. Also, some of them seem to have been included on the basis of a thematic connection with the plot. See G. A. A. Kortekaas, *Commentary on the Historia Apollonii Regis Tyri* (Leiden: Brill, 2007), 707–8. For an edition of these riddles in the *Historia Apollonii* (cc. xlii–xliii), see Kortekaas, *The Story of Apollonius*, 214–23. For further information on these riddles, see Elizabeth Archibald, *Apollonius of Tyre: Medieval and Renaissance Themes and Variations* (Cambridge: Brewer, 1991), 23–26.
146. The earliest vernacular translation of this work is the Old English text appearing in Cambridge, Corpus Christi College 201 (mid-eleventh century). Unfortunately, the section corresponding to the riddles is missing. An edition and translation of this version is found in Elaine Treharne, ed. and trans., *Old and Middle English c. 890–c. 1450: An Anthology* (Oxford: Blackwell, 2000), 234–53.

a mid-seventh-century alphabetical compendium of Latin terms with their grammatical gender and illustrative citations from other works.[147]

It has also been pointed out that Symphosius's *Enigmata* have been used as a source in *Fecunda ratis* (The well-laden ship),[148] an early-eleventh-century poetic miscellany composed by Egbert of Liège and with clear pedagogic aims.[149] Knowledge of Symphosius's Riddle 26 (crane) is also perceived in one of the riddles included in Arnulf's *Delicie cleri* (The delights of the clerics), a further didactic work composed between 1054 and 1056.[150] In addition, the *Ecbasis cuiusdam captivi per tropologiam* (The flight of the captive through allegorical exposition), an allegorical beast poem probably dating from the mid-eleventh century, also offers two passages that are clearly derivative of Symphosius's *Enigmata*.[151] Further citations from these riddles are found in the early-thirteenth-century *Prouerbia rustici* (the rural/plain proverbs), which comprises 76 proverbs

---

147. Line 3 of Symphosius's Riddle 19 (frog) is partially cited in this work ("nullus mea carmina laudat") but attributed to some Valentinus. See *CCSL*, vol. 133A, 771 (no. 129). See also Bergamin, *Aenigmata Symposii*, lix and 108.
148. See Manitius, *Geschichte der lateinischen Literatur des Mittelalters*, vol. 2 (Munich: Beck'sche, 1923), 537, and Archer Taylor, *The Literary Riddle before 1600* (Berkeley: University of California Press, 1948), 66.
149. For this text, see Robert Gary Babcock, ed. and trans., *The Well-Laden Ship: Egbert of Liège* (Cambridge, MA: Harvard University Press, 2013).
150. An edition of this text is Johann Hümer, "Zur Geschichte der mittellateinischen Dichtung. *Arnulfi delicie cleri*," *Romanische Forschungen* 2 (1886): 211–46. Cf. line 1 of Symphosius's Riddle 36, which alludes to the cranes in flight displaying a *lambda* (Λ) and *Delicie cleri* (780–84), ibid., 242–43.
151. As explained by Ziolkowski, *Talking Animals*, 44, in the *Ecbasis captivi* the hedgehog says he belongs to "Cato's clan" ("gente Catonis," 661), which clearly recalls the reference to the pig as being "de gente Catonis" (1) in Riddle 86. In the case of Symphosius's riddle, the clue plays on the name of the animal (Latin *porcus*) and the full name of the Roman censor Marcus Porcius Cato. In *Ecbasis captivi* (1002), the fox is described as "versuta dolis" (versed in stratagems), a phrase that also occurs in Symphosius's line 2 of Riddle 34 dealing with that animal. See Ernst Voigt, ed. *Ecbasis Captivi, das älteste Thierepos des Mittelalters* (Strassburg, 1875), 109 and 129.

in Latin hexameters.[152] Finally, the *Gesta romanorum* (The exploits of the Romans), a collection of Latin anecdotes and legends assembled in the late thirteenth or early fourteenth century, includes three riddles of Symphosius in the version of *Apollonius of Tyre* contained in this work.[153]

After the introduction of the printing press, interest in Symphosius's *Enigmata* did not wane. The collection proved once more to be a successful work in the post-medieval era, as the riddles were edited in various European countries. The *editio princeps* was issued by Joachim Périon in Paris in 1533 and later reprinted in 1537.[154] German humanist Liebhard Kammerer provided a selection of some of Symphosius's Riddles in Greek translation which were published in Basel around 1541.[155] Symphosius's collection also appeared in printed format thanks to Giuseppe Castalio's edition (Rome, 1581), followed by two reprints in 1597 and 1607.[156] The riddles were also edited in Pierre Pithou's *Epigrammata et poematia vetera* (Old epigrams

---

152. The *Prouerbia rustici* are extant in Leiden, Universiteitsbibliotheek, Vulc. 48. Lines 61 and 62 of this work correspond to the opening lines of Riddle 16 (moth) and 25 (mouse), respectively. See the edition found in Ernst Voigt, "Prouerbia rustici," *Romanische Forschungen* 3 (1887): 639.

153. The three riddles included in this version are nos. 12 (river and fish), 13 (ship), and 90 (bath-house). For an edition of this work and these three riddles, see Charles Swan, *Gesta romanorum*, revised and corrected by Wynnard Hooper (London: Bell, 1905), no. 153, 292–93.

154. Joachimus Perionius, *Simphosii ueteris poetae elegantissimi erudita iuxta ac arguta et festiua aenigmata* (Paris, 1533). For more information on post-medieval versions of Symphosius's Riddles, see Ohl, "The Enigmas," 24–25. Also, a comprehensive list of the earliest printed versions of these riddles is found in *CCSL*, vol. 133A, 616–18.

155. Joachimus Camerarius, *Elementis Rhetoricae* (Basel, 1541). The second and third editions appeared in Leipzig in 1562 and 1600, respectively.

156. Iosephus Castalio, *Aenigmata Symphosii poetae* (Rome, 1581). For a study of this edition and Castalio's comments on Symphosius's Riddles, see Javier Pizarro Sánchez, "Notas críticas del humanista Iosephus Castalio a los *Aenigmata Symphosii*," *Cuadernos de filología clásica, Estudios latinos* 17 (1999): 219–28. Castalio's second edition was issued in 1597 and was followed by a third in 1607.

and poetic compositions), first published in Paris in 1590 and later reprinted in Lyons in 1596 and Geneva in 1619. All these publications show that Symphosius's Riddles had a continuing popularity well beyond the medieval period.

3.2.2 The Organization of Symphosius's Enigmata

In terms of subject matter, Symphosius's Riddles are extremely varied, since they describe human utensils, meteorological phenomena, and the natural world.[157] This apparently disjointed appearance has made scholars think that the riddles were not organized according to any definite plan.[158] However, as observed in Appendix III, the majority of the riddles are grouped in well-defined thematic clusters.[159] The resulting sections disclose orga-

---

157. The order of the Latin riddle collections that will be considered throughout this monograph is that found in the *CCSL* editions. In the case of Tatwine and Eusebius it is exactly the same order in both Cambridge, Gg.5.35 and London, Royal 12.C.xxiii, the only two manuscripts in which their collections are extant. However, order variations are common in the case of collections that appear in numerous manuscripts, as illustrated with the anchor riddle in Symphosius's *Enigmata*. The omission of Riddle 96 (tightrope walker) is, for example, the major feature of family B to which St Gall, Stiftsbibliothek, Cod. Sang. 196 is associated. For further distinctive features of the two recensions, see Finch's "Symphosius" and "Codex Vat. Barb. Lat. 721." As regards Aldhelm's *Enigmata*, Riddle 23 (pair of scales) occurs after no. 50 (yarrow) in both Cambridge, Gg.5.35 and London, Royal 12.C.xxiii. Given the limitations of the present research, variations of this kind are not going to be taken into account. The *CCSL* order will therefore conveniently be taken as a paradigm and only occasionally will I refer to significant alterations to this ideal organization.
158. This view is for instance illustrated by Whitman: "Concerning the subject matter, the riddles are a disparate lot." *Old English Riddles*, 23.
159. A somewhat different appreciation of these groupings is found in Pizarro Sánchez, "Estructura y tipología," 242. Moreover, he does not associate them with encyclopedic organizational principles. A review of the different thematic segments discerned in this collection is also found in Bergamin, *Aenigmata Symposii*, xxxii–xxxix. By contrast with Pizarro Sánchez, Bergamin recognizes the encyclopedic character of Symphosius's Riddles,

nizing principles that resemble those found in encylopedic works. Apart from section 2 on meteorological subjects, which was briefly discussed at the beginning of this book, orderly arrangement is discernible in section 1, dealing with tools. Further evidence of encyclopedic organization can be observed in sections 3 and 4, which distribute biological topics into two separate groups: animals and plants. Section 5 in turn returns to the initial instrumental subject, whereas section 6 offers a representation of wonders or prodigies. Finally, Riddle 100 (tombstone) constitutes a fitting coda for the collection and another return to the initial writing subject,[160] as the inscription on stone reflects on the usual way to keep the memory of a deceased person by means of an epitaph. The writing subject therefore produces an enveloping structure for the rest of the topics in the collection.

Even if the exact date of Symphosius's *Enigmata* is not possible to ascertain, this collection in all likelihood antedates Isidore's *Etymologiae*. It may then be assumed that Symphosius drew his classification method from an encyclopedia other than Isidore's *Etymologiae*. Pliny's *Naturalis historia* thus stands as a possible model of organization.[161] However, as explained before, Pliny's encyclopedia cannot function as a touchstone against which to evaluate the degree of organization observed in Symphosius's *Enigmata*, since the organization is diffuse in the extreme.[162] As noted above, Bergamin has argued that Symphosius's collection shares some parallelisms with Eucherius of Lyons's *Formulae*, a tract from the first half of the fifth century.[163] Indeed, the underlying structure of the zoological sequence and the choice of subjects offered in

---

which she attributes to the influence of Eucherius of Lyons's *Formulae*. See her "Eucherio di Lione," and pp. 98–100 of this book.
160. This has also been noted by Bergamin, *Aenigmata Symposii*, xxxiii.
161. The list of Plinian echoes in the *CCSL* (vol. 133A, 866–68) leave no room for doubt that Symphosius, as well as Aldhelm, used the *Naturalis historia* as a source.
162. See above, p. 96.
163. See Bergamin, "Eucherio di Lione," 315–29.

Eucherius's Book IV evoke the contents and the layout of Symphosius's section 3.[164]

Still, the fact that Symphosius might have used an encyclopedia with a Christian-oriented classification similar to that found in the *Etymologiae* as a source should not be ruled out. However, such an encyclopedia, hypothetically earlier than Isidore's work, has not been preserved.[165] On the other hand, the order of Symphosius's Riddles as they stand, say, in the Salmasian codex—containing the earliest version of this collection (c. 800)—may differ significantly from the organization originally envisaged by the author in the late fifth or early sixth century. As mentioned above, it is evident that the contents of the riddles in the Salmasian version were considerably altered, as was their layout, as illustrated with the anchor piece in codices belonging to Recension D. All these modifications clearly suggest the constant presence of Christian compilers at work. On the basis of its resemblance to other Carolingian florilegia, it has been argued that the Salmasian codex was probably commissioned by learned Carolingian petitioners.[166] According to this, it is reasonable to assume that Symphosius's *Enigmata*, as well as the other works from the Latin Anthology in that manuscript, would have been adapted to the contemporary Carolingian taste. In her thorough analysis of the contents of the Salmasian manuscript, Spallone concludes that the primary sources employed by Isidore for the composition of the *Etymologiae* were probably the same as those used by the compilers of late Roman handbooks from which the Salmasian assemblage derives.[167] As the *Etymologiae* formed an important part of the Carolingian school curriculum,[168]

---

164. See ibid., 322–24.
165. I owe this idea to Prof. Juan Gil Fernández.
166. See Socas Gavilán, *Antología Latina*, 10; Spallone, "Il Par. Lat. 10318 (Salmasiano)," 71. For the study of a similar handbook, see E. K. Rand, "A Vade Mecum of Liberal Culture in a MS of Fleury," *PQ* 1 (1922): 258–77.
167. See Spallone, "Il Par. Lat. 10318," 70.
168. For example, Brown defines both the *Etymologiae* and the *De natura rerum* as "key texts" in the Carolingian school curriculum. Giles Brown,

it may therefore be inferred that Symphosius's collection could have been adapted by then to the influential model of Isidore's work. In any case, whether Symphosius's *Enigmata* were planned on a Christian basis at their inception or later modified according to Christian encyclopedic patterns, the parallelisms observed in the organization of these riddles and the structural principles of the *Etymologiae* are so evident that their analysis in light of Isidorean categorization is in order.

3.2.2.1 Section 1 *(*Enigmata *1–6)*

As regards internal structure, Symphosius's *Enigmata* also present a notable degree of cohesion in some parts, a notion that supports my assumption that the compilation aims at encyclopedic classification. To begin with, section 1 presents two thematically related subgroups: first, Riddle 1 (stylus) is followed by Riddle 2 (reed)—i.e., the plant from which papyrus was made.[169] The foremost position of these two topics in the collection thus denotes their prominent role in the compilation as the writer's main tools. Further in section 1, Riddles 3 (ring with gem), 4 (key), and 5 (chain) all describe round metal objects. *Enigma* 3 is also related to the topic of writing, since, as Bergamin explains, the text probably alludes to a signet ring.[170] Ohl in turn points out that a further possible association may be underlying the juxtaposition of Riddles 3 and 4: "There is a close connection between *anulus* and *clavis*, for anciently the combination of key and ring in one must have been quite popular, to judge from the number of such objects that has come down to us and which may be seen in almost any museum of Roman antiquities."[171] Also, in a typically Isidorean gradation, of the three consecutive metallic items (3–5) the ring comes first, we may infer, on account

---

"Introduction: The Carolingian Renaissance," in McKitterick, *Carolingian Culture*, 37.
169. See also Pizarro, "Estructura y tipología," 242–43, for the recognition of similar pairs in the collection.
170. Bergamin, *Aenigmata Symposii*, xxxii and 84.
171. Ohl, "The Enigmas," 38.

of its being made of gold or silver. In fact, with the exception of the reed and the roof-tile, section 1 manifests an interest in metallic objects.[172]

3.2.2.2 Section 2 (Enigmata 7–11)

This series opens with Riddle 7 (smoke) which, as commented above, is meaningfully associated with the subsequent Riddle 8 (fog).[173] The remainder of the topics of section 2 deal with atmospheric phenomena and seem to evoke Isidore's display of meteorological subjects as found in Book XIII of the *Etymologiae*.[174] Bergamin has pointed out that this group suggests the cycle of water.[175] Indeed, these riddles are thematically bound in a sort of cause-effect chain: clouds, as represented by fog, produce rain; ice is rainwater that has frozen; finally, ice is compact snow.[176]

3.2.2.3 Section 3 (Enigmata 12–39)

At first sight, section 3 seems to offer an indiscriminate representation of animals, but, on closer inspection, we can perceive that it abounds in thematic interconnections that suggest a concern with encyclopedic systematization, as observed in the following outline (see also Appendix III):[177]

---

172. As explained by Ohl, "ancient *styli* were often of iron or bronze, but are found more often of bone" (ibid., 34). In the case of the roof-tile (no. 6), the clues leave no room for doubt that the object is made from fired clay: "Terra mihi corpus, uires mihi praestitit ignis" (1) [The earth supplied my body; fire, my strength (my hardness)]. But it might be worth adding that, as noted by Ohl, "In later times, metal tiles were used on some of the larger public buildings in Rome" (ibid., 40).
173. See on p. 128.
174. See comparative tables on p. 3 as illustrative of cosmological groups in riddle collections.
175. Bergamin, *Aenigmata Symposii*, 92.
176. For significant parallels observed in Eucherius's cosmological subjects offered in Book II (*De supernis creaturis*, On the superior parts of Creation), see Bergamin, "Eucherio di Lione," 317–18.
177. For an analysis of stylistic and structural similarities detected in the

Symphosius's Subgroup A	Isidore's *Etymologiae*
A) Animals in General	
12. River and fish	—
13. Ship	—
14. Chicken in egg	—
B) Snakes/"Worms"	*De serpentibus/De vermibus*
15. Viper	XII.iv.10–11
16. Bookworm	XII.v.11[178]
17. Spider	XII.v.2
C) Aquatic Animals	*De piscibus*
18. Snail	XII.vi.48[179]
19. Frog	XII.vi.58
20. Turtle	XII.vi.56
D) Small Quadrupeds/Insects	*De minutis animantibus/volatilibus*
21. Mole	XII.iii.5
22. Ant	XII.iii.9
23. Fly	XII.viii.11
24. Weevil	XII.viii.17
25. Mouse	XII.iii.1
E) Birds	*De avibus*
26. Crane	XII.vii.14–15
27. Crow	XII.vii.44
28. Bat	XII.vii.36
29. Hedgehog	**XII.iii.7**

zoological subjects offered by Eucherius's Book IV of the *Formulae*, see ibid., 322–24.

178. In *Etymologiae* XIII.v.11, Isidore actually refers to the clothes moth, but what is relevant for our study here is that this insect is also called *tinea* —"a gnawing worm, in clothes, books, etc., a moth, bookworm, etc." It is therefore classified as a worm.

179. The snail (*cochlea*) is alluded to in *Etymologiae* XII.vi.48 and is said to belong the category of shellfish (*conchae*).

Symphosius's Subgroup A	Isidore's *Etymologiae*
30. Louse	XII.v.14
31. Phoenix	XII.vii.22
F) Big Quadrupeds/Wild Beasts	*De pecoribus et iumentis/ De bestiis*
32. Bull	XII.i.29
33. Wolf	XII.ii.23–24
34. Fox	XII.ii.29
35. She-Goat	XII.i.15–16
36. Pig	XII.i.25
37. She-Mule	XII.i.57
38. Tigress	XII.ii.7
39. Centaur	XI.iii.37

Though somewhat imperfect, a well-defined zoological classification emerges. As inferred from the headings that I have included, there are six different subdivisions, which reveal the acknowledgment of the eight principal zoological categories found in the *Etymologiae*. Besides, the groupings clearly take into account size and physiognomy as further organizational criteria.

As regards the first three riddles of this series—nos. 12 (river and fish), 13 (ship), and 14 (chicken in egg)—they seem to me a corrupt version of an introductory series similar to that observed in Eusebius's Riddles 37–40, of which nos. 38 (chicken) and 40 (fish) partially recall the topics of Symphosius's Riddles 14 and 12. Also importantly, this initial mini-group accords with the representation of animals of air and water, as well as with the small size of the subjects of this part of section 3. Subgroup B (nos. 15–17) incorporates subjects dealt with by Isidore in chapters iv (*De serpentibus*) and v (*De vermibus*), while subgroup C offers aquatic animals, corresponding to topics treated by Isidore's chapter vi (*De piscibus*). Subgroup D combines small animals and insects, which correlate with creatures described in Isidore's chapters iii (*De minutis animantibus*) and viii (*De minutis volatilibus*). In turn, subgroup E includes birds, thus concurring with with Isidore's chapter vii (*De avibus*). Despite exceptional Riddles 29 (hedgehog) and 30 (louse), the series offers further evidence of a consistent organization with the choice of the phoenix (31)—incidentally, a traditional symbol of Christ's resurrection—as the final topic.

Subgroup F provides a mixture of two further categories—quadrupeds and wild animals of great size—which occur in chapters i (*De pecoribus*) and ii (*De bestiis*) of the *Etymologiae*. This final series jointly deals with male and female creatures (she-goat, she-mule, and tigress),[180] the latter absent from the other subgroups. In addition to this, domestic animals (bull, she-goat, pig, and she-mule) are amalgamated with wild quadrupeds (wolf, fox, tigress). The fact that the bull is leading subgroup F may reflect a further attempt to endow the collection with typical Christian orderly principles such as the pre-eminence of domestic creatures if we assume that it is the domestic bull that Symphosius is referring to.[181] Nevertheless, as Ohl has pointed out, the bull was "always regarded as the choicest sacrificial animal,"[182] a notion that could also explain its prominent position in an originally pagan collection.

As observed in the outline, all the animal motifs offered in section 3 have a corresponding entry in Isidore's Book XII, the only exception being the centaur (no. 39), which appears in Book XI (*De portentis*, on prodigies). Also importantly, with Riddle 39 Symphosius resumes the mythic mood of the opening bull riddle. The location of this topic at the end of the zoological sequence, which evidently parallels the presence of the phoenix at the close of the ornithological series, seems to

---

180. Note that in *Enigma* 34, the fox is alluded to with a feminine adjective: "uersuta dolis" (versed in stratagems, 2).
181. The clues of the riddle refer to the myth of Pasiphaë, the name of a mountain in Cilicia, and the constellation of Taurus. It is therefore not possible to ascertain whether the animal meant in the first line is a domestic or a wild bull. However, it is worth noting that in other versions of the myth, the animal alluded to is an ox or a bullock. Note, for example, that Virgil's sixth Eclogue alludes to Pasiphaë finding comfort in the love of a white bullock: "Pasiphaen niuei solatur amore iuuenci" (46). Robert Coleman, ed., *Vergil: Eclogues* (Cambridge: Cambridge University Press, 1977), 58.
182. Ohl, "The Enigmas," 67.

reflect Symphosius's recognition of this animal as having the status of a prodigy. The wondrous nature of this hybrid animal, with the upper part of a human and the lower of a horse, is made clear in Riddle 39, where the creature is described as "insignis" (1, extraordinary), an adjective that, as Ohl explains, may also have monstrous connotations.[183] This idea thus adds weight to the assumption that the thematic layout observed in this collection evinces the observance of encyclopedic principles of organization, notably those found in the *Etymologiae*, where prodigies are set apart in the last two chapters of Book XI.[184]

As a whole, an oppositional pattern arises in section 3, since the first five subgroups represent creatures of small size whereas subgroup F offers animals that are comparatively larger. Furthermore, subgroups B, D, and F offer a rather balanced combination of two different zoological categories, while the remainder of the subgroups provide a representation of a sole class of animals. By the same token, the typical encyclopedic recognition of the three elements (land, water, and air) is also evident, although subgroup D offers a blending of creatures of land and air.[185]

Symphosius's Section 3	
Subgroup B	Earth
Subgroup C	Water
Subgroup D	Earth/Air
Subgroup E	Air
Subgroup F	Earth

183. Ibid., 72.
184. One also wonders if Symphosius equivocally connected the centaur to the minotaur, the prodigious offspring of Pasiphaë and the bull, thus further relating Riddles 32 and 39. Besides, the obscure etymology of Greek κένταυρος, which inevitably conjures up Latin *taurus*, could have given rise to this association. Note, for example, that the centaur and the minotaur are consecutive entries in the *Etymologiae* (XI.iii.37–38).
185. The distinction of the three elements and size as organizational criteria in Symphosius's collection are also considered by Pizarro Sánchez, "Estructura y tipología," 243.

As observed in this outline, these five subgroups delineate a circular pattern, starting and ending with earth. The pre-eminence of land animals thus seems to be acknowledged in the order of nature, a notion that is present in both Pliny's *Naturalis historia* and Isidore's *Etymologiae*.

If we consider the Isidorean distinction of clean and unclean creatures in Symphosius's section 3, the disposition of the subjects might also be revealing. It is remarkable that both the crane and the bull, which are clean animals, are the opening subjects of the subgroups on birds and big quadrupeds, respectively. Also importantly, in the case of subgroup E, the crane opposes the other unclean "birds" of the sequence—i.e., the crow, the bat, and the phoenix.[186] By the same token, the bull contrasts with the quadrupeds, all of which are unclean with the only exception of the she-goat (no. 35). The oppositional roles of the bull and the crane are certainly striking, as they tentatively suggest a compilation based on Christian principles.[187] Whether this was part of Symphosius's plan we cannot prove, but it is at least feasible that a later compiler might have altered an originally pagan-oriented disposition in the manner, say, of Pliny's *Naturalis historia* in order to align it in the best way possible to Christian principles of organization.

Symphosius's section 3 also displays interesting interconnections that need to be assessed. Sometimes the association is based on the principle of analogy, which is typical of encyclopedias, and is

---

186. The crane is not mentioned as an unclean bird in Leviticus or in Deuteronomy. By process of elimination, it is thus inferred that it is a clean creature. On the crane as a clean animal, see George Soper Cansdale, *Animals of Bible* Lands (Exeter: Paternoster Press, 1970), 159. The phoenix, like any other mythic creature not appearing in these biblical lists, would be likewise assumed to be unclean, regardless of the fact it was a well-known Christian allegory.
187. Still, this assumption must be made with caution, since this differentiation is not even fully consistent in Isidore's *Etymologiae*, as commented above p. 102 (n. 27). Besides, the crane appears in this encyclopedia among unclean birds (XII.vii.21), following the entry for the ostrich.

explicitly presented in the riddles' clues. Thus, Riddle 15 alludes to the destructive way in which the viper is born: "Non possum nasci, si non occidero matrem" (1) [I cannot be born, if I do not murder my mother]. Similarly, *Enigma* 16 offers paradoxical clues, which explain that the existence of the moth depends on its "devouring" the Muses, in other words, on the feeding on books: "Exedi Musas, nec adhuc tamen ipsa profeci" [I have eaten up the Muses, and yet I myself have not accomplished much so far]. Just as the viper must kill its own mother in order to be born, so must the moth kill the Muses to live on. The lives of the two creatures thus rely on the death of others.

Apart from the pair formed by Riddles 22 (ant) and 23 (fly) mentioned above, there are further cases in which the clues reveal a particular connection between two texts. For example, the clues used for the description of the fly (23) and the weevil (24) characterize the two insects as extremely greedy. In Riddle 23, the fly boastfully proclaims the power of its "gula":[188] "quid enim gula turpe ueretur?" (1) [for what nasty thing should my gullet fear?]. By the same token, the etymological clue of Riddle 24 alludes to the gluttonous nature of the weevil: "nec recto nomine dictus" (2) [nor am I rightly named]. As conjectured by Ohl, this part seems to focus on the fact that the name *curculio* should actually be spelled as *gurgulio*,[189] which would thus hint more effectively at the weevil's insatiable throat (Latin *guttur*) and proverbial greed at devastating crops.[190]

In turn, a further clue in *Enigma* 24 relates the weevil to the mouse, which follows next in the zoological series: "Nec gratus Cereri—, sed

---

188. This term means "gullet, weasand, throat" but it can also refer to "the palate, i.e., gluttony, gormandizing, appetite."
189. Indeed, several manuscripts adopt the form "Gurgulio" as a heading. See, for example, Vatican *Enigma* 92 (Appendix IX). See Glorie, *CCSL*, vol. 133A, 645, for other manuscripts offerering this reading.
190. Ohl, "The Enigmas," 57. This etymological connection is, for example, explained by Isidore in the *Etymologiae*: "Gurgulio dicitur, quia pene nihil est aliud nisi guttur" (XII.viii.17) [The weevil is called so because it is almost nothing but a throat].

multa uiuo sagina" (3) [(I am) not pleasant to Ceres, but I live from a large amount of food]. The mouse in *Enigma* 25 is described in similar terms: "Exiguo sumptu furtiua uiuo sagina" (2) [I live at the scanty expense of stolen food]. The two animals are consequently defined by their common parasitical relationship to humans, the only difference being that the weevil can eat a great amount of food whereas the mouse lives on a more modest provision.

The frog of Riddle 19 is said to be a frustrated singer: "Cumque canam semper, nullus mea carmina laudat" (3) [And even though I am always singing, nobody praises my songs]. The subsequent riddle offers clues that point to the double meaning of the term *testudo* as both the turtle and the lyre made of this animal's shell: "Viva nihil dixi, quae sic modo mortua canto" (3) [When alive, I did not speak at all; once dead, I sing in this way]. *Enigmata* 19 and 20 are thus connected by the singing abilities of the two creatures. Here, analogy is also subtly mixed with antithesis, as one of them is a terrible singer whereas the other one, the turtle, excels in musical skills when turned into a lyre.

Symphosius's *Enigmata* also indulge in further veiled connections. For example, Riddles 21 (mole) and 22 (ant) hint at an underlying common factor: the two creatures can live under the earth. In the case of the mole, this is overtly expressed in the textual clues: "malo tegi terra" (3) [I prefer to be covered by dirt]. On the other hand, the mole's blindness—"caeca mihi facies" (1) [My face is blind]—contrasts with the foresight of the ant, who is characterized as "prouida" (1).[191] The prickly hedgehog (29) and the sting-bearing louse (30) may have also been juxtaposed on purpose. Riddles 25 and 26 playfully bring up the pair *mus/grus*, two terms that were usually employed to illustrate final-*ūs* in Latin.[192] An antithetical duo is

---

191. The term is thus connected to the verb *prouideo*, "to see forwards or before one's self, to see in the distance, to discern," and also "In respect of time, to see or perceive beforehand, to foresee; to see before or earlier."
192. Ælfric's *Grammar* (XXXIII), for instance, reads: "on langne *us* geendjað þás naman: *hic mus* þeos mûs, *huius muris; COMMVNIA: hic et haec sus* swyn, *huius suis; hic et haec grus cran, huius gruis*" ["on long -ūs end the

detected in Riddles 33 and 34; in Ziolkowski's words, Symphosius here "juxtaposes the wolf and the fox, a fact which suggests that he knew of their enmity from either fables or folktales."[193]

Further links are discerned in the Riddles describing the pig (no. 36) and the she-mule (37). While the former alludes to the hog as being born in the fertile womb of the sow ("fecunda natus in alvo," 1), the clues of the latter refer to the she-mule as belonging to a race unfit for offspring ("generi non apta propago," 2). The mule therefore represents infertility as a result of the crossing of a horse and a donkey. In turn, line 3 of *Enigma* 36 playfully alludes to the fact that the term *porcus* (pig) is close to *Orcus*, the god of the underworld. A further case of atypical closeness of an animal to the world of gods is brought up with the allusion to the she-goat of Riddle 35 as the nourishing nurse of Jupiter ("Alma Iouis nutrix," 1).[194] The tigress similarly exemplifies an anomalous case of motherhood, since the clues of *Enigma* 38 allude to the traditional belief that this animal could be impregnated by the wind: "Et mihi dat uentus natos nec quaero maritum" (3) [The wind gives me offspring; I do not seek a husband].

Being a hybrid of a human and a horse, the centaur of Riddle 39 could be regarded as an instance of the results of anomalous mating and, therefore, a suitable topic with which to close section 3F. Even if the clues do not explicitly refer to this creature as the offspring of Ixion and a cloud with Juno's appearance, Symphosius might have had this mythological tale in mind, as inferred from the juxtaposition of Riddle 39 to the preceding riddle describing the conception of the tigress by the wind. In fact, Riddles 35–39 have in common an interest in atypical mating and parenthood. Furthermore, the transgressing of boundaries in nature's established order is represented in some of these riddles in which unusual relations between humans/

---

following nouns: this mouse, this mouse, of this mouse; commons: this swine, this swine, of this swine; this crane, crane, of this crane"]. The citation is from Zupitza, *Ælfrics Grammatik und Glossar*, 59, and the translation is from Perrello, "An Undiscovered Riddle," 11.
193. Ziolkowski, *Talking Animals*, 42.
194. In Greek mythology, Jupiter was fed with the milk of a she-goat.

gods and animals are suggested in the clues. This idea also accords with the opening riddle (32), which alluded to Pasiphaë and the bull. The continuous concatenation of related features and subjects therefore reveals Symphosius's concern with providing cohesion throughout the zoological series.

3.2.2.4 Section 4 (Enigmata 40–49)

Symphosius's section 4 is also worth analyzing in detail. Again, from its comparison with Isidore's *Etymologiae* interesting implications arise. Accordingly, this subgroup offers a combination of topics that are dealt with by Isidore in chapters viii (*De aromaticis arboribus*, On aromatic trees), ix (*De herbis aromaticis sive communibus*, On aromatic or common herbs), and x (*De oleribus*, On vegetables) of Book XVII (*De rebus rusticis*, On rural things).[195] As with the preceding zoological group, it is thus clear that Symphosius was culling from an encyclopedic source with a division into three botanical categories: aromatic trees, herbs, and vegetables.[196] This encyclopedic design is thus similar to that observed in Isidore's Book XVII. The balanced number of selected subjects corresponding to each internal subcategory seems to corroborate this.

As offered in the standard compilation that we are analyzing, the different topics of section 4 can be categorized into several subgroups. The following outline offers headings to indicate the possible subcategories that Symphosius may have had in mind:

---

195. Pliny's *Naturalis historia* also offers a similar distinction of these three major botanical categories in Books XII–XXI but, as with the chapters on animals, the information is much more diffuse. Pliny's Books XXII–XXVII in turn offer plants from a pragmatic point of view as products and medicines for human beings.

196. Pizarro Sánchez incorporates further riddles into this botanical series, thus including Riddles 50 (hay) and 53 (vine). "Estructura y tipología," 243. However, I prefer to consider these topics as part of the typical instrumental categories. Furthermore, they are clearly linked to the other agricultural topics found in that part: nos. 51 (millstone) and 52 (flour).

Symphosius's Section 4	Isidore's *Etymologiae*
A) Medicinal plants	
40. Poppy	XVII.ix.31
41. Mallow	XVII.x.5
B) Vegetables	*De oleribus*
42. Beet	XVII.x.15
43. Gourd	XVII.x.16
44. Onion	XVII.x.12
C) Ornamental/garden flowers	*De herbis aromaticis sive communibus*
45. Rose	XVII.ix.17
46. Violet	XVII.ix.19
D) Aromatic trees	*De aromaticis arboribus*
47. Frankincense	XVII.viii.2–3
48. Myrrh	XVII.viii.4
49. Ebur ivory	XII.ii.14

The coherent organization of the botanical series adds weight to the assumption that Symphosius's *Enigmata* constitute a carefully planned collection. The first two riddles correspond to the poppy and the mallow, two plants which also have in common their medicinal properties.[197] A triad of vegetables follows, which also share the fact that they are typical food for human beings and also have a roundish shape, as noted by Javier Pizarro Sánchez.[198] The beet, as inferred by Ohl, may have also been juxtaposed to the preceding plants on account of its medicinal virtues—notably, its purgative properties, similar to those of the mallow.[199] As for the gourd, the plant served as a drinking vessel.[200]

---

197. The poppy's sleep-inducing effects are traditionally well-known. As regards the mallow, the plant had various medicinal uses. See Ohl, "The Enigmas," 72–74.
198. "Estructura y tipología," 243–44.
199. Ohl, "The Enigmas," 74. The mallow is in turn connected to subgroup B, since it is included in the category of vegetables, as is found in *Etymologiae* XVII.x.5.
200. Pliny, for example, largely expounds on contemporary experiments

On the other hand, as pointed out above, frankincense and myrrh constitute a pair based on analogy: the riddles describe the much-valued product of two aromatic trees. This collocation is also typical of encyclopedic works, as observed in Isidore's *Etymologiae* (XVII. viii.2–4). On a similar basis, ivory occurs next as a luxury item, also coming from distant lands. The three riddles therefore suggest a triad based on the description of sophisticated articles. The fact that ivory is, by contrast, an animal product thus distinguishes Riddle 49 from the other pieces of this botanical series. It was probably intended to mark the conclusion of this group. This emphasis on the uses of plants sets the botanical subgroup in line with the encyclopedic treatises like Pliny's *Naturalis historia*, which has an outstanding concern with practicality. The notable pragmatic focus observed in the botanical subjects, which is also shared by the subsequent instrumental topics, however, contrasts with the choice of animals in the preceding series. Only in the last subgroup of quadrupeds does Symphosius offer some domestic animals.

3.2.2.5 Section 5 (Enigmata 50–92)

Section 5 is the longest and most miscellaneous of Symphosius's collection. Yet, this heterogeneous assemblage seems to correspond to instrumental topics that are dealt with by Isidore in Books XVII–XX of the *Etymologiae*. In this light, it is perfectly understandable that human-made tools such as the saw (no. 60) and the anchor (61) should co-occur with food and drinks—as with spiced wine (83), wine turned to vinegar (84), apple (85) and ham (86)—as well as footwear (military shoe, 56), domestic utensils (broom, 80), and subjects related to human craft such as bridge (62), window pane (68), water-clock (70), and well (71). Section 5 is therefore a good illustration of the instrumental category, which obviously has a regular representation in encyclopedic works.

The instrumental motifs also show interesting thematic intercon-

---

with the shapes of gourds and their practical uses as pitchers and other drinking vessels. Pliny, *Naturalis historia* XIX.xxiv.71–74. Ohl, "The Enigmas," 74–75.

nections. Riddles 50 to 53 convey agricultural topics, as mentioned above. The association of these riddles is thus based on analogy. As noted before, *Enigma* 51 (millstone) describes the movement of one of the stones and the lack of movement of the other during the process of grinding corn. Subsequently, Riddle 52 alludes to flour as the product that emerges from the action of the two stones: "Inter saxa fui quae me contrita premebant" (1) [I was ground between stones that crushed me]. Symphosius's *Enigmata* indulge in pairs of this kind.

An obvious connection exists between Riddles 56 and 57. The former deals with a shoe (*caliga*) and the latter a hob-nail (*clauus caligaris*) used for this kind of military footwear. *Enigma* 58 describes hair (*capillus*), while Riddle 59 alludes to a ball (*pila*) stuffed with hair. Riddles 54 (hook) and 55 (needle) similarly present sharp pointed metal utensils. As regards the saw (60) and the anchor (61), their description is based on the typical riddling technique of personification. Thus, the saw is said to have innumerable teeth ("dentibus innumeris," 1), with which it feeds on wood by biting it sharply ("morsu depascor acuto," 2). In the following riddle, the anchor is said to bite the earth ("mordeo terras," 3). In turn, the anchor and the bridge are significantly connected on the basis of their firm resistance against the power of water. The anchor is thus described as continually waging war against the elements: "Cum uento luctor, cum gurgite pugno profundo" (2) [I struggle against the wind, I fight with the deep raging sea]. In Riddle 62, Symphosius uses a similar parallel contruction to refer to the heroic resistance of the wooden bridge against the water current: "Stat nemus in lymphis, stat in alto gurgite silua, / et manet in mediis undis inmobile robur" (1–2) [A forest arises over the waters; the woods arise on the high seas and an oak remains motionless in the middle of the waves]. Here, the phrasing resembles that used in the preceding riddle so as to highlight the underlying connection.[201] Further links are observed

---

201. Cf. "cum gurgite ... profundo" (2) and "aquas medias" (3) in Riddle 61 and "in alto gurgite" (1) and "in mediis undis" (2) in *Enigma* 62.

in Riddles 63 (sponge) and 64 (trident), as the two texts describe objects related to the sea.[202]

Riddles 67 (lantern) and 68 (window pane) are linked on the basis of their being made of translucent materials. The lantern is described as "perlucida" (1) or transparent and as having a light within ("lumen habens intus," 2). Similarly, the clues of Riddle 68 allude to the window pane as allowing the light to go through.[203] Actually Riddles 67–69 make a triad on the basis of the object's capacity to deal with light. A similar concatenation is observed in water-clock (70), well (71), and pipe (72), which describe objects that have to do with water. The pipe and the well also share the fact that they are both long structures created to carry water. The pipe in turn is associated with the bellows (73), as the former channels water and the latter air. By the same token, the stone (74), the lime (75), and the two flint riddles (76–77), which have been defined by Bergamin as "a brief lapidary,"[204] denote elements used in the construction industry.[205] The juxtaposition of Riddles 83 (spiced wine) and 84 (wine turned to vinegar) suggests a cause effect relationship. Similarly, Riddle 82 is related to 83, as the first describes an earthenware jar or flagon (Latin *lagena*), typically used to contain wine. The triad formed by Riddles 87 (hammer), 88 (pestle), and 89 (bronze strigil) seems to recognize that these are all metallic objects, the first two being related to the action of hitting. Finally, Riddles 89 (bronze strigil)[206] and 90 (bathhouse) are no doubt interconnected, as are 91 (die) and 92 (money).

Analogy is therefore a pervasive ruling principle in Symphosius's

---

202. Apart from being the symbol of Neptune, the trident was used to hunt fish. See Ohl, "The Enigmas," 94.
203. Also, in some manuscripts the window glass is referred to as *specular*, so that it can be related to the subsequent subject (*speculum*, mirror) on the basis of their having a similar nomenclature. See *CCSL*, vol. 133A, 689 (*Codices*).
204. Bergamin, *Aenigmata Symposii*, xxxii.
205. Lime was an essential component of concrete, and flint was used for "paving roads and streets." Ohl, "The Enigmas," 106 and 107.
206. "An instrument with a curved blade, for scraping the sweat and dirt from the skin in the hot-air bath or after gymnastic exercise." *OED*, s.v. "strigil."

section 5. Instead of offering a subclassification as in the case of the biological subjects of sections 3 and 4, the instrumental riddles are rather intertwined in an endless chain of connections based on the resemblance of outward characteristics (e.g., the metaphorical "teeth" of the saw and the anchor), their having similar components (hair and ball), or their being used with a similar purpose (bronze strigil and bath-house). All in all, section 5 is concerned with offering a representation of objects that form part of everyday life. The section's broad scope clearly aims at being encyclopedic with the description of modest simple objects (needle, ball), provisions (flour, spiced wine, wine turned into vinegar), and housewares (lantern, bellows, mirror, broom, jar). But there is also an interest in offering a sketch of human technology, as illustrated by agriculture and farming (hay, millstone, vine, whip, apple), as well as the exploitation of marine resources (hook, sponge, trident). Section 5 also touches on the military profession (arrow, military shoe, hob-nail, gouty soldier), the judicial system (water-clock), as well as leisure and entertainment (bronze strigil, bath-house, die).[207] Finally, there is a clear aim at providing an insight into late Roman civilization through engineering (bridge, well, pipe, wheels), construction (saw, stone, lime, flint, hammer), and buildings (window pane, stairs).[208]

3.2.2.6 Section 6 (Enigmata 93–99)

The focus of section 6 seems to be wonders or prodigies. In the case of Symphosius's Riddle 93, the mother of twins is described as a creature with three souls: "tres animas habui, quas omnes intus habebam" (2) [I had three souls, all of which I had inside]. Subsequently, Riddle 94 depicts a soldier as a six-footed creature ("sex qui pedes

---

207. For the water-clock as a way to measure the time of the speeches in a trial as illustrated by Symphosius's Riddle 70 and Martial's two epigrams on the clepsydra from Books VI (no. 36) and VIII (no. 7), see James Ker, "Drinking from the Water-Clock: Time and Speech in Imperial Rome," *Arethusa* 42.3 (2009): 279–302.
208. See Zoja Pavlovskis, "The Riddler's Microcosm: from Symphosius to St. Boniface," *Classica et Mediaevalia* 39 (1988): 223–24.

habui," 2), in other words, the man's two feet plus the four legs of his horse. The final clue playfully alludes to a dramatic physical change, suggesting that some sort of metamorphosis has taken place: "Nunc mihi uix duo sunt; inopem me copia reddit" (3) [Now I hardly have two; abundance turned me into a destitute]. This clue dwells on the paradox that an excess of quality food (i.e., meat) has provoked the soldier's gout, thus depriving him of his former livelihood and his military profession. By indirectly hinting at feet deformed by the disease, Riddle 94 therefore further indulges in the grotesque, the common denominator of section 6.

Like the soldier suffering from gout, the garlic seller of *Enigma* 95 is described in similarly monstrous terms: "Unus inest oculus, capitum sed milia multa" (2) [Just one eye there, but many thousands of heads]. In Riddle 96 the funambulist is described as a marvelous creature that is capable of sustaining itself between heaven and earth: "Inter luciferum caelum terrasque iacentes, / aera per medium docta meat arte uiator" (1–2) [Between light-bringing heaven and the lands lying below, the traveler passes through the air thanks to his learned skill]. It is also worth noting that these four riddles share the fact that they are concerned, on the one hand, with human "deformities"—the woman's multiple pregnancy, the soldier's gouty feet, and the garlic seller's visual handicap—and, on the other, with superhuman activities, as represented by tightrope walker.

Riddles 97, 98, and 99 entail non-human topics (shadow, echo, and sleep) that might have been included at this point as further wondrous phenomena. This series also presents evident thematic connections among its components as, for example, with Riddles 97 (shadow) and 98 (echo), since the first entails the reflection of an image and the second implies the reverberation of sound. In the same manner, *Enigma* 99 (sleep) is followed by Riddle 100 (tombstone), as if evoking the commonplace association of sleep and death. Finally, the tombstone riddle seems to have been intentionally located at the end as a fitting conclusion to the collection. The section as a whole therefore seems to provide a representation of prodigies in both human and non-human dimensions. Also interestingly, all these motifs occur at the close of the collection, a notion that recalls the location of the two sections on prodigies at the end of Isidore's Book XI.

3.2.2.7 Final Considerations on Symphosius's Enigmata

On the basis of this analysis, the organizing criteria employed in Symphosius's *Enigmata* clearly go beyond the sporadic occurrence of thematic groups. The overall design of Symphosius's collection seems to deploy a twofold subdivision similar to that discerned in Isidore's second decade of the *Etymologiae*. Thus, with the exception of framing sections 1 and 6 (plus the coda), the remainder of the collection reveals a typical "Opera-Dei" series (covering cosmology, animals, and plants with sections 2, 3, and 4) and an "Opera-hominis" sequence (comprising human-created artifacts, food, and drinks, as reflected in section 5). Further support for this hypothesis is the fact that these two symmetrical subdivisions appear to be numerically balanced, with the "Opera-Dei" and the "Opera-hominis" groups amounting to exactly 43 riddles each.[209] Even if this organization may not be exactly as Symphosius first devised it, as this arrangement was no doubt subject to variation in the course of manuscript transmission, the resulting well-balanced structure of the collection does suggest a Christian coloring. With these ideas in mind, it may be conjectured that the compilation of Symphosius's *Enigmata*, at least in its current state, could have been based on organizational parameters akin to those found in Isidore's *Etymologiae* or any other early Christian encyclopedia with a similar structural scheme.[210] It is hard to ascertain if

---

209. The peripheral sections are also roughly balanced, with "Tools I" offering six pieces and "Wonders" comprising seven riddles.

210. This twofold subdivision is not perceptible in Pliny's *Naturalis historia*, which is nevertheless an unquestionably important source for the composition of Symphosius's Riddles. For the influence of Pliny's *Naturalis historia* in the contents of Symphosius's collection, especially in the section on animals, see notes (*fontes et imitat.*) of the *CCSL*, vol. 133A. Though comparatively much fewer in number than Pliny's excerpts, it is worth noting that the *CCSL* editor has also pointed out some excerpts from Isidore's *Etymologiae* as possible parallels for some passages found in Symphosius's Riddles.

Symphosius was responsible for this Christian-oriented plan or if the compilation of the riddles was rather the outcome of later manipulation. The notable homogeneity of the *enigmata* in terms of style, metrical structure, and thematic design seems to favor the hypothesis that Symphosius's Riddles were initially conceived with this twofold structure as part of the original plan. Yet the second conjecture should not be ruled out, since the observance of the Isidorean binary scheme might have been extremely helpful for medieval compilers aiming at concealing a possible pagan outlook of the original collection.

3.3. Aldhelm's Pioneering Enigmata

3.3.1 Introduction to Aldhelm and His Works

Being the author of the most influential riddle collection after Symphosius's, Aldhelm is the second enigmatist to take into account. Unlike his predecessor, we have access to details of his life thanks to two late biographies,[211] some letters,[212] and other related

---

For example, Isidore's XII.iii.5 and XII.ii.7 are indicated in relation to nos. 21 (mole) and 38 (tigress), respectively. Also interestingly, an Isidorean echo from *Etymologiae* XI.iii.38 (on the definition of the Minotaurus) seems to be present in Riddle 32 (bull). Two further passages—notably, from two eminently instrumental Books of the *Etymologiae* (XVIII.viii.1 and XX.x.7)—are pointed out for *Enigmata* 65 (arrow) and 67 (lantern). For this, see the notes (*fontes et imitat.*) for these riddles in *CCSL*, vol. 133A.

211. One of Aldhelm's biographers was Faricius of Arezzo (d. 1117), who became abbot of Abingdon in 1100. Probably composed between 1093 and 1099, Faricius's *Vita sancti Aldhelmi* is edited in J. A. Giles, *Sancti Aldhelmi opera* (Oxford, 1844), 354–82. The other biographer, William of Malmesbury (c. 1090–c. 1142), was a monk at the monastery with the same name. Aldhelm's *vita* forms part of William's *Gesta pontificum anglorum* (c. 1125), of which Book V is wholly devoted to him. For an edition of this work, see Winterbottom, *William of Malmesbury*, vol. 1, 498-663.

212. There are thirteen extant letters that were either authored by Aldhelm or addressed to him. Some of these letters (nos. 2, 3, 9, 10, 11, 12, and 13) have survived only as excerpts in William of Malmesbury's *Gesta pontificum anglorum*, but all of them are regarded as authentic by scholars, with

documents that have been preserved. It is generally assumed that he was born either in 639 or 640 on the basis of a reference found in Malmesbury's *Gesta pontificum anglorum* (V.188.3), which states that he was probably a seventy-year old man ("septuagenario") when he died.[213] Both Bede's *Historia ecclesiastica* (V.18) and the *Anglo-Saxon Chronicle* report his death, which took place around 709.[214]

It has been traditionally assumed that Aldhelm was related to the West-Saxon royal family, although the identity of his father is still doubtful.[215] Accordingly, Aldhelm received an outstanding education. The high standards of Irish scholarship attracted many English students at that time, and Aldhelm was no exception. In Malmesbury's *Gesta pontificum anglorum* (V.189.1–2), it is reported that, after an initial period of training at the school of Theodore and Hadrian at Canterbury, Aldhelm returned to Wessex and became a monk at Malmesbury. At this monastery, he studied with an Irish teacher named Maíldub.[216] This piece of information is partly corroborated by a letter from an unknown Irishman who refers to Aldhelm as someone who has been "nourished" ("nutritus") by a certain holy

---

the exception of no. 13. Aldhelm's letters 4, 6, 7, and 8 have come down to us in a complete form in Vienna, Österreichische Nationalbibliothek, Cod. 751. Letter 5 occurs in seven other manuscripts, which are listed in Ehwald, *Aldhelmi Opera*, 486–87. See the introduction to Aldhelm's letters in Michael Lapidge and Michael Herren, eds. and trans., *Aldhelm: The Prose Works* (Cambridge: Brewer, 1979), 136–51, and their translation, 152–70. For an edition of the letters, see Ehwald, *Aldhelmi Opera*, 475–503.

213. Winterbottom, *William of Malmesbury*, vol. 1, 502–3.

214. Colgrave and Mynors, *Bede's Ecclesiastical History*, 514–15. Bately, *The Anglo-Saxon Chronicle*, vol. 3, 33.

215. As recorded in Malmesbury's *Gesta pontificum anglorum* (V.188.2), Aldhelm's father was possibly named Kenten. For this passage, see Winterbottom, *William of Malmesbury*, vol. 1, 502–3. Lapidge recently recognized this name as "a corrupt spelling of the OE name Centwine," and therefore as a possible reference to King Centwine of Wessex (676–85). Michael Lapidge, "The Career of Aldhelm," *ASE* 36 (2007): 17.

216. On Maíldub's elusive identity, see Barbara Yorke's "Aldhelm's Irish and British Connections," esp. 166–67.

man of that nationality ("sancto viro de nostro genere").²¹⁷ It is probably due to this Irish tutelage in the early stages of his instruction that Aldhelm acquired his idiosyncratic Latin style, endowed with sentences of extreme syntactic complexity and length, as well as with the obscure learned vocabulary that was characteristic of Hiberno-Latin literature.²¹⁸ Given the essential role that Isidore's *Etymologiae* played in the Irish curriculum,²¹⁹ Aldhelm probably became acquainted with this encyclopedia during this phase.

There is evidence that Aldhelm eventually went back to the school at Canterbury, which probably offered the best academic "program" of the early Middle Ages.²²⁰ The excellence of the Canterbury education, from which Aldhelm surely drew further knowledge of Isidore's *Etymologiae*,²²¹ might have triggered Aldhelm's critical views on his earlier—presumably Irish—training, for example, in Letter 1 to Bishop Leutherius.²²² In turn, Letter 2 (c. 675) by Aldhelm addressed to Hadrian proves that he was a student at Canterbury.²²³ The same text alludes to the fact that Hadrian's tui-

---

217. Ehwald, *Aldhelmi opera*, 494. For a full translation of this letter (no. 6), see Lapidge and Herren, *Aldhelm: The Prose Works*, 164.
218. This literary trend reached its maximum splendor with the *Hisperica Famina*. See above, p. 66.
219. For the relevance of Isidore's *Etymologiae* in Irish culture, see above, p. 66 (n. 231).
220. In the *Historia ecclesiastica* (IV.2), Bede gives an account of the high level of the studies at Canterbury. Colgrave and Mynors, *Bede's Ecclesiastical History*, 332–35.
221. For evidence of the thorough use of the *Etymologiae* in the Canterbury curriculum, see above p. 67 (n. 235).
222. Ehwald, *Aldhelmi opera*, 475–77. For the exact passage, see 477. For further comments on this passage, see Lapidge and Herren, *Aldhelm: The Prose Works*, 138. In Letter 5 to Heahfrith, an English acquaintance, Aldhelm recommends Canterbury as a place to pursue his studies instead of Irleand, where Heahfrith had already spent six years. Ehwald, *Aldhelmi Opera*, 488–94; Lapidge and Herren, *Aldhelm: The Prose Works*, 160–64.
223. This letter (no. 2), of which only an excerpt is preserved in Malmesbury's *Gesta pontificum anglorum*, is edited in Ehwald, *Aldhelmi Opera*, 478. Also, see its translation in Lapidge and Herren, *Aldhelm: The Prose Works*, 153–54.

tion was interrupted for almost three years on account of a serious illness ("corporeae fragilitatis"), which prevented Aldhelm from resuming his elementary studies ("prima elementa") there.[224] In addition, it might be inferred that, among the diverse obstacles and impediments ("diversa impedimentorum obstacula"), his appointment for the abbacy of Malmesbury about 675 could have marked the end of this instruction.[225]

Apart from his Irish training and his stay at the Canterbury school, Aldhelm's trip to Rome (c. 689)[226] seems to have had a significant impact on some of his works, including the *Epistola*.[227] With this exceptional educational background, Aldhelm managed to amass a huge amount of knowledge, deriving from both classical and Christian authors, which can be appreciated throughout his literary production. His extraordinary wisdom and his experience as abbot of Malmesbury might have played an important role in his eventual consecration as Bishop of Sherborne, which is mentioned in Bede's *Historia ecclesiastica* (V.18) as occurring in 705 or 706.[228]

Lapidge has repeatedly pointed out that Aldhelm was "the first

---

224. Ehwald, *Aldhelmi Opera*, 478. As Lapidge and Herren point out, this period under Hadrian's supervision should be between 670 and 672. *Aldhelm: The Prose Works*, 138.

225. This date is provided by William of Malmesbury in the *Gesta pontificum anglorum* (V.199.6). See Winterbottom, *William of Malmesbury*, 526–27. But, as Lapidge points out, "there is no reliable means of dating Aldhelm's becoming abbot of Malmesbury." *ODNB*, s.v. "Aldhelm," by Michael Lapidge.

226. For the exact passage ("quia tu Romae advena fuisti") in Letter 6, see Ehwald, *Aldhelmi opera*, 494, and Lapidge and Herren, *Aldhelm: The Prose Works*, 164. Lapidge offers further details of the special circumstances of this pilgrimage, in which Aldhelm accompanied his kinsman, King Ceadwalla of Wessex. See his "The Career of Aldhelm," 58–59.

227. For this trip and the possible implications it had for Aldhelm's works, see Joanna Story, "Aldhelm and Old St Peter's, Rome," *ASE* 39 (2010): 7–20. See also Lapidge, "The Career of Aldhelm," 52–64.

228. This appointment took place after Bishop Hædde's death, when the West-Saxon see was split up into the dioceses of Winchester and Sherborne. Colgrave and Mynors, *Bede's Ecclesiastical History*, 514–15.

English man of letters."[229] When composing his works, he was no doubt a forerunner who was paving the way for future Anglo-Saxon authors.[230] Aldhelm's pioneering force is thus attested to in the so-called *Carmen Rhythmicum*.[231] This brief composition in continuous octosyllabic verse[232] narrates the effects of a storm on Aldhelm, his companions, and a church, presumably in the area of Sherborne.[233] Aldhelm's interest in further poetic formats is also observed in his *Carmina ecclesiastica*,[234] which comprises five poems or *tituli*, dedicated to several churches and altars that might have been inaugurated by Aldhelm.[235]

Following the model of Caelius Sedulius's *Carmen paschale* (The

---

229. Note, for example, Lapidge and Rosier, *Aldhelm: The Poetic Works*, 1.

230. For Aldhelm's own awareness of his contribution as a pioneering writer, see Michael Lapidge, "Aldhelm's Latin Poetry and Old English Verse," *Comparative Literature* 31.3 (1979): 210–11.

231. The title was given by Ehwald in *Aldhelmi opera*, where the work is edited (524–28). For an introduction to this poem, see Lapidge and Rosier, *Aldhelm: The Poetic Works*, 171–76, and for the translation, see 177–79. The text and three different translations of it appear in Barker and Brooks, eds., *Aldhelm and the See of Sherborne*, 271–89. Further study of this poem is found in Andy Orchard, *The Poetic Art of Aldhelm* (Cambridge: Cambridge University Press, 1994), 19–28; David R. Howlett, "Aldhelmi Carmen rhythmicum," *Archivum Latinitatis Medii Aevi* 53 (1995): 119–40; and Katherine Barker, "*Usque Domnomiam*: the Setting of Aldhelm's *Carmen rhythmicum*, literature, language and the liminal," in Barker and Brooks, *Aldhelm and the See of Sherborne*, 15–54.

232. Lapidge and Rosier, *Aldhelm: The Poetic Works*, 175. On Anglo-Latin octosyllabic meter, see also Orchard, *The Poetic Art*, 19–72.

233. For this poem as autobiographical, see Lapidge and Rosier, *Aldhelm: The Poetic Works*, 171, and Barker, "*Usque Domnomiam*."

234. The title derives from Ehwald's edition of these poems. Ehwald, *Aldhelmi opera*, 11–32. For an annotated translation, see Lapidge and Rosier, *Aldhelm: The Poetic Works*, 46–58, and for an introduction, 35–45.

235. Aldhelm contributed to the spread of Christianity in Wessex by building and consecrating churches. For this task, a *titulus* or short inscription in verse was often issued in order to provide a verbal testimony of the church's consecration. As Aldhelm was particularly active in this evangelical task, he probably composed many of these *tituli* himself, most of which have been lost, although, as noted by Lapidge and Rosier, not all of them "may

Easter poem), Aldhelm tested his own proficiency as a writer with a challenging poetic format: the *opus geminatum* or "twin work."[236] The result of this literary endeavor was the treatise known as *De virginitate* (On virginity), in its verse and prose versions, which have been dated to some time after 675 or 680.[237] Interestingly, the prose *De virginitate* was dedicated to the nuns at the monastery at Barking (Essex),[238] by then ruled by Abbess Hildelith. The prose treatise was no doubt conceived for such an audience,[239] as it expounds on *virginitas* as a capital virtue, as well as on its theological implications and variants, among which Aldhelm stressed *castitas* as a mode of virginity that applies to the state of a woman who, having previously had a marital experience, has committed herself to an ecclesiastical life.[240]

The introductory discussion is accompanied in the prose *De virginitate* by a set of hagiographical chapters, first on male saints and then on female. Aldhelm probably offered these saints because they set a valuable example for the monastic community at Barking. The poetic *De virginitate* follows a pattern similar to that of the prose treatise, providing the corresponding poetic sections on saints. However, it is remarkable that the poetic work offers a concluding part

---

have been composed for actual dedications." Lapidge and Rosier, *Aldhelm: The Poetic Works*, 10.

236. For further information on this type of composition, see Peter Godman, "The Anglo-Latin 'Opus Geminatum': from Aldhelm to Alcuin," *Medium Aevum* 50 (1981): 215–29.

237. On this dating, see Lapidge and Rosier, *Aldhelm: The Poetic Works*, 12–13.

238. The monastery "was probably founded after the conversion of the East Saxons, possibly during the years 665 x 675." Ibid., 12.

239. Aldhelm was no doubt taking into consideration the special circumstances of some of the women of the Barking institution—among them Cuthburg, formerly King Aldfrith's wife—who played an essential role in the christianization of the area. See Lapidge and Herren, *Aldhelm: The Prose Works*, 51-52.

240. For Aldhelm's peculiar handling of the term *castitas*, as a state of womanhood, in comparison to its uses in prior patristic literature, see Lapidge and Herren, *Aldhelm: The Prose Works*, 55–56. For this passage in the prose *De virginitate* (XIX), see Ehwald, *Aldhelmi opera*, 248–49.

that dwells on the allegorical fight between vices and virtues.²⁴¹ This section is missing, however, in the prose version.

As pointed out above, the *Enigmata*, Aldhelm's most famous work, were initially part of the *Epistola ad Acircium*, a dense work addressed to some Acircius, who has been convincingly identified with King Aldfrith of Northumbria, a learned man and a personal acquaintance of Aldhelm's.²⁴² There is a reference to Aldfrith at the beginning of the *Epistola,* where Aldhelm alludes to a ceremony in which he acted as the monarch's godfather.²⁴³ This fact enables one to infer the approximate date of composition of the *Epistola* and, hence, of the *Enigmata* as well, since the letter was probably sent by Aldhelm soon after Aldfrith acceded to the throne in 686.²⁴⁴ After the initial exordium, Aldhelm expounds on the significance of the number seven. This is in turn followed by a metrical treatise, which

---

241. Godman described this section as "a miniature *psychomachia*" functioning as a poetic excursus. "The Anglo-Latin '*Opus Geminatum*,'" 221.
242. As Lapidge has pointed out, the name "derives from a+circio (*Circius* = the northwest wind, hence 'someone from the region of the northwest')." "The Career of Aldhelm," 24.
243. For the exact passage, see Ehwald, *Aldhelmi opera*, 61, and its translation in Lapidge and Herren, *Aldhelm: The Prose Works*, 34. On Lapidge's comments on this excerpt, see "The Career of Aldhelm," 25. For further information on this ceremony, see Joseph H. Lynch, *Christianizing Kinship. Ritual Sponsorship in Anglo-Saxon England* (Ithaca, NY: Cornell University Press, 1998), 112–16, and Barbara Yorke, "Adomnán at the Court of King Aldfrith," in *Adomnán of Iona: Theologian, Lawmaker, Peacemaker*, ed. Jonathan M. Wooding et al. (Dublin: Four Courts Press, 2010), 36–50.
244. On the dating of Aldhelm's collection, see Bolton, *A History*, vol. 1, 77. See also Lapidge and Rosier, *Aldhelm: The Poetic Works*, 11–12, and Lapidge, "The Career of Aldhelm," 24–25. Story has recently detected some verbal echoes in the *Epistola* that derive from some epigrams that Aldhelm might have known first-hand from his visit to Rome. The passage in question is "Claviger aetherius qui portam pandit in aethram," which is line 2 of the epigram entitled "De Petro." The line is quoted three times in the *Epistola*. See Ehwald, *Aldhelmi opera*, 68, 314, 485. See also Story, "Aldhelm and Old St Peter's, Rome," 18–19. If Story's conjecture is correct, the dating of the *Epistola*, as well as of some of the other works, should be placed some time after 688–689.

has been conveniently entitled by editors *De metris* (On meter).[245] This part concerns the basics of the Latin hexameter, offering an illustration of different kinds of metrical feet and its possible combinations. There follows the *Enigmata*, which might have been an earlier work that was later incorporated into the *Epistola* in order to exemplify the explanations on the hexameter contained in the *De metris*.[246] After the *Enigmata*, a second treatise on meter, *De pedum regulis* (On the metrical feet), is included.[247] This final part offers a description of the main metrical feet and is accompanied by a list of Latin words that help illustrate the different types.

Aldhelm soon gained a reputation as a learned scholar, and his works eventually achieved a remarkable popularity both in England and the Continent. The fact that books containing his works were required by Aldhelm's contemporaries is evidence of the way this author was appreciated by "colleagues" such as Cellanus of Péronne, an Irish monk.[248] Among his works, Aldhelm's *Enigmata* became seminal for subsequent enigmatists such as Tatwine, Eusebius, Boniface, Pseudo-Bede, as well as the author of the Lorsch Riddles.[249] Apart from the notable influence of this work on Anglo-Saxon and Conti-

---

245. *De metris* is edited in Ehwald, *Aldhelmi opera*, 77–96. A translation of *De metris* is found in Lapidge and Rosier, *Aldhelm: The Poetic Works*, 191–211.
246. Lapidge and Rosier, *Aldhelm: The Poetic Works*, 11.
247. For an edition of *De pedum regulis*, see Ehwald, *Aldhelmi opera*, 150–201. A translation is found in Lapidge and Rosier, *Aldhelm: The Poetic Works*, 212–19.
248. In Letter 9 Cellanus, for instance, explains that he is well aware of the magnificent quality of Aldhelm's *latinitas* from the reading of his works and urges him to send him a few little sermons (*"sermunculos"*). For this letter, see Ehwald, *Aldhelmi opera*, 498–99, and Lapidge and Herren, *Aldhelm: The Prose Works*, 167. These sermons have not survived, however. On Cellanus, see ibid., 149.
249. Parallels from Aldhelm's riddles can be found in the collections by all these authors, as indicated in the notes of the *CCLS* edition, vols. 133 and 133A. In the case of Pseudo-Bede's *Collectanea*, five of Aldhelm's riddles occur in this collection. Notably, nos. 103, 200, 242, 243, and 244 of the *Collectanea* (as numbered in Bayless and Lapidge's edition) correspond to

nental riddling, the popularity of Aldhelm's *Enigmata* is also attested to in other literary genres. For example, Lapidge and Rosier point out that the charters issued from King Athelstan's period onwards are virtually "Aldhelmian centos."[250]

In England, the heyday of Aldhelm's influence can be traced back as early as the 940s or 950s when the Benedictine reformers started to turn to Aldhelm's works, which were thoroughly scrutinized, glossed, and imitated.[251] The presence of two vernacular adaptations of Aldhelm's *Enigmata* 33 and 100 in Exeter Riddles 35 and 40 is proof of this keen interest, which might have to do with the profound cultural renewal promoted by Benedictinism. Aldhelm's imprint is also everywhere discernible in Byrhtferth of Ramsey's hagiographies on St Ecgwine and St Oswald, the latter being one of the main leaders of the Benedictine movement. Byrhtferth entirely quotes Aldhelm's *Enigma* 46 (nettle) and offers the first two lines of Riddle 59 (pen) in his *Vita sancti Oswaldi*.[252] Similarly, the initial part of the *Historia Regum*, which Lapidge attributes to this author,[253]

Aldhelm's nos. 3 (cloud), 90 (woman giving birth to twins), 2 (wind), 4 (nature), and 9 (diamond).
250. Lapidge and Rosier, *Aldhelm: The Poetic Works*, 4. Also, see D. A. Bullough, "The Educational Tradition in England from Alfred to Ælfric: Teaching *utriusque linguae*," *Settimane di studio del centro Italiano di studi sull'alto Medioevo* 19 (1971): 453–94, esp. 466–73.
251. As mentioned above (pp. 28–29, n. 81), Gretsch has convincingly claimed that Bishop Æthelwold and his circle were responsible for the glosses found in Aldhelm's prose *De virginitate* from Brussels, Bibliothèque Royale, 1650. *The Intellectual Foundations*, 4–5.
252. For these two passages, see Lapidge, *Byrhtferth of Ramsey*, 52–53 (ii.10 and iii.1), and for further echoes of Aldhelm's *Enigmata* in the *Vita sancti Oswaldi*, see ibid., 27, 56, 102, and 146.
253. Nowadays scholars agree that this first part, which was thought to be integral to the *Historia regum* by Symeon of Durham (d. 1130), is actually a separate work, which was at some point incorporated into the larger *Historia*. Michael Lapidge, "Byrhtferth of Ramsey and the Early Sections of the *Historia Regum* attributed to Symeon of Durham," *ASE* 10 (1981): 97–98.

cites from Aldhelm's Riddle 6 (moon).²⁵⁴ In addition, a thorough knowledge of Aldhelm's *De virginitate*, particularly of the poetic version, is also observed in Byrhtferth's *Enchiridion*.²⁵⁵ All these instances bring us to the conclusion that the influence of Aldhelm was strong, far-reaching, and long-standing in the early Middle Ages.

3.3.2 Introduction to Aldhelm's Enigmata

Aldhelm's Riddles appear in more than thirty codices, although not all of them present the collection in a complete form. Probably introduced in the Continent by Boniface and his circle, Aldhelm's *Enigmata* were eventually "absorbed into the Carolingian school curriculum to judge by the number of extant later eighth- and ninth-century Carolingian copies of that work," as Joanna Story affirms.²⁵⁶ By way of example, in Vatican City, Biblioteca Apostolica Vaticana, Pal. Lat. 1719 (early ninth century),²⁵⁷ which originated at the monastery of St Nazarius at Lorsch,²⁵⁸ Aldhelm's collection (fols. 1v-14v) reaches up to line 3 of Riddle 84 and precedes that of Symphosius. A further product of the Lorsch scriptorium offering a complete version of Aldhelm's *Enigmata* (fols. 87r-92r), which is inserted in the *Epistola ad Acircium* and followed by Symphosius's Riddles, is Vatican City, Pal. Lat. 1753 (c. 800). Another codex including the entire collection (fols. 15r-23r) within the *Epistola* is Karlsruhe, Badische Landesbiblio-

---

254. On the influence of Aldhelm's *Enigmata* on Byrhtferth's works, see Lapidge, "Byrhtferth of Ramsey," 113.
255. For the passages in question, see Lapidge, "Byrhtferth of Ramsey," 113 (n. 40). See also Baker and Lapidge, *Byrhtferth's Enchiridion*, lxxxiii-lxxxiv.
256. Story, "Aldhelm and Old St Peter's, Rome," 13. For the presence of Aldhelm's Enigmata in the Carolingian school curriculum, see Irvine, *The Making*, 356-57.
257. On paleographical grounds, this codex has been dated by Lagorio to some time before 820. Valerie M. Lagorio, "Aldhelm's *Aenigmata* in Codex Vaticanus Palatinus Latinus 1719," *Manuscripta* 15 (1971): 24. For further information on this manuscript, see Pellegrin, et al., *Les manuscrits classiques*, vol. 2, Part 2, 386-88.
258. As Finch has pointed out, the manuscript displays twice the "ex libris" of this monastic house on the flyleaves. Finch, "Symphosius," 6.

thek, Aug. 85, which was produced at Reichenau in the early ninth century. Once more jointly with Symphosius's *Enigmata*, Aldhelm's Riddles (fols. 123r-35r) are included in Vatican City, Reg. Lat. 2078 (tenth century) from Rheims. The presence of Aldhelm's *Enigmata* in all these manuscripts therefore illustrates the relevance of this work in monastic centers with Anglo-Saxon connections during the Carolingian period.

The collection has also been preserved in several codices of English provenance. An early version occurs in the so-called "Miskolc fragment" from Hungary (Miskolc, Lévay József Library, s.n.), which was dated by Z. Mády to the mid-eighth century on paleographical grounds.[259] This snippet contains lines 28–42 and 56–71 from Aldhelm's *Enigma* 100 plus a portion from the *De pedum regulis*. With Bischoff's assistance, Mády concluded that this copy originated somewhere in southern England, probably at Canterbury.[260] The Miskolc fragment may therefore be the earliest testimony of Aldhelm's *Enigmata* and *De pedum regulis* that has come down to us. A further early English manuscript is St Petersburg, Q.v.I.15 (fols. 71v-79r), which, as mentioned above, was produced at some southwestern scriptorium at the beginning of the eighth century and later taken to Corbie, where, we may assume, Aldhelm's *Enigmata* were copied into it.[261] Interestingly, the copying of the riddle collection was probably planned when the manuscript was in England, as inferred from the presence of a list of the solutions occurring on folio 52v.[262]

Apart from the Miskolc fragment, there are two other English manuscripts in which Aldhelm's collection has survived. Together

---

259. Z. Mády, "An VIIIth Century Aldhelm Fragment in Hungary," *Acta Antiqua Academiae Scientiarum Hungaricae* 13 (1965): 445.
260. Mády established the provenance on the basis of a personal communication with Bernhard Bischoff. Ibid., 444.
261. According to McKitteridge, "The book [St Petersburg, Q.v.I.15] is written in insular minuscule for the most part, but from f. 71 the work was continued in the Corbie eN script." "The Diffusion of Insular Culture," 413. See also Ganz, *Corbie in the Carolingian Renaissance*, 130.
262. Ibid.

with Symphosius's Riddles, Aldhelm's *Enigmata* occur in both London, Royal 12.C.xxiii (fols. 79v-103v) and Cambridge, Gg.5.35 (fols. 394r-407r), two codices with a Canterbury affiliation, as pointed out above.[263] In these two copies, Aldhelm's *Enigmata* are profusely glossed,[264] a circumstance suggesting that these texts were thoroughly studied. Apart from these two well-known codices, Aldhelm's Riddles occur separately from those of Symphosius in two Frankish books—London, Royal 15.A.xvi (fols. 60r-73v) and Oxford, Rawlinson C.697 (fols. 1r-13v and 14v-16r)—"which were probably brought to England to replenish libraries depleted during the ninth century."[265] Like the Miskolc fragment and the two English riddle compendia, these two Continental manuscripts have a connection to Canterbury, a notion implying that Aldhelm's *Enigmata* were particularly appreciated in the metropolitan diocese.[266]

Aldhelm's *Enigmata*, which, like those of his predecessor Symphosius, amount to one hundred pieces, were most likely designed to practice metrics, as explained above.[267] Whereas in Symphosius's work the tristich was the only poetic format employed, Aldhelm's *Enigmata* by contrast present a considerable variety in terms of length. Actually, as noted by Bolton, the riddles increase the number of lines in "a rough kind of progression" that culminates in the Creation poem (no. 100), by far the longest composition.[268] Aldhelm's collection was so successful that it probably started to circulate in manuscripts independently from the metrical tracts of the *Epistola* at an early stage.[269] But the

---

263. See pp. 35–36 of this book.
264. According to Stork, *Through a Gloss Darkly*, 12, the number of glosses in the London manuscript is 1,286, and 575 in the case of the Cambridge codex.
265. O'Brien O'Keeffe, "The Text of Aldhelm's *Enigma* no. C," 66. As pointed out by Gretsch, "Aldhelm's works were among the earliest books which were re-imported from the Continent for the restocking of English libraries from the times of King Alfred onwards . . ." *The Intellectual Foundations*, 333.
266. See above, pp. 30-32.
267. See p. 75 (n. 272).
268. Bolton, *A History*, vol. 1, 83.
269. As Boyer notes, the exclusions of the *Capitula*, the prologue, and the preface in various codices "are indications that on the Continent at an early

prosodic element was surely part of the original plan, so, even in a separate format, Aldhelm's Riddles still reflect a compilation based on metrical criteria.

A further outstanding difference with regard to Symphosius's *Enigmata* is the fact that Aldhelm articulated his preface in the form of acrostics and telestichs that spell out "Aldhelmus cecinit millenis versibus odas" [Aldhelm sang (i.e., composed) poems in a thousand lines].[270] Despite these notable divergences, scholars agree that Aldhelm's *Enigmata* are indebted to Symphosius's collection.[271] Aldhelm himself acknowledged this influence in the prologue to the *Enigmata*: "Simfosius poeta, uersificus metricae artis peritia praeditus, occultas enigmatum propositiones exili materia sumpta ludibundis apicibus legitur cecinisse et singulas quasque propositionum formulas tribus uersiculis terminasse"[272] [It is well-known that poet Symphosius, the verse-maker, gifted with the knowledge of metrical art, sang obscure enigmatic puzzles on simple matters which were gathered in the highest playful style, restricting each of these puzzles to three-line formulas]. The fact that Aldhelm thoroughly studied Symphosius's *Enigmata* is also attested to by the numerous citations that he brought up from twelve of these riddles to illustrate the metrical theory in the *Epistola*.[273]

---

date the *Aenigmata* [of Aldhelm], considered inapposite to a treatise on meter but popularly received *per se*, went into circulation separately—contrary to the author's intention." Blanche Boyer, "Insular Contribution to Medieval Literary Tradition on the Continent," *Classical Philology* 42 (1974): 218.

270. As Pitman notes, "since the riddles contain only 800 verses, Aldhelm here, as elsewhere, is using 'thousand' merely as a round number." James Hall Pitman, ed. and trans., *The Riddles of Aldhelm* (New Haven, CT: Yale University Press, 1925), 68.

271. As stated by Lapidge and Rosier, *Aldhelm: The Poetic Works*, 63, "Aldhelm clearly modelled his collection of one hundred *Enigmata* on that of Symphosius's."

272. All citations from Aldhelm's prologue are from Glorie, *CCSL*, vol. 133. Unless indicated otherwise, the translations of all these excerpts are mine.

273. In *De metris*, Aldhelm quotes from Symphosius's Riddles 47 (1), 98 (2), 72 (1), 17 (2), 85 (3), 92 (3) and in *De pedum regulis*, he cites Riddles 58

A notable aspect of Aldhelm's collection is the explicit and ubiquitous presence of Christian ideas, a feature that strongly contrasts with that of Symphosius. To take an example, his preface to the *Enigmata* opens with a lengthy solemn invocation to God—alluded to in his role of judge ("Arbiter," 1)—for inspiration. While Symphosius apologizes for his appealing to a "drunken Muse" ("ebria Musa," 15) for the composition of his Saturnalian riddles, Aldhelm further detaches himself from his predecessor's pagan stance by uncompromisingly stating that he will not turn to the Muses to accomplish his writing task:[274]

> Castalidas nimphas non clamo cantibus istuc
> examen neque spargebat mihi nectar in ore;
> Cynthi sic numquam perlustro cacumina, sed nec
> in Parnasso procubui nec somnia uidi.
> Nam mihi uersificum poterit Deus addere carmen
> inspirans stolidae pia gratis munera menti
> tangit si mentem, mox laudem corda rependunt. (10–16)
>
> [I do not invoke the Castalian nymphs thither with my songs (i.e., poems), nor a swarm of bees has spread nectar in my mouth[275];

(3, twice), 22 (3), 53 (3), 24 (3), 36 (2), 52 (2). For these citations, see Ehwald, *Aldhelmi opera*, 93, 94, 95, 96, 154, 157, 160, 167, and 197. Note that some of the riddles' numbers are different from those offered by Ehwald, as I follow throughout the numbering of the *CCSL* edition. Some of these citations are not identical to the ones offered in the *CCSL* edition because Glorie's text occasionally departs from Ehwald's readings. Aldhelm also quotes Pseudo-Symphosius's Riddle 5 (ice) in *De metris*. For this, see Ehwald, ibid., 77.
274. For a similar formulaic rejection of the Muses, see Adlhelm's poetic *De virginitate* (23–35). Ehwald, *Aldhelmi opera*, 353.
275. On the basis of the gloss accompanying line 11 of the preface in London, Royal 12.C.xxiii (fol. 83r), Thornbury reads this line as a reference to the legend of St Ambrose, "whose divine eloquence was miraculously foretold by a swarm of bees that lit upon his mouth as an infant." She therefore interprets it as a "modesty topos." Emily V. Thornbury, "Aldhelm's Rejection of the Muses and the Mechanics of Poetic Inspiration in Early Anglo-Saxon England," *ASE* 36 (2007): 80. For the gloss ("sicut legimus de sancto ambrosio"), see Stork, *Through a Gloss Darkly*, 94.

I never wander on the summits of Cynthus[276]; I have not slept on Parnassus nor seen any dream (there). For (only) God will be able to increase pious gifts by freely inspiring my brutish mind with a verse song; If He touches my mind, my heart at once will give praise in return (for these gifts)].

By saying what he will not do, Aldhelm thus categorically affirms that the Christian spirit will permeate the riddles and will therefore set this work apart from its literary pagan antecedents. But at the same time these lines also offer Aldhelm the opportunity to display his outstanding knowledge of classical culture.[277]

Aldhelm continues the verse preface by identifying himself with Old Testament figures who have been capable of similar heroic "literary" exploits, such as Moses (17–20), traditionally considered to be the author of the Pentateuch, and David as the author of the Psalms (21 and 34). Through his writing skills, Aldhelm is therefore positioning himself as an intermediary between God and humans, just as Moses and David did before him. Moses is thus presented as a poet ("uatem," 17) who has composed "metrica . . . carmina" (17)[278] while David is described as the psalmist, singing metrical songs with his voice ("et psalmista canens metrorum cantica uoce," 21).[279] The author similarly compares

---

276. Mount Cynthus is found on the island of Delos, the birthplace of Apollo. Traditionally considered the god of poetry and music, Apollo was also the leader of the Muses in classical mythology.

277. For the reference to the Muses and other ideas deriving from the classical and patristic sources employed by Aldhelm in composing the preface as an illustration of the typical "cultural omnivorousness" of Anglo-Saxon poetry, see Thornbury, "Aldhelm's Rejection of the Muses," 92. See also Lapidge and Rosier, *Aldhelm: The Poetic Works*, 248 (n. 2).

278. As Thornbury explains, lines 17–20 allude to Moses' triumphal song after leading the Israelites through the Red Sea (Exodus 15.1–18). See her "Aldhelm's Rejection of the Muses," 74 (n. 11).

279. Also, David is referred to as having composed ("cecinit quod carmine," 34) a particular psalm (78.13–16) recalling Moses' heroic crossing of the Red Sea and the flowing of water out of a dry rock. On the references to David's reputation as a singer in the Bible and the allusion to the Psalms in Aldhelm's preface, see ibid., 74 (n. 12).

his literary endeavor with the Israelites' crossing the Red Sea and the desert (33–34), probably on account of the tremendous effort and the huge size of the undertaking that he is setting out to accomplish with the composition of the *Enigmata*. In addition, with the reference to Job (30), Aldhelm also establishes a parallelism with this Old Testament character. Described as belligerent ("belligero," 30) in the text, Job constituted a well-known illustration of courageous and unyielding perseverance against adversity. Aldhelm's own strenuous writing task, adjusting scrupulously to metrical requirements (25–27) and avoiding *rusticitas* (26), is thus presented as an exercise of Christian faith that will have its reward with the achievement of divine inspiration.

With the allusion to the biblical beast known as Behemoth (4) in the preface,[280] the author brings up the idea of a a great chaotic force that can be controlled only by God, who appears as the only one who is capable of restoring order in nature.[281] By the same token, only divine power can enable Aldhelm to reveal in verse the secret mysteries of (created) things—"rerum / uersibus enigmata queam clandistina" (7–8)—so that the allegedly random appearance of Creation can be disclosed. By using the term "enigmata," Aldhelm is, on the one hand, referring to the literary genre that he has chosen to describe God's Creation; on the other, the term and the context in which it appears are reminiscent of St Paul's verse ("Videmus nunc per speculum in aenigmate")[282]—which was frequently used by medieval writers to explain God's obscure ways as reflected in nature.

3.3.3 The Organization of Aldhelm's Enigmata

As a whole, Aldhelm's *Enigmata* do not present the distribution into clear-cut sequences that is observed in Symphosius's work. Despite

---

280. The sources of this passage are Job 40.10 and Gregory the Great's *Moralia in Job* (XXXII.x.16). See *CCSL*, vol. 133, 377 (*Fontes*).
281. For the same idea used throughout Exeter Riddle 1-2-3, see further on pp. 292–93.
282. "For we now see in a mirror dimly" (1 Corinthians 13.12). Latin text from Robert Weber, ed., *Biblia sacra: iuxta vulgatam versionem* (Stutgart: Deutsche Bibelgesellschaft, 1969).

this, Aldhelm's collection seems to be at least partially organized from a thematic point of view (see Appendix IV). With manifest cosmological character, the initial homogeneous sequence (nos. 1–8) introduces the *Enigmata*. Section 2 dwells mainly on the description of animals and stones, while section 3 offers a miscellany. Section 4 on wonders precedes the final long poem on Creation, which constitutes an appropriate conclusion and obviously connects with the ideas presented in the preface. It is therefore evident that the first section and the Creation riddle constitute a framework encapsulating a large amalgam of zoological, lapidary, botanical, instrumental, and cosmological motifs. All in all, Aldhelm's subjects would no doubt correspond to topics included in Isidore's second decade.

*3.3.3.1 Section 1 (*Enigmata *1–8)*

Aldhelm's section 1 clearly offers a compendium of cosmological topics. It is thus worthwhile comparing the thematic layout of the riddles with the equivalent passages from Isidore's *Etymologiae*:

Aldhelm's Section 1	Isidore's *Etymologiae*
1. Earth	XIV.i.1–2
2. Wind	XIII.xi.1
3. Cloud	XIII.vii.2
4. Nature	XIII.v.6[283]
5. Rainbow	XIII.x.1
6. Moon	XIII.xv.1 (*oceanus*)[284]

---

283. The reference to *Etymologiae* XIII.v.6 actually alludes to a gloss added in London, Royal 12.C.xxiii (fol. 84v) to explain "conuexa" (3), describing the arched shape of the high celestial vaults ("alta poli," 4). See Stork, *Through a Gloss Darkly*, 104. The term *natura* is also explained in *Etymologiae* XI.i.1. The same can be said about the source indicated for Riddle 5 (rainbow), since a gloss from *Etymologiae* XIII.x.1 accompanies the text in the London manuscript. See Stork, ibid., 105.
284. The description of the "ocean" in *Etymologiae* XIII.xv.1 obviously

Aldhelm's Section 1	Isidore's *Etymologiae*
7. Fate	—
8. Pleiades	III.lxxi.13[285]

Aldhelm decided to open his series with "earth," which is the subject introducing Isidore's Book XIV (*De terra et partibus*, On the earth and its parts). As discussed above, the corresponding encyclopedic passage is also included as a gloss that co-occurs with Riddle 1 in London, Royal 12.C.xxiii (fol. 84r).[286] The reading of the riddle would no doubt be accompanied by the perusing of the Isidorean excerpt in this manuscript. As illustrated in the chart, Aldhelm might have used at least two further passages from Isidore's Book XIII (*De mundo et partibus*, On the world and its parts) as a source of inspiration for the composition of Riddles 5 and 6.[287] The association of these riddles and the *Etymologiae* therefore suggests that Aldhelm culled some topics from this encyclopedia, particularly from Book XIII, which similarly handles cosmological topics.

Section 1 as a whole presents the different subjects as being in constant conflict with the environment. From Aldhelm's perspective, nature seems to be at odds with the surrounding elements. For example, in Riddle 1 the earth is personified as the nurse of all creatures ("Altrix cunctorum," 1). Subsequently, human beings are compared to wicked infants ("pignora ... inproba," 2–3) who tear ("lacerant," 3) the mother's breasts ("maternas dente papilla," 3) with their teeth, a notion that metaphorically suggests the plowing of land. The earth is thus presented as patiently enduring human mistreatment. By the same token, the wind in Riddle 2 is an invisible and untouchable force (1), which can destroy oaks ("confringere quercus," 3) with its

does not correspond thematically to Aldhelm's *Enigma* 6 (moon), but it has been included as it has been recognized as a source for the riddle. See the note for this (*fontes*) in *CCSL*, vol. 133, 389.
285. This passage from the Isidorean source (III.lxxi.13) is found in the bottom margin of folio 84v. Stork, *Through a Gloss Darkly*, 108.
286. See above, p. 82, and Stork, *Through a Gloss Darkly*, 100.
287. See *CCSL*, vol. 133, 387 and 389 (*fontes*).

horrible-sounding power ("uiribus horrisonis," 3).[288] The cloud is personified as a fugitive in *Enigma* 3: "Versicolor fugiens caelum terramque profundam relinquo, / non tellure locus mihi, non in parte polorum est: / exilium nullus modo tan crudele ueretur" (1–3) [Of varying color as I flee, I leave behind the sky and the deep earth; there is no place for me on earth nor anywhere in the skies; no one fears an exile as cruel as this]. Aldhelm thus sets the cloud against heaven and earth. Riddle 4 describes nature as an invisible god-like entity, which recalls the description of the wind in Riddle 2: "Crede mihi, res nulla manet sine me moderante / et frontem faciemque meam lux nulla uidebit" (1–2) [Believe me, nothing remains (alive) without my control; yet no light (i.e., no one) will see my forehead and my face].[289]

Aldhelm also seems to be concerned with presenting the cosmological topics as being tightly interrelated. Thus, in Riddle 5 the rainbow is said to be born from the sun and a watery cloud ("nubis aquosae," 3). Together with the ocean, the moon in Riddle 6 is said to be subject to a cyclical rule decreed by fate: "Nunc ego cum pelagi fatis communibus insto / tempora reciprocis conuoluens menstrua cyclis" (1–2) [I now pursue a common fate with the sea, rotating periodic monthly cycles of time]. In turn, fate is dealt with in subsequent Riddle 7, in which it is described as a woman (*Fortuna*)[290]: "Me ueteres falso 'dominam' uocitare solebant, / sceptra regens mundi dum Christi gratia regnet" (3–4) [Mistakenly, the ancients used to call me "mistress,"

---

288. This line recalls Isidore's description of the wind in the *Etymologiae* (XIII.xi.1): "Dictus autem ventus quod sit vehemens et violentus. Vis enim eius tanta est ut non solum saxa et arbores evellat, sed etiam caelum terramque conturbet, maria commoveat" [It is called wind because it is severe and violent, for its strength is such that it not only roots stones and trees out but also upsets the sky and the earth and agitates the oceans].
289. The concept *Natura* is similarly associated with God in Isidore's *Etymologiae* (XI.iii.1): "gentiles Deum modo Naturam, modo Deum appellant" [the pagans refer to God sometimes as "Nature," sometimes as "God"].
290. In the preceding line, by means of a citation from Virgil's *Aeneid* (XII.677), fate is alluded to as "Fortuna" (2), thus fitting the subsequent designation as *domina*. Note also how *fortuna*, representing the pagan concept of fate, is presented as the antagonist of "gratia" (4) or Christian grace.

ruling the scepters of the world until Christ's grace started to rule]. The inclusion of this topic in this cosmological section can be explained by the association with the allusion to both the moon and the sea being under the influence of fate in the preceding riddle. Furthermore, it may be assumed that fate would suit this series, since from a medieval perspective this concept was tightly linked to the stars.

In fact, *Enigma* 7 would be connected to the subsequent Riddle 8 describing the Pleiades, a cluster of seven stars ("septena cohors," 2). The number seven, which was an important topic at the beginning of the *Epistola*, makes this riddle a meaningful conclusion for the cosmological section.[291] Also, the Pleiades are mentioned twice in the Book of Job (9.9 and 38.31), which played a prominent role in the verse preface. One of these passages (38.31) is cited in relation to the Pleiades in *De metris* (III),[292] where these stars are said to prefigure the sevenfold distribution of the God-given presents of the universal church ("universalis ecclesiae septinariam charismatum distributionem"),[293] in other words, the seven sacraments. The allegorical significance of this final subject might have triggered its position at the end of section 1. Finally, Riddle 8 is also distinguished in the series on a metrical basis, since it is the only composition with five lines instead of four.

3.3.3.2 Section 2 *(*Enigmata 9–39*)*

Section 2 comprises seventeen animals,[294] seven instruments,[295] and five stones.[296] There is only one cosmological topic (water) and one

---

291. One also wonders if *Enigma* 1 should be excluded from the section, as with Riddle 100, so as to consider section 1 as a group composed of seven pieces, with the Pleiades symbolizing number seven at the close.
292. Ehwald, *Aldhelmi opera*, 72. See Lapidge and Herren, *Aldhelm: The Prose Works*, 42.
293. Ehwald, *Aldhelmi opera*, 72; Lapidge and Herren, *Aldhelm: The Prose Works*, 43.
294. Dog, silkworm, peacock, salamander, squid, pinna, ant-lion, bee, nightingale, rooster, stork, locust, night owl, midge, crab, pond-skater, and lion.
295. Bellows, organ, file, pair of scales, alphabet, writing-tables, and breastplate.
296. Diamond, salt, dragon-stone, magnet, and whetstone.

prodigy (minotaur). Despite these miscellaneous contents, there is a clear predominance of zoological riddles which offer clues that are related to the characteristics recorded in Isidore's Book XII for some of those animals. Also interestingly, as observed in the following outline, there are seven subjects that correspond to topics that Isidore treated in Book XVI (*De lapidibus et metallis*, On stones and metals).[297]

Aldhelm's Section 2	Isidore's *Etymologiae*
9. Diamond	XVI.xiii.2[298]
10. Dog	—
11. Bellows	—
12. Silkworm	XII.v.8
13. Organ	—
14. Peacock	XII.vii.48
15. Salamander	XII.iv.36
16. Squid	XII.vi.47
17. Pinna[299]	XII.vi.50[300]
18. Ant-lion	XII.iii.10

---

297. In the following outline, I am mainly considering entries from the *Etymologiae* that are mentioned as probable sources in *CCSL*, vol. 133. Some of them are also found as glosses in Aldhelm's *Enigmata* in London, Royal 12.C.xxiii. For the Isidorean excerpts in the riddles of this section, see Stork, *Through a Gloss Darkly*, 110–48.

298. The *CCSL* edition (391, *Fontes*) also mentions *Etymologiae* XII.i.14, which offers a passing reference to goat's blood being capable of dissolving a diamond, as a possible source. The same idea is later taken up again in XVI.xiii.2.

299. "A bivalve mollusc of the genus *Pinna*, having a large silky byssus; a fan mussel" (*OED*, s.v. "pinna"). Cameron proposes this term as a translation from Latin *perna*, the title-solution of this riddle. See Cameron, "Aldhelm as Naturalist" 120.

300. According to the *CCSL* edition (399, *Fontes*), the source for this riddle might be Pliny's *Naturalis historia* but note that in London, Royal 12.C.xxiii (fol. 86r) *Enigma* 17 is accompanied by a gloss from *Etymologiae* XII.vi.50, which mentions the purple dye that can be obtained from the mollusk known as *murex* or *concilium* (purple-fish). See Stork, *Through a Gloss Darkly*, 118.

Aldhelm's Section 2	Isidore's *Etymologiae*
19. Salt	XVI.ii.3
20. Bee	XII.viii.1
21. File	**XIX.vii.4**[301]
22. Nightingale	XII.vii.37, 74
23. Pair of scales	XVI.xxv.4
24. Dragon-stone	XVI.xiv.7 (*dracontites*)
25. Magnet	XVI.iv.1
26. Rooster	—
27. Whetstone	XVI.iii.6 (*cos*)[302]
28. Minotaur	**XI.iii.38**
29. Water	—
30. Alphabet	**I.iv.10, 11–15**
31. Stork	XII.vii.16–17
32. Writing-tables	—
33. Breastplate	—
34. Locust	—[303]
35. Night owl	XII.vii.40–41
36. Midge	XII.viii.13–14
37. Crab	XII.vi.51[304]
38. Pond-skater	—
39. Lion	XII.ii.3, 5

---

301. In this case, I am using bold letters only for the reference to the source in the *Etymologiae*, as the clues of the riddle derive from Book XIX (see *CCSL*, vol. 133, 403, *Fontes*). However, the file as a topic is perfectly suitable for the series, as I will later explain.
302. The whetstone (*cos*) is described by Isidore in Book XVI, although it is not to be regarded as a possible source, as in the other cases. But I am including this reference in order to show the parallel occurrence of subjects in Aldhelm's section 2 and Book XVI of the *Etymologiae*.
303. For Pliny's *Naturalis historia* as a probable source for this riddle, see *CCSL*, vol. 133, 419 (*Fontes*).
304. The *CCSL* edition (vol. 133, 421, *Fontes*) also offers *Etymologiae*

Apart from disclosing the outstanding relevance of Isidore's influence in the composition of these riddles, the outline suggests that Aldhelm intentionally devised a section combining animals with minerals and thus drew subjects contained in Books XII and XVI. In this sense, "salt" (no. 19) is accordingly a logical topic, since it occurs in *Etymologiae* XVI.ii.3. The pair formed by dragon-stone (no. 24) and magnet (25), two lapidary subjects, is also noteworthy. Furthermore, section 2 includes some tools that are clearly associated with metalwork such as the bellows (11),[305] the file (21), the pair of scales (23),[306] and the whetstone (27).[307] In the case of the breastplate (33), the item can be understood as a product from the forge.

Being the most powerful and enduring stone in nature, the diamond (no. 9) was appropriately chosen as a suitable topic to open section 2:

En ego non uereor rigidi discrimina ferri
flammarum neu torre cremor, sed sanguine capri
uirtus indomiti mollescit dura rigoris.
Sic cruor exsuperat, quem ferrea massa pauescit.

---

lll.lxxi.26, which describes the constellation of Cancer but also alludes to the crab's crawling backwards, as a source for this riddle.

305. In London, Royal 12.C.xxiii (fol. 85r), the title of this riddle—"De poaleis id est follibus fabrorum" [On the *poalum*, that is, on smiths' bellows] evinces this association. See Stork, *Through a Gloss Darkly*, 112.
The title was probably meant to explain the arcane term *poalum*, which probably derives from a glossary. See Lapidge and Rosier, *Aldhelm: The Poetic Works*, 249 (n. 9).
306. The pair of scales is treated among the items of Book XVI, as indicated in the preceding outline. The position of this topic here is therefore consistent with the section's concern with metalwork, since the scales were used for weighing metal in the forge. However, whereas in the other instrumental topics (whetstone, bellows, and file) the connection to the forge context is explicit, the clues of Riddle 23 dwell mainly on the scales as the allegorical representation of justice.
307. As pointed out above, the whetstone (*cos*) is treated among the common stones (*De lapidibus vulgaribus*) in *Etymologiae* XVI.iii.6.

[Behold, I do not fear the severing of hard iron, nor am I consumed by the firebrand of the flames, but the hard quality of this fierce stiffness softens with goat's blood. Thus blood overpowers that which frightens a mass of iron].

The clues of this riddle allude to the unwavering strength of the diamond, which is not surpassed by iron but is paradoxically destroyed by goat's blood.[308] With the allusion to the diamond, iron, and the goat, *Enigma* 9 thus effectively embraces the zoological and mineral orders—the latter comprising stones and metals—which confirm the composite subject of section 2. Apart from this, the special status of this riddle is supported by the fact that a learned reader[309] would know about the allegorical significance of the diamond representing Christ's invincibility as well as the firmness of the Christian faith.[310]

Given that the dominant thematic category of section 2 is the zoological one, in the following pages I will focus on the way its components are displayed. To begin with, there are two zoological strings that need to be analyzed. The first one comprises five subjects, all of which have a correspondence with animals treated in Isidore's Book XII, as observed in the following outline:

---

308. See above (p. 182, n. 298) for Aldhelm's use of two passages from the *Etymologiae* as a source for this riddle.
309. The allegorical function of the diamond is, for example, attested to in Boniface's poem to his student Duddo, in which an intricate set of acrostics is displayed in the shape of a diamond. A facsimile version of this poem appears in Gebauer and Löfsted, *CCSL*, vol. 133B, 1. For the edited text, see 4–6. Also, see Irvine, *The Making*, 300–301. Alcuin's "De sancta cruce" (On the holy cross) similarly contains the figure of a diamond as a visual pattern. See Godman, *Poetry*, 138-43.
310. Since it is a typical motif in the *Physiologus*, Baxter notes that the pre-eminence of the diamond over the other stones compares to "Christ's dominion over death and hell." Baxter, *Bestiaries*, 60.

Aldhelm's Section 2	Isidore's *Etymologiae*
14. Peacock	XII.vii.48
15. Salamander	XII.iv.36
16. Squid	XII.vi.47
17. Pinna	XII.vi.50
18. Ant-lion	XII.iii.10

Thus, Aldhelm's first mini-series offers four different zoological categories: birds (peacock), snakes (salamander),[311] fish (squid and pinna), and small land animals (ant-lion). The size criterion, with the peacock as the largest animal leading the sequence, also seems to apply. It is also noteworthy that the peacock, a clean bird, contrasts with the remainder of the animals of the series, all of them being unclean, a notion that undoubtedly recalls the Isidorean method of organization.[312]

As a hybrid animal, the ant-lion constitutes an apt conclusion to

---

311. For the notable parallels between this riddle and the entry on the salamander found in Isidore's *Etymologiae* (XII.ix.36), see Henry Mayr-Harting, *The Coming of Christianity to Anglo-Saxon England* (University Park: The Pennsylvania State University Press, 1972; repr. 1991), 203–4.

312. Also noteworthy is the fact that Aldhelm's concern with clean and unclean animals may derive from the instruction period with Theodore, whose *Penitential* also manifests a keen interest in this issue. As Mayr-Harting points out, there is a significant digression in the section on the spondee in *De pedum regulis* (CXIV), in which Aldhelm mentions the African buffalo (*bubalus*) and the chamois (*tragelaphus*), which are classified in Deuteronomy 14.5 as clean animals. See Ehwald, *Aldhelmi opera*, 155. Mayr-Harting affirms that knowledge of these two animals could come from Theodore's first-hand regional lore. As he affirms, "Aldhelm's passage looks as if it had its origins in a very characteristically Theodoran gloss on the Deuteronomy animals." *The Coming of Christianity*, 208. Still, the interest in discriminating between clean and unclean animals could stem from Isidore's appreciation of zoology as observed in the *Etymologiae*, a work which was well known at the school of Canterbury. See David W. Porter, "Isidore's *Etymologiae* at the School of Canterbury," *ASE* 43 (2014): 7–44. For the reference to unclean meat in Theodore's *Penitential*, see A. W. Haddan and W. Stubbs, eds.,

this mini-series, thus recalling the centaur in Symphosius's quadruped subgroup. From a Christian perspective, the peacock's incorruptible flesh is also a suggestive opening topic,[313] as it could be associated with Christ's resurrection. The pre-eminent position and the implicit allegory similarly remind us of the occurrence of the phoenix at the end of Symphosius's subgroup 3E. These five zoological riddles no doubt reflect an attempt at encyclopedic classification, since the animals are representative of the four elements: air (peacock), fire (salamander), water (squid, pinna), and land (ant-lion).[314]

This sequence also manifests an interest in extraordinary creatures. Riddle 14 thus presents the peacock as an incredibly beautiful bird, whose flesh does not rot when it dies: "et moriens mea numquam pulpa putrescit" (4). Similarly, the clues of Riddle 15 dwell on the salamander's remarkable capacity to live unharmed in the middle of flames ("Ignibus in mediis uiuens non sentio flammas," 1). In the case of Riddle 16, the squid is presented as an animal that

---

Councils and Ecclesiastical Documents relating to Great Britain and Ireland, vol. 3 (Oxford, 1881), vii.6–7 (183) and XI.1–9 (198).

313. In the *Civitate dei* (XXI.iv), St Augustine himself marvels at the incorruptible nature of this bird: "Quis enim nisi Deus creator omnium dedit carni pavonis mortui ne putesceret?" ["For who if not God, the creator of all things, has granted to the flesh of the dead peacock immunity from decay?"]. Edition and translation from William M. Green, *St Augustine: The City of God against the Pagans*, vol. 7 (Cambridge, MA: Harvard University Press, 1972), 14–15. Aldhelm explicitly refers to this source when alluding to the peacock in the prose *De virginitate* (IX) and the poetic version of the latter work (231-35). See Ehwald, *Aldhelmi opera*, 237 and 362.

314. Lapidge and Rosier similarly appreciate Aldhelm's interest in the four elements as a constitutive principle of his *Enigmata*: "The relationship between *enigmata* involves one of the four cosmic elements (earth, air, fire, water). Thus the aquatic Salamander (xv), which can also inhabit fire, is paired with the Squid (xvi), which though aquatic also inhabits the air. The aquatic Crab (xxxvii) walks on the sea-shore but also climbs the heavens (in a manner of speaking), whereas the Pond-skater (xxxviii) walks on both water and earth. The feathers in the Pillow (xli) can swell up to the clouds, whereas the feathered Ostrich (xlii) is earth-bound." Lapidge and Rosier, *Aldhelm: The Poetic Works*, 64.

can move in the water and in the air alike:[315] "Cum grege piscoso scrutor maris aequora squamis, / Cum uolucrum turma quoque scando per aethera pennis . . ." (2–3) [I search the sea expanse with a school of fish with scales; I also ascend in the air with a crowd of birds with feathers]. The paradoxical implication is that the squid is deprived of scales and feathers but, despite this, it can rank with fish and birds thanks to its extraordinary skill to navigate in two different media. As regards Riddle 17, the clues allude to the pinna's twin shells ("geminis . . . concis," 1)[316] and its double use, since it can produce a purple dye for clothes and is also edible (2–3). This animal is thus said to pay a twofold tribute to fate ("sic duplex fati persoluo tributum," 4). On the other hand, Riddle 18 (ant-lion) alludes to the animal's compound name (*myrmicoleon*): "Dudum compositis ego nomen gesto figuris: / ut leo, sic formica uocor sermone pelasgo . . ." (1–2) [From long ago I have had a name with a composite form: just as "lion," thus am I called "ant" in Greek language].

Enigma 18 therefore dwells on the twofold nature of the ant-lion—note "compositis" (1), "duplis" (3), and "gemino" (5)—hence linking this creature to the duality of the squid in terms of locomotion and to the bivalved and doubly useful pinna. This mini-series consequently seems to be based primarily on analogy, a typical Isidorean structuring principle, for the clues of the riddles generally concern the creatures' double qualities, which make them extraordinary if they are compared to other animals.

The second zoological string of Aldhelm's section 2 similarly offers a selection of subjects, most of which are also handled in Isidore's Book XII.

---

315. For the squid's actual capacity to propel out of the water, see Cameron, "Aldhelm as Naturalist," 119.
316. As Lapidge and Rosier explain, the pinna is "shaped like a ham: hence Aldhelm's title *Perna*." *Aldhelm: The Poetic Works*, 249 (n. 15).

Aldhelm's Section 2	Isidore's *Etymologiae*
34. Locust	—
35. Night Owl	XII.vii.40–41
36. Midge	XII.viii.13–14
37. Crab	XII.vi.51
38. Pond-skater	—
39. Lion	XII.ii.3, 5

Here the outline discloses typical Isidorean categories such as animals of air, including small flying creatures (locust and midge) and nocturnal birds (night owl); water (crab and pond-skater); and land (lion). But, as with the preceding zoological mini-series, this group suggests a juxtaposition based on similar characteristics, in other words, on analogy. For example, the clues of some of these riddles allude to the animals' negative reputation. This is the case of the locust (no. 34), as this insect provoked one of the Egyptian plagues;[317] the night owl or *nycticorax* (35), which etymologically associates this bird with darkness;[318] the midge (36) that lives on the blood of four-footed beasts and is also related to the biblical plagues;[319] and the crab (37), which is said to hunt the defenseless oyster by means of a cunning trap.[320]

Also interestingly, this second zoological mini-section resembles the first one, since it opens with a clean animal—the locust is one of the few edible insects, according to Mosaic law;[321] the other ani-

---

317. Exodus 10.14–15.
318. As Scott points, the allegorical significance of the night owl (or night-raven) as symbolizing the Jewish people, who preferred darkness instead of light, occurs in the *Physiologus* (vii.3–4, *De nicticorace*), which might have inspired some of the clues of Aldhelm's *Enigma* 35. Scott, "Rhetorical and Symbolic Ambiguity," 131. See also Francis J. Carmody, ed., "Physiologus Latinus Versio Y," *University of California Publications in Classical Philology* 12 (1941): 107.
319. Exodus 8.16–18.
320. See my "The Oyster and the Crab" and pp. 109–10 and 411–13 of this book.
321. In Leviticus 11.22, it is established that the only exceptions are the

mals of the series are unclean.[322] The closing motif also seems to have been chosen on account of the supremacy of the lion over the other animals and his traditional royal character: "Ora cruenta ferens morsus rictusque luporum / horridus haud uereor regali culmine fretus" (4–5) [Endowed with a bloodthirsty mouth, I am not frightened by the bites and the jaws of wolves; supported by my royal head, I am indeed a frightful creature]. Given that the first zoological string ended with the ant-lion, the occurrence of the lion as the last subject of the second mini-series may not be haphazard. The underlying philological association—*myrmicoleon* and *leo*—recalls that offered by the bull (*taurus*) and the centaur (*centaurus*), being the first and the last subjects of Symphosius's quadruped subgroup.[323]

If we consider all the zoological topics of section 2 as a whole, including those that are not present in the two animal mini-sections that have just been discussed, it is reasonable to assume that Aldhelm intended to offer an illustration of at least seven of the eight Isidorean categories of animals.

1. Cattle and beasts of burden: none
2. Big wild animals: dog, lion
3. Small animals: ant-lion
4. Snakes: salamander
5. Worms: silkworm, pond-skater
6. Fish: squid, pinna, crab

---

locust, the cricket, and the grasshopper. Note, for example, that locusts and honey were the basic elements of John the Baptist's diet as mentioned in the Gospel (Matthew 3.4; Mark 1.6). A gloss alluding to this appears next to Aldhelm's *Enigma* 33 in London, Royal 12.C.xxiii (fol. 88r). See Stork, *Through a Gloss Darkly*, 140. Aldhelm also includes the reference to locusts as part of St John's daily food in the poetic *De virginitate* (399–400). Ehwald, *Aldhelmi opera*, 369.

322. Although it was technically prohibited by both Leviticus and Deuteronomy, the crab was however typical food at monasteries, as attested to by the list provided by the fisherman in Ælfric's *Colloquy*. See G. N. Garmonsway, *Ælfric's Colloquy* (London: Methuen, 1947), 29.

323. See above pp. 148–49 and n. 184.

7. Birds: peacock, nightingale, cock, stork, night owl
8. Small flying animals: bee, locust, midge

Still, the absence of clean quadrupeds is no doubt remarkable, but this was probably compensated for with the presence of the bullock (no. 83) toward the end of the collection. Also importantly, from this list it can be deduced that Aldhelm was interested primarily in unclean animals. Furthermore, a special attention to animals of small size is discerned, the only exceptions being the peacock, the stork, and the lion. Section 2 offers only a prodigy, the minotaur (28), which would also count as a large creature; besides, its position in the collection is anomalous, if compared to Symphosius's practice. In short, the representation of the majority of the Isidorean zoological categories, the observance of the size criterion, the occurrence of contrastive patterns as regards clean and unclean animals, and the pervasive concern with the four elements all jointly support my contention that Aldhelm structured section 2 on the basis of Isidorean organizing criteria.

Nevertheless, section 2 does present some outstanding thematic digressions that need to be taken into consideration. For example, the occurrence of a musical instrument such as the organ (no. 13) is most striking at this point, but the key to understanding its position in the collection may be found in the riddle's clues: "Centenos tamen eructant mea uiscera cantus; / me praesente stupet mox musica chorda fibrarum" (3–4) [But my entrails burp with a hundred songs; being present, the music of string instruments (i.e., made of tripe strings) is right away stunned]. Riddle 12 (silkworm) offers clues that resemble those used in the description of the organ: "Annua dum redeunt texendi tempora telas, / lurida setigeris redundant uiscera filis" (1–2)[324] [When the yearly season for weaving webs returns, my wan entrails overflow with bristly strings]. Riddles 12 and 13 therefore share the reference to strings as connected to entrails and the allusion to the creature's *uiscera* as producing music, on the

---

324. Cf. line 1 of Symphosius's preface: "*Annua* Saturni *dum tempora* festa *redirent*" (emphasis mine).

one hand, and silken threads, on the other. Riddle 11, which alludes to the bellows' breath ("flatibus," 1) and its air-hole ("spiracula," 2), similarly dwells on prosopopeia and is close to the clues describing the organ, whose entrails are said to burp ("eructant," 3).

As is usual with exceptional motifs, the occurrence of pairs offers a reasonable explanation for the presence of some of these riddles. This is the case of water (no. 29) and alphabet (no. 30). The inclusion of water in section 2 can be justified on the basis of the following clue: "Nam uolucres caeli nantesque per aequora pisces / olim sumpserunt ex me primordia uitae" (4–5) [The birds of the sky and the fish that swim in the ocean formerly obtained the origins of their life from me]. Here water is described as producing two zoological categories that are represented in section 2. Furthermore, the allusion to a needle as being capable of piercing the surface of water seems to connect this motif with the mineral world that also has a representation in section 2: "Ast acus exilis mox tanta gestamina rumpit!" (3) [but a thin needle breaks through such a (mighty) covering right away!].[325] The description of water thus parallels that of the diamond riddle (no. 9), in which an insignificant thing such as goat's blood can however have such a potent effect on a creature belonging to a different natural order. The subsequent riddle (no. 30) offers Latin *elementa* as the solution, a term that actually refers to the letters of the alphabet: "Nascimur ex ferro rursus ferro moribundae /

---

325. A different reading of this line is offered by Ehwald, *Aldhelmi opera*, 109 (note to line 3), who considers that *acus* refers to a sharp rock that may cause a shipwreck. This idea is accepted by Lapidge and Rosier, *Aldhelm: The Poetic Works*, 75 and 250 (n. 26). Pitman, *The Riddles of Aldhelm*, 70, discards Ehwald's interpretation, as he argues that "this riddle has nothing to do with either the fragility or the strength of ships." My own reading, and that of Stork's translation (*Through a Gloss Darkly*, 133), support Pitman in considering line 3 as a literal reference to a needle that can easily break through ("rumpit") the surface of water (*gestamen*, meaning "that which is borne or worn, a burden, load; ornaments, accoutrements, arms, etc."). Note that the previous line decribes water as being extremely strong because it can bear ("fero") a thousand oaks from the woods ("siluarum robora mille"). For a similar reading of "gestamina," see Pitman, ibid., 70–71.

necnon et uolucris penna uolitantis ad aethram" (3-4) [We are born from iron, and return to death by iron; also, from the feather of a bird flying in the sky]. In this case, the metal stylus is a decisive element in allowing letters to be born—by being written with its point on the wax tablet—or to die—by being erased by its flat part. Iron is thus presented as taking an active part in the origin of letters. In turn, the sharp stylus piercing the wax evokes the needle penetrating the water in Riddle 29 (3). In addition to this, the clue alluding to letters as being born from the feather of a bird in *Enigma* 30 recalls the reference to the birds having their origin in water in Riddle 29.

It may be argued that Aldhelm's perception of the letters as the basic elements of speech may have triggered the pairing of Riddles 29 (water) and 30 (alphabet), as well as the use of the word *elementa* for alphabet.[326] This idea seems to be rooted in Isidore's discussion of the indivisible quality of atoms and elements, as he compares them to letters: "Sic et littera: nam orationem dividis in verba, verba in syllabas, syllabam in litteras. Littera, pars minima, atomus est, nec dividi potest" (XIII.ii.4) [Thus (is it) with the letter, since you divide the sentence into words, words into syllables, syllables into letters. A letter, the minimal part, is an atom which cannot be divided].[327] It is therefore fairly reasonable to assume that Aldhelm envisaged Riddle 30 as a companion to Riddle 29: just as the letter constitutes the smallest component of speech, so it is with water as the source element of all the creatures on earth.

Section 2 abounds in interconnections of this kind, even among riddles that are not juxtaposed. Riddle 32 is, for example, indirectly related to Riddle 20 (bee) on account of the wax of the writing

---

326. Note that Isidore uses the term twice in the *Etymologiae* (I.iii.4) when referring to the 22 characters of the Hebrew alphabet ("Hebraei viginiti duo elementa litterarum") and the 23 Latin letters ("viginti tria elementa").
327. Interestingly, the subsequent section of the *Etymologiae* (XIII.iii) deals with the "elements" proper (i.e., earth, wind, air, and fire). Irvine similarly comments on this excerpt from the *Etymologiae* and states that letters, "as minimal units, are also *elementa*, the irreducible constituents of written discourse." *The Making*, 215.

tablets: "Melligeris apibus mea prima processit origo" (1) [My origin proceeded from the honeybees]. In turn, the writing tablets interact with the world of metals, since the waxen surface is carved by the point of the stylus ("ferri stimulus," 4) and the holy crop ("sancta seges," 8) is eventually destroyed by cruel weapons ("diris extinguitur armis," 8); in other words, the written text is erased. The reference no doubt recalls the description of the letters of the alphabet (no. 30), which issue from the iron-pointed stylus, and that of water (no. 29) being pierced by a slender needle. By the same token, *Enigma* 33 plays on the idea that the breastplate is not woven by silkworms, the latter being the topic of Riddle 12: "Nec crocca Seres texunt lanugine uermes" (4) [nor do Chinese worms weave me with their saffron-colored woolly substance]. Unlike the writing tablets (no. 32), the breastplate in Riddle 33 is not affected by metal: "Spicula non uereor longis exempta faretris" (7) [I do not fear the arrows released from long quivers]. This is thus an illustration of how the riddles are intricately interwoven by means of two major encyclopedic principles: analogy and difference.

Some of the clues present in the riddles of section 2 were probably meant to suggest the dynamic interaction between the different natural orders. For example, the dragon-stone (no. 24) is said to be drawn from the head of a living dragon. The clues of Riddle 19 initially describe salt as water containing living fish and eventually being transformed into a lifeless substance. Being a hybrid of a woman and a bull, the minotaur (no. 28) in turn provides evidence of the fact that humans may also trespass the established natural order by mixing themselves with animals. This topic was probably inspired by Symphosius's Riddle on the bull (no. 32), alluding to the myth of Pasiphaë, and that on the centaur (39). With the minotaur of Aldhelm's *Enigma* 28, the outcome of the relationship between Pasiphaë and the bull is presented.

From Aldhelm's perspective, the *Enigmata* describe a world that is in a continuous conflict, in which animals, minerals, and tools are in competition with one another. Thus, the organ (no. 13) contends with the string instruments; the melodious warbling of the nightingale (22) is set in opposition to the harsh irritating sound of the file (21). The antagonism of the seventeen legitimate letters and the six "bastards"[328] is evident in the description of the alphabet (30). In the same riddle, the flat part of the metal stylus is involved in the "death" of letters. The stork (31) is said to be the snake's foe; the cunning crab (37) is inimical to the oyster; the midge (36) parasitizes quadrupeds; the magnet (25) is said to be powerless when facing the diamond. And so we could go on offering examples.

Aldhelm probably considered the inclusion of some of the riddlic subjects on the basis of their being reminiscent of the Scriptures. Explicit references to the plagues as recorded in Exodus are offered in the locust and midge riddles (nos. 34 and 36). In turn, the juxtaposition of the breastplate (33) to the locust (34) evokes the reference to these insects in the Book of Revelation (9.9), where they are said to have "scales like iron breastplates."[329] The rooster (26) may have also been included on a similar basis even if there is no explicit reference to the significant role played by this animal in the Gospels.[330] It is also worth noting that some of the topics of this section—salamander, ant-lion, magnet, night owl, and lion[331]—are found in the *Physiologus*.[332] This work, which was at some point tightly associated with

---

328. Accordingly, h, k, q, x, y, and z are thus presented as the illegitimate sisters ("nothas," 2) because, as Pitman explains, these "are not native Latin letters," as expounded in *Etymologiae* I.iv.10. Pitman, *The Riddles of Aldhelm*, 71.
329. In Riddle 34, the locust is described on the basis of its having the heart encased in a natural corselet, in other words, the insect's outer shell: "Cor mihi sub genibus: nam constat carcere saeptum" (6) [My heart is under my knees, for it is protected by a cage].
330. As Pitman has noted, "the crowing cock is a familiar figure in Latin hymns." *The Riddles of Aldhelm*, 70.
331. See the corresponding chapters in Carmody's edition of the *Physiologus*: i (lion), vii (night-raven), xxiv and xlvii (diamond), xxxiii (ant-lion), xlv (salamander), and xlvi (magnet). Carmody, "Physiologus Latinus Versio Y."
332. Lapidge and Rosier, *Aldhelm: The Poetic Works*, 247, state that "perhaps an early recension of the Latin *Physiologus*" might have been available as a literary source for Aldhelm's *Enigmata*.

Isidore's *Etymologiae*,[333] contained descriptions of animals to which an allegorical interpretation was added.[334]

There is no doubt that Aldhelm was aware of the inherent symbolic potential of some of the riddlic themes. As with Isidore in the *Etymologiae*, Aldhelm only occasionally and vaguely alludes to the allegorical interpretation the riddle subjects. Evidence of the allegorical character of some of the subjects explicitly arises in the riddle on the pair of scales (no. 23), which refers to this tool as the emblem of justice. In the case of the ant-lion (18), the clues state that the animal's twofold name will consequently conjure up a double figurative meaning: "tropica nominibus signans praesagia duplis . . ." (3).[335] On the other hand, the implicit presentation of the bee (18) as a symbol of chastity, as suggested by the reference to its being born from no seed ("sine semina creta," 1), could hardly escape a learned reader.

The selection of some of these subjects seems to respond to their having a special significance in the monastic context. For example, in Riddle 22 the nightingale's profuse singing throughout the night could evoke the diligent monk singing compline, that is, the nocturnal service of the Divine Office: "Sic non cesso canens fato terrente futuro" (4) [Thus, in spite of the scary future fate, I do not stop singing].[336] The presence of some of these topics that are prone to

---

333. See above, p. 69.
334. It is also noteworthy that some themes of section 2 occur in the *Liber monstrorum*—particularly, salamander (Riddle 15), minotaur (28), and lion (39). This intriguing coincidence is pointed out in Orchard, *Pride and Prodigies*, esp. 98. For the possible connection between the *Liber monstrorum* and Aldhelm's *Enigmata*, see Lapidge, "*Beowulf*," 271–312.
335. Indeed, readers were expected to discern the allegorical role of the two animals, as suggested by the interlineal gloss offered in London, Royal 12.C.xxiii (fol. 86r): "i. leo peccatores. et formica sanctos significat" [that is, the lion (stands for) the sinners and the ant symbolizes the saints]. The text of the gloss is from Stork, *Through a Gloss Darkly*, 119.
336. Although this clue only opaquely touches on the metaphorical comparison with the monk, Scott has similary detected this faint allusion in Aldhelm's riddle; he offers Eugenius of Toledo's poem on the nightingale (no. 33) as an example of this typical analogy. Scott, "Rhetorical and Symbolic

allegorical reading is also reminiscent of Aldhelm's use of them in other works. For example, the bee, which is dealt with in Riddle 20, figures prominently in the prose *De virginitate* (IV–VI) as an example of this cardinal virtue. At the beginning of this work, the Barking nuns are thus compared to bees wandering far and wide throughout the blossoming fields of the Scriptures ("per florulenta scripturarum arva late vagans").[337] The image of the peacock similarly recurs in the poetic *De virginitate*, where it symbolizes virginity's scorn of the putrefaction of the flesh ("putridine carnis," 235).[338] Also in the verse *De virginitate* (1115–16), the twin saints Cosmas and Damian are compared to the salamander as they emerge unharmed out of the fiery furnace.[339] For Aldhelm, as well as for his medieval readership, the animals described in the riddles would therefore evoke either a capacity to endure torment that would be suggestive of the heroic behavior of saints, or a particular virtue such as diligence in the performance of monastic duties and virginity.[340]

Ambiguity," 126 and 140 (n. 24). For Eugenius's poem, see *Eugenii Toletani episcopi carmina et epistulae, MGH, Auctores antiquissimi*, ed. Friedrich Vollmer, vol. 14 (Berlin: Weidmann, 1905), 254 (no. 33). For further information on this motif, see my comments on Exeter Riddle 8 and Alcuin's "De luscinia" on pp. 303–04.

337. Ehwald, *Aldhelmi opera*, 232 (IV). For a study of Aldhelm's use of this allegory, which is based on patristic literature, see Augustine Casiday, "St Aldhelm's Bees (*De uirginitate prosa* cc. IV–VI): some Observations on a Literary Tradition," *ASE* 33 (2004): 1–22.

338. Ehwald, *Aldhelmi opera*, 362. For the equivalent reference to the peacock in the prose *De virginitate* (IX), in which the bird symbolizes the vain trappings of beauty that virginity wisely scorns, see Ehwald, ibid., 237. Given the paramount importance of this virtue in Aldhelm's works, one also wonders if the purity of the diamond in Riddle 9 should also be read as representing virginity.

339. Ehwald, *Aldhelmi opera*, 400. See also the reference to the salamander in the same episode of the prose *De virginitate* (XXXIV), 276.

340. This is also so with instrumental riddles. For a similar moralizing reading of the heroic endurance of flames and boiling water in the case of the cauldron (49) and the two millstones (66), which stoically accept their unequal lot, see Pavloskis, "The Riddler's Microcosm," 237 and 240.

In Aldhelm's section 2, the allegorical dimension reaches beyond the scope of a single riddle. For example, *Enigma* 38 describes the pond-skater's extraordinary capacity to walk on water, as offered in the following clues: "Pergo super latices plantis suffulta quaternis . . ." (1) [I walk on the waters sustained by my four soles (feet)][341] and "pedibus gradior super aequora siccis" (6) [with my dry feet I step on the surface of the water]. As Scott has pointed out, this phrasing parallels that found in the poetic *De virginitate*: "Ut populus domini liquit[342] Memphitica sceptra / umida cum siccis pervadens caerula plantis . . ." (2477–78) [Just as the Lord's people abandoned the Egyptian scepters (kingdom), penetrating (pervading) the wet blue (sea) with their dry soles (feet) . . .].[343] The description of the pond-skater in Riddle 38 thus brings up the biblical allusions of the verse preface (33) with the suggestion of the Israelites crossing the Red Sea. This may conveniently explain Aldhelm's reasons for including this topic, for which no encyclopedic source has been found.[344]

It should also be noted that the pond-skater riddle is juxtaposed with that of the lion, a well-known allegory of Christ. That Aldhelm might have been thinking of the lion from an allegorical point of view is supported by the following clue: "Dormio nam patulis, non claudens lumina, gemmis" (6) [For I sleep with my eyes (literally, gems or jewels) wide open, without closing these lights]. This line alludes to what was habitually referred to as the lion's "second nature," a characteristic of this animal that was traditionally associated with Christ. Thus, when Christ died on the cross and was buried, his body was asleep but his spirit was always awake thanks to his divine

---

341. As Scott explains, "One can by poetic licence call the water-spiders 'four-footed,' since the two front feet are inconspicuous." "Rhetorical and Symbolic Ambiguity," 139 (n. 21).
342. From *linquo*, "To leave, quit, forsake, depart from something," but with a pun on *liqueo*, "to be fluid or liquid."
343. Scott, "Rhetorical and Symbolic Ambiguity," 139 (n. 21); Ehwald, *Aldhelmi opera*, 454.
344. For Cameron, the clues of this riddle must have been based on direct observation. "Aldhelm as Naturalist," 121–22.

nature. The fact that readers should be aware of the allegorical significance of this clue is supported by the presence of a long excerpt expounding on the three natures of the lion from the *Physiologus* in London, Royal 12.C.xxiii (fol. 89r).[345] With this gloss, a reader could not miss the relationship between the information given by line 6 of Riddle 39 and its allegorical interpretation. In this light, the juxtaposition of Riddles 38 (pond-skater) and 39 would conform a pair with allegorical connotations. Apart from evoking the crossing of the Red Sea, the pond-skater could similarly suggest the image of Christ walking on Lake Galilee.[346] This is an illustration of how Aldhelm probably envisaged the riddles as being allegorically interconnected.

3.3.3.3 Section 3 (Enigmata 40–80)

Compared to the thematically unified sections of Symphosius's *Enigmata*, the forty-one riddles of Aldhelm's section 3 look rather loosely assembled. By contrast with section 2, there is a clear predominance of instrumental topics, with a total of eighteen. Furthermore, section 3 omits lapidary subjects and introduces instead botanical topics— pepper (no. 40), nettle (46), yarrow (50), heliotrope (51), yew-tree (69), apple-tree (76), and fig-tree (77). A faint attempt at encyclopedic classification is thus observed in the choice of a vegetable, three herbs, and three trees. Section 3 also includes eleven zoological topics—ostrich (42), leech (43), swallow (47), beaver (56), eagle (57), unicorn (60), raven (63), dove (64), cat (65), fish (71), and hornet (75). A selection of five Isidorean categories seems to be present here with five birds (with the ostrich as the biggest of them at the head), three quadrupeds (beaver, unicorn,[347] and cat), a fish, a worm (leech),[348]

---

345. For this passage as found in this manuscript, see Stork, *Through a Gloss Darkly*, 148. The lion similarly figures prominently in the Bible, particularly in Job 4.10–11.
346. Matthew 14.25–26, Mark 6.48–49, and John 6.19.
347. Note that the unicorn is described by Isidore in the chapter concerning quadrupeds (XII.ii.12–13), and so are the beaver (XII.ii.21) and the cat (XII.ii.38).
348. The leech forms part of the chapter on vermin in Isidore's *Etymologiae* (XII.v.3).

and a representative of small flying animals (hornet).[349] Even if the layout is somewhat disjointed, the binary system that was observed in both Isidore's second decade and Symphosius's *Enigmata* clearly pervades Aldhelm's miscellany. Section 3 thus seems to have been devised as a combination of subjects created by God—animals, plants, and some cosmological motifs such as Movement of the Heavens (48), the Great Bear (53), evening star (58), spring of water (73), and sun and moon (79)—as well as man-made artifacts such as pillow (41), spindle (45), cauldron (49), dagger (61), trumpet (68), and so forth.

Riddle 40 starts the section with the presentation of pepper, which, as with the diamond, functions as a sort of boundary mark distinguishing this group of riddles from those of section 2:

Sum niger exterius rugoso cortice tectus,
sed tamen interius candentem gesto medullam.
Dilicias, epulas regum luxusque ciborum,
ius simul et pulpas battutas condo culinae;
sed me subnixum nulla uirtute uidebis,
uiscera ni fuerint nitidis quassata medullis.

[I am black outside, protected by a wrinkled bark, but inside I have a white kernel. I season the exquisite and sophisticated meals of kings, as well as the gravy and minced meats of the kitchen; but you will not see me relying on any power if the entrails with my bright marrow have not been crushed].

The special status of this subject is manifested in the clues, which dwell on the description of pepper as worthy of royal meals. As a product imported from India, this vegetable was a costly luxury item. As such, pepper was frequently used as a gift and as tax payment.[350] For example, the final lines of a letter (dated 739–741) addressed by

---

349. The hornet is described in Isidore's chapter on small flying animals (*De minutis volatibus*), notably XII.viii.4.
350. See Erika von Erhardt-Siebold, *Die lateinischen Rätsel der Angelsachsen* (Heidelberg: Carl Winter, 1925), 148.

Lull and two other ecclesiastics to Abbess Cuniburg mention "turis et piperis et cinnamomi"—frankincense, pepper, and cinnamon—as "munusculorum" or small gifts that are sent along.[351] Furthermore, we learn from Cuthbert's "Epistola de obitu Bedae" (Letter on Bede's death) that pepper was among the valuable items that Bede bequeathed to his fellow monks before he died: "Quaedam preciosa in mea capsella habeo, id est piperum, oraria et incensa" [I have a few treasures in my box, some pepper, and napkins, and some incense].[352] It is therefore due to the high worth of pepper that Aldhelm chose it as the starting motif of section 3.

Although there are no clear subgroups in section 3, this miscellany indulges in riddling associations that are worth taking into account. As with section 2, the thematic links range from the simplest—based on elementary analogy or difference—to intricate correspondences among the riddles. A typical analogical association is observed in the pair formed by the double-cooking pot (no. 54) and the ciborium (55).[353] These two riddles depict containers, the first being a modest double cooking pot and the latter a richly adorned ciborium that serves to keep the Eucharist.[354] Also, while the pot carries fire and water in the innards of its belly ("in uiscere uentris," 3),

---

351. Tangl, *S. Bonifatii et Lullii Epistolae*, vol. 1 (no. 49), 80. Erhardt-Siebold mentions this letter and two more from Boniface's correspondence, in which pepper figures as a gift. See *Die lateinischen Rätsel*, 148, and Tangl, ibid., 128 (no. 62) and 189 (no. 84).
352. Edition and translation from Colgrave and Mynors, *Bede's Ecclesiastical History*, 584–85.
353. As Erhardt-Siebold explains, this container—also known as *authepsa* (or "self-boiler")—corresponds to the modern tea-urn or *samovar*." Erika von Erhardt-Siebold, "An Archaeological Find in a Latin Riddle of the Anglo-Saxons," *Speculum* 7 (1932): 254. See also her "Aldhelm's Chrismal," *Speculum* 10 (1935): 270–76.
354. As Ehwald explains, the pot is said to be double because the upper vessel contains water, and the lower fire or coals. My translation from Ehwald's note to this *enigma*: "duplex dicitur, quoniam vas superius aquam, inferius ignem vel carbones continet." Ehwald, *Aldhelmi Opera*, 121 (note to Riddle 55 [54 in Ehwald's edition]).

the ciborium's coarse entrails burn within with the beautiful sight of Christ ("uiscera crassa / intus, qua species flagrat pulcherrima Christi," 6–7).

A further case of analogy is observed in the pair formed by Riddles 66 and 67, respectively describing the millstones and the sieve, which are artifacts associated with the production of flour. This juxtaposition also suggests a chronological scheme, whose first phase consists of the crushing of the corn by the millstones in Riddle 66; the second phase corresponds to the straining with the sieve, which gives way to flour, which is described in Riddle 67 as "pruinosam . . . niuem" (1–2) or frosty snow that paradoxically never melts even if set on the burning coals of the furnace (8–9). Later, Riddle 70 offers the loaf of bread as the result of cooking the "niue fecunda" (2), the productive snow, in the oven.[355]

Though separate by another text, Riddles 78 and 80 provide a similar two-phase approach. Thus, the initial clues of Riddle 78 (wine cask) allude to the effects of alcohol and the processing of wine:

> En, plures debrians impendo pocula Bacchi,
> uinitor expressit quae flauescentibus uuis
> pampinus et uiridi genuit de palmite botris,
> nectare cauponis complens ex uite tabernam. (1–4)[356]
>
> [Behold, I intoxicate many when I distribute Bacchus's cups (with wine), which the vineyard worker pressed from the yellow (ripe) grapes and the young vine produced in bunches from the green shoot (i.e., the green or unripe ones), supplying the innkeeper's tavern with nectar from the vine].

In turn, Riddle 80 describes the manufacturing of glass that will be used to drink wine from: "De rimis lapidum profluxi flumine lento, / dum frangant flammae saxorum uiscera dura / et laxis ardor fornacis

---

355. Note that the end of Riddle 67 (8–9) already alludes to the baking of dough in the oven.
356. For a parallel reference to the vineyard worker, see the poetic *De virginitate* (177–79). Ehwald, *Aldhelmi opera*, 360.

regnat habenis" (1–3) [From cracks in stones I flowed in a slow river, as flames broke the hard entrails of the rocks, and the furnace gave free rein to fire]. As the product of this process, the glass goblet is then presented as follows: "Nunc mihi forma capax glacieque simillima lucet" (4) [Now my ample form glitters just like ice]. As typical with riddles involving the manufacturing of an object, the clues offering the final product are introduced by the adverb "nunc."

Throughout section 3, Aldhelm makes use of analogy and difference in order to incite comparison between God's macrocosm and human microcosm, a method that is typically illustrated in a Christian-oriented encyclopedia such as Isidore's *Etymologiae*. Thus, the sharp spindle (no. 45), a human-made tool, seems to be deliberately paired with the stinging nettle (46) in Aldhelm's collection. By the same token, the unicorn (60) is juxtaposed with the dagger (61), as if comparing the mighty horn of this mythological animal with the weapon created by man. Some of these binary associations are clearly based on a dramatic contrast of size, as with Riddles 52 (candle) and 53 (the Great Bear), whose juxtaposition suggests an underlying comparison between the modest light of a human-made object and that emitted by the great constellation created by God.

Aldhelm makes the most of the didactic potential of this encyclopedic approach, as illustrated with the juxtaposition of Riddles 48 and 49. The clues of Riddle 48 explain the complex notion of the movement of the heavens in the following terms:

> Sic me formauit naturae conditor almus:
> lustro teres tota spatiosis saecula ciclis;
> latas in gremio portans cum pondere terras
> sic maris undantes cumulos et coerula cludo. (1–4)

[The bountiful Creator of nature shaped me thus: (being) round, I move over the whole world in ample circles, carrying in my bosom the burden of the vast lands; in the same way, I enclose the flowing masses of the seas and the oceans].

The presentation of this cosmological subject, which is no doubt intended to illustrate one of the marvels of divine Creation, is unexpectedly juxtaposed by the description of a coarse cauldron:

> Horrida, curua, capax, patulis fabricata metallis
> pendeo nec caelum tangens terramue profundam,
> ignibus ardescens necnon et gurgite feruens;
> sic geminas uario patior discrimine pugnas,
> dum latices limphae tolero flammasque feroces.

[Made of flattened metal, I hang horrible, round and spacious, without touching heaven nor the deep earth. I am burning with fire and boiling in a whirlpool of water. I suffer the double fight of a variable opposition, as I endure the streams of water and fierce flames].

The two riddles display parallels that seem to urge readers to compare the two objects. Thus, the human-made implement overtly contrasts with the perfect "object" created by God. Also, both the cauldron and the sphere of heavens are said to be between heaven and earth. In addition to this, the cauldron must endure opposing elements (water and fire), whereas the vault of heaven bears the lands and oceans within its expanse. It may be inferred that the earth was considered to be flat so that the vault of heaven would possibly be imagined as a sort of bubble (cut in the middle) that was capable of firmly sustaining the earth with its oceans. In the context of a monastic school, one can easily imagine the *magister* using a real cauldron to explain to the students the shape of the vault of heaven and its movement.[357] The humble cooking pot representing human craft would thus serve to shed light on one of the wonders of divine Creation.

Two riddles that seem to be initially based on difference are nos. 71 and 72.[358] In Riddle 71, the fish is presented as an underprivileged creature of nature: "Me pedibus manibusque simul fraudauerat

---

357. For the intense pedagogic focus of medieval *enigmata*, see Lendinara, "The World of Anglo-Saxon Learning."
358. The contrastive relationship between these two riddles had already

almus / Arbiter, immensum primo dum pangeret orbem" (1–2) [The bountiful Judge deprived me of feet and hands at the same time when He first established the immense world]. The fish similarly lacks the capacity to breathe air, a characteristic that was traditionally understood as typical of superior beings:[359] "Spiritus alterno uegitat nec corpora flatu" (4) [the air does not enliven my body by means of alternating breaths]. Yet the riddle explains next how God compensated for this lack by allowing the fish to be the star constellation of Pisces and to swim in the water: "Quamuis in caelis conuexa cacumina cernam, / non tamen undosi contemno marmora ponti," 5–6) [Although I behold the arched summits of the heavens, I do not contempt the expanse of the flowing sea]. Contrasting the fish, the colossus (no. 72) is endowed with a fully equipped body: "Omnia membra mihi plasmauit corporis auctor ..." (1) [The maker of my body made all my limbs]. These limbs are however useless, since the colossus cannot walk with his feet nor see with his eyes: "Pergere nec plantis, oculis nec cernere possum ..." (3). Furthermore, like the fish, the colossus cannot breathe air: "Nullus anhelanti procedit uiscere flatus ..." (5) [No breath proceeds from my lungs (literally, my breathing entrails)]. The riddle then concludes with the colossus's bitter reflection on the pointlessness of his enormous body ("corpus inorme," 7) and the total numbness of all his limbs.

Aldhelm thus skillfully uses *differentia* by establishing a contrast between the small size of the fish and the impressive magnitude of the colossus, the presence or absence of limbs, as well as the advantages of a creature created by God which dramatically oppose the

---

been noted by Bolton, *A History*, vol. 1, 84, and Lapidge and Rosier, *Aldhelm: The Poetic Works*, 65.

359. This idea derives from the Aristotelian notion of the degrees of perfection in animals, according to which creatures endowed with lungs belong to the upper hierarchy of nature. As explained by French, "possession of lungs also implies a greater degree of heat, the possession of blood (and a brain to cool it)." *Ancient Natural History*, 60. See also A. L. Peck, ed. and trans., *Aristotle: History of Animals, Books I–III* (Cambridge, MA: Harvard University Press, 1965, repr. 2001), xv–xvi.

futility of a statue created by a human artist. From this comparison, subsequent parallels arise in the form of analogies: the two creatures can neither walk nor breathe. As with encyclopedias, thematic adjacency is usually meant as a didactic strategy. By juxtaposing the fish, apparently a disanvantaged creature of nature, with the colossus, the implicit lesson is that even the most underprivileged creature of God's Creation surpasses by far the greatest example of human craft.[360]

As with the preceding series, some of the subjects offered in section 3 have special figurative connotations, since, as pointed out above, Aldhelm probably got part of the inspiration for these subjects from the *Physiologus*, which offers allegorical explanations for each topic. For example, the final lines of Aldhelm's Riddle 57 allude to the way in which the eagle renews its youth: "Corpora dum senio corrumpit fessa uetustas, / fontibus in liquidis mergentis membra madescunt; / post haec restauror praeclaro lumine Phoebi" (6–8) [When old age has corrupted my exhausted body with senile condition, my limbs get wet by plunging into clear water; after this, I am restored by the bright light of Phoebus (i.e., the sun)]. The *Physiologus* (viii.7) offers a similar description and adds the following allegorical explanation: "Ergo et tu, si uestitum habes ueterem, et caliginant oculi cordis tui, quere spiritalem fontem dominum" ["Therefore, you also, if you have the old clothing and the eyes of your heart have grown dim, seek out the spiritual fountain who is the Lord"].[361] The bird was accordingly considered to be a symbol of spiritual regeneration and, in addition, was traditionally associated with St John. The motif, for example, occurs in Wulfstan Cantor's *Vita sancti Æthelwoldi* (xx),

---

360. For a similar appreciation of the colossus riddle as representing human vain "attempts to emulate the only true Creator," see Pavlovskis, "The Riddler's Microcosm," 235. See also Lapidge and Rosier, *Aldhelm: The Poetic Works*, 65.

361. The edition of this excerpt is from "Physiologus Latinus Versio Y," 108. The translation is by Curley, *Physiologus*, 13. The idea is based on Psalm 103.5, which is cited at the beginning of the entry on the eagle in the *Physiologus*: "your youth is renewed like the eagle's."

in which the saint is styled "Christi aquila" (Christ's eagle).[362] Similarly, in Byrhtferth's *Vita sancti Oswaldi* (viii), Oswald is described as "being renewed daily 'like an eagle'"—"cotidie renouatus 'more aquilino.'"[363] The comparison with the eagle is here used to express the renewal of the faith that was constantly sought by the saint.

The fact that the eagle riddle is preceded by that on the beaver (no. 56) in Aldhelm's collection is also noteworthy. Apart from offering a zoological pair, the two riddles seem to be related on the basis of analogy. The clues of Riddle 56 offer the following piece of information about this animal: "Humidus in fundo, tranat qua piscis, aquoso / saepe caput proprium tingens in gurgite mergo" (5–6) [I often dive, soaking my own head in the flood, in the watery bottom where the wet fish swims]. Like the eagle, the beaver thus plunges into the water. Although Aldhelm's riddle does not offer any reference to the allegorical role of the beaver, this animal was thought to be an emblem of chastity, Latin *castitas*. In *Etymologiae* XII.ii.21, Isidore, for example, associates Latin *castor* (beaver) with *castrare*. This was supported by the belief that the beaver castrated himself when being chased by hunters, as further explained in the same passage from the *Etymologiae* and the *Physiologus* (xxxvi.4).[364] Even if this idea is not present in Aldhelm's riddle, readers were probably expected to know about the beaver's connection with chastity, as inferred from the occurrence of a gloss from Isidore's entry on the beaver next to *Enigma* 56 in London, Royal 12.C.xxiii.[365] Riddles 56 and 57 are therefore interconnected by their possible allegorical roles,

---

362. Cited from Lapidge and Winterbottom, *Wulfstan of Winchester*, 36–37. See also 6–7 (iii), in which the comparison of Æthelwold with an eagle once more occurs.
363. The edition and translation of this passage are from Lapidge, *Byrhtferth of Ramsey*, 48–49. As explained by Lapidge, the phrase "more aquilino" stems from a poem by Abbo of Fleury.
364. For this reference, see Carmody, "Physiologus Latinus Versio Y," 128.
365. For the exact text of the gloss, occurring on the bottom margin of folio 92r of this manuscript, see Stork, *Through a Gloss Darkly*, 170.

which would suggest spiritual renewal and chastity, two qualities that might have been in consonance with monastic life.

Scholars have similarly pointed out that the pairing of some of Aldhelm's Riddles is undoubtedly suggestive of allegorical reading, as occurs with nos. 63 (raven) and 64 (dove).[366] Apart from presenting two ornithological topics, both texts start by alluding to the episode of the Flood in Genesis in a chronological order[367] and make a clear distinction about the roles played by the raven and the dove. The clues of Riddle 63 focus on the raven's disobedience to Noah and the consequent rupture of God's pact: "Primus uiuentum perdebam foedera iuris / imperio patris contemnens subdere colla" (4–5) [I was the first of living creatures to break the covenant of the law by refusing to bow my head (lit. to bend my neck) to the patriarch's command]. Conversely, the dove is described as complying with Noah's command in Riddle 64: "Prima praecepti compleui iussa parentis / portendens fructu terris uenisse salutem" (3–4) [I was the first to comply with the orders of the precepts (given by) the patriarch, foretelling with the fruit (i.e., the olive branch) that salvation had come to earth].

As I have explained elsewhere,[368] the two motifs would call to mind the first bird that departed from Noah's Ark, the treacherous raven, which did not come back, and the second one, the trustworthy dove, which returned to the ark. A discussion on the symbolic and allegorical

---

366. Erhardt-Siebold considers the two riddles as opposite pieces on account of the roles played by the two birds in Genesis 8.6–12. See her *Die lateinischen Rätsel*, 185. Lapidge and Rosier affirm that "Aldhelm's *Enigmata* explore hidden and subtle relationships between objects of the visible world. Sometimes the relationship is immediately clear from Aldhelm's juxtaposition of two *enigmata*: thus Raven (lxiii), the first animal dispatched from the Ark, alongside Dove (lxiv); or Apple-tree (lxxvi), the source of man's downfall, alongside Fig-tree (lxxvii), which supplied the covering for his shame; or Sling (lxxiv) alongside Hornet (lxxv)." *Aldhelm: The Poetic Works*, 63–64.
367. The raven was first released by Noah (Genesis 8.7) and then the dove (8.8).
368. See my "The Oyster and the Crab," 415.

significance of the two birds might thus have accompanied the reading of these texts.[369] According to exegetical tradition, these birds had well-known antithetical roles. The dove was the long-established representation of the Holy Ghost and, as indicated by Riddle 64, had a further feature that distinguished it from the raven and the other birds: "Et felix praepes nigro sine felle manebo" (6) [and I will (always) be a blessed winged creature without black gall].[370] The dove's lack of a gall bladder was therefore considered a symbol of its purity. Aldhelm thus characterized the two birds by applying the principle of *differentia*. As Beryl Rowland notes, "the Church Fathers all assumed the raven to be a shameless defector" and "the sinner expelled from the church," thus contrasting the saintly dove.[371] Accordingly, Aldhelm's riddles on the raven and the dove would most likely be discussed as presenting antagonistic motifs, which could also suggest positive and negative models of behavior for human beings.[372]

A further contrastive pattern is observed in Riddles 76 and 77,

---

369. This oppositional relationship is also well illustrated in a substantial passage from *Genesis A* (1438–82). For this excerpt, see Daniel Anlezark, ed. and trans., *Old Testament Narratives* (Cambridge, MA: Harvard University Press, 2011), 102–6. Also, see my "Allegorizing and Moralizing Zoology in Aldhelm's *Enigmata*," *Revista canaria de estudios ingleses* 68 (2014): 212, where I discuss the passage of *Genesis A* in relation to Aldhelm's Riddles 63 and 64.
370. A similar reference to the dove, which is said to be the only bird that lacks the bile of cruel venom ("crudelis felle veneni," 436), is found in Aldhelm's poetic *De virginitate*. Ehwald, *Aldhelmi opera*, 371.
371. Beryl Rowland, *Birds with Human Souls: A Guide to Bird Symbolism* (Knoxville: University of Tennessee Press, 1978), 146. Rowland illustrates the symbolic role of the raven with a passage from Pseudo-Hrabanus Maurus's *Allegoriae in universam sacram scripturam* (Allegories in the entire sacred Scriptures): "Corvus, contumax quilibet et procax, ut in Genesi: 'Emisit corvum, qui non est reversus,' quod eiicitur ab Ecclesia procax et contumax, et damnatur" [The raven (symbolizes) whoever (is) contumacious and shameless, as (told) in Genesis: "He (Noah) sent forth a raven that did not come back," because the shameless and the contumacious are driven out of the Church and are damned (my translation)]. The text is from *PL*, vol. 112 (col. 903A).
372. For a similar appreciation of the moralistic overtones underlying Aldhelm's *Enigmata*, see Pavloskis, "The Riddler's Microcosm," 237 and 240.

whose juxtaposition responds to the traditional interpretation of the reference to the trees in Genesis 3.4–7. In Riddle 76, the apple-tree is presented as follows: "Ex me tunc priscae processit causa ruinae, / dulcia quae rudibus tradebam mala colonis" (3–4) [The cause of that primeval fall (i.e., the original sin) came from me, who handed over sweet apples to those ignorant farmers (i.e., Adam and Eve)]. The term "mala" (4) would thus refer to the apples but would similarly conjure up the origin of evil (*malum*) on earth.[373] The final lines of the riddle (5–7) clearly allude to the apple-tree prefiguring the cross or the tree of Salvation. As regards Riddle 77, the clues present the fig-tree as producing the first robes for mankind, thus continuing the allusion to man's downfall started in the preceding composition: "Primitus in terra proprio de corpore peplum, / ut fama fertur, produxi frondibus altis" (4–5) [I was the first on earth to produce, so rumor tells, from my own body a robe with my high leaves]. Riddles 76 and 77 are therefore interconnected by the traditional association of these two trees with the story of the fall.

Finally, Riddle 80 (glass goblet) probably features as the closing composition of section 3 on account of its allegorical connotations:[374]

> Nempe uolunt plures collum constringere dextra
> et pulchre digitis lubricum comprendere corpus;
> sed mentes muto, dum labris oscula trado
> dulcia compressis impendens basia buccis,
> atque pedum gressus titubantes sterno ruina. (5–9)

[Many (men) wish to hold my neck with their right hand and seize my fine supple body with their fingers; but I change their minds (i.e., I intoxicate them), when I offer my mouth to their lips;[375] by

---

373. See above for my comments on Symphosius's Riddle 85 (apple), pp. 126–27.
374. For an analysis of the double entendres of this riddle, see my "The Sexual Riddle Type in Aldhelm's Enigmata," 370–71.
375. Note that *labrum* can punningly refer to both the brim of the goblet and the lips of a person.

giving sweet kisses to their tightly-pressed mouths, I provoke their fall (or ruin), causing their faltering footsteps].

The female characterization of the goblet as a voluptuous woman leading men astray by means of her charm and alcohol is unquestionably suggestive of the Whore of Babylon, who, as reported in Revelation 17.4, holds in her hand "a golden cup full of abominations and the impurities of her fornication." The motif is also used by Aldhelm in a passage from the prose *De virginitate* (XVII), in which the author expounds on the difference between divine love and carnal love, the latter being associated with the married woman who dresses "after the fashion of that woman handing over the deadly drink of the brothel in a golden goblet" ("adinstar illius mulieris aureo calice prostibuli poculum letiferum propinantis").[376] As "a powerful image for the lethal seductions of the world,"[377] the goblet riddle therefore dovetails with Aldhelm's concern with drunkenness[378] and lechery as two sins that seriously endanger virginity, a virtue of crucial importance for ecclesiastics.[379]

One also wonders if the evocation of the Whore of Babylon at this point may explain the separation of Riddle 80 (glass goblet) from Riddle 78 (wine cask). Indeed, *Enigma* 79 (sun and moon) offers clues that seem to be in consonance with the apocalyptic flare of

---

376. Ehwald, *Aldhelmi opera*, 246.
377. Hugh Magennis, "The Cup as Symbol and Metaphor in Old English Literature," *Speculum* 60 (1985): 519.
378. Aversion to drunkenness (*ebrietas*) in the monastic context may also explain the prominence of this topic as the closing motif of section 3. For a similar sanction of drunkenness, see Boniface's *Enigma* 6 (*De ebrietate*) from the Vices, *CCSL*, vol. 133, 331.
379. In the final section of the verse *De virginitate* (2501–14), which presents the allegorical fight between virtues and vices, Aldhelm illustrates the effects of alcohol with the example of Noah, who showed himself naked in front of his sons after he drank wine from the vine he had planted after the Flood. Aldhelm next refers to the terrible consequences of indulging in *ebrietas* by alluding to Lot, who unknowingly slept with his own daughters when he got drunk (2515–24). Ehwald, *Aldhelmi opera*, 455.

Riddle 80: "Ni soror et frater uaga saecula iure gubernent, / heu! chaos immensum clauderet cuncta latebris / atraque nunc Erebi regnarent Tartara nigri" (9–11) [If we, brother and sister, did not govern the roving world by right, alas! immense chaos would enclose everything with darkness and the infernal regions of black Erebus would then reign]. The darkening of both the sun and moon is a well-known apocalyptic sign.[380] Accordingly, it may not be far-fetched to assume that Riddles 79 and 80 form a pair on the basis of their apocalyptic resonances. Furthermore, as a valuable costly object equivalent to the diamond and pepper above, the glass goblet could have been chosen as an outstanding representative of human manufacturing skills and, therefore, as a fitting conclusion for section 3.[381]

3.3.3.4 Section 4 (Enigmata 81–99)

After section 3, a further block, based roughly on the description of wonders, can be discerned. For this Aldhelm was most probably inspired by Symphosius's corresponding group on wonders or Isidore's chapters on prodigies in Book XI of the *Etymologiae*. This thematic category might have specially attracted Aldhelm's interest due to the traditional notion that prodigies were didactic and exemplary from a Christian viewpoint.[382] Section 3 thus opens with Lucifer (no. 81), which is the name of the morning star—actually, the planet Venus—but the clues also allude to the transformation of the angel into Satan, whose Hebrew etymology is "enemy": "O felix olim seruata lege Tonantis! / Heu! post haec cecidi proterua mente

---

380. See Revelation 6.12. Also, see Revelation 12.1 for the description of the woman clothed with the sun and the moon at her feet.
381. As Erhardt-Siebold explains, the glass industry in Britain was not yet known at the beginning of the eighth century. *Die lateinischen Rätsel*, 30. The glass goblet must have therefore been an imported luxury item. For further information, see Vera I. Evison, "Glass Vessels in England AD 400-1100," in *Glass in Britain and Ireland AD 350–1100*, ed. Jennifer Price (London: British Museum, 2000), 47–104.
382. This is, for instance, expounded by Isidore in his *Etymologiae* (XI. iii.4).

superbus; / ultio quapropter funestum perculit hostem" (6–8) [Oh, I was blessed when divine law was kept! Alas, proud and with this shameless mind, I later fell; vengeance thus struck down the deadly foe]. On the basis of this allusion to Lucifer's previous angelic condition and his subsequent transformation into a fallen angel or devil, it is quite reasonable to assume that—among the different prodigies, monsters, and metamorphosed beings of this section—this topic was selected as a suitable motif to introduce this group. In this chain of thought, we may also infer that Aldhelm could have similarly been interested in pointing to the "anomalous" polysemic nature of the word *Lucifer*, referring both to the fallen angel and the morning star.

The section on prodigies continues with Riddle 82, in which the weasel is said to be capable of fighting dragons, an extraordinary quality that might well have triggered its inclusion in the cluster of wonders: "Discolor in curuis conuersor quadripes antris / pugnas exercens dira cum gente draconum" (1–2) [A variegated four-footed, I live in winding caves, training (myself) in combats with the fierce race of dragons]. This feature also clearly links this motif to the preceding "Lucifer," since *draco*, meaning "snake," was the traditional representation of the devil.[383] A further peculiarity of the weasel is the fact that this animal was believed to conceive and give birth through the ear, an idea that is developed in lines 3–4 of the riddle.[384] This exceptional quality led patristic writers to equate this

---

383. The connection between the dragon or serpent and Lucifer, for example, typically occurs in medieval bestiaries. See, for example, T. H. White, *The Book of Beasts* (New York: Putnam, 1954), 167. Another illustration of this is found in Boniface's Riddle 4 (*De superbia*): "Serpens angelicus genuit me in culmine caeli, / viperea spirans et crimina noxia cordi" (1–2) [the angelic serpent gave birth to me in the summit of heaven, while breathing sins into the heart with viperish crimes]. The association is also made explicit in Vatican City, Reg. Lat. 1553 (fol. 6r), containing a version of Boniface's Riddles, in which the term "serpens" in this passage is glossed as "demon." See *CCSL*, vol. 133, 325 (*glossae*).
384. Interestingly, Isidore discredits this belief in his *Etymologiae* XII.iii.3: "Falso autem opinantur qui dicunt mustelam ore concipere, aure effundere partum" [Those who say that the weasel conceives through its mouth and

animal to the Virgin Mary on account of her conceiving Christ as she listened to the angel's words. In this sense, it may be assumed that the weasel riddle was possibly juxtaposed with the preceding enigma as a symbol of chastity and humility as a contrast to Lucifer's pride and lust.

Among the themes of this section, some of the riddles deal with extraordinary and unusual birth phenomena. Apart from the weasel's anomalous impregnation through the ear, the expectant sow (no. 84) and the woman in labor with twins (90), the latter probably inspired in Symphosius's *Enigma* 93, are both described as monsters with multiple limbs and eyes. In turn, the man blind from birth (85) clearly constitutes a further freakish example of nature and recalls Symphosius's riddle on the one-eyed garlic seller (95). Similarly, there are other riddles whose clues play on the notion of either unusual birth or pregnancy in inanimate objects. An example of this is *Enigma* 89: "Nunc mea diuinis complentur uiscera uerbis / totaque sacratos gestant praecordia biblos" (1–2) [Now my entrails are pregnant with divine words and all my vitals bear sacred books]. The notion of "multiple pregnancy" clearly makes *Enigma* 89 an apposite companion to Riddle 90 (woman giving birth to twins). Apart from this, the riddle's initial lines also clearly invite us to compare the book chest with the Virgin Mary, who became pregnant by listening to the words of Archangel Gabriel. Furthermore, Aldhelm's handling of this topic recalls the reference to the weasel's virginal impregnation "ex aure" (6), as commented above with regard to Riddle 82. A similar use of "pregnancy" imagery is observed in Riddle 93 (spark): "letum proprii gestant penetralia uentris" (5) [the innermost parts of my own belly bear death].[385] Also, the spark is said to be born from the cold stony womb of its mother, the flint: "Frigida dum genetrix dura generaret ab aluo / primitus ex utero producens pignora

---

gives birth through its ear however express a false opinion]. This example is illustrative of Aldhelm's idiosyncratic treatment of the encyclopedic materials that he perused for the composition of the *Enigmata*.

385. Note the occurrence of "gestant" as in the preceding book-chest riddle (89).

gentis" (10–11) [when my cold mother delivered me from her hard womb, she originally produced all the progeny of this race (i.e., fire in its different forms)]. In turn, the elephant, the topic of Riddle 96, must have looked like a monstrous beast to medieval people and, as such, it is said to have been created repulsive by God from birth ("me turpem nascendi fecerit auctor," 7).

A further interesting motif of this series is provided by Riddle 97 (night), in which motherhood images recur: "Et nil fecundum stereli de uiscere promo . . ." (2) [I cannot generate any fertile thing with my sterile womb]. Further on, Aldhelm personifies *nox* as the mother of infernal creatures: "carmine uates / Tartaream partu testentur gignere prolem" (3–4) [in their songs poets testify to the fact that I engendered the offspring of Tartarus (i.e., the underworld]. Like the book chest, this creature is said to have a protective bosom: "Diri latrones me semper amare solebant, / quos gremio tectos nitor defendere fusco" (9–10) [Cruel thieves always used to love me, (thieves) whom I try to guard by having them covered in my dark womb]. But there are further reasons for including this riddle in this series. The following lines of Riddle 97 are devoted to describing *fama* (fame or reputation), a sister of night, which is in turn depicted by means of a citation from Virgil's *Aeneid* (IV.177, 181–84) as a hideous flying monster with innumerable eyes, mouths, and tongues:

> Vergilium constat caram cecinisse sororem:
> "Ingrediturque solo et caput inter nubila condit
> monstrum horrendum, ingens, cui quot sunt corpore plumae,
> tot uigiles oculi subter, mirabile dictu,
> tot linguae, totidem ora sonant, tot subrigit aures;
> nocte uolat caeli medio terraeque per umbras." (11–16)[386]

---

386. Note that these lines have been considered a separate riddle on fame in several manuscripts; for example, in Oxford, Rawlinson, C.697 (fol. 13v). As Stork explains, "This 'extra' riddle was created by a gloss that became a title." *Through a Gloss Darkly*, 45.

[It is well-known that Virgil of my dear sister sang thus: "She advances on land and conceals her head in the clouds, an enormous, dreadful monster, who has many feathers on her body, with so many vigilant eyes below, and, extraordinary to tell, so many tongues, so many mouths resound, so many ears are uplifted; she flies between heaven and earth through the shadows by night"].

From this description, it can be inferred that night formed part of this section by analogy with other monster motifs, such as the woman in labor with twins or the pregnant sow. Incidentally, Lapidge and Rosier have pointed out the presence of "night" as a subject in the *Liber monstrorum* (I.42),[387] an idea that supports my assumption that "night" could have functioned as a further suitable topic in this group on wonders.

As observed in Isidore's chapter iv (*De transformatis*) of Book XI of the *Etymologiae*, some of the topics of Aldhelm's section 3 describe creatures undergoing dramatic transformations. Thus the metamorphosed Scylla (no. 95), whose lower half-body was transformed into terrible barking dogs, was no doubt considered a remarkable monstrous creature with both human and animal characteristics.[388] This physical transformation is explicitly alluded to in the riddle: "Femora cum cruribus, suras cum poplite bino / abstulit immiscens crudelis uerba uirago" (5–6) [Mingling words (i.e., by means of a spell), the cruel woman (Circe) stole two by two, my thighs and my shanks, as well as my calves and my knees]. The resulting multiple monstrous shape, a hybrid human and animal, is thus described in a way similar to that found in the preceding riddles: "Pignora nunc pauidi referunt ululantia nautae / . . . auscultare procul, quae latrant inguina circum" (7–11) [Now the frightened sailors report that . . . they hear from a distance my yelling children as they bark around my privy parts]. Note again the presence of "nunc" to in-

---

387. Lapidge and Rosier, *Aldhelm*, 254, n. 88; for the passage in the *Liber monstrorum*, see Orchard, *Pride and Prodigies*, 280–81, and see 98–101 for Orchard's comments on this excerpt and Aldhelm's night *enigma*.
388. This story is found in Ovid's *Metamorphoses* XIV.40–67.

dicate that transformation has already taken place, and the usual reference to offspring.

A more modest metamorphosis seems to be alluded to in Riddle 88 with the description of the serpent's shedding of its skin: "Namque senescenti spoliabor pelle uetustus / atque noua rursus fretus remanebo iuuenta" (6–7) [When I grow old, I will be stripped of my decrepit skin and will once more continue (living) thanks to my renewed youth]. The riddle in turn explicitly associates this animal with Satan and the origins of evil: "Late per mundum dispersi semina mortis; / unde horrenda seges diris succreuit aristis, / quam metit ad scelera scortator falce maligna" (2–4) [I have widely dispersed the seeds of death throughout the world, where a dreadful crop has grown up with its cruel grain, which the fornicator (Satan) reaps as sins with his mischievous scythe]. These lines thus provide clues that are in line with the offspring/pregnancy imagery and thematically connect the description of the serpent in Riddle 81 (Lucifer).

A further example of "transformation" can be observed in Aldhelm's Riddle 86, in which the creature in question is described as unusually multiform—the title-solution "Aries" referring to the animal, the constellation, and the battering ram. This riddle thus seems to focus on the "anomalous" quality of the Latin term *aries*, which is endowed with an outstanding polysemic character.[389] It may be tentatively inferred that, rather than considering the ram as a wondrous animal, the riddle seems to be concerned with presenting the term *aries*, like *Lucifer* in Riddle 81, as a further illustration of a grammatical prodigy: polysemy. The juxtaposition of Riddles 86 (battering ram) and 87 (shield) is also noteworthy, since these subjects are treated as consecutive sections of Isidore's *Etymologiae*—namely, chapters xi (*De ariete*) and xii (*De clypeis*) of Book XVIII.

---

389. This typical reflection on a polysemic word is also found, for example, in Symphosius's Riddle 32, in which Latin *taurus* refers to a Cilician mount and the constellation. It is therefore quite clear that Aldhelm could have been inspired by riddles such as this for his own collection.

The remainder of the riddles of this section also possibly suit the wonder category, as the presence of exotic plants (palm tree, no. 91) and animals from foreign lands—elephant and camel (96 and 99, respectively)—seem to indicate. In this series the high lighthouse (92) represents a prodigy of human creation, and its pairing with the tall palm tree (91) prompts comparison.[390] In short, the majority of the topics contained in section 3 of Aldhelm's *Enigmata* seem to comply with the wonder category. Also importantly, three motifs of this section (night, Scylla, and elephant) similarly occur in the *Liber monstrorum*.[391] Even in the case of some topics, whose ascription to the wonder category is clearly more doubtful—as in the case of bullock (83), shield (87), and spark (93)—the clues of these texts describe these creatures as surpassingly special, since in one way or another they are extraordinarily resistant to death. Thus, when dead, the bullock's proverbial strength survives in the form of leather bonds that are used to handcuff men; the shield in turn is alive after mortal battle wounds;[392] and, despite its lifeless condition, the spark is endowed with an incredible strength and devouring power.

As a whole, the underlying rationale of section 3 suggests a concern with offering a variety of prodigies representing typical encyclopedic fields of knowledge: cosmological (Lucifer, night), zoological (weasel, bullock, the pregnant sow, serpent, elephant, camel), botanical (palm tree, wallwort, woody nightshade), instrumental (shield, book chest, high lighthouse), human (man blind from birth, woman

---

390. Note that I consider the title-solution of this riddle (Latin *palma*) as the tree. The description of the palm tree as an emblem of victory ("uictrix," 2) and the implicit allusion to its Isidorean etymology (from *palma*, also meaning palm) in line 2, which suggests the hand holding the branch and the outstretched fingers as symbols of victory is also found in *Etymologiae* XVII.vii.1. On the riddle's etymological clue, see Howe, "Aldhelm's *Enigmata*," 44–45.
391. For a comparative chart of topics appearing in Aldhelm's *Enigmata* and the *Liber monstrorum*, see Orchard, *Pride and Prodigies*, 98.
392. We may conjecture that the shield might have also been viewed by Aldhelm as an example of a prodigious human creation.

giving birth to twins, Scylla),[393] and possibly grammatical (Aries and Lucifer).[394] All of these topics in turn re-examine the thematic categories presented in section 2. A distinctive characteristic of this final section is the fact that human subjects are included: Lucifer, man blind from birth, and the woman in labor with twins. It seems that Aldhelm consciously relegated these illustrations of "human" anomalies to the end of the *Enigmata*.

3.3.3.5 Final Considerations on the Organization of Aldhelm's Enigmata

The contents of Aldhelm's collection follow a pattern similar to that found in Isidore's second decade in the *Etymologiae*, thus providing a representation of the following subjects: cosmological, zoological, lapidary, botanical, and instrumental, relegating the "monstrous" creatures to the end—just as Symphosius also did. The analysis of the riddle sequences observed in Aldhelm's *Enigmata* therefore highlights diverse associative patterns that this author may have taken into account when compiling the contents of the riddle collection. The position of a particular topic seems to have been determined on the basis of the encyclopedic principles of analogy and difference as established among the clues of the surrounding riddles, the allegorical interconnections, and the metrical requirements.[395] Apart from this, the cumulative effect sought in cosmological, zoological, and wonder sequences reveals a concern with encyclopedic organization.

With such a variegated combination of structural criteria, it is therefore quite clear that Aldhelm pursued an ambitious plan. Undoubtedly, he was using the format established by Symphosius, where these organizing patterns are also present, as the discussion found in the preceding chapter has demonstrated. Aldhelm,

---

393. The latter being an example of the transformation of a human-like goddess into a monster.
394. In the case of Riddle 81, the title-solution *Lucifer* seems to draw upon both the metamorphosis topic and the "grammatical prodigy."
395. In section 1, for example, the rule seems to be four-line riddles with the exception of Riddle 8.

however, took a step further and developed his predecessor's model to its utmost possibilities by fully adapting it to Christian ideology and to the teaching of Latin metrics. But all this was done at a cost. With its monotonous use of the tristich and more limited allegorical interconnections, Symphosius's *Enigmata* is well organized, whereas Aldhelm's combined observance of the encyclopedic, allegorical, and metrical requirements inevitably results in a much looser structure and a substantial miscellany (section 3).

Apart from this, Aldhelm's collection differs significantly from that of Symphosius in the presence of an underlying comparative pattern in which small or great objects, made either by God or by human beings, are constantly contrasted. As pointed out by Lapidge and Rosier, Aldhelm explains his own *modus operandi* in a passage from the *Epistola ad Acircium* (V): "praesertim veterum auctoritate provocatus de diversis rerum qualitatibus modo caelestium modo terrestrium materiam nanctus nunc grandem nunc gracilem creaturarum naturam considerans strictim summatimque defloravi" [Having been particularly stimulated by the authority of the old (writers) (and) having found material dealing with the diverse qualities of things, either heavenly or terrestrial, I culled them briefly and summarily, considering sometimes the great, sometimes the slender nature of creatures].[396] This excerpt suggests that Aldhelm used his sources—the *Etymologiae* and Symphosius's *Enigmata* being major ones—to provide the contents of his riddles and apply to them this contrastive pattern.

This binary system responds to Aldhelm's concern with infusing his *Enigmata* with a prominent Christian character and is also reflected in the concluding riddle on Creation: "Grandior in glaucis ballena fluctibus atra / et minor exiguo, sulcat qui corpora, uerme / aut modico, Phoebi radiis qui uibrat, atomo" (65–67) [(I am) greater than the black whale in the blue flood, and smaller than the little worm which tunnels through bodies, or the small atom

---

396. Ehwald, *Aldhelmi Opera*, 75. See Lapidge and Rosier, *Aldhelm: The Poetic Works*, 65.

which glitters in Phoebus's rays (i.e., the sun's rays)]. This associative structure unmistakably recalls the binary approach found in Isidore's second decade of the *Etymologiae* and Symphosius's *Enigmata*. However, instead of providing a separate subdivision into the "Opera Dei" and the "Opera hominis," Aldhelm took the initiative to apply a continuous contrastive pattern that would permeate the whole collection.

3.4. *The Continuation of the Riddling Tradition in England: Tatwine and Eusebius*

3.4.1 *Tatwine's* Enigmata

Tatwine, to whom a forty-riddle collection is traditionally ascribed, is the next author to take into account. There are only a few known facts about his life. Originally from Mercia, he was a priest in the monastery at Breedon on the Hill (Leicestershire). Apart from this, the only significant piece of information is supplied by Bede in his *Historia ecclesiastica* (V.23), where it is stated that "He was a man renowned for his devotion and wisdom and excellently instructed in the Scriptures" ("uir religione et prudentia insisgnis, sacris quoque litteris nobiliter instructus").[397] In the *Anglo-Saxon Chronicle*, Tatwine's appointment as Archbishop of Canterbury in 731 and his death in 734 are reported.

As mentioned above, Tatwine is also known as the author of the grammatical treatise *Ars Tatuini*, which has been preserved in four different manuscripts. Of these, the earliest is Paris, Bibliothèque Nationale, MS. 17959, a composite codex, whose second part, also containing Boniface's grammar, dates from the late eighth or early ninth century.[398] Together with those of Eusebius, Tatwine's Riddles have survived only in London, Royal 12.C.xxiii (fols. 121v-27r) and

---

397. Colgrave and Mynors, *Bede's Ecclesiastical History*, 558–59.
398. See Williams, "The Riddles of Tatwine and Eusebius," 27. For the other three manuscripts containing the *Ars Tatuini*, see 27–28.

Cambridge, Gg.5.35 (fols. 374v-77v). On the basis of a rubric appearing right after his *Enigmata* in London, Royal 12.C.xxiii (fol. 127r), W. F. Bolton has established the composition of Tatwine's *Enigmata* to before his consecration as archbishop in 731.[399]

Tatwine's collection presents clear evidence of having been modeled on the *Enigmata* of his older contemporary Aldhelm.[400] Like his predecessor, Tatwine made use of the acrostic technique. But, compared to Aldhelm's *Enigmata*, where this device was restricted to the preface, Tatwine took a step further by joining all the riddles of his collection by means of acrostics and telestichs. By linking the first and the last letter of each line, a distich introducing the collection is thus spelled out: "Sub deno quater haec diuerse enigmata torquens / stamine metrorum extructor conserta retexit" [By turning these forty riddles linked below backward, the author discloses them by means of the warp of the meters]. The first line of the distich is provided by the first letter of the first line of each riddle; the second line of the distich is in turn supplied by the last letter of the first line of each riddle, beginning with the last riddle. The key to read the acrostics and telestichs is explained in the possibly spurious verse epilogue that was appended to the *Enigmata* in both the Cambridge and London codices:[401]

---

399. The rubric seems to point to the fact that Tatwine was not yet archbishop when he wrote the collection. See Bolton, *A History*, vol. 1, 216, for a discussion of the passage in question.
400. By contrast, Tupper considers that the Aldhelmian influence in Tatwine's collection is but "a small debt." Frederick Tupper, ed. and trans., *The Riddles of the Exeter Book* (Boston: Ginn, 1910), xxxiv. His opinion is at odds with scholars like Lapidge and Rosier, who have noted that in Tatwine's *enigmata* "the influence and inspiration of Aldhelm is everywhere discernible." *Aldhelm: The Poetic Works*, 66. Also, Orchard affirms that Tatwine's Riddles "are informed by a thorough knowledge of Aldhelm's *Carmen de virginitate* and in particular his *Enigmata*." *The Poetic Art*, 242.
401. As Williams, "The Riddles of Tatwine and Eusebius," 156, explains, these lines are not to be attributed to Tatwine; they were probably later added as "an afterthought" by a scribe.

Versibus intextis uatem nunc iure salutat,
litterulas summa capitum hortans iungere primas,
uersibus extremas hisdem, ex minio corolatas;
conuersus gradiens rursum perscandat ab imo!

[With woven verses, one now duly salutes the poet,[402] exhorting (the reader) to link the first small letters of the top of the headings (i.e., of the first line of each riddle), and (do) the same with the last letters of the lines, which are colored with red lead (i.e., the rubrics).[403] Going backwards, (the reader) will climb from the bottom! (i.e., do the same again from the end of the collection to the beginning)].

The use of the acrostic technique, which is rather frequent in medieval literature, is particularly significant as far as the compilation of Tatwine's Riddles is concerned. As Whitman has noted, "What is important is that the acrostic assures that the riddles are preserved in faithful order and so permits an examination of the organizing principles at work in collections of this sort."[404] Accordingly, Tatwine's

---

402. The line is syntactically problematic, since the subject of "salutat" seems to be missing. Following Williams, "The Riddles of Tatwine and Eusebius," 156, I have provided a subject ("one"), which tentatively implies the involvement of the scribe who congratulates the poet on his skillful handling of the lines in the acrostic-telestich technique and urges the reader to properly follow the instructions in order to do a correct reading. For a similar translation licence, see Erhardt-Siebold's rendering of these lines in *CCSL*, vol. 133, 208.
403. In fact, the scribal practice in both Cambridge, Gg.5.35 and Royal 12.C.xxiii is to use rubrics only for the first letter of the first line of the riddle and the solutions.
404. Whitman, "Aenigmata Tatwini," 15. Although Whitman acknowledges the importance of the acrostics for the study of the compilation, he fails to discern any trace whatsoever of arrangement of the riddling material: "But thereafter [i.e., apart from the structuring of the collection by means of acrostics] any principle of organization is hard to detect. The ordinary things of life seem haphazardly mixed in with the religious or specifically monastic" (ibid.).

collection offers us a great opportunity to investigate the compilation modes ruling medieval riddle collections.

With respect to structural cohesion, the general design of Tatwine's *Enigmata* comparatively surpasses that of Aldhelm's collection. Like his predecessor, Tatwine organized his *Enigmata* on the basis of a metrical criterion (see Appendix V). Following the Aldhelmian pattern, though in a decreasing manner, Tatwine's riddles are assembled in a consistent metrical arrangement. The collection thus starts with a twelve-line poem on philosophy. There follows a sequence of six-line riddles ending in Riddle 10 (lectern). The subsequent metrical series is made of twenty riddles of five lines each (up to no. 30), ending in a final group of four-line poems. The metrical principle therefore divides the collection into three well-defined sections: leaving aside the opening and concluding riddles (nos. 1 and 40), a first block of riddles (2–10), all of them comprising six lines, stands out; the second subdivision (11–30) dwells on five-liners, and the third (31–39) offers four-line compositions. Not surprisingly, the closing riddle (rays of the sun) is metrically distinguished, as its length is slightly enlarged by an extra line.

Apart from the metrical criterion, Tatwine also clearly structured his collection on an encyclopedic basis. To start with, a theological triad functions as an introductory section to Tatwine's *Enigmata*. This initial riddle—and, notably, the longest of all—describes philosophy, a theme that occupies a significant first position in the collection. As pointed out above, the subjects of section 1 would therefore correspond to topics dealt by Isidore's first decade. As Whitman affirms, this first riddle functions as a topic that encompasses all the following ones and is thus comparable to Aldhelm's *Enigma* 100 (Creation): "In Aldhelm's riddles this structuring force is provided by the long final riddle, *De Creatura*, which embraces all things; in Tatwine's, by the opening riddle, *De Philosophia*, signifying the culmination of human wisdom."[405] Also importantly, as regards contents and phraseology, Tatwine's first riddle owes much to that

---

405. Whitman, "Aenigmata Tatwini," 16.

of Aldhelm. Thus Philosophy, as with Creation in Aldhelm's Riddle 100, is presented in superlative terms:

> Sum Salomone sagacior et uelocior euro,
> clarior et Phoebi radiis, pretiosior auro,
> suauior omnigena certe modulaminis arte,
> dulcior et fauo gustantum in faucibus ęso. (4–7)

[I am more sagacious than Solomon, swifter than the eastern wind, brighter than Phoebus's rays, worthier than gold, certainly more pleasant than any kind of art of melody (i.e., music), and sweeter than honey when eaten in the mouths of those who taste it].

The thematic focus of this introductory section continues with the second riddle on the Theological Virtues (faith, hope and charity) and the third dealing with the four levels of biblical interpretation (historical, spiritual, moral, and allegorical).

As with Symphosius's *Enigmata*, the writing motif also occupies a pre-eminent place in Tatwine's collection, since three riddles are devoted to this topic in section 2: nos. 4 (letters), 5 (parchment), and 6 (pen). This first thematic triad is followed by diverse objects of religious cult such as bell (7), altar (8), cross (9), lectern (10), and paten (12). As a whole, the items of this section have in common the fact that they are related to the ecclesiastical profession. Apparently two thematic exceptions occur in this series: nos. 11 (needle) and 13 (embroidery needle). However, those two topics do not imply a rupture of the sequence, for needles were typical utensils in the ecclesiatical milieu. Indeed, they were employed to embroider vestments,[406] as well as cloth for the altar or for church relics, among other uses.[407]

---

406. For a commentary on Tatwine's needle riddles, see Erhardt-Siebold, *Die lateinischen Rätsel*, 48–54. A comprehensive account of the Anglo-Saxon embroidery industry is found in Gale R. Owen-Crocker, *Dress in Anglo-Saxon England* (Woodbridge: Boydell, 2004), 308–15.

407. The relationship between embroidering activity and monastic life is well attested. Erhardt-Siebold, for example, mentions a spurious passage occurring at the end of Aldhelm's *Enigmata* included in Paris, Bibliothèque

The presence of these topics next to the writing motifs might thus be suggesting the widespread employment of needles to produce inscriptions on cloth.[408]

Although section 2 concludes with an abstraction (no. 14, charity), which significantly contrasts with the consistent presentation of ecclesiastical implements, this motif does not break the general cohesion of the group. Rather, though partly overlapping the theme of *Enigma* 2, it conveys an appropriate reflection on the religious concept of charity, which very fittingly brings this thematic sequence to an end. Besides, like Riddle 4 (letters), the abstract motif of *Enigma* 14 clearly contrasts with the other instrumental topics of the section, thus aiming at distinctiveness, as usual with opening and closing themes.

Tatwine's section 3 is composed of six riddles on diverse topics with no apparent cohesion, but, on closer observation, the components of this group, though certainly varied, seem to comply with the category of wonders as analyzed in the case of Symphosius's and Aldhelm's collections. However, the position of this series is not at the end of the collection, as is the case in Symphosius's *Enigmata*. Interestingly, there are also two factors shared by most of the pieces included in this series: the clues are based on family links, and the riddling objects are said to be subject to the strict laws of fate. Thus, snow, hail, and ice are described in Riddle 15 as three sisters ("ternas . . . sorores," 1–2) whose ethereal father ("Aethereus . . . genitor," 1), Heaven, begot them under the fate of

---

Nationale, Lat. 8440, in which there is a comparison of the poet's own writing skills with those of a nun's dexterous hands at embroidering: "Aurea dum exili Christo fila virgo acu dedicata / manu pallida torquet æreo tum ego calamo / crinigeris pingo paginas lacrymis" (1–3) [Just as the virgin consecrated to Christ twists with her pale hand the golden threads with her thin needle, I embellish these pages with a bronze pen with tears (running along my face)]. The text is from Giles, *Sancti Aldhelmi opera*, 273. See also Ehwald, *Aldhelmi opera*, 149. For Erhardt-Siebold's comments on this passage, see her *Die lateinischen Rätsel*, 52.

408. Also, note the metaphorical comparison of the writer's own task with weaving in the distich spelled out by the acrostic technique mentioned on p. 222.

an unfortunate law ("sub miserae fato legis," 2). Also, this description entails a metamorphosis, as is typical of sections on wonders, since the riddle alludes to the three sisters' hope to return soon to the royal womb of their mother ("Quod mox regalem matris remeamus in aluum," 5); in other words, they will eventually become water. Possibly representing a grammatical "prodigy," the prepositions ruling two cases are said to be four sisters ("bis binae . . . sorores," 4–5) who must yield to strict grammatical laws in Riddle 16: "Emerita gemina sortis sub lege tenemur" (1) [We are kept under a long-standing double law of fate (i.e., the two possible states)]. The resulting semantic transformation depending on the case that the preposition takes is thus apparently viewed as a suitable topic for a section on wonders: "Nam tollenti nos stabiles seruire necesse est, / causanti[409] contra cursus comitamur eundo" (2–3) [for, when at rest, we must serve the one (the case) that removes (i.e., the ablative); when in motion, conversely, we accompany the one pleading a cause (i.e., accusing; hence, accusative) on his course].[410] In this sense, this riddle recalls Aldhelm's *Enigma* 86, in which the allusion to multiple-meaning *aries* was probably considered as illustrative of a grammatical "wonder."

As with the preceding riddles of Tatwine's section 3, the last three pieces of this series make use of family clues, playing on the well-known commonplace that eyes are brothers. Interestingly, these three riddles seem to be arranged in a sort of gradation (from the

---

409. I here include "causanti" (Williams, "The Riddles of Tatwine and Eusebius," 126) instead of Glorie's "causantis" (*CCSL*, vol. 133, 183). The dative form is preferable because "comitamur" (3) requires that case; besides, "causanti" parallels "tollenti" in the preceding line.

410. As pointed out by Williams, this passage parallels Tatwine's own explanation of the ablative and accusative cases in *Ars Tatuini* (I.54). See her "The Riddles of Tatwine and Eusebius," 126. The term "tollenti" (2) alludes to the etymology of *ablatiuus*, which is connected to *sublatus*, the participle of *tollo* ("to lift or take up, to raise, always with the predom. idea of motion upwards or of removal from a former situation"). I owe this idea to Pablo Toribio Pérez, who kindly drew my attention to it.

most regular type of eyes to the most defective), recalling the unifying principle observed, for example, in Isidore's Book XI, in which the anomalous aspects of Creation (prodigies and metamorphosed beings) occupy a secondary place.[411] Thus, Tatwine's sequence provides the following order: eyes (no. 18), squinting eyes (19), and the one-eyed (20). It is also notable that Riddle 18 alludes to the laws of nature affecting the eyes, a trait linking this text to the preceding riddles: "Discernens totum iuris, natura locauit / nos pariter geminos una de matre creatos" (1–2) [Discerning every law, nature arranged it for us to be identical twins born from the same mother]. Tatwine's notable interest in ocular themes probably testifies to the conspicuous ecclesiastical stamp pervading his collection. The eyes were no doubt regarded as extremely valuable "tools" for someone belonging to the ecclesiastical profession.[412] But, apart from this natural concern with the topic, the description of ocular anomalies (nos. 19 and 20) evidently recalls the typical description of human deformities in sections on wonders, as illustrated with Symphosius's Riddles 94 (gouty soldier) and 95 (one-eyed man selling garlic), as well as Aldhelm's *Enigma* 85 (man blind from birth). As with Aldhelm's series on wonders discussed above, Tatwine's section 3 therefore seems to offer a representation of prodigies falling into four different categories of encyclopedic knowledge: cosmological (snow, hail, and

---

411. See the chart and comments on the internal structure of Isidore's Book XI offered on p. 92.

412. Blindness was considered a major physical defect that could hinder the practice of priesthood, as established in Leviticus 21.16–20: "And the Lord said to Moses, 'Say to Aaron, one of your descendants throughout their generations who has a blemish may approach to offer the bread of his God. For no one who has a blemish shall draw near, a man blind or lame . . . or a man with a defect in his sight.'" Also, blindness was considered a major impediment to kingship. As noted by Waugh, "According to the *Anglo-Saxon Chronicle*, Earl Godwine blinds King Æthelred's son Alfred in 1036 (C), most likely to destroy Alfred's candidacy for the throne." Robin Waugh, "Literacy, Royal Power, and King-Poet Relations in Old English and Old Norse Compositions," *Comparative Literature* 49 (1997): 302.

ice), grammatical (prepositions with two cases), zoological (squirrel),[413] and human (the eyes triad).

The initial theological mood of the collection is revived with section 4, whose components are also thematically intertwined. There is a first clear link between nos. 21 (evil) and 22 (Adam), since their juxtaposition alludes to the traditional notion that Adam and Eve are the source of evil on earth. Furthermore, as the title-solution of Riddle 21 is "De malo," the juxtaposition of the two riddles playfully evokes the well-known wordplay on the Latin term *malum*, which can either mean "apple" or "evil."[414] Riddle 23 in turn presents the immediate result of Adam's sin, that is, death,[415] whereas Riddles 24 (humility) and 25 (pride) constitute a related thematic pair. Closing this section, *Enigma* 26 provides a further theological concept associated with the idea of Adam's Fall, since the five senses were traditionally considered as the gates through which sin entered the body.

Section 5 comprises instrumental motifs that are typically bound in riddle couplings. For example, the tongs and anvil (nos. 27 and 28) are tools used by the smith, as are charcoal and whetstone (38

---

413. In this sense, it may be tentatively argued that Riddle 17 (squirrel) could have been provided by Tatwine on the grounds of the supernatural "flying" skills of this animal: "Sum petulans agilisque, fera insons; corporis astu / ardua ceu pennis *conuexa* cacumina scando . . ." (3–4) [I am an unruly, swift, and harmless animal; I climb the steep vaulted summits by means of my body's craft as if with wings]. Note that I have preferred the reading "conuexa," as provided by Giles, *Anecdota Bedae*, 29, and Adolf Ebert, ed., "Über die Räthselpoesie der Angelsachsen, insbesondere die Aenigmata des Tatwine und Eusebius," *Berichte über die Verhandlungen der Königlich-sächsischen Gesellschaft der Wissenschaften zu Leipzig, Philologisch-Historische* Classe 29 (1877): 36 (n. 15). *CCSL*, vol. 133, 184, offers instead "conuecta," as found in both Cambridge, Gg.5.35 (fol. 376r) and London, Royal 12.C.xxiii (124r).

414. For a similar association, see Symphosius's Riddle 85 (apple) and Aldhelm's *Enigma* 76 (apple-tree), discussed above on pp. 126–27 and 210.

415. For various scholarly hypotheses on the description of death as being threefold (note the title "De trina morte"), see Williams, "The Riddles of Tatwine and Eusebius," 136.

and 39). By the same token, Riddles 36 (winnowing fork) and 37 (sower) share their agricultural subject. The thematic connections are not only discernible in pairs as in the preceding examples, since further associations should be noted among the remainder of the riddles. A clear illustration of this can be observed in Riddles 31 (spark), 33 (fire), and 35 (ember), which allude to fire in three different phases: first as a spark from the flint, then as fire proper, and finally as embers. In fact, *Enigma* 33 provides a clue on this, as fire is said to exist in a threefold form: "Testatur simplex triplicem natura figuram / esse meam, haut mortales qua sine uiuere possunt" (1–2) [Though single, my nature testifies to my existing triple shape, without which mortal beings cannot live]. As some of the topics of this section are concerned with the smith's profession and the forge, this suggests that fire, in its three different states, was probably viewed as a fitting instrumental topic.

Considered as a group, the riddles of section 5 therefore provide topics that are typically found in the three instrumental books *par excellence* of the *Etymologiae*: Book XVIII, concerning topics related to war and entertainment; Book XIX, including chapters vi and vii on the smith's tools; and Book XX, corresponding to provisions and diverse domestic and agricultural implements.[416] The presentation of the following outline, which was also offered at the beginning of this book to illustrate an instrumental sequence,[417] can be helpful for comparing the contents of Tatwine's section 5 with the corresponding entries offered by Isidore in these books.

Tatwine's Section 5	Isidore's *Etymologiae*
27. Tongs	XIX.vii.3
28. Anvil	XIX.vii.1
29. Table	—

---

416. See my discussion of Isidore's instrumental books on pp. 105–06.
417. For the conspicuous presence of erotic imagery and double entendre in the riddles of this sequence, see my "The Sexual Riddle Type in Aldhelm's *Enigmata*," 363–65.

Tatwine's Section 5	Isidore's *Etymologiae*
30. Sword and sheath	XVIII.vi.1 (sword); XVIII.ix.2 (sheath)
31. Spark	XIX.vi.6
32. Arrow	XVIII.viii.1
33. Fire	XIX.vi.5
34. Quiver	XVIII.ix.1
35. Ember	XIX.vi.7
36. Winnowing fork	XX.xiv.10
37. Sower	—
38. Charcoal	XIX.vi.7
39. Whetstone	**XVI.iii.6**[418]

Tatwine's section no doubt calls to mind Aldhelm's interest in subjects related to metalwork in section 2 of his *Enigmata*.[419] Apart from this, the comparative outline suggests that the composition of section 5 offers a combination of topics occurring in Isidore's instrumental books. These riddling themes clearly represent three major instrumental subdivisions observed in Isidore's encyclopedia: first, the smith's "tools" (tongs, anvil, spark,[420] fire, ember, charcoal, and whetstone), all of them being topics dealt with in Book XIX, with the exception of whetstone; second, agricultural and domestic artifacts (winnowing fork, sower, and table), which convey subjects from Book XX[421]; third, military implements (sword and sheath, arrow, and quiver), which correspond to entries handled in Book XVIII.

---

418. In this case, bold letters indicate that the exceptional status relates to the source (Book XVI), not the subject (whetstone).
419. Hahn explains Tatwine's concern with metalwork on the basis of his being from a part of Mercia where the iron industry was prominent. Heinrich Hahn, "Die Rätseldichter Tatwin und Eusebius," *Forschungen zur deutschen Geschichte* 26 (1886): 609.
420. In Isidore's *Etymologiae*, the term *scintilla* is not actually an entry but part of the explanation of the ash (*favilla*) that is produced in the smith's furnace.
421. The only exception being *seminante* (sower), which is not dealt with in Isidore's *Etymologiae*.

After the instrumental series, Riddle 40 (rays of the sun) appropriately brings Tatwine's collection to a close:

Summa poli spatians dum lustro cacumina laetus,[422]
dulcibus *allecti*[423] dapibus sub culmine curuo
intus ludentem sub eodem temporis ortu
cernere me tremulo possunt in culmine caeli.
Corporis absens plausu quid sum pandite sophi!

[While I happily go walking through the highest summits of heaven, those who have been invited to the sweet banquets under its curved zenith can see me, tremulous, playing within, at the very moment of sunrise on the highest part of the sky. Wise men, with a round of applause, say what I, lacking body, am!][424]

From the point of view of the compilation, this topic constitutes an effective coda to the *Enigmata*, since the rays of the sun form part of the traditional iconography related to God.[425] The reference to the divine blessings awaiting the elect (the good Christians) in heaven (line 2) is thus a clue that is consistent with the special significance of this subject. If we take into account the theological implications of the sun motif, it may then be assumed that section 1 and Riddle 40 thus provide a framework for Tatwine's collection.

---

422. I am here supplying a comma that is not present in the CCLS version.
423. Following Williams, "The Riddles of Tatwine and Eusebius," 155, I have modified "allectis" in line 2 as found in *CCLS*, vol. 133, 207, for "allecti," which is offered in the London codex (fol. 127r). A variant reading is offered in the Cambridge manuscript with "at lectis" (fol. 377v). As explained by Williams (ibid.), "the form ["allecti"] could be the participle from either 'allego' ('to admit by election') or 'allicio' ('to attract')," but the former is preferable, since "the reference is to the souls in Heaven."
424. For the incorporeal quality of the sunbeams as offered by this riddle, see Leslie Lockett, *Anglo-Saxon Psychologies in the Vernacular and Latin Traditions* (Toronto: University of Toronto Press, 2011), 265.
425. As Ferguson states, "the eye within the triangle, surrounded by a circle and radiating rays of light, is used to suggest the infinite holiness of the Triune God." George Wells Ferguson, *Signs and Symbols in Christian Art* (Oxford: Oxford University Press, 1954; repr. 1961), 47.

With respect to the general scheme of the collection (see appendix V), Tatwine possibly envisaged his *Enigmata* as conveying an internal twofold subdivision, in which two parts composed of 20 riddles each can be discerned. According to this, the first part would cover sections 1–3 and the second would include sections 4–5 plus the coda. In this light, following the Symphosian model, the collection seems to have been designed as a sort of "dyptich" in which the two major subdivisions are to be contrasted. With a clear emphasis on learning, "Theological Motifs I" would thus mirror the presentation of "Theological Motifs II," the latter offering a meditation on the original causes of sin and death. By the same token, "Tools I," with its focus on implements that are typical of the monastic environment, provides an interesting counterpoint to "Tools II," which dwells on craftsmanship and sexual double entendre.[426]

Apart from this reading, the overall structure of Tatwine's collection may be approached in a slightly different way, such that the section on prodigies may be tentatively understood as a sort of "hinge" for the dyptich described above. The following scheme may help clarify this second interpretation of the collection's structural design:

Theological Motifs I (emphasis on learning and spiritual life)

Tools I (implements associated with the monastic environment)

Wonders

Theological Motifs II (emphasis on the origins of sin and death)

Tools II (implements associated with the smithy and the farm)

This outline reveals Tatwine's peculiar handling of the section on wonders that is situated in the middle rather than at the end, as observed in Symphosius's and Aldhelm's collections. The result is a well-balanced compilation, whose twofold structure seems to urge readers to compare the topics located at the two sides of the

---

426. See my "The Sexual Riddle Type," 363–65.

"dyptich." In this sense, it is quite clear that Tatwine managed to successfully combine the encyclopedic and the metrical principles.

3.4.2 Eusebius's Enigmata

The name Eusebius appears as referring to the author of a collection of riddles occurring in both Cambridge, Gg.5.35 (fols. 370r-74v) and London, Royal 12.C.xxiii (fols. 113v-21v). In Bede's preface to the fourth book of his commentary on Samuel (c. 716),[427] it is stated that Hwætberht, abbot of Wearmouth-Jarrow, earned the cognomen Eusebius because of his great spiritual merits.[428] Indeed, Eusebius's intellectual reputation must have been high during his own lifetime, since he figures as the dedicatee of Bede's commentaries on Revelation (c. 703) and Acts (c. 709), as well as of his treatise *De temporum ratione* (c. 726).[429] On the basis of this association, scholars have usually conjectured that Hwætberht could be the author of these *enigmata*[430] and, therefore, a contemporary of Bede.[431]

---

427. For the reference to Hwætberht in this work, see *In primam partem Samuhelis libri IIII*, CCSL, vol. 119, ed. David Hurst (Turnhout: Brepols, 1962), 212.
428. Eusebius in Greek derives from εὐ (good) and σέβας (piety).
429. All these excerpts from Bede's commentaries are cited, translated, and discussed in Williams, "The Riddles of Tatwine and Eusebius," 44–57. For further information on Bede's commentaries, see Alan Thacker, "Bede and the Ordering of Understanding," *Innovation and Tradition in the Writings of the Venerable Bede*, ed. Scott DeGregorio (Morgantown: West Virginia University Press, 2006), 54–60.
430. It has been suggested that Hwætberht/Eusebius may also be the author of the anonymous *Vita Ceolfridi*. Hwætberht succeeded Ceolfric as abbot of Wearmouth-Jarrow around 716. For this, see Ian Wood, *The Most Holy Abbot Ceolfrid*, Jarrow Lecture, 1995, and Alan Thacker, "Bede and the Ordering of Understanding," 41 and n. 22.
431. See Giles, *Anecdota Bedae*, x, and Bolton, *A History*, vol. 1, 219. This inference has however been contested by Neil Wright in "The Anglo-Latin Hexameter: Theory and Practice c. 600–c. 800" (Unpublished PhD Dissertation, Cambridge, 1981). On the basis of the closeness of Eusebius's metrical practice to that of Aldhelm and Tatwine, Wright concludes that Eusebius was probably an unknown Southumbrian author and, consequently, not

On the basis of his having being ordained priest in 704 and other biographical details, Tupper deduces that 680 could be the date of Eusebius's birth.[432] Also, as this scholar notes, "That he [Eusebius] was still living in the forties of the eighth century is proved by a letter addressed to him by the missionary bishop Boniface between 744 and 747."[433] In this letter, Boniface urged Abbot Hwætberht to assist him and his fellow missionaries in Germany by sending them Bede's works. As Lendinara has pointed out, the fact that Boniface addressed Hwætberht, allegedly the Eusebius who wrote the riddle collection, is significant in that it gives us an insight into a potential network of ecclesiastical writers, all of them followers of Aldhelm and Bede, with a special regard for riddle composition.[434] A further detail supporting the idea of an intellectual circle of writers with a common interest in this literary genre is the general acceptance that Eusebius's sixty riddles were meant to complete the forty riddles of a fellow ecclesiastic, Tatwine, in both Cambridge, Gg.5.35 and London, Royal 12.C.xxiii in order to offer a one-hundred piece compilation in the manner established by Symphosius and Aldhelm.[435]

As with Aldhelm's and Tatwine's collections, Eusebius's *Enigmata*

---

the Hwætberht mentioned by Bede. See Michael Lapidge, "The Present State of Anglo-Saxon Studies," in *Insular Latin Studies: Papers on Latin Texts and Manuscripts of the British Isles: 550–1066*, ed. Michael Herren (Toronto: Pontifical Institute of Mediaeval Studies, 1981), 52. By contrast, Orchard, *The Poetic Art*, 254, considers the metrical characteristics of Eusebius's *Enigmata* akin to the practice of Northumbrian poets.

432. See Tupper, *The Riddles of the Exeter Book*, xxxv. See also Lapidge's entry for "Hwætberht" in Lapidge et al., *The Wiley Blackwell Encyclopedia*, 250–51.

433. Tupper, *The Riddles of the Exeter Book*, xxxv. For this letter, see Tangl, *S. Bonifatii et Lullii Epistolae*, vol. 1, 158–59 (no. 76).

434. See Patrizia Lendinara, "Gli Aenigmata Laureshamensia," *PAN* 7 (1981): 74.

435. As Lapidge and Rosier have affirmed, Eusebius "took the step of extending Tatwine's collection from forty to one hundred, the number canonized by Symphosius and Aldhelm." *Aldhelm: The Poetic Works*, 66. The custom of assembling riddles from diverse sources might have been

seem to be arranged on a metrical basis (see Appendix VI). Thus the first forty riddles are four-line poems, the only exception being Riddle 34 (river) with six lines. From Riddle 41 onwards, in the part devoted to animals the number of lines increases, although the metrical progression is rather loose and four-line poems still occur. Together with this metrical differentiation, the fact that these last twenty riddles are remarkably dependent on Isidore's Book XII has led Tupper and Whitman to conjecture that the second part might be the work of another author.[436] Regardless of whether this hypothesis is correct,[437] the important issue here is that the two parts thematically complement each other, as the following analysis shows.

Eusebius's Riddles[438] open with a group organized on the basis of a hierarchical principle, which follows the traditional Great Chain of Being, a unifying principle that is also present in Isidore's *Etymologiae*.[439] Accordingly, God appears in the first place and the following topics range from the immediately inferior categories—angel (no. 2) and fallen angel (3)—to man (4). An internal criterion based on priority therefore also applies in this part. This hierarchical principle continues in section 2 with the description of the following cosmological topics: heaven (5), earth (6), wind and fire (8), sun (10), and moon (11). Here the Isidorean classification of cosmology on the basis of the three main elements is evident. As discussed above,[440] the two thematic irregularities—letters (7) and alpha (9)—could be viewed as belonging to the idea of God's Creation. By including

---

common practice in the Middle Ages, as deduced from the composite collection extant in Vatican City, Reg. Lat. 1553.
436. See Tupper, *The Riddles of the Exeter Book*, xxxvii, and Whitman, *Old English Riddles*, 33.
437. Tupper's and Whitman's arguments in favor of a different authorship for the last 20 riddles seem to me inconclusive.
438. Part of the discussion of the structure of Eusebius's riddles, particularly those devoted to zoological subjects, has already been included in my "Clean and Unclean Animals."
439. For the relevance of this orderly parameter in the compilation of this treatise, see Barney et al., *The Etymologies*, 20.
440. See p. 8.

these two topics in a cosmological section, Eusebius prioritized them on the grounds of their Christian significance, since letters are the basic components of the speech, just as the elements are the primary constituents of the other cosmological concepts of the series.[441]

Eusebius's section 3 is certainly a miscellany, although several thematic pairings can be detected.[442] For example, Riddles 12 (bullock) and 13 (cow) offer a meaningful correlative order. Further in this section, Riddles 17 (cross) and 18 (iniquity and justice) are juxtaposed, as the former describes the cross as an instrument of justice to punish outlaws. Similarly, Riddle 25 (heart) is preceded by *Enigma* 24 (death and life). After this miscellany, the thematic plan seems to be resumed, with a group on writing tools (section 4): inkhorn (no. 30), wax (31),[443] parchment (32), book chest (33),[444] and pen (35). Despite the general cohesion of this series, two exceptional themes—34 (river) and 36 (sword)—convey a remarkable rupture of thematic consistency for which I have found no reasonable explanation.

With respect to section 5, I have detected four subgroups, of which A comprises three animals: calf (no. 37), chicken (38), and fish (40).

---

441. The presence of these two subjects among the cosmological topics of section 2 therefore recalls the reference to the letters of the alphabet as *elementa* in Aldhelm's Riddle 30. See above on p. 193.

442. For a discussion of some of Eusebius's oppositional patterns, see Emily V. Thornbury, *Becoming a Poet in Anglo-Saxon England* (Cambridge: Cambridge University Press, 2014), 58.

443. This riddle alludes to the wax writing tablets used in schools. Cf. Aldhelm's Riddle 32 on the same subject. See also Williams, "The Riddles of Tatwine and Eusebius," 199.

444. The term "sceta" is explained by Du Cange as being equivalent to Latin *armarium*, "a closet, chest, or safe, for food, clothing, money, etc." (*L&S*). The clues allude to the object possessing abundant wisdom of different sorts ("multigena sapientia . . . habunde," 1), which come forth through its mouth ("processerit ore," 3). Accordingly, "book chest" seems to me preferable to Erhard-Siebold's "book-wallet" (*CCSL*, vol. 133, 243), Williams's "bookcase" (*The Riddles*, 202–3), and Ebert's "Bücherschrank" ("Die Rätselpoesie," 49, n. 4). For further comments on Eusebius's Riddle 33, see pp. 362–63 of this book.

These topics are apparently disconnected, but, on closer inspection, they actually reveal a typically Isidorean categorization suggesting three of the four elements: land, air, and water. A size criterion also applies here, since the calf, the chicken, and the fish contrast with the bullock (12) and cow (13) of section 3, as well as with the subsequent bigger animals of subgroup 5B. Furthermore, given that these animals are of use to human beings, they are clearly prioritized. As a representative of clean cattle, the calf thus fittingly opens section 5—in the same way that the bullock and the cow introduce section 3. The calf is then followed by the chicken, a clean bird, and the fish; the latter, we may assume, is also a clean animal, since it at least has one of the characteristics mentioned in Leviticus and Deuteronomy: "me pennula fulcit" (2) [the fin (literally, the little wing) sustains me].[445] With this selection of small clean animals, subgroup 5A therefore functions as an introduction to the subsequent larger zoological series, which, as will be explained below, comprises mostly unclean specimens. The Isidorean principle of contrast is therefore no doubt at work here.

Despite this fairly coherent arrangement, the order as we find it in Isidore's Book XII is significantly changed to land, air, and water in Eusebius's subgroup A. Besides, a notable exception occurs with Riddle 39 (the letter i), whose inclusion at this point can be explained, as I have argued elsewhere,[446] if we take into account a possible connection with the subsequent fish riddle. It is well known that the Greek acronym ΙΧΘΥΣ, the Greek word for "fish," contains the first letters of the phrase "Ἰησοῦς Χριστός, Θεοῦ Υἱός, Σωτήρ" (Jesus Christ, God's Son, Savior). The knowledge of the fish symbol in Anglo-Saxon England is also evinced from the *Sibylline Acrostic*, a Latin translation of a Greek poem on the Last Judgement whose lines spell out the equivalent phrase, "Iesus Christus Dei filius

---

445. Note, for example, Leviticus 11.9: "Everything in the waters that has fins and scales, whether in the seas or in the rivers, you may eat." Cf. Deuteronomy 14.10.

446. See my "Patterns of Compilation," 350, and "Clean and Unclean Animals," 576–77.

saluator."⁴⁴⁷ The poem, which is uniquely preserved in Leipzig, Stadtbibliothek, Rep. I.74, has been associated with the Canterbury school of Theodore and Hadrian, where the Latin translation might have been produced.⁴⁴⁸ The fact that Aldhelm quotes from this poem three times in the *Epistola* led Walther Bulst to argue that we owe the Latin version of the *Sibylline Acrostic* to Aldhelm.⁴⁴⁹ This hypothesis has not, however, found support among scholarship,⁴⁵⁰ but the association of the fish acrostic and riddling is underpinned by the co-occurrence of Aldhelm's *Enigmata* and the full Latin version of the *Sibylline Acrostic* in Leipzig, Rep. I.74.⁴⁵¹

The juxtaposition of Eusebius's Riddles 39 and 40 would similarly conjure up the Latin acronym INRI—standing for "Iesus Nazarenus Rex Iudaeorum" (Jesus the Nazarene, King of the Jews). In addition, Adolf Ebert suspects that the first line of Riddle 39 alludes to the fact that the letter i alone was used as an abbreviation for *imperator* or *imperium*: "Effigie gracilis, sum usurpans famina regum" [Having a slender figure, I usurp (i.e., substitute,

---

447. In the *De civitate Dei* (XVIII.xxiii), St Augustine had previously contributed to the popularity of the *Sibylline Acrostic* by claiming its authenticity as a prophecy of the Erythraean Sybil related to Christ. On St Augustine's comments on the fish and the Greek acronym in the *Sibylline Acrostic*, see Eva Matthews Sanford and William McAllen Green, *St Augustine: The City of God against the Pagans* (Cambridge, MA: Harvard University Press, 1965), vol. 5, 446–47. For the fish as a traditional symbol of Christ, see Everett Ferguson, Michael P. McHugh, and Frederick W. Norris, eds., *Encyclopedia of Early Christianity* (New York: Garland, 1997; repr. 1999), s.v. "fish," by Everett Ferguson, 431–32.
448. On this, see Lapidge and Rosier, *Aldhelm: The Poetic Works*, 16; Bischoff and Lapidge, *Biblical Commentaries*, 185; and Walther Bulst, "Eine anglo-lateinische Übersetzung aus dem Grieschichen um 700," *ZfdA* 75 (1938): 105–11.
449. See Bulst, ibid. For Aldhelm's citations of this poem, see Ehwald, *Aldhelmi opera*, 79 (23) and 93 (18 and 29).
450. See Lapidge and Rosier, *Aldhelm: The Poetic Works*, 16.
451. For this, see Filippa Alcamesi, "The *Sibylline Acrostic* in Anglo-Saxon Manuscripts: The Augustinian Translation and the Other Versions," in Bremmer and Dekker, eds., *Foundations of Learning*, 147–73, esp. 152–58.

abbreviate) the words of kings (i.e., the word for king)].[452] Probably on account of the scepter-like shape of its capital version (I), the last clue of Riddle 39 describes the letter i as endowed with imperial power, a notion that seems to corroborate the symbolic connotations of the Christ-fish pair: "sola duarum / et regimen hominis aliaque sceptra patrabo" (3–4) [Alone of two (i.e., only letter i), I will accomplish the rule of one man and other scepters (i.e., the power of a monarch and that of an emperor)]. Besides, as pointed out by Ebert, the two letters ("duarum," 3) are possibly IC or IX, the initials of *Iesus Christus*.[453] Accordingly, it seems to me that the compiler, most likely Eusebius himself, deliberately broke encyclopedic order—which in the Isidorean source is land, water, and air—and offered a thematic digression (the letter i) because this gave him an opportunity to teach a Christian symbol that was of interest to Anglo-Saxon writers.

Considered as a whole, the arrangement of Eusebius's section 5 is far from orthodox scientific taxonomy. But an internal classification seems to be at work with the subsequent three subgroups—serpents/quadrupeds (B), fish (C), and birds (D)—which clearly adopt the Isidorean threefold element distribution (land, water, and air), as illustrated in the outline below:

Eusebius's Section 5	Isidore's *Etymologiae*
A) Animals in General	
37. Calf	—
38. Chicken	—
39. The letter i	I.iv.17
40. Fish	—

---

452. Adolf Ebert, "Über die Räthselpoesie," 50 (n. 5). Cf. the description of letter i in *Versus*, *CCSL*, vol. 133A, 733.
453. Ebert, " Über die Rätselpoesie," 50 (n. 8). Erhardt-Siebolt supports this view in *Die lateinischen Rätsel*, 255. See also Williams, "The Riddles of Tatwine and Eusebius," 211.

Eusebius's Section 5	Isidore's *Etymologiae*
B) Animals of Land	*De bestiis/De serpentibus*
41. Chelydros snake and hydra	**XI.iii.34** (hydra); XII.iv.23–24 (hydra, chelydros)
42. Dragon	XII.iv.4
43. Tiger	XII.ii.7
44. Panther	XII.ii.8–9
45. Giraffe and chameleon	XII.ii.18 (chameleon); XII.ii.19 (giraffe)
46. Leopard	XII.ii.10 (pard); XII.ii.11 (leopard)
47. Scytale	XII.iv.19
48. Day and night	–
49. Amphisbaena	XII.iv.20
50. Lizard	XII.iv.37
51. Scorpion	**XII.v.4**
52. Chimaera	**XI.iii.36**
C) Animals of Water	*De piscibus*
53. Hippopotamus	XII.vi.21
54. Remora	XII.vi.34
55. Electric ray	XII.vi.45
D) Animals of Air	*De avibus*
56. Stork	XII.vii.16–17
57. Ostrich	XII.vii.20
58. Night Owl	XII.vii.40–41
59. Parrot	XII.vii.24
60. Horned Owl	XII.vii.39

In the case of subgroup B, this compendium of unclean land animals combines both quadrupeds (43, 44, 45,[454] and 46) and snakes

---

454. As explained above (p. 112), in Isidore's Book XII, *camelopardus* (giraffe) and *cameleon* appear as successive entries in chapter ii (18–19), mainly devoted to quadrupeds of great size, probably because of Isidore's conviction about the etymological propinquity of the two words.

(41, 42, 47, 49, and 50), denoting a concern with the exotic and the wondrous. As observed in the chart above, these topics correspond to subjects that Isidore deals with separately in chapters ii (*De bestiis*) and iv (*De serpentibus*) of Book XII. When composing this part of the *Enigmata*, Eusebius selected from the Isidorean source a group of snakes of great size: chelydros/hydra, dragon, scytale, and amphisbaena.[455] To these, three smaller unclean crawling animals—lizard, chameleon, and scorpion[456]—were added, thus following a rough gradation principle. The fact that both the chameleon and the scorpion possess special skills suggests they were selected on the basis of their having a prodigious status.[457] By the same token, felines and carnivores in general were traditionally viewed as unclean because they fed on the flesh of other animals; hence, tiger, panther, and leopard would be suitable for subgroup B.

A clear exception, however, is Riddle 45, since this text describes the giraffe, a clean quadruped according to Mosaic law. The reference to this animal as having "pedesque buballo" (2), the feet of an ox (i.e., parted hoof), seems to acknowledge this condition. Yet the title occurring in the two extant manuscripts (*De cameleone*) suggests that Eusebius actually had a double solution in mind: giraffe

---

455. None of these fabulous animals appears in the biblical lists but, since "Whatever goes on its belly" (Leviticus 11.42) is considered to be unclean; it is quite logical that medieval authors like Isidore and Eusebius would include all kinds of snakes in this subcategory.

456. Also, it is noteworthy that Eusebius does not slavishly follow Isidore's classification of this insect among vermin; by contrast, in Riddle 51 he admits the possibility that the animal may belong to either serpents or worms: "Vermibus ascriptus nec non serpentibus atris..." (1) [I am included among worms or black (poisonous) snakes]. Cf. *Etymologiae* XII.v.4: "Scorpio vermis terrenus, qui potius vermibus adscribitur, non serpentibus" [The scorpion is an earthly worm, which is considered preferably among vermin rather than among the serpents].

457. The chameleon's ability to change its skin color and the scorpion's venomous stinger probably triggered their inclusion as wonders in subgroup B.

(Latin *camelopardus*) and chameleon (Latin *cameleon*).[458] The inclusion of this subject in the series was therefore probably motivated on account of the etymological connection with the pard, which is an animal of the feline type and, hence, unclean. It is thus not surprising that the first clue of Riddle 45 relates the physical appearance of the giraffe to that of the pard: "Muneror orbiculis ut pardus discolor albis . . ." (1) [Like the variegated pard, I have been given white spots]. On the other hand, line 4 clearly alludes to the chameleon, an animal that is classified as unclean:[459] "Respectaeque rei cuiusque resumo colorem" (4) [I pick up the color of the thing I am gazing at]. The association with these two unclean animals, the pard and the chameleon, may therefore have led Eusebius to include the giraffe among the other unclean creatures of section 5.

Riddle 41 also seems to be thematically anomalous, since it offers a double solution with a joint treatment of the hydra (a water-snake) and the chelydros, the latter described by Isidore as a serpent that dwells both in the water and on land.[460] Rather than viewing this riddle as an irregularity, it seems to me that Eusebius was simply following once more the Isidorean source, where the hydra appears in chapter iv, that is, among land animals.[461] Furthermore, the hydra could well have been considered as a suitable topic to mark the beginning of subgroup A because of its inclusion in Isidore's Book XI (*De portentis*).[462] By the same token, the chimaera riddle appropriately brings subgroup B to a close, since this threefold beast—with the face of a lion, the middle part of a goat, and the rear of a dragon—partakes of the two categories ruling this subgroup: the quadruped and the snake types. The author's choice therefore reveals a clear attempt at achieving coherence for subgroup B by providing a prodigy at the start with the hydra, and again at the end

---

458. Lines 1–3 describe the giraffe and line 4 refers to the chameleon.
459. Leviticus 11.30.
460. Also, note that the hydra and the chelydros are dealt with subsequently in XII.iv.23–24.
461. XII.iv.23.
462. XI.iii.34–35.

with the chimaera.⁴⁶³ Besides, Eusebius's decision to close the zoological sequence with a prodigy recalls Symphosius's *modus operandi* with the centaur (no. 39) as the last topic of the latter's animal series.

Eusebius's *Enigma* 48 (day and night) in subgroup B is a further thematic exception that needs to be dealt with.

> Non sumus aequales, quamuis ambaeque sorores:
> Tetrica nam facie est una, stans altera pulchra;
> Horrida sed requiem confert, et grata laborem.
> Non simul et semper sumus, at secernimur ipsi.

> [Although we are both sisters, we are not similar: one of us has a gloomy appearance, the other one is beautiful; but the horrible one conveys rest and the pleasing one (brings) work. We are never together at the same time but rather always separate].

Here, day and night are described as two sisters that are radically different. In a clear parallel construction, one sister (night) is said to be gloomy ("tetrica," 2) and hideous ("horrida," 3), while the other sister (day) is described as fair ("pulchra," 2) and pleasing ("grata," 3). The clues then play on the paradox that the fair sister offers hard toil for human beings while the horrible one affords rest.

The riddle constitutes such an abrupt interruption of the zoological series that Glorie suspected that the order of the collection might have been disturbed at this point.⁴⁶⁴ However, if we consider Aldhelm's Riddle 97 (night), which was discussed above among the topics that can be classified as portents, a better explanation can be found for this thematic digression. In Aldhelm's riddle, night is characterized as a bizarre creature by means of negative features such as dark complexion ("nigrantem," 1) and barrenness ("stereli de uis-

---

463. The hydra and the chimaera are the only topics of section 5 whose source is Isidore's Book XI, where they appear as successive entries—XI.iii.34-35 and XI.iii.36, respectively. Interestingly, the chimaera is also described in the *Liber monstrorum* (II.11). See Orchard, *Pride and Prodigies*, 294-95.

464. Glorie, *CCSL*, vol. 133, 258 (note).

cere," 2). As pointed out above, further in this riddle (lines 11–16) *nox* is said to be a sister of *fama* (rumor), which is in turn presented as a horrifying monster. Accordingly, both Eusebius's Riddle 48 and Aldhelm's Riddle 97 share the motif of the two wondrous sisters. It is therefore probable that the day-and-night topic was included in Eusebius's section 5 by analogy with Aldhelm's treatment of *nox* as a portent. Also importantly, night is a subject in the *Liber monstrorum* (I.42),[465] an idea that supports my contention that Eusebius's Riddle 48 could have been considered as a fitting topic for subgroup B, where creatures of the prodigy kind predominate.

As regards Eusebius's subgroup C, the topics included in this series clearly illustrate unclean wondrous "fish." The opening motif, the hippopotamus (no. 53), no doubt was viewed as an aquatic monster by medieval people and, as such, it was included in the *Liber monstrorum* (II.9, 17).[466] Even though the hippopotamus is said to graze in the fields ("rura . . . depascor," 6), this animal was traditionally assumed to be unclean.[467] As regards the subject of Riddle 54, the remora is a fish with no scales—hence, unclean—and endowed with an extraordinary sucking disk on its head with which it attaches to boats. The last of this series, the electric ray (no. 55), shares with

---

465. For this passage, see Orchard, *Pride and Prodigies*, 280–81.
466. See ibid., 294-95 and 298-99. Also, note the proximity of the reference to the chimaera in the same work (II.11), ibid., 294–95. A further possible reference to hippopotami may be found in *The Letter of Alexander the Great*: "Þæt wæs þonne nicra mengeo on onsione maran & unhyrlicran þonne ða elpendas . . ." (86–88) ["It was a multitude of water-monsters (i.e., hippopotami), larger and more terrible in appearance than the elephants"]. Text and translation from R. D. Fulk, ed. and trans., *The Beowulf Manuscript* (Cambridge, MA: Harvard University Press, 2010), 48–51. Information within parentheses is mine. Also, see Norman Davis, "'Hippopotamus' in Old English," *RES* 4 (1953): 141–42.
467. As pointed out by Cansdale, *Animals of Bible Lands*, 101, "By the Mosaic classification, therefore, it [the hippopotamus] divides the hoof but does not chew the cud; in fact, it goes half-way to doing this, having a complex three-chambered stomach for dealing with the large masses of coarse food that it must work over."

the preceding animal the characteristic of having no scales and a wondrous ability: it can produce an electric shock. Apart from belonging to the genus of fish, the three riddles of Eusebius's subgroup C also denote a common interest in the etymological connection between the name of the animal in question and its main characteristics. The hippopotamus thus shares some of the features of the horse ("equo," 3) and some of the fish (note "pisce" in the title), thus illustrating the etymology of the Greek word (ἱπποπόταμος, river-horse). The echenais or remora of Riddle 54 is said to be so called because it constitutes a hindrance ("moram," 6) to ships, thus alluding to the Greek origin of the term.[468] By the same token, the clues of Riddle 55 insist on the paralyzing effect—note "torpescere" (1) and "torpescerent" (6)—that the electric discharge of the torpedo or electric ray can produce on other creatures. Considered as a whole, the three riddles of this series are linked by an interest in the etymological origin of the name of these animals, as observed in the clues that clearly derive from the Isidorean excerpts that inspired them. The aquatic triad is also meaningfully organized on the basis of the size of its components, thus opening with the largest aquatic specimen, the hippopotamus.

Eusebius's subgroup D parallels the preceding series with its selection of unclean birds—all of them are classified as such in the biblical lists.[469] A contrastive pattern based on size seems to apply, for the stork and the ostrich are comparatively bigger than the remainder of the birds of the series. On the other hand, when analyzing the structure of Isidore's Book XII, Jacques André has pointed out the presence of a group of exotic birds (mainly, vii.20–33) and a string of nocturnal birds (vii.38–42).[470] In this sense, the following chart listing four of the topics from Eusebius's subgroup D can shed light on its internal organization.

---

468. As explained by Williams, "The Riddles of Tatwine and Eusebius," 237, the term used by Eusebius in the title "De ocheano pisce" is probably a corrupt version of Greek ἐχενηΐς, meaning ship-retaining fish.
469. Leviticus 11.13–19; Deuteronomy 14.11–18.
470. André, *Isidore de Séville*, 12.

57. Ostrich (exotic/diurnal)
58. Night Owl (common/nocturnal)
59. Parrot (exotic/diurnal)
60. Horned owl (common/nocturnal)

The fact that Eusebius was aware of Isidore's distinction of these two ornithological subcategories is therefore evident from the alternative display detected in subgroup D.

Further internal cohesion can be discerned in this section. The ornithological series opens with the stork riddle (no. 56), which incidentally is distinguished as the longest of the collection with 13 lines. The clues of this riddle describe the bird's extraordinary diligence at raising its offspring: "sic sollicitudo / circa communis cunctis stat tam pia multos / natos, sic ut alentes hos uestimine carnes / nostras nudemus" (9–12) [For all of us our common loving concern with our many children is such that, when we nurse them, we strip our flesh of its garment (i.e., feathers)]. By contrast, in a typically alliterative fashion the clues of subsequent Riddle 57 put the emphasis on the ostrich's carelessness with its chicks: "et conceptum neglego foetum / forte fouere meum, sed fotu pulueris oua[471] / sparsa fouentur uel potius animantur in illo" (3–5) [I neglect to brood my offspring (i.e., sit on the eggs) that were conceived by chance, but the heat of the dust keeps warm my dispersed eggs, or rather they are given life in it].[472] In fact, this oppositional pattern is set between the stork riddle and the remainder of the ornithological themes of this section,

---

471. Following Williams, "The Riddles of Tatwine and Eusebius" (244), I have slightly modifed the punctuation offered in Glorie's version of this riddle (*CCSL*, vol. 133, 268).

472. The proverbial carelessness of the ostrich and its figurative illustration of bad parenthood are also present in Job 39.13–17: "The wings of the ostrich wave proudly; but are they the pinions and plumage of love? For she leaves her eggs to the earth, and lets them be warmed on the ground, forgetting that a foot may crush them, and that the wild beast may trample them. She deals cruelly with her young, as if they were not hers; though her labor be in vain, yet she has no fear; because God has made her forget wisdom, and given her no share in understanding."

since the other birds might have been likewise regarded as examples of negative conduct for human beings, as the darkness-loving night owl (no. 58), the garrulous parrot (59), and the lazy horned owl (60) suggest.

In spite of the overall thematic plan ruling the *enigmata*—and unlike the other three collections analyzed so far—Eusebius's Riddles strikingly do not end in a typically concluding coda, as might be expected to match the initial theological series. Conversely, the collection ends with Riddle 60 (horned owl), a bird whose negative characteristics are emphatically offered in the textual clues by means of alliteration: "Ignaua uolucris uenturi nuntia luctus / pigraque perseuerans uertor prae[473] pondere plumae" (1–2) [An idle bird announcing the coming of grief, I am persistently inclined to laziness because of the weight of my feathers]. The fondness for darkness as well as the bird's reputed sloth made this bird a negative example in medieval literature, as Hrabanus Maurus's passage from *De rerum naturis* (VIII.vi.961–62) illustrates: "Bubo tenebris peccatorum deditos, et lucem iustitiae fugientes significat, unde inter inmunda animalia in Leuitico deputatur"[474] [The horned owl symbolizes those who, fleeing the light of justice, are devoted to the darkness of sins; that is why they are considered among the unclean animals in Leviticus]. The presentation of an unclean bird illustrating a negligent conduct as a closing motif is at best intriguing, since this implies that the *enigmata* are unfinished and imperfect according to the compilation standards observed in the previously analyzed collections.

The absence of an appropriate conclusion in Eusebius's *Enigmata* can however be satisfactorily explained if we consider that this collection precedes Tatwine's in both Cambridge, Gg.5.35 and London,

---

473. I here accept Williams's modification of Glorie's "pre pondere," which is the reading offered by the Cambridge codex (fol. 374r). The reading in the London manuscript is "prepondere (fol. 121r)." Williams, "The Riddles of Tatwine and Eusebius," 249.
474. Cited from Schipper, *Hrabani Mauri*. I have supplied a comma after "significat" that is not present in Schipper's edition of this passage.

Royal 12.C.xxiii.[475] It might be inferred that Tatwine's concluding motif—no. 40 (rays of the sun)—functions as a coda to both collections, which could well have been regarded as a unified lot. Indeed, the sun-rays motif, with the well-known iconographic associations pointed out above, perfectly dovetails with Eusebius's initial riddle on God, thus extending the theological framework to the composite assemblage. Apart from this, there are still other significant aspects which suggest that the two collections complement one another. From an encyclopedic point of view, Tatwine's *Enigmata* are clearly faulty, as they do not offer a zoological group—the only representative animal being the squirrel (no. 17), which is inserted in a section on wonders. However, Tatwine's missing zoological part is supplied by Eusebius's comprehensive section on animals. Also, since Tatwine's collection offers no cosmological series, Eusebius's section 2 remedies this lack. The resulting assemblage of Eusebius's and Tatwine's *enigmata* therefore adds to the encyclopedic scope of the individual collections by covering all the typical themes dealt with in these treatises.

As the analysis of Eusebius's *Enigmata* has shown, the initial arrangement following the orderly criterion of the Great Chain of Being, the subsequent cosmological string, the instrumental sequence, and, especially, the coherent zoological series all prove that this collection was organized according to traditional encyclopedic principles. As regards section 5, Eusebius did not only derive the contents of this part from Isidore's Book XII but also closely reproduced its classification method in terms of the tripartite distribution of animals, the distinction between domestic and wild creatures, and the adoption of size and priority criteria. As with the Isidorean source, Eusebius not only adhered to the zoological taxonomy of Leviticus and Deuteronomy but also maintained the differentiation

---

475. Notably, in Cambridge, Gg.5.35, Eusebius's collection appears on fols. 370r–74v, followed by Tatwine's occurring on 374v–77v. In London, Royal 12.C.xxiii, Eusebius's Riddles appear on fols. 113v–21v, and Tatwine's on 121v–27r.

between clean and unclean animals in a quite consistent way. On the other hand, the inclusion of the letter i as well as the day-and-night topic in the zoological series reveals an idiosyncratic handling of the source material. In the case of Riddles 39 and 40, Eusebius made encyclopedic organization subsidiary to the pedagogic potentiality of the juxtaposition of the letter i and the fish. In turn, the choice of day and night as a subject and the section's remarkable concern with the wondrous reveals a knowledge of previous riddling tradition—notably, Aldhelm's *Enigmata*—and catalogues of marvels such as the *Liber monstrorum*. All this suggests that Eusebius carefully selected the Isidorean material and skillfully adapted it to the riddle-collection format with a clear didactic aim in mind.

3.5. Medieval Riddle Collections by Other Authors

There are still three further medieval Latin collections that can be brought forth to illustrate riddle compilations based on Isidorean encyclopedic patterns: the Bern Riddles, the Lorsch *Enigmata*, and the Vatican assemblage. There is, however, no space in this monograph to deal with all of them in a detailed way, as has been done with the preceding collections. For this reason, I will go through them briefly and expound on the thematic structures that may be relevant for our later study of the Exeter Book Riddles. As has been done so far, I will offer a chronological approach.

3.5.1 The Bern Riddles

The *Enigmata Bernensis* or Bern Riddles have come down to us in twelve manuscripts,[476] of which the earliest is a late eighth-century

---

476. For a brief description of the manuscripts in which the Bern *Enigmata* are extant, see Finch, "The Bern Riddles in Codex Vat. Reg. Lat. 1553," 145. See also the list of manuscripts in *CCSL*, vol. 133A, 544–45, and *Aenigmata Hexasticha*, *MGH*, *PLAC*, ed. Karl Strecker, vol. 4.2 (Berlin: Weidmann, 1923), 733–37. To Glorie's list of nine manuscripts, Finch added Vatican City, Cod. Barb. Lat. 1717, a codex from the sixteenth century. See Chauncey E. Finch, "The Riddles in Cod. Barb. Lat. 1717 and Newberry Case MS

codex known as Bern, Burgerbibliothek, Cod. 611 (fols. 73r–80v),[477] from which the name derives.[478] At its maximum length, the collection comprises sixty-three hexastich riddles in rhythmical hexameters as found in Leipzig, Rep. I.74 (fols. 15v-24r), manuscript from the Loire region.[479] This codex, which probably originated in an Insular-influenced environment in the first half of the ninth century, also contains Aldhelm's *Enigmata* and the *Sibylline Acrostic*, as was mentioned above.[480] Fifty-two of the Bern riddles apppear in combination with pieces by Aldhelm and Symphosius in a single collection in Vatican City, Reg. Lat. 1553 (fols. 8v-21v) from the early ninth century.[481]

---

f. 11," *Manuscripta* 17 (1973): 3–11. To these we should add Zwettl, Zisterzienserstift, Cod. 53 (second half of the twelfth century), which also offers a complete version of the Bern Riddles (fols. 153r–58r) and had not been taken into account so far. A brief description of the manuscript contents is found in Stephan Rössler, *Verzeichniss der Handschriften der Bibliothek des Stiftes Zwettl* (Vienna, 1891), 322. A similar case is that of Graz, Universitätsbibliothek, Cod. 85 (thirteenth century), containing a version of the Bern *Enigmata* (fols. 266v-69v), which scholars have failed to notice.

477. For a detailed account of the contents of this manuscript, see Hermann Hagen, *Catalogus codicum bernensium (Bibliotheca Bongarsiana)* (Bern, 1885), 479–83.

478. As with the other Latin collections, all references to the Bern Riddles are from Fr. Glorie, *Aenigmata in Dei nomine Tullii*, CCSL, vol. 133A, with a German translation by K. J. Minst, 541–610. I have also consulted Wilhelm Meyer, ed., "Über die Beobachtung des Wortaccentes in der altlateinischen Poesie," *Abhandlungen der Philosophisch-Philologischen Classe der königlich Bayerischen Akademie der Wissenschaften* 17 (1886), 412–30, and *Gesammelte Abhandlungen zur mittellateinischen Rythmik*, vol. 2 (Berlin: Weidmann, 1905), 155–79 by the same author; Buecheler and Riese, *Anthologia Latina*, vol. 1.1, 351–70 (no. 481), and Strecker, *Aenigmata Hexasticha*, 732–59.

479. On this manuscript, see *Bischoff, Katalog, Teil II*, 69 (no. 2272), and M. Haupt, "Über eine Handschrift der Leipziger Stadtbibliothek," *Berichte über die Verhandlungen der Königlich Sächsischen Gesellschaft der Wissenschaften zu Leipzig, Philologisch-Historische Classe* 2 (1850): 1–15. See also Lapidge and Rosier, *Aldhelm: The Poetic Works*, 16, and Bischoff and Lapidge, *Biblical Commentaries*, 185.

480. See on p. 239 of this book.

481. Also significantly, this hybrid assemblage is preceded in this

Symphosius's Riddles 59 (ball, first two lines), 63 (sponge), and 69 (mirror) are also appended at the end of the Bern *Enigmata* in Berlin, Phillipps 1825 (fols. 37v-45r),[482] a further early-ninth-century codex which probably originated in Saint-Aubin of Angers.[483]

Max Manitius, who has dated the Bern *Enigmata* to the seventh century,[484] argues that these riddles might be the work of an Irish monk at Bobbio.[485] However, there is no evidence to support this conjecture and no other scholar has adhered to this hypothesis. On the basis of the presence of topics related to Italian flora as well as Mediterranean food, Archer Taylor conjectures that the riddles might the work of an Italian poet.[486] Zoja Pavlovskis, on the other hand, speculates about a possible female authorship on account of

---

manuscript by Boniface's *Enigmata*. See Finch, "The Bern Riddles," 146.

482. On this, see Valentin Rose, *Verzeichniss der Lateinischen Handschriften der Königlichen Bibliothek zu Berlin*, vol. 1 (Berlin, 1893), 379-80 (no. 167). This codex preserves two more riddles that are edited as additional pieces of the Bern collection as nos. 50a (*De charta*, on papyrus sheet) and 56a (*De penna*, on the pen) in Buecheler and Riese, eds., *Anthologia latina*, vol. 1.2, 380. Also, Glorie included Riddle 50a in *CCSL*, vol. 133A, 597. Bern Riddle 56a is followed by the first two lines of Symphosius's *Enigma* 59 (ball) on folio 44v of this manuscript. See Rose, ibid., 380. A similar blending of Symphosius's Riddles and arrangement is observed at the end of the Bern collection in Chicago, MS f.11. For this, see Finch, "The Riddles in Cod. Barb. Lat. 1717," 9-10.

483. Formerly known as Meermann 167, this manuscript is fully described in Rose, *Verzeichniss*, 374–80 (no. 167). See also Bernhard Bischoff, *Katalog der festländischen Handschriften des neunten Jahrhunderts (mit Ausnahme der wisigotischen), Teil I: Aachen-Lambach* (Wiesbaden: Harrassowitz, 1998), 91 (no. 433) and Lapidge and Rosier, *Aldhelm: The Poetic Works*, 39.

484. *Geschichte der lateinischen Literatur*, vol. 1, 193. So does Glorie, *CCSL*, vol. 133, 149, although the date of the Bern *Enigmata* is far from being clear. Note that Buecheler and Riese, *Anthologia latina*, vol. 1.1, xlvii, consider that these riddles may have been composed in late antiquity.

485. *Geschichte der lateinischen Literatur*, vol. 1, 193.

486. Taylor, *The Literary Riddle before 1600*, 59. Also, see Pavlovkis, "The Riddler's Microcosm," 229–30 and 232; and Meyer, "Über die Beobachtung," 416.

the poet's strong familiarity with kitchen objects and a keen interest in riddle clues related to childbirth.[487] Although the hypothesis is certainly attractive, we will probably be unable to offer solid evidence of this. Besides, clues related to progeny are very frequently used by male writers like Aldhelm.[488]

In Berlin, Phillipps 1825, the collection is introduced with the following title: "ENIGMATA IN DEI NOMINE TULLII" (fol. 37v) [In the name of God, the riddles of Tullius]. On this basis, Glorie and other editors traditionally refer to the Bern Riddles as *Enigmata Tullii*. As an author's name, Tullius is as suspicious and unreliable as Symphosius, since, as noted earlier in this book, it was probably simply meant to evoke Roman statesman and rhetorician Marcus Tullius Cicero rather than to identify the actual author. As discussed above, the connection of these riddles with grammar, notably with rhetoric, is clear from the *incipit* introducing the *enigmata* in seven manuscripts.[489] A further intriguing aspect that might be related to the authorship of the Bern collection is offered by *Enigma* 63 (wine), which displays the name *Paulus* in acrostics. According to Andy Orchard, this riddle constitutes a later addition by a different poet, since it is "in fact an acrostic evidently composed by one 'Paulus' that is appended to the collection in two manuscripts."[490] Indeed, *Enigma* 63 appears in a final position in Leipzig, Rep. I.74 (fol. 24r),[491] but in the case of Vatican City, Reg. Lat. 1553 (fol. 14r), the

---

487. As Pavlovskis adds, "perhaps too he [the author of the Bern Riddles] was a monk in charge of, or mainly occupied in, a monastery kitchen." "The Riddler's Microcosm," 230 (n. 35).
488. See above, pp. 214–15.
489. See p. 78 (n. 284).
490. Andy Orchard, "Enigma Variations: The Anglo-Saxon Riddle-Tradition," in *Latin Learning and English Lore: Studies in Anglo-Saxon Literature for Michael Lapidge*, ed. Andy Orchard and Katherine O'Brien O'Keeffe (Toronto: University of Toronto Press, 2005), vol. 1, 287.
491. After the sixty-two riddles, there follows a prose enigma entitled "Item de ove," which precedes *Enigma* 63 in the Leipzig codex. The same prose enigma is extant and accompanied by a further prose piece without a title in Chicago, MS f.11, Zwettl, Cod. 53, and Vienna, Cod. 67. These two

text occurs as no. 43 among the agricultural topics that I have designated as section 3 (see Appendix IX).

Karl Neff has affirmed that the *Paulus* acrostic of Bern *Enigma* 63, as offered in the Leipzig codex, is indicative of the authorship of Paul the Deacon (c. 720–799), the Carolingian scholar from Pavia.[492] To demonstrate this, Neff adduces that in this manuscript further poems by this author are found and that parallels between the Bern riddle and Langobardic poetry have been detected.[493] The acrostic of Bern *Enigma* 63 might however be a further spurious ascription like that of Tullius.[494] It is well known that Paul the Deacon participated in an exchange of epistolar riddles with Peter of Pisa, another

---

prose riddles are edited in F. Mone, "Zweite Räthselsamlung," *Anzeiger für Kunde der deutschen Vorzeit* 8 (1839): 228-29, and Finch, "The Riddles in Cod. Barb. Lat. 1717," 6-7. Also, see Glorie, *CCSL*, vol. 133A, 610 (note after Riddle 63). Probably on account of the Paulus acrostic, *Enigma* 63 is followed by the *Sibylline Acrostic* in the Leipzig manuscript.

492. Karl Neff, *Die Gedichte des Paulus Diaconus: Kritische und erklärende Ausgabe* (Munich: Beck'sche, 1908), 82–83.

493. Notably, folios 35v–37v offer "Ordiar unde tuas laudes, o maxime Lari?" [Where shall I start your praises, o great Como?] by Paul the Deacon and other poetic pieces attributed to him. Neff, *Die Gedichte des Paulus Diaconus*, xvii. See also Haupt, "Über eine Handschrift," 6–9. Meyer similarly suspects that Paul the Deacon might be the author of Riddle 63, arguing that this piece is closely related in form and content to other rhythmical poems from Lombardy. See Meyer, "Über die Beobachtung," 416, and *Gesammelte Abhandlungen*, vol. 2, 155.

494. In the context of Charlemagne's intellectual circle, it was frequent that authors would have nicknames recalling classical or canonical authors. For example, Moduin of Autun's nickname was Naso, evidently conjuring up the name of Ovid, and Angilbert's was Homer. Charlemagne himself was frequently referred to as David, evoking the biblical king and allegedly the author of the Psalms, in the literature of court poets. On this, see Mary Garrison, "The Social World of Alcuin: Nicknames at York and at the Carolingian Court," in Luuk A. J. R. Houwen and Alasdair A. MacDonald, eds., *Alcuin of York: Scholar at the Carolingian Court* (Groningen: Egbert Forsten, 1998), 59–79; Godman, *Poetry*, 18; and Irvine, *The Making*, 312–13.

scholar of Charlemagne's court, between 782 and 786.[495] In the first half of the ninth century, when the two manuscripts containing Bern Riddle 63 were compiled, Paul would no doubt have already become an iconic author, renowned for his mastery of rhetoric. Seen in this light, the *Paulus* acrostic could simply be an attempt at providing a canonical status to a collection which, as inferred from the introductory phrase found in seven of the surviving manuscripts, was meant to teach the art of rhetoric.[496] If the attribution to Paul the Deacon was intended with the acrostic, this would clearly associate the Bern *Enigmata* with the learned elite of Charlemagne's court, in which riddle making was much appreciated.

Scholars have generally considered a possible connection between the Bern *Enigmata* and Insular riddling tradition. Manitius, for example, affirms that Aldhelm was acquainted with the Bern collection, which was a major source of inspiration, together with that of Symphosius, for the composition of his own *Enigmata*.[497] Tupper, however, tones down the relevance of these riddles as a major influence on Aldhelm's collection.[498] Still, the fact that various Bern Riddles present noteworthy parallels with some of Aldhelm's compositions has led Tupper to conclude that there is a "direct literary connection" and that "the Bern enigmas belong to the same circle of thought as the Anglo-Latin problems."[499] A cursory look at the collection confirms Tupper's inference. For example, in Bern Riddle 5 the table is presented as a mother who willingly gives away everything she bears in her breast to all ("cunctis trado quicquid libens in pectore gesto," 2) but is still treated most unkindly by her children: "quos lactaui, nudam me pede per angula uersant" (6) [those whom

---

495. For these texts, see Neff, *Die Gedichte des Paulus Diaconus*, 60–62 and 64–68. See also Godman, *Poetry*, 9–10 and 82–86; and Garrison, "The Emergence of Carolingian Latin Literature," 121–22.
496. See above on p. 78.
497. See his *Geschichte der christlich-lateinischen Poesie, bis zur mitte des 8. Jahrhunderts* (Stuttgart, 1891), 487–88.
498. Tupper, *The Riddles of the Exeter Book*, xlvii (note).
499. Tupper, *The Riddles of the Exeter Book*, xlvii.

I nursed, turn me upside down naked with my leg[500] in a corner].[501] Apart from paralleling the description of the table in Tatwine's Riddle 29,[502] these clues recall Aldhelm's *Enigma* 1, which characterizes the earth as a nurse whose generous services are unfairly repaid, for her breasts are severely torn by the babies' teeth.[503] A further notable resemblance is found in Bern Riddle 6, in which the goblet, like that of Aldhelm's *Enigma* 80, is personified as a woman readily kissing many men: "et amica[504] libens oscula porrego cunctis" (6) [as a willing girlfriend, I dole out kisses to everyone]. Although the Bern Riddles are preserved only in Continental manuscripts, it is worth noting that the version found in Berlin, Phillipps 1825, also containing Aldhelm's *Carmina ecclesiastica*, might derive from an Insular exemplar. As pointed out by Lapidge and Rosier, "From various orthographical errors it is clear that the Angers scribe was copying from a manuscript of Insular origin, but this has not survived."[505] The connection of the Bern Riddles with an Anglo-Saxon cultural milieu and their possible influence on authors like Aldhelm therefore deserves further analysis.

Interestingly for this study, four of the manuscripts containing the Bern *Enigmata* offer either excerpts of the *Etymologiae* or the entire encyclopedia, thus providing further evidence of the close connection between riddle collections and Isidore's work. Indeed, Bern, Cod. 611 contains some fragments from the *Etymologiae*.[506]

---

500. Note "pede" in singular; the description seems to be that of a one-legged table.
501. Once used, the tablecloth was removed (i.e., leaving the table "naked"), while the leg(s) and board could be dismantled.
502. The correspondences between Tatwine's Riddle 29 and Bern Riddle 5 have been pointed out by Glorie, *CCSL*, vol. 133A, 551, and Williams, "The Riddles of Tatwine and Eusebius," 144.
503. See above, p. 179.
504. The term *amica*, which consistently applies to the woman in the Song of Songs (for example, 1.14), could also conjure up the meaning "concubine, mistress, courtesan."
505. Lapidge and Rosier, *Aldhelm: The Poetic Works*, 39. See also 246 (n. 37).
506. See Strecker, *Aenigmata hexastica*, 734, and Hagen, *Catalogus codicum*

In the case of Vienna, Cod. 67 and Zwettl, Cod. 53—both from the second half of the twelfth century and Graz, Universitätsbibliothek, Cod. 85 (thirteenth century), the Bern collection is preceded by the complete encyclopedia. By the same token, in Chicago, Newberry Library, MS f.11 (first half of the twelfth century), these riddles are followed by an incomplete version of Isidore's *Etymologiae*.[507]

With respect to the compilation of the Bern *Enigmata*, it is necessary to note that the collection usually appears in a fragmentary form. The only manuscript containing all sixty-three riddles is Leipzig, Rep. I.74, and, as Pavlovskis notes, "it is entirely possible that the set was at some point longer."[508] On the other hand, the order of the riddles differs considerably in the codices in which they have been preserved.[509] It is also worth noting that the Bern collection abounds in thematic repetitions, as observed, for example, in Riddles 55–57, all three of which deal with the sun,[510] and Riddles 58 and 59 describing the moon.

In spite of all these irregularities, the Bern *Enigmata* no doubt present an encyclopedic layout (see Appendix VII). The collection opens with an instrumental series revealing a clear emphasis on domestic implements (a cooking pot, lamp, table, goblet, and bag). Most of these objects are vessels or containers that Isidore describes

---

bernensium, 479–80.

507. See Strecker, *Aenigmata hexastica*, 735 (no. 6) and Paul Saenger, *A Catalogue of the Pre-1500 Western Manuscript Books at the Newberry Library* (Chicago: The University of Chicago Press, 1989), 21-22.

508. Pavlovskis, "The Riddler's Microcosm," 229.

509. For discrepancies in the layout of the riddles as found in several manuscripts, see the comparative tables offered in Glorie, *CCSL*, vol. 133A, 542–45. As with Symphosius's and Aldhelm's collections, I follow the ideal order offered in Glorie, *CCSL*, vol. 133A, 542–610, which in turn uses the edition of Strecker, *Aenigmata hexastica*, 732–59 and complements it with the collation of Vatican City, Reg. Lat. 1553, a codex that was not employed by the latter editor.

510. However, as Socas Gavilán, *Antología latina*, 403 (n. 352), points out, the clues of Riddle 55 rather fit the cloud, although the title-solution is "De sole."

in Book XX of the *Etymologiae*. The pot (*olla*) of Bern Riddle 1, for example, is dealt with by Isidore in chapter viii (*De vasis coquinariis*, On cooking vessels), and the lamp (*lucerna*) of Riddle 2 corresponds to an entry in chapter x (*De vasis luminariorum*, On light vessels) of Book XX.[511] The juxtapostion of the cooking pot and the lamp suggests the analogical pairing of the two objects, as both are meant to keep liquids.[512] There are further correspondences of this kind, as with Riddles 6 (goblet) and 7, the latter describing an animal bladder (*uesica*) as a bag that can keep liquid, air (i.e., as a balloon or a ball) or solid things (e.g., as a sausage).[513] The series also includes salt (3) and egg (8), probably as typical elements that could be found in a kitchen, and ends with Riddle 11 (ship), which may have been regarded as a suitable topic because of its relevance to supplying food and provisions of all kinds. With this clear pragmatic concern, the Bern author clearly followed in the footsteps of Symphosius.[514]

Section 2 offers a group of plants and trees, again with a clear focus on their usefulness. Four of these topics appear in Book XVII (*De rebus rusticis*, On rural things) of the *Etymologiae*. As explained earlier in this book, the chapters of Isidore's Book XVII are organized on the basis of a priority principle and a size criterion. Probably acquainted with this distribution, the Bern compilers possibly viewed the bulk of the Isidorean botanical material as being divided into two blocks, selecting a minimum representation of the following categories:

1. cereal (chapter iii), vines (v), trees (vii)
2. aromatic trees (chapter viii), herbs (ix)

Block 1 would thus correspond to topics dealt with in section 2, whereas block 2 represents subjects treated in section 4. The following

---

511. Respectively, XX.viii.2 and XX.x.2.
512. Note that lamps were filled with oil.
513. See Socas Gavilán, *Antología latina*, 389 (ns. 247, 248, 249 and 250).
514. The influence of Symphosius's *Enigmata* on the Bern Riddles is noted, for example, by Ohl, "The Enigmas," 21. Pavloskis has also pointed this out in "The Riddler's Microcosm," 229.

comparative outline can help elucidate the rationale underlying the second series of riddles:

Bern Section 2	Isidore's *Etymologiae*
12. Grain	XVII.iii.4[515]
13. Vine	XVII.v.2
14. Olive tree	XVII.vii.62, 65[516]
15. Palm tree	XVII.vii.1
16. Citron fruit[517]	XVII.vii.8

Grain and vine are clearly prioritized, as both subjects refer to essential food and drink for human beings. Riddles 14–15 describe two trees, thus complying with the contrastive size criterion, if compared to the preceding topics. The two riddles evidently form a pair, since both texts describe fruit trees. In Riddle 16, the clues seem to focus on the fruit of the citron tree, whose medicinal properties were much appreciated.[518] It was possibly the knowledge of the Asian origin of

---

515. This entry actually deals with wheat (*triticum*) but also describes the milling of the grain (*granum*).
516. In the case of the olive tree and the palm tree, Glorie's edition also offers these passages from the *Etymologiae* as the possible sources of some of the clues of these riddles. See *CCSL*, vol. 133A, 560–61.
517. Instead of Glorie's "De cedride" (*CCSL*, vol. 133A, 562), I am here adopting the title-solution "De cedria" offered by Buecheler and Riese, *Anthologia latina*, vol. 1.1, 356, Meyer, "Über die Beobachtung," 420, and Strecker, *Aenigmata Hexasticha*, 743. Also, note that in *CCSL*, vol. 133A, Minst translates "Die Zeder" (cedar tree, ibid., 562), but the riddle seems to refer to the fruit of the citron tree. Socas Gavilán notes the presence of a poetic triad on this fruit in the Latin Anthology; see his *Antología latina*, 392 (n. 274). For these poems, see Buecheler and Riese, ibid., 150–51 (nos. 169–71), and N. M. Kay, ed. and trans., *Epigrams from the Anthologia Latina: Text, Translation and Commentary* (London: Duckworth, 2006), 295–99. Apart from the poems of the Latin Anthology, the knowledge of the citron tree may also derive from Virgil's *Georgics* (II.126–35), a passage alluded to by Isidore (*Etymologiae*, XVII.vii.8).
518. This is, for example, alluded to in Epigram 170 of the Latin Anthology.

the tree that made the Bern compilers regard it worthy of becoming the closing subject of the series.[519]

An interesting textual variant occurs in Vatican City, Reg. Lat. 1553 (fol. 15r), where the title-solution of Bern Riddle 16 is "cedrus" (cedar). Although the riddle clues rather allude to the citron fruit, the compilers probably thought that the reference was to the cedar because of the presence of the palm tree in the preceding riddle.[520] In this sense, the pairing of the two riddle subjects in this manuscript version (see Appendix IX, nos. 49-50) would find a correspondence in Psalm 92.12: "The righteous flourish like the palm tree, and grow like a cedar in Lebanon."[521] This figural analogy would be reinforced by the last line of Bern Riddle 15, in which the palm branch is alluded to as the symbol of the martyrs: "Et amata cunctis flore sum socia iustis" (6) [I am the blooming companion loved by all the righteous]. In the Vatican codex, Bern Riddles 14–16 therefore convey a thematic triad, in which three trees with biblical symbology are offered.[522] Bern section 2 suggests an interest in botanical subjects connected to the Bible, since the grain, the vine, and the olive tree

---

See Socas Gavilán, *Antología latina*, 203 (n. 491) and Kay, *Epigrams from the Anthologia Latina*, 298. Also, see *Etymologiae*, XVII.vii.8.

519. Note that the species is known as *citrus medica*, the latter adjective alluding to the Median or Persian origin of the tree. In *Etymologiae* XVII. vii.8, Isidore alludes to the origin of this name.

520. The close connection between Latin *cedria* and *cedrus* could have originated the confusion of the citron tree and the cedar. As explained by Isidore (*Etymologiae*, XVII.vii.8), the name *citria* stems from the fact that the fragrance expelled by the tree's fruit and leaves resembles that of the cedar (*cedrus*). Also in *Etymologiae* XVII.vii.33, Isidore explains that the *cedria* is the name of the cedar resin used to preserve books. This reference may have similarly contributed to the garbling of the original reference to the citron fruit.

521. The biblical reference is indicated as a source of Riddle 15 (palm tree) in *CCSL*, vol. 133A, 561.

522. For an illustration of the profuse occurrence of the cedar in the Bible, see Lytton John Musselman, *Figs, Dates, Laurel, and Myrrh: Plants of the Bible and the Quran* (Portland, OR: Timber), 90–92.

are also frequently mentioned in the Scriptures.[523] Considered as a whole, the series complies with a typically Isidorean gradation principle, starting with the grain as the smallest item and ending with the cedar, the biggest botanical representative, as might have been mistakenly understood.[524]

Section 3 returns to the intrumental motif of the initial series, although the emphasis is now on the ways in which human beings make the most of the natural resources at hand. The adjacency of Riddles 19 (pitch)[525] and 20 (honey) seems to acknowledge the relationship of two substances that are drawn from nature for the use of human beings. A thematic pair related to apiculture follows—honey (20) and bees (21). The juxtaposition of parchment (24) and letters (25) similarly denotes a duo based on writing motifs. A further pairing is that offered by Riddles 26 (mustard) and 27 (papyrus wick),[526] as the two texts describe the product of a plant. In turn, Riddles 27 and 28 are connected,[527] since the shape of the candle wick can

---

523. On the numerous biblical references to the vine, see Hans Arne Jensen, *Plant World of the Bible* (Bloomington, IN: AuthorHouse, 2012), s. v. "vine." On the prominence of the olive tree in the Scriptures, see Musselman, *Figs, Dates, Laurel, and Myrrh*, 210–13, and for biblical references to grain, see 290–91.

524. As King and Stager point out, "The biblical reference is usually to the stately 'cedar of Lebanon' (Cedrus libani), which may grow as high as thirty-five meters." Philip J. King and Lawrence E. Stager, *Life in Biblical Israel* (Louisville, KY: Westminster John Knox Press, 2001), 110.

525. Instead of "De cera," as provided by Glorie, *CCSL*, vol. 133A, 565, I follow the reading of the title-solution "De pice," which is offered in Buecheler and Riese, *Anthologia latina*, vol. 1.1, 357, Meyer, "Über die Beobachtung," 421, and Strecker, *Aenigmata Hexasticha*, 744. The clues seem to refer to the processing of pitch by heating the resin of a tree in the oven. The last line clearly alludes to the resulting black-colored pitch.

526. Latin *papyrus* is used for the wick of a candle or a lamp (Du Cange, s. v. *papyrus*). The name derives from the papyrus reed from which the fabric for wicks was produced. See Socas Gavilán, *Antologia latina*, 395 (n. 297).

527. Note that the title of *Enigma* 28 is "De serico" (*CCSL*, vol. 133A, 574), where the term *sericus* refers to the silk alluded to in lines 5 and 6, but the initial speaker of the riddle is no doubt the worm (1–3) which describes

be compared to that of the silkworm;[528] also, the wick made from the papyrus plant resembles the silk thread produced by the worm. Finally, the series is closed with Riddles 30–32, three subjects connected to water: fish, water container[529] and sponge.

Section 4, to which I made passing reference at the beginning of this book,[530] is devoted to plants and flowers, with the exception of Riddle 38 (ice).

Bern Section 4	Isidore's *Etymologiae*
33. Violet	XVII.ix.19
34. Rose	XVII.ix.17
35. Lilies	XVII.ix.18
36. Saffron flower[531]	XVII.ix.5
37. Pepper	XVII.viii.8
38. Ice	—
39. Ivy	XVII.ix.22

Accordingly, the series offers subjects included by Isidore in chapter ix (*De herbis aromaticis sive communibus*, On aromatic or common

---

its transformation into a moth (4) and later into luxurious clothes after its death has taken place. See Socas Gavilán, *Antologia latina*, 395 (n. 301).
528. Cf. *Etymologiae* XX.x.2: "Licinius autem quasi lucinius; est enim cicindela lucernae" [(We say) *licinius* (*lychnus* from λύχνος, lamp) but it is close to *lucinius* (glowworm), for it (the wick) is the glowworm of the lamp].
529. As Socas Gavilán, *Antologia latina*, 396 (n. 308), notes Latin *nympha* means "water" but the clues clearly refer to a some kind of vessel to keep water. Also, Du Cange defines *nympæum* as "aquarum receptaculum" (a water container).
530. See p. 4.
531. At the beginning the clues allude to the bulb being buried ("sepulto," 2) in the ground ("sub tellore," 2), but later on, the flower is clearly suggested: "pluchra mihi domus manet" (5) [my beautiful house remains (i.e., after the stigma has been harvested)]. Socas Gavilán, *Antologia latina*, 398 (n. 319). The inclusion of the riddle among flower plants similarly supports the reading of *crocum* as "saffron flower" rather than saffron, the spice.

herbs) of Book XVII. The initial four riddles are clearly interconnected, the first three of which follow very closely the Isidorean order as found in chapter ix. With the exception of the lily, the other three species seem to have been chosen on account of their multiple uses, since the rose, the violet, and the saffron flower were much appreciated for both their fragrance and their beauty as ornamental plants. Besides, they had culinary, medicinal, and cosmetic properties. On the other hand, it might be inferred that the first pair recognizes the rose and the violet as species that are normally propagated either from seeds or from leaf/stem cuttings, whereas the second duo offers the lily and the saffron flower, which originate from a bulb.

Section 5 is a miscellany with no particular common link but several thematic connections can be observed. For example, Riddles 41 (wind) and 42 (ice) are obviously linked on the basis of their being comological subjects. In the case of Riddles 43 (silkworms) and 44 (pearl), the two texts share an interest in describing products deriving from an animal.[532] Toward the end of the Bern *Enigmata*, cosmological subjects predominate conveying a series (no. 6) that was probably meant to bring the collection to a close, although in most codices, as commented above, further pieces were added after Riddle 62 (stars). In fact, despite the presence of clear-cut thematic sections, the Bern *Enigmata* are imperfect in many ways. As mentioned above, even in its most complete version in Leipzig, Rep. I.74 the collection is numerically faulty, as it does not offer a round number. Notwithstanding the representation of cosmological, botanical, and instrumental subjects, it evidently lacks the traditional section on animals. Indeed, only a few zoological motifs are interspersed among the other topics as, for instance, the bees (no. 21) and the sheep (22). It is therefore no surprise to see that the Bern *Enigmata* were subsumed into the Vatican collection, together with some of Symphosius's and Aldhelm's riddles, not only to reach the canonical

---

532. The full title-solution of Riddle 43 is "De uermibus bombycibus sericas uestes formantibus" (On the silworms that make silken clothes). Glorie, *CCSL*, vol. 133A, 589.

hundred but also to provide a more accomplished assemblage with a zoological section and thus conform to the Isidorean compilation model.[533]

3.5.2 The Lorsch Riddles

The Lorsch *Enigmata* constitute a collection of twelve anonymous verse riddles that are uniquely extant in Vatican City, Pal. Lat. 1753 (fols. 115r/v, 117r/v).[534] This codex was most probably compiled in the late eighth century at the Benedictine Abbey of St Nazarius at Lorsch.[535] Founded in 764, this monastic house had well-known Anglo-Saxon affiliations.[536] As discussed above, the codex shows a

---

533. Cf. the final zoological sequence offered by the Vatican collection, including riddles by Aldhelm and Symphosius. See my comments on this further on pp. 281–83.
534. For information on this codex, see Finch, "Symphosius," 6–8 and Pellegrin, et al., *Les manuscrits classiques latins*, vol. 2, Part 2, 400–404.
535. An inventory offered in Vatican City, Biblioteca Apostolica Vaticana, Pal. Lat. 1877 (fol. 30v) lists the contents of a codex, which closely parallel the texts found in the manuscript where the Lorsch Riddles have been preserved. It has therefore been generally assumed that the book described in that catalogue is Vatican City, Pal. Lat. 1753, which was thus most likely produced at St Nazarius at Lorsch. In the sixteenth century many of the codices from this monastery were transferred to Heidelberg and, eventually, confiscated as war booty in 1623 to be carried to Rome. Since then, they have formed part of the Palatine Latin collection of the Vatican Library. For the inventory contained in Vatican, Pal. Lat. 1877 (fols. 1r–34r), see August Wilmanns, "Der Katalog der Lorscher Klosterbibliothek aus dem 10. Jahrhundert," *Rheinisches Museum für Philologie* 23 (1868), 385–410. A commentary on this catalogue is found in Angelika Häse, *Mittelalterliche Bücherverzeichnisse aus Kloster Lorsch: Einleitung, Edition und Kommentar* (Wiesbaden: Harrassowitz, 2002), 71–75. See also Lendinara, "Gli Aenigmata Laureshamensia," 73, n. 3, and Chauncey E. Finch, "Catalogues and Other Manuscripts from Lorsch," *Transactions and Proceedings of the American Philological Association* 99 (1968): 165–79.
536. For the history of Lorsch Abbey and its scriptorium, see Bernhard Bischoff, *Die Abtei Lorsch im Spiegel ihrer Handschriften*, 2nd rev. ed. (Lorsch: Laurissa, 1989), 17–135, and W. M. Lindsay, "The (Early) Lorsch

typical mixture of grammatical texts such as Marius Victorinus's *Ars grammatica* and metrical treatises such as Boniface's *Caesurae versuum*, as well as Aldhelm's *De metris* and *De pedum regulis*. Apart from the Lorsch Riddles, the manuscript includes the *Enigmata* of Symphosius and Aldhelm. The presence of these two collections in a further codex from Lorsch—Vatican City, Pal. Lat. 1719[537]—allows us to conjecture that there may have been a special interest in riddles in the Lorsch scriptorium. This idea seems quite reasonable, since this monastery was an important focus of Anglo-Saxon culture due to permanent contact with Anglo-Saxon missionaries.[538]

As with the Bern collection, some scholars view the Lorsch *Enigmata* as an Anglo-Saxon literary product. In his first edition of the Lorsch Riddles, Ernst Dümmler considered the possibility that these texts could have been composed at Lorsch by imitating earlier collections that had already attained great popularity.[539] He alternatively surmised that they might have been produced in England and later brought from there to Germany.[540] In his second edition of the Lorsch Riddles, Dümmler took a step further and included them among the poems attributed to Boniface under the title *Aenigmata anglica*.[541] In turn, Ebert argued that the Lorsch *Enigmata* betray an acquaintance not only with Aldhelm's Riddles but also with those by Tatwine and Eusebius, consequently proposing an Anglo-Saxon authorship for them.[542] Indeed, some of the clues of the Bern *Enig-*

Scriptorium," in his *Palaeographia latina, Part III* (Oxford: Oxford University Press, 1924), 5–48.
537. On this codex, see Finch, "Symphosius," 6, and Lagorio, "Aldhelm's *Aenigmata*," 23–24.
538. See above pp. 54 (n. 198) and 136.
539. Dümmler, "Lorscher Rätsel," 262.
540. Ibid.
541. Ernst Dümmler, ed., *Aenigmata anglica*, MGH, PLAC, vol. 1 (Berlin: Weidmann, 1881), 20–23.
542. Adolf Ebert, "Zu den Lorscher Rätseln," *ZfdA* 23 (1879): 200–202. See also, for example, the multiple correspondences provided for some of these riddles in Dümmler, ed., *Aenigmata anglica*, 23 (ns. 1, 2, 3, 4, 5, and 6), and Lendinara, "Gli Aenigmata Laureshamensia," 80–85. In *Aldhelm:*

mata are merely borrowings from the riddles of these other authors. To take an example, the description of the beaker of wine offering sweet kisses to the drinking mouths in Lorsch Riddle 5 ("Dulcia quin bibulis tradunt et bassia buccis," 5)[543] closely resembles line 8 of Aldhelm's Riddle 80 on the same subject ("Dulcia compressis impendens basia buccis") and basically paraphrases line 2 of Tatwine's Riddle 4 ("Dulcia quod bibulis prestamus pocula buccis"), in which the letters are compared to sweet cups offered to thirsty mouths.[544]

Further evidence of the connection with Insular riddling is illustrated with Lorsch *Enigma* 8 (egg),[545] which offers a notable resemblance to Pseudo-Bede's *Collectanea* (no. 18), as has been pointed out by several scholars.[546] This text also presents striking affinities with the second Latin enigma extant in St Gall, Cod. Sang. 196 (p. 389), a manuscript which was mentioned earlier in this book.[547] By the same token, in Lorsch Riddle 5 the metaphorical reference to the five fingers holding the cup as the branches of a tree ("Lucidus et laetus quinis considere ramis/ saepe solent . . . ," 1–2) echoes the initial clue offered by riddle no. 2 (cup of wine) as found in St Gall, Cod. Sang. 446 (p. 1), which was also discussed above: "Lucidus et

---

The Poetic Works, 68, Lapidge and Rosier have similarly affirmed that the author of the Lorsch collection "evidently drew inspiration from Aldhelm's *Enigmata*."

543. All citations and references to the Lorsch Riddles are from Fr. Glorie, *Aenigmata Laureshamensia*, *CCSL*, vol. 133, with a German translation by K. J. Minst, 346–58.

544. These parallels have also been noted by Dümmler, ed., *Aenigmata anglica*, 22 (n. 1), and Glorie, *Aenigmata Laureshamensia*, *CCSL*, vol. 133, 351 (Loci paralleli).

545. Note that I here adopt Dümmler's title-solution "De ouo," as offered in *Aenigmata anglica*, 22, instead of "De fetu" (embryo), as proposed by Glorie, *CCSL*, vol. 133, 354.

546. Bayless and Lapidge, *Collectanea*, 122–23 and 205–6; Lendinara, "Gli Aenigmata Laureshamensia," 80.

547. See above, p. 49. For the text of this riddle, see Daly and Suchier, *Altercatio Hadriani*, 144 (n. 91); see also Lendinara, "Gli Aenigmata Laureshamensia," 81.

placidus sedebant in quinque ramis: luci(d)us sedit, placidus pertransiit"⁵⁴⁸ [Lucidus (i.e., the shiny one, the goblet) and Placidus (the gentle one, the wine) were sitting on five branches: the shiny one remained; the gentle one passed through (the throat)].⁵⁴⁹ A similar version of Lorsch Riddle 7, which plays on the closeness of the noun *castanea* (chestnut) and the adjective *casta* (chaste), is offered in St Gall, Cod. Sang. 446.⁵⁵⁰ The fact that further variants of this text have been detected by Dümmler suggests that the chestnut logogriph could have enjoyed much popularity in Continental tradition.⁵⁵¹ On the other hand, Andrew Galloway has commented on the remarkable similarities observed in a Latin version included in an extant collection from the mid-fifteenth century in London, British Library, MS. Harley 3362 (fol. 33r).⁵⁵² The presence of this riddle in the Harley manuscript suggests that the chestnut enigma could have evolved in English tradition from an early medieval specimen similar to that found in the Lorsch collection.

It is worth noting that the scriptorium in which Vatican City, Pal. Lat. 1753 originated was under the direction of Ricbod, a former student of Alcuin at Charlemagne's court (c. 780), who held the abbacy of Lorsch between 784 and 804. Interestingly, Bischoff considers this manuscript among the group of twenty-five surviving codices from Ricbod's scriptorium.⁵⁵³ A further important aspect to

---

548. See p. 49. This text is cited from Ernst Dümmler, "Lateinische Rätsel," 422.
549. In other words, the wine disappeared and only the goblet remained. My translation. I take the first "lucidus" and "placidus" as proper names, but in the second part of the riddle these terms function as adjectival predicatives that punningly refer to the goblet and wine. I thank María del Mar Gutiérrez-Ortiz for kindly pointing this out to me.
550. For this text, see Dümmler, "Lateinische Rätsel," 422.
551. For other Continental versions, see ibid., 421, and *Aenigmata anglica*, 22 (n. 5). Also, see Glorie, *CCSL*, vol. 133, 353. The case of the chestnut enigma may thus be compared to that of the turtle-dove riddle, mentioned earlier in this book.
552. Galloway, "The Rhetoric of Riddling," 100, no. 23 (n. 121).
553. Bischoff, *Manuscripts and Libraries*, 95–96.

take into account is the fact that two other codices offering works by Anglo-Saxon authors form part of this group—notably, Vatican City, Pal. Lat. 1746, which contains the *Ars Tatuini* and the *Ars Bonifatii*,[554] and Paris, Bibliothèque Nationale, Lat. 16668, which includes Bede's *De arte metrica* and Aldhelm's poetic *De virginitate*.[555] W. M. Lindsay has pointed out that these two manuscripts, together with Vatican, Pal. Lat. 1753 and other codices of Lorsch provenance, display outstanding similarities in their script, arguing that these resemblances are probably due to the influence exerted by Anglo-Saxon missionaries at St Nazarius.[556] Given that significant parallelisms with Aldhelm's works, particularly from the verse treatise on virginity and the Riddles, have been noted by Glorie and Lendinara in the Lorsch *Enigmata*,[557] it is reasonable to assume that Vatican City, Pal. Lat. 1753 was certainly in the Anglo-Saxon sphere of influence.

The lack of homogeneity of the Lorsch Riddles has led scholars to think that they may be the work of various authors. Lendinara, for example, comments that the Lorsch collection seems to be a florilegium or anthology by diverse writers.[558] Indeed, the varied length—ranging from fourteen lines as observed in Riddle 2 to only two in the case of Riddle 8—might be an indication of multiple authorship. Lendinara suggests comparing the method of compilation of Vatican City, Pal. Lat. 1753 with that of Pal. Lat. 1746 (late eighth or early ninth century), the latter described by M. de Marco as a mixed assemblage combining various grammatical treatises, with Tatwine's

---

554. As Irvine has pointed out, the final part of this manuscript, offering Tatwine's and Boniface's grammatical treatises, constitutes "a distinctively Insular corpus," suggesting "an Anglo-Saxon line of textual transmission to the Lorsch scriptorium of the late eighth or early ninth century." *The Making*, 349.
555. See Bischoff, *Manuscripts and Libraries*, 96.
556. Lindsay, "The (Early) Lorsch Scriptorium," 45–46.
557. For Aldhelm's influence, see specially Lendinara, "Gli Aenigmata Laureshamensia," 85–89. See also Dümmler's notes in *Aenigmata anglica*, 20–23, and those present in *CCSL*, vol. 133, 347–58.
558. Lendinara, "Gli Aenigmata Laureshamensia," 76. This hypothesis has been recently corroborated by Lockett, *Anglo-Saxon Psychologies*, 276.

and Boniface's *Artes* among them, from diverse areas and periods, which were at some point put together and studied at Lorsch.[559]

Before dealing with the compilation of the Lorsch *Enigmata* in particular, it is necessary to comment on the eclectic presentation of the Riddles as they are displayed in Vatican City, Pal. Lat. 1753. Like the preceding riddles from the collections of Aldhelm and Symphosius extant in this codex,[560] Lorsch Riddles 1–4 and 7 occur in a continuous format; in other words, the lines are presented without verse separation being marked. As Leslie Lockett has noted, this is most unusual for Latin poetry and points to a connection with early Anglo-Saxon practice.[561] Conversely, Riddles 5, 6, 8, and 9–12 adhere to the convention of presenting line breaks. This may suggest either that the scribe was experimenting with the two formats as (s)he copied the texts or, alternatively, that (s)he copied Riddles 5–12, probably with the exception of 7,[562] at a later time when the presentation in lines of verse had become the norm.

---

559. Lendinara, "Gli Aenigmata Laureshamensia," 76; M. de Marco, "Letture grammaticali a Lorsch," *Aevum* 31 (1957): 273–77, esp. 275 and 277. For a detailed account of the contents of Vatican City, Pal. Lat. 1746, see Irvine, *The Making*, 345–49.
560. Note, for example, that Aldhelm's preface (fols. 87r–87v) is presented in the usual format of Latin verse, probably on account of the acrostics and telestichs. By contrast, the end of poetic lines is marked only by means of punctuation in the remainder of the riddles in this collection (fols. 87v–92r). Symphosius's preface and riddles are displayed in a similar way (fols. 110v–13r).
561. Lockett, *Anglo-Saxon Psychologies*, 276. As O'Brien O'Keeffe explains, "From the eighth century on, Latin poetry in England was copied in lines of verse." Katherine O'Brien O'Keeffe, *Visible Song: Transitional Literacy in Old English Verse* (Cambridge: Cambridge University Press, 1990), 26. Among the early illustrations of this practice, she mentions St Petersburg, Q.v.I.15, which offers Aldhelm's *Enigmata* in separate verse lines and has been directly associated with Boniface by several scholars. See ibid., 26 (n. 9) and in this book (p. 79).
562. Written in a significantly smaller script and marked with a cross (fol. 117r), Riddle 7 might have been copied earlier, as if the scribe were waiting to obtain more material to continue the collection.

The second conjecture is supported by the fact that the Lorsch collection does not present the riddles in a continuous sequence in the manuscript. In fact, these texts were combined in the Vatican compilation with two other works: the *Caesurae versuum*, attributed to Boniface, and the poem known as "Dombercht's Epitaph." Riddles 1 and 2 are the only two poems offered on folio 115r, right after the *Caesurae versuum*, which is interrupted at the end of folio 114v.[563] On account of the majuscules offered at the final phrase ("quare poetae") at the right bottom of folio 114v, it seems that the scribe deliberately interrupted the copying of the metrical tract and introduced the first two riddles on folio 115r and two more (nos. 3 and 4) on 115v. Interestingly, the *Caesurae versuum* resumes on the following leaf (fol. 116r) with an excerpt from Isidore's *Etymologiae* (VIII.vii.3), offering the explanation of *uates* (poet), probably on account of "poetae," the term at which the tract stopped on folio 114v. The metrical treatise is unfinished, but the scribe left enough blank space, we may infer, to continue it at some point.[564]

On folio 116v, "Dombercht's Epitaph,"[565] which presents neither verse delimitation nor an *incipit*, follows the *Caesurae versuum*.[566]

---

563. The metrical tract begins on folio 114r, where the name "*Sancti* Bonifatii" occurs next to the *incipit*.
564. Note that in this codex the final passage ends with "*per* simplici" (fol. 116r), which corresponds to "per simplices" in line 124 of Gebauer and Löfsted, *CCSL*, vol. 133B, 113. A short passage on the description of the main metrical feet (i.e., lines 125–31 of this edition) is therefore missing.
565. This poem is edited in Ernst Dümmler, ed., *Bonifatii carmina*, *MGH*, *PLAC*, vol. 1 (Berlin: Weidmann, 1881), 19–20 (no. 7).
566. On the basis of the passage written in majuscules at the end of this poem (116v)—"Rogo te domine pater ut emendas (sic) et corrigas" [I beg you father to emend and correct]—Lindsay conjectures that the scribe of Vatican City, Pal. Lat. 1753 could be the author of "Dombercht's Epitaph," possibly himself a pupil of the latter. Lindsay, "The (Early) Lorsch Scriptorium," 45. Neff in turn considers that the closing passage could indicate that the author was a novice writer. Arguing that the epitaph presents the typical style of Carolingian poetry of this period, this scholar speculates that the writer might be a student of Peter of Pisa on account of the verbal

Dombercht was an Anglo-Saxon student of Boniface who eventually became a priest and a teacher at Lorsch, thus adding further weight to the hypothesis of the Anglo-Saxon connection of this manuscript and some of its contents. In this poem, Dombercht is described as well versed in the study of grammar and the principles of metrics,[567] two of the disciplines that are represented in Vatican City, Pal. Lat. 1753. This might have triggered the inclusion of this poem honoring Dombercht at this point. On the other hand, the combination of grammatical works, riddles, and an obituary poem found in the Vatican codex recalls the early-eleventh-century Antwerp flyleaf in which Bishop Ælfric was honored in a similar way.[568]

After "Dombercht's Epitaph," Riddles 5–8 occur on folio 117r and are followed by nos. 9–12 on folio 117v. The wide blank spaces left in folios 115r/v and 117r suggest that the compilers expected to add more pieces but at some point the collection was left incomplete.[569] Several riddles—notably, 3 and 4 (fol. 115v) plus 6 and 7 (fol. 117r)— are accompanied by a cross, a sign that, we may infer, intended to mark the place where the text should later be added. The prospect of inserting further texts for the collection may also explain why the first four riddles do not offer verse separation. Once the compilers realized that they could not provide more pieces, they started to mark verse lines in what are now the final riddles of the series, as there was not much else to be added. It may thus be reasonably assumed that the Lorsch *Enigmata* represent a faint attempt at offering a riddle collection, the progress of which was possibly hampered because the compilers failed to supply—or maybe to compose— enough riddles to offer a larger collection. The empty space of folio 115v was eventually filled in with pen-trials, which seems to indicate

---

parallels found in the works of the latter poet. *Die Gedichte des Paulus Diaconus*, 178–80.
567. "Grammaticae studio, metrorum legibus aptus" (11). Dümmler, *Bonifatii carmina*, 20.
568. See above, pp. 46–47.
569. Lendinara similarly suspects that the collection was unfinished. "Gli Aenigmata Laureshamensia," 76.

that the prospective incorporation of further pieces was ultimately abandoned. All in all, the assemblage no doubt suggests improvisation and, possibly, the composition of riddles at the same time the compilation was produced.

Embedded between two parts of Boniface's metrical treatise, the Lorsch Riddles imitate the presentation of Aldhelm's *Enigmata* located between *De metris* and *De pedum regulis* in the preceding part of Vatican City, Pal. Lat. 1753.[570] The deliberate emulation of this pattern might have occasioned the interruption of the *Caesurae versuum*, thus introducing the first batch of riddles. If the insertion of the initial four Lorsch Riddles was intended to indicate that they were thought to be by Boniface or, like "Dombercht's Epitaph," by a student of the same school is an interesting conjecture but is, however, hard to prove.

As extant in the manuscript, the Lorsch Riddles are not accompanied by the title-solutions;[571] these were supplied by Dümmler's first edition.[572] As regards their compilation, the collection shows signs of having been arranged in an encyclopedic way, at least in the first part (see Appendix VIII). The first thematic section conveys the two opening riddles, which were initially solved by Dümmler as man and soul, respectively.[573] Gaston Paris proposed Latin *cor* for *Enigma* 2 on the basis of the biblical passage "I slept, but my heart was awake" (Song of Songs 5.2),[574] which seems to be echoed in the firt line:

---

570. In this manuscript, *De metris* begins on folio 82v, the *Enigmata* occupy folios 87r-92r, and *De pedum regulis* starts on folio 92v.
571. The collections of Symphosius and Aldhelm in the same manuscript are, by contrast, preceded by the *capitula*, which offer the title-solutions to the riddles.
572. Dümmler, "Lorscher Rätsel." In his second edition of the Lorsch Riddles (*Aenigmata anglica*), Dümmler modified some of the solutions; later on Ebert provided a revision of some of them in his "Zu den Lorscher Rätseln," 200–202.
573. Dümmler, "Lorscher Rätsel," 262.
574. Gaston Paris, review of *ZdfA* 22 (1878), *Romania* 8 (1879): 139. Lockett has recently supported Paris's solution, arguing that Riddle 2 should be solved as *cor* or Old English "*breostsefa* (the mind-in-the heart)." *Anglo-Saxon Psychologies*, 277.

"Dum domus ipsa mea dormit, uigilare suesco . . ." [When my own house sleeps, I usually remain awake]. This solution was accepted by Dümmler in his second edition of the Lorsch Riddles.[575] The term *cor* could be suitable as an answer, as it also signifies "heart, soul, feeling"; in other words, it includes the concept "soul." Glorie, however, offers "De anima," thus maintaining Dümmler's first proposal "menschliche Seele" (the human soul), which is thus offered in K. J. Minst's translation for the *CCSL* edition.[576] The mini-section therefore seems to parallel Isidore's explanation of *homo* and *anima*, two concepts that occur jointly at the beginning of chapter 1 of Book XI (*De homine et partibus eius*, On the human being and his parts).[577] Given that there is a large blank space in folio 115r containing these riddles, it may be tentatively conjectured that further pieces dealing with parts of the human body might have been intended to be inserted in this section.

The second group of riddles is clearly composed of cosmological motifs, starting with the description of water (no. 3) and ice (4), which might have been designed as a pair. After the second part of the *Caesurae versuum* and "Dombercht's Epitaph," section 2 resumes with Riddles 5 (cup of wine) and 6 (snow). With the exception of Riddle 5, the components of the cosmological series arise: water (rain),[578] ice, and snow. Though interrupted, this triad recalls the meteorological subjects of Symphosius's section 2, which was similarly based on the cycle of water.[579] The third section is no doubt a miscellany, as it offers no coherent organization. Though separated

---

575. Dümmler, *Aenigmata anglica*, 21.
576. Glorie, *CCSL*, vol. 133, 348. Dümmler, "Lorscher Rätsel," 262.
577. The two concepts are defined in *Etymologiae* XI.i.4–8.
578. Dümmler, *Aenigmata anglica*, 21, proposed the editorial solution "De nube" for this riddle, although Glorie's "De aqua" (*CCSL*, vol. 133, 349) seems to me preferable, for the clues of Lorsch *Enigma* 3 are entirely devoted to describe the cycle of water, as it evaporates from the ocean and later falls down on both land and sea in the form of rain.
579. See above (p. 145) and Bergamin, *Aenigmata Symposii*, 92. Riddle 3 (water) is therefore most appropriate to head this cosmological mini-series.

by a large empty space in folio 117r, the subsequent presentation of Riddles 7 (chestnut) and 8 (egg) might have been meant to acknowledge the relationship of two objects possessing a a hard shell. Riddle 12 (ink), a writing topic, brings the collection to an end. As in the case of Symphosius's opening topic (stylus), the closing of the Lorsch collection reveals some concerns with structural coherence.

What makes the Lorsch *Enigmata* most interesting for this study is the fact that the lack of solutions, the varied length, and the discontinuous layout recall the case of the Exeter Book Riddles. The analysis of the structure of the Lorsch *Enigmata* has also illustrated that the compilation of a riddle collection was not always a lineal process but could instead be subject to occasional breaks, which could motivate the inclusion of non-riddling works, as observed in *Caesurae versuum* and "Dombercht's Epitaph." Finally, as the layout of the Lorsch *Enigmata* suggests, it should be borne in mind that the riddling materials could be simultaneously provided as the manuscript was copied.

3.5.3 The Vatican Collection

Vatican City, Biblioteca Apostolica Vaticana, Reg. Lat. 1553 is a manuscript from Lorraine, whose first part, dating from the early ninth century, contains Boniface's *Enigmata* (fols. 1r-8v) and a composite riddle collection that I have called the Vatican *Enigmata* (fols. 8v-21v).[580] Finch has demonstrated that the version of Boniface's Riddles in this manuscript is very close to that found in St Petersburg, F.v.XIV.1,[581] a late-eighth-century codex from Corbie, which was mentioned before.[582] As the Anglo-Saxon connections with both Corbie and

---

580. For information on this manuscript, see Finch, "The Bern Riddles in Codex Vat. Reg. Lat. 1553"; Élisabeth Pellegrin, et al., *Les manuscrits classiques latins de la Bibliothèque Vaticane*, vol. 2, Part I (Paris: Éditions du Centre national de la recherche scientifique, 1982), 263–64; and Henry Marriott Bannister, *Monumenti vaticani di paleografia musicale latina* (Leipzig: Harrassowitz, 1913), 99–100.
581. Chauncey E. Finch, "The Text of the Aenigmata of Boniface in Codex Reg. Lat. 1553," *Manuscripta* 6 (1962): 25.
582. See above pp. 17 and 137.

Lorraine are well-known,[583] we should not preclude the possibility that the Vatican collection may have originated in an Insular milieu.

The Vatican assemblage offers fifty-two pieces from the Bern *Enigmata*, forty-five from Symphosius's, and five from Aldhelm's.[584] This riddle collection thus illustrates a traditional medieval method of compilation, which involved the culling and rearranging of pre-existing material into a new format. As Bischoff explains, this was a typical practice in the context of the Carolingian revival of education:

> when specific textbooks had not yet been adopted, the teachers' personal collections of materials for instruction must have played a significant role in instruction at school. Extant manuscripts which fall outside the normal categories indicate that the school master had considerable freedom in deciding what and how to teach.[585]

The hybrid riddle collection of Vatican City, Reg. Lat. 1553 therefore illustrates the idiosyncrasies of a compilation process, in which texts from three different sources were used. Accordingly, the particular didactic interests of a given *magister* could have guided the Vatican compilation. In this sense, we must not forget the conspicuous educational character of riddle collections, as well as their close relation to both grammatical treatises and encyclopedias, as discussed earlier in this monograph.[586]

In its current state, the Vatican collection comprises one hundred two riddles, but it must be noted that the scribe did not count thematic repetitions. Following *Enigma* 7 (ice), Vatican Riddle 8 (ice), for example, has no Roman numeral, although the title-solution "Glaties" clearly marks it out as an independent text (fol. 10r). After

---

583. See above pp. 17-19 and 27.
584. The collection offers the following heading (fol. 8v): "Incipit prologus Symphosii super enigmata quaestionum artis retoric*ae*." This is a variant of the phrase that typically introduces the Bern Riddles in six other manuscripts (see above, p. 78, n. 284).
585. Bischoff, *Manuscripts and Libraries*, 100. For a similar discussion of the phenomenon of medieval compilation, see Irvine, *The Making*, esp. 428–29.
586. See above pp. 74–87.

Riddle 42 (wine), *Enigma* 43—actually, Bern no. 63 (wine) with the *Paulus* acrostic—similarly bears no numeral but is clearly differentiated from the other texts with the title "uinum" (fol. 14r). In the two cases, the numbering resumes after Riddles 8 and 43.[587] The scribe consistently adhered to this practice, for (s)he did not assign a number when two adjacent riddles with an identical answer were offered.[588] But on one occasion, the textual boundaries were clearly misinterpreted, as appreciated in Riddles 77 (fire) and 78 (sun), which occur as a single text with the title "ignis" and the Roman numeral LXVIII (fol. 18v) for both of them. A further solution appears as "ignis sintilla (sic)" (spark of fire) next to line 6 of Riddle 77 on the right margin of folio 19r,[589] probably in an attempt to distinguish the two texts once the erroneous blending had already taken place.[590]

---

587. Riddle 7 (ice) is, for example, assigned the numeral VII (fol. 9v) but *Enigma* 9 (snow) counts as number VIII (fol. 10r) for the Vatican scribe, thus obviously not counting the second ice version. By the same token, Riddle 42 (wine) occurs as number XXXVIII (fol. 13v) and *Enigma* 44 (honey) is assigned number XXXVIIII in the manuscript (fol. 14r).

588. Note, however, that Vatican Riddles 68 (garlic) and 69 (onion) are both numbered (fol. 17v). Even though the two texts describe an onion, the solution "Alium" occurring as a heading of Riddle 68 probably made the scribe think it had a different answer from that of *Enigma* 69. In the case of Riddles 84 (lantern) and 85 (lamp), the scribe again distinguishes the two texts by providing numerals for each one (fols. 19v-20r).

589. The use of this redundant solution suggests a certain degree of improvisation in the Vatican assemblage. Also, note that the editorial formula for the headings changes from folio 10r onwards. The initial title-solutions are offered as "De + noun" (e. g., "De caelo") in the first seven riddles, but from *Enigma* 8 on a single noun consistently occurs (e.g., "Glaties").

590. The collection offers further errors of appreciation, but these do not affect the numbering of the riddles. For example, the scribe mistakenly assigns the heading "Edera" (ivy) to Vatican Riddle 53 (fol. 15v), which corresponds to Bern *Enigma* 31 ("De nympha," On the water container, as offered in *CCSL*, vol. 133A, 577). Obviously, this heading was anticipating the solution of Riddle 54, which is subsequently introduced as "Edere." Again, we observe the same problematic interpretation with Riddle 81 (fol. 19r), entitled "Verbum" (word), although the clues allude to the sun, the

With this scribal numbering practice, the Vatican assemblage comprises a total of ninety-one pieces. The numeral LXXXXII, however, occurs at the bottom of folio 21v. It may thus be inferred that this number was probably meant for the subsequent riddle, which has however not been preserved, even though the numeral is not accompanied by a title-solution, as is common in the manuscript.[591] As Finch conjectures, it is therefore possible that the Vatican Riddles originally amounted to one hundred pieces and that the final part of the manuscript, with at least nine further riddles, was probably "lost by mutilation."[592] This hypothesis may also be supported by the fact that the collection evidently lacks a coda.

As Finch notes further, "The riddles of the three different collections represented have been rearranged by subjects, with those dealing with the same topic grouped together."[593] In this rearrangement, analogy once more played an essential role. After Symphosius's preface, which the Vatican compilers adopted as an introduction to the *Enigmata*, there follows a typical cosmological section composed of ten riddles, seven of which are from the Bern collection and the last three from Symphosius's (see Appendix IX). The series offers evident analogical connections, as illustrated with the pair formed by sun and moon (nos. 2 and 3), as well as the meteorological string—wind (5), rain (6), ice (7 and 8), snow (9), and fog (10)—which clearly recalls Symphosius's second section as well as Lorsch section 2.

A miscellany occurs next, although a general common factor

---

subject and text corresponding to Bern *Enigma* 56 (*CCSL*, vol. 133A, 603). This heading was probably intended as the solution for subsequent Riddle 81 (letter), which is introduced on folio 19v with the title "littera." We may conjecture that the scribe was copying the material from an exemplar with a different editorial practice regarding title-solutions, which may have been presented in the margins or in some other place, thus consequently provoking the erroneous assigment of some of the headings.

591. As illustrated with *Enigma* 4, number IIII and the title "De stellis" occur on folio 9r; the text of the riddle follows next on 9v. This is similarly done with Riddles 12, 16, 21, and 77.

592. Finch, "The Bern Riddles in Codex Vat. Reg. Lat. 1553," 146.

593. Ibid.

seems to be at work here, since most of the subjects of section 2 have to do with water in some way or another: water (and) fish (no. 11),[594] fish (12), hook (13), salt (14), bridge (15), ship (16 and 17), anchor (18), frog (19), and so forth. The first six riddles of this series consistently alternate pieces deriving from the Bern and Symphosius's collections. On the other hand, the compilers offered thematic duplications, clearly aiming at contrasting two versions of the same topic from the two main sources. This is the case of the ship in Riddles 16 and 17, correlating with Bern *Enigma* 11 and Symphosius's Riddle 13, respectively. This is also observed in the two sponge versions (nos. 27 and 28), which offer Bern *Enigma* 32 and Symphosius's Riddle 63. The Vatican *Enigmata* provide some interconnections that simply reproduce thematic links observed in the original sources, as illustrated with Riddles 19–21, which offer frog, turtle, and snail, three subjects that correspond to Symphosius's *Enigmata* 19, 20, and 18. Another example of this is provided by the pairing of Vatican Riddles 23 (pipe) and 24 (well), respectively Symphosius's *Enigmata* 72 and 71. Further thematic clusters based on analogy have been devised by the Vatican compilers, such as the triad formed by Riddles 11 (fish [and] river), 12 (fish), and 13 (hook). Similarly, the juxtaposition of Riddles 25 and 26 associates the skin bag (Latin *uesica*) used to keep liquids or solids[595] with the bellows, an object that is also made of animal skin (*uter*) and filled with air.

In the third section, agricultural topics clearly predominate. As in the preceding series and throughout the collection, the compilers indulge in duplication by presenting riddles with identical solutions from different sources. That is the case of the pairing of Riddles 33 (earth) and 34 (earth), which link Bern Riddle 45 and Aldhelm's *Enigma* 1; a further doublet is given by the juxtaposition of the two wine pieces (42 and 43), relating Bern Riddles 50 and 63; by the

---

594. Note that the solution of Riddle 11 is slightly different from Symphosius's counterpart (no. 12), as the Vatican manuscript offers the heading "Aqua piscis" (water [and] fish) on folio 10r.

595. See above, p. 258 for the explanation of Bern Riddle 7 on that subject.

same token, Riddles 55 and 56 offer two enigmas on the broom that correspond to Bern Riddle 18 and Symphosius's *Enigma* 80. The components of section 3 also provide analogical interconnections that have been directly drawn from the original collections in which these riddles appear. This is the case of the botanical trio formed by the mallow, the beet, and the gourd, as observed in Vatican *Enigmata* 30–32, which slavishly reproduce the cluster offered by Symphosius's Riddles 41–43. The pair formed by Vatican nos. 44 (honey) and 45 (bee) actually conveys Bern Riddles 20 and 21; *Enigmata* 46 (spiced wine) and 47 (wine turned to vinegar) simply repeat the duo offered by Symphosius's Riddles 83 and 84. By the same token, the trio formed by nos. 48–50 provide the olive tree, the palm tree, and the cedar in the same order as found in the Bern collection (nos. 14–16).[596] The Vatican compilers also sought to yield new riddlic associations in section 3, as exemplified with the farm subjects offered by *Enigmata* 36 (millstone) and 37 (grain), 39 (flour) and 40 (sieve), as well as 41–43 linking the vine and its product, wine.

Despite the occurrence of three exceptional motifs, section 4 offers a rather cohesive selection of botanical subjects, drawn mainly from the Bern *Enigmata*. A choice of flower plants is thus illustrated: rose (nos. 57 and 58), lily (59), saffron flower (60), violet (63), mustard (64),[597] and poppy (65), all of them useful to human beings in multiple ways. The series then presents two further plants which were similarly selected from a pragmatic point of view: the papyrus (66),[598] which was employed to make candle wicks, and hay (67), which was used as cattle fodder. Finally, a representation of two vegetables is offered with onion (68 and 69) and pepper (70 and 71).

---

596. Note that Bern Riddle 16 actually describes the citron fruit. See my discussion (pp. 259–61) of the variant solution offered by Vatican Riddle 50, whose heading ("cedrus") clearly indicates that the compilers understood that the cedar tree was meant.
597. Here probably viewed as a flower plant.
598. Note that in the manuscript, the title-solution of *Enigma* 66 is "paparium," which may be a misreading of "Pap[irum igni]arum," the candle wick produced from the papyrus plant, as inferred by Glorie, *CCSL*, vol. 133A, 573.

With the exception of the silkworm pair (nos. 61 and 62), the botanical topics of section 4 mostly correspond to themes dealt with by Isidore in Book XVII, notably from chapters ix (*De herbis aromaticis sive communibus*, On aromatic or common herbs) and x (*De oleribus*, On vegetables), as observed in the table below:

Vatican Section 4	Isidore's *Etymologiae*
57. Rose (B34)[599]	XVII.ix.17
58. Rose (S45)	XVII.ix.17
59. Lily (B35)	XVII.ix.18
60. Saffron flower (B36)	XVII.ix.5
61. Silkworms (B43)	—
62. Silkworm (B28)	—
63. Violet (B33)	XVII.ix.19
64. Mustard (B26)	XVII.x.9
65. Poppy (S40)	XVII.ix.31
66. Papyrus wick (B27)	XVII.ix.96
67. Hay (S50)	XVII.ix.107
68. Onion (B51)	XVII.x.14
69. Onion (S44)	XVII.x.12
70. Pepper (B37)	XVII.viii.8
71. Pepper (A40)	XVII.viii.8

Interestingly, pepper, for which two versions from the Bern collection and Aldhelm's *Enigmata* are offered, occupies a prominent position as Vatican Riddles 70 and 71, the closing topics of the series. This vegetable is further distinguished in section 4 as the only subject that has been drawn from chapter viii (*De aromaticis arboribus*, On aromatic trees) from Isidore's Book XVII.[600] The pattern

---

599. Here, as in Appendix IX, abbreviations indicate the sources from which the compiler drew the riddles. Thus, S stands for Symphosius; A, for Aldhelm, and B, for Bern.
600. Cf. pepper as the opening motif in Aldhelm's section 3 (see above, pp. 200-01).

therefore follows previous models of compilation, in which the most sophisticated or exotic themes were used either to introduce or to close a section.

Section 5 is rather miscellaneous, but there are still typical pairings such as Riddles 72 (bench) and 73 (table), 82 (letter) and 83 (parchment), and so forth. The series also seems to offer a faint attempt at providing some subjects that are usually classified as wonders. This is the case of Vatican Riddle 80, offering Symphosius's *Enigma* 95 (one-eyed man selling garlic), and Vatican nos. 86 and 87—actually, Bern Riddle 61 and Symphosius's Riddle 97, both on the shadow. Finally, the Vatican collection, like that of Eusebius, presents zoological topics at its close. When rearranging the zoological material drawn from Symphosius's and Aldhelm's collections, the Vatican compilers used several Isidorean criteria of subclassification, also observed in Symphosius's section 3:

Vatican Section 6	Isidore's *Etymologiae*
A) Small animals/insects	*De minutis animantibus/volatilibus*
89. Bee (A20)	XII.viii.1
90. Ant (S22)	XII.iii.9
91. Fly (S23)	XII.viii.11
92. Weevil (S24)	XII.viii.17
B) Birds	*De avibus*
93. Crane (S26)	XII.vii.14–15
94. Rooster (A26)	XII.vii.50
95. Peacock (A14)	XII.vii.48
96. Crow (S27)	XII.vii.44
97. Bat (S28)	XII.vii.36
C) Big Quadrupeds/Wild Beasts	*De pecoribus et iumentis/De bestiis*
98. Centaur (S39)	**XI.iii.37**
99. Bull (S32)	XII.i.29
100. Phoenix (S31)	**XII.vii.22**
101. She-Mule (S37)	XII.i.57
102. Wolf (S33)	XII.ii.23–24

There are three clear-cut subdivisions, starting with the smallest creatures, continuing with birds, and ending with larger four-footed beasts. A gradation principle based on size was therefore applied.

In addition, an implicit moralization guided the layout of Vatican subgroup 6A, which, following the model of Symphosius,[601] distributes the creatures in contrastive pairs:

    89. Bee (A20)
    90. Ant (S22)
    91. Fly (S23)
    92. Weevil (S24)

By adding the bee from Aldhelm's collection, the Vatican compilers appropriately complemented the triad offered by Symphosius's Riddles 22–24. The bee, the Christian symbol of chastity, thus heads the series and is paired with the ant, a further creature embodying positive qualities. The subgroup was clearly structured in two pairs, in which industrious creatures such as the bee and the ant oppose two parasites, the fly and the weevil.

In the subsequent zoological subgroup, two further riddles from Aldhelm's collection were added to the birds selected from Symphosius's section 3. The Isidorean differentiation between clean and unclean categories can be thus discerned in the twofold structure of subgroup 6B:

    Clean Birds

    93. Crane (S26)
    94. Rooster (A26)
    95. Peacock (A14)

    Unclean Birds

    96. Crow (S27)
    97. Bat (S28)

---

601. Note that the Vatican compilers offered Symphosius's triad in the same order as it was probably found in the source they were using.

In addition, the bat opposes the other birds of the series as it is the only nocturnal bird. These distinctive dichotomies were no doubt devised by the Vatican compilers to instigate the moralizing reading of this part of the collection.

As regards the last zoological series, subgroup 6C is primarily composed of quadrupeds, the only exception being the phoenix (no. 100), which would rather suit the preceding bird mini-series. As a representative of prodigies, the centaur (98) occupies a prominent position leading the quadrupeds. Also, by pairing Riddles 98 and 99, which correlate with Symphosius's Riddles 39 and 32, the compilers recognized the centaur as the resulting offspring from the relationship between Pasiphaë and the bull. As mentioned above, the collection was probably made of one hundred riddles, considering that at least nine pieces may be missing. These lost riddles, we may infer, could have focused on the description of further animals, in all likelihood, aquatic. Also tentatively, a final riddle dealing with a cosmological subject might have been present.

Despite its fragmentary state at the end, the Vatican *Enigmata* therefore illustrate a collection based on an encyclopedic compilation method, which comprises the major subjects covered by Isidore's second decade: cosmology (section 1), instruments (sections 2 and 5), botanical subjects (3 and 4), and zoological motifs (6). The Vatican assemblage therefore constitutes an interesting compilation model, which can be particularly helpful to compare with the Exeter Book Riddles.

Chapter Four

The Compilation of the Exeter Book Riddles

4.1. An Introduction to the Exeter Book Riddles

The Exeter Book Riddles display a number of textual idiosyncrasies that have strongly conditioned scholarly approaches to them. Whereas all the major Latin collections appear in at least two different codices in which solutions are frequently offered in the form of titles, the Old English Riddles have survived only in the Exeter Book with no solutions. For this reason, a great deal of scholarly effort has been put into the solving of these texts. In addition to this, the flawed punctuation that is occasionally observed in some parts of the manuscript has deterred scholars from knowing securely the exact number of pieces that are extant in the manuscript, with the consequent variable numbering of modern editions.[1]

---

1. As will be discussed further in this section, the total number of riddles is still subject to debate. Krapp and Dobbie's edition, for instance, provides ninety-five riddles, while Williamson's offers ninety-one and Muir's ninety-four. George Phillip Krapp and Elliott van Kirk Dobbie, *ASPR*, vol. 3 (New York: Columbia University Press, 1936), 180–243. I have preferred to adopt Krapp and Dobbie's edition and numbering, which I use throughout this book, but I also occasionally adopt different editorial readings when I consider it necessary. By the same token, I have provided modifications of this edition's numbering according to the advances that research has

Toward its conclusion, the manuscript is partially damaged by a diagonal burn that has obliterated some of the riddles contained in the last fourteen folios. Also importantly, there are two substantial textual lacunae that need to be taken into account. A bifolium from Quire XIV (fols. 106–11) was lost, thus affecting the end of Riddles 20 and 40.[2] Similarly, Riddle 70 was considered a single composition until a gap was detected at the end of Quire XVI (fols. 119–25).[3] These incomplete quires and the burn have therefore provoked a considerable loss of text that has hindered our understanding of some of the Exeter Book Riddles in that manuscript area.

A further characteristic of the Exeter compilation that distinguishes it from the Latin collections is that the riddles appear in a discontinuous form in the manuscript. There are two main sequences, Riddles 1–59 (fols. 101r–15r) and 61–95 (fols. 124v–30v), which are separated by a series of poems on diverse subjects.[4] This seems to suggest that the two blocks were actually treated by the

---

produced in the past decades. I have also benefited significantly from the use of Tupper's *The Riddles of the Exeter Book*, W. S. Mackie's *The Exeter Book, Part II*, EETS, o.s. 194 (London: Oxford University Press, 1934), Williamson's *The Old English Riddles*, and Muir's *The Exeter Anthology*.

2. For information on this lacuna, see below, pp. 339–40.

3. See further on pp. 393–94.

4. The material occurring after the first riddle sequence includes the following poems in order of appearance: *The Wife's Lament*, *The Judgment Day I*, *Resignation*, *The Descent into Hell*, *Alms-Giving*, *Pharaoh*, *The Lord's Prayer I*, *Homiletic Fragment II*, *Riddle 30b*, *Riddle 60*, *The Husband's Message*, and *The Ruin*. The titles of these poems accord with Krapp and Dobbie's *ASPR*, vol. 3. In this poetic series, *Riddle 30b* and *Riddle 60* occur on folios 122v and 123r. These two poems have traditionally been considered part of the riddle collection. As Liuzza has demonstrated, *Riddle 30b* is a rhetorically improved version of the piece appearing in the first sequence. For this, see Roy Michael Liuzza, "The Texts of the Old English Riddle 30," *JEGP* 87 (1988): 1–15. Thus, being an isolated riddle variant, I will not consider it for this research. As for *Riddle 60*, the majority of scholars follow Strobl and take this text as the first part of *The Husband's Message*. Joseph Strobl, "Zur Spruchdichtung bei den Angelsachsen," *ZfdA* 31 (1887): 54–64. For these reasons, *Riddle 30b* and *Riddle 60* have not been included in Appendix X

Exeter compilers as two riddle collections.⁵ However, the fact that the two groups add up to almost one hundred poems, the canonical number established by Symphosius and Aldhelm, has led scholars to think that the Exeter Riddles might be a single one-hundred piece collection. However, no significant effort has been carried out in the past decades to determine if this assumption is correct.

The Exeter Riddles are also conspicuous for their formal and stylistic variety, which strongly contrasts with the homogeneity of most Latin compilations. In terms of length, for example, there are riddles that are extremely brief, as is the case with Riddle 75–76 (only two lines), whereas Riddle 40 reaches up to one hundred seven lines in its current fragmentary state. By contrast, as we have seen in the preceding chapters, while formal variation is also typical of Latin collections, this phenomenon is fairly regularly structured on the basis of prosodic principles. In the Exeter Riddles, the treatment of the subjects is equally varied. To take an example, some of the poems display sexual imagery and a vocabulary that is close to the colloquial register (e.g., Riddle 42), while some others deal with more serious matters that are handled with the solemnity the topic requires—for instance, Riddle 26 (Gospel book). The texts similarly range from simple jokes, as in the case of Riddle 75–76 (piss), to erudite puzzles such as Riddle 1-2-3, which virtually consists of a test of encyclopedic meteorological science. These poems thus interestingly exhibit a considerable heterogeneity in terms of form and style while posing diverse degrees of intellectual difficulty for the audience. However, no serious attempt to analyze the underlying reasons for this great diversity has been carried out.

All these features have contributed in one way or another to deflect scholarship from viewing the Exeter Book Riddles as a whole. Thus, the critics' great concern with finding solutions for some of

---

and will not be taken into account with regard to the calculation of the total number of riddles.

5. In the upcoming chapters, I will be referring to the compilers in the plural, as I infer that a team might have collaborated in the task of gathering so many texts for the massive Exeter Book miscellany.

these texts has made them center on the treatment of individual pieces. Not surprisingly, there are hundreds of articles devoted to the solving of particular riddles,[6] but only a few publications deal with riddle sequences or the whole compilation.[7] By the same token, a substantial part of most editions inevitably dwells on the discussion of possible answers for the different riddles.

The discontinuous occurrence of the Exeter Riddles in the manuscript has also contributed to a somewhat fragmentary view of the compilation. Indeed, with the exception of the editions, practically no books have been fully devoted to the research of the Exeter Riddles as a whole. The extreme heterogeneity of the compilation has in turn provoked a preference for some pieces. The bookworm riddle (no. 47), for instance, has always been a favorite of scholarly publications and anthologies of Anglo-Saxon literature.[8] Conversely,

---

6. A notorious example is Riddle 74, to which all these solutions have been proposed: quill pen, cuttlefish, sea-eagle, siren, water, soul, swan, barnacle-goose, ship's figure-head, and boat made of oak wood. For the textual complexities that have made this riddle specially challenging for critics, see my "Direct and Indirect Clues: Exeter Riddle no. 74 Reconsidered," *NM* 99 (1998): 17–29, and Daniel Donoghue, "An Anser for Exeter Book Riddle 74," in *Words and Works: Studies in Medieval English Language and Literature in Honour of Fred C. Robinson* (Toronto: University of Toronto Press, 1998), 45–58.
7. The exceptions are Foley's study of the sequence formed by nos. 53–55, Blakeley's comments on the possible pairing of nos. 21 (plough) and 22 (Charles's Wain), and Meaney's ideas on the tight connection of the bird group (nos. 7–10). See John Miles Foley, "Riddles 53, 54, and 55: An Archetypal Symphony in Three Movements," *Studies in Medieval Culture* 10 (1976): 25–31; Blakeley, "Riddles 22 and 58 of the Exeter Book;" and Audrey L. Meaney, "Birds on the Stream of Consciousness: Riddles 7 to 10 of the Exeter Book," *Archaeological Review from Cambridge* 18 (2002): 120–52. I have dealt with the thematic patterns observed in the sexual riddles in my "The Key to the Body." Also, see my "The Oyster and the Crab" and "Patterns of Compilation."
8. Among other articles, this riddle is the focus of attention of Fred C. Robinson's "Artful Ambiguities in the Old English 'Book-Moth' Riddle," in *Anglo-Saxon Poetry: Anglo-Saxon Poetry: Essays in Appreciation for John C. McGalliard*, ed. Lewis E. Nicholson and Dolores Warwick Frese (Notre

there are other riddles, especially those at the end of the manuscript, that have received hardly any critical attention.

The reliance on the individual treatment of the Exeter Riddles has also deflected our attention from important issues that were brought up by earlier scholars. For example, their cleft occurrence in the poetic anthology gave rise to the question of the unity of the Exeter Riddles.[9] The alleged integrity of the collection was soon ruled out by subsequent scholars on the basis of the enormous heterogeneity observed in the compilation. By discarding the assumption of the unity of the collection, the question of the diverse provenance of the Exeter Book Riddles was raised. Certainly, there is not much uniformity among the riddles of each block; it would therefore be reasonable to suspect that the two main sequences are respectively the result of a coalescence of riddles from different collections and manuscripts carried out by the compilers, who eventually shaped the two groups of riddles into their current layout. Further supporting evidence for this hypothesis is the presence of frequent thematic duplications. Agop Hacikyan has already pointed out that this feature, which rarely occurs in Latin collections,[10] is indicative of the use of various sources for the compilation of the riddles,[11] but no scholar seems to have taken up the challenge to go deeper into this issue.

Dame, IN: University of Notre Dame Press, 1975), 355–62; Ann Harleman Stewart's "Old English Riddle 47 as Stylistic Parody," *Papers in Language and Literature* 11 (1975): 227–41; Geoffrey Russom's "Exeter Riddle 47: A Moth Laid Waste to Fame," *PQ* 56 (1977): 129–36; and John Scattergood's "Eating the Book: Riddle 47 and Memory" in *Text and Gloss: Studies in Insular Language and Literature*, ed. Helen Conrad-O'Briain, Anne Marie D'Arcy, and V. J. Scattergood (Dublin: Four Courts, 1999), 119–127.
9. As discussed by Tupper, *The Riddles of the Exeter Book*, lxxv–lxxix.
10. Only the Bern and Vatican Riddles have showed an interest in providing duplicated subjects, but this is due to the employment of different sources in the compilation process. By contrast, repetition is only occasionally attested in collections by a single author as, for example, illustrated with the two flint riddles (nos. 76 and 77) in Symphosius's *Enigmata*.
11. Agop Hacikyan, *A Linguistic and Literary Analysis of Old English Riddles* (Montreal: Mario Casalini, 1966), 22.

Similarly, modern scholarship seems to have given up the search for the general purpose of a compilation that includes, on the one hand, riddles with notable playful ingredients and, on the other, remarkable intellectual puzzles. The traditional separate assessment of riddles has probably prevented any endeavor to discover if the compilation as a whole was meant for entertainment or rather had a didactic function. Furthermore, with the exception of Patrick W. Conner's insightful comments on the Riddles in *Anglo-Saxon Exeter* (1993),[12] only occasional reference has been made to what their place in the cultural context of the second half of the tenth century might have been.

The formal and stylistic peculiarities of the Exeter Riddles have also had an impact on the way in which scholars have applied different research methods at hand. Investigation in this field has traditionally relied on the search for Latin parallels for the Exeter Book Riddles, with scholars seeking analogues, especially in the earlier riddle counterparts found in the collections by Symphosius, Aldhelm, Tatwine, and Eusebius. This methodological approach has frequently been regarded by critics as a useful way of dealing with the numerous textual challenges posed by the vernacular riddles.[13] Yet, with the exception of a few riddles for which a definite Latin analogue has been detected, no conclusive parallels have been proposed for the remainder of the vernacular collection. On the other hand, most alleged analogues have proved to be useless for the interpretation of obscure or fragmentary passages, nor have they provided any help for solving especially elusive riddles.[14] Besides, this emphasis

---

12. See Conner's *Anglo-Saxon Exeter*, esp. 159–62. For a publication offering a reference to the Riddles in a period-centered study of the manuscript, see Butler, "Glastonbury," 198–99.
13. A classic illustration of this research method is Tupper, "Originals and Analogues of the Exeter Book Riddles."
14. For example, Bitterli compares Exeter Riddle 75 to Aldhelm's Riddle 10 (dog) only to admit the pointlessness of the comparison with the alleged analogue: "For once the Old English Riddle and its Latin counterpart may have little in common." Bitterli, *Say What I Am Called*, 109.

on the vernacular dimension of riddling has consigned Anglo-Latin *enigmata* to a subsidiary position. This traditional stand has thus frequently contributed to undermining our perception of Anglo-Saxon literature as an eminently bilingual culture in which Latin and Old English literary modes intermingled in a more natural way than has been suspected so far. However, publications like F. H. Whitman's *Old English Riddles* (1982), which studies these poems in the context of the preceding Latin riddling trend and the medieval encyclopedic genre, have opened up new channels of investigation, advancing our understanding of the riddling genre.[15] Yet only recently has this view gained any scholarly support. In *Old English Enigmatic Poems and the Play of the Texts* (2006), for example, John D. Niles contemplates the possibility that many of the puzzles posed by the Exeter Riddles might have had an answer in both Old English and Latin.[16]

The absence of solutions in the manuscript has similarly urged scholars to compare the Exeter Riddles with medieval encyclopedias, especially Isidore's *Etymologiae*. Many excerpts of this work have been frequently brought up in an attempt to clarify the interpretation of problematic passages found in the Exeter Riddles. An illustration of this approach is Craig Williamson's admirably learned *The Old English Riddles of the Exeter Book* (1977), in which the contents of these texts are usually contrasted with passages from diverse medieval encyclopedic works. From the appearance of this seminal edition, much scholarly effort has been made in that direction. However, subsequent publications following this methodological approach tend to rely on the parallels observed in the contents and

---

15. Whitman, *Old English Riddles*. This approach is also illustrated in Orchard, "Enigma Variations," in which the author affirms that most of the formal and stylistic features of the Exeter Riddles find an echo in Anglo-Latin riddle collections.

16. For this, see especially his list of solutions for the Exeter Riddles in *Old English Enigmatic Poems and the Play of the Texts* (Turnhout: Brepols, 2006), 141–44. Also, a recent study of the Exeter Book Riddles, Latin *enigmata*, and the folklore roots of these texts is Patrick J. Murphy, *Unriddling the Exeter Riddles* (University Park: Penn State Press, 2011).

pay little attention to the internal organizing principles that seem to be shared by both riddle collections and encyclopedias.¹⁷

In light of this discussion, in the following sections I aim to provide an overall view of the compilation of the Exeter Riddles in an attempt to address issues that have been neglected due to a marked focus on the individual treatment of these texts. This research is not so much a proposal of a new methodology but rather a significantly different approach that will consider the Exeter Riddles in their entirety, both from a structural point of view and in relation to the organizational patterns observed in Latin riddle compilations and Isidore's *Etymologiae*.

4.2. An Encyclopedic Source Collection: Group 1 (Riddles 1–40)

4.2.1 Section 1 (Riddles 1–6)

4.2.1.1 Riddle 1-2-3: An Encyclopedic Test

The thematic focus of the Exeter Book collection can already be perceived in Riddle 1-2-3, formerly known as the "Storm Riddles," a nomenclature that was based on F. Dietrich's interpretation of the text as three separate riddles conveying the description of diverse natural disturbances.¹⁸ Since the appearance of Williamson's edition, most scholars have agreed that Riddle 1-2-3 is a lengthy composition in which three major subdivisions, detailing various meteorological phenomena provoked by the wind, can be detected.¹⁹ Thus, Riddle 1

---

17. In his *Say What I Am Called*, Bitterli provides a discussion of a selected group of riddles that are frequently checked against passages from encyclopedic works. See my review of this book in *Kritikon Litterarum* 39 (2012): 243–48.
18. Dietrich considered Riddle 1 as a description of a storm on land, Riddle 2 as a sea storm, and Riddle 3 as a storm affecting land, sea, and air. Dietrich, "Die Räthsel des Exeterbuchs: Würdigung, Lösung und Herstellung," 459–61.
19. Actually, this riddle had traditionally been printed as three separate

provides a description of a storm on land and Riddle 2 a seaquake. Riddle 3 in turn has three internal subdivisions that successively depict an earthquake (lines 1–16), a sea storm (17–35), and a thunderstorm (36–66).[20] The final lines of Riddle 3 (67–74) function as a recapitulation of the phenomena described in Riddle 1-2-3, since all those natural convulsions seem to be understood as a "storm" that is manifested in three different media: on earth, at sea, and finally in the air.

On the basis of the meteorological information found in various encyclopedic treatises, Williamson convincingly argues that all the natural phenomena depicted throughout Riddle 1-2-3 are actually the varying manifestations of an earthquake.[21] He thus adds that the answer "wind" should also be taken into account for nos. 1 and 2 as well as for the three sections of no. 3, in all of which the wind is always the first-person speaker and the carrier of the various "burdens" (water, land, houses, human beings, and the like).[22] By the

---

texts until Moritz Trautmann edited them as a single composition in *Die altenglischen Rätsel (Die Rätsel des Exeterbuchs)* (Heidelberg: Carl Winter, 1915), 1–4 and 65–68. With the exception of Muir, who has printed the three riddles separately, most scholars have maintained Trautmann's views. See Muir, *The Exeter Anthology*, vol. 1, 287–91 and vol. 2, 576–80. Krapp and Dobbie's first three riddles will likewise be treated here as one text (hence Riddle 1-2-3), although I will also conveniently allude to the three separate sections as nos. 1, 2, and 3, since, as I intend to show, they function as autonomous riddling pieces.
20. According to medieval meteorological lore, all these phenomena were thought to be produced through the agency of wind. See Williamson, *The Old English Riddles*, esp. 132–33.
21. Notably, Pliny's *Naturalis historia* (II.xxxviii.102–3), Lucretius's *De rerum natura* (VI.577–84), Isidore's *De natura rerum* (xlvi), and Bede's *De natura rerum* (xlix). For this, see Williamson, *The Old English Riddles*, esp. 130–32.
22. Before Williamson, Kennedy argued that Riddles 2 and 3 constituted a single composition, with "wind" as the solution, since medieval meteorological lore regarded the wind as responsible for various natural disasters such as storms, seaquakes, and earthquakes. Charles W. Kennedy, *The Earliest English Poetry* (Oxford: Oxford University Press, 1943), 364ff. Williamson

same token, God, as the divine entity controlling the wind, should form part of the triple answer, since the rhetorical questions posed throughout Riddle 1-2-3 seem to point to both the wind as the producer of earthquakes, characterized by harsh "storms" in different media, and to God as the wind's master. The solution of Riddle 1-2-3 therefore involves a three-phase process in which the solver must first determine the type of "storm" (be it on land, at sea or in the air), an intellectual task that would certainly require the knowledge of encyclopedic treatises describing these phenomena as the typical accompaying effects of an earthquake; second, identify the wind as the cause of those atmospheric disturbances; and third, be able to answer that God is the omnipotent force behind those awesome events.[23]

This solving process can be illustrated with Riddle 1, in which the clues clearly allude to the devastating effects of a violent storm. The text thus describes the burning of people's houses: "[ic] folcsalo bærne" (5b); the ravaging of trees: "þonne ic wudu hrere, / bearwas bledhwate, beamas fylle..." (8b-9) [when I stir the wood, the fruitful groves, I destroy the trees];[24] and the flooding affecting both houses and their dwellers: "hæbbe me on hrycge þæt ær hadas wreah / foldbuendra, flæsc ond gæstas, / somod on sunde" (12-14a) [I have on my back what once covered the people, both the flesh and spirits (alike) of the earth-dwellers, all together in the water current]. In this light, it is quite clear that associating the clues' imagery with the description of a storm is the solver's first task.

---

extends Kennedy's proposal to Riddle 1-2-3, which in his view should thus be understood as a single text whose solution is "wind." See his *The Old English Riddles*, 127-41.

23. An interesting parallel is found in the Welsh riddle found in the *Book of Taliesin*. This composition similarly describes the wind as a whimsical creature provoking devastation as it moves throughout the earth. As Haycock points out, this riddle also betrays "a fleeting decoy 'solution,' God." Marged Haycock, ed. and trans., *Legendary Poems from the Book of Taliesin* (Aberystwyth: CMCS, 2007), 329. For an edition of this text, see 332-37. My thanks to Paul Russell for bringing this riddle to my attention.

24. Unless indicated otherwise, the translations of the excerpts from the Exeter Riddles provided in this chapter are mine.

But a riddle always implies a question, either implicit or explicit in the text, which needs to be answered, and the solving process is not complete until a specific word is found for the solution. As Niles has argued, an Old English riddle cannot be solved "until one arrives not just at a *thing* that satisfies all the requisite conditions, but also *a word that designates that thing* in the vocabulary that was current in Anglo-Saxon England during the general period when the Exeter Book poems were compiled and written down."[25] In the case of Riddle 1, the question is expressly provided by the poet and evidently alludes to two entities, whose relationship is metaphorically presented as that of a master and a servant: "Saga hwa mec þecce, / oþþe hu ic hatte, þe þa hlæst bere" (14b–15) [Say who covers me (i.e., God), or what I am called, (I) who bear those burdens (i.e., the wind)]. In view of this discussion, the complete answer to Riddle 1 is therefore threefold: "storm on land," as the question about the natural phenomenon is posed implicitly in the text, plus "wind" and "God."

Riddle 2 should be solved by applying the same method. The reader is thus required to provide three answers, the first of which is "seaquake," as suggested by the description given by the clues:

> streamas staþu beatað, stundum weorpaþ
> on stealc hleoþa   stane ond sonde,
> ware ond wæge,   þonne ic winnende,
> holmmægne biþeaht,   hrusan styrge,
> side sægrundas. (6–10a)

[The streams beat the coasts, and violently throw stone and sand, seaweed and water on the steep cliffs, when I, covered by the power of the ocean, strive to stir the ground, the wide bottom of the sea].

The other two answers, "wind" and "God," simply derive from the explicit question found in the text: "Saga, þoncol mon, / hwa mec bregde of brimes fæþmum, / þonne streamas eft stille weorþað, / yþa geþwære, þe mec ær wrugon" (12b–15) [Say, wise man, who draws (i.e., God) me (i.e., the wind) from the bosom of the sea when the

---

25. Niles, *Old English Enigmatic Poems*, 109; italics in original.

streams, the troubled waves that covered me before, again grow calm].
The reader's encyclopedic knowledge is therefore tested once more.

The internal subdivisions present in Riddle 3—which will henceforth be referred to as sections A (lines 1–16), B (17–35), and C (36–66)—require individual treatment, since a solver should concentrate on the clues depicting three different "storm" phenomena and then on various questions posed throughout. Thus, as with Riddles 1 and 2, Riddle 3A continues the metaphorical presentation of the two responsible agents as master and servant:

> Stille þynceð
> lyft ofer londe ond lagu swige,
> oþþæt ic of enge up aþringe,
> efne swa mec wisaþ se mec wræde on
> æt frumsceafte furþum legde,
> bende ond clomme, þæt ic onbugan ne mot
> of þæs gewealde þe me wegas tæcneð. (10b–16)

[The air looks still over the land and the water silent, until I urge out of my confined place, even as He (God) guides me (wind), (He) who at first, at the beginning of time, laid straps, bonds and fetters, on me, so that I may not escape from His control, (He) who marks the paths out for me].

In this passage, "wind" and "God" are again clearly suggested as answers. Similarly, in Riddle 3B, which reflects on the dramatic consequences of a sea storm with the description of a shipwreck, the wind is once more characterized as a servant who must follow orders: "Þær bið egsa sum / ældum geywed . . . / . . . þara þe ic hyran sceal / strong on stiðweg" (33b–35a) [A certain terror will be revealed to men there . . . which I (the wind) must obey while strong on my rough way].[26] Also importantly, Section B ends with

---

26. Ellipses in this excerpt acknowledge Mackie's inference that "at least two half-lines appear to have been omitted in the MS." *The Exeter Book*, 92. For other alternative readings, see Krapp and Dobbie, *ASPR*, vol. 3, 323.

the explicit question "Hwa gestilleð þæt?" (35b) [Who calms that?], which again underpins the solution "God."

Finally, Section C returns to the master-and-servant clues in the following passage: "þonne hnige eft / under lyfte helm londe near, / ond me on hrycg hlade þæt ic habban sceal, / meahtum gemagnad mines frean" (63b–66) [I then descend again closer to the land under the protection of the air, and, strengthened by the power of my Lord, I bear on my back that which I must have]. The closing section of Riddle 3 (67–74) in turn characterizes the wind as God's "mighty servant" ("þrymful þeow," 67a) and similarly provides an explicit question that directs the reader to the twofold answer "wind/God": "Saga hwæt ic hatte, / oþþe hwa mec rære, þonne ic restan ne mot, / oþþe hwa mec stæðþe, þonne ic stille beom" (72b–74) [Say what I am called, or who lifts me up when I am not allowed to rest, or who holds me so that I am still]. As a whole, lines 67–74 offer a summary of the natural disasters expounded in Riddle 1-2-3, an idea that has been taken by Williamson and other critics as a proof of the rhetorical integrity of these texts.

In view of this analysis, the internal structure of Riddle 1-2-3 reveals that the text virtually functions as various autonomous riddling pieces whose answers need to be sought separately but are also closely interconnected. This reading therefore suggests that Riddle 1-2-3 might have originally constituted separate poems that were at some point fused into a larger piece in order to provide a typically lengthy cosmological (and even also theological) opening, as is characteristic of Latin *enigmata*. This hypothesis is supported by the scribe's inconsistent use of punctuation and capitalization, which reveals a somewhat defective conflation that does not totally conceal the possible composite origin of Riddle 1-2-3. On folio 101r, the typical end-punctuation sign :— occurs at the close of Riddle 1, namely after the word "bere" (15b). At the end of Riddle 2, there is a simple dot after the word "wrugon" (15b), but this mark coincides with the end of the manuscript folio and, as Williamson indicates, "The placing of a simple point after the last word on a MS. page does not indicate the end of a riddle. The manuscript end-page point is a kind of carry-over sign used at the scribe's discretion."[27] Also on folio 101r, a capital H occurs in "Hwylc" (Riddle 1, 1a) and a smaller H in "Hwilum" (Riddle 2, 1a). Besides, the H of Riddle 1 is slightly adorned, whereas the capital in Riddle 2 is unadorned. As Williamson and other scholars have pointed out, this absence of ornamentation and the significantly smaller size of the second H suggest that Riddle 2 is actually a section of a larger poem.[28] These paleographical features led Bernard J. Muir to conclude that "either Riddles 2 and 3 were composed as a single riddle originally, or that at some stage in their transmission, prior to their being copied into the MS, they had fallen together."[29] The hypothetical composite origin of Riddle 1–2-3 may similarly explain the evident overlapping of some of the themes occurring in this text. Indeed, Riddles 1 and 3C deal with the same type of phenomenon, a storm on land, the main difference being the reference to thunder and lightning in the latter. Similarly, Riddles 2 and 3B basically provide a description of a harsh sea storm with the allusion to the shipwreck in the latter as the major thematic divergence between them.

With its introductory role, Riddle 1–2-3 resembles other Latin riddles that appear in similar initial positions. For example, Eusebius's *Enigma* 1 offers an interesting parallel to the Old English composition, as one of the clues characterizes God as a powerful destructive entity: "Agmina deuastans auertor, laesus ab uno" (4) [Harmed by one, I ruin and put to flight armies]. Interestingly, Aldhelm's *Enigma* 2 provides a description of the devastating power of the wind that recalls some passages of Riddle 1–2-3: "Viribus horrisonis ualeo confringere quercus; / nam superos ego pulso polos et rura peragro" (3–4) [I am strong (enough) to crush oaks with my dreadfully sounding might, for I strike the high celestial vaults and travel over

---

27. *The Old English Riddles*, 127. Williamson here cites fols. 101v, 102r, 102v, and 105r as an example of simple dots being used in the same way.
28. See folio 101r of the manuscript in Bernard J. Muir, ed., *The Exeter DVD: The Exeter Anthology of Old English Poetry* (Exeter: Exeter University Press, 2006).
29. Muir, *The Exeter Anthology*, vol. 2, 575.

the fields].³⁰ The affinities with the God/wind topic and the fact that both Eusebius's and Aldhelm's poems occur at the beginning of their respective collections therefore support my contention that Riddle 1-2-3 conforms to the structural and thematic requirements of a collection that was at least initially meant to follow the encyclopedic patterns observed in Latin *enigmata*. Also importantly, the encyclopedic principle underlying the presentation of the storm topics is evident, since the internal sections of this initial composition involve a description of natural phenomena evoking the distinction of the four elements: earth (Riddles 1 and 3A), water (Riddles 2 and 3B), fire, and air—the latter two as suggested in the description of the thunderstorm in Riddle 3C.

4.2.1.2 Riddles 4–6

The thematic coherence of the cosmological introduction is abruptly interrupted, however, with the presence of Riddle 4, which seems to describe a domestic tool of some kind.³¹ Despite this thematic disruption, the object in question and the person manipulating it are described in terms of a master-and-servant relationship, a notion that recalls the clues employed throughout Riddle 1-2-3. Interestingly, the creature is said to have a ring or a band around its neck ("halswriþan," 4a), which echoes the description of the wind in Riddle 3A (lines 13–16), as it was said to be chained with fetters. The co-occurrence of the master-and-servant clues in Riddle 4 might have caused the placing of this composition next to Riddle 1-2-3. It may therefore be conjectured that at some stages of the assembling

---

30. Cf. Riddle 1 (lines 8b–9) cited above on p. 293.
31. Given the great obscurity of the clues, Williamson and other editors classify this riddle as "uncertain." As the compilers of the Exeter Book offered no solutions, some of the riddles are still subject to debate. The compilation issue being the main concern of this monograph, I will avoid any discussion related to controversial solutions unless strictly necessary. A thoroughgoing revision of the Exeter Riddles' answers has been recently provided by Niles in *Old English Enigmatic Poems*. Some of the solutions considered in this monograph are based on Niles's interpretation of the corresponding riddles.

process the compilers possibly sacrificed basic thematic principles of cohesion for the sake of analogical associations of this kind.

Riddle 5 (shield) in turn maintains the thematic rupture, but the cosmological focus is intriguingly retaken with Riddle 6 (sun), suggesting that two exceptional instrumental topics could have been inserted in an originally cohesive cosmological section. In light of this assumption, there are significant links between Riddles 5 and 6 that may explain the presence of the first in this section. To begin with, in the two poems the clues share a typical war context. The shield is personified as a warrior who must endure terrible injuries in combat: "Ic eom anhaga iserne wund, / bille gebennad, beadoweorca sæd, / ecgum werig" (1–3a) [I am a solitary creature, wounded by iron, injured by the sword, sated with battle-work, weary of (fighting against) swords]. The sun in turn is characterized as a warrior commanded by Christ to attack human beings:

Mec gesette soð   sigora waldend
Crist to compe.   Oft ic cwice bærne,
unrimu cyn   eorþan getenge,
næte mid niþe,   swa ic him no hrine,
þonne mec min frea   feohtan hateþ. (1–5)

[The true Ruler of victories, Christ, made me for combat. I often burn the living, and, when near the earth, I fiercely afflict innumerable creatures without touching them at all, when my Lord orders me to fight].

In addition, Riddle 6 seems to be analogically linked to Riddle 1-2-3, since the clues of the two texts describe the wind and the sun as destructive creatures that oppress mankind when God and Christ, respectively, urge them to do so.

However, the connection of Riddles 5 and 6 may go beyond their offering clues based on heroic tradition. Interestingly, the Old Icelandic *Rune Poem* presents a definition of *sól*, the runic equivalent to Old English *sigel*, which alludes to the resemblance of the sun and a shield: "(sól) er skýja skjöldr / ok skínandi röðull / ok ísa aldrtregi" ["(sun) is shield of the sky and shining ray and destroyer of the ice"].³² The juxtaposition of the shield and the sun in the Exeter collection thus similarly suggests a simple analogical pattern linking two round objects. But one also wonders if the pairing of Riddles 5 and 6 responds to their offering two subjects that are representative of traditional Christian symbology. Even though the allegorical connotations are not explicit in Riddle 5, the image of the "shield of faith" was well known from St Paul's reference to it in his Epistle to the Ephesians (6.16), where he urged Christians to defend themselves from the "flaming darts of the evil one." The idea is clearly retaken by the author of *Juliana* in the Exeter Book, as the steadfast Christian is said to protect himself with the holy shield ("haligne scyld," 386b) when the devil directs a storm of arrows ("flanþræce," 384a) against him.³³ On the other hand, the comparison of Christ with a shield was a popular literary motif, as illustrated, for instance, in the following excerpt from a Latin poem attributed by Lapidge to an author related to Theodore's school: "Pater, parme, procul arma / arce hostis ut e costis / imo corde sine sorde" (19–21) ["O Father, O shield, drive afar the Enemy's weapons, as from my ribs, from the depth of my heart, free from filth"].³⁴ In Riddle 6, the implicit association of Christ with the sun is also to be taken into account, as the *sol iustitiae* cliché seems to be hinted at in the cited passage above. This idea could therefore offer a reasonable explanation for the occurrence of a thematic irregularity such as Riddle 5 in a sequence starting with a conspicuous cosmological stamp.

---

32. Text and translation from Maureen Halsall, ed., *The Old English Rune Poem: A Critical Edition* (Toronto: University of Toronto Press, 1981), 185.
33. Unless indicated otherwise, all citations from Anglo-Saxon poems other than the Exeter Book Riddles in this book have been taken from the editions provided in *ASPR*.
34. The equation Christ/shield is used several times throughout this text. Edition and translation from Lapidge, "Theodore and Anglo-Latin Octosyllabic Verse," in his *Anglo-Latin Literature, 600–899,* 241–44; for this passage, 241.

4.2.2 Section 2 (Riddles 7–15)

The subsequent series of riddles denotes an underlying encyclopedic subclassification at work. The texts are distributed into two groups describing, on the one hand, birds and, on the other, quadrupeds. The following outline evinces this internal structure:

Subgroup A (Birds)

7. Swan
8. Nightingale
9. Cuckoo
10. Barnacle goose
11. **Cup of wine**

Subgroup B (Quadrupeds)

12. Ox
13. **Ten chickens**
14. Aurochs
15. Vixen

Though in a somewhat imperfect way, the structuring of the zoological sequence reveals an encyclopedic method of organization: animals of air (birds) and animals of land (quadrupeds)[35]—the water subcategory evidently missing.[36] As I will discuss next, an internal binary subdivision can be discerned in both subgroups. The

---

35. Sorrell has similarly pointed out that the contents of the Exeter zoological riddles, whose clues describe the animal's habitat or means of locomotion, clearly acknowledge the Levitical/Isidorean threefold view of zoology. Illustrating this with Aldhelm's *Enigma* 48 (movement of the heavens), he adds that this knowledge was directly transmitted from Latin *enigmata*. See Paul Sorrell, "Like a Duck to Water: Representations of Aquatic Animals in Early Anglo-Saxon Literature and Art," *Leeds Studies in English* 25 (1994): 29–68, esp. 35–36.
36. However, as explained further on pp. 402–13, two aquatic animals are the subject of Riddles 77 and 78 in Group 3.

ornithological series is clearly made of two pairs, and subgroup B parallels that twofold distribution by offering a distinction between farm animals (the ox and the ten chickens) and wild beasts (the aurochs and the vixen).

4.2.2.1 Subgroup A (Riddles 7–11): Birds

The first ornithological motif of subgroup A, Riddle 7 (swan), alludes to the bird's musical capacity, as expressed by the onomatopoetic verbs "swogað" (7a) and "swinsiað" (7b), and "singað" (8a),[37] which represent the sound of the feathers in the air and provide an Isidorean-like clue suggesting Old English *swan*.[38] As for Riddle 8, A. J. Wyatt's proposal "nightingale" is based on his reading the term "æfensceop" (5a) as an etymological clue alluding to Old English *nihtegale* (literally, "the night-singer").[39] According to this, the juxtaposition of Riddles 7 and 8 in the manuscript reveals further evidence of the thematic design observed in this first part of the collection. Indeed, it could be inferred that the adjacency of these two riddles is probably due to the fact that they offer etymological clues that describe the two birds' musical skills. At the same time, a typical contrastive pattern arises if we consider that the swan

---

37. Cf. "swinsað ond singeð" (124a), "singeð swa ond swinsað" (140a), and "swinsað" (618a) in *The Phoenix*.
38. As mentioned above (p. 85), Frank notes this etymological connection in Riddle 7: "alliteration again uncovers a correspondence between name and essence, word and thing: a swan (OE *swan*) is destined to soar aloft, to make melody (OE *swinsian*) . . . If the riddler's audience knew the traditional Latin etymology deriving *cygnus* 'swan' from *canendo* 'singing,' the more graceful convergence of *swan* and *swinsian* would have seemed to them to confirm the fitness of their native tongue to discover truths, to be an instrument of prophecy." Frank, "The Unbearable Lightness," 493–94. For the etymology of *cygnus* as deriving from Latin *canere*, see Isidore, *Etymologiae* XII.vii.18.
39. Wyatt, *Old English Riddles*, 69; Williamson, *The Old English Riddles*, 154 (see above, pp. 85–86). I support Wyatt's and Williamson's interpretation in my "The Evening Singer of Riddle 8 (K-D)," *SELIM* 9 (1999): 57–68.

produces music with its feathers during the day and the nightingale is a nocturnal songbird.

Riddle 9 has unanimously been solved as "cuckoo," since the text alludes to a parasitic fowl that abandons its eggs in another bird's nest. As for the subsequent Riddle 10, the solution is based on the belief that the barnacle goose is born at sea, and by seizing on to a piece of wood it finally comes out of a mollusk shell.[40] Following this train of thought, Riddles 9 and 10 probably appear consecutively because the two birds undergo an unnatural birth process, a fact that distinguishes them from the pair formed by the swan and the nightingale.

As with the possible allegorical resonances of the preceding shield/sun pair, the four bird riddles might have been juxtaposed on the basis of traditional medieval symbology.[41] On the one hand, the swan's singing and flying over the sea are often likened to the tribulations of the solitary soul in search of redemption. An illustration of this symbolism is found, for instance, in *The Seafarer*, in which the reference to the "ylfete song" (19b) also suggests this allegorical reading.[42]

---

40. As Kitson points out, "the barnacle goose nests in arctic islands further north than Iceland. In Anglo-Saxon times, therefore, its true breeding-habits were unknown." Peter Kitson, "Swans and Geese in Old English Riddles," *ASSAH* 7 (1994): 81.
41. Anglo-Saxon concern with bird symbology is well attested, for instance, in Alcuin's letters. As Scott notes, "Alcuin did have a pupil whom he addressed in his letters as Cuckoo, just as their friend Bishop Arne was an eagle, and Alcuin himself a goose, a swallow, or a swan." Peter Dale Scott, "Alcuin's *Versus de Cuculo*: The Vision of Pastoral Friendship," *Studies in Philology* 62 (1965): 512. The use of bird symbology in the ecclesiastical circles is well-known, as illustrated with Hugh of Fouilloy's *Aviarium* (composed c. 1132–52). As Clark explains, this work was "written expressly for a monastic audience, and contains lessons in Christian thought and behavior in addition to its avian lore." Willene B. Clark, ed. and trans., *The Medieval Book of Birds: Hugh of Foilloy's Aviarium* (Binghamton, NY: Medieval and Renaissance Texts and Studies, 1992), 1–2.
42. For an analysis of this passage, see Juan Camilo Conde Silvestre, *Crítica literaria y poesía elegíaca anglo-sajona: las ruinas, el exiliado errante y el*

On the other hand, the nightingale has been traditionally reputed to sing endlessly during the night, a characteristic that prompted the comparison of the bird with a devout monk fulfilling the nightly service by chanting in praise of the Lord. The analogy is, for example, made explicit in Alcuin's "De luscinia": "Felix o nimium, dominum nocteque dieque / qui studio tali semper in ore canit" (15–16) ["How happy is he who both day and night with such zeal always has songs for the Lord on his lips!"].[43] Here, the characteristic behavior of the bird overtly encourages comparison with human beings.

The pairing of Riddles 8 and 9 seems to suggest a concern with parental duties,[44] as evinced by the allusion to the reproachable conduct of the cuckoo's progenitors at the beginning of Riddle 9: "Mec on þissum dagum deadne ofgeafun / fæder ond modor" (1–2a) [On these days my father and my mother left me while still dead (i.e., still in the egg)].[45] Further in the same riddle, this initial reference dramatically differs from the description of the behavior of the adoptive bird-mother, personified as a dutiful kinswoman ("welhold mege," 4a), who acts as graciously with the cuckoo as with her own children ("swa arlice swa hire agen bearn," 6).

In medieval bestiaries, the nightingale is traditionally represented as the embodiment of maternal care.[46] Apparently, the clues of Riddle

---

navegante (Murcia: Universidad de Murcia, 1994), 100–01. On the contemplative mood offered by *The Seafarer*, see María José Mora's "The Invention of the Old-English Elegy," *English Studies* 76 (1995): 136–37, and "Un invierno entre los hielos: los paisajes de la poesía anglo-sajona," *Cuadernos del CEMYR* 7 (1999): 235–42. For further information on the symbolic role of birds in this poem, see Margaret E. Goldsmith, "*The Seafarer* and the Birds," *RES* 5 (1954): 225–35.

43. Godman's text and translation from *Poetry*, 144–45 (no. 13).
44. For the prominence of childraising as a subject in Riddle 9, see Jennifer Neville, "Fostering the Cuckoo: Exeter Book Riddle 9," *RES* 58 (2007): 434–36.
45. On "dead/alive clues" as typical of bird riddles, see my "Direct and Indirect Clues," 22–23. For the notion of birds being born twice, see Neville, "Fostering the Cuckoo," 434. See also Isidore, *Etymologiae* (XII.vii.79).
46. Rowland, *Birds with Human Souls*, 109.

8 focus on the description of the bird's extraordinary singing skills. But a controversial passage of this poem, which has not yet been convincingly explained by editors, could actually give us an insight into the nightingale's conscientious breeding: "þonne ic bugendre / stefne styrme, stille on wicum / sittað nigende" (6b–8a). In this excerpt, George Phillip Krapp and Elliott van Kirk Dobbie emended manuscript "siteð" (fol. 103r) to "sittað," as they understood this part as a possible allusion to people ("eorlum," 5b) being silently enraptured by the bird's singing. However, "sittað" is unacceptable from a metrical point of view, since this form would give rise to a D* pattern, which demands double alliteration.[47]

A further alternative reading of this excerpt is worth taking into account: "Þonne ic bugendre / stefne styrme, stille on wicum / *siteð* nigende"[48] (6b–8a) [When I (the male nightingale) cry aloud with my modulating voice, the quiet/still one (the female) sits brooding in the dwellings (i.e., in the nest)]. This interpretation maintains manuscript "siteð," thus assuming that this verb specifically alludes to the female nightingale being quiet or still[49] as she incubates the eggs while the male keeps singing, an idea that might be based on the observation of the bird's actual nesting habits.[50] This variant form would give way to a D-type metrical pattern, thus avoiding the double-alliteration requirement of the other editorial reading. As regards the term "nigende" (8a), it is close to *eacnigende*, "bringing forth," and *bearn-eacnigende*, "being with child, pregnant."[51] In addition,

---

47. And so is Trautmann's proposal "sitte" in *Die altenglischen Rätsel*, 6 and 71. My thanks to Rafael J. Pascual for his insightful comments on this part.
48. Note that I have modified Krapp and Dobbie's punctuation by assuming that "Þonne ic bugendre" is the initial part of this sentence and by placing a comma after "styrme." Krapp and Dobbie, *ASPR*, vol. 3, 185.
49. *BT* (s.v. "stille"): "without motion, at rest, not moving from a place, not disturbed."
50. "When the building (of the nest) is complete, and she (the female nightingale) has laid her portion of eggs, incubation immediately takes place. The male is now heard loud again, but not near so frequently as at first." Philip Henry Gosse, *Popular British Ornithology* (London, 1849), 31.
51. *BT* (s.v. "eacnigende" and "bearn-eacnigende"). Also, see *DOE* (s.v.

hnigan—meaning "to bend, bow down, incline, descend, decline, sink"—probably alludes to the bird's position while brooding.[52]

Although grammatical gender is not always fully reliable in the Exeter Riddles for the purpose of finding solutions,[53] the reference to the nightingale as "æfensceop" (5a) seems to be incompatible with subsequent feminine terms "scirenige" (9a) and "sceawendwisan" (9b) in Riddle 8. A possible explanation arising from the preceding discussion is that the female nightingale is in fact alluded to from line 8b onwards.[54] However, the use of the first-person singular form of "onhyrge" (10a) and the possessive "minre" (11b) should rather apply to the male nightingale who, supposedly, is the speaker from the beginning. The exact meaning of these two controversial hapax legomena is hard to ascertain, but, as I have argued elsewhere,[55] *scirenige* might be the poet's own coinage, which can be translated as "brightly declining" or "the bright one (i.e., the sun) descending;"[56] hence, it is an etymological clue related to Latin *luscinia* and the nightingale's

---

"(ge)eacnıan," meanings nos. 4–6, and "bearn-ēacniende").
52. *BT* (s.v. "hnigan"). The term "nigende" has been read by most scholars as a reference to the people listening to the nightingale with reverence, hence leaning their heads or being silent. See Tupper, *The Riddles of the Exeter Book*, 85, and Williamson, *The Old English Riddles*, 157–58.
53. See my "The Oyster and the Crab," 412–14, and further on p. 410 (n. 373).
54. As observed in Latin riddles, the choice of female animals as solutions for riddles is quite common, as Symphosius's Riddles 35 (she-goat) and 37 (she-mule) exemplify. Other possible female solutions are found in Exeter Riddles 15 (vixen, see further on p. 318, n. 89) and 24; in the latter riddle, the jay is described as "glado" (7a), a feminine form of the adjective meaning "glad, cheerful, joyous in disposition" (*DOE*, s.v. "glæd"). See below on p. 328.
55. See my "The Evening Singer," 63–66.
56. *BT* (s.v. "scire," I): "of light, clearly, brightly." A completely different interpretation was provided by Cosijn, who thought that this term was a variation of *scericge*, meaning "actress," an idea supported by Tupper, Mackie, Trautmann, and Krapp and Dobbie. P. J. Cosijn, "Anglosaxonica. IV," *Beiträge* 23 (1898): 128. For further information on "scirenige," see Williamson, *The Old English Riddles*, 158.

habit of singing at dusk,[57] an idea which complements the reference to the "evening singer" (5a). Besides, the second compound "nige" might simultaneously pun on the idea of the female bird's crouching position for brooding as suggested by "nigende" (8a).

By analogy with *sceawendsprac*,[58] the term *sceawendwise* in turn has been interpreted as implying the imitative capacity of the bird, similarly suggested by the verb "onhyrge" (10a), which also occurs as part of the clues describing the jay in Riddle 24 (4a).[59] Nevertheless, as Williamson explains, the term could be translated as "showing words or words that reveal a story"[60] in consonance with the identification of the bird as a poet or minstrel in line 5a. Besides, given the prodigious warbling repertoire of the nightingale, it might not be too rash to assume that the bird's voice emulates the artistic skills of a man ("æfensceop") and those of a woman ("sceawendwisan"), thus providing a logical explanation for the verb "onhyrge" (10a) and conveying a typical misleading clue to puzzle readers.[61] Williamson suspects that "heafodwoþe" (3a), a hapax legomenon used to allude to the ample register of the bird's voice, could in fact be a reference to "a minstrel poet singing beautiful falsetto songs."[62] Indeed, a passage from Pliny's *Naturalis historia* (X.xliii.82–85) highlights the

---

57. Cf. Isidore, *Etymologiae* XII.vii.37 discussed above (p. 111). "The Evening Singer," 65. Another possibility is that "scirenige" might be a further reference to the bird's modulating skills, as if referring to the clear voice bending or twisting (cf. *hnigan*). *BT* (s.v. "scire," II): "of the voice, clearly." Hence, it parallels "bugendre," which means "with varying pitch." *DOE* (s.v. "būgan," 11).
58. *BT* (s.v. "sceawendsprac"): "Buffoonery, the speech of the theatre."
59. *BT*, s.v. "onhyrian," meaning "to imitate, emulate." On this basis, Tupper, *The Riddles of the Exeter Book*, 85, discarded "nightingale" in favor of "jay," because the latter "possesses the power of mimicry." Similarly, W. S. Mackie proposed "chough" or "jackdaw" in "Notes on the Text of the 'Exeter Book,'" *MLR* 28 (1933): 76.
60. Williamson, *The Old English Riddles*, 154.
61. For the paradoxical reference to the creature as being male and female at the same time as a typical misleading clue in riddles, see my "Direct and Indirect Clues," 17–18 and 21–22.
62. Williamson, *The Old English Riddles*, 157.

extremely varied pitch of the nightingale's voice: "infuscatur ex inopinato, interdum et secum ipse murmurat, plenus, gravis, acutus, creber, extentus, ubi visum est vibrans—summus, medius, imus" ["it (*sonus*, the sound) is suddenly lowered, and at times sinks into a mere murmur, loud, low, bass, treble, with trills, with long notes, modulated when this seems good—soprano, mezzo, baritone"].[63] This description is no doubt consistent with the riddle's initial reference to the bird's "many voices" ("mongum reordum," 1b) and the allusion to its singing "with modulated tones" ("wrencum singe," 2a).[64]

In any case, with the alternative reading proposed for lines 6b–8a above, Riddle 8 offers the image of the female nightingale as a dedicated mother incubating her eggs while the male stands singing powerfully by her side. The nightingale couple would thus convey a positive example of parenthood, since, as known from actual observation, the two birds take care of their eggs before they hatch and later feed their fledglings once they are born. Even though no contemporary text can be brought up, an excerpt from the bestiary (c. 1200), contained in Aberdeen, University Library, MS 24 (fol. 52v) may serve to illustrate this idea: "Est enim pervigil custos cum ova quodam sinu corporis et gremio fovet, insompnem longe[i] noctis laborem cantile ne suavitate solatur" ["It (*lucinia*, the nightingale) is an ever-watchful sentinel, warming its eggs in a hollow of its body, relieving the sleepless effort of the long night with the sweetness of its song"].[65] It is probable that this traditional role of the female night-

---

63. Text and translation from Rackham, *Pliny: Natural History*, vol. 3, 344–45. For Williamson's comments on this passage in connection with the clues found in Exeter Riddle 8, see *The Old English Riddles*, 155.
64. *BT* (s.v. "wrenc," II). Williamson, *The Old English Riddles*, 156.
65. I am citing the transcription and translation from this passage from the chapter on the nightingale as found in the official website of *The Aberdeen Bestiary* (http://www.abdn.ac.uk/bestiary/index.hti). A further illustration of the nightingale's dedicated singing while brooding is found, for example, in the twelfth-century bestiary extant in Cambridge, Cambridge University Library, Ii.4.26. The bird is there described as follows: "She tempers the sleepless labour of her long night's work by the sweetness of her song, and hence it is seen that the summit of her ambition is to cherish her young

ingale as a caring mother is alluded to in Riddle 8, thus conveying a notion that is clearly in consonance with the loving foster-mother of Riddle 9; likewise, it contrasts with the reference to the cuckoo's neglectful parents in the latter riddle. The pairing of the nightingale and the cuckoo in section 2 may therefore respond to a long-established symbology of this sort antedating medieval bestiaries. The contrastive pattern also calls to mind Eusebius's Riddles 56 and 57, in which the stork and the ostrich had similar antithetical roles, exemplifying good and bad parenthood in each case.[66]

The cuckoo and the barnacle goose, the two birds described in Riddles 9 and 10, have traditionally symbolized ungratefulness to one's own kin. The cuckoo is said to betray its foster-mother by knocking the legitimate fledgelings out of the nest, as suggested in the last part of Riddle 9: "heo hæfde swæsra þy læs / suna ond dohtra, þy heo swa dyde" (11b-12) [She (i.e., the bird mother) had fewer of her own sons and daughters because she did so (i.e., because of fostering the cuckoo)]. Jan M. Ziolkowski has also pointed out that the term *cuculus* "carried connotations of slothfulness" and probably "denoted, in early medieval monastic parlance, a foolish young monk."[67] Taking this into account, the bird-riddle pairs of the Exeter Book could have a special significance in the monastic context in which they were probably generated and read. The cuckoo,

---

and to warm the eggs, to the best of her ability, not less by her sweet tones than by the heat of her body." Cited from White, *The Book of Beasts*, 139-40. For a similar passage in another Latin bestiary, see Richard Barber, trans., *Bestiary: Being an English Version of the Bodleian Library, Oxford, MS Bodley 764* (Woodbridge: Boydell, 1993; repr. 2006), 158. In these three versions, the chapter is accompanied by a picture of the nightingale hatching the eggs.
66. See above pp. 247-48.
67. *Talking Animals*, 56. Ziolkowski also mentions two poems from Froumund of Tegernsee's *Carmina* (second half of the tenth century) as a further illustration of the cuckoo as a symbol of sloth and folly in the monastic milieu. For these poems, see Karl Strecker, ed., *Codex epistolarum tegernseensium (Froumund), MGH, Epistolae selectae*, vol. 3 (Berlin: Weidmann, 1925), 53-55 (no. 19, 1) and 93 (no. 35, 4). For an English translation of poem 19, see Ziolkowski, ibid., 248-49.

who could represent the truant monk neglecting his duties, was thus probably set as the antithesis of the unwavering nightingale described in the preceding riddle.

Alcuin's "Versus de cuculo" can illustrate the symbolic connotations that were typically associated with this bird's negative conduct: "Heu mihi, si cuculum Bachus dimersit in undis, / qui rapiet iuvenes vortice pestifero. / Si vivat, redeat, nidosque recurrat ad almos . . ." (17–19) [Woe to me, if the cuckoo has been drowned in the waves by Bacchus, who seizes youths in his destructive whirlpool. If he is (still) alive, let him come back, hasten to the nourishing nest].[68] Here the cuckoo is the metaphorical representation of the novice who eventually abandons the monastic school (the nest), neglecting the spiritual training that has been granted to him by the *magister* (the lamenting foster-father) and choosing secular life as he is led astray by Bacchus, who symbolizes the devil.[69]

The idea of the cuckoo as an ungrateful foster-child also finds a counterpart in the traditional role of the barnacle goose in late Anglo-Saxon literature. In the anonymous *Vita Ædwardi regis (I.2)*, composed in the late 1060s, there is a poem on Godwine's children, in which one of them, possibly Sweyn, is compared to a barnacle goose:

> Illa profunda petit tranans inimica uoratrix,
> dampna suę stirpis faciens truncumque parentem
> pendit ab ore tenens, dum certo tempore uitę
> flatus uiuificans animal de non animata
> matre creat; studet inde suis resoluta rapinis. (17–21)

> ["The other (bird), gulping monster, seeks the depths, attacks its root and mouths the parent trunk, and holds, until, as doomed,

---

68. My translation. Edition from Dümmler, *Carmina, MGH, PLAC*, vol. 1, 269 (no. 57). On the metaphorical reading of this passage, see Scott, "Alcuin's *Versus de Cuculo*," 517–19.

69. For further allegorical implications of the cuckoo in Riddle 9 and for information about Anglo-Saxon fostering practices, see Neville, "Fostering the Cuckoo," esp. 436.

the breath of life creates a creature from a lifeless dam; and losing grip, pursues again its prey"].⁷⁰

Sweyn—who killed his cousin Beorn, i.e., he was hostile to his own family—is thus compared to the treacherous barnacle goose who must parasitize a trunk in order to survive.⁷¹ The Latin excerpt therefore attests to the reputation of the barnacle goose as an ungrateful parasitic bird in Anglo-Saxon tradition. Hence, these symbolic correspondences shared by Riddles 9 and 10 might be a further reason why the compilers chose to juxtapose the two texts, since these two birds have traditionally been considered as treacherous to their kin.⁷² Analogy once more proves to be a crucial encyclopedic device to achieve cohesion in section 2.

In light of this analysis, it should come as no surprise that the Exeter compilers offered this binary structure, because these riddles were expected to be treated in a similar way to joint entries in Isidore's *Etymologiae*, in which the allegorical associations were equally implicit. Indeed, the ornithological duos recall the combination of the principles of analogy and difference as exemplified with the pairing of the nightingale and the bat, as well as with that of the crab and the oyster in the *Etymologiae*.⁷³ It is also quite clear that

---

70. Text and translation from Frank Barlow, ed., *The Life of King Edward who Rests at Westminster* (Oxford: Oxford University Press, 1992), 26–27.

71. According to Barlow, Sweyn might be the treacherous bird from Godwine's kin on the grounds that he "abducted for his pleasure the abbess of Leominster in 1046 (could she have been a kinswoman?) and in 1049 murdered his cousin Earl Beorn." Ibid., 27, n. 57. On the problematic identification of the barnacle goose in this poem, see Rhona Beare, "Earl Godwin's Son as a Barnacle Goose," *N&Q* 44 (1997): 4–6; "Which of Godwin's Sons Was Called a Barnacle Goose?," *N&Q* 46 (1999): 5–6; and "Is the Barnacle Goose Selfish, and Is It Harold?," *N&Q* 50 (2003): 10–11. Also, see entry for Sweyn by Ann Williams in *ODNB* (s.v. "Swein [Sweyn]").

72. On the basis of a different argumentation, Meaney, similarly acknowledges the thematic links of the four riddles in "Birds on the Stream of Consciousness."

73. See my discussion above on pp. 109–12.

the Exeter bird riddles follow the encyclopedic patterns that have been studied in the case of Aldhelm's pairing of the dove and the raven (nos. 63–64), Eusebius's juxtaposition of the stork and the ostrich (56–57), and the contrast between the bat (97) and the other diurnal birds (93–96) in the Vatican collection.[74] Apart from this, the distribution in pairs also resembles the chapters of a *Physiologus*, in which the description of the different animals usually entails the illustration of a particular conduct for human beings. In the case of the Exeter Book *Physiologus*, for example, it is quite evident that the chapters on the panther and the whale constitute an oppositional pair. Among other parallels, the panther and the whale are said to attract other animals by emitting an extremely delightful scent. The allegorical interpretation that accompanies the description of each animal reinforces this binary construction, as the panther, the positive model to follow, is said to represent Christ, and the whale, the devil.[75] The Exeter *Physiologus* therefore testifies to the employment of animal allegory and the pairing of zoological motifs for didactic purposes. Like the panther and the whale in the *Physiologus*, the four Exeter bird riddles were probably compiled in pairs, so that they could be read as polarized examples of behavior for human beings.

The structural cohesion of the ornithological series is seemingly broken with the presence of Riddle 11 (cup of wine), whose description of the negative effects of alcohol on human behavior might rather be pointing to an instrumental topic. But the opening lines of this text deserve careful attention as they present two clues that might explain the occurrence of this riddle at this point in the compilation: "Hrægl is min hasofag, hyrste beorhte, / reade ond scire on reafe minum" (1–2) [My outfit is gray, and on my garment (there

---

74. See my comments of these riddles on pp. 208–09, 247–48, and 282–83 of this book.

75. For a fine review of the characteristics of each animal in the *Physiologus* and their allegorical significance in medieval tradition, see Michael D. C. Drout, "'The Partridge' is a Phoenix: Revising the Exeter Book *Physiologus*," *Neophilologus* 91 (2007): 487–503.

are) red and shiny trappings].[76] Interestingly, the terms "hrægl," "hyrste," and "reafe" found in Riddle 11 form part of a group of terms that are typically used in Exeter bird riddles, as observed in the following comparative outline:

Riddle 7 (swan): hrægl (1a), hyrste (4a), and frætwe (6b)

Riddle 10 (barnacle goose): hrægle (7b) and hyrste (8b)

Riddle 13 (ten chickens): reafe (7a),[77] hrægl (9b), and frætwe (10b)

Besides, the adjective "hasofag" (1a) in Riddle 11 could well have been mistaken for a reference to the color of a bird, as *haso* often applies to birds in Old English poetry.[78] In short, given that riddles usually occurred with no solutions in manuscripts, it is not rash to assume that, in the course of copying from one manuscript to another, a scribe might have read the first two lines of Riddle 11 as being suitable for the ornithological contents of subgroup A. It is therefore possible that Riddle 11 could have been confused with another bird motif, as the compilers seem to have regarded it as a suitable piece for the zoological series.

4.2.2.2 Subgroup B (Riddles 12–15): Quadrupeds

Subgroup B includes a series of four-footed animals starting with Riddle 12, which has been solved as "ox" by most critics. The riddle is based on the well-known paradox that is also present in several Latin analogues: while alive, the animal is said to cut through the

---

76. Krapp and Dobbie, *ASPR*, vol. 3, 186, supplied "minum," which is absent in the manuscript, to complete the second half-line. For other alternative readings of this line, see ibid., 327. See folio 103v of the manuscript in Muir's *The Exeter DVD*.
77. With the exception of *frætwe* and *reafe* in Riddle 13, which refer to the egg-shell, the remainder of the terms allude to bird feathers.
78. Note, for example, that the dove of Noah's Ark in Genesis is referred to as "haswe culufran" (1451b). Similarly, the eagle in Riddle 24, as one of the animals that the jay can imitate, is alluded to as "þone haswan earn" (4b).

earth, evidently alluding to its contribution to the plowing of land; when dead, its leather serves as binding material, among other uses expressed in the clues.

Fotum ic fere,	foldan slite,
grene wongas,	þenden ic gæst bere.
Gif me feorh losað,	fæste binde
swearte Wealas,	hwilum sellan men. (1–4)

[I move on feet (and) slit the earth, the green plains, while I am alive. If life escapes from me, I tightly bind the dark Welsh, and sometimes better men].

However, the allusion to the living ox is reduced to the first two lines (and a short reference at the end), the remainder of the text being used to describe the multiple uses of leather. This has made some critics think of "oxhide" or "leather" as a more satisfactory solution than ox.[79] Latin analogues—such as Aldhelm's Riddle 83 (bullock) and Eusebius's Riddle 37 (calf)—certainly do not display such detailed post-mortem descriptions of the animal. But, as Williamson points out, "The conditional beginning with Gif in line 3 and extending through all possible futures (hwilum . . . hwilum) seems to indicate the live beast musing upon his roles as a servant to men."[80] Following Williamson's argument in favor of "ox," it is worth considering the prominent position of this motif as the first item among the four-footed animals of the sequence. Apart from being the symbol of one of the four evangelists, the ox or the bullock was a traditional allegory of the monk. A passage from Alcuin's "Versus de cuculo," for

---

79. Trautmann proposed "leather," and this solution has been supported by most scholars. *Die altenglischen Rätsel*, 74–75. Niles has interestingly combined the two concepts in his proposal *oxa and oxan-hyd* (an ox and its hide), *Old English Enigmatic Poems*, 125. For a recent review of this riddle and its layers of signification in terms of class and gender, see Jennifer Neville, "Speaking the Unspeakable: Appetite for Deconstruction in Exeter Book Riddle 12," *ES* 93 (2012): 519–28.
80. Williamson, *The Old English Riddles*, 167.

instance, illustrates this: "En tondent nostri librorum prata iuvenci, / solus abest cuculus, quis, rogo, pascit eum?" (29–30) [Behold, our bullocks graze in the meadows of books. The cuckoo alone is missing. I ask, who feeds him?].[81] These lines allegorically allude to the monastic companions (the bullocks) of the idle novice (the cuckoo) peacefully "ruminating" the sacred texts. Having abandoned the monastery, the wayward defector will not be able to receive this spiritual food. The presentation of the bullock and the cuckoo as contrastive allegorical figures in Alcuin's poem therefore adds further weight to my assumption that contemporary readers of the Exeter zoological series were expected to note the implicit presence of these well-known symbols.

Close to the bird section but inserted among four-footed animals, Riddle 13 stands out for its anomalous position. The riddle was convincingly solved by Moritz Trautmann as "ten chickens," and his proposal has been supported by most scholars since then.[82] Apart from the use of conventional terms alluding to feathers,[83] the clues in this composition no doubt comply with the typical elements found in other ornithological pieces. For example, the phrase "Ic seah turf tredan" (1a) [I saw (them) step on the ground] alludes to the chickens' capacity to move on land. Further emphasis on this idea is made with "gewitan lond tredan" (11a), which insists on the physical activity once they are alive ("hæfdon feorg cwico," 3a) after hatching out from the apparently lifeless egg.[84] The latter expression recalls the clues offered in Exeter Riddles 9—"ne wæs me feorh þa gen" (2b)—and 10—"Hæfde feorh cwico" (6a)—to refer to the cuckoo and the barna-

---

81. My translation. Text cited from Dümmler, *Carmina, MGH, PLAC*, vol. 1, 270 (no. 57). On the metaphorical reading of this passage, see Scott, "Alcuin's *Versus de Cuculo*," 517–19.
82. Trautmann, *Die altenglischen Rätsel*, 76. See Williamson, *The Old English Riddles*, 168–69.
83. See above p. 313.
84. This expression is typical of bird riddles and stems from the assumption that the creatures were initially dead, as the egg looks like a lifeless object. It is only after hatching that the chickens are said to be fully alive.

cle goose, respectively. It is therefore reasonable to assume that Riddle 13 has been accidentally displaced from the ornithological series.

Despite the unexpected occurrence of Riddle 13 at this point, the zoological focus continues with Riddle 14, which, as with the ox piece discussed above, presents a problematic interpretation due to its ambivalent beginning: "Ic wæs wæpenwiga. Nu mec wlonc þeceð / geong hagostealdmon golde ond sylfore, / woum wirbogum" (1–3a) [I was an armed warrior. Now a lively young man covers me with gold and silver, with twisted ornamental wires]. As observed in this passage, the extinct aurochs or wild ox is clearly alluded to in line 1a, but henceforth the drinking-horn deriving from the dead animal is the first-person speaker. On the basis of this notable imbalance of textual clues, most scholars have preferred "horn" as the solution. Still, even if the majority of the clues are devoted to describing the object as an ornamented drinking vessel, the poem clearly starts with a reference to the living bull as "wæpenwiga."[85] The lengthy description of the horn is actually logical, since the bull's impressive horns are the most remarkable feature of this animal, but this does not necessarily preclude the answer "aurochs."[86]

---

85. The manuscript form "wæpen wiga" (armed warrior) has been emended by Williamson and most editors to "wæpen wigan" (the weapon of a warrior) in an attempt to make it consonant with the preferred solution "horn." Williamson, *The Old English Riddles*, 171. By contrast, Krapp and Dobbie's edition retains manuscript "wæpenwiga." See *ASPR*, vol. 3, 329, and folio 104r of the manuscript in Muir's *The Exeter DVD*. In view of this analysis, maintaining the answer "aurochs" supports Krapp and Dobbie's reading and makes the editorial emendation unnecessary. I owe this idea to María José Mora, who generously pointed this out for me.
86. Note, for instance, the emphatic reference to the aurochs's horns in the Old English *Rune Poem*: "(ūr) byþ anm ōd and oferhyrned, / felafrēcne dēor,—feohteþ mid hornum—/ mære mōrstapa; þæt is mōdig wuht" (4–6) ["The aurochs is courageous and has huge horns, a very fierce beast—it fights with its horns—a notorious moor-stalker; that is a brave creature!"]. Halsall, *The Old English Rune Poem*, 86–87. For a commentary on this passage, see Inmaculada Senra Silva, "The Names of the U-Rune," *Futhark: International Journal of Runic Studies* 1 (2010): 109–22, esp. 110–11.

As with Exeter Riddles 12 and 14, Latin *enigmata* similarly lack transitional clues to help distinguish living animals from lifeless objects stemming from them. Note, among others, Aldhelm's *Enigma* 86 (ram), in which the description of the animal as an armed warrior recalls the characterization of the aurochs as a "wæpenwiga" in Exeter Riddle 14: "Sum namque armatus rugosis cornibus horrens . . ." (1) [I am armed with terrifying wrinkled horns]. Further on, the reference to the living ram is likewise surpassed by the allusion to various lifeless objects—all of them speaking in the first person—related to the word *Aries*: the constellation, a battering ram, a woollen cloth, and a wall—the latter playfully connecting Latin *Aries* with *paries*. Similarly, in Aldhelm's Riddle 96 (elephant), the first-person speaker is equivocally presented as the living creature and the ornamented ivory horn from the dead animal:

Quamquam me turpem nascendi fecerit auctor,
editus ex aluo dum sumpsi munera uitae,
ecce tamen morti successit gloria formae,
letifer in fibras dum finis serpat apertas;
bratea non auri fuluis pretiosa metallis,
quamuis gemmarum constent ornata lucernis,
vincere, non quibunt falerarum floribus umquam. (7–13)

[Even though God made me (i.e., the living elephant) ugly at birth when I was issued from the womb and obtained the gifts of life; behold, the glory of my shape (i.e., ivory) however follows after my death, when the fatal end glides into my open inwards; precious leaves of gold, tawny metal—even if they are adorned with the light (literally, the lamps) of gems, the flowers of ornaments—will never be able to conquer me (i.e., surpass the beauty of ivory)].

Aldhelm's text therefore offers a valuable parallel to Exeter Riddles 12 and 14, since the ultimate answer, as expressly indicated in the title-solution in some manuscripts, is "elephant," not "ivory." Apart from the similar treatment of the dead/alive clues in Latin *enigmata*, this assumption is likewise supported by the occurrence of the aurochs motif among the other zoological items of the series, in which four-footed animals clearly predominate.

As regards Riddle 15, most scholars agree that its solution must be some four-footed creature, the physical features of which are condensed in the first lines of the text:

Hals is min hwit	ond heafod fealo,
sidan swa some.	Swift ic eom on feþe,
beadowæpen bere.	Me on bæce standað
her swylce swe on hleorum.	Hlifiað tu
earan ofer eagum.	(1–5a)

[My neck is white and my head yellowish-red, matching my sides. I am swift-footed; I bear battle-weapons. Hair stands on my back and also on my cheeks (face); two ears are uplifted above my eyes].

In view of this description, the solutions "badger" and "hedgehog" have been put forward, since these animals have prominent "battle-weapons."[87] However, the fox's claws and teeth could likewise be considered "beadowæpen." Furthermore, the characteristic swiftness and the color description rather favor the solution "fox."[88] Also importantly, the animal's courageous defense of its offspring, as expressed in lines 6b–15a, led Jean I. Young to propose "vixen," a solution that seems to me more accurate than "fox."[89]

As regards the compilation issue, Riddle 15 was probably meant

---

87. The latest proponent of this solution is Dieter Bitterli, "Exeter Book Riddle 15: Some Points for the Porcupine," *Anglia* 120 (2002): 461–87.
88. This was first proposed by Brett and later supported by Williamson. Cyril Brett, "Notes on Old and Middle English," *MLR* 22 (1927): 257–64; Williamson, *The Old English Riddles*, 173–74.
89. Jean I. Young, "Riddle 15 of the Exeter Book," *RES* 20 (1944): 304–6. Audrey L. Meaney supports Young's "vixen" in "The Hunted and the Hunters: British Mammals in Old English Poetry," *ASSAH* 11 (2000): 95–105, as does Marijane Osborn, "Vixen as Hero: Solving Exeter Book Riddle 15," in *The Hero Recovered: Essays on Medieval Heroism in Honor of George Clark*, ed. Robin Waugh and James Weldon (Kalamazoo, MI: Medieval Institute Publications, 2010), 173–87.

to be a companion to Riddle 14, as both texts allude to "armed animals"—cf. "wæpenwiga" (1a)[90] and "beadowæpen" (3a), respectively. Also interestingly, Riddle 15 describes how the animal in question is pursued by some kind of predator, which is referred to as "wælgrim wiga" (cruel warrior, 8a),[91] or a hunting dog—"wælhwelpes wig" (the combat of a slaughter-hound, 23a).[92] The presentation of the different animals involved as fierce warriors seems to have prompted the juxtaposition of Riddles 14 and 15 in the collection. In addition, the occurrence of Riddle 15 at this point could have been occasioned by analogy with the neighboring ox motif (no. 12), the tame counterpart of the aurochs.[93] But the adjacency of Riddles 14 and 15 arguably responds to the negative allegorical role shared by both the aurochs and the fox. For example, Isidore's explanation of the buffalo and the aurochs in the *Etymologiae* (XII.i.33–34) is complemented by Hrabanus Maurus's *De rerum naturis* (VII.viii.990–92) with the following passage: "In bubalis autem uel uris possunt accipi superbi doctores uel dominatores plebis, qui habentes similitudinem bonorum doctorum in gradu uel officium quod gestant, sed superbia tumentes" [Aurochs and buffaloes can be understood as

---

90. Note that the reputation of the wild ox as being extremely fierce and having fearsome horns is also present in Psalm 22.21: "Save . . . my afflicted soul from the horns of the wild oxen!"
91. In "Riddle 15 of the Exeter Book," 306, Young, for example, considers that the predator could be a snake and thus offers "weasel" as a further possible answer.
92. I am here using Williamson's translation for this phrase in *The Old English Riddles*, 177. He also notes that the word may also refer to a wolf. Niles in turn has interpreted these clues as an allusion to a hound pursuing the fox and has therefore proposed the solution *fox ond hund* in *Old English Enigmatic Poems*, 122 and 144–45, n. 4.
93. Interestingly, the aurochs and the common ox are contrasted in Job 39.9–12: "Is the wild ox willing to serve you? Will he spend the night at your crib? Can you bind him in the furrow with ropes, or will he harrow the valleys after you? Will you depend on him because his strength is great, and will you leave to him your labor? Do you have faith in him that he will return, and bring your grain to your threshing floor?"

arrogant teachers or as rulers of the people, who have an appearance similar to that of good teachers in their status and the office they hold, but are actually swelling with pride].⁹⁴ In like manner, the fox is described in the same work as a cunning creature with an extraordinary capacity to deceive people (VIII.i.249–50): "Vulpis enim mistice diabolum dolosum uel hereticum callidum, siue peccatorem hominem significat" [Indeed, the fox symbolically represents the cunning devil or the crafty heretic, or the sinful man]. The fox is thus allegorically understood as a person that can lead others astray, a notion that dovetails with the description of the aurochs as falsely representing a good teacher. Riddles 14 and 15 therefore subtly allude to the crucial duties of the *magister*, thus conveying an insightful allegorical complement to the notion of good parenthood and the idea of fosterage that were raised in the bird riddles.

4.2.2.3 A Final Reflection on Section 2

In light of this discussion, Exeter section 2 reveals an attempt at providing internal cohesion by applying organizational principles akin to those found in both Isidore's Book XII and Latin *enigmata*. Considered as a whole, section 2 follows the pattern offered by the collections of Symphosius and Eusebius, as well as that found in the Vatican assemblage. In all of them, a basic distinction between animals of air and animals of land is similarly observed. Apart from the pairing of the riddles on the basis of the Isidorean principles of analogy and difference, a contrastive size criterion is discernible throughout the zoological sequence:

Subgroup A (Birds)	Subgroup B (Quadrupeds)
7. Swan (big)	12. Ox (big)
8. Nightingale (small)	**13. Ten chickens (small)**
9. Cuckoo (small)	14. Aurochs (big)
10. Barnacle goose (big)	15. Vixen (small)

---

94. Text for this and the subsequent extract from Schipper, *Hrabani Mauri*. My translation.

Disregarding the exceptional inclusion of Riddle 11, the result is a well-balanced series, in which a big animal is consistently contrasted with a small one. However, in Exeter section 2, birds are given priority of place, whereas in Isidore's Book XII, land animals come first.[95] The fact that birds can fly and thus be close to heaven and God might have occasioned this initial position. But this noteworthy divergence could also be explained on the basis of a concern with ecclesiastical dietary habits as prescribed in St Benedict's Rule.[96] The notion that bird flesh was preferable to that of four-footed animals can help further elucidate the internal organization of Exeter section 2.

The choice of the barnacle goose (no. 10), for example, seems to support the assumption of an ecclesiastically oriented compilation. The absence of this animal in the Mosaic lists—quite logically, since it is a species that is geographically located in northern Europe—might have generated the assumption that it was a clean bird. Gerald of Wales's *Topographia Hiberniae* (c. 1188) offers an enlightening passage that seems to support this inference. After describing the bird's unnatural birth process, Gerald establishes a connection between the barnacle goose and the clergy's dietary customs: "Unde et in quibusdam Hiberniæ partibus, avibus istis, tanquam non carneis quia de carne non natis, episcopi et viri religiosi jejuniorum tempore sine delectu vesci solent" (I.xv) ["Accordingly in some parts of Ireland bishops and religious men eat them (barnacle geese) without sin during a fasting time, regarding them as not being flesh, since they were not born of flesh"].[97] Although Gerald's reference to the barnacle goose is chronologically distant from Exeter Riddle 10, it is fairly

---

95. Cf. the scheme of the contents of Isidore's Book XII on pp. 93–94.
96. As Hagen explains, "After the Regularis Concordia, abstinence from flesh meat was general throughout the monasteries of England until well after the Conquest. . . . The flesh of birds and fish could normally be consumed while still keeping to the letter of the law." Anne Hagen, *A Handbook of Anglo-Saxon Food: Processing and Consumption* (Hockwold-cum-Wilton: Anglo-Saxon Books, 1992), 120.
97. The edition is from James F. Dimock, *Topographia Hibernica, Giraldi Cambrensis Opera*, Rolls Series xxi.5 (London, 1867), 48. The translation of

reasonable to deduce that the inclusion of the barnacle goose in section 2 could have been triggered by a conceptualization of this bird as being doubtfully suitable for consumption[98] in the theoretically restricted monastic context of the second half of the tenth century,[99] when, at some point, the Anglo-Saxon poem was incorporated into the Exeter Book.

The presence of the ox as the introductory subject of the quadruped section similarly suggests the compilers' acquaintance with the Isidorean zoological model. Indeed, the ox is classified as a clean animal in both Leviticus and Deuteronomy and, as discussed above, in medieval symbology it was often regarded as a representation of the monk. Accordingly, it may be surmised that this topic could have been chosen to lead the quadruped series on account of its clean status—even if this riddle indulges in sexual double entendres.[100]

The zoological series therefore seems to dwell on the clean or unclean status of its components, thus offering a well-delineated structure:

Clean Birds (natural birth process)	Clean Domestic Quadrupeds
7. Swan	12. Ox
8. Nightingale	13. Ten chickens

this passage is from John O'Meara, *The History and Topography of Ireland* (Harmondsworth: Penguin, 1951), 460.
98. When commenting on Gerald's passage, Beare explains that "In Lent and on Fridays when Christians ate fish instead of flesh, shellfish counted as fish. If the barnacle goose started life as a goose-barnacle, it ought perhaps to count as fish." Rhona Beare, "Gerald of Wales on the Barnacle Goose," *N&Q* 44 (1997): 460.
99. As was illustrated above with the riddle known as "Æthelwold's bowl" (p. 45, n. 152), the restrictions were not as harsh as one might have expected.
100. For a thorough revision of the erotic clues found in this riddle, see Sarah Higley, "The Wanton Hand: Reading and Reaching into Grammars and Bodies in Old English Riddle 12," in Withers and Wilcox, *Naked Before God*, 29–59.

Unclean Birds (unnatural birth process)	Unclean Wild Quadrupeds
9. Cuckoo	14. Aurochs[101]
10. Barnacle goose	15. Vixen

As illustrated in this outline, cleanness seems to be implicitly associated with birds that undergo a normal birth process, as in the case of the swan and the nightingale. A further implied idea is that these fowls hatch their eggs; in other words, they have regular incubatory habits. By contrast, unclean birds such as the cuckoo or the barnacle goose are unfavorably characterized by their refusal to incubate their eggs, thus giving rise to their parasitic customs, all of which was traditionally viewed as contrary to the laws of nature. The plea can be compared to Eusebius's *Enigma* 57, which similarly illustrates neglectful motherhood by explaining how the female ostrich refuses to sit on the eggs and instead covers them with sand, where the chicks will eventually hatch out.[102]

With quadrupeds, a similar pattern arises with domestic animals being prioritized on the basis of their being classed as clean creatures, thus opposing unclean animals such as the aurochs and the vixen. The anomalous presence of Riddle 13 suggests that a small clean quadruped should be in its place, but, we may conjecture, the compilers probably did not have such a riddle at hand and supplied the ten-chickens subject instead. Strongly contrasting Eusebius's exotic zoological string, Exeter section 2 stands out for its choice of

---

101. As noted by Cansdale, *Animals of Bible Lands*, 83, "The OT [Old Testament] passages . . . make it clear that the biblical writers knew it [the aurochs], yet it is not included among the animals whose flesh could be eaten, though technically it was 'clean' [i.e., it was cloven-hoofed and chewed the cud]." I have not found any reference in Anglo-Saxon texts to the aurochs as being either clean or unclean but, from the layout of this sequence, this animal, like the barnacle goose, might have been viewed at least as doubtfully clean.
102. See my comments on Eusebius's Riddle 57 above (p. 247).

homely species, possibly intending to generate a pragmatic debate among readers—or a brainstorming session in the classroom—so as to determine which of the animals should be ascribed to clean or unclean categories. If this assumption is correct, the idea would no doubt accord with contemporary preoccupations in the context of the Benedictine reform.

4.2.3 Section 3 (Riddles 16–39)

The instrumental sequence is comparatively larger and more miscellaneous than the preceding sections. However, these riddles share some common features that suggest that this series was viewed by the compilers as a thematic section. To begin with, as A. N. Doane has noted, the clues found in instrumental riddles frequently put the emphasis on the object's usefulness: "Implement riddles tend to present the object in a dynamic state, concentrating not on its visual makeup or total formal/structural aspect but on its *use*, from the point of view of the user and the thing used."[103] The reference to the object's utility or value is thus normally presented by means of a simple statement, as observed for instance at the beginning of Riddle 27 (mead)—"Ic eom weorð werum" (1a) [I am of worth to men]—or in the description of the rake in Riddle 34—"Hafað fela toþa; / nebb biþ hyre æt nytte . . ." (2b–3a) [It has many teeth; its nose is of use]. This idea is sometimes provided in a more elaborate way, as with Riddle 32 (ship):

fereð foddurwelan,	Moncynne nyt,
wist in wigeð,	folcscipe dreogeð,
gaful geara gehwam	ond werum gieldeð
rice ond heane. (9b–13a)	þæs þe guman brucað,

[Useful to mankind, it carries abundance of food, works for the people, brings their sustenance, and every year to men it pays tribute, of which both rich and poor make good use].

---

103. A. N. Doane, "Three Old English Implement Riddles: Reconsiderations of Numbers 4, 49, and 73," *MP* 84 (1987): 243. Emphasis Doane's.

The onion of Riddle 25 is similarly described from this pragmatic point of view: "Ic eom wunderlicu wiht, wifum on hyhte, / neahbuendum nyt" (1–2a) [I am a wonderful creature, the joy of women, and of use to neighbors]. Understood as a product of agricultural toil, the onion was probably meant to be part of the instrumental section. Riddle 26 (Gospel book) in turn illustrates the characteristic reference to the object's utility, listing the numerous benefits gained by human beings (20–26a) if they are willing to use ("brucan willað," 18b) this object. The riddle further insists on this idea in the final challenge to the reader: "Frige hwæt ic hatte, / niþum to nytte. Nama min is mære, / hæleþum gifre ond halig sylf" (26b-28) [Figure out what I, of use to men, am called. My name is well-known, and I myself (am) useful to men and holy]. As observed in these riddles, expressions associated with the utility of the objects are typically found: *nyt* (nos. 25, 26, 32, and 34) and *brucan* (nos. 26 and 32).

A further feature shared by some of the instrumental riddles of this series is the description of the processing and consumption of a particular object. This is the case for Riddles 26 (Gospel book), 27 (mead), and 28 (ale), all three of which seem to be linked on this basis.[104] The initial part of Riddle 27 alludes to the way in which honey is produced by the bees and fetched by people who will turn it into mead by allowing fermentation to take place: "Hæleð mec siþþan / baþedan in bydene" (5b-6a) [Later men washed me in a vat].[105] As regards Riddle 28, the processing of barley is described in a passage in which rhyme and alliteration join to suggest this routine in a most effective way:

corfen, sworfen, cyrred, þyrred,
bunden, wunden, blæced, wæced,
frætwed, geatwed, feorran læded
to durum dryhta. (4-7a)

---

104. The solutions of Riddles 26 and 28 are based on Niles's reading of these texts in *Old English Enigmatic Poems*, 114–19.
105. A detailed account of the clues of this riddle is found in ibid., 125–26.

[Cut, polished, turned, dried, bound, wrung, bleached, weakened, seasoned, made ready; it is (then) brought from a distance to the doors of the people].[106]

Riddle 26 similarly provides a lavish description of the various stages involved in the production of parchment and the manufacturing of a Gospel book:

Mec feonda sum	feore besnyþede,
woruldstrenga binom,	wætte siþþan,
dyfde on wætre,	dyde eft þonan,
sette on sunnan,	þær ic swiþe beleas
herum þam þe ic hæfde.	Heard mec siþþan
snað seaxses ecg,	sindrum begrunden. (1–6)

[An enemy deprived me of my life (and) took away my physical strength; (he) then soaked me, dipped me in water; (he) took me out of there again, put me in the sun, where I rapidly lost the hairs that I had. The hard edge of a knife then cut me, once I had been polished with slag].[107]

This passage thus alludes to the slaughtering of the animal and the various tasks that are needed to transform its skin into parchment.[108] The subsequent lines (7–11a) provide an insight into the stages of

---

106. Niles offers the following reading for this passage: "The barley is then cut and malted, and reference is made to the process by which it is harvested, then dried, threshed, and turned, then soaked and allowed to germinate before being fermented in the malting Old English *mealt-hūs*)." Ibid., 115.

107. As regards "sindrum begrunden" (6b), I follow the reading offered by Laurence K. Shook, "Riddles Relating to the Anglo-Saxon Scriptorium," in *Essays in Honour of Anton Charles Pegis*, ed. J. Reginald O'Donnell (Toronto: Pontifical Institute of Mediaeval Studies, 1974), 220. Also, Niles, *Old English Enigmatic Poems*, 118 (n. 34), reads this half-line as possibly referring to "the smoothing of the tanned hide using an abrasive tool."

108. For a detailed description of the process, see Niles, *Old English Enigmatic Poems*, 118. Tatwine's Riddle 5 and Bern Riddle 24 similarly present clues alluding to the preparation of parchment.

writing, illuminating, and binding. As illustrated with this excerpt and the other passages that have been analyzed, the riddles of this instrumental section clearly share a concern with describing the uses of the object in question and the processes involved in its production.

4.2.3.1 Thematic Exceptions: Riddles 22, 24, 29, 33, 38, and 39

As a whole, section 3 offers a representation of domestic utensils (jug, bellows), agricultural subjects (plow, rake, onion), war gear (sword, bow, mail coat), drinks (mead, ale), musical instruments (bagpipe), navigation topics (anchor, ship), and monastic implements (Gospel book). Most of these subjects have a corresponding entry in Isidore's instrumental Books XVIII, XIX, and XX.[109] Despite this general cohesion, there are several outstanding thematic digressions that need to be dealt with. As anticipated at the beginning of this book,[110] the exceptional occurrence of Riddle 22 among instrumental topics can be explained as a further case of thematic pairing. In Riddle 22, the term "wægn" (waggon, 9a), which also occurs in the description of the plow in Riddle 21 (8a), is a crucial clue that was intended to help readers find out the solution. Citing a passage from Virgil's *Georgics* (I.169–75), B. Colgrave identified the different parts of the plow alluded to in Riddle 21, thus reading "wægne" (8a) as "the fore-carriage which Virgil calls the 'currus.'"[111] Riddle 22 therefore suggests the constellation "Charles's Wain," commonly known as Old English *Carles wægn*[112] and Latin *plaustrum* (plow), the latter designating both the agricultural tool and the cosmological concept. The juxtaposition of Riddles 21 and 22 no doubt was meant

---

109. Note, for example, that mead is dealt with in *Etymologiae* XX.iii.13. The entry "cepa" (onion), however, occurs among other vegetables in XVII.x.12.
110. See p. 9.
111. B. Colgrave, "Some Notes on Riddle 21," *MLR* 32 (1937): 282. For Virgil's excerpt, see R. A. B. Mynors, ed., *Virgil: Georgics* (Oxford: Clarendon, 1990), xxiv; for the explanatory notes on these lines and further information on the Roman plough, 37–39.
112. *DOE* (s.v. "carles wæn").

as a didactic strategy similar to that observed in the adjacency of Aldhelm's *Enigmata* 48 and 49, in which the vault of heaven was subtly compared to a cauldron.

As for Riddle 24 (jay), this text apparently does not present any thematic association with the other neighboring riddles to justify its presence in an instrumental section. The solution is based on Dietrich's reading of the runes as *garohi*, which, once reversed, stand for *higora*, a term that can actually mean "jay" or "magpie,"[113] which are both birds with a mimicking capacity. Nevertheless, as Charles H. Whitman has pointed out, the etymology of the Old English word suggests some bird name close to present-day German *Häher* (jay), in other words, "a laugher."[114] The idea is corroborated by the expression "þær ic glado sitte" (7a) [where I sit cheerfully].[115] On the other hand, the presence of verbal parallelisms with regard to Riddle 8 (nightingale) has also been pointed out.[116] It is therefore logical to assume that the inclusion of Riddle 24 at this point responds to a misplacement like that of Riddle 11, for it is quite evident that the clues betray a bird subject. The fact that this text is juxtaposed with Riddle 23 (bow), another logogriph in which the solution *boga* (bow) is to be decoded, is worth taking into account. After all, the two riddles could have been brought together because they share spelling clues.

Riddle 29 (sun and moon) constitutes a further intriguing case that deserves our attention. As with the preceding exceptions, the

---

113. Dietrich, "Die Räthsel des Exeterbuchs: Würdigung, Lösung und Herstellung," 466. Trautmann's proposal *higoræ*, the feminine form of *higora*, is based on a more accurate reading of the runic codes of the riddle. See his *Die altenglischen Rätsel*, 86. The presence of the feminine adjective "glado" (7a) supports this interpretation.
114. Charles H. Whitman, "The Birds of Old English Literature," *JEGP* 2 (1898): 161.
115. Niles, *Old English Enigmatic Poems*, 146 (n. 8), however, prefers "magpie," on the basis that this bird "is a great mimic and so has the desired vocal characteristics."
116. See above p. 307.

presence of this theme at this point can be clarified if we consider the subsequent composition (no. 30a), which was convincingly solved by F. A. Blackburn as Old English *beam*, a polysemic term meaning "tree, log, ship and cross."[117] Williamson similarly notes that the riddle "treats the various aspects and uses of a tree,"[118] a notion that accords with the fact that this text was probably understood by the compilers as an instrumental motif. Also importantly, the majority of scholars agree that the final passage alludes to the rood, as the most outstanding by-product: "Þonne ic mec onhæbbe, ond hi onhnigaþ to me / monige mid miltse, þær ic monnum sceal / ycan upcyme eadignesse" (7–9) [When I raise myself up, and many prostrate before me with reverence, I will increase the growth of (heavenly) bliss there for the people]. Contrasting with the description of the congregation fervently kneeling ("onhnigaþ," 7b) in front of the object, the playful emphasis on the actions of rising ("onhæbbe," 7a) and increasing ("ycan," 9a) leaves no room for doubt that the image of the exalted cross is meant. The traditional iconography that frequently accompanies the cross in pictorial representations may help elucidate the occurrence of this riddle among the items of this instrumental series. The cross usually co-occurs with images of the sun and the moon, symbolizing the natural convulsion caused by the crucifixion, as described in Matthew 27.51.[119] With the juxtaposition of Riddles 29 and 30a, the compilers probably aimed at reproducing this well-known joint motif, even if this meant a momentary break in thematic cohesion.[120]

---

117. F. A. Blackburn, "*The Husband's Message* and the Accompanying Riddles of the Exeter Book," *JEGP* 3 (1900): 4.
118. Williamson, *The Old English Riddles*, 231.
119. "And behold, the curtain of the temple was torn in two, from top to bottom; and the earth shook, and the rocks were split."
120. In this sense, this thematic pairing recalls Eusebius's doublet formed by Riddles 39 (the letter i) and 40 (fish). For a discussion of the combined occurrence of the cross and the sun and the moon, see especially Barbara C. Raw, *Anglo-Saxon Crucifixion Iconography and the Art of the Monastic Revival* (Cambridge: Cambridge University Press, 1990), 86–87.

The anomalous position of Riddle 33 (iceberg) can also be elucidated on the basis of riddlic pairing. The opening lines of this text describe a magnificent iceberg drifting at sea. The direct observation of a calving mass of ice approaching the coast might have triggered the comparison with a ship carrying a boisterous crew, bearing swords and inspiring terror on the inhabitants on land:[121] "Wiht cwom æfter wege wrætlicu liþan, / cymlic from ceole cleopode to londe, / hlinsade hlude; hleahtor wæs gryrelic, / egesful on earde, ecge wæron scearpe" (1–4) [a splendid creature came sailing on the water; the stately one cried out to land from its keel, loudly resounded; its laughter was terrifying, fearful on earth; the edges were sharp]. A didactic intent is here perceived, for the different clues—the horrible sound, the keel, and the sword edges—all need to be assessed as metaphorical references alluding to the iceberg, thus helping readers learn the characteristics of a natural phenomenon through the comparison with the ship. The analogy with the preceding text is also evident, as the noisy sound of the vessel when it reaches the shore is also described in Riddle 32: "Siþum sellic ic seah searo hweorfan, / grindan wið greote, giellende faran" (3–4) [I saw a wonderful device go on journeys, grind against the sand (and) move yelling]. The reference to the iceberg "crying out from its keel" in Riddle 33 could similarly be interpreted as an allusion to the mass of ice grinding the pebbles of the shore, thus paralleling the presentation of the ship in the preceding riddle. This juxtaposition also reveals a meaningful contrastive aim, since Riddle 32 describes a ship in positive terms by referring to its function as a supplier of provisions, whereas the iceberg of Riddle 33 metaphorically alludes to a ship carrying warriors who intend to launch an imminent attack on land. Once more, it seems that thematic coherence was sacrificed in an attempt to produce a suggestive riddle duo.

Solved by critics as "bullock" or "young ox," Riddle 38 is a further exception that needs to be assessed. The fact that this riddle is both

---

121. On the comparison of the iceberg with a ship, see Williamson, *The Old English Riddles*, 240.

a thematic irregularity and a repetition makes it doubly anomalous from the point of view of the compilation.[122] As discussed above with regard to Riddle 12, the allegorical role of the animal symbolizing the apostle or the monk might have prompted the compilers' special interest in this motif to the extent that the Exeter collection offers three different versions.[123] Still, its exceptional status in an instrumental series and its condition as a thematic repetition might respond to a connection with Riddle 39, as the following dicussion might help elucidate.

The solution of Riddle 39 needs to be considered here in order to understand its role in the compilation. In my view, among the numerous proposals that have been put forward for this riddle, "cloud" is the answer that best complies with all the conditions established in the text.[124] The clues of this riddle describe a creature that travels all over the world but paradoxically lacks feet or any other animate attribute that could justify such extraordinary capacity to move: "Ne hafað hio[125] fot ne folme, ne æfre foldan hran, / ne eagena ægþer twega, / ne muð hafaþ, ne wiþ monnum spræc, / ne gewit hafað . . ." (10–13a) [It has neither foot nor hand, nor does it ever reach the earth, nor has it either of the two eyes, nor has it a mouth, nor does it speak with human beings, nor has it intelligence].[126] The riddle con-

---

122. Repeated motifs rarely occur in Latin *enigmata*. However, the Bern and Vatican collections are an exception to the rule, since they offer abundant thematic repetitions probably due to the assembling of riddling material from disparate sources.

123. Note that Exeter Riddle 72 conveys a third "ox" motif.

124. Among other solutions, day, moon, time, Creature Death, dream, and speech have been offered for Riddle 39. The answer "cloud" was put forward by Christopher B. Kennedy, "Old English Riddle No. 39," *ELN* 13 (1975): 81–85, and supported by Paul Meyvaert, "The Solution to Old English Riddle 39," *Speculum* 51 (1976): 195–201.

125. Although gender clues are not wholly reliable in the Exeter Riddles, it is worth noting that the poet consistently uses "hio" (she) for the creature, an idea that may accord with *wolcne* being feminine just as Latin *nubes*; the form *wolcn* or *wolcen*, neuter, is however also common. See *BT* (s.v. "wolcen").

126. As Taylor indicates, the clue "moves without legs" frequently applies

tinues by stating that the creature lacks soul or life ("Ne hafað hio sawle ne feorh," 16a) as well as blood or bones ("Ne hafaþ hio blod ne ban," 18a). Nevertheless, it is endowed with a great capacity for traveling: "ac hio siþas sceal / geond þas wundorworuld wide dreogan" (16b-17) [but it will make journeys widely throughout this wondrous world]. An interesting parallel for Riddle 39 is Bern *Enigma* 55,[127] in which the cloud is described in a similar way: "Vestigia nulla figens perambulo terras. / Anima nec caro mihi nec cetera membra . . ." (4-5) [I wander throughout the regions without leaving any tracks behind. I do not have a soul, nor flesh, nor the rest of the limbs]. In addition to this, the opening lines of Exeter Riddle 39 offer an important hint that might be specific to the cloud motif only: "Gewritu secgað þæt seo wiht sy / mid moncynne miclum tidum / sweotol ond gesyne" (1-3a) [Writings say that the creature is manifest and visible for human beings at important times]. Meyvaert suggests that "Gewritu" (1a) in this passage could refer to the Scriptures on the basis of the numerous instances in which the phrase "Us gewritu secgað" alludes to the Bible in Anglo-Saxon literature.[128] In this light, the solution "cloud" gains ground, as the expression "miclum tidum" (2b) most likely points to the presence of clouds on relevant occasions, as found in various biblical episodes.[129]

However, the following passage has often been regarded as an obstacle to the solution "cloud":[130]

---

to closely related themes such as "a cloud, smoke, fire, wind, or a windmill." Archer Taylor, *English Riddles from Oral Tradition* (Berkeley: University of California Press, 1951), 87.

127. Note that the title-solution of Bern *Enigma* 55 is "De sole" although the clues clearly describe a cloud. On this, see Socas Gavilán, *Antología latina*, 403 (n. 352).

128. Meyvaert, "The Solution," 198-99.

129. A substantial passage from the Old English *Exodus* (71b-97) describing the cloud-pillar that protected the Israelites on their way to the Promised Land, for example, typically illustrates this. See Peter J. Lucas's comments to these lines in his *Exodus* (London: Methuen, 1977), 71-91.

130. This clue has been used by some scholars to support the answer "dream." See Stanley B. Greenfield, "Old English Riddle 39 Clear and

maran micle, Sundorcræft hafað
Heo wile gesecan þonne hit men witen.
feorhberendra, sundor æghwylcne
 gewiteð eft feran on weg. (3b–6)

[It has a much greater special power than men know of. It will seek every living creature separately; it then sets out again on a journey].

According to Bosworth and Toller, "sundorcræft" (3b) means "a special power or art, one possessed or exercised by an individual or a class."[131] It is clear that the creature is capable of performing an extraordinary task that is essential for mankind—"bearnum wearð / geond þisne middangeard mongum to frofre" (18b–19) [(it) has become a comfort to many people throughout this world]. None of the other solutions that have been proposed can really fit these clues, which most likely allude to the cloud's capacity to produce rain.

By touching on the special task performed by the cloud, readers might be implicitly urged to consider the cloud's traditional symbolism, as Meyvaert has already suspected: "Could the author be alluding to the numerous allegorical interpetations found in the patristic commentaries (Nubes = prophets, apostles, etc.)?"[132] For example, in *De natura rerum* (xxxii.1), Isidore explains that the clouds symbolize the apostles disseminating the Christian doctrine throughout the world: "Nubes autem sancti praedicatores intelleguntur, qui uerbi diuini pluuiam credentibus fundunt" [Clouds are understood as the saintly apostles, who spread the rain of God's word over the believers].[133] An interesting illustration of this idea is present in a passage from St Æthelwold's *Benedictional* in the following blessing for

---

Visible," *Anglia* 98 (1980): 95–100; Antonina Harbus, "*Exeter Book* Riddle 39 Reconsidered," *SN* 70 (1998): 139–48. For a recent reassessment of this solution, see Niles's proposal *swefn* (Lat. *somnium*), "auspicious dream" in his *Old English Enigmatic Poems*, 142 and 147 (n. 13).
131. *BT* (s.v. "sundorcræft").
132. Meyvaert, "The Solution," 199, n. 19.
133. My translation. Text from Fontaine, *Isidore de Séville: Traité de la nature*, 287.

Advent, "Aperi domine ianuas caeli, et uisita plebem tuam in pace, et mitte spiritum tuum de alto, et irriga terram nostram, ut germinet nobis spiritualem fructum" ["Open O Lord, the gates of heaven, and visit your people in peace, and send your spirit from above, and irrigate our earth, so that it may bring forth spiritual fruit for us"].[134] The passage recalls the clues of Riddle 39, as God is here urged to seek His people and send them spiritual rain from heaven.

Taking into account the traditional symbology associated with the ox and the cloud, it may be deduced that a medieval learned reader could interpret Riddles 38 and 39 as allegorically intertwined compositions, since the two topics were frequently linked to the figures of the apostle and the monk. Furthermore, with its cosmological character Riddle 39 could well have been inserted at this point as a fitting prelude to the subsequent Creation riddle. Also importantly, the instrumental section opens with Riddle 16 (anchor), whose solution would similarly bear metaphorical overtones with its traditional symbology as the hope and steadfastness of the Christian faith. As discussed above with regard to Symphosius's Riddle 61, the anchor was the last subject in several manuscripts in which this collection is extant, thus suggesting the compilers' acknowledgment of its allegorical significance.[135] Interestingly, the Old English terms *ancor/ancra* equally designate the anchorite or the ship tool,[136] so it can be inferred that the solution *ancor* might have been charged with suggestive allegorical connotations that could be easily grasped by a learned audience. In this sense, it might tentatively be assumed that Riddle 16 was deliberately chosen by the compiler as a meaningful opening for the instrumental sequence, since it constitutes a fitting allegorical counterpart to the cloud motif of Riddle 39 at the end of

---

134. The transcription of this passage is by G. F. Warner and H. A. Wilson, eds., *The Benedictional of St Æthelwold, Bishop of Winchester 963–984* (Oxford: Roxburghe Club, 1910), 2; translation by Deshman, *The Benedictional of Æthelwold*, 15. For further information on the symbology of the cloud in the Benedictional iconography and related texts, see 13–19 in the latter work.
135. See above, pp. 130-31.
136. See *DOE* (s.v. "ancor, ancra").

section 3. The opening and closing motifs of the instrumental series therefore point to a consciously arranged compilation.

4.2.4 Riddle 40: A Misplaced Coda?

An essential piece for understanding the compilation process, Riddle 40 shares some features with Riddle 1-2-3. Like the wind in that initial composition, Creation is presented in Riddle 40 as an extraordinarily mighty creature that can be controlled only by God:

> Nis under me ænig oþer
> wiht waldendre on worldlife;
> ic eom ufor ealra gesceafta,
> þara þe worhte waldend user,
> se mec ana mæg ecan meahtum,
> geþeon þrymme, þæt ic onþunian ne sceal. (86-91)

[Below me, there is no other mightier creature in this life on the world; I am above the whole of Creation which was made by our Ruler, who alone by His eternal power can subdue me with His strength so that I shall not exceed my confines].

As with the description of the various destructive aspects of the wind in the opening poem, Riddle 40 similarly hints at the negative qualities of Creation, as it also subjects human beings to extreme situations:

> Heardra ic eom ond caldra þonne se hearda forst,
> hrim heorugrimma, þonne he to hrusan cymeð;
> ic eom Ulcanus up irnendan
> leohtan leoman lege hatra. (54-57)

[I am harder and colder than the hard frost or the savage frozen rain when it comes to the ground; I am hotter than the bright blazing of Vulcan's fire when it rises up].[137]

---

137. For an analysis of the reference to Vulcan and other classical allusions in Riddle 40, see Janie Steen, *Verse and Virtuosity: The Adaptation of Latin*

But, as a whole, Riddle 40 represents God's benevolence manifested in the Creation, such that it constitutes an interesting counterpoint to the descriptions of massive natural destruction offered in Riddle 1-2-3.

Riddle 40 is a close translation of Aldhelm's *Enigma* 100,[138] a fact that can enlighten the study of the compilation. As Robert DiNapoli has pointed out, Aldhelm's poem "forms a comprehensive summary and recapitulation of the entire sequence that precedes it."[139] Several researchers, Janie Steen most recently, have noted that the Anglo-Saxon translator took pains to recreate the extremely learned contents and the aural devices of the Latin original.[140] Being the conspicuous summarizing quality and the concluding effect of the Latin riddle exactly the same in the Old English version, one wonders why the Exeter compilers—or, rather, earlier compilers—would decide at this point to add more riddles after a text that was clearly expected to be a coda.[141] As DiNapoli further observes, with the appending of further poems, Exeter Riddle 40 "has lost its authoritative position as the all-encompassing closure of the collection."[142] It might therefore be inferred that, prior to its incorporation into the Exeter Book, Riddle 40 could originally have functioned as an ending motif in the source collection from which it was drawn.

Paleographical evidence shows that the special status of Riddle 40 was acknowledged by the Exeter scribe, since it has been clearly regarded as a distinctive piece in the compilation. As observed in

---

Rhetoric in Old English Poetry (Toronto: University of Toronto Press, 2008), 103–8.

138. For a constrastive analysis of Aldhelm's *Enigma* 100 and Exeter Riddle 40, see ibid., 98–109.

139. Robert DiNapoli, "In the Kingdom of the Blind, the One-Eyed Man is a Seller of Garlic: Depth-Perception and the Poet's Perspective in the Exeter Book Riddles," *ES* 81 (2000): 439.

140. See Steen, *Verse and Virtuosity*, 100–08.

141. As Fulk has pointed out, "the position of this riddle is better explicable as the choice of a compiler than of a poet making and shaping a collection." Fulk, *A History*, 404.

142. DiNapoli, "In the Kingdom of the Blind," 439.

folio 110r of the manuscript, the scribe left a blank line between Riddles 39 and 40, an unusual feature, since that never occurs with the other riddles.[143] Similarly, Riddle 40 starts with a considerably large, adorned capital E, a further characteristic that possibly suggests the prominence of this piece in the collection. The unusual length of Riddle 40 (107 lines), which, even in its incomplete form, surpasses the extension of Riddle 1-2-3 (104 lines) also distinguishes this Creation poem from the other items of the assemblage. All this suggests that Riddle 40 was meant to mark the end of the collection in the exemplar that the Exeter scribe was using and that (s)he probably simply reproduced the visual design of the text as found in the copy (s)he had at hand.

In addition to these paleographical idiosyncrasies, we should take into account some valuable scholarly research that can shed light on our study of the role of Riddle 40 in the compilation of this first part of the collection. To begin with, O'Brien O'Keeffe has suggested that Exeter Riddle 40 could date to approximately the mid-tenth century on the basis of its stylistic parallels with the version of Aldhelm's *Enigma* 100 extant in Oxford, Rawlinson C.697, a manuscript containing annotations by Hand D, which has universally been accepted as Dunstan's. Apart from showing a similar arrangement of lines as that offered in the Latin *enigma*,[144] some of the terms used in Riddle 40 reveal a dependence on various glosses accompanying Aldhelm's Creation riddle found in Oxford, Rawlinson C.697. The most significant case is the rendering "ealdum þyrse" (63b, old giant) in Exeter Riddle 40, which translates Latin "lurconum more Ciclopum" (33) [in the way greedy cyclopes] from Aldhelm's *Enigma* 100. The Old English translation is therefore based on an understanding of "Ciclopum," which is actually a plural, as a singular form, as found in a gloss above Aldhelm's phrase, which reads "inmensum gigan-

---

143. See folio 110r in Muir's *The Exeter DVD*.
144. As O'Brien O'Keeffe has noted, Riddle 40 shows a shift of lines that is observed in Oxford, Rawlinson C.697 and other six Continental codices. "The Text of Aldhelm's *Enigma* no. C," 64 (and n. 10).

tem" (an enormous giant), in the Rawlinson manuscript (fol. 15v).¹⁴⁵ O'Brien O'Keeffe's hypothesis was confirmed by Fulk, who demonstrated that the language and meter of the poem evinced that it was composed later than the rest of the riddles.¹⁴⁶ In view of this, it is fair to conclude with O'Brien O'Keeffe that Riddle 40 was rendered into English from the source contained in Oxford, Rawlinson C.697 and copied into the exemplar of the Exeter Book not much earlier than the time the latter manuscript was compiled.

In addition, Steen has lately noted the probable glossarial origin of the Anglo-Saxon translator's misinterpretation of the Latin adjective *pernix*¹⁴⁷ as found in Aldhelm's *Enigma* 100—"plus pernix aquilis" (35) [faster than eagles]. The Latin phrase is clearly rendered as a reference to a bird in Exeter Riddle 40: "Ic mæg fromlicor fleogan þonne pernex / oþþe earn oþþe hafoc æfre meahte" (66–67) [I can fly faster than the pernex or the eagle or the hawk has ever been capable of]. The proximity of *pernix* to Latin *perdix* (partridge) might have given rise to this mistake. The latter word is vaguely glossed as "auis quaedam" (some bird) in the *Corpus Glossary*, "which preserves interpretations ultimately derived from the school of Theodore and Hadrian at Canterbury."¹⁴⁸ To this it should be added that Steen has also detected some rhetorical affinities in the mythological references of Riddle 40¹⁴⁹ with the glosses offered in the third glossary copied in London, Cotton Cleopatra A.iii in the second quarter of the tenth century.¹⁵⁰ As was pointed out above (pp. 31-32),

---

145. See ibid., 72.
146. See Fulk, *A History*, 408–9.
147. Meaning "striving or pressing through, nimble, brisk, active, agile, quick, swift, fleet." The term appears in Exeter Riddle 40 as "pernex" (66b). This misunderstanding had already been pointed out by Dietrich, "Die Räthsel des Exeterbuchs: Würdigung, Lösung und Herstellung," 455.
148. Steen, *Verse and Virtuosity*, 103. Also see Lapidge, "The School of Theodore and Hadrian," 152–54. For *perdix* and its gloss, see Lindsay, *The Corpus Glossary*, 137 (P377).
149. See Steen, *Verse and Virtuosity*, 107–9.
150. This text offers glosses to Aldhelm's prose and verse *De virginitate*. See Rusche, "Isidore's *Etymologiae*," 444–45.

the latter work contains annotations that were carried out by the St Augustine scribe who included some corrections in Oxford, Rawlinson C.697.

Evidence supplied by both O'Brien O'Keeffe and Steen therefore connects the Exeter Riddles to glossarial activity at Canterbury. It was probably there that the translation of Aldhelm's Riddle 100 was carried out at the initial stages of the cultural revival instigated by Archbishop Dunstan (959–88), who himself annotated Oxford, Rawlinson C.697 and, together with Æthelwold, was the driving force behind the intense lexicographic research that the Benedictine reform brought about.[151] The production of a translation like that of Exeter Riddle 40 might have therefore originated at Canterbury, where Aldhelm's *Enigmata* were no doubt thoroughly studied, as the glosses and annotations found in Oxford, Rawlinson C.697, London, Royal 12.C.xxiii, and Cambridge, Gg.5.35 all suggest.[152]

4.2.5 Some Final Thoughts on Group 1

The continuation of the riddles up to no. 59 is at best a contradictory fact that powerfully calls our attention. Besides, the solemnity of the Creation poem strongly contrasts with the dynamic presentation of brief pieces that follow, notably the so-called "sexual riddles."[153] In short, from the point of view of the compilation, the anomalous position of Riddle 40 in the Exeter collection constitutes a further irregularity that needs to be analyzed. In order to throw light on this, it is worth taking into account the existence of two textual lacunae in Quire XIV (fols. 106–11) of the manuscript, in which a bifolium

---

151. As demonstrated by Gretsch, *The Intellectual Foundations*, 5 and passim.
152. I am not alone in suspecting this, since, as conjectured by Steen, *Verse and Virtuosity*, 99, "It is thus tempting to speculate that Riddle 40 was composed at tenth-century Canterbury, whence several manuscripts of the *Enigmata* [of Aldhelm] derive, and where the *Enigmata* were no doubt studied, as evidenced by glosses in three Anglo-Saxon manuscripts of that period."
153. Fulk, *A History*, 404, has similarly noted the striking disparity of the learned contents of Riddle 40 when compared to the "more mundane verses surrounding it."

was lost, thus affecting the final part of Riddles 20 and 40.[154] Given that Quire XIV is ruled for twenty-two lines, the missing folio after Riddle 20 thus constitutes a loss of forty-four. Having reached line 35 (equivalent to twenty-three manuscript lines), we can infer that Riddle 20 might have been close to its conclusion. As for Riddle 21, this poem opens with a capital letter, so no text seems to be missing. Since riddles are quite extensive at this point of the manuscript, particularly after Riddle 20, we can conjecture that the missing folio contained the last part of no. 20 and at least two more riddles of considerable length.[155]

In view of this, it is possible to estimate the number of riddles that might have constituted the initial block that has just been analyzed. Given that Riddle 1-2-3 seems to have been treated as a single composition in the manuscript, the total number of riddles preserved in this first sequence is thirty-eight. We should then add the two riddles that were possibly lost between Riddles 20 and 21. As regards the total quantity of riddles in a collection, medieval compilers normally offered round numbers such as one hundred, forty or sixty. This tentatively leads us to deduce that this initial Exeter sequence might have originally comprised forty units, like Tatwine's *Enigmata*, which probably served as a model. Just as Tatwine's forty riddles were complemented by the sixty of Eusebius, the compilers eventually appended more riddles after no. 40 in an attempt to enlarge this first block and turn it into a sixty-riddle collection up to

---

154. The gap affecting Riddles 20 and 40 was first detected by Benjamin Thorpe, ed., *Codex Exoniensis: A Collection of Anglo-Saxon Poetry, from a Manuscript in the Library of the Dean and Chapter of Exeter* (London, 1842), 402 and 428. See also Chambers, *The Exeter Book*, 59.
155. Riddle 20 itself occupies the whole of folio 105v; it also has one manuscript line on the preceding folio. As indicated by the numbers between brackets offered in Appendix X, riddles are quite lengthy after no. 20. Note, for example, nos. 21 (15 lines), 22 (21), and 23 (16). The extension is actually quite regular if we compare riddles contained in the same section. This is, for instance, illustrated by the ornithological cluster: nos. 7 (9 lines), 8 (11), 9 (12), and 10 (11).

no. 59, or perhaps up to no. 66.¹⁵⁶ The second batch of riddles (nos. 61–95) would then probably amount to forty. Though separate, the two main riddlic blocks would reach the canonical one hundred, thus clearly following the tandem compilation model of Tatwine and Eusebius, as found in London, Royal 12.C.xxiii and Cambridge, Gg.5.35. This fact relates Group 1 to Canterbury, where these two manuscripts, the only surviving codices containing Tatwine's and Eusebius's collections, are from.

Even if this analysis is inevitably conjectural, it suggests that the first 38 riddles form a collection that, prior to the loss of a bifolium in present-day Quire XIV (fols. 106–11), comprised forty items at some point. My suspicion is that this collection constituted a single source that was copied as an entire block into the Exeter Book. This hypothesis concurs with that of Wim Tigges, who has surmised that the Exeter Riddles could stem from a smaller collection that was later enlarged:

> As some folios are clearly missing (as can be ascertained from gaps in the text), and as the Latin riddle collections tended to comprise round numbers of 100, 60 or 40 items, it may not be too speculative to assume that at some stage in the compilation an "editor" was trying to either eke out an extant collection from the smaller to the greater number, or to make up a native collection by culling items from the native (oral?) as well as from the learned Latin (written) tradition, until an orderly figure of one hundred was reached.¹⁵⁷

Fulk's linguistic study of the riddlic string up to Riddle 40 similarly supports this contention: "Even if the riddles are of diverse origins, undoubtedly small groups of them stem from a single source."¹⁵⁸ This

---

156. See my discussion of Riddle 66 further on pp. 386–90.
157. Wim Tigges, "Snakes and Ladders: Ambiguity and Coherence in the Exeter Book Riddles and Maxims," in *Companion to Old English Poetry*, ed. Rolf H. Bremmer and Henk Aertsen (Amsterdam: VU University Press, 1994), 97.
158. Fulk, *A History*, 406.

might be so for the cluster formed by Riddles 1–40. Interestingly, Fulk has also highlighted the occurrence of variant formulas of the kind "ic eom wunderlicu wiht" in the initial batch of poems, the latest illustration being Riddle 29 (7a), thus concluding that "This small group, then, is very likely by a single poet."[159] All these considerations therefore reinforce the hypothesis that Group 1 was probably a separate collection. As anticipated above, Riddle 40 is most probably a poem whose rendering into the vernacular was roughly contemporary with the compilation of this source collection included in the exemplar of the Exeter Book. It may be tentatively inferred that the translation of Aldhelm's *Enigma* 100 was expressly carried out to convey a coda to a collection of riddles of earlier creation.

As a whole, the sequence formed by Riddles 1–40 evinces a characteristic arrangement into sections, which reflects a deliberate imitation of the encyclopedic patterns observed in the *enigmata* of Symphosius, Aldhelm, Tatwine, and Eusebius. This initial cluster, which constitutes the nucleus of the Exeter Riddles, therefore seems to have been originally designed as an independent collection, comprising forty items (like Tatwine's), to which the other riddles were eventually appended. The thematic plan of this source collection seems to follow the twofold encyclopedic pattern found in Isidore's second decade: on the one hand, the "Opera-Dei" motifs that include the cosmological and zoological themes; on the other, the "Opera-hominis" themes that are represented by the long instrumental section. Ending with an undoubtedly appropriate coda (Riddle 40), the structure of this source collection thus echoes Symphosius's twofold subdivision and Aldhelm's scheme aiming to cover the whole of God's Creation. Despite the thematic inconsistencies offered by Riddles 4 and 5, the initial cosmological section and the final Creation riddle therefore function as a framework enclosing the different themes of the source collection. Apart from these parallels with the Symphosian and Aldhelmian models, the Exeter compilation also seems to be structurally close to the thematic distribution observed

---

159. Ibid.

in the composite assemblage of Tatwine and Eusebius, especially with respect to the zoological and instrumental clusters.

Despite this conscious reproduction of riddling compilation models, the extent of the imitation of Latin patterns is not great, since there are clear signs pointing to an attempt to offer a vernacular collection with an innovative stamp. This is observable, for instance, in the compiler's choice of the storm motifs to fulfill the traditional requirements of a cosmological (and theological) opening and in the presence of homely species in the animal section. The study of the thematic organization of Exeter Riddles 1–40 has also revealed that, like Latin *enigmata*, their compilation was ruled by a manifest didactic intent. The cosmological framework suggests a conscious effort to endow the collection with a notable instructional character. Furthermore, the distribution of the zoological riddles into birds and four-footed animals clearly supports this didactic approach. The oppositional pairings of the ornithological series in turn suggest that a contemporary audience should have been aware of the allegorical dimension of the different topics, just as the polarization of the stork (no. 56) and the subsequent bird riddles in Eusebius's homologous section hints at. The internal twofold subdivision of the ornithological series therefore not only points to a possible didactic plan but also collections a moralizing reading of these riddles.

The didactic component is not restricted to the cosmological and zoological sections, since the analysis of the instrumental sequence has similarly revealed an interest in catalogues of implements as found in Symphosius's and Tatwine's collections—as well as in Isidore's Books XVIII–XX of the *Etymologiae*. Thematic exceptions in this series also indicate a conspicuous concern with pedagogic purposes; for example, the pairing of Riddles 21 (plow) and 22 (Charles's Wain) presupposes an audience well-read in the basics of medieval cosmology. Similarly, the juxtaposition of Riddles 29 (sun and moon) and 30a (tree) would require an acquaintance with the joint motif of the cross flanked by the celestial bodies in pictorial art, a notion suggesting the scriptural account of the Crucifixion.

Despite the general thematic design and the evident didactic component pervading the collection, there are several ruptures of orderly coherence, as nos. 4, 5, 11, 13, 22, 24, 29, 33, 38 and 39 have illustrated. The exceptions surpass by far those observed in Latin *enigmata* collections. Furthermore, there are some texts that seem to provide an ambivalent role, for example Riddle 11, whose ascription to the zoological category cannot be conclusive. All this seems to imply that, in the course of transmission, the original thematic arrangement might have been disorganized or corrupted due to subsequent acts of compilation. As was customary, riddle collections often circulated in manuscripts either without the solutions or with a minimum indication of the answers by means of initial letters or codes. Owing to this practice, it is not surprising that the usual absence of solutions, together with the frequent handling of riddling material from disparate sources, might have resulted in a possible distortion of orderly arrangement. A revealing example of this is Riddle 11 (cup of wine), whose first two lines could well have motivated its inclusion in the ornithological series, as I have argued above. Also significant is the exceptional occurrence of Riddle 24 (jay), which is clearly displaced from the zoological series. In this sense, the sequence of Riddles 1–40 denotes a somewhat imperfect imitation of Latin structural patterns. It may be conjectured, then, that in its current state the compilation of riddles in the Exeter Book derives from an exemplar executed by a scribe who either was not well acquainted with the custom of organizing riddles in thematic sequences or simply did not always understand the texts (s)he was copying, so that riddling materials were consequently intermingled with one another in a somewhat haphazard arrangement. In spite of this, Riddles 1–40 preserve much of the original organization inspired by the Isidorean model of compilation as transmitted in the *enigmata* of Symphosius, Aldhelm, Tatwine, and Eusebius.

4.3. An Addition Based on Analogy: Group 2 (Riddles 41–59)

The next sequence that I am going to discuss covers Riddles 41 to 59, at which point the Exeter collection was temporarily stopped. As noted above, the uncommon length of Riddle 40 and its particular paleographical features most probably indicate that this composition was meant as a closing topic for the collection, at least in the exemplar from which the Exeter scribe was copying. But maybe, we may speculate, these visual elements were at some point produced in order to make Riddle 40 an appropriate coda for the Exeter collection as well. However, the brevity of this initial assemblage did not satisfy the compilers, who eventually decided to extend the initial forty-piece assemblage up to Riddle 59. For this, it may be inferred, further pieces from a different collection were provided, of which Riddle 41 (water), a cosmological subject, was probably the opening text.

4.3.1 Section 4 (Riddles 42–46)[160]

As with Tatwine's section 5, one of the cohesive factors of the riddles comprising Exeter section 4 is, with the exception of Riddle 43, the presence of sexual imagery and/or double entendre.[161] As this is a non-encyclopedic criterion of organization, I will make only passing reference to these elements in this chapter,[162] focusing instead on the ways in which the riddles of this series are interrelated by means of analogy.

---

160. The discussion of the riddles forming part of this section is based on my analysis of these texts in "The Key to the Body."
161. These pieces were formerly known as "obscene riddles," a nomenclature that has been replaced by "sexual" in the past decades because of the first's strongly negative connotations. For further information on the Exeter sexual riddles, see Reinhard Gleissner's *Die "zweideutigen" altenglischen Rätsel des Exeter Book in ihrem zeitgenössischen Kontext* (Frankfurt: Peter Lang, 1984); D. K. Smith's "Humor in Hiding: Laughter Between the Sheets in the Exeter Book Riddles," *Humour in Anglo-Saxon Literature*, ed. Jonathan Wilcox (Cambridge: Brewer, 2000), 79–98; and Jorge Luis Bueno Alonso, "Actitudes anglosajonas hacia el humor: la caracterización del humor obsceno y sexual en los acertijos de Exeter Book," *Cuadernos del CEMYR* 12 (2004): 17–36. More recently, Murphy, *Unriddling*, esp. 175–219, has explored the popular roots of the Exeter sexual riddles.
162. For this, see my "The Sexual Riddle Type in Aldhelm's *Enigmata*."

The first poem of section 4, Riddle 42, famously starts with the description of the rooster and the hen coupling:

Ic seah wyhte	wrætlice twa
undearnunga	ute plegan
hæmedlaces;	hwitloc anfeng
wlanc under wædum,	gif þæs weorces speow,
fæmne fyllo. (1–5a)	

[I saw two splendid creatures openly having sex outside; if the act turned out well, the lustful bright-haired girl took on plumpness under her garments].

Apart from the explicitness of the opening image, critics have pointed out the presence of words that possibly form part of the colloquial register—notably, "plegan" (2b) and "hæmedlaces" (3a).[163] Indeed, by contrast with other riddles of this series, Riddle 42 lacks double entendre, probably because the two creatures committing the sin of fornication are animals, not human beings. The clues of Riddle 42 insist on the irrational quality of these creatures. In this sense, the paronomastic pair "wihta"/"witan" is here used to underline the difference between beasts—"wihta" (8a)—indulging openly in sexual pleasure, and human beings who know about books—"þe bec witan" (7a)—in other words, the ones characterized by reason.

Scholars have also pointed out the learned character of Riddle 42, as perceived in the names of the two creatures, which are spelled out by means of transliterated clues, giving rise to the double solution *hana* (rooster) and *hæn* (hen):

---

163. Julie Coleman has listed both *plegan* and *hæmed* among other Old English terms alluding to sex that have been traditionally affected by editorial euphemism in dictionaries: "Sexual Euphemism in Old English," *NM* 93 (1992): 93–94. For an assessment of the advances of the Dictionary of Old English in this semantic field, see Roberta Frank, "Sex in the Dictionary of Old English," in *Unlocking the Wordhord: Anglo-Saxon Studies in Memory of Edward B. Irving, Jr.*, ed. Mark C. Amodio and Katherine O'Brien O'Keeffe (Toronto: University of Toronto Press, 2003), 302–12.

twega oþer
an an linan,
Hægelas swa some. (8b-11a)

Þær sceal Nyd wesan
ond se torhta Æsc
Acas twegen,

[Need (N) will be there twice, and the beautiful Ash (Æ), only one in a row, two Oaks (A), and the same (amount) of hail (H)].

In a way that recalls the encyclopedic principle of *differentia*, the riddle seems to focus on the striking resemblance of the two words and how the same letters can basically spell two different concepts by providing a minimum variation (runic Æ). The physical union of the two fowls thus symbolizes this philological connection.[164] Also, in a typically Isidorean fashion, the poet has created an etymological clue *ad hoc* by describing the two birds as "heanmode" (low-minded, 17a),[165] an adjective that playfully relates the names of the two animals—*hana* and *hæn*—and their basic instincts at the end of the text.

Further on, the clues of Riddle 42 state that only by means of the power of a key—"cægan cræfte" (12a)—can the solution be achieved. This phrase obviously refers to the fact that the solving of this riddle depends on the correct decoding of the runes. But it also alludes to the commonplace notion that letters are the key to knowledge—and, by extension, of spiritual life. The metaphorical implication goes beyond the solving of the riddle and implicitly suggests that literacy leads to salvation. As discussed above with regard to other riddles from the Latin collections, the choice of the rooster and the hen may also hide further allegorical significance, as it might have been intended to represent the traditional conflict between carnal desire and spiritual aspirations. The two creatures involved in the sexual act could therefore evoke the allegorical representation of the body and soul, the subject of the subsequent riddle.

---

164. DiNapoli has similarly appreciated that "the cock and hen are if anything even more intimately and thoroughly united than they are by their physical union on the literal level." DiNapoli, "In the Kingdom of the Blind," 448.
165. *BT*, "dejected, cast down, humiliated" (s.v. "heanmod").

The opening lines of Riddle 43 stress the superior nature of the soul, which is said to be unaffected by the torments that the body, on the contrary, must endure:

Ic wat indryhtne   æþelum deorne
giest in geardum,   þam se grimma ne mæg
hungor sceððan   ne se hata þurst,
yldo ne adle. (1–4a)

[I know an aristocratic, noble, bold guest at home,[166] whom severe hunger cannot damage, nor hot thirst, nor old age nor illness].

As observed in this excerpt, the term "frea" designates the soul, which is thus fittingly characterized with adjectival class-markers such as "indryhtne" (1a)[167] and "æþelum" (1b). Conversely, "esne"— meaning "man of low social status"[168] or simply "servant"—is used three times further in the poem (5a, 8b, and 16a) as an allusion to the body. This verbal distinction highlights the idea of the subservience of the body to the soul, the latter being the intellectual and spiritual part of human beings.

The instructional overtones of Riddle 43 are particularly evident in lines 4b–10a, which emphasize the positive effect of a life grounded in spiritual aims, not in carnal interests, a plea that also finds an echo in the preceding composition. In this sense, Riddle 43 also warns potential readers of the disastrous consequences that will be faced by those who allow the body to rule their lives, just as in Riddle 42 lechery and irrational behavior in general were contrasted with spiritual life based on learning. Riddle 43 clearly continues the carnal/spiritual reflection initiated in the preceding composition. We may therefore infer that Riddle 43 was juxtaposed with the preceding composition owing to their ostensible thematic connection and the instructional overtones

---

166. *DOE* (s.v. "geard," 1): "*in geardum*, 'at home.'"
167. I here follow Neville's reading of *dryht* and its derivatives as conveying primarily the "the idea of nobility." See her "Speaking the Unspeakable," 525. Also see *DOE* (s.v. "dryht").
168. *DOE* (s.v. "esne").

shared by the two texts. Just as the rooster and hen of Riddle 42 allegorically represent the battle between fleshly desires and spiritual aspirations, Riddle 43 offers this conflictive duality in a literal plane. Also importantly, Riddle 42 appears on folio 112r of the manuscript with no strong punctuation or blank space at the end to separate it from Riddle 43—even if the latter begins with a small capital.[169] The omission of end-punctuation may be due to the compilers' acknowledgment of the allegorical links connecting these two compositions.

With the reference to the key and the lock alluding to male and female pudenda, Riddle 44 contributes to the display of the metaphorical dichotomies and analogies initiated with Riddle 42. The sexual connotations of key imagery are well known from the Song of Songs and medieval lyrics.[170] In this sense, the association of the metaphorical penis (the key) and the "cuþe hol" (5b)—the well-known hole or lock—of Riddle 44 correspond to the copulating rooster and hen of Riddle 42, as well as to the soul-and-body union of Riddle 43.

As regards Riddle 45, the clues present the process of kneading and baking the dough as being suggestive of the sexual act. Thus, "banlease" (boneless, 3a) and "þrindende þing" (swelling thing, 5a), which ambiguously apply both to the dough and to the male sexual organ, favor the double entendre. The term "hygewlonc" (4a), which characterizes the woman kneading the dough, parallels the use of similar expressions in other sexual riddles in which the meaning is assumed to be "wanton" or "lustful."[171] Despite the sexual innuendo, the clues of Riddle 45 would surely remind an ecclesiastical audience of a well-known parable, in which the growing and spreading

---

169. See folio 112r in Muir's *The Exeter DVD*.
170. Song of Songs 5.2 and 5.4–6. See, for example, Cambridge Song 49. Ziolkowski, *The Cambridge Songs*, 126–27, and my comments in "The Key to the Body," 77. Also, for the key as a metaphorical allusion to the Virgin Mary as the "closed gate," see Exeter Advent Lyric 9 (328–34) and Robert B. Burlin's comments in *The Old English Advent: A Typological Commentary* (New Haven, CT: Yale University Press, 1968), 147–49.
171. Bogislav V. Lindheim, "Traces of Colloquial Speech in OE," *Anglia* 70 (1951): 35. For example, the hen in Riddle 42 is described as "wlanc" (4a).

of God's kingdom is expressed in similar terms: "The kingdom of heaven is like leaven which a woman took and hid in three measures of flour, till it was all leavened."¹⁷² The image of the lady of Riddle 45 covering the dough under her clothes thus conjures up that of the biblical woman hiding the leaven in the flour:¹⁷³ "hrægle þeahte / þrindende þing þeodnes dohtor" (4b-5) [the prince's daughter concealed the swelling thing with her garment]. On the other hand, the negative connotations of leaven in St Paul's first letter to the Corinthians (5.6) are also worth exploring in connection with Riddle 45: "Do you not know that a little leaven leavens the whole lump?" Sinful behavior spreading in a Christian community is thus represented in the Pauline text with the powerful image of a small amount of yeast fermenting a whole piece of dough. A similar metaphorical allusion is used in the devil's speech in *Juliana* to illustrate the secretive ways in which Satan corrupts the weaker Christian:

         ac ic geomor sceal
secan oþcrnc   ellenleasran,
under cumbolhagan,   cempan sænran,
þe ic onbryrdan mæge   beorman mine,
agælan æt guþe. (393b-97a)

["but (I, the devil), downcast, must seek out another (warrior), a baser soldier whom I can puff up with my leaven and hinder in the fray"].¹⁷⁴

---

172. Matthew 13.33. Also, see Luke 13.20–21. For further biblical resonances in Riddle 45, see Winfried Rudolf, "Riddling and Reading: Iconicity and Logogriphs in Exeter Book Riddles 23 and 45," *Anglia* 130 (2012): 499–525, esp. 517–18.
173. Translation from S. A. J., Bradley, trans., *Anglo-Saxon Poetry* (London: Dent, 1981), 311. Words within parentheses for clarification are mine. Also, see my comments on *Vainglory* (23–25), in "The Key to the Body," 83.
174. Translation from S. A. J., Bradley, *Anglo-Saxon Poetry* (London: Dent, 1981), 311. Words within parentheses for clarification are mine. Also, see my comments on parallel images of swelling and fermentation in *Vainglory* (23-25) in "The Key to the Body," 83–84.

The reading of the clues of Exeter Riddle 45 alluding to the swelling of the dough might therefore prompt similar allegorical resonances.

A popular theme in both literary and folklore tradition, Riddle 46 would no doubt remind learned readers of the episode found in Genesis 19.30–38. Having lost his wife as he escaped the destruction of Sodom with his family, Lot took refuge in a cave with his daughters. Once there, the daughters contrived a plan to seduce their father in order to bear him offspring; they made him become drunk and slept with him. As a result, two sons, Moab and Ammon, were born. Exeter Riddle 46 presents the outcome of this incestuous relationship, which ends up in a confusing family structure: "Wer sæt æt wine mid his wifum twam / ond his twegen suno ond his twa dohtor, / swase gesweostor, ond hyra suno twegen, / freolico frumbearn" (1–4a) [a man sat at wine with his two wives, and his two sons and his two daughters, sisters of their own, and their two sons, handsome firstborn children]. These clues subtly hint at the negative consequences of wine inebriation and illicit sexual behavior.[175] As pointed out by Reinhard Gleissner, Riddle 46 would probably conjure up the traditional exegetical interpretation of this biblical episode, as illustrated in Bede's commentary on Genesis, in which Lot's daughters are said to represent the carnal thoughts ("carnales . . . cogitationes") with which eminent men ("sublimium uirorum") are sometimes tempted.[176] Seen in this light, Lot's sons would thus symbolize the sins and vices generated by these thoughts.[177]

As can be gathered from this discussion, section 4 as a whole might have been devised as a warning for readers to beware of the dangers of relying too much on the flesh.[178] The components of this

---

175. For a reference to Lot as an illustration of the consequences of immoderate sexual behavior in Aldhelm's poetic *De virginitate*, see above, p. 211 (n. 379).
176. Gleissner, *Die "zweideutigen" altenglischen Rätsel*, 321 (n. 557). The text from Bede's commentary is cited from Charles W. Jones, ed., *In principium Genesim*, CCSL, vol. 118A (Turnhout: Brepols, 1967), 230.
177. Gleissner, *Die "zweideutigen" altenglischen Rätsel*, 321–22.
178. Rudolf, "Riddling and Reading," 522, has similarly detected in Riddle

section are thus tightly interrelated, fittingly starting with Riddle 42, which establishes the difference between animal irrational behavior and the wisdom of letters as represented by humans. In turn, this riddle constitutes an allegorical prelude to the soul and the body in the subsequent piece (no. 43), in which the surpassing spiritual qualities of the soul are extolled and contrasted with the weak, corruptible nature of the body. The veiled plea in the two riddles seems to be that the spiritual part should prevail over the bodily part and the carnal instincts, as illustrated by animal conduct. In turn, Riddles 44 and 45 are linked by their use of sexual double entendre and their evocation of biblical imagery, the latter a characteristic that is also shared by Riddle 46.[179] Being the last piece of the series, the Lot riddle was probably selected as a coda for the series because it illustrates a conduct that is doubly anomalous, since, apart from incest, it entails bigamy.

As a whole, section 4 evinces a notable cohesiveness and a concern with offering subjects entailing double solutions.

42. Rooster and hen
43. Soul and body
44. Key and lock
45. Dough and oven
46. Lot and his family

The first four texts of this series thus allude directly or indirectly to a pair of creatures, which are clearly assigned male and female roles. In the case of Riddles 44 and 45, the literal reading entails the allusion to a pair of domestic items such as the key and the lock, as well as the dough and the oven—even if the latter is only vaguely suggested by the expression "on wincle" (1a, in a corner). The two texts also make use of double entendre to evoke the description of sexual intercourse and suggest the implicit solution "penis" and "vagina."

---

45 a "warning to male audiences" against women's seductive ways.
179. Rudolf also regards Riddle 45 as "a fitting companion and a chronological predecessor to Riddle 46." Ibid., 518.

It is also noticeable that three of the riddles of section 4 conjure up pregnancy or offspring as a result of the sexual intercourse hinted by the clues. In Riddle 42, the hen is said to grow plump, as suggested by the term "fyllo" (5a), under her garments ("under wædum," 4a). In Riddle 45, the dough swelling in the oven metaphorically stands for the pregnant woman. Furthermore, Winfried Rudolf has also recently interpreted the obscure reference to the dough being in the corner ("on wincle") as punning on "OE *wencel*, meaning 'child (of either sex).'"[180] Finally, Lot's sons are explicitly mentioned in Riddle 46 as the result of the incestuous relation. In sum, section 4 offers subjects that are intertwined by means of analogy, sexual imagery, double entendre, allegory and biblical allusion.

4.3.2 Section 5 (Riddles 47–66)

Riddle 47 initiates an instrumental series whose components share several characteristics evincing the fact that they constitute a separate thematic sequence, which I have designated as "Tools II" in Appendix X. This series recalls Exeter section 3 (Tools I), which offered a similar illustration of topics. But, unlike the former, Tools II seems to have been distributed into three subgroups, two of which form part of Group 2; a third one, as will be discussed later, is included in Group 3.

4.3.2.1 Subgroup A (Riddles 47–51)

The cluster of riddles that I have designated as subgroup A of section 5 provides subjects that are either directly or indirectly related to the notion of written culture, thus bringing to mind the thematic string observed in Eusebius's section 4. The initial piece of this sequence, Riddle 47, is undoubtedly one of the most popular texts of the Exeter Book.[181] On the basis of its parallelisms with Symphosius Riddle 16, which is generally acknowledged as a source, it has been assumed that Exeter Riddle 47 describes a bookworm eating some parchment.

---

180. Ibid., 513.
181. See above, pp. 287–88 (n. 8).

Moððe word fræt.	Me þæt þuhte
wrætlicu wyrd,	þa ic þæt wundor gefrægn,
þæt se wyrm forswealg	wera gied sumes,
þeof in þystro,	þrymfæstne cwide
ond þæs strangan staþol.	Stælgiest ne wæs
wihte þy gleawra,	þe he þam wordum swealg.

[A moth devoured words. When I found out about this wonder, a surprising event, I thought that the worm, a thief in darkness, swallowed the poem (made) by some man, his glorious speech (i.e., the words) and its firm foundation (i.e., the parchment). The thievish guest was not at all wiser by swallowing these words].

Fred C. Robinson has pointed out the numerous layers of wordplay observed in Riddle 47, arguing that there are "successions of interconnected puns organized around a central subject."[182] There is thus a particular insistence on terms starting with *w* that accompany the pivotal term "word" (1a), a metonymic reference to parchment and, therefore, a representation of written wisdom or books: "wrætlicu wyrd" (2a), "wundor" (2b), "wyrm" (3a), "wera" (3b), "wihte" (6a), and "wordum" (6b). Some of these terms relate to one another in a playful way, as in the case of the pair "wera"/ "wyrm" in line 3.[183] Further punning words are "þystro" (4a), which means darkness but also carries overtones of ignorance, and "cwide" (4b), meaning

---

182. Fred C. Robinson, "Artful Ambiguities," 356.
183. A further pair is *word/wyrd*, whose paronomastic possibilities were well known in Old English poetry. Frank illustrates this conceptual association in the Old English *Genesis*, namely in the episode narrating God's reply to Sarah's distrust, when Isaac's birth was announced to her: "Ne wile Sarran so gelyfan / wordum minum. Sceal seo wyrd swa þeah / forð steallian swa ic þe æt frymþe gehet" (2390–92) ["Sarah does not want to believe the truth in My words. Nevertheless, that destiny must take place which I promised you in the beginning"]. See Roberta Frank, "Some Uses of Paronomasia in Old English Scriptural Verse," *Speculum* 47 (1972): 214. See also 214–15 for further examples. The text and translation from the *Genesis* excerpt are also from this article.

"utterance, voice, speech; something said,"[184] which Robinson interpreted as a wordplay on *cwidu*, literally, "what is chewed."[185] On the basis of this assumption, "cwide" therefore alludes to the fact that vellum is merely food for the ignorant bookworm, just as fodder is for animals. The attribution of irrationality and lack of intelligence to animals therefore recalls Riddle 42, in which the distinction between bookish human beings and the fowls indulging in sex was established in a similar way.

A puzzling aspect of Riddle 47 is the fact that the poem opens with the word "moððe" (1a),[186] a term that is usually found as a gloss of Latin *tinea*.[187] Although it is actually in the larval phase that the insect can devour vellum,[188] the riddler did not seem to attach much importance to the fact that he had mentioned the solution, or at least part of it, in the first line. With regard to this, Robinson states that Riddle 47 "seems embarrassingly unproblematic," adding that "since it begins and ends by stating the answer to the riddle . . . it appears to be no riddle at all."[189] Apart from the fact that the solution could include parchment as well,[190] it might be surmised that the image of the bookworm eating vellum may be a metaphorical reference to something else. Given that the interpretation of Riddle 47 strongly depends on the reading of punning terms, this seems quite logical. As discussed above, the riddle insists on the combined idea of liter-

---

184. *DOE* (s.v. "cwide").
185. Robinson, "Artful Ambiguities," 358. *BT* (s.v. "cwidu") and *DOE* (s.v. "cwudu, cudu").
186. On "moððe" and the different occurrences of this term in Anglo-Saxon literature, see John Van Zandt Cortelyou, *Die altenglischen Namen der Insekten, Spinnen- und Krustentiere* (Heidelberg: Carl Winter, 1906), 55–57.
187. For example, as offered in Ælfric's *Glossary*: "tinea moððe." Zupitza, *Ælfrics Grammatik und Glossar*, 310. See the same correspondence in Porter, *The Antwerp-London Glossaries*, vol. 1, 61 (547).
188. As explained by Niles, *Old English Enigmatic Poems*, 120, it is at this stage that the moth is "equipped by nature to eat its way through the organic tissue in which it had been deposited when in the form of an egg."
189. Robinson, "Artful Ambiguities," 356.
190. See Niles, *Old English Enigmatic Poems*, 122.

acy, as represented by "word" (1a) / "wordum" (6b), and the action of eating. The closeness of the term "cwide" (speech) to *cwidu* (what is chewed), as noted by Robinson, thus helps establish this connection. Furthermore, there is a literal allusion to the bookworm devouring words—"Moððe word fræt" (1a)[191]—and to its swallowing them—"forswealg" (3a) and "wordum swealg" (6b)—which leads us to suspect that these expressions could also be interpreted figuratively.

After studying the frequent occurrence of images of eating and swallowing in medieval illuminated manuscripts, Michael Camille concluded that this widespread phenomenon was related to the concept of *ruminatio* in the monastic context.[192] Indeed, *ruminatio*, which literally refers to how cattle and other animals digest their food, became a powerful metaphor for the assimilation of the Scriptures and other texts. A well-known example is that of Cædmon, who is described in Bede's *Historia ecclesiastica* (IV.24) as "ruminating" his daily lessons on sacred history at Whitby "like some clean animal chewing the cud" ("et quasi mundum animal ruminando").[193] It is therefore with the concept of *ruminatio* in mind that we should approach the clues of Exeter Riddle 47.[194] In this light, one wonders if the key word "moððe"—which was probably meant to translate Latin *tinea* from Symphosius's Riddle 16—might have had a contemporary meaning similar to the colloquial usage of PDE "bookworm,"[195] so

---

191. On the use of *fretan*, see Hugh Magennis, *Anglo-Saxon Appetites: Food and Drink and Their Consumption in Old English and Related Literature* (Dublin: Four Courts, 1999), 74, and further in this book (pp. 404–05).
192. Michael Camille, *Image on the Edge: The Margins of Medieval Art* (Cambridge, MA: Harvard University Press, 1992), 63–64.
193. Text and translation from Colgrave and Mynors, *Bede's Ecclesiastical History*, 418–19. See also Philip J. West, "Rumination in Bede's Account of Cædmon," *Monastic Studies* 12 (1976): 217–26, and Gernot Wieland, "Cædmon, the Clean Animal," *American Benedictine Review* 35 (1984): 194–203.
194. A further study considering *ruminatio* as being essential for the understanding of the clues of Riddle 47 is Scattergood, "Eating the Book," especially 120–23.
195. Although evidence of colloquial speech in Old English is very difficult to prove, Lindheim demonstrated the existence of possible colloquial

that the Old English term could equally be a metaphorical reference to a monk or a student.[196] The image of the bookworm tunneling books would no doubt be familiar to the medieval readers of Exeter Riddles and could have prompted a caricature for a slow-witted monk[197] unsuccessfully "ruminating" the contents of excellent learned books.[198] Furthermore, Niles argues that the terms used in the riddle point to the psalms as the "glorious speech" ("þrymfæstne cwide," 4b) or the song ("gied," 3b) that the bookworm is eating.[199] The common knowledge that the psalms were authored by King David—possibly the man ("wera . . . sumes," 3b) alluded to in the poem—also adds further weight to this assumption. This idea suits the school context of the riddle, since students were expected to thoroughly scrutinize and memorize the psalter.[200]

---

expressions in poetry, especially in the Exeter Riddles. Lindheim, "Traces of Colloquial Speech in OE."

196. When commenting on Symphosius's *Enigma* 16, Bergamin, *Aenigmata Symposii*, 102, points out the universal character of this association: "The image of the moth which is portrayed here corresponds to that of Italian 'topo di biblioteca,' and of English 'bookworm'" (my translation). Pavlovskis, "The Riddler's Microcosm," 226, likewise considers Symphosius's bookworm riddle as "an allegory for an unsuccessful student."

197. I am not alone in suspecting that a human being could be behind the clues of this riddle. See Martin Foys, "The Undoing of Exeter Book Riddle 47: 'Bookmoth,'" Festschrift (title confidential) (Tempe, AZ: ACMRS, forthcoming).

198. The association of *ruminatio* with Riddle 47 was kindly pointed out to me by Andrew Galloway. I thank Prof. Galloway for this and for other insightful readings he shared with me while I was a student at Cornell University. For further information on the concept of *ruminatio*, see Mary Carruthers, *The Book of Memory: A Study of Memory in Medieval Culture* (Cambridge: Cambridge University Press, 1990), esp. 164–67.

199. The solution he proposes is thus "maða ond sealm-boc" (maggot and psalter) for Riddle 47. Niles, *Old English Enigmatic Poems*, 120–21 and 142.

200. For the crucial role of the psalter in the medieval system of education, see George Hardin Brown, "The Dynamics of Literacy in Anglo-Saxon England," *Bulletin of the John Rylands University Library* 77 (1995): 122, and "The Psalms as the Foundation of Anglo-Saxon Learning," in *The Place of*

This interpretation of "moððe" may not seem far-fetched if we take into account that riddles from the Exeter collection only occasionally mention the solution and, when they do, this is usually provided by means of codes, as, for instance, in the case of Riddle 23, in which "Ago*b*" (1a) is spelled backward in order to hide its solution, Old English *boga* (bow).[201] On the other hand, the metaphorical resonances detected in the study of the pairing of the Exeter bird riddles in section 2 leave no room for doubt that an allegorical reading was applied to these subjects. In this sense, the bookworm of Riddle 47 recalls the negative connotations of the cuckoo in Riddle 9, whose solution, Old English *geac* (Latin *cuculus*), might have carried similar colloquial reminiscences suggesting a wayward student.[202]

Tupper drew attention to Riddle 13 of the Holme collection (c. 1640)[203] as an analogue of Exeter Riddle 47:

> Q[estion]. l[e]arning doth feed me yet j know no letter
> j have lived among books yet am never the bet-
> ter j have eaten up the muses yet j know not a
> verse what student that is j prey y^u rehearse

A[nswer]. a worme bred in a booke.[204]

Apart from its evident resemblance to Symphosius's *Enigma* 16, the Holme piece is also noteworthy because of the metaphorical allusion

---

the Psalms in the Intellectual Culture of the Middle Ages, ed. Nancy van Deusen (Albany: State University of New York Press, 1999), 1–24. Also, see Niles, *Old English Enigmatic Poems*, 168.

201. Actually, the manuscript reading is "Agof," a form that is retained by Krapp and Dobbie, *ASPR*, vol. 3, 192. See Muir, *The Exeter DVD* (fol. 106v). The hypotheses provided by different scholars for the occurrence of this mispelling are conveninently gathered in Williamson, *The Old English Riddles*, 204–05.

202. See above, p. 309.

203. See Frederick Jr. Tupper, "The Holme Riddles (MS. Harl. 1960)," *PMLA* 18 (1903): 211–73.

204. The edition is from ibid., 221–22 (no. 13). Interestingly, the collection also includes a riddle on Lot and his daughters (221, no. 10).

to the bookworm as a "student." It is similarly remarkable that here the "booke" forms part of the solution, just as "parchment" may be part of the answer to Exeter Riddle 47, as Niles has argued.[205] In Symphosius's collection, however, the bookworm motif appears in zoological section 3 (see Appendix III). Although Riddle 47 was no doubt inspired by the Latin source, the clues clearly dwell on the reference to words or speech that are put on parchment, thus suggesting that the Exeter piece rather functions as a writing motif.[206]

Subgroup A of section 5 continues with Riddle 48. Most scholars agree that its solution is an object of Christian cult that has been identified as either a chalice or a paten. The description of the hidden object as a "hring" (1b) can certainly apply to both objects: "Ic gefrægn for hæleþum *hring gyddian*,[207] / torhtne butan tungan, tila þeah he hlude / stefne ne cirmde, strongum wordum" (1–3) [I have heard of a bright ring speaking rightly before men without a tongue, although it did not shout in a loud voice with strong words]. Tupper favored *huseldisc* or paten, a solution that has also been supported by Niles.[208] Riddle 48 presents the typical paradoxical description

---

205. Niles, *Old English Enigmatic Poems*, 122. By contrast with Exeter Riddle 47 and the Holme piece, the title-solution "De tinea" in Symphosius's *Enigma* 16 clearly leaves out what the moth is eating. Furthermore, the clues do not mention the insect.

206. For an analysis of Riddle 47 as a representative of the writing themes of the Exeter collection, see Shook, "Riddles Relating to the Anglo-Saxon Scriptorium." For a similar appreciation of Riddle 47 as a writing topic, see Helga Göbel, *Studien zu den altenglischen Schriftwesenrätseln* (Würzburg: Würzburger Wissenschaftliche Schriften, 1980), 226–55.

207. Krapp and Dobbie, *ASPR*, vol. 3, 205, offer "hring endean" (1b) on the basis of manuscript "hringende an" (fol. 113r), but other editors have replaced this meaningless word for "hring ærendean," referring to the ring bringing a message. See, for example, Mackie, *The Exeter Book*, 142. Williamson however emended this term as "hring gyddian," as he interpreted the phrase to be a scribal mistake. See his comments on *The Old English Riddles*, 288–89. This interpretation has been accepted by Muir, *The Exeter Anthology*, vol. 2, 610. I here follow Williamson's and Muir's reading.

208. Tupper, *The Old English Riddles*, 179–80; Niles, *Old English Enigmatic*

of a dumb creature—"butan tunga" (2a)—which can however speak at some point: "Sinc for secgum swigende cwæð: / 'Gehæle mec, helpend gæsta'" (4–5) [while being silent, the treasure said before men: "Heal me, Helper of souls"]. Williamson explains that this clue surely refers to an inscription on the object and that line 5 might be identified as "the last petition of the *Pater Noster* before the fraction or breaking of the bread: *libera nos a malo*"; hence, "the creature of the riddle could be the paten and not the chalice."[209] However, Williamson finally does offer "paten or chalice" as a possible solution, which I have similarly adopted here, as none of the clues seems to help us discern which of the two vessels is alluded to.[210] Whether a paten or a chalice, the object's inscription clearly connects it to the writing topic offered by Riddle 47, thus contributing to the thematic coherence of the section.

A further interesting aspect of Riddle 48 is that there is no end-punctuation between this text and the preceding composition. Instead, a simple dot after "swealg" occurs at the end of Riddle 47 (fol. 113r). The beginning of Riddle 48 is, however, marked with the capitalization of I in the word "Ic," although this letter is unadorned and much smaller than the capitals offered in the neighboring riddles of this part of the manuscript.[211] The lack of punctuation might have been intended as a visual acknowledgment of the relationship between the two subjects dealt with in Riddles 47 and 48. The case no doubt recalls that of Riddles 42 and 43.[212]

Poems, 112.
209. Williamson, *The Old English Riddles*, 288.
210. Aldhelm's poem 3 ("On a church of St Mary built by Bugga") from the *Carmina ecclesiastica* offers a description of the silver paten and the golden chalice found in that church. For this passage from Aldhelm's poem (70–76), see Ehwald, *Aldhelmi opera*, 18 (no. 3), and its translation in Lapidge and Rosier, *Aldhelm: The Poetic Works*, 49. As Williamson, *The Old English Riddles*, 288, points out, the fact that patens might have customarily been made of silver seems to be an obstacle to finally accepting paten as the solution of Riddle 48.
211. See Muir, *The Exeter DVD* (fol. 113r).
212. Anderson has sought to link Riddles 47 and 48, assuming that these

As with Riddle 48, the paradox of the tongueless creature that is capable of speaking is also one of the clues of Riddle 49 (book chest): "Ic wat eardfæstne anne standan, / deafne, dumban, se oft dæges swilgeð / þurh gopes hond gifrum lacum" (1–3) [I know about (a certain) deaf and dumb one that is stuck to the ground, (a creature) who often during the day swallows beneficial gifts from a servant's hand]. The meaning of the obscure term *gop* has been deduced to mean "servant" or "slave" from the context of these clues.[213] Andrew Breeze validates this general assumption by providing evidence that the word could be a loan from Irish meaning "beak- or snout-faced menial."[214] The image would thus be that of a book chest characterized as an animal that is liberally fed by an animal-looking servant.

Further on, the riddlic object is described as "unwita" (11a), in other words, as an ignorant creature, a motif that reminds us of the witless bookworm of Riddle 47. Similarly, the adjective "eorp" (11a)—meaning "dark, dusky, swarthy"[215]—is used in a metaphorical sense, echoing the term "þystro" (darkness, 4a), which introduced the idea of ignorance in Riddle 47. The bookworm was also said to swallow the words—"forswealg" (3a) and "swealg" (6b)—which parallels the use of "swilgeð" (2b) and "forswilgeð" (11b) in Riddle 49 in

---

two texts present thematic associations similar to those of Riddles 42 (rooster and hen) and 43 (soul and body), which are not separated by conventional end-punctuation in the manuscript either. Although Riddles 47 and 48 can be considered as thematically bound due to the fact that they both present a topic related to writing, Anderson's joint reading of these two poems is not convincing and has found no scholarly support. James E. Anderson, "Two Spliced Riddles of the Exeter Book," *In Geardagum* 5 (1983): 57–75.

213. See *DOE* and *BT* (s.v. "gop").

214. Andrew Breeze, "Old English *gop* 'Servant' in Riddle 49: Old Irish *gop* 'Snout,'" *Neophilologus* 79 (1995): 671–73. Hough corroborates Breeze's arguments by offering examples of *gop* with the general meaning of "servant" in place-names. Carole Hough, "Place-names and the Provenance of Riddle 49," *Neophilologus* 82 (1998): 617–18.

215. *DOE* (s.v. "earp, eorp").

the context of a chest keeping books. The paradox of a creature that devours books but is no wiser for it also forms part of the clues in Aldhelm's *Enigma* 89 (book chest), which is usually brought up by scholars as an analogue to Exeter Riddle 49.[216] As discussed above,[217] Aldhelm's book chest is described as having its entrails ("uiscera," 1) crowded with divine words ("diuinis . . . uerbis," 1) and holy books ("sacratos . . . biblos," 2) in Riddle 89. Employing a similar paradox, the object is said to assimilate no knowledge at all: "At tamen ex isdem nequeo cognoscere quicquam: / infelix fato fraudabor munere tali, / dum tollunt dirae librorum lumina Parcae" (3–5) [But yet I cannot learn anything whatsoever from them (the books). Unhappy (creature), I am deprived of such a gift by fate, as long as the cruel Parcae steal the light (or the enlightenment) of books]. Like the book chest of Aldhelm's *Enigma* 89 or the bookworm of Exeter Riddle 47, the creature of Old English Riddle 49 is unable to absorb any knowledge even though it literally "swallows" books.

Some scholars have pointed out an even closer parallel with Eusebius's *Enigma* 33 (book chest):

> In me multigena sapientia constat habunde,
> nec tamen illud scire quid est sapientia possum.
> Cum prudentia forte meo processerit ore,
> tunc quod ab internis uenit, intus habere nequibo.

[In me there is wisdom of different sorts in abundance although I cannot understand what wisdom is. Even if knowledge has perhaps gone through my mouth, I cannot then hold inside what comes from my inwards].

Like Exeter Riddle 49, the clues of the Latin *enigma* therefore dwell on the description of a creature that stores books but cannot retain

---

216. Aldhelm's Riddle 89 is, for example, listed among the possible sources of Exeter Riddle 49 in Michael J. B. Allen and Daniel G. Calder, *Sources and Analogues of Old English Poetry: the Major Latin Texts in Translation* (Cambridge: Brewer, 1976), 171.
217. See p. 214 for my discussion of Adlhelm's riddle.

any knowledge.²¹⁸ Even if "þurh gopes hond" (3a) makes perfect sense, as explained above, as a reference to the servant's hand "feeding" the book chest in the Old English text, the verbal parallels observed in Eusebius's analogue bring up the assumption that the phrase could be a scribal-corrupted version of a clue describing the object's metaphorical "gaping mouth." However, as pointed out by the *OED*, "An Old English **gapian* may have existed . . . but is not recorded."²¹⁹ Still, the use of the preposition "þurh" in Riddle 49 supports this reading, as it could be equivalent to the reference to knowledge going through ("processerit") the book chest's mouth ("ore") in line 3 of the Latin enigma.²²⁰

As for the thematic groups in which the Latin counterparts appear, it is worth noting that Aldhelm's *Enigma* 89 (book chest) occurs among wonder motifs such as Riddles 88 (serpent) and 90 (woman giving birth to twins). By contrast, Eusebius's *Enigma* 33 (book chest) is preceded by Riddle 32 (parchment) and forms part of a sequence, which is clearly devoted to writing subjects. As with Eusebius's section 4, the writing topic seems to be the common factor linking Exeter Riddle 49 to the preceding texts of the series.²²¹

As is typical of instrumental compositions, the opening lines of Riddle 50 allude to the usefulness of the object: "Wiga is on eorþan wundrum acenned / dryhtum to nytte, of dumbum twam / torht atyhted . . ." (1–3a) [There is on earth a warrior begotten in a curious way for the use of men, (a warrior who is) made bright from two

---

218. Note also the insistence on the idea of wisdom as represented by "sapientia" (twice, 1 and 2) and "prudentia (3)," the latter meaning "Sagacity, good sense, intelligence, prudence, practical judgment, discretion" (*L&S*).
219. *OED* (s.v. "gape").
220. I am not alone in suspecting this, since Holthausen also regarded this possibility. See F. Holthausen, "Zu altenglischen Dichtungen," *Englische Studien* 74 (1940): 325.
221. Interestingly, Ælfric's *Glossary* combines writing tools and liturgical implements in the section entitled "Nomina domorum" (household nouns). Thus, the Old English term "scrîn," glossed as Latin *arca*, appears close to the entry "calic" (Latin *calix*). Zupitza, *Ælfrics Grammatik und Glossar*, 313.

dumb creatures].²²² Actually, the description of fire as an essential element for people's lives occupies the greatest part of Riddle 50:

>   Forstrangne oft
> wif hine wrið;   he him wel hereð,
> þeowaþ him geþwære,   gif him þegniað
> mægeð ond mæcgas   mid gemete ryhte,
> fedað hine fægre;   he him fremum stepeð
> life on lissum. (4b–9a)

[(Though) very strong, a woman often covers it (i.e., with a cooking pot). It obeys them well, and serves them gently if (both) women and men deal with it in an appropriate and measured way, feeding it nicely; it will reward them with the benefits and comforts of life.]

The inclusion of this motif here could seem incongruous from a thematic point of view. Yet it must be noted that "fire" appears as a riddlic topic in instrumental sections of Latin collections. For instance, Tatwine's fire triad (ns. 31, 33, and 35) occurs in an instrumental cluster (section 5), among the smith's tools.²²³ By the same token, in the Bern collection *Enigma* 23 (fire spark) is included in instrumental section 3.²²⁴ Apart from this, Exeter Riddle 50 shares

---

222. The two dumb creatures (2b) are "the flint and the steel used to engender the fire," as explained by Williamson, *The Old English Riddles*, 292. There are several Latin riddles that allude to the process of producing fire by this method. Aldhelm's *Enigma* 93 (spark) refers to the stone as the mother from whose icy womb the spark is born. Similarly, Tatwine's Riddle 31 (spark) describes the flint as a cold mother, the spark being buried in the stone's womb. Also, see Bern *Enigma* 23 (fire spark).
223. On the other hand, there is a direct reference to "fire" as one of the "tools" used by a smith in the forge as it appears in Exeter Riddle 71 (sword): "nu eom wraþra laf, / fyres ond feole . . ." (3b–4a) [Now I am what is left by the wrathful fire and file].
224. Finally, "fire" also appears as a motif among different houseware implements, as a further tool for cooking, in Ælfric's *Glossary*: "*ignis* [*ve]l focus* fŷr; *flamma* lîg; *pruna* glêd; *andena* brandîsen; *titio* brand; *olla* crocca." Zupitza, *Ælfrics Grammatik und Glossar*, 316.

several aspects with the companion subjects included in subgroup 5A. For example, the reference to the two dumb creatures (2b), the flint and the steel used to produce fire, finds an echo in the description of the paten or the chalice of Riddle 48 as having no tongue (2a) and that of the book chest of Riddle 49 as being dumb (2a and 10b). Also significantly, Riddle 50 presents fire as serving human beings—"þeowaþ" (6a)—while they wait on him as well ("þegniað," 6b). Furthermore, fire is said to be fed ("fedað," 8a) by both men and women, an idea that calls up the image of the servant "feeding" (i.e., filling) the book chest in Riddle 49 (3a).

As regards Riddle 51, the solution is based on the description of the three fingers holding the quill pen, as they write on parchment: "Ic seah wrætlice wuhte feower / samed siþian; swearte wæran lastas, / swaþu swiþe blacu" (1–3a) [I saw four splendid creatures traveling together; their footsteps were black, their tracks very dark]. Being a typical metaphor of writing subjects, the allusion to the quill ("fugles wyn," literally, the bird's delight, 7b) traveling and leaving black tracks ("siþade sweartlast," 11a) on the parchment is also a motif found in Riddle 26 (Gospel book). Furthermore, Tatwine's *Enigma* 6 (pen) and Aldhelm's Riddle 30 (alphabet) offer clues hinting at the three fingers involved in the activity of writing.[225] In Exeter Riddle 51, the expression "winnende wiga" (6a), the struggling warrior, could be a reference to the copyist's thumb.[226] The motif of the richly ornate manuscript already appeared in Riddle 26 (Gospel book)—"gierede ... mid golde" (13a)—and is also present in Riddle 51, in which the pen moves over ornamental gold ("ofer fæted gold," 7a). On the basis of these parallelisms, Riddle 51 is clearly a suitable component of a section whose major thematic link is the writing subject.

Apart from a concern with topics related to writing, the riddles of subgroup 5A share an interest in the paradox of an object that is silent but can however speak. This is the case of the paten/chalice

---

225. See Williamson, *The Old English Riddles*, 293.
226. In *The Old English Riddles*, 294, however, Williamson reads this phrase as an allusion to "the hand or arm of the scribe."

(no. 48), an inscribed tongueless object which is capable of speaking. The book chest (no. 49) is portrayed as being deaf and dumb. It is also said to swallow books without any profit, just as the bookworm of Riddle 47 can devour vellum pointlessly. In Riddle 50, the creature is presented as the offspring of two dumb creatures, the two pieces of flint and steel that are used for lighting fire. All in all, the components of Exeter section 5A seem to focus on the different ways in which written culture is produced (pen and fingers), preserved (on either parchment or on a metal object such as a paten or a chalice), kept (book chest), and even destroyed (bookworm,[227] fire).[228]

4.3.2.2 Subgroup B (Riddles 52–59)

Subgroup B of section 5 continues the instrumental subject but is clearly differentiated from the preceding cluster in its description of tools or gadgets in which wood is a primary component, with the exception of Riddles 57 (swallows)[229] and 59 (chalice). Riddle 52, whose clues hide a flail (an agricultural tool[230]), opens this series.[231]

---

227. Other scholars have viewed Riddle 47 as a reflection on the perishable nature of written culture. For example, DiNapoli, "In the Kingdom of the Blind," 427, has defined this riddle as "a strikingly modern conundrum about the fragility of the written word."
228. Even if it is not overtly mentioned in the clues, one wonders if fire was included in this section as a further creature that devours parchment purposelessly.
229. Among the different solutions that have been proposed, Dietrich's "swallows" seems to me the one that fulfills most of the conditions expressed in the clues of Riddle 57. Dietrich, "Die Räthsel des Exeterbuchs: Würdigung, Lösung und Herstellung ," 477. This riddle thus raises a similar problem as Riddle 24 (jay), which was considered an intriguing thematic irregularity above.
230. *OED* (s.v. "flail"): "An instrument for threshing corn by hand, consisting of a wooden staff or handle, at the end of which a stouter and shorter pole or club, called a swingle or swipple, is so hung as to swing freely."
231. In *Die altenglischen Rätsel*, 110–11, Trautmann proposed "flail," a solution which has been generally accepted even if the clues of the riddle do no offer much information. Williamson labels this riddle as "flail" with a question mark, noting that Old English *fliegel* (flail) is listed among other

Riddle 53 has been interpreted by some scholars as a description of a battering ram on the basis of the following lines: "Nu he fæcnum weg / þurh his heafdes mægen hildegieste / oþrum rymeð" (8b-10a) [Now it treacherously makes way for another enemy (literally, battle-guest) by means of the power of its head]. This solution however has been contested by Jonathan Wilcox, who argues that the adjective *fæcne* "seems inappropriate for one making such an open assault."[232] He further adds that "The characterization of the 'battle-guest' as *fæcne* is more appropriate for one on the receiving-end of the action of an instrument of punishment."[233] Accordingly, Wilcox considers "gallows," Old English *gealga*, as the best answer for Riddle 53, with "heafod" being a literal reference to the head of the criminal who is characterized as *fæcne*, meaning "deceitful, treacherous; fraudulent."[234]

However, as I indicate in the translation of this passage, "fæcnum" (8b) could be interpreted as a dative plural functioning as an adverb. This reading suggests the unwilling involvement of the tree, which has been transformed into a sophisticated assault weapon, in the criminal act of ravaging a city as an accomplice of the warrior who is launching the attack. This moralizing tone is very typical of instrumental motifs in which the creature is said to suffer a radical and painful transformation. The tree, in this case, "is taken from a state of innocence and treated savagely to create an instrument of destruction," as Wilcox explains.[235] With this reading, the subsequent clue similarly supports the answer "battering ram": "Oft hy an yste strudon / hord ætgædre" (10b–11a) [Together, they (i.e., both the warrior and the battering ram) have often violenty (literally, as

---

agricultural tools in the text know as the *Gerefa*. *The Old English Riddles*, 295. Also, see Felix Liebermann, ed., "Gerefa," *Anglia* 9 (1886): 264 (17.5).
232. Jonathan Wilcox, "New Solutions to Old English Riddles: Riddles 17 and 53," *PQ* 69 (1990): 399.
233. Ibid.
234. *DOE* (s.v. "fæcne, fācne").
235. Wilcox, "New Solutions," 398.

if in a storm)²³⁶ plundered the hoard].²³⁷ The tone is no doubt that of reproval. Even if the solution "battering ram" seems to me the preferable one, Wilcox's analysis nevertheless has demonstrated that the description of the battering ram suspiciously parallels that of another "gallows," the cross of Riddle 55 in the same series.

A further instrumental motif, Riddle 54 alludes to the process of churning and, as with Riddle 45 (dough and oven), describes this domestic task by means of double entendre:

Hyse cwom gangan,	þær he hie wisse
stondan in wincsele,	stop feorran to,
hror hægstealdmon,	hof his agen
hrægl hondum up,	hrand under gyrdels
hyre stondendre	stiþes nathwæt,
worhte his willan;	wagedan buta. (1–6)

[A young man came walking by where he knew she was standing by a corner. The vigorous warrior stepped forth to her from far off, raised his own clothes with his hands, and pushed something stiff under her belt where she was standing; he carried out his desire; both of them shook].²³⁸

In a way that recalls Riddle 42, in which the hen's literal pregnancy was alluded to (4–5), the last lines of this riddle refer to the barrel's

---

236. On "yste" (10b), see Williamson, *The Old English Riddles*, 298.
237. For example, note the parallel use of *strudan—BT*, "To spoil, ravage, plunder, pillage, defraud"—in *Beowulf* (3126) as a reference to the usual custom of casting lots to establish the order of the pillaging of the hoard that the dragon's death has made accessible for the Geats: "Næs ðā on hlytme hwā þæt *hord strude*. . ." Text cited from R. D. Fulk, Robert E. Bjork, and John D. Niles, eds., *Klaeber's Beowulf and the Fight at Finnsburg* (Toronto: University of Toronto Press, 2008), 106 (emphasis mine).
238. Foley, for example, notes the explicitness of the double entendre: "The plunge-stick becomes personified as a man ('hyse' in 1a; 'hægstealdmon' in 3a), and the barrel as a woman ('hie' in 1b). The 'thane,' or 'servant' as he is called (7a, 8a), approaches and enters the woman and they perform the procreative act (4b-6)." Foley, "Riddles 53, 54, and 55," 27–28.

metaphorical impregnation as a result of churning: "Hyre weaxan ongon / under gyrdelse þæt oft gode men / ferðþum freogað ond mid feo bicgað" (10b-12) [what good men frequently love in their hearts and procure with money began to grow under her belt]. These lines no doubt allude to butter, which is certainly appreciated and valued as the product of churning.[239]

As regards Riddle 55, the problematic interpretation of some of its clues has given rise to several solutions, of which Tupper's proposal "cross" seems to me the most plausible.[240] According to Tupper, this riddle alludes to a well-known medieval topos which asserts that the cross was made of four different kinds of trees: "þær wæs hlin ond acc ond se hearda iw / ond se fealwa holen" (9–10a) [There was the maple-tree and the oak and the hard yew-tree, and the tawny holly]. As an illustration of the four-tree motif, Tupper provided Pseudo-Bede's *Collectanea* 372, whose beginning reads as follows: "Crux Domini de quatuor lignis facta est, quae uocantur cypressus, cedrus, pinus et buxus" ["The cross of the Lord was made from four woods, which are called cypress, cedar, pine and boxwood"].[241] This idea derives from the Old Testament (Isaiah 60.13) and, as William O. Stevens points out, patristic authors soon began to associate the biblical theme of the four trees to the four parts of the cross.[242] Exeter Riddle 55 no doubt stems from this tradition.

As other scholars have indicated, the terms used in Exeter Riddle 55 to describe the hidden object are similar to those employed

---

239. As Williamson indicates, "the creature described in the last lines of the riddle is the O.E. *butere*, the child of the churn." *The Old English Riddles*, 299.
240. Tupper, *The Riddles of the Exeter Book*, 189.
241. Edition and translation from Bayless and Lapidge, *Collectanea*, 178–79. Further parallels from medieval Irish literature are brought up in Hildegard Tristram, "In Support of Tupper's Solution of the Exeter Book Riddle (Krapp-Dobbie) 55," in *Germanic Dialects: Linguistic and Philological Investigations*, ed. Bela Brogyanyi and Thomas Krömmelbein (Amsterdam: John Benjamins, 1986), 592–93.
242. William O. Stevens, *The Cross in the Life and Literature of the Anglo-Saxons* (New Haven, CT: Yale University Press, 1904), 10.

in Old English poems in which the cross plays an important role. The expressions "wudutreow" (a tree of the woods, 3a), "rode tacn" (the sign of the cross, 5a), and "beames" (tree, 7b) found in this text can compare to "rode treo" (rood tree, 643a) in *The Phoenix*, as well as "syllicre treow" (excellent tree, 4b) and "beama beorhtost" (the brightest of trees, 6a) in *The Dream of the Rood*.[243] Another outstanding feature of Riddle 55 is that the cross is said to be profusely ornate: "wunden gold" (twisted gold, 3b), "sinc searobunden" (treasure intricately bound, 4a), and "seolfres dæl" (a part of silver, 4b). In the same way, the cross of *The Dream of the Rood* is said to be covered with gold—"begoten mid golde" (7a) and "gegyred mid golde" (16a).[244] These citations point to the well-known custom of ornamenting crosses in churches, since, as Barbara Raw explains, these were "a favourite gift to monasteries."[245] Indeed, kings, noblemen, and bishops used to donate richly elaborate crosses. Exeter Riddle 55 seems to describe one of these costly specimens that were housed in Anglo-Saxon churches.

However, Riddle 55 presents a rather obscure passage: "[Ic seah] rode tacn, þæs us to roderum up / hlædre rærde, ær he helwara / burg abræce" (5–7a) [(I saw) the sign of the cross, of him who lifted us up to the skies by a ladder, before He conquered the fortress of the inhabitants of hell]. These lines were interpreted by Tupper as a reference to the Harrowing of Hell,[246] an idea that interestingly parallels the allusion to plundering with the description of the battering ram in Riddle 53 (10b-11a). Moreover, the term "hlædre" (6a) suggests the comparison of the cross with a ladder, which is commonplace in exegetical literature.[247] In Christian iconography and

---

243. Tupper, *The Riddles of the Exeter Book*, 190; Tristram, "In Support of Tupper's Solution," 594.
244. The cross is described in similar terms in *Elene* (1022b–26a).
245. Raw, *Anglo-Saxon Crucifixion Iconography*, 41.
246. Tupper, *The Riddles of the Exeter Book*, 190.
247. As Ferguson points out, "the ladder is one of the instruments of the Passion and is frequently shown in scenes of the Descent from the Cross." Ferguson, *Signs and Symbols*, 176.

literature, the cross is said to be a ladder leading the pious to heaven.[248] In this sense, it is worth noting that line 5 of this riddle also contains the well-known paronomastic pair *rodor* (heaven) and *rod* (rood), which is frequently found in allusions to the cross. As Frank points out, this wordplay is used at least fifteen times in Old English poetry, twelve of which appear in *Elene*, as with, for instance, "rode under roderum" (the cross under the skies, 1234a).[249]

A further elusive passage in Riddle 55 has been interpreted as an allusion to a "sword-rack" by Felix Liebermann and other scholars:[250] "wulfheafedtreo, þæt oft wæpen abæd / his mondryhtne, maðm in healle, / goldhilted sweord" (12–14a) [the gallows (literally, the wolfhead-tree), which often received a weapon, a treasure in the hall, a gold-hilted sword for its lord].[251] In this sense, this passage could be a reference to a sword attached to the crucifix. Churches and cathedrals have traditionally been furnished with swords and other weapons from kings and noblemen, as these also constituted a frequent donation. Raw, for example, mentions an example of this joint display of the cross and a sword: "At Harold's church of Holy Cross, Waltham, a figure of the crucified Christ carved out of flint, or possibly black marble, stood near the altar. . . . Tovi, Cnut's standard-bearer, had attached his own sword to it and then fixed the

---

248. This theme, which is traditionally known as "Jacob's ladder," stems from Jacob's vision in Genesis 28.12: "And he dreamed that there was a ladder set up on the earth, and the top of it reached to heaven; and behold the angels of God ascending and descending on it."
249. See Frank, "Some Uses of Paronomasia," 210, for further examples in *Elene*, *Juliana*, and *Christ*.
250. By using the first letters of the names of the four trees alluded to, Liebermann proposed "gallows" or "sword-rack." See Felix Liebermann, "Das anglesächsische Rätsel 56: 'Galgen' als Waffenständer," *Archiv* 114 (1905): 163–64. The idea has not found much support, although some scholars have maintained the answer "sword-rack." For instance, in *Old English Enigmatic Poems*, 75, Niles offers *wæpen-hengen or weapon-rack.
251. Note that I follow the explanation offered at *DOE* (s.v. "abiddan," B.1.d) that "abæd" (12b) in Riddle 55 is a form of *abiddan* in the sense of "obtain" or "receive." For a similar reading, see Williamson, *The Old English Riddles*, 304.

body to a wooden cross with silver bands."[252] The custom of affixing weapons to crosses could therefore explain this passage.

As for the reference to the object as "wulfheafedtreo" (12a), John Miles Foley states, "cross and gallows are interchangeable terms for the instrument and symbol of Christ's crucifixion in Anglo-Saxon poetry."[253] An illustration of this is found at the beginning of *The Dream of the Rood*, in which the poet explains that the cross of his vision was not the gallows of the criminal ("fracodes gealga," 10b).[254] Further in the poem, a reference is made to Christ ascending the vile gallows ("on gealgan heanne," 40b) and to his suffering on the gallows-tree ("gealgtreow," 146a) for the sins of men.[255]

As for the function of Riddle 55 in the compilation, it is clear that the cross is an instrumental motif—just as with the cross of Riddle 30a found in section 3. However, the fact that Riddle 54 (churn), which presents blatant double entendres, precedes such a significant religious theme is striking at best. Nonetheless, the juxtaposition of these two riddles can be explained on the basis of analogy. Riddles 53 (battering ram), 54 (churn), and 55 (cross) have in common the fact that they all describe long wooden implements.[256]

---

252. Raw, *Anglo-Saxon Crucifixion Iconography*, 41.
253. Foley, "Riddles 53, 54, and 55," 28. In *The Riddles of the Exeter Book*, 191, Tupper explains that the term *wulfes-hēafod* "is the legal expression for an outlaw, who may be killed like a wolf, without fear of penalty. . . ."
254. Eusebius's Riddle 17 similarly plays on the paradox that the cross is worshipped by the virtuous but at the same time dreaded by sinners and criminals.
255. This theme also appears in *Christ and Satan* (509a and 548a) and *Menologium* (86b).
256. Foley takes this a step further and contends that these three riddles are thematically bound: "riddles fifty-three through fifty-five describe through three distinctly different metaphors precisely one archetypal process—the act of entry and impregnation." "Riddles 53, 54, and 55," 27. Accordingly, Riddle 53 (battering ram) could be understood as a description of a weapon whose main function is "to make possible forceful entry and 'impregnation' of the enemy's enclosure" (ibid.). In the case of Riddle 54 (churn), the sexual act and resulting pregnancy are quite evident in the clues. Finally, this

The solution "web and loom" has been accepted by all scholars for Riddle 56 since Dietrich first proposed it.[257] There is general agreement on the fact that the opening lines of this riddle describe the activity of a loom during the process of weaving:

Ic wæs þær inne	þær ic ane geseah
winnende wiht	wido bennegean,
holt hweorfende;	heaþoglemma feng,
deopra dolga.	Daroþas wæron
weo þære wihte,	ond se wudu searwum
fæste gebunden. (1–6a)	

[I was in there, where I saw a piece of wood, a turning beam, injure a striving creature; it received battle injuries, deep wounds. Darts were a cause of misery to that creature, and the wood was intricately and firmly bound].

As conveniently explained by Erika von Erhardt-Siebold, "the struggling creature, the true subject of the riddle is a web still in the loom; it receives battle-scars and gashes because the needle or shuttle passes right through its body."[258] The act of weaving, in which the creature is presented as enduring a most cruel torture,[259] is thus

---

theme is also present in Riddle 55, especially in the Jacob's Ladder theme, by which heaven is said to be filled or impregnated with the souls of the pious ones. The fact that Wilcox ("New Solutions," 400), similarly associated the gallows subject with Riddle 53 (see above, p. 367) reinforces the notion that the latter text is thematically akin to Riddle 55.

257. Dietrich, "Die Räthsel des Exeterbuchs: Würdigung, Lösung und Herstellung," 476. This solution has been supported by the majority of editors. See Tupper, *The Riddles of the Exeter Book*, 192–95; Mackie, *The Exeter Book*, 241; Krapp and Dobbie, *ASPR*, vol. 3, 350; Williamson, *The Old English Riddles*, 305; and Muir, *The Exeter Anthology*, vol. 2, 614.

258. Erika von Erhardt-Siebold, "The Old English Loom Riddles," in *Philologica: The Malone Anniversary Studies*, ed. Thomas A. Kirby and Henry Bosley Woolf (Baltimore: The Johns Hopkins University Press, 1949), 15.

259. For a recent analysis of images of torture and warfare in this text, see Megan Cavell, "Looming Danger and Dangerous Looms: Violence

the central clue of Riddle 56, and, as with Riddle 35 (mail coat), its vocabulary dwells on the different parts of a loom. According to Erhardt-Siebold, the "daroþas" (4b) stand for "the teeth of the batten penetrating through the warp" and "se wudu" (5b) corresponds to "the needle or shuttle."[260]

Riddle 56 seems to be a continuation of the thematic sequence initiated with Riddle 52 (flail), for the description of the riddlic object is again that of a wooden implement, as the words "holt" (3a), "wudu" (5b), and "treow" (9a) evince. Like the cross in Riddle 55, the loom of Riddle 56 is also depicted as a tree-shaped object: "Treow wæs getenge þam þær torhtan stod / leafum bihongen" (9–10a) [The tree was close to that which stood there with bright hanging leaves]. As we have seen with other riddles from the Exeter collection, the juxtaposition of the web and loom to the preceding cross enigma might have been intended on purpose. In fact, the comparison of the cross with long wooden objects was frequent in exegetical literature.[261] Also interestingly, when compared, Riddles 55 and 56 exhibit outstanding verbal parallels, which underpin a connection of the two subjects:[262]

> Riddle 55: "Ic seah in healle, þær hæleð druncon, / on flet beran feower cynna . . ." (1–2) [I saw in the hall, where men were drinking, four kinds (of wood) being carried on the floor].
>
> Riddle 56: "Ic lafe geseah / minum hlaforde, þær hæleð druncon, / þara flana,[263] on flet beran" (10b–12) [I saw what was left by the

---

and Weaving in Exeter book 'Riddle 56,'" *Leeds Studies in English* 42 (2011): 29–42.

260. Erhardt-Siebold, "The Old English Loom Riddles," 15. Also, for a detailed description of the parts of the medieval loom, see Owen-Crocker, *Dress in Anglo-Saxon England*, 286–91.

261. Ferguson, McHugh, and Norris, eds., *Encyclopedia of Early Christianity*, 303, mention the loom, among other objects, as a typical cruciform symbol used by Christian writers.

262. Most recently, Cavell has pointed out the notable links existing between these two texts in "Looming Danger and Dangerous Looms," 40.

263. The manuscript reading is "flan" (fol. 114r), which Krapp and Dobbie, *ASPR*, vol. 3, 208, complemented as "flana geweorc." The addition of

arrows (i.e., the woven cloth) being carried on the floor to my lord, where men were drinking].

The reference to the loom as a wooden object, its possible allegorical reading as the cross, and the notable verbal traits shared with the preceding composition all suggest that Riddles 55 and 56 are thematically related.

In Riddle 58, the reference to the bucket traversing the well's pit is an essential piece of information for its solving: "eorðgræf pæþeð" (9b) [(it) goes through a hole dug in the earth]. The paradoxical statement that the creature does not drink but carries water in the air adds further layers of signification to the preceding idea: "Wætan ne swelgeþ ne wiht iteþ, / foþres ne gitsað, fereð oft swa þeah / lagoflod on lyfte" (10–12a) [(it) does not swallow liquid, nor does it eat anything; (it) does not crave for food; however, it often conveys water in the air]. The final lines of the riddle have been read by most editors as a spelling clue similar to those offered by Riddle 42: "Þry sind in naman / ryhte runstafas, þara is Rad foran" (14b–15) [(if written) correctly, there are three letters in its name; of them Rad is the first]. This clue has been understood as an allusion to runic *rad*, which would then constitute either the first letter or the first compound of the solution. According to this, Christian W. M. Grein proposed *radpyt*, i.e., "riding-well."[264] However, Williamson offered *radrod* on the basis that "it is the pole and not the pit that is the subject,"[265] an idea that is supported and further elaborated by Niles.[266] I agree with the latter two scholars that the focus is evidently on the well's pole, which lifts the bucket in the air, as suggested by the clues. The

---

"geweorc" seems to me unnecessary, as reflected in Tupper, *The Riddles of the Exeter Book*, 195; Mackie, *The Exeter Book*, 148; Williamson, *The Old English Riddles*, 307; Hans Pinsker and Waltraud Ziegler, eds., *Die altenglischen Rätsel des Exeterbuchs* (Heidelberg: Carl Winter, 1985), 278; and Muir, *The Exeter Anthology*, vol. 2, 614.
264. Christian W. M. Grein, "Kleine Mittheilungen," *Germania* 10 (1865): 309.
265. Williamson, *The Old English Riddles*, 312.
266. Niles, *Old English Enigmatic Poems*, 89–92.

riddle therefore seems to fit well in subgroup 5B, whose components are clearly concerned with the description of long wooden objects of diverse kinds.[267] It may thus be inferred that the shape of the well pole in Riddle 58 mirrors the flail (no. 52), the battering ram (53), the stick of the churn (54), the cross (55), and the loom (56).

Scholars have pointed out that Riddle 59, the last piece of subgroup B, is clearly a companion to Riddle 48, since the treatment of the clues is very similar in both compositions. To begin with, the allusion to the ring-shaped creature, which was present in Riddle 48, also appears in Riddle 59, in which the object is twice designated as "hring" (1b and 6a) and once as "beages" (11b). The text leaves no room for doubt that the hidden object is another ecclesiastical implement, since it is said to be a golden token—"goldes tacen" (10a). This expression recalls the way in which the cross of Riddle 55 was described as being made of twisted gold—"wunden gold" (3b)—and was similarly referred to as "tacn" (5a).

As with Riddle 48 and other components of section 5, Riddle 59 also introduces the paradox of the dumb creature that is however able to speak:

                            word æfter cwæð
hring on hyrede,   hælend nemde
tillfremmendra.   Him torhte in gemynd
his dryhtnes naman   dumba brohte
ond in eagna gesihð . . . (5b–9a)

[Afterwards, the ring spoke words to the community, named the Savior of the righteous. (Though) dumb, it brought the Lord's name clearly into their minds and into the sight of their eyes].

The description of the dumb object, as if compared to human beings endowed with speech, finds an echo in a passage from the *Vita sancti Æthelwoldi* (xxix), in which Wulfstan Cantor uses the phrase "muta metalla" (dumb metals) to refer to the silver vessels and other

---

267. Note too that Symphosius's Riddle 71 (well) also appears in an instrumental series (no. 5).

church implements used by St Æthelwold in order to turn them into money to save his congregation from a harsh famine.[268]

On the other hand, the ring of Riddle 59 is said to have "wounds," a further metaphorical clue that has generally been understood as a reference to the fact that the chalice bears an inscription. This idea is presented twice in the text: "swa þæs beages / benne cwædon" (11b–12a) [as the wounds of the ring spoke], and further on as "Ræde, se þe wille, / hu ðæs wrætlican wunda cwæden / hringes to hæleþum . . ." (15b–17a) [Let the one who is willing to solve the riddle (say) how the wounds of that splendid ring talked to men]. The clues thus evince a notable resemblance to those found in Riddle 48.

With its description of a chalice with a capacity to speak, Riddle 59 would clearly suit subgroup 5A, in which the other church vessel handled in Riddle 48 is included, and futher topics related to writing similarly make use of paradoxical statements of this kind.[269] It may be conjectured that Riddle 59 was regarded as thematically very close to the preceding piece to be included in the same series, and this circumstance probably caused its displacement. In this sense, it is worth comparing with the exclusion of Riddle 30b from the two main blocks on account of its being practically identical with Riddle 30a.[270] Generally, we can see that the Exeter collection abounds in thematic repetitions, but these texts are always significantly differ-

---

268. Text from Lapidge and Winterbottom, *Wulfstan of Winchester*, 44–45. In the preface to the *Narratio metrica de sancti Swithuno*, the same author alludes to dumb metals ("mutis . . . metallis," 110) being used for the worship of false gods. Cited from Michael Lapidge, *The Cult of St Swithun* (Oxford: Clarendon Press, 2003), 406–7.

269. As a golden object, the chalice would also be more suitable for subsequent subgroup C, in which further metal implements such as helmet and borer appear.

270. Patrick W. Conner explains the displacement of Riddle 30b on similar grounds in "Four Contiguous Poems in the Exeter Book: A Combined Reading of *Homiletic Fragment III, Soul and Body II, Deor, and Wulf and Eadwacer*," in *The Genesis of Books: Studies in the Scribal Culture of Medieval England in Honour of A. N. Doane*, ed. Matthew Hussey and John D. Niles (Turnhout: Brepols, 2011), 129–30.

ent, as illustrated with Riddles 48 and 59. It might be inferred that including a duplicate such as Riddle 30b could have been viewed as unorthodox.[271] In the case of Riddles 48 and 59, the compilers simply decided to separate the two pieces by adding ten more between them. But resorting to similar subjects clearly suggests that the Exeter compilers encountered difficulties at this stage of the process. Kenneth Sisam suspected that the material at their disposal was not sufficient: "It seems that the collection was put together by tacking on new groups or items as codices or single pieces came to hand."[272] Fulk corroborates Sisam's hypothesis as he affirms that "the compiler of the Exeter Book or its exemplar . . . seems to have added riddles to the collection as they became available," further noting that this assumption "derives support from the insertion of several lyrics after *Riddle 59*."[273] From this we can deduce that the compilers were simply running out of material, so they felt compelled to interrupt the assembling task until more riddles could be gathered.

If this inference is accepted, Riddle 59 was chosen to function as a sort of "provisional" coda, a hypothesis that was anticipated by Baum, as he noted that this text "might have been regarded as a fitting Christian conclusion."[274] From a paleographical point of view, it is worth noting that the capital I of "Ic" is considerably larger and more elaborate than that of preceding Riddle 58 (fol. 114v), which bears no ornament at all. But, apart from this, Riddle 59 does not present any other special feature, as the text ends with the typical punctuation symbol 7: and there is no blank space between this riddle and the beginning of the next poem, *The Wife's Lament* (fol.

---

271. The repetition of the same riddle in a collection is a rare phenomenon and usually suggests a poor compilation. An illustration of this is the second part of London, Royal 15.B.xix (fols. 79r-82r), which, among other anomalies, offers Symphosius's Riddle 78 (stairs) twice. See Bergamin, *Aenigmata Symposii*, lxxxv.
272. Kenneth Sisam, *Studies in the History of Old English Literature* (Oxford: Clarendon Press, 1953), 97.
273. Fulk, *A History*, 404.
274. Baum, *Anglo-Saxon Riddles*, xx.

115r). These paleographical features imply that the scribe did not particularly bother to mark the limits between the first riddlic block and *The Wife's Lament*, although none of the non-enigmatic poems separating the riddles displays a blank space at the beginning either. Being the longest composition of the sequence with eighteen lines, Riddle 59 apparently reveals the compilers' aim of interrupting the assembling process, while further riddles to complete the core assemblage (Group 1) were searched for. This inference also points to the fact that the compilation of the riddles, at least in the exemplar from which they were copied, was guided at this stage by a notable degree of improvisation.[275]

4.4. Striving for the Canonical Century: Group 3 (Riddles 61–95)

I have given the name "Group 3" to this final set of riddles that were added to the initial core collection in what I suspect was a third phase of the compilation process. As I will show next, Group 3 offers a continuation of the instrumental sequence, henceforth referred to as subgroup C from section 5, which broke off after Riddle 59.

4.4.1 Section 5 (A Continuation)

4.4.1.1 Subgroup C (Riddles 61–66)

As the upcoming analysis will illustrate, subgroup 5 was most likely devised as a complement to the preceding two clusters of section 5, since its components offer a reflection of human craftsmanship in a variety of ways. The first element of this series, Riddle 61, was solved by Wyatt as "helmet" on the basis of two clues, which seem to describe a man putting on a helmet: "Siðþan me on hreþre heafod sticade, / nioþan upweardne, on nearo fegde" (5–6) [Afterwards he stuck his head into my bosom; (he) firmly pulled the one turning

---

275. As pointed out by Sisam, *Studies*, 97, "it is unlikely that the compilation was first made in the Exeter Book, whose stately, even style indicates that it was transcribed continuously from a collection already made."

upwards from below in the narrow place (i.e., adjusted the helmet to the head)]²⁷⁶ and "mec frætwedne fyllan sceolde / ruwes nathwæt" (8–9a) [something hairy must fill me, the ornamented one]. As Williamson notes, both helmet and mailshirt are probable solutions, for the phrase "ruwes nathwæt" (9a) may refer to either a chest or a head.²⁷⁷ However, as the information within parentheses that I have added for clarification indicates, I understand the clues of this riddle as referring to a man putting on an elaborate helmet.

The clues alluding to the action of adapting the narrow helmet to the head give rise to double entendre, as has been generally reported by scholarship. Accordingly, "upweardne" (6a) seems to accord with the helmet, whose shape, as well as that of the implied erect penis, is understood as either pointing upwards or having a protuding ornament of some kind on its top. The adjective, also meaning "turned upwards,"²⁷⁸ could similarly allude to the action of inverting the position of the helmet when the man puts it on by seizing the base (from below, "nioþan") and thus making it look upwards ("upweardne").²⁷⁹ By contrast, the adjective does not fit so well the mailshirt context because this would imply describing the man's head, rather than the object, as point-shaped—unless we assume the man is already wearing a helmet. Moreover, "upweardne" and "frætwedne" (8a) are both masculine accusative, and could well have been meant as a hint for Old English *helm* (helmet), which is a masculine noun, whereas *byrne* (mailshirt) is feminine.²⁸⁰

---

276. Wyatt, *Old English Riddles*, 110. I thus read line 2 as referring to the man properly adjusting the helmet to his head, in other words, making it fit. Note that Old English *fegan* can mean "to put together, join, unite; bind, fit (something acc.)." *DOE* (s.v. "fegan"). I therefore understand "nioþan" as pleonastically complementing the action of pulling down the helmet and as a verbal contrast with "upweardne."
277. Williamson, *The Old English Riddles*, 320.
278. *BT* (s.v. "upweard").
279. I am indebted to Rafael J. Pascual for bringing my attention to this.
280. Niles, however, solves this problem by proposing the masculine noun *cyrtel* (shirt). See his *Old English Enigmatic Poems*, 106. Still, the solution

As is usual with battle gear, the helmet is no doubt a suitable topic for the instrumental series starting at this point. However, as the first composition of the second large block, Riddle 61, a text with evident double entendres, seems to be inappropriate for beginning a collection. Sexual riddles are typical of instrumental sequences, as I have elsewhere illustrated with some of the components of Tatwine's sections 2 and 5;[281] yet no riddle of this kind has been found as an initial or final topic in any of the collections that I have discussed earlier in this book. As I anticipated above, we may infer that the compilers kept on including riddle material from the point where they had stopped before and thus considered subgroup C as a continuation of the instrumental sequence that had been interrupted at Riddle 59.[282] This compilation process therefore suggests that this part was viewed as a sequel of preceding section 5B rather than the beginning of a second collection.

The solution "poker" for Riddle 62 has gained the support of some editors,[283] but Dietrich's proposal "borer" has been accepted by most scholars.[284] As with the preceding subject, the riddler once more took advantage of the description of an instrumental subject[285] to present another double-entendre composition:

"shirt" does not fit so well the double entendre. On grammatical gender in the riddles, see Niles, ibid., 103–10, and further on p. 410 (n. 373).
281. See my "The Sexual Riddle Type in Aldhelm's *Enigmata*," 363–65.
282. We must remember that the Bern *Enigmata* start with an instrumental series, whose first component is a cooking pot.
283. Tupper, *The Riddles of the Exeter Book*, 202; Mackie, *The Exeter Book*, 241; and Krapp and Dobbie, *ASPR*, vol. 3, 366.
284. Dietrich, "Die Räthsel des Exeterbuchs: Würdigung, Lösung und Herstellung," 477–78.
285. The borer appears as Old English "nauegâr" or "borige"—glossed as Latin "terebro" or "terebrum"—in Ælfric's *Glossary*, where it is is listed among other tools such as the axe, the spade, and the saw. Zupitza, *Ælfrics Grammatik und Glossar*, 318. The catalogue of implements found in the *Gerefa* includes the term "næfeborg." See Liebermann, "Gerefa," 263 (15.3). In *Etymologiae* (XIX.xix.15), Isidore mentions the "taratrum" among the tools used by carpenters.

> wade under wambe ond me weg sylfa
> ryhtne geryme. Rinc bið on ofeste,
> se mec on þyð æftanweardne,
> hæleð mid hrægle; hwilum ut tyhð
> of hole hatne, hwilum eft fareð
> on nearo nathwær, nydeþ swiþe
> suþerne secg. (3–9a)

[I go under a belly and I make a straight way for myself. The warrior is in a hurry, the man who presses me from behind with a garment. Sometimes he pulls me out hot from the hole, sometimes again takes me somewhere into a narrow place; the southern man strongly pushes].

The sexual mood of this poem is evident, particularly as the text mentions the narrow place ("on nearo," 8a), a phrase that is identically found in Riddle 61 (6b). As regards the phrase "suþerne secg" (9a), Tupper associated this clue with the references to the dark Welsh servants involved in other sexual riddles.[286] Williamson took a step further in the interpretation of "suþerne," stating that this term could possibly "indicate somewhat obliquely the direction of the thrust," adding that this type of clue is frequent in sexual jokes.[287] This second reading, as well as the reference to the object going under the belly ("under wambe," 3a), thus parallels the riddler's concern with detailing the position of the helmet in the preceding text with the expressions "upweardne" and "nioþan," which are equally suggestive of sexual innuendo.

Dietrich proposed "beaker" as the solution to Riddle 63 on the basis of this text's resemblance to Aldhelm's *Enigma* 80 (glass

---

286. Tupper, *The Riddles of the Exeter Book*, 203. On the figure of the darkskinned slave in the Exeter sexual riddles, see John W. Tanke, "*Wonfeax wale*: Ideology and Figuration in the Sexual Riddles of the Exeter Book," *Class and Gender in Early English Literature: Intersections*, eds. Britton J. Harwood and Gillian R. Overing (Bloomington: Indiana UP, 1994), 21-42.
287. Williamson, *The Old English Riddles*, 323.

goblet), an inference that has been accepted by most scholars.[288] To start with, the "kissing" clue offered by Riddle 63 is a typical element of those riddles that allude to drinking from a vessel of some kind:[289]

Hwilum mec on cofan   cysseð muþe
tillic esne,   þær wit tu beoþ,
fæðme on folm[. . . . .]grum þyð,
wyrceð his willa[. . . . . .]ð l[. . . . . . .
. . . .] fulre,   þonne ic forð cyme. (4–8)

[Sometimes in a room, where the two of us are together, a capable young man kisses me with his mouth; with his hand clasp, (he) presses (me) with his (fingers) . . . carries out his desire . . . full, when I come forth.][290]

Riddle 63 clearly shares with Aldhelm's *Enigma* 80 the reference to the kissing mouth ("labris oscula," 7, and "basia buccis," 8), the grasping hand ("constringere dextra," 5), and the fingers ("digitis," 6).[291] It is therefore quite probable that the Anglo-Saxon poet used the Latin text as a source.[292]

---

288. "Die Räthsel des Exeterbuchs: Würdigung, Lösung und Herstellung," 478–79. I have slightly modified Dietrich's original answer as referring to a glass goblet on account of the upcoming examination of the riddle's clues. Also, note that Niles, *Old English Enigmatic Poems*, 143, proposes Old English *glæs-fæt* (glass vessel).
289. Cf. Exeter Riddle 14 (aurochs, 3b). However, logical exceptions to this metaphorical interpretation of kissing as drinking are Riddle 30a (cross) and Riddle 55 (cross), where this expression should be taken literally.
290. I here follow Mackie's reconstruction of this passage, as offered in *The Exeter Book*, 203–4.
291. See above pp. 210–11.
292. As pointed by Tupper, *The Riddles of the Exeter Book*, 203, "in both poems [i.e., Riddle 63 and Aldhelm's *Enigma* 80] the drinking-vessel is a woman who yields readily to caresses." Also, see Wyatt's comments on the striking parallelisms observed in these two compositions. Wyatt, *Old English Riddles*, 110–11. However, the notable double entendre of Exeter Riddle 63 has surprisingly been downplayed by some scholars. For example, Gleissner recognized the unquestionable sexual character of this text but he

The allusion to the goblet being full ("fulre," 8a) in Riddle 63 brings to mind the hen of Riddle 42, which was said to become pregnant with a similar expression ("fyllo," 5a).[293] Combined with double-entendre clues, the metaphorical reference to pregnancy continues in the fragmentary last lines of Riddle 63:

Ne mæg ic þy miþan,   [............
................]an on leohte
[.................................]
swylce eac bið sona   [............
..]r[.]te getacnad,   hwæt me to [.....
....]leas rinc,   þa unc geryde wæs. (10–15)

[I cannot hide it.... (when) in the light.... just as it is also soon.... (clearly) shown what the.... warrior ... to me, when it was agreeable to the two of us].[294]

The transparent quality of the goblet, which allows one to see the wine in its interior, is thus presented as a veiled reference to pregnancy resulting from sexual intercourse.[295] Riddle 63 therefore is an apt companion to the preceding pieces in which the description

---

concluded that, despite these overtones, this piece could not be considered within the sexual category. See his *Die "zweideutigen" altenglischen Rätsel*, 396.
293. Clues suggestive of pregnancy are typical of double-entendre riddles. Note, for example, the description of the dough rising in the oven in Riddle 45 and the allusion to butter as being the "offspring" of churning in Riddle 54. For further examples in the Exeter Riddles and Aldhelm's *Enigmata*, see my "The Sexual Riddle Type," 373.
294. As before, words between parentheses acknowledge Mackie's reconstruction of this passage, where the phrase "[siþþ]an on leohte" (11b) and "[to]r[h]te getacnad" (14a) seem to be plausible readings. Mackie, *The Exeter Book*, 204.
295. On this, see my "The Sexual Riddle Type," 372. Note, by contrast, the reference to transparency in Aldhelm's *Enigma* 80: "Nunc mihi forma capax glacieque simillima lucet" (4) [Now my ample form glitters just like ice]. See my comments on this riddle above, p. 203.

of the helmet and the borer was also articulated by means of double-entendre clues.

Being the most frequent motif of the Exeter collection, the ship recurs as the subject of Riddle 64. As with nos. 19 and 36, the cryptographic codes must be spelled out in order to uncover partial clues similar to those employed in these riddles. F. Hicketier was the first scholar who managed to decode the runic pairs conveying the first two letters of several words that were expected to be completed by the solver: wi(cg), be(orn), ha(foc), þe(gn), fæ(lca), and easp(or).[296] On the basis of this code, Williamson demonstrated that Riddle 64 is a variant of the other previous ship motifs of the Exeter collection. According to his interpretation, the term "wicg" alludes to the horse as a typical compound of kennings referring to ships; "beorn" and "þegn" correspond to the man on the ship; "hafoc" and "fælca" both refer to the sails, whereas "easpor" stands for "water-track, the wake of the ship."[297] Williamson concluded that "the man is a sailor, the horse is a ship, and the hawk is a sail."[298] Thus, the ultimate solution for this riddle is "ship," but, as one of the runic clues suggests, a more precise answer could be a kenning such as *brim-hengest, mere-hengest* or *sæ-hengest*, as Niles has argued.[299]

Riddle 65 has been unanimously interpreted as "onion," and its resemblance to Symphosius's *Enigma* 44 (onion) has generally been acknowledged. The central clue of the Old English riddle is clearly based on the "bitten biter" ("mordeo mordentes," 1) motif of the Latin counterpart: "Monnan ic ne bite, nymþe he me bite" (5) [I do not bite a man unless he bites me]. The passage is thus equivalent to the following clue of Symphosius's riddle: "Sed sunt mordentem me multi mordere parati" (2) [yet many are ready to bite me even if they will be bitten]. As regards the compilation issue, Exeter Riddle

---

296. F. Hicketier, "Fünf Rätsel des Exeterbuches," *Anglia* 10 (1888): 597. The transliteration follows Williamson's interpretation of the runes in *The Old English Riddles*, 325–30.
297. Williamson, *The Old English Riddles*, 329.
298. Ibid., 327.
299. Niles, *Old English Enigmatic Poems*, 147 (n. 18).

65 is the last instrumental motif of section 5. The components of subgroup C seem to have been brought together as an illustration of human craftsmanship. The helmet thus represents the smith's work, while the borer is the carpenter's tool. By the same token, the goblet is an example of a glass artifact of human creation, whereas the ship exemplifies building and engineering. Finally, the onion stands for agriculture. The series therefore seems to have been thematically organized so that each riddle illustrates a facet of human accomplishment. The same mood is certainly observed in Latin collections such as that of Symphosius, and it also clearly evinces the encyclopedic focus of the Exeter collection.

Subgroup C is brought to a close with Riddle 66, which is a puzzling choice because of its anomalous location in the collection. Though significantly shorter than Exeter Riddle 40 or Aldhelm's *Enigma* 100, Riddle 66 is unquestionably a cosmological subject. As such, it constitutes a conspicuous thematic irregularity that needs to be dealt with. Dietrich proposed "Creation" as a solution for this riddle on the basis of several parallels observed in Aldhelm's *Enigma* 100.[300] He thus argued that Riddle 66, like no. 40 in the Exeter collection, was another translation of Aldhelm's Creation piece, notably of lines 61–66.[301] Georg Herzfeld, in turn, claimed that Riddle 66 was a more compact variant of Exeter Riddle 40.[302]

An illustration of the closeness of these two compositions is observed in the way Riddle 40 introduces the notion that Creation encompasses all things, which seems to be highlighted by the choice of two terms whose first compound is *ymb-*: "þisne ymbhwyrft utan ymbclyppe" (15) [I embrace all this world from outside]. This idea is clearly retaken and expanded in Riddle 66: "Sæs me sind ealle / flodas on fæðmum ond þes foldan bearm, / grene wongas" (3b-5a)

---

300. "Die Räthsel des Exeterbuchs: Würdigung, Lösung und Herstellung," 480.
301. F. Dietrich, "Die Räthsel des Exeterbuchs: Verfasser; Weitere Lösungen," *ZfdA* 12 (1865): 235.
302. Georg Herzfeld, *Die Räthsel des Exeterbuches und ihr Verfasser* (Berlin, 1890), 6–7.

[I surround all the seas, the oceans and the bosom of the earth, the green plains]. On the other hand, the resemblance between Riddle 66 and Aldhelm's *Enigma* 100 is also evident in the opening line of the Old English text which exhibits the same comparative technique of the Latin: "Ic eom mare þonne þes middangeard" (1) [I am bigger than this world]. The Latin counterpart in turn offers: "Latior, en, patulis terrarum finibus exto" (27) [Lo, I am larger than the wide-spreading ends of the earth].[303]

Exeter Riddle 66 maintains the comparative mood with the allusion to a particular kind of "worm" representing one of the tiniest creatures on earth—"(ic eom) læsse þonne hondwyrm" (2a) [(I am) smaller than the itch-mite].[304] This line corresponds to Aldhelm's "et minor exiguo, sulcat qui corpora, uerme . . ." (66) [and I am smaller than the meager worm which tunnels its way through bodies]. Latin "uerme" in this passage refers to a corpse worm. Riddle 40 returns to the key idea of Aldhelm's text but alludes to the itch-mite instead, offering a more detailed description than that observed in Riddle 66: "swylce ic eom on mægene minum læsse / þonne se hondwyrm, se þe hæleþa bearn, / secgas searoþoncle, seaxe delfað" (95–97) [just as I have less force than the itch-mite which the children of warriors, wise men, delve with a knife].[305] The fact that the specific reference to

---

303. These verbal similarities made Whitman conclude that Riddle 66 "was influenced by Aldhelm's 'De creatura,' though probably only indirectly." Whitman, *Old English Riddles*, 124. A contrastive table listing the parallels is found on the same page in Whitman's work.

304. "An insect supposed to produce disease in the hand." *BT* (s.v. "handwyrm"). Also, see Charles H. Whitman, "The Old English Animal Names: Mollusks; Toads, Frogs; Worms; Reptiles," *Anglia* 30 (1907): 387. Cortelyou, *Die altenglischen Namen der Insekten*, 114, specifically proposed to read "hondwyrm" as a reference to the itch-mite or itch-acarus, "a small parasitic arachnid (*Sarcoptes scabiei*) of the family Acaridæ, which burrows in the human skin, and gives rise to the disease called itch or scabies" (*OED*, s.v. "itch," C2).

305. Pinsker and Ziegler, *Die altenglischen Rätsel des Exeterbuchs*, 253, explain that this passage possibly originated in the misunderstanding of the Anglo-Saxon translator who thought that the reference to the worm's

the "hondwyrm" is also shared by Riddle 40 (96a) thus underscores a connection between the two Exeter Creation riddles.[306]

But why do Riddles 40 and 66 specifically allude to the itch-mite if Latin *uermis* is usually simply glossed as "wyrm"?[307] The case is particularly intriguing if we consider that the Anglo-Saxon translator apparently did not bother to render Latin "tippula" (pond-skater) in Aldhelm's *Enigma* 100 (41) and offered "wyrm" (76b) in an earlier passage of Exeter Riddle 40: "leohtre ic eom micle þonne þes lytla wyrm / þe her on flode gæð fotum dryge" (76–77) [I am much lighter than the small insect that walks here on the water by means of its dry foot].[308] Interestingly, the term "uerme" of Aldhelm's *Enigma* 100 (66) is glossed as ".i. briensis, hondweorm" in London, Royal 15.A.xvi (fol. 73r) and as "handwyrme" in Cambridge, Gg.5.35 (fol. 407r),[309] two codices with verifiable ties to St Augustine's, Canterbury.[310] The term further appears as "honduyrm" and "hondwyrm" in the *Corpus Glossary*,[311] which, as pointed out above (p. 338), might also be affili-

---

tunneling in the Latin *enigma* was actually alluding to the cure carried out by the physician by severing the crust produced by the itch-mite on the skin with a knife.

306. See Williamson's comments on "hondwyrm" in *The Old English Riddles*, 274.

307. For example, in Ælfric's *Glossary: "uermis wyrm."* Zupitza, *Ælfrics Grammatik und Glossar*, 309.

308. Note that the reference to the insect walking on water with its dry feet is not present in Aldhelm's riddle on Creation but in *Enigma* 38, in which the pond-skater is described walking on its dry feet (1 and 6). Also, cf. the allusion to the Israelites crossing the Red Sea in the verse *De virginitate* (2477–78). See above, p. 198.

309. See Arthur S. Napier, ed., *Old English Glosses, chiefly Unpublished* (Oxford: Clarendon, 1900), 23.50 and 25.1.

310. See above on pp. 30-31 and 35-36.

311. See Lindsay, *The Corpus Glossary*, 28 (B179), where "Briensis" is glossed as "honduyrm," and 104 (L93), where "Ladasca" is glossed as "piae, Briensis: id est hondwyrm." The interpretation of line 66 of Aldhelm's *Enigma* 100 as a reference to the itch-mite burrowing into a person's body seems to have been transferred to Continental Leipzig, Rep. I.74, in which "uerme" is glossed as "bariensis." See Ehwald, *Aldhelmi opera*, 148, and Glorie, *CCSL*,

ated with Canterbury. Similarly, the term "handwyrm" occurs in the one of the glossaries offered by London, Add. 32246, which both Ker and Porter associated with Abingdon.[312] But, as Philip G. Rusche has noted, the sources of the Antwerp-London glossaries "all seem to derive from Canterbury exemplars."[313] Seen in this light, the presence of "hondwyrm" in Exeter Riddle 66 suggests that, like Riddle 40, this text possibly derives from a translation produced at the metropolitan see.

As regards its role in the compilation, the conspicuous cosmological character of Riddle 66 contrasts with the primarily instrumental subjects of Group 2 as if inviting readers to compare God's Creation with human craftsmanship. This pattern mirrors the one observed in Group 1, in which Riddle 40 brought section 3, a long instrumental series, to a close. Whether Riddle 66 derives ultimately from Exeter Riddle 40 or from Aldhelm's *Enigma* 100 is hard to tell, but it is clear that this topic constitutes a second Creation poem and is therefore an evident case of repetition. This thus reinforces the hypothesis that the compilers were drawing material from a second assemblage from which the expansion of the core collection (Group 1) was made. Just as Riddle 40 might have been the closing motif of an originally independent collection, Riddle 66 may have also functioned as the cosmological coda of that hypothetical second collection of riddles before this was copied into the Exeter Book. If we assume that Riddle 1–2-3 is just one text and take into account the manuscript losses around Riddles 20 and 40, plus the texts for which no clear delimitation has been provided (namely, 42 and 43 as well as 47 and 48), it can be inferred that the Exeter assemblage would have probably reached sixty pieces with Riddle 66. It can therefore be deduced that this text was inserted here

---

vol. 133, 537. Cf. ".i. briensis, hondweorm" in London, Royal 15.A.xvi, which is also of Continental provenance. For the occurrence of *hondwyrm* in glossaries and the *Leechdoms*, see Williamson, *The Old English Riddles*, 274.

312. Cf. "Surio. Et briensis. 7 Sirincus. handwyrm" from Porter, *The Antwerp-London Glossaries*, 61 (560). Also, see above, p. 46 and n. 160.

313. Rusche, "Isidore's *Etymologiae*," 452 (n. 38).

because the compilers were evaluating the possibility of closing the collection at this point for the second time—the first time was with Riddle 59. The conspicuous cosmological character of Riddle 66 could not have passed unnoticed to the compilers, but it seems that, once more, they decided to continue, probably because their priority was to reach the canonical hundred rather than to comply with thematic requirements.

4.4.1.2 A Final Word on Section 5

As a whole, section 5 offers a variety of topics, including subjects related to written culture (bookworm and parchment, pen and fingers), objects of religious cult (paten?, cross, chalice), furniture (book chest), agricultural subjects (flail, onion), weapons (battering ram, helmet), tools (borer), domestic implements (churn, web and loom), and samples of human craftsmanship (well-sweep, glass goblet, ship). All of them clearly fit into the instrumental category. It is noteworthy that the section offers a threefold subclassification, a characteristic that was mainly observed in the case of Latin zoological clusters. An example of an instrumental series based on a specific subject is Tatwine's section 5, which includes topics related to the forge, but separate instrumental subdivisions within the same section, as observed in the following outline, have not been attested in the Latin collections.

Section 5: Tools II

A) Writing
47. Bookworm and parchment
48. Paten or Chalice
49. Book chest
50. Fire
51. Pen and fingers

B) Wooden objects
52. Flail
53. Battering ram

54. Churn
55. Cross
56. Web and loom
57. **Swallows**
58. Well sweep
59. **Chalice**

C) Crafstmanship
61. Helmet
62. Borer
63. Glass goblet
64. Ship
65. Onion
66. **Creation**

As observed in this scheme, the three subgroups offer a quite regular quantity of riddles, with A including five items, B eight, and C six. Also importantly, the line number is fairly balanced, ranging from six to eighteen lines, with Riddle 59 being the longest (see Appendix X)—maybe because this text functions as a coda, assuming the compilation had to be interrupted at this point. With its description of an elaborate golden chalice, Riddle 59 could certainly function as a fitting end to the instrumental series, thus offering a representative of finest human craftsmanship and paralleling Aldhelm's *Enigma* 80 (glass goblet), which also served to close a section. The majority of the topics of section 5, as is common with instrumental riddles, correspond to subjects included in Books XVIII, XIX, and XX of Isidore's *Etymologiae*. As with Exeter subgroup A, the occurrence of a sequence on a specific type of instrument is also observed is Eusebius's section 4, which focuses on subjects connected to the task of writing. By the same token, the subclassification of instrumental subjects was pointed out, for example, with regard to Tatwine's *Enigmata*, in which section 2 is clearly devoted to ecclesiastical tools. Exeter section 5 therefore shows that this first stage of the expansion of the core collection (Group 1) was executed in a rather carefully planned way. Furthermore, section 5 suggests that the compilers continued to apply encyclopedic subclassification in this part of the collection.

4.4.2 Section 6 (Riddles 67–94)

Section 6 represents a typical miscellany, some cases of which have already been observed in Latin *enigmata*. With the only exception of Symphosius's and Tatwine's Riddles, the other collections offer a potpourri in which all thematic categories appear indiscriminately. Exeter section 6, which was placed at the end of the collection, seems to be a hodgepodge of this kind.[314] Indeed, the components of this final eclectic series do not seem to share any particular thematic link, but the study of this miscellany can still shed light on the final stages of the process of compilation. I will therefore provide an analysis of a selected group of riddles from section 6 that can help us understand how this last part of the assemblage was carried out.

4.4.2.1 Fragmentariness and Manuscript Loss: Riddles 67, 70a, and 70b

The solving of Riddle 67, the opening piece of section 6, is a particularly complex task because of the textual gap caused by fire damage affecting this composition and the other pieces that occur at this part of the manuscript. Trautmann's proposal "Bible" was accepted by most editors, although some scholars, Niles most recently, have preferred to leave this piece unanswered.[315] The notable parallelisms observed in Riddles 67 and 26 have been generally acknowledged. Like Riddle 26 (Gospel book), the writing motif of Riddle 67 is said to have rich ornaments, a feature pointing to a religious book of some kind: "Ic þæt oft geseah / golde gegierwed, þær guman druncon, / since ond seolfre" (13b–15a) [I have frequently seen it ornamented with gold, jewels and silver, where warriors were

---

314. Cf. Aldhelm's section 3, Eusebius's section 3, and Vatican section 5. Only the Lorsch *Enigmata* offer a miscellany at the end (section 3).
315. Niles, *Old English Enigmatic Poems*, 143.

drinking].³¹⁶ As noted by Niles in the case of Riddle 26, complete Bibles were seldom produced in the medieval period,³¹⁷ whereas the manufacture of separate parts—particularly, the Gospels—was common practice in scriptoria.³¹⁸ Accordingly, this scholar contends that the lavish illumination of the specimen described in Riddle 26 suggests the answer "Gospel book," which I have tentatively adopted for Riddle 67 as well.

Among the surviving clues of Riddle 67, the paradox of the mouthless speaker stands out: "nænne muð hafað" (6b) [it has no mouth]. As discussed above, this is a typical characteristic of subjects related to writing. Furthermore, the text offers two clear references to wisdom as the main feature of the hidden creature: "snytt[...]" (3a) and "wisdome" (5a). Further on, the object speaks in the first-person singular form and refers to itself as "leoda lareow" (10a) or the teacher of the people, an idea that could fit the Gospel, which was thought to contain Christ's teaching.³¹⁹ As for the function of Riddle 67 in the compilation, the topic might have seemed appropriate to initiate section 6.

Exeter Riddle 70 was considered a single composition until John C. Pope detected a lacuna between folios 125 and 126 of the manuscript,³²⁰ thus demonstrating that the four lines that constitute the final passage of the last leaf of Quire XVI were actually a different

---

316. The expression "þær guman druncon" (14b) has been interpreted either as a formula or as an allusion to the eucharist.
317. Niles, *Old English Enigmatic Poems*, 118–19.
318. Niles's argument is in turn based on that of Richard Marsden's assertion that "complete Bibles were a rarity in Anglo-Saxon England." See Lapidge et al., *The Wiley Blackwell Encyclopedia*, s.v. "Bible," 68.
319. As Williamson states, "the great teacher, *leoda lareow* (line 10), which speaks to men without a mouth (line 6) and which is richly adorned with gold and silver (lines 14–15), can only be a religious book, presumably the Bible." *The Old English Riddles*, 334.
320. John C. Pope, "An Unsuspected Lacuna in the Exeter Book: Divorce Proceedings for an Ill-matched Couple in the Old English Riddles," *Speculum* 49 (1974): 615–22.

text from the two lines of the first leaf of Quire XVII.³²¹ The presence of this lacuna could be deduced from certain textual irregularities that had already been pointed out by other critics, who attributed them to scribal mistakes. As observed in most editions antedating Pope's article, Riddle 70 offers verbs in the third-person singular up to line 5b, in which "stonde" occurs.³²² This first-person singular form therefore suggests that the text is actually two different compositions, which will henceforth be referred to as Riddles 70a and 70b. Pope's argumentation has been endorsed by editors such as Williamson and Muir, who have printed the two passages as separate texts.³²³

As for the solving of Riddle 70a, there is general agreement on the fact that the text describes a musical instrument of some kind:

Wiht is wrætlic   þam þe hyre wisan ne conn.
Singeð þurh sidan.   Is se sweora woh,
orþoncum geworht;   hafaþ eaxle tua
scearp on gescyldrum.   His gesceapo dreogeð . . .

[The creature is beautiful to the one who does not know its ways. It sings through its sides; its neck is curved and intricately made; it has two shoulders with ornaments (?) on the two shoulders. It (suffers) its fate . . .].³²⁴

Following Trautmann, Pope proposed "lyre" or "harp."³²⁵ Williamson accepted this interpretation, arguing that "the lyre sings through its sides; it has a crooked or curved neck that is skillfully wrought."³²⁶

---

321. For a study of the structure of these quires, see Conner, *Anglo-Saxon Exeter*, 107–10.
322. See Krapp and Dobbie, *ASPR*, vol. 3, 231–32; also, see their comments on the verbal discrepancy on 369.
323. See Williamson, *The Old English Riddles*, 107 (nos. 67–68), and Muir, *The Exeter Anthology*, vol. 1, 366 (nos. 69–70).
324. Note that "dreogeð," which is not present in the manuscript, was supplied by Krapp and Dobbie, *ASPR*, vol. 3, 232.
325. Trautmann, *Die altenglischen Rätsel*, 125. Pope, "An Unsuspected Lacuna," 621.
326. Williamson, *The Old English Riddles*, 338. Considering the two

I concur with Williamson that the description offered by the clues of Riddle 70a fits that of a lyre, but the reference to the two pairs of shoulders is at best intriguing. In a way, we could assume that two of the shoulders correspond to the two round edges of the musical instrument, but the lyre or the harp would be sustained by only one human shoulder, not two. Also, manuscript "scearp" (4a) does not seem to accord with the reference to the shoulders. As argued by Pope, the word that was probably meant was *sceorp* (apparel), arguing that "scearp" might be a dialectal variant.[327] He thus proposed to emend this passage to *scearpan gescyldru*, accusative plural, as a variation on "eaxle tua" (3b). The reading is still unconvincing but, to my knowledge, no better alternative interpretation has been provided.

As regards Riddle 70b, the only two lines that have been preserved seem to contain the essential clues to solve this composition: "þe swa wrætlice be wege stonde / heah ond hleortorht hæleþum to nytte" [as I stand so beautifully by the way, high, bright of face and of use to men]. The riddle thus apparently refers to the function of the object as indicating the way,[328] standing high, and possessing a light-emitting capacity. The phrase "hæleþum to nytte" in turn establishes the utility of the object, a feature that usually fits instrumental topics. The term "hleortorht" is a hapax legomenon which has been translated as "bright of face" or "bright-cheeked."[329] The

---

fragments as one composition, Dietrich solved Riddle 70 as "shepherd's pipe" or "shawm," a solution that has been accepted by most scholars. "Die Räthsel des Exeterbuchs: Würdigung, Lösung und Herstellung," 480.
327. Pope, "An Unsuspected Lacuna," 620–21.
328. Pope pointed out that "be wege" could be interpreted as either "by the water" (Old English *wēg*) or "by the way" (*weg*). He finally supported the second reading because it is metrically preferable and may be understood as a reference to the lighthouse marking the way to sailors. "An Unsuspected Lacuna," 622 (n. 25). This reading is endorsed by Williamson, *The Old English Riddles*, 340, and Muir, *The Exeter Anthology*, vol. 2, 665.
329. Pope proposed to read it as "bright of face" in "An Unsuspected Lacuna," 619. Williamson, *The Old English Riddles*, 431, similarly offers "bright-cheeked" in his glossary. Cf. Mackie's translation "bright of hue" in *The Exeter Book*, 209. On the basis of a literal reading of "hleortorht" as a possible reference

attribution of human features to the lighthouse in Riddle 70b brings to mind the flame-bearing ("flammiger," 9) high tower ("turribus altis," 9), which is personified as a human guide ("index," 4)—or maybe as a pointing finger[330]—marking the path for the ships in Aldhelm's *Enigma* 92 (high lighthouse).[331] A combined reference to height, brightness, and human characteristics is similarly present in Wulfstan Cantor's portrayal of the tower of the Old Minster at Winchester in a passage from his *Narratio metrica sancti Swithuni* (c. 996): "Turris ab axe micat qua sol oriendo coruscat / et spargit lucis spicula prima suae" (179–80) ["From the summit of heaven a tower gleams, on which the rising sun shimmers and sprinkles the first rays of its light"].[332] The tower is subsequently described as having five storeys ("segmenta," 181) which are said to be "oculata" (181), in other words, with eyes as a reference to the gaping windows ("patulis . . . fenestris," 181). The phrase "heah ond hleortorht," high and bright of face, in Riddle 70b therefore seems to be in line with the personification of the lighthouse in Aldhelm's *Enigma* 92 and that of the Old Minster tower in Wulfstan's *Narratio*.

The presence of the lighthouse as a topic in section 6 is noteworthy. As discussed above (p. 218), Aldhelm's counterpart was probably included as an example of human extraordinary craftsmanship among other riddles that can be ascribed to the wonder category.

---

to a human face, a radically different solution has been put forward in Colette Stévanovitch, "Exeter Book Riddle 70A: Nose?" *N&Q* 240 (1995): 8–10.

330. Note that Latin *index* can either refer to "the forefinger, index-finger" or to "one who indicates or discloses, a discoverer, director, guide, informer, discloser, witness."

331. As noted by Pope, "An Unsuspected Lacuna," 619, the clues of Aldhelm's riddle were probably based on Isidore's description of the famous lighthouse of Alexandria (*Etymologiae* XV.ii.37). But, as he further infers, Aldhelm might have known this type of construction from personal experience, for there were two Roman lighthouses in Dover and a few more on the other side of the English Channel. The same might have been the case for the Exeter riddler.

332. Text and translation from Lapidge, *The Cult of St Swithun*, 386–87. On this work, see further on p. 416.

Interestingly, Exeter Riddle 86 (one-eyed garlic seller), which has been generally acknowledged to be indebted to Symphosius's *Enigma* 95, is a further composition that could be classified as a wonder.[333] Like Aldhelm's *Enigma* 92 (high lighthouse) and Symphosius's *Enigma* 95, Exeter Riddles 70b (lighthouse) and 86 (one-eyed garlic seller) occur toward the end of the collection. The presence of these two subjects at this point of Exeter Group 3 suggests the compilers' awareness of the fact that they were including two wonder motifs in an attempt to imitate Latin compilation patterns.

The discovery of the textual lacuna between folios 125 and 126 of the Exeter Book by Pope also has further implications on our study of the compilation of Group 3, as it is probable that some other riddles could have been lost in the missing folio. As Conner explains, "The lost folio would have contained the rest of Riddle 70A, probably one or two other unknown riddles, and the beginning of the now-truncated Riddle 70B."[334] However, the textual gap might be even larger, since the first leaf of Quire XVII may also be wanting, as Conner conjectures that this final gathering could have originally had eight folios, instead of seven, as Förster conversely had thought.[335] Thus, these two missing folios might have contained several riddles. Given that these quires were pricked and ruled for twenty-two lines, the loss possibly did not entail much text. However, the length of riddles at this point varies exceedingly, as observed in Appendix X, so that it is almost impossible to deduce the amount of poems that may have been lost in this manuscript gap. Still, a tentative guess of approximately six or seven riddles may be put forward.

---

333. See Jonathan Wilcox, "Mock-Riddles in Old English: Exeter Riddles 86 and 19," *Studies in Philology* 93 (1996): 180–87.
334. Conner, *Anglo-Saxon Exeter*, 107.
335. See ibid., 109, for a reconstruction of Quire XVII. See also Förster's description this quire in Chambers, *The Exeter Book of Old English Poetry*, 59. See also John C. Pope, "Paleography and Poetry: Some Solved and Unsolved Problems of the Exeter Book," in *Medieval Scribes, Manuscripts and Libraries: Essays Presented to N. R. Ker*, ed. M. B. Parkes and Andrew G. Watson (London: Scolar, 1978), 29.

4.4.2.2 A Careless Compilation: Riddles 68–69, 79–80, and 75–76

There is evidence that the assembling of the riddles included in Group 3 was done in a rather careless way and that, as pointed out above, the compilers increasingly resorted to opportunistic improvisation in place of planned arrangement. The extreme brevity of some of the pieces of Group 3—note, for example, Riddle 75–76 (piss) with only two lines—dramatically contrasts with the notable length of texts such as Riddle 84 (water) with fifty-six lines. Also, this imbalance strikingly differs from the homogeneity observed in Symphosius's collection or the Bern *Enigmata*. As with Riddle 1-2-3 and other cases, one wonders if the compilers really understood where the textual boundaries of some of the riddles were.[336]

An illustration of this general carelessness is Riddle 68–69, which corresponds to the following three lines: "Ic þa wiht geseah on weg feran; / heo wæs wrætlice wundrum gegierwed. / Wundor wearð on wege; wæter wearð to bane" [I saw the creature travel on the water; it was magnificently and wonderfully adorned. An amazing thing happened on the sea; the water became bone]. On paleographical grounds, Krapp and Dobbie interpreted the first two lines as an independent riddle (no. 68), since there is a conventional end-punctuation symbol (:7) occurring after the term "gegierwed" (2b) on folio 125v; as for the subsequent line, which begins with a capital W ("Wundor," 3a), Krapp and Dobbie edited it as Riddle 69. Tupper, Wyatt, Mackie, Williamson, and most recently Muir, however, all read these three lines as a single composition, whose first two lines are merely formulaic. The text evidently resembles Exeter Riddle 33 (iceberg), and it has been generally accepted that line 3 constitutes the crucial clue on which the solution "ice" or "iceberg" is based.[337] This second

---

336. This problem is not only observed in the Exeter Riddles. As reported by Conner in "Four Contiguous Poems," 120, further "sliding boundaries" can be detected in some of the poems separating the two main riddle blocks.
337. Dietrich, "Die Räthsel des Exeterbuchs: Würdigung, Lösung und Herstellung," 480, first proposed this possible answer for Riddle 68–69.

view seems to me the most convincing. The fact that Riddle 68–69 is made of three lines could be regarded as average length, if we use Symphosius's *Enigmata* as a touchstone of riddlic format. But, compared to the other Exeter riddles in the area (see Appendix X), this text is extremely short.[338] Besides, it is rhetorically very poor, giving the impression that it was left incomplete and, maybe, not correctly punctuated in the exemplar that was being copied by the Exeter compilers. It could consequently be surmised that Riddle 68–69 was simply incorporated into Group 3 for the sake of enlarging the collection and making up the numbers.

Riddle 79–80 (horn) is a further interesting case that can give us insight into how the final phase of the compilation of the Exeter Riddles was carried out. Krapp and Dobbie considered the line preceding Riddle 80—"Ic eom æþelinges æht ond willa" [I am the property and will of a prince]—as a separate composition.[339] Once more, this editorial decision is grounded on the occurrence of end-punctuation after "willa" and the beginning of the next line with a capital "IC."[340] However, printing this single line as an independent composition makes no sense, as it provides no distinctive clue to elicit a particular solution. Dietrich accurately noted that this line was simply a variant of subsequent Riddle 80: "Ic eom æþelinges eaxlgestealla" (1) [I am a prince's close comrade].[341] Wyatt agreed with Dietrich, adding that the line could probably be "a false start unerased."[342] This idea supports my inference

---

338. Noting the exceptional brevity of some of the pieces of this part of the collection, Murphy states that "the average number of lines per Exeter riddle is roughly fourteen (as edited by Krapp and Dobbie)." See his *Unriddling*, 10 (n. 33).
339. Krapp and Dobbie, *ASPR*, vol. 3, 235. Muir accepts this reading in *The Exeter Anthology*, vol. 1, 371 and vol. 2, 670.
340. See Muir, *The Exeter DVD* (fol. 127r).
341. "Die Räthsel des Exeterbuchs: Würdigung, Lösung und Herstellung," 483.
342. Wyatt, *Old English Riddles*, 116. For a similar opinion, see Trautmann, *Die altenglischen Rätsel*, 129. Williamson agrees with this interpretation and reads this line as part of the subsequent text, thus editing Riddle 79–80 as one composition. He further argues that this case represents a similar

that this phase of the compilation was carried out in a rather awkward and rushed way. It seems to me that the scribe of the Exeter exemplar was probably rewriting and improvising as (s)he copied the riddles from the sources at hand, as deduced from the insertion of a variant reading of line 1. The occurrence of end-punctuation was probably simply intended to indicate that the riddle proper started next.

As we advance in section 6, there are further signs of the compilers' disregard for selectiveness in the low literary quality and the terseness of some of the riddles that were incorporated into this part of the collection. The two lines, separated by four runes, that Krapp and Dobbie considered as two independent riddles (nos. 75 and 76), are a good illustration of this:

> Ic swiftne geseah   on swaþe feran
> ·ᛞ ᛣ ᛚ ᚻ·
> Ic ane geseah   idese sittan.

[I saw a swift one traveling on the path (DNLH). I saw a woman sitting alone].

As with the preceding cases, the separate printing of these two lines is based on the presence of an end-punctuation mark (:7) after the runes and on the fact that the second line begins with a capital letter (fol. 127r). Williamson, however, edits these two lines as a single riddle, arguing that they both constitute a structurally unified composition. As regards the punctuation mark after the first line, Williamson contends that "the scribe has mistakenly copied one riddle as two."[343] Following Williamson, Muir likewise prints these two lines as a single text and compares this case to that of Riddles 68–69.[344]

---

scribal error as that observed in Riddles 42 and 43, 47 and 48, 68 and 69, and 75 and 76. Additionally, Williamson considers the possibility that, "alternatively, the scribe could have been copying a defective exemplar, in which a missing leaf or some other defect caused all but the first line to be lost." *The Old English Riddles*, 360.
343. Williamson, *The Old English Riddles*, 353.
344. See Muir's comments in *The Exeter Anthology*, vol. 2, 669–70.

Considering this runic passage in relation to the consonantal codes embedded in Exeter Riddle 36, Muir concludes that *DNLH* constitutes "an interpolation, an encoded, cryptic (and correct) solution offered by an early reader which has subsequently been incorporated into the main text."[345] In fact, in both Riddles 36 and 75–76 the position of the codes seems to have been understood by the scribe as being extra-textual material. Given the natural limitations deriving from the copying on parchment, the concept of what marginal space meant for a medieval scribe differs considerably from what this could be in a printed book. Accordingly, the marginal character of *DNLH*, situated to the right of the word "feran," seems quite logical. In a present-day publication, this could compare to the occurrence of the solution to a given puzzle at the bottom of the page or at the end of the book.

The runic passage in Riddle 75–76 is particularly hard to decode, however, as it only presents consonants and the solver is expected to supply the missing vowels. This situation has produced some disparate solutions such as *hund* (dog) and *Hælend* (Savior).[346] Williamson decoded the runic passage as *hland* (urine), usually glossed as Latin *lotium*, pointing out that this term "is normally listed as a neuter noun, but in its unmodified occurrences it could be confused with the masculine."[347] Runic *hland*, therefore, could accord with the term "swiftne" (1a). The key to understand the riddle therefore lies in the suggestion of the two different positions in which men and women urinate: standing and sitting. Despite the gender crux, Williamson's arguments seem to me the best explanation that has been offered for these lines so far.[348]

---

345. Muir, *The Exeter Anthology*, vol. 2, 670.
346. Old English *hund* is Thorpe's proposal (*Codex Exoniensis*, 487) for the first line (Riddle 75). This obviously entails the emendation of the runic code and the assumption that the third line (Riddle 76) is insoluble. Even though this proposal is highly speculative, it has recently gained support from Bitterli, *Say what I am Called*, 106. Mackie, on the other hand, proposed *Hælend* as an allusion to Christ. See Mackie, "Notes on the Text," 77.
347. Williamson, *The Old English Riddles*, 354.
348. As he explains, "The swift pissing of man is seen to travel on the

Interestingly, Riddle 75–76 is the only scatological composition of the Exeter Book. To my knowledge, there is only one more case that has been reported in early medieval English literature.[349] As early Latin collections do not offer scatological themes, the presence of this riddle providing a vulgar subject is remarkable and confirms the idea that the compilers were not particularly selective at this stage of the assembling process: they did not mind including a coarse joke, as long as its inclusion helped to move the collection toward the canonical number of one hundred items.

4.4.2.3 Riddles 77 and 78: An Aquatic Duo

The study of Riddles 77 and 78 can shed some light on the compilation history of this part of the Exeter collection.[350] Though partially obliterated due to the diagonal burn that affects the last folios of the manuscript, Riddle 77 has universally been solved as "oyster."[351] By contrast, Riddle 78 has puzzled scholars for a long time, since the same burn affected this text more severely than the preceding one.

---

road or track. The piss of woman by implication is hidden. The riddler does not see the *hland* of woman; he merely sees the woman 'sitting alone' (*ane . . . idese sittan*)." Williamson, *The Old English Riddles*, 355.
349. The scatological character of a query found in Pseudo-Bede's *Joco-Seria* 10 was pointed out by Orchard: "Littera queque culum facit ut uideat uelut oc[u]lus? / (Gloss.) Etque culus—ani dorsi que minime uidet, antepone o littera et uidebit ut oc[u]lus utpote quia erit oculus" ["'How do you make an ass-hole see?' (answer: add the letter 'o,' to transform *culus* (ass-hole) into *oculus* (eye)]." Cited from Tupper, "Riddles of the Bede Tradition," 569. I am here offering Orchard's translation of this query from "Enigma Variations," 287. In later English medieval riddle collections, several scatological pieces have been detected. Note, for example, a logograph (no. 26) whose solution is *latrina*, "A water-closet, privy," and another piece from a different collection (no. 3) probably suggesting *mentula*, penis, as the answer. Galloway, "The Rhetoric of Riddling," 101 (ns. 124 and 127).
350. The upcoming discussion on Riddles 77 and 78 is a re-elaboration of the main ideas offered in my "The Oyster and the Crab."
351. Dietrich first proposed "oyster" in "Die Räthsel des Exeterbuchs: Würdigung, Lösung und Herstellung," 483. Since then, this solution has been unquestioned.

Tupper and Trautmann, however, noted outstanding parallels in these two riddles, concluding that "oyster" should also be the solution of Riddle 78.[352] F. Holthausen similarly noticed these textual correspondences and thus accepted "oyster" as a possible answer but added two other possible solutions: "oyster? crab? fish?"[353] Mackie in turn listed "oyster" as a probable solution to this riddle.[354]

The presence of two consecutive riddles on the same topic is nevertheless questionable, since this phenomenon is not very common in medieval riddlic tradition.[355] Instead of attributing the similarities observed in Riddles 77 and 78 to their sharing the same solution, it might be safer to assume that these parallels stem from the fact that these two texts convey a zoological pair, just as we have frequently seen in Latin *enigmata* and earlier in the Exeter collection. On the basis of the well-known connection between the oyster and the crab in medieval encyclopedic lore, Holthausen's second suggestion, "crab," seems to me the answer that best suits the fragmentary clues of Riddle 78 and can best explain the verbal parallels observed in the two compositions.

As editors have convincingly argued, the clues of Riddle 77 describe an oyster:

---

352. Tupper, *The Riddles of the Exeter Book*, 217; Trautmann, *Die altenglischen Rätsel*, 129.
353. As translated from Ferdinand Holthausen, "Zu alt- und mittelenglischen Dichtungen. XV," *Anglia* 24 (1901): 265.
354. Mackie, *The Exeter Book*, 242. By contrast, Muir, *The Exeter Anthology*, vol. 2, 688, classifies this riddle as "uncertain."
355. With the exception of the Bern and Vatican Riddles, repetition occurs only rarely in the other Latin collections that have been analyzed. For example, Symphosius's *Enigmata* offer two contiguous versions of the "flint" riddle (nos. 76 and 77) in the Salmasian codex (pp. 152–53). The first "flint" riddle offers the word "aliter"—meaning "otherwise, differently"—as a title, thus suggesting that the scribe clearly acknowledged the fact that this was a variant of the subsequent text. On this case of repetition, see Bergamin, *Aenigmata Symposii*, 174–75. As pointed out above (p. 378, n. 271), a further case of repetition is found in London, Royal 15.B.xix (fols. 79r–82r), in which Symphosius's *Enigma* 78 (stairs) occurs twice. See ibid., lxxxv.

Sæ mec fedde, sundhelm þeahte,
ond mec yþa wrugon eorþan getenge
feþelease. Oft ic flode ongean
muð ontynde. Nu wile monna sum
min flæsc fretan, felles ne recceð,
siþþan he me of sidan seaxes orde
hyd arypeð, [. . .]ec hr[.]þe siþþan
iteð unsodene ea[. . . . .]d.

[The sea fed me, the water covered me, and, close to the land, the waves sheltered me. Without the power to walk, I frequently open my mouth to the flood. Now some man wishes to devour my flesh; (he) does not care for my shell when he tears off the skin from my side (i.e., removes the shell) with the point of a knife, when (he quickly) eats (me) uncooked, and also . . .]

The creature is presented as a passive eater, as there is an external agent (the sea) that feeds it (1a). The passivity of this animal is further emphasized through its characterization as lacking the power to move ("feþelease," 3a). Besides, the oyster's modest defense, its shell, alluded to metaphorically as the animal's skin ("felles," 5b), is easily broken through by means of a knife.

The role of the oyster as a victim of man's ravenous act is strongly suggested by the use of "fretan" (5a). As Hugh Magennis explains, "in referring to eating by people and animals, Old English distinguishes between the senses of its two basic verbs 'to eat,' *etan* and *fretan*," adding that "*fretan* is nearly always used of beasts."[356] But this scholar also notes that there are occasional uses of this verb in a human context. After discussing several passages in which *fretan* applies to people, Magennis concludes that this verb does not only refer specifically to animal feeding but that its meaning should also be extended to the notion of "voracious or eager eating, and completeness of eating."[357] Indeed, this verb appears in literary excerpts

---

356. Magennis, *Anglo-Saxon Appetites*, 74.
357. Ibid., 76.

in which, regardless of animal or human context, there are moralistic overtones that explicitly or implicitly disapprove of the action that is being described. In Exeter Riddle 47, which was discussed above, the bookworm (or the witless student) is said to devour written words on parchment: "Moðð e word fræt" (1a). In this sense, the use of *fretan* emphasizes the uselessness of the eroding activity (or that of the inefficient *ruminatio*), by which no wisdom or spiritual benefit can be obtained. In *The Wonders of the East, fretan* occurs when the cannibalistic habits of tribes from remote lands such as the gigantic Hostes are mentioned: "Cuþlice swa hwylcne man swa hy gelæccað, þonne fretað hi hyne" (53–54) ["Evidently, whatever person they get hold of, they eat him"].[358] In the case of Exeter Riddle 77, the poet most likely chose *fretan* to convey similar deontological resonances, censuring the man's gluttonous conduct as well as his violent attitude toward a defenseless creature like the oyster.

Now that the textual peculiarities of Riddle 77 have been analyzed, we should concentrate on the reasons that made the compilers include an oyster motif in the collection. We may concur with Williamson and other scholars that the Anglo-Saxons simply knew this animal quite well, as there are several literary passages that attest to the Anglo-Saxons' familiarity with the oyster and could justify its presence in the Exeter Riddles.[359] But, as I have earlier argued with regard to some of the zoological riddles of Group 1, the connection of the oyster with the food restrictions established by the Benedictine Reform might be a satisfactory explanation for the presence of

---

358. Text and translation from Fulk, *The Beowulf Manuscript*, 22–23. For other passages in which *fretan* is used for human beings, see Magennis, *Anglo-Saxon Appetites*, 75–78.

359. As noted by Tupper, *The Riddles of the Exeter Book*, 216, the oyster is listed among the animals of the fisherman's catch in Ælfric's *Colloquy* (106–8). Garmonsway, *Ælfric's Colloquy*, 29. For the oyster in medicinal recipes, see Rev. Thomas Oswald Cockayne, ed. and trans., *Leechdoms, Wortcunning and Starcraft of Early England*, vol. 2 (London: The Holland Press, 1961), 194–95 and 254–55. As regards the employment of oysters for culinary purposes, see Hagen, *A Handbook of Anglo-Saxon Food*, 55, 62, 118, and 150.

this theme in the collection. This association is certainly worth exploring, since it could contribute to understanding the context in which Riddles 77 and 78 were read.

Together with other mollusks, fish, and poultry in general, the oyster was included in the diet allowed by the relatively strict monastic regulations, which prescribed a moderate consumption of red meat or even total abstinence from it.[360] The presence of the oyster in clerical dietary practices is attested to, for example, in a passage from an Anglo-Saxon monastic sign list with verifiable Benedictine affinities:[361] "Gif þu ostran habban wylle þonne clæm þu þinne wynstran hand ðam gemete þe þu ostran on handa hæbbe and do mid sexe oððe mid fingre swylce þu ostran scenan wylle" ["If you want an oyster, then close your left hand, as if you had an oyster in your hand, and make with a knife or with your fingers as if you were going to open the oyster"].[362] Incidentally, the simulation of the opening of the animal's shell with a knife, the gesture described to refer to this mollusk, recalls one of the clues of Riddle 77. The oyster is also clearly associated with monastic food consumption in a passage from *The Seasons for Fasting*:

Hwæt! Hi [þa sacerdas] leaslice   leogan ongynnað
and þone tæppere   tyhtaþ gelome,

---

360. *The Rule of St Benedict*, for instance, permitted meat consumption only in cases of illness or extreme weakness. See H. Logeman, ed. *The Rule of St. Benet*, EETS, o.s. 90 (1888, Kraus repr., 1975), 68 (xxxvi). See also Arthur S. Napier, ed., *The Old English Version of the Enlarged Rule of Chrodegang, together with the Latin Original*, EETS, o.s. 150 (London: Kegan Paul, 1916; repr. Kraus, 1988), 47–48 (xxxviii).
361. The contents of London, Cotton Tiberius A.iii (mid-eleventh century) are clearly associated with the Benedictine revival. Apart from the sign list and other texts related to the reformist movement, this codex offers one of the only two surviving copies of the *Regularis Concordia*, and the Old English translation of St Benedict's Rule. Debby Banham, ed. and trans., *Monasteriales Indicia: The Anglo-Saxon Monastic Sign Language* (Pinner: Anglo-Saxon Books, 1991; repr. 1993), 7. Also see above, p. 39 (n. 126).
362. Text and translation from ibid., 36–37 (no. 72).

secgaþ þæt he synleas syllan mote
ostran to æte and æþele wyn
emb morgentyd þæs þe me þingeð"
þæt hund and wulf healdað þa ilcan
wisan on worulde and ne wigliað
hwæne hie to mose fon, mæða bedæled. (216–23)

["Behold, they (the priests) falsely begin to lie and often persuade the tapster, telling him that he may without sinning give them oysters to eat and excellent wine in the morning-time, to the extent that it seems to me that the dog and the wolf act in the same way in the world and do not foresee when they may get food, lacking in moderation"].[363]

From the point of view of the author, the priests' gluttonous conduct equates them with proverbially ravenous animals such as dogs or wolves. This idea finds an echo in the way in which "lack of moderation," as befits irrational creatures such as the rooster and the hen in Riddle 42, can easily affect human beings, too.

In *The Seasons for Fasting*, further reference is made to the priests as frequent consumers of oysters and other aquatic animals ("ostran eac and oþerne / fisc of flode," 229–30a). As this work is known to be strongly affiliated with the reformist ideology of the late tenth century,[364] it is not surprising to find this allusion in a passage where the dietary abuses of the clergy are denounced. Even if the oyster was theoretically classified as an unclean animal, that is, a "fish" with no scales or fins, it seems that the flesh of mollusks was not considered prohibited food, as inferred from this text in which the speaker alludes to the clerics taking advantage of this and yielding to gluttony. The case no doubt brings to mind Gerald of Wales's comments

---

363. The text is from Elliott Van Kirk Dobbie, *ASPR*, vol. 6, 104. Note that Dobbie's "þingað" (220b) has been altered to "þingeð," as adopted by Magennis for this passage in his *Anglo-Saxon Appetites*, 89 (n. 15). The translation of this excerpt is also from Magennis, 90.

364. For further information on this poem's association with the Benedictine reform, see Sisam, *Studies*, 47–48, and Magennis, *Anglo-Saxon Appetites*, 86.

on the clerics' sinless indulgence in the meat of the barnacle goose and Exeter Riddle 10 on this bird in Group 1.[365]

The Benedictine context in which the Exeter Riddles were probably read might thus contribute to elucidating the moralistic overtones that were detected in the reference to man's voracious appetite in Riddle 77. The term "unsodene" (8a)—i.e., "uncooked," alluding to the raw oyster being eaten—clearly increases the dramatic connotations of the first-person experience presented.[366] Since the oyster is eaten alive, the description might have also been intended to convey further nuances of reprobation with regard to the man's sinful conduct, which, as in the passage from *The Seasons for Fasting*, could be even more significant in a monastic milieu.[367] The combined use of "fretan" (5a) and "unsodene" (8a) in Riddle 77 similarly suggests that the man devouring the oyster ranks equally with the uncivilized people who eat raw meat, as depicted in works such as *The Wonders of the East*.[368] Seen in this light, the occurrence of the oyster motif in the Exeter collection cannot be haphazard, as this mollusk most likely formed part of the monastic diet in the reformist context of the late tenth and early eleventh centuries. The riddle theme would therefore be a well-known subject for an ecclesiastical audience, as the passages from the monastic sign list and the *Seasons for Fasting* also demonstrate.

As regards fragmentary Riddle 78, most critics have inferred that the riddlic creature should be another aquatic animal of some kind.

Oft ic flodas   [............
.....................]s   cynn[.] minum
ond [.......................................

---

365. See above, pp. 321–22.
366. *BT*, "To cook in a liquid, seethe, boil" (s.v. "ge-seóþan").
367. It is worth noting that *The Rule of St Benedict* makes clear that the midday meal should consist of two cooked dishes: "twa gesodene syflian." Logeman, *The Rule of St. Benet*, 70 (c. xxxviii).
368. Note, for example, this passage (94–95): "ond þær syndon men þe be hreawum flæsce ond be hunie hy lifiað" ["and there are people there who live on raw meat and on honey"]. Text and translation from Fulk, *The Beowulf Manuscript*, 28–29.

.]yde me to mos[. . . . .
. . . .]   swa ic him [. . . . .
. . . .]   ne æt ham gesæt
[. . . . .]   flote cwealde
þurh orþonc [. . . . .]   yþum bewrigene.

[[I often . . . on the flood . . . to my kin, and. . . . I had for my food. . . . so that I . . . to it. . . . (it) did not remain at home. . . . killed in the water in a skillful way. . . . covered by the waves].

The expressions "oft ic flodas" (1a), "flote" (7b), and "yþum bewrigene" (8b) leave no room for doubt that sea is the creature's habitat.[369] As noted above, Tupper drew attention to phrases that clearly echo those found in Riddle 77, in which the oyster is also described as a sea animal, covered by the waves.[370]

The fourth line of Riddle 78—".]yde me to mos[. . ."—is the first of a sequence of clues that will prove crucial for unveiling the solution. For the missing parts of this phrase, Tupper proposed "[d]yde me to mos[e]," a reading that I will henceforth adopt, on the basis of a parallel passage from *Andreas*,[371] in which the phrase is used to describe the Mermedonians' cannibalistic customs:

	Swelc wæs þeaw hira
þæt hie æghwylcne	ellðeodigra
dydan him to mose	meteþearfendum,
þara þe þæt ealand	utan sohte. (25b–28)

["Such was their practice, that they turned into food for the hungry each foreigner who visited the island from abroad"].[372]

---

369. For a detailed reflection on aquatic animals in Anglo-Saxon literature, see Sorrell, "Like a Duck to Water."
370. Cf. lines 1–2a and 3b–4a of Riddle 77 above (p. 404).
371. Holthausen, "Zu alt- und mittelenglischen Dichtungen. XV," 265, had previously read "[h]yde me to mos[e]," but Tupper's proposal (*The Riddles of the Exeter Book*, 217) seems to be more appropriate on the basis of the analogy with the passage from *Andreas*.
372. The translation is by Bradley, *Anglo-Saxon Poetry*, 112.

This initial passage of *Andreas* serves to set a contrast between the uncivilized heathen Mermedonians and St Andrew, the Christian hero. A similar expression is used in the excerpt cited above from *The Seasons for Fasting*, in which the ravenous attitude of the dog and the wolf was brought up and compared to the behavior of gluttonous priests ("ne wigliað / hwæne hie to mose fon," 222b–23a). On the basis of the textual analogy found in these two passages from *Andreas* and *The Seasons for Fasting*, the phrase "[d]yde me to mos[e]" in Riddle 78 therefore points to a creature with a particularly rapacious instinct. This idea establishes a further interesting parallel with Riddle 77, in which the man eating the oyster was presented with a similar predatory attitude. Also, it suggests an oppositional relationship between the creature of Riddle 78 and the oyster, which was clearly portrayed in the preceding text as a helpless victim of man's greed.

The subsequent clues of Riddle 78 seem to deal with this animal's special method when hunting for food at sea. Following the context established by "[d]yde me to mos[e]," "flote cwealde" (7b) most likely refers to an aquatic predator. According to this, "him" (5b) could be an allusion to this animal's usual prey.[373] Furthermore, the phrase "þurh orþonc" (8a) possibly points to the predator's cunning method of hunting. As deduced by Williamson, this creature "kills its wave-covered victims (*ypum bewrigene*) with a special power or

---

373. There is a possible objection to this hypothesis, as the pronoun "him" (5b) does not fit the feminine form of Old English *ostre* or Latin *ostrea*. However, further cases of gender irregularities are found in the Exeter Riddles, an example being Riddle 40 in which the solution is alluded to indistinctively as feminine and masculine throughout the text. On this, see Tupper, *The Riddles of the Exeter Book*, 164; Wyatt, *Old English Riddles*, xxxv–xxxvi; Williamson, *The Old English Riddles*, 274; and my "The Oyster and the Crab," 413. Latin riddles also illustrate gender inconsistencies of this kind. Williams reports three such cases in Tatwine's collection. For example, the spark (*scintilla*) of Tatwine's Riddle 31 is said to be buried ("sepultus," 4) in the flint's "womb." See Williams, "The Riddles of Tatwine and Eusebius," 143, 146, and 151.

adaptation (*cwealde / þurh orþonc*)."³⁷⁴ The only clue that is left, "ne æt ham gesæt" (6b), as Williamson also noted, is the key to determining the type of animal involved. Reading "gesæt" as a first-person singular form, Williamson proposed the lamprey, as he contended that this clue alludes to the migratory character of this fish.³⁷⁵ Still, he was not completely convinced of the accuracy of this proposal, as he added a question mark to the solution "lamprey" in his edition.³⁷⁶ However, the crux can be resolved if we assume that "ne æt ham gesæt" refers to the victim, which is not allowed to remain "at home" because of the cunning snare set by the predator.³⁷⁷

We should also take into account the fact that "house" is a traditional metaphor for the shells of animals such as turtles, snails, and oysters. An example of this is the Old English gloss "gehused snægl" (537) for Latin *testudo* (turtle), which occurs in one of the Antwerp-London glossaries.³⁷⁸ In the marine context of Riddle 78, this clue clearly favors the oyster, an idea that is supported by the fact that this animal appropriately fits the passive role of victim, just as Riddle 77 has shown. In light of this, the oyster might thus be the victim that the predator of Riddle 78 devours, an assumption that could explain the conjecture offered by Tupper and the other editors that this animal might be the sea-covered creature alluded to as "yþum bewrigene." Yet the ultimate solution, the skillful predator, might rather be the crab, which was traditionally reputed to be the enemy of the oyster, as mentioned in one of the clues of Aldhelm's

---

374. Williamson, *The Old English Riddles*, 358. On the basis of this reading, Williamson argues against Tupper's proposal "oyster," as this animal "exhibits no special power of killing. . . . It sits and sifts particles of food from the seawater" (357).
375. As noted by Williamson, ibid., 358, the lamprey "travels from stream to sea and back to its stream again to spawn a new generation."
376. Ibid., 357.
377. See my discussion of this clue in "The Oyster and the Crab," 409–10.
378. From Porter, *The Antwerp-London Glossaries*, vol. 1, 60. For further examples, see Tupper, *The Riddles of the Exeter Book*, 216, and my "The Oyster and the Crab," 410 (n. 34).

Riddle 37: "ostrea quem metuit duris perterrita saxis" (6) [Frightened by the hard stones (that I throw at it), the oyster dreads me]. Aldhelm's text alludes to the traditional belief that the crab used a stone to open the tight valves of the oyster.[379]

Apart from Aldhelm's *enigma*, Bede's *De ortographia* bears witness to the knowledge of the crab's hunting method. A short passage from St Ambrose's *Hexameron* (V.viii.22) is cited in Bede's work to exemplify the phrase "Appetens cibum, et appetens cibi" as referring to the crab's keen appetite: "Ambrosius: 'Cancer . . . ut appetens cibi ita prospiciens est periculi'" (57–58) [Ambrose: "just as the crab is anxious for food, he is also cautious about the danger"].[380] Accordingly, it is very likely that a learned audience would know about the connection between the oyster and the crab in encyclopedic literature. On this basis, "ne æt ham gesæt" seems to be a reference to the oyster, which cannot close its shell because of the artful device ("þurh orþonc") employed by the crab to eat its flesh.

Since all editors agree that the solution of Riddle 77 is "oyster," and since it is also generally accepted that Riddle 78 hides a cunning aquatic predator of some kind, we cannot discard the well-known connection between the oyster and the crab, as presented in Aldhelm's *Enigma* 37, and medieval encyclopedic lore, as illustrated by the passage from Isidore's *Etymologiae* (Xii.vi.51) that was discussed earlier in this book.[381] The parallels noted by Tupper and other scholars thus point to the fact that Riddles 77 and 78 could have been juxtaposed in the manuscript with the idea of offering a thematic pair. The two texts would thus present antagonistic creatures: inactive versus active, victim versus predator, and trustworthy versus treacherous. In this sense, the pairing of the oyster and the crab recalls the juxtaposition of Aldhelm's Riddles 63 (raven) and 64 (dove), Exeter Riddles 8 (nightingale) and 9 (cuckoo), as well

---

379. See above (p. 110).
380. Jones, *CCSL*, vol. 123A, 9. My translation. For the citation of the full passage from St Ambrose's *Hexameron* and its significance for the understanding of Riddle 78, see my "The Oyster and the Crab," 410–11.
381. See above, pp. 109–10.

as the polarization of the panther and the whale in the Exeter *Physiologus*,[382] as discussed above (p. 312) with regard to the zoological string in Group 1. The oyster and the crab could well represent good and bad Christians for a monastic audience. Read as a thematic pair, Exeter Riddles 77 and 78 provide positive and negative examples of conduct for the ecclesiastical readers: the pious, defenseless Christian and the covetous wicked sinner, who usually takes advantage of the former's naivety.

What becomes clear from the discussion of these two riddles is that the Exeter compilers evidently attempted to complement zoological section 2 appearing in Group 1 with some pieces on aquatic animals, an idea that favors the inference that they viewed the two main riddle blocks as a unified collection. Despite its eminently miscellaneous character, Group 3 therefore reveals the compilers' efforts to produce as cohesive a collection as possible. Indeed, there seems to be no other aquatic animal as a subject in Groups 1 and 2. Also importantly, the inclusion of the oyster and the crab suggests the compilers' preoccupation with dubiously lawful food, an idea that finds an echo in the concerns underlying the zoological series offered in Group 1, as well as in the plea offered in the excerpt from *The Seasons for Fasting*, a work that is demonstrably in the orbit of the Benedictine reform. The presence of the oyster and the crab as riddlic motifs in Group 3 therefore implies a parallel interest in food prescriptions, a notion that accords with the reformist context in which the Exeter riddle compilation was produced. In addition, the choice of these subjects also humorously suggests typical food subterfuges, since Riddles 77 and 78 describe animals that were considered neither strictly clean nor tolerable for consumption but that were still frequently allowed in monasteries.

---

382. The crab's cunning stratagem, designed to trap the oyster, resembles the whale's treacherous ways of entrapping sailors and smaller fish as described in the Exeter *Physiologus*. Notably, the whale is said to be versed in trickery ("facnes cræftig," 24b) and, further in the poem, this animal is compared to the devil, who ensnares human beings by cruel deceit ("þurh sliþen searo," 42a).

4.4.2.4 Riddle 81: A Contemporary Touch

A further text that deserves our attention is Riddle 81, which was solved by Trautmann as "weathervane," an answer that has been universally accepted since then.[383] This riddle offers a passage in which the creature, as is typical of instrumental motifs, is personified and laments its having to put up with terrible weather conditions:

Ic eom bylgedbreost,[384]	belcedsweora,
heafod hæbbe	ond heane steort,
eagan ond earan	ond ænne foot,
hrycg ond heardnebb,	hneccan steapne
ond sidan twa,	sag*ol* on middum,[385]
eard ofer ældum.	Aglac dreoge,
þær mec wegeð	se þe wudu hrereð,[386]

---

383. Moritz Trautmann, "Die Auflösungen der altenglischen Rätsel," *Anglia Beiblatt* 5 (1894): 46–51.
384. Following Tupper and Mackie, Williamson, *The Old English Riddles*, 111, emended manuscript "by led breost" (fol. 127v) to "bylgedbreost" (1a). Also, see Williamson's comments on this term (ibid., 362). I have adopted this reading instead of Krapp and Dobbie's "byledbreost" (*ASPR*, vol. 3, 235 and 372), which is based on Trautmann's interpretation of this term as referring to *bȳl(e)*, "boil." See Trautmann, *Die altenglischen Rätsel*, 130. However, the definition offered by *DOE* (s.v. "bylged-brēost")—"puff-breasted, having a breast which is swollen (? with pride)"—seems to me preferable and is clearly in consonance with the subsequent adjective "belcedsweora" (1b), meaning "swollen-necked, having a neck which is puffed up with pride (*DOE*, s.v. "belced-swēora")."
385. Krapp and Dobbie, *ASPR*, vol. 3, 235, provide manuscript "sag" (fol. 127v). BT offers this hapax legomenon with no meaning and a question mark (s.v. "ság"). Following Tupper and Mackie, Williamson emended this word to *sagol*, usually glossed as Latin *fustis*, "a knobbed stick, a cudgel, staff, club" (L&S), explaining that "sagol on middum" refers to "a pole in the middle." Williamson, *The Old English Riddles*, 111 and 363. See *BT*, "A staff, cudgel, club" (s.v. "ságol"). Also, see Ælfric's *Grammar* (XXVIII), "*fustis* sâgol oððe stæf," cited from Zupitza, *Ælfrics Grammatik und Glossar*, 55.
386. Note the resemblance with the introduction of the wind as the one shaking the woods in Riddle 1 ("þonne ic wudu hrere," 8b). See above, p. 293.

ond mec stondende   streamas beatað,[387]
hægl se hearda,   ond hrim þeceð,
[.]orst [.....]eoseð,   ond fealleð snaw
on þyrelwombne,   ond ic þæt [.]ol[.........
............] mæ[.]   wonsceaft mine.

[I am puff-breasted and neck-inflated; I have a head and a high tail, eyes and ears and one foot, a back and a tough beak, a long neck and two sides, a staff in the middle, and a home above human beings. I endure torture when the one that stirs the wood (i.e., the wind) moves and while standing, torrential rains and the hard hail beat me, and frozen mist covers me, (f)rost (f)reezes and snow falls on (me), the one with a pierced stomach; and I (suffer all) that,[388] (for I) can(not change) my miserable condition].

This riddle plays on the ambivalent description of the living rooster and the meteorological implement. Without taking into account the reference to a single foot ("ænne foot," 3b), the catalogue of anatomical parts mentioned in lines 2–5 of the poem suggests a living animal. The subsequent clues point to the metallic nature of the object with the adjective "þyrelwombne" (11a), which describes it as "having the stomach pierced,"[389] but they also typically contribute to misleading readers into thinking that it may refer to the animal being injured by a spear. Once the clues are appropriately decoded,[390] the text portrays a one-footed implement, which is situated above the people's houses, thus effectively conveying the picture of a weathervane.[391]

---

387. Cf. "streamas staþu beatað" (6a) in Riddle 2. See above, p. 294.
388. As reflected in the translation, I here accept Mackie's reasonable restoration of this part as "[þo]l[ige eall]" (11b). *The Exeter Book*, 218–19.
389. *BT* (s.v. "þyrelwomb").
390. On misleading clues in the Exeter Riddles, see Anita Riedinger, "The formulaic style in the Old English Riddles," *SN* 76 (2004): 30–43, and my "Direct and Indirect Clues."
391. A roughly contemporary picture of a weathervane can be found in Deshman, *The Benedictional of Æthelwold* (plate 35, fol. 118v). See also Williamson, *The Old English Riddles*, 362.

The terms "bylgedbreost" (1a) and "belcedsweora" (1b) in Riddle 81 have customarily been considered to allude to the characteristic arrogant pose of a rooster.[392] The bird's tail and neck are equally said to be high—"heane steort" (2b) and "hneccan steapne" (4a)—and help transmit the image of the rooster's proverbial haughtiness. By means of prosopopeia, the characterization allows a glimpse into the paradoxical situation of the weathervane, which is placed in a position of privilege with respect to human beings ("eard ofer ældum," 6a) but must nevertheless suffer the negative consequences of this distinction ("wonsceaft mine," 12b). The term "sagol" (5b), meaning "staff," similarly adds further equivocal information to readers, who may think that a crosier or scepter held as a sign of authority is meant.[393] It may reasonably be assumed that Exeter Riddle 81 was intended to metaphorically evoke the hardships encountered by the one who holds office.

As Lapidge has pointed out,[394] Riddle 81 shares remarkable verbal parallels with a passage from Wulfstan Cantor's *Narratio metrica sancti Swithuni*, a hagiography dedicated to Bishop Ælfheah[395] and produced at Winchester (c. 996), where the author served as precentor of the Old Minster.[396] Notably, in the *Epistola specialis*, an introductory verse letter to this work, the golden weathervane of the tower of the Old Minster is lavishly described as follows:

---

392. Note that *DOE* includes the idea of pride in the definition of these two adjectives; in the case of "bylged-brēost" with a question mark.
393. As pointed out above, *sagol* is often glossed as Latin *fustis*, a term for which L&S offer *sceptrum* as a close synonym.
394. Lapidge, *The Cult of St Swithun*, 389 (note to lines 201–4),
395. On Ælfheah, see below, pp. 420-21 and n. 411.
396. As explained by Lapidge, *The Cult of St Swithun*, 338 (n. 13), the term *cantor* (precentor), as Wulfstan was usually styled in contemporary records, was an ecclesiastical office that "included responsibility for liturgical services, especially the chant, as well as for the institutional library." For further information on Wulfstan's scanty biographical data, see Lapidge, ibid., 337–39, and Lapidge and Winterbottom, *Wulfstan of Winchester*, xiii–xiv.

Imperii sceptrum pedibus tenet ille superbis,
stat super et cunctum Wintoniae populum.
Imperat cunctis euectus in aera gallis,
et regit occiduum nobilis imperium.
Impiger imbriferos qui suscipit undique uentos,
seque rotando suam prebet eis faciem;
turbinis horrisonos[397] suffertque uiriliter ictus,
intrepidus perstans, flabra niues tolerans. (197–204)[398]

["It ('gallus,' the weathervane) holds the sceptre of rule in its proud talons and stands above the entire populace of Winchester. Thus raised aloft this noble fowl commands all other birds, and rules the western domain. It is eager to receive the rainy winds from all directions and, turning itself, it offers its face to them; bravely it endures the violent blasts of the wind, standing unafraid, tolerating gales as well as snowstorms"].

As the Exeter weathervane, the Winchester implement is similarly said to occupy a prominent position. But without the logical constraints of the more condensed format of the riddle, Wulfstan developed the rhetorical possibilities offered by the use of prosopoeia to a greater extent. The Latin excerpt thus clearly emphasizes the idea of how the elevated location of the weathervane metaphorically compares to that of a high dignatary. The *gallus* is said to stand over all the people of Winchester ("stat super et cunctum Wintoniae populum," 198), which recalls the reference to the Exeter implement as having its home over human beings (6a). The phrase similarly echoes the introductory lines of the *Epistola specialis*, in which Ælfheah is alluded to as the Lord Bishop ("Domno pontifici," 5) who rules the Church of Winchester ("Wentanam . . . / qui regit ecclesiam . . . ," 5–6).[399] It is also worth noting that at the beginning of the excerpt

---

397. Cf. "viribus horrisonis" (3) for the dreadful-sounding force of the wind in Aldhelm's Riddle 2. See above, pp. 179-80.
398. Text and translation from Lapidge, *The Cult of St Swithun*, 388–89.
399. Text and translation from ibid., 372–73.

describing the Old Minster tower, Bishop Ælfheah is addressed in the second-person plural ("fecistis," 177) as the one who had it built. The image of the weathervane and the tower itself therefore symbolize the dignity and the moral stance of the bishop, who is described as the embodiment of power and authority. As in Exeter Riddle 81, the notion of power is also further supported by Wulfstan's description of the weathervane as being endowed with a physical appearance that suggests pride, since the creature is said to possess "proud talons" ("pedibus . . . superbis," 197). Wulfstan insists on this idea, as illustrated in his choice of terms alluding to the bird's authoritative stance: "imperii sceptrum" (197),[400] "imperat" (199), "regit" (200), "nobilis" (200), and "imperium" (200).[401]

Like Exeter Riddle 81, the Latin excerpt offers a passage on the meteorological hardships endured by the weathervane that can similarly be open to a metaphorical interpretation. The Winchester *gallus* thus stoically accepts ("suscipit," 201) raging stormy winds coming

---

400. That the image of the weathervane represents human power is also supported by the parallel expressions used by Wulfstan to allude to Edgar as king of the English in the preface to the *Narratio*: "Eadgar et inuictus, / sublimia sceptra gubernans, / omnibus Anglorum feliciter imperitando / gentibus, Arcturi quae uertice sidera cernunt. . ." (162–64) ["at that time the great and unconquerable King Edgar wielded royal authority, possessing the highest sceptre of office, blessedly ruling all the English peoples who behold the stars beneath the zenith of Arcturus. . ."]. Text and translation from ibid., 408–09. Cf. the description of the weathervane in the excerpt cited above and in the following passage: "Despicit omne solum, cunctis supereminet aruis, / signiferi et Boreae sidera pulchra uidens" (195–96) ["It gazes down on the entire countryside, soars over all the fields, able to behold the bright constellations of the starry North"]. Ibid., 388–89. See also the description of a golden eagle flying over Winchester in the premonitory dream of Æthelwold's mother, foreseeing the future of her son as bishop of that city, in Wulfstan's biography of the saint. Lapidge and Winterbottom, *Wulfstan of Winchester*, 4–7 (ii–iii).

401. Note that the Latin text refers to the rooster/weathervane holding the scepter of power ("imperii sceptrum," 197) with its feet ("pedibus," 197). Cf. the reference to the staff ("sagol," 5b) placed in the middle ("on middum," 5b) of the bird's sides ("on sidan twa," 5a) in Exeter Riddle 81.

from anywhere ("imbriferos . . . undique uentos," 201). The use of the adjective "impiger" (201), which rhetorically connects to "imperium" (200), continues the personification of the weathervane as indefatigable and diligent in its struggle against the elements, a notion that suggests the qualities of a good ruler—possibly with Ælfheah in mind—tenaciously confronting adversity. The description of the weathervane as an undaunted ("intrepidus," 204) creature valiantly ("uiriliter," 203) offering its face ("prebet eis faciem," 202) and standing ("perstans," 204) impervious to the weather conditions adds to these metaphorical resonances. In sum, the diction and the rhetorical elements of this excerpt from Wulfstan's *Epistola specialis* no doubt have a clear correspondence in Riddle 81, thus providing us with further evidence of a connection between the Exeter collection and the cultural context of the Benedictine reform.

But further important implications can be drawn from the association of Riddle 81 with Wulfstan's work. Several scholars have identified Wulfstan's version of the *Te Deum*, as offered in the *Narratio* (i.984–1021), among the contents of Cambridge, Gg.5.35 (fols. 423r/v),[402] the monumental compilation produced at St Augustine's, Canterbury. Interestingly, the *Te Deum* comes after two medical riddles (fols. 422v–23r) and is also close to the anonymous Latin *enigmata* on the Seven Liberal Arts known as *Bibliotheca magnifica* (fol. 423v–25r).[403] A further work, an abecedarian hymn for All Saints ("Aula superna poli"), very likely by Wulfstan, is also extant in this manuscript (fols. 362v–63v).[404] On the other hand, a triad of hymns

---

402. Peter Dronke, Michael Lapidge, and Peter Stotz, "Die unveröffentlichten Gedichte der Cambridger Liederhandschrift (CUL Gg.5.35)," *Mittellateinisches Jahrbuch* 17 (1982): 55. Also, see Rigg and Wieland, "A Canterbury Classbook," 128 (no. 41). For the edited text of the *Te Deum* in the *Narratio*, see Lapidge, *The Cult of St Swithun*, 458–61; also, see Lapidge's comments, 365 and 459 (n. to lines 984–1021).
403. See above p. 48.
404. Lapidge and Winterbottom, *Wulfstan of Winchester*, xxxviii; Dronke, Lapidge, and Stotz, "Die unveröffentlichten Gedichte," 59–65, where the poem is edited and translated into German.

devoted to St Augustine,[405] which have survived only in Durham, Cathedral Library, B.iii.32 (fols. 29r-30r), a codex produced at Christ Church (Canterbury) in the first half of the eleventh century, are suspected to be of Wulfstanian authorship.[406]

All this suggests a direct or indirect association of Wulfstan with Canterbury, a place where the riddling genre had burgeoned, as we know from the importation of at least two codices from Francia—London, Royal 15.A.xvi and Rawlinson, C. 697—and the translation of Exeter Riddle 40 from Aldhelm's *Enigma* 100 in the latter. This connection with Canterbury may well explain Wulfstan's use of Exeter Riddle 81 or an earlier version as a source for the excerpt describing the Old Minster weathervane in the *Epistola specialis*. But the possibility that Wulfstan may have had at hand a copy of Riddle 81 or that from the Exeter Book exemplar at Winchester should not be ruled out. Even if it is scanty evidence, the survival of an Old English prose riddle in a Winchester manuscript—London, Cotton Vitellius E.xviii—containing a Latin version of the psalter suggests that vernacular riddling might have been cultivated in the monastic milieu there.[407]

The fact that Ælfheah, Bishop of Winchester (984–1006) and later Archbishop of Canterbury (1006–12),[408] is the dedicatee of

---

405. St Augustine was venerated as the patron saint of Canterbury. As noted by Gneuss, it seems unlikely that a parallel cult of St Augustine would have developed at Winchester as well. See Helmut Gneuss, *Hymnar und Hymnen im englischen Mittelalter: Studien zur Überlieferung, Glossierung und Übersetzung lateinischer Hymnen in England* (Tübingen: Niemeyer, 1968), 248.
406. See Lapidge and Winterbottom, *Wulfstan of Winchester*, xxxvii-xxxviii.
407. On the Vitellius riddle, see above p. 43.
408. Ælfheah, who might have formerly been prior of Glastonbury, was Æthelwold's successor at the Winchester bishopric, a position he gained at Dunstan's behest. He is well known for his enlarging and improving the buildings forming part of the Old Minster, as lavishly described in Wulfstan's *Epistola specialis*. The information provided in this work has been largely confirmed by archeological discoveries in the past few decades. See *ODNB*, s.v. "Ælfheah," by Henrietta Leyser.

the *Narratio* provides a further interesting link between Wulfstan's literary production and the metropolitan see. The hypothesis that this poet may have accompanied Ælfheah to Canterbury on his promotion to the archbishopric in 1006 is no doubt tantalizing, but solid proof of this has not yet been found.[409] Nevertheless, there is evidence that Ælfheah brought with him "a number of liturgical and artistic practices,"[410] among which may well have been the literary production of Winchester authors. Even if Wulfstan remained in Winchester after 1006, the notable parallels observed in Exeter Riddle 81 and the excerpt from the *Narratio* can also be explained on the grounds of the natural cultural exchange produced between Winchester and Canterbury. Besides, Wulfstan's connection to the metropolitan see antedates Ælfheah's appointment, since he alludes to Sigeric, Archbishop of Canterbury (990–994),[411] in a passage of the *Epistola specialis* (217–22),[412] in which the latter is said to have

---

409. Lapidge, *The Cult of St Swithun*, 338.
410. Cited from *ODNB*, s.v. "Ælfheah," by Henrietta Leyser.
411. For this passage, see Lapidge, *The Cult of St Swithun*, 390–91. Sigeric, Ælfheah, and Wulfstan were no doubt significantly involved in the Benedictine movement. Sigeric expelled the secular clerks from Christ Church, replacing them with monks instead. See *ODNB*, s.v. "Sigeric," by Emma Mason. With a Glastonbury background, Ælfheah became abbot of Bath some time in the 960s and was actively involved in the refoundation of this monastic house according to the Benedictine system. See Lapidge et al., *The Wiley Blackwell Encyclopedia*, s.v. "Ælfheah," by Simon Keynes, 7–8, and *ODNB*, s.v. "Ælfheah," by Henrietta Leyser. As regards Wulfstan, he was a student of Æthelwold and the author of the *Vita sancti Æthelwoldi*, a biography of the latter (996). See *ODNB*, s.v. "Wulfstan Cantor," by Michael Lapidge.
412. This piece of information is adduced by Lapidge to suggest that the *Narratio* might have been composed before Sigeric's death (994). *The Cult of St Swithun*, 336. As Lapidge further points out, "these lines [221–22] were clearly written while Sigeric was still alive" (391, n.). For further information on Sigeric and his significance during Æthelred's reign, see Simon D. Keynes, *The Diplomas of King Æthelred "The Unready" (978-1016): A Study in their Use as Historical Evidence* (Cambridge: Cambridge University Press, 1980), 191.

attended the rededication of the Old Minster together with seven other distinguished prelates. It is worth noting that Sigeric, formerly a monk at Glastonbury and abbot of St Augustine's (c. 980), was a predecessor of Ælfric, who was mentioned above in relation to "Æthelwold's bowl," a riddle that accompanies a poem commemorating Ælfric's death.[413]

All this brings to mind the hypothesis expressed at the beginning of this book that the production of riddles at Canterbury could have been under the auspices of successive generations of archbishops with a Glastonbury background, Sigeric and Ælfheah being a further illustration of it. Whether it was at Canterbury or at Winchester that Wulfstan came across a version of Riddle 81 or a similar text we will probably never know. But the references to Sigeric in the *Epistola specialis*, the dedication of the *Narratio* to Ælfheah, and the presence of Wulfstan's *Te Deum* among riddles in Cambridge, Gg.5.35 are all enlightening facts that once more link vernacular riddling with the literary concerns of the Benedictine reform, episcopal patronage, and the intellectual circles of Winchester, Glastonbury, and Canterbury.

4.4.2.5 Thematic Duplications and Textual Variants: Riddles 84, 87, 88, 93, and 94

A remarkable aspect of Group 3 that deserves our attention is the presence of numerous repetitions, particularly of topics that were already handled by riddles occurring in Group 1. A contrastive table of these thematic coincidences as found in the three groups that have been defined can give us an idea of the relevance of this phenomenon:

Group 1	Group 2	Group 3
R. 7 (swan)	—	R. 74 (swan)
R. 11 (cup of wine)	—	R. 63 (glass goblet)
R. 12 (ox) and 38 (bullock)	—	R. 72 (ox)

---

413. On this, see above, pp. 46–47.

Group 1	Group 2	Group 3
Rs. 19, 32 and 36 (ship)	—	R. 64 (ship)
R. 20 (sword)	—	R. 71 (sword)
R. 25 (onion)	—	R. 65 (onion)
R. 26 (Gospel book)	—	R. 67 (Gospel book)
R. 33 (iceberg)	—	R. 68–69 (iceberg)
R. 37 (bellows)	—	R. 87 (bellows)
R. 40 (Creation)	R. 66 (Creation)	R. 94 (Creation)
—	R. 41 (water)	R. 84 (water)
—	R. 44 (key)	R. 91 (key)

It is clear that most of the repeated subjects belong to Groups 1 and 3. From this, it can tentatively be deduced that the compilers were drawing material from a second source collection in which some of the topics were the same as those found in Group 1. Some of these texts share such notable verbal parallels with their counterparts in Group 1 that one might suspect that the compilers were using variant riddles which were distributed in Groups 1 and 3, probably in an attempt to avoid including repetitions in neighboring parts.

Some of these correspondences are so remarkable that it may be alternatively be inferred that various texts of Group 1 were the source of some others from Group 3. For example, Riddle 41 presents water as the mother of many races ("moddor monigra cynna," 2), a clue that is basically paraphrased in Riddle 84: "Modor is monigra mærra wihta" (4) [it (water) is the mother of many well-known creatures]. As only a fragment of Riddle 41 has been preserved, further correspondences might have been shared by these two poems, although this idea must remain a conjecture.

An even more outstanding case is observed in Riddle 87, which shows evident verbal echoes of the previous bellows composition (no. 37). The striking resemblance was first pointed out by Tupper, who solved Riddle 87 as "bellows" on the basis of the likeness observed in the clues of Riddle 37, which he considered a "companion-piece" to the former.⁴¹⁴ Williamson took a step further and argued that the initial lines of the two texts are "so similar as to indicate that one riddlic beginning was probably used as a source for the other."⁴¹⁵ If we contrast the two compositions, the correspondences are no doubt intriguing:

Riddle 37

Ic þa wihte geseah;	womb wæs on hindan
þriþum aþrunten.	Þegn folgade,
mægenrofa man,	ond micel hæfde
gefered þæt hit felde,	fleah þurh his eage. (1–4)

[I saw the creature. Extremely swollen, its belly was behind. It was attended by a servant, a very strong man; and what filled it (i.e., the air) had traveled much (and) flew out through its eye].⁴¹⁶

Riddle 87

Ic seah wundorlice wiht;	wombe hæfde micle,
þryþum geþrungne.	Þegn folgade
mægenstrong ond mundrof;	micel me þuhte
godlic gumrinc,	grap on sona
heofones toþe	. . . . .⁴¹⁷
bleowe on eage. (1–6a)	

[I saw a wonderful creature. It had a big belly, extremely swollen. It was attended by a mighty and strong-handed servant. He seemed

---

414. Tupper, *The Riddles of the Exeter Book*, 227.
415. Williamson, *The Old English Riddles*, 378.
416. I here follow Barnow's explanation for this part, which is that of Krapp and Dobbie's (*ASPR*, vol. 3, 342), too. See A. J. Barnouw, Review of *Die altenglischen Rätsel (Die Rätsel des Exeterbuchs)* by Moritz Trautmann, *Neophilologus* 3 (1917): 77–78.
417. As Mackie, *The Exeter Book*, 226, points out, "A half-line appears to have been omitted by the scribe." For "heofones toþe" (5a) as a reference to the "biting" capacity of wind and a parallel in Bern *Enigma* 41 (4), see Tupper, *The Riddles of the Exeter Book*, 227.

to me big, an excellent warrior. He soon grabbed it and blew through its eye thanks to heaven's tooth (i.e., the wind)].

Indeed, the idea of the "swollen belly" and the allusion to the smith as a strong servant using the bellows is shared by the two texts. In both cases, the clues clearly display double entendre, as the smith's handling of the bellows can be suggestive of the sexual act. In addition, the allusion to the action of blowing and the metaphorical reference to the "eye" as the hole through which the air passes similarly co-occur in the two riddles.

These parallels evidently go far beyond the natural correspondences deriving from the handling of the same riddlic subject. As the case of the two bellows riddles suggests, it seems that the compilers progressively encountered such difficulties in gathering material that they started to reuse pieces from Group 1, including them with some slight changes in Group 3. Brian O'Camb has studied the verbal parallelisms observed in *Maxims I* and other poems from Quire XI of the Exeter Book, inferring a similar reworking of the material at hand, stating that "one can imagine that the scribe found the repeated statements in *Exeter Maxims* while flipping back and forth through quire XI or its exemplar as he copied out the poem."[418] The striking similarity of the two Exeter bellows riddles could also be explained by a deliberate transfer of text from Group 1 to Group 3—notably, from Quire XIV to Quire XVII.[419]

A further case in point is given by the two "inkhorn" riddles occurring in Group 3. As scholars have noted, Riddle 93 is a companion piece to no. 88 on the same subject.[420] These two riddles display a similar set of clues. A description of the living stag (and its two antlers) in its natural habitat is thus provided in both texts:[421]

---

418. Brian O'Camb, "The Inscribed Form of *Exeter Maxims* and the Layout of Quire XI of the Exeter Book," in Hussey and Niles, *The Genesis of Books*, 157.
419. Riddles 37 and 87 occur on folios 109v and 129r, which are found in each of those quires, respectively.
420. See, for example, Williamson, *The Old English Riddles*, 393.
421. The whole equivalent passage in Riddle 88 is too severely damaged,

Riddle 88

wudubeama helm
scildon wið scurum. (12b–14a)

Ful oft unc holt wrugon,
wonnum nihtum,

[Very frequently the wood, the protection of the forest, covered us both on dark nights (and) shielded us from storms].

Riddle 93

hwilum stealc hliþo
up in eþel,
in deop dalu
strong on stæpe . . . (9–12a)

[Frea min]
stigan sceolde
hwilum eft gewat
duguþe secan

[sometimes (my lord, i.e., the stag) had to climb the steep hills up to his homeland; sometimes, strong on his step, (he) left again for the deep valleys to look for the herd].[422]

As is usual with instrumental riddles, these clues offer an insight into the primeval state of the creature before the transformation into an object takes place.

By centering on the pivotal verb *stondan*, Riddle 88 dwells on the reference to the antler's lofty site which is initially determined by nature to be on the stag's head: "Ic weox þær ic s[. . . ." (1a) [I grew where I (stood)], " . . .]d ic on staþol" (5a) [I (stood) on my fixed spot],[423] and "ic uplong stod" (9a) [I stood tall]. Further on, the verb *stondan* recurs, as if to insist on the idea that fate maintains

---

however, to be brought up here for comparison, so I am offering only the part that is best preserved in the manuscript. See Krapp and Dobbie, *ASPR*, vol. 3, 239.

422. For "duguðe" in Riddle 88 "as the stag's *comitatus*, i.e., the herd," see Williamson, *The Old English Riddles*, 394, and *DOE* (s.v. "duguð," 4.a.iv).

423. I here follow Mackie's reasonable reconstruction of the text, assuming that "stod" was present in the obliterated passages. See *The Exeter Book*, 228.

the object firmly anchored just as before—only that it is a different place: "ic on wuda stonde / bordes on ende" (19b-20a) [I stand on wood at the end of a table] and "ac ic sceal broþorleas bordes on ende / staþol weardian, stondan fæste" (21–22) [but I, brotherless, must guard my fixed place at the end of the table and stand still]. The clues thus affirm that the creature's state has apparently not changed much. Note that both "wuda" (19b) and "bordes" (board, plank, 20a and 21b) playfully echo "holt" (12b), the latter term meaning both "wood" and "grove" alike.[424] However, the perception of the creature's sad lot is only fully grasped when the antler laments the fact that he has lost his brother who used to dwell high by his side ("se me ær be healfe heah eardade," 25). By repeatedly offering *stondan*, Riddle 88 was therefore meant to make readers reflect on how the notion of standing high—which recalls the lighthouse and the weathervane's privileged positions in Riddles 70b and 81, respectively—is paradoxically unchanged in the two phases undergone by the creature, only to finally realize that the situation is utterly different in each case.

In Riddle 93, *stondan* is similarly used to allude to the inkhorn on the table: "ic stonde" (26b)—but, as the opening part is badly damaged (fol. 130r), it is not possible to discern if there is the same contrastive use of the verb before and after the transformation takes place. Still, we find the same reference to the antlers standing high ("heah," 4a) on the stag's head ("gleawstol," 15a), and the renewal of horns is handled in a similar way as in the other inkhorn piece.

Riddle 88

Nu unc mæran twam   magas uncre
sculon æfter cuman,   eard oðþringan
gingran broþor. (15–17a)

[Now our two well-known kinsmen (i.e., the new antlers) will come after us; our younger brothers shall take (our) home].

---

424. *BT* (s.v. "holt").

Riddle 93

oþþæt him þone gleawstol	Ic on fusum rad
min agnade	gingra broþor
	ond mec of earde adraf. (14b–16)

[I rode upon the fast one (i.e., the hart) until my younger brother seized the seat of wisdom (i.e., the head), and drove me from my home].

By means of prosopopeia, the fresh antlers replacing the older ones are thus referred to as the "younger brothers," and the head on which they are fixed as their home (*eard*) in the two cases, thus metaphorically suggesting a family dispute over land ownership.

In Riddle 88 the subsequent clues offer the dramatic outcome of the conflict by referring to the inkhorn as a creature condemned to endless solitude separated from its twin brother: "Eom ic gumcynnes / anga ofer eorþan" (17b–18a) [I am the only one of my kind on earth].[425] Riddle 93, by contrast, explores more deeply the dire consequences of the creature's change of status by giving free rein to the notion of feud: "ne wrecan meahte" (21b) [I was not able to avenge] and "ac ic aglæca ealle þolige, / þæt [. .]e bord biton" (23–24a) [but I suffer all the torments that pierced the shield].[426] Whereas the replacement of the horns is presented in Riddle 88 as a case of exile close to the elegiac mood of other Exeter poems, Riddle 93 dwells on the desolation caused by the loss of property and the physical injuries produced by the human "malefactor."

The subsequent lines in both compositions make reference to the painful transformation of the antler into an inkhorn:

---

425. For this reading of "anga" as exemplified in this riddle, see *DOE* (s.v. "ānga").
426. Cf. "aglace" (7a) and "aglac" (6b) in Riddles 3 and 81, where the tortures endured by the wind and the weathervane are alluded to, respectively. For an interpretation of "aglæca" (23a) in Riddle 93 as either "attack, conflict" (i.e., as a partitive genitive of *āglāc*) or as "an awesome opponent" (i.e., āglǣca as nominative), see *DOE* (s.v. "āg-lāc").

Riddle 88

Nu mec unsceafta[427] innan slitað,
wyrdaþ mec be wombe; ic gewendan ne mæg. (29–30)

[Now cruel creatures tear me inside, injure me in my stomach; I cannot run away].

Riddle 93

Siþþan mec isern   innanweardne
brun bennade;   blod ut ne com,
heolfor of hreþre,   þeah mec heard bite
stiðecg style. (17–20a)

[Afterwards burnished[428] iron injured my interior; no blood nor gory liquid came out from my bosom, even though the hard, stiff-edged steel pierced[429] me].

The two riddles thus present the commonplace allusion to human beings as the cause of the creature's grief and change of state, which is marked in both cases, as is usual with instrumental subjects, by means of the adverb "nu." By the same token, the term *womb* alluding to the antler's inwards, which are cruelly plundered by men in Riddle 88 (30a), is equivalent to *hreþer* in Riddle 93 (19a). In addition, *womb* is further used in Riddle 93 (25b and 30a)[430] to refer to

---

427. I here adopt Mackie's reading for "unsceafta" (29a), which he translates as "cruel creatures" (*The Exeter Book*, 231). The reference is to the human beings who hollow out the antler in order to turn it into an inkhorn. Tupper, on the other hand, interpreted "unsceafta" as a reference to "the iron and steel weapons" used in that process. Tupper, *The Riddles of the Exeter Book*, 229.
428. Note that I accept the definition of *brun* as "in poetry, of forged metal: traditionally interpreted as 'shining, gleaming, burnished.'" *DOE* (s.v. "brun").
429. *DOE* (s.v. "bītan," 2). Cf. "heardecg heorscearp, hondweorc smiþa, / bitað in burgum" (8–9a) in Riddle 5 for the reference to the shield being pierced by the sword.
430. The term "wombe" (25b) is Mackie's reconstruction in *The Exeter Book*, 234.

the ink ("min hord," 28a), the treasure kept in the inkhorn's belly which is stolen by the quill pen ("hiþende feond," 28b), the ravaging enemy.

Apart from having a similar structure and using parallel clues, the length of the two inkhorn riddles is also worth noting. Riddle 88 has thirty-two lines, and Riddle 93 has thirty-five. The two texts therefore seem to be variants of the same motif. On the other hand, the fact that only four riddles separate the two "inkhorn" motifs is also significant.[431] The case may be compared to Riddle 66, whose likeness to Riddle 40 was pointed out above and accounts for the most notable case of repetition in Group 2. Even though thematic recurrence is also observed in Group 1, in particular with the ship riddles (nos. 19, 32, and 36), it should be pointed out that the clues of these three texts differ substantially from one another and, as suggested by several scholars, their solutions probably entail three different kinds of ship. Note, for example, that Niles considered Riddle 19 as conveying the answer *snac(c)*, "light warship," on the basis of Mark Griffith's proposal to read the initial letter of each runic code in order to spell out that word.[432] As for Riddle 32, Niles offered a more specific solution than that offered by Dietrich[433] by inferring that the answer is *cēap-scip* or "merchant ship," an idea that accords with the clues presenting the object as carrying the provisions for the people in lines 9b–13a.[434] Riddle 36, in turn, seems to be a variation of Riddle 19, possibly offering *scip* as a solution, for no special clue is provided in this case to determine a further kind of

---

431. In its current state in the Exeter Book, Riddle 88 is on folio 129r/v and Riddle 93 occurs on folios 130r/v. The proximity between the two compositions is thus remarkable, as one can see part of the two riddles at the same time.
432. See Niles, *Enigmatic Poems*, 142, and Mark Griffith, "Riddle 19 of the Exeter Book: SNAC, an Old English Acronym," *N&Q* 237 (1992): 15–16.
433. Dietrich, "Die Räthsel des Exeterbuchs: Würdigung, Lösung und Herstellung," 469–70, proposed "ship," a solution that has been generally accepted since then.
434. This passage was cited and discussed above (p. 324).

vessel. The same can be said of Riddles 12 (ox) and 38 (bullock), in which the solution and the treatment of the clues are not alike. The high degree of similarity observed in the bellows riddles (nos. 37 and 87) and the inkhorn pieces (88 and 93) is therefore unparalleled in the repetitions observed in Group 1, thus further supporting the hypothesis that the compilers were short of riddlic material as they reached Group 3.

Riddle 94 (Creation) is a further case of thematic repetition. Owing to the severe damage affecting this part of the manuscript, this riddle has been subject to much editorial speculation, successive textual reconstructions, and emendations. I will not enter the usual editorial debate, but for our purposes the most important issue concerning Riddle 94 is that the intelligible fragments suggest that this poem provides another "Creation" subject, just like Riddles 40 and 66.[435]

Smeþr[...]ad,
hyrre þonne heofon[.......................................
..............................] glædre þonne sunne,
[..]style,
smeare þonne *sealt ry*[......................................][436]
leofre þonne þis leoht eall,   leohtre þon w[............]

[(I am) smoother (than).... higher than the heaven(s),.... shinier than the sun,.... (than) steel, more penetrating than salt.... dearer than all this light, brighter (lighter?) than ...].

---

435. As Tupper, *The Riddles of the Exeter Book*, 238, pointed out, "the few surviving phrases of this badly damaged fragment exhibit a striking likeness to the comparatives of the 'Creation' riddles." On the basis of the extreme fragmentariness of this riddle, however, some scholars have opted for labeling the riddle as unsolvable. See, for example, Pinsker and Ziegler, *Die altenglischen Rätsel des Exeterbuchs*, 335.

436. My emphasis. I here concur with Mackie, Williamson, and Muir, among other scholars, in that the reading should be "sealt ry-" because it represents the space that can be observed on folio 130v. See Mackie, *The Exeter Book*, 237, Muir, *The Exeter Anthology*, vol. 1, 382, and Williamson, *The Old English Riddles*, 120 and 397.

There is little doubt that Riddles 40, 66, and 94 convey the same approach to the subject. They evince a similar employment of imagery, of grammatical structures such as comparatives, of parallel syntactic construction with the characteristic contrastive pattern,[437] as well as the presence of common rhetorical elements as observed in the combined use of paradox and antithesis.

With these remarkable similarities, Riddle 94 no doubt constitutes a thematic companion to nos. 40 and 66. For example, "hyrre þonne heofon[.]" (2a) in Riddle 94 clearly echoes the phrase "Hyrre ic eom heofone" (38a) in Riddle 40 and is also close to "heofonas oferstige" (6b) [I climb the heavens] in Riddle 66. In turn, "glædre þonne sunne" (3b) in Riddle 94 parallels "swiftre þonne sunne" (3a) [faster than the sun] in Riddle 66.[438] By the same token, "leohtre þon w[." (6b) in Riddle 94 brings to mind "leohtre ic eom micle þonne þes lytla wyrm" (76) [I am much lighter than this little worm] in Riddle 40—or maybe "leohtre þonne mona" (2b) [brighter than the moon] in Riddle 66.

On the basis of these outstanding parallelisms, it is quite clear that Riddle 94 constitutes a shorter variant of Riddles 40 and 66. As inferred from the three Exeter Creation riddles, it is possible that different attempts at translating Aldhelm's *Enigma* 100 might have been made, since it was no doubt a text that had a great impact on Anglo-Saxon poets. This would also justify the use of several English versions to provide as accurate a translation as possible. Even if fragmentary Riddle 94 is not as extensive as Riddle 40, its cosmological subject makes it suitable for the position it occupies, almost at the end of the collection, following the pattern set by Aldhelm's *Enigmata*. But it is evident that Exeter Riddle 94 does not act as a

---

437. This is obviously not so clear in the case of Riddle 94, but that is probably due to the extreme fragmentariness of the text.
438. This reading, which is also accepted by Williamson and other editors, is based on Trautmann's comment in *Die altenglischen Rätsel*, 139, that the adjective *glæd* resembles the references "glædum gimme" (92a) and "gimma gladost" (289a), which describe the sun as a shining gem in the Exeter *The Phoenix*. See *DOE* (s.v. "glæd").

cosmological coda, as it is followed by a further piece. The compilers clearly treated it as a regular topic, as they had similarly done with Riddle 66.[439]

4.4.2.6 Riddle 95: A Final Coda?

Even though Riddle 95 does not present particularly complicated clues, scholars have put forward many different interpretations.[440] As Michael Korhammer notes, among the varied set of proposals, the writing topics clearly stand out.[441] Erhardt-Siebold proposes "quill pen,"[442] arguing that the key to solve the riddle is the kenning "hiþendra hyht" (5a)—which she translates as "the joy of plunderers."[443] She contends that this phrase is similar to the expression "hiþende feond" (28b) found in Riddle 93 (inkhorn), which, as discussed above, is identified with the personified quill pen "stealing" ink from the inkhorn. Williamson, on the other hand, interpreted Riddle 95 as a description of a book, taking "hiþendra hyht" as a kenning for "gold" on the basis that this expression refers to "the gold used to gild the leaves and to ornament the bindings of medieval books."[444] He thus reads this phrase as a further conventional

---

439. Even if Riddle 40 is followed by other riddles, this text seems to have been treated as a special composition, as the paleographical features pointed out above (p. 337) suggest.
440. A convenient summary of the numerous proposals offered for this text is found in Michael Korhammer, "The Last of the Exeter Book Riddles," in *Bookmarks from the Past. Studies in Early English Language and Literature in Honour of Helmut Gneuss*, ed. Lucia Kornexl and Ursula Lenker (Frankfurt: Peter Lang, 2003), 69. See Donald K. Fry's long list of solutions for this riddle in "Exeter Book Riddle Solutions," *OEN* 15 (1981): 25.
441. Korhammer, "The Last of the Exeter Book Riddles," 70. For a monographic study of the writing subject in the Exeter Riddles and in the context of the Middle Ages, see Göbel, *Studien zu den altenglischen Schriftwesenrätseln*, esp. 54–150.
442. Erika von Erhardt-Siebold, "Old English Riddle No. 95," *MLN* 62 (1947): 558–59. See also Williamson, *The Old English Riddles*, 397.
443. Erhardt-Siebold, "Old English Riddle No. 95," 559.
444. Williamson, *The Old English Riddles*, 401. He cites a passage from

allusion to the ornamentation of books, as found in other texts related to writing such as Exeter Riddles 26 (13a), 51 (7a), and 67 (14a). Helga Göbel also included Riddle 95 in the writing sub-category and offered "(holy) text" as a possible answer for it.[445] She read "hiþendra hyht" as a reference to parchment, arguing that the phrase recalls the allusion to human beings "plundering" the skin of the animal (a sheep or a calf) in order to produce vellum, as found in the initial clues of Riddle 26 (1–2a).[446] This interpretation has been accepted by Korhammer with some minor modifications.[447]

The remainder of the clues of this text support the idea that the riddlic object is a writing implement. As Erhardt-Siebold states, "the many mediaeval riddles dealing with either the quill or other things relating to the art of writing draw on essentially the same repertoire of ideas."[448] Indeed, apart from the allusion to gold that is present in other Exeter riddles entailing a book solution, the hidden object of Riddle 95 is said to bring knowledge to men, a clue that also features in the two preceding "Bible" pieces (nos. 26 and 67). "Nu snottre men swiþast lufiaþ / midwist mine; ic monigum sceal / wisdom cyþan" (7–9a) [Now learned men very much love my company; I will announce wisdom to many]. A further clue shared by writing subjects is the reference to the tracks left by the quill pen on the vellum, which is also found in Riddle 95:

                           Þeah nu ælda bearn
londbuendra   lastas mine

Andreas where the term "hyht" is used in a similar context: "næs him to maðme wynn, / hyht to hordgestreonum" (1113b-14a) ["for them there was no pleasure in wealth nor joy in hoarded treasures"]. Translation by Bradley, *Anglo-Saxon Poetry*, 139.

445. Göbel, *Studien zu den altenglischen Schriftwesenrätseln*, 538–606.
446. Cited and discussed above, p. 326.
447. As pointed out by Korhammer in "The Last of the Exeter Book Riddles," 77, Göbel's proposal could be narrowed down as "the Holy Scriptures." Also, see Williamson's discussion of this text for which he proposed the solution "book" in *The Old English Riddles*, 397–402.
448. Erhardt-Siebold, "Old English Riddle No. 95," 558.

swiþe secað,   ic swaþe hwilum
mine bemiþe   monna gehwylcum. (10b–13)

[Even though now the children of men, the inhabitants of the earth, keenly search for my footsteps, I sometimes hide my way from everyone].[449]

Thus, these lines could be read as a reference to the challenges met by those who try to read books, or rather the Scriptures, whose interpretation sometimes escapes the most learned.

Being a writing subject and the last piece of the Exeter Book collection, Riddle 95 could have functioned as a coda. There are Latin antecedents that may support this idea. For example, Symphosius's *Enigma* 1 (stylus) clearly occupies a prominent position at the head of the collection. By the same token, the Lorsch *Enigmata* are brought to a close with Riddle 12 (ink). However, as Pope has pointed out, on folio 130v there is no *explicit* nor any other conventional graphic sign indicating that with Exeter Riddle 95 the collection has come to an end.[450] Following the same line of thinking, Conner conjectures that Quire XVII, comprising from Riddle 70b to 95, lost three leaves, one at the beginning and two at the end.[451] Accordingly, Riddle 95 might have been followed by a few more riddles and a final lengthy poem acting as a coda, none of which has survived.

Conner also considers the possibility that the last part of the manuscript could have had a further quire.[452] If his inference is right, this missing quire would have probably contained other non-riddlic poems. Taking into account the manuscript losses produced in Quires XIV and XVI, a few more texts were possibly included after Riddles 20, 40, and 70a. If we assume that Williamson's editorial in-

---

449. Cf. Riddle 51 (pen and fingers), "swearte wæran lastas, / swaþu swiþe blacu" (2b–3a) and "siþade sweartlast" (11a) in Riddle 26 (Gospel book), as discussed above on p. 365.
450. Pope, "Paleography and Poetry," 29.
451. Conner, *Anglo-Saxon Exeter*, 108–9.
452. "We cannot be sure that yet another gathering was not part of the original book." Conner, *Anglo-Saxon Exeter*, 109.

terpretation—that Riddles 1-2-3, 68-69, 79-80, and 75-76 are unified texts—is correct, the resulting number of riddles is ninety-one.[453] Given that the scribe did not include end-puntuation either after Riddle 42 or after Riddle 48, we should substract two from ninety-one, which gives us eighty-nine. This implies the Exeter compilers would be adding more riddles than they actually needed to reach one hundred, a situation that brings to mind the case of the Vatican assemblage in which similar errors of appreciation made the compilers add two extra pieces, thus unwittingly surpassing the canonical century.[454] The number of the extant riddles, as the scribe/compilers possibly visualized it, is thus eighty-nine. This tentatively suggests that at least eleven riddles are missing, of which several might have been lost in the manuscript lacunae affecting Quires XIV and XVI, along with some others as well as, we may infer, a long solemn piece after Riddle 95.

4.4.3 Some Final Thoughts on Group 3

From the analysis of Group 3 (see Appendix X), we can conclude that at least the first six riddles (nos. 61–66) may have constituted the continuation of section 5 on the basis of their presenting diverse kinds of craftsmanship. Section 6 in turn seems to have been devoted primarily to instrumental riddles: Gospel book, lyre, lighthouse, sword, spear, horn, weathervane, bellows, inkhorn (twice), bottle, and key. The compilers also incorporated some zoological topics: ox, swan, oyster, crab, and fish (and river). As has been pointed out above, there seems to be an aim at supplementing zoological section 2, which offered animals of air and land, with the presentation of some aquatic motifs. There are also three cosmological topics (water, iceberg, Creation), a botanical subject (beech), and a "lapidary" motif (gold). In addition, the sequence reveals a faint attempt at

---

453. Note that this number is based on Williamson's acceptance of Pope's reading of Riddles 70a and 70b as different pieces.
454. As explained above (pp. 275-77), the compilers simply left some riddles unnumbered in Vatican City, Reg. Lat. 1553. This possibly triggered the addition of the two extra riddles.

providing a sample of wonder topics, as inferred from the presence of the lighthouse and the one-eyed seller of garlic. Even if the result is generally poor, the choice of these subjects reveals the compilers' desire to endow Group 3 with an equally encyclopedic character. All in all, the series is clearly a miscellany, although the wide range of instrumental topics suggests that a concern with enlarging the preceding tool sequences might have principally guided the third phase of the compilation.[455]

The study of Group 3 has also revealed a considerable level of improvisation in this part of the manuscript, as the inclusion of brief pieces with no special literary quality indicates. This is the case for Riddles 68–69 and 75–76, whose incorporation can be explained by the compilers' haste to reach the century. By the same token, the rewriting of the first line of Riddle 79–80 implies that the compilers probably had their doubts as to what version should be included. Besides, the numerous cases of duplication point to a possible reuse of the material found in Group 1. Finally, at least one of the pieces in Group 3, Riddle 81, betrays a connection with late-tenth-century literature, an idea that supports my analysis of Riddles 77 and 78 as being consonant with contemporary Benedictine ideology.

---

455. DiNapoli, "In the Kingdom of the Blind," 440, has pointed out the overwhelming prominence of this subject if compared to the other topics treated in the Old English Riddles, concluding that the Exeter collection seeks to present "secret affinities and identities between the acts of human and divine creation, establishing implicit analogies between *homo faber* and *deus conditor*."

Chapter Five

Conclusions

5.1. The Compilation of the Exeter Book Riddles and Latin Enigmata

Sisam opened his discussion about the Exeter Book by pointing to one of the crucial challenges that this manuscript has posed for scholars: "shall we ever know more about the way in which this miscellany was compiled?"[1] This monograph has aimed to contribute to answering this question, as the study of the compilation of the Old English Riddles has provided us with valuable information about how the material of the last part of the Exeter Book was put together and organized. My analysis of the Exeter Riddles, however, needed to be preceded by an examination of the internal structural organization of Isidore's *Etymologiae*, as this work established some patterns of compilation that were subsequently imitated by riddle collections in general. This monograph then offered a detailed study of Latin *enigmata*, which are often brought up as parallels to the Exeter Riddles but have only recently been considered with regard to the ordering of the vernacular counterparts. Some scholars had already noted thematic connections among *enigmata*, but these were thought to be a sporadic phenomenon. Nevertheless, this book has presented sufficient evidence to demonstrate that Latin collections

---

1. Sisam, *Studies*, 97.

distributed their riddles in thematic sections in the manner of encyclopedias, among which Isidore's *Etymologiae* was a major model.

The seven Latin collections that I have studied here all reveal a structure that appears in the form of sections, as well as thematic pairs or triplets. As I have demonstrated, these associative patterns are usually formulated according to the encyclopedic organizing principles of the kind observed in Isidore's *Etymologiae*. Latin *enigmata* therefore exhibit some common features. To begin with, the cosmological sections have proved to be an essential constituent, as these appear in almost all of these medieval collections. Cosmological sections or individual riddles on this subject normally occupy a prominent position, either at the beginning or at the end. In the case of Aldhelm's *enigmata*, on the one hand, this subject forms part of the introductory series and, on the other, it functions as a coda, the lengthy *Creatura* poem, which encompasses all the aspects of Creation. Aldhelm's cosmological topics therefore delineate an enveloping pattern that includes the remainder of the riddles. In turn, Eusebius's collection provides a set of cosmological motifs, as do the Bern, Lorsch and Vatican Riddles. Even if much shorter than Aldhelm's prototypical *Creatura*, Tatwine's *Enigma* 40 (rays of the sun) is a further illustration of a cosmological coda. Equally significant has proved to be the writing subject, which sometimes occupies salient places in a collection, either at the beginning, as in the case of Symphosius's *Enigmata*, or at the end, as with the Lorsch Riddles.

As this study has showed, the zoological groupings play an important role in most riddlic assemblages, a characteristic that tightly links riddling with Isidore's *Etymologiae*, from which authoritative Book XII has proved to be a determining influence. In this sense, Symphosius's, Eusebius's, and the Vatican zoological sections stand out as the most extensive and organized ones. In all of them—including Symphosius's—Isidorean influence has been detected. The study of the subgroups offered by zoological sequences suggests that their compilation was probably carefully planned ahead. In turn, the analysis of Aldhelm's section 2 has also showed that this series was conceived mainly as a sort of encyclopedic chapter on animals.

Latin collections also present substantial instrumental sequences, as, for example, in both Symphosius's and Tatwine's *Enigmata*, as well as in the Bern Riddles. Instrumental groupings in general include a varied range of themes that seem rather miscellaneous from our contemporary point of view. However, these sections comply with the characteristics of heterogeneous assemblages like those found in Books XVIII-XX of Isidore's *Etymologiae*, which include all kinds of utensils, weapons, food, drinks, clothes, and vehicles. Instrumental clusters sometimes dwell on a specific thematic field, as Tatwine's section on ecclesiastical motifs or the Bern group on agricultural subjects reveal.

Sections devoted to prodigies have also proved to be an important component of Latin riddle collections, an idea that is quite logical since these topics constitute a separate category in Isidore's *Etymologiae*. As this study has demonstrated, Symphosius, Aldhelm, and Eusebius each present a section of this kind. Even in the Vatican *enigmata*, in which no series on prodigies has been preserved,[2] we find two wondrous animals, as a minimum representation of this riddlic category, in the last section. Although the sequences of wonders offer motifs that are peculiar to each author, there are certain themes that are common to the three collections. For example, both Aldhelm and Eusebius include "night," which might be equivalent to Symphosius's Riddle 97 (shadow), in their groupings on wonders. In addition to this, Symphosius, Aldhelm, and Tatwine share an interest in birth processes and human anomalies of diverse kinds in their respective sections on prodigies. It is also worth noting that in the case of Aldhelm's and Eusebius's *Enigmata*, some of these motifs also occur in catalogues of marvels such as the *Liber monstrorum*.

---

2. As discussed above (p. 277), the collection is incomplete owing to manuscript loss. For this reason, the possibility that a section on wonders might have followed after Riddle 102 should not be precluded.

The logical conclusion that can be drawn from this discussion is that medieval Latin collections were conceived as encyclopedias on a small scale. Symphosius's and Aldhelm's *Enigmata*, as well as the hybrid compilation of the Vatican Riddles, all comprise God's Creation—understood as cosmological motifs, plants, and animals—and human-made tools. This overall scheme is similarly perceived in the tandem formed by Tatwine's and Eusebius's *Enigmata*, even if the botanical realm has no representation in them. The possibly incomplete Bern and Lorsch Riddles also reflect an attempt at offering a compilation based on encyclopedic models. In a clear imitation of the organizing patterns observed in the second decade of Isidore's *Etymologiae*, an ideal riddle collection should at least have an illustration of what I have defined as cosmological, biological, and instrumental subjects. Evidence of this is offered by the Bern *Enigmata*, in which the lack of representation of the zoological topics probably triggered their combination with some of Symphosius's and Aldhelm's riddles in the Vatican assemblage.

In this book I have aimed to show that the concept of encyclopedic compilation is much more important than has been considered so far, as it pervades medieval riddle collections in general. My analysis of the organization of Latin *enigmata* has similarly revealed an interest in the presentation of the different topics into smaller thematic segments such as pairs and triplets, some of which had already been detected by other scholars. The basic pattern in pairs has pointed to a close connection with the structures used in encyclopedias, particularly the principles of analogy and difference, which are exploited by Isidore *ad infinitum* throughout the *Etymologiae*. All in all, riddle collections, like encyclopedias, are eminently didactic products and thus "frame knowledge for consumption" for a specific audience at a particular time.[3] In the same way encyclopedists did, authors of riddle assemblages conscientiously organized and

---

3. I am here borrowing Murphy's timely description of Pliny's *Naturalis historia* as a cultural artifact that was expressly created with the audience of the Roman Empire in mind. Murphy, *Pliny*, 29.

distributed their materials into "parcels" of knowledge,[4] as if, so to say, they were "pills" for potential consumers, usually in an educational milieu.

The analysis of the organization of the Exeter Riddles in the manuscript shows that there is solid evidence of their having been arranged in thematic sections like those found in Latin *enigmata*. Moreover, the sequences observed in the Exeter Riddles denote certain boundaries, confirming the assumption made by earlier scholars that this is not the work of a sole author, but rather the result of a conflation of at least two, possibly even three, different riddle collections. This was probably done in an attempt to produce a vernacular collection with one hundred pieces. The analysis of the sequence that I have designated as Group 1 (from Riddles 1-2-3 to 40) has evinced a consistent thematic organization, which no doubt illustrates the threefold encyclopedic components—cosmological, biological, and instrumental—that can be observed in Latin *enigmata*. In spite of several irregularities that have been pointed out, the three sections of Group 1 exhibit a notable cohesiveness, revealing a thematic plan that follows the twofold pattern established by Symphosius. Group 1 thus presents, on the one hand, the "Opera Dei" motifs, including cosmological and zoological themes and, on the other, the "Opera hominis" subjects. This imitation of the Symphosian model, which in turn follows the basic twofold thematic pattern of Isidore's second decade in the *Etymologiae*, is a distinctive feature of Group 1, which evinces organizational divergences suggesting different provenance and authorship when compared to Groups 2 and 3.

At the end of the instrumental sequence of Group 1, there are two cosmological subjects—Riddles 39 (cloud) and 40 (Creation)—which seem to mark the end of what I have identified as a source collection. Riddles 1-2-3 and 40 therefore delineate a cosmological framework that comprises the other subjects dealt with in Group 1, a notion that underscores the unity of this initial batch and its originally independent character. The enveloping pattern offered by the

---

4. Here again I am using Murphy's expressions, ibid., 13.

cosmological subjects is similar to that observed in Aldhelm's *Enigmata*, whose direct influence can also be perceived in Exeter Riddles 35 and 40. Aldhelmian traces can also be discerned in some of the texts included in Exeter Groups 2 and 3—most notably, with Riddle 63 (glass goblet) and the Old English Creation riddles (nos. 66 and 94). But the outstanding dependence on Aldhelm's *Enigmata*, both in form and content, differentiates Group 1 from the other two riddle groups. By the same token, the imitation of Symphosius's structural layout is also a characteristic of Group 1. On this basis, I have concluded that Group 1 could be a sort of source collection that was entirely incorporated into the Exeter Book in the first stage of the compilation of the riddles.

The consideration of the manuscript losses has resulted in an approximate estimate of the riddles that the core collection (Group 1) might have originally had. The lacunae affecting the end of Riddles 20 and 40 thus point to the fact that a few more riddles could have formed part of this hypothetical source collection. As the number of riddles in Group 1 is close to forty, we may tentatively conclude that this core collection could have been initially composed of forty units, like Tatwine's *enigmata*. It is evident, however, that the compilers considered this number to be insufficient, and the expansion of the source collection thus started with Riddle 41. Group 2 (nos. 41–59) represents a second phase of the compilation in which the enlarging of this initial source collection was undertaken. Further riddles were appended after Riddle 40, possibly in an attempt to create a one-hundred riddle collection. With the detailed study of the compilation of the Exeter Riddles and its comparison to the preceding Latin models, I have therefore tried to offer solid evidence of what some scholars had already suspected.

According to this analysis, Group 2 possibly represents a second phase of the compilation process in which material from a different source was brought forth. The idiosyncrasy of this second batch is clearly manifested in the predominance of analogy, a major organizing principle that was "inherited" from encyclopedism. Even if section 5 (Tools II) is split into two parts due to the interruption that was most likely occasioned by the scarcity of material, it seems that this instrumental sequence was organized into three subgroups. This is a major difference with regard to section 3 (Tools I) of Group 1, which offers an indiscriminate assemblage of subjects with the exception of some thematic pairs. This also supports my earlier assumption that Group 1 was based primarily on the model set by Symphosius's *Enigmata*, in which section 5 offers a similar mixture of instrumental topics. Furthermore, the analysis of the underlying subgroups observed in Exeter section 5 suggests the compilers' concern with specifity and subclassification, a notion that recalls the instrumental sequences offered in Tatwine's and Eusebius's *Enigmata*. Notably, subgroup A of Exeter section 5 resembles Eusebius's section 4, which shows a similar interest in writing topics.

However, the compilers carried out the expansion of Group 1 in a rather unorthodox way, as evinced by the co-occurrence of Riddle 40 (Creation) and the sexual riddle series in Group 2. The resulting juxtaposition is rather awkward, especially if we take into account the marked elevated tone of Riddle 40 as a Christian reflection on God's Creation. The compilers just placed Riddle 41 (water) as a transitional piece bridging Riddle 40 and the sexual pieces, which themselves constitute a cohesive series. In turn, the presence of Riddle 59 has been interpreted here as a provisional coda marking the end of the first riddlic block in the manuscript.

The study of Group 3 (nos. 61–95) reveals that the material included in this part of the Exeter manuscript corresponds to a third phase of the compilation. As the analysis of the first five riddles suggests, the compilers envisioned what I have called subgroup C as a continuation of section 5 (Tools II). The thematic relationship of these five riddles to those of the preceding series in Group 2 therefore implies that the compilers added more instrumental topics to section 5. The presence of Riddle 66, a short Creation poem that was probably the cosmological coda of the second source collection, marks a further turning point in the compilation process.

The next group of riddles (section 6) is clearly differentiated from the preceding sequences for a number of reasons. To begin with, if compared to the other parts of the collection, section 6 is strongly miscellaneous, since it presents a disparate mixture of cosmological, biological, and instrumental topics. The botanical, lapidary, and wonder motifs also add to the heterogeneous character of section 6. Furthermore, the occurrence of a short scatological subject (no. 75–76), the other extremely brief pieces found in this area, and the remarkably faulty Latin riddle (no. 90)[5] all suggest that the compilers' priority was to comply with the traditional requirement of the canonical hundred.[6] The presence of numerous scribal mistakes in punctuation also reveals a certain degree of carelessness and improvisation. In addition to this, section 6 offers a notable amount of duplication and even suggests that some of the riddles included at this point are merely reworkings of various poems offered in Group 1, as the case of "bellows" Riddles 37 and 87 have illustrated. In turn, the inclusion of at least two aquatic animals in Riddles 77 and 78 discloses an attempt at maintaining the encyclopedic standards of the preceding groups, as these motifs would complement section 2 in Group 1, which deals with animals of air and land.

The thematic and structural differences observed in the three major riddle groups confirm my hypothesis that the compilation process had at least three distinctive phases. In the first stage, the compilers copied what seems to be an early independent collection, to which Riddle 40, a mid-tenth-century translation of Aldhelm's *Enigma* 100 of probable Canterbury provenance, was added. The

---

5. Most editors have consequently labeled this composition as "uncertain." For this reason, I have not considered it for this study. Whitbread attributes some of these mistakes to the natural problems arising from changing from one language to another. See L. Whitbread, "The Latin Riddle in the Exeter Book," *N&Q* 190 (1946): 156–58. On the other hand, Anderson considers that the poem could be incomplete. James E. Anderson, "Exeter Latin Riddle 90: A Liturgical Vision," *Viator* 23 (1992): 76.

6. I therefore concur with Tigges, who states that "The final group in particular has a few mysterious one- and two-liners (Krapp-Dobbie 66, 67, 75, 76 and 79) and an item in Latin (86 [90]), which may be evidence of hurried half-recollection as the compilation neared its completion." Tigges, "Snakes and Ladders," 97.

resulting forty-unit assemblage evinces an imitation of the Tatwinian format, while the binary encyclopedic distribution of the contents into the "Opera Dei" and the "Opera hominis" motifs reproduces the Isidorean/Symphosian model. All this implies that the source collection adhered to compilation patterns that were no doubt known at Canterbury, as shown by the presence of the *enigmata* of Aldhelm, Symphosius, Tatwine, and Eusebius in several manuscripts associated with the metropolitan see.

In the second phase, Group 1 was extended by appending to it further pieces deriving from another collection. The arrangement of the added pieces suggests that this second source, by contrast with the one used for Group 1, was probably governed by the encyclopedic principle of analogy. The presence of the term "hondwyrm" in Riddle 66 might establish a connection with Canterbury, since the word glosses Latin "uerme" in Aldhelm's *Enigma* 100 in London, Royal 15.A.xvi and Cambridge, Gg.5.35. This inference would interestingly accord with the idea that the second assemblage employed to produce Group 2 was possibly coeval with—as well as geographically akin to—the source collection of Group 1. However, the hypothesis of a Canterbury provenance for Riddle 66 cannot rest on a firm ground, since the occurrence of "hondwyrm" in this text may simply derive from a recycling of Riddle 40 rather than from a translation from Aldhelm's *Enigma* 100.

In the third phase, the compilers continued to enlarge the collection by supplying five more riddles to instrumental section 5 and then a miscellany. The possible reusing of some pieces from Group 1, the abundant cases of repetition, and the presence of numerous textual errors and imprecisions found in Group 3 all confirm the validity of previous scholarly assumption that this last part of the collection was ruled by improvisation and the need to comply with the traditional century. As evinced by the study of Riddle 81, the outstanding parallels with Wulfstan's *Narratio* suggest that the weathervane piece aligns with the literary concerns of late-tenth-century authors in the Benedictine sphere, just as previously inferred from the moralistic nuances underlying the clues of Riddles 77 and 78 and the zoological string of Group 1. In addition, the connection of Riddle 81 to Wulfstan's *Narratio*—a work that offers a version of the *Te Deum* by this author, which is also included in Cambridge, Gg.5.35, as well as references to Sigeric and Ælfheah—associates the Exeter collection with the Benedictine intellectual circles of Winchester, Glastonbury, and Canterbury.

5.2 Some Final Thoughts on Early Medieval Riddling

Michael W. Herren describes "The last quarter of the seventh century and, perhaps, the opening decades of the eighth" as a "mini-renaissance," characterized by the adoption of features deriving from classical culture in Anglo-Saxon literature.[7] Running parallel to the rapid spread and promotion of the *Etymologiae* in Anglo-Saxon England, this renaissance coincides for the most part chronologically and geographically[8] with the emergence and splendor of Insular Latin *enigmata* and vernacular riddles, as inferred from Fulk's dating of the majority of the pieces contained in the Exeter collection.[9]

---

7. Herren, "The Transmission," 102.
8. This renaissance may also have a geographical correspondence with the first flourishing of riddling in Anglo-Saxon England. As explained by Herren, ibid., "The mini-renaissance I speak of was localized and short-lived. It was basically limited to the area of Southumbria, specifically Kent and Wessex, and faded away probably in the second decade of the eighth century." Interestingly, authors of *enigmata* were based mainly in the area pointed out by Herren. A Mercian by birth, Tatwine probably developed part of his literary career at Canterbury, where he occupied the bishopric from 731 to 734. In turn, Aldhelm was West-Saxon and so was Boniface, the latter first educated at the monastery of Exeter and later on at the monastic school at Nhutscelle, which has been identified as Nursling (Hampshire, near Southampton), of which he eventually became headmaster. Eusebius might have been a Northumbrian colleague of Bede, although his identification as a native of Southumbria instead has also been suggested, as pointed out above pp. 234–35 (n. 431).
9. One should bear in mind that Fulk favors the same timespan (c. 685–825) that he proposed for *Beowulf* and early biblical narratives for the Exeter Riddles, particularly for the first large block. *The History*, 408.

Conclusions

In the context of this early cultural flowering, riddling no doubt played a major role, since it permitted authors to effectively channel knowledge of grammar, rhetoric, encyclopedic lore, lexicography, metrics, and other disciplines into a compact literary format. Riddle collections consequently became an ideal vehicle for didactic and instructional purposes, as this study has demonstrated. Isidore's *Etymologiae* in turn constituted a successful reference book that, as explained above, was instrumental in the development of early medieval riddling. Both riddle collections and the *Etymologiae* thus emerged side by side in Anglo-Saxon England in a period of intellectual flourishing that was drastically truncated by the outbreak of the Danish invasions. But this brief Anglo-Saxon renaissance was effectively transferred to the Continent, where it continued its natural development and would eventually form part of the Carolingian *renovatio*. Together with Isidore's *Etymologiae* and other works, the *Enigmata* of Symphosius and Aldhelm were thus included in the Carolingian literary canon and enjoyed a widespread circulation in a vast geographical area.

In the late ninth century, Anglo-Saxon England started to recover from the cultural decline provoked by the Scandinavian occupation. Thanks to the endeavors carried out during Alfred's and Æthelstan's reigns, a re-establishment of the cultural standards of the renaissance described by Herren started to materialize. In this context, the Carolingian cultural program, to which Boniface's and Alcuin's contributions were crucial, began to be absorbed in Anglo-Saxon England, but with a distinctive emphasis on the vernacular that was unparalleled in the Continent. The recovery and development of education continued and achieved its peak in the Anglo-Saxon period with Edgar's and Æthelred's reigns, during which the Benedictine reform contributed decisively to this second cultural flourishing and to the reinstatement of the earlier literary canon. Part of the cultural renovation launched by the reform also involved the reintroduction of literary genres such as riddling. Manuscripts were thus imported and Latin *enigmata* contained in them were thoroughly scrutinized, particularly at Canterbury, where the arrival of two

Frankish codices—London, Royal 15.A.xvi and Oxford, Rawlinson C.697—probably stimulated the translation of Latin riddles and the composition of new ones in the vernacular. In addition, it is mainly in Anglo-Saxon codices from the late tenth century onwards that we find evidence of the anthologizing of the *enigmata* of Symphosius and Aldhelm, the canonical riddle authors *par excellence*, as well as those of Tatwine and Eusebius.

As the study offered in Chapter 4 of this book has showed, the Exeter Book riddle collection presents several aspects that may have a relation to the cultural and ideological background of the second half of the tenth century, when the manuscript was compiled. This seems to be so with the particular choice of animals in section 2, the aquatic duo formed by Riddles 77 and 78, as well as the verbal correspondences observed in Riddle 81 and Wulfstan's *Narratio*. In addition, the notable Aldhelmian imprint of the Exeter collection, particularly in Group 1 with the two translations from this author's *Enigmata* and its cosmological framework, similarly points to a relationship with the reform period, during which Aldhelm was regarded an iconic writer. Besides, the sixty-plus-forty structure observed in the Exeter collection evinces the imitation of the tandem compilation of Tatwine's and Eusebius's *Enigmata* as found in London, Royal 12.C.xxiii and Cambridge, Gg.5.35, the two grand Canterbury riddle compendia. This comes as no surprise to us, since, with the reformists' endeavors to consolidate a new educational program mirroring the successful past one, the literary achievements of Aldhelm's literary "heirs" would similarly have been in the spotlight, particularly at Canterbury.

In view of these findings, it can be deduced that the Exeter Riddles constitute the literary product of a team of compilers from a reform-oriented scriptorium, most likely Canterbury, as suggested by the presence of Riddle 40 in the collection and the observance of compilation patterns deriving from Latin *enigmata* associated with manuscripts that were either studied or produced at the metropolitan see. Still, Glastonbury, Winchester, and Exeter cannot be ruled out, since there is evidence that riddling was appreciated in these

Benedictine foundations as a literary genre. Probably under episcopal patronage, the Exeter compilers endeavored to put together a collection of riddles that could live up to the high standards of the golden period of the late seventh and early eighth centuries. Admittedly, the result was far from brilliant, especially as revealed by the awkward patchwork joining cosmological Riddles 40 and 41 to the sexual-riddle series and the general slovenly outlook of Group 3. However, the study of the compilation of the Exeter Riddles has allowed us to glimpse that there was at least a serious attempt to recover this literary genre under the auspices of the Benedictine reform.

The encyclopedic layout of the Exeter Riddles therefore suggests that their compilation originated in a monastic center, in which they were probably used for teaching purposes. The learned contents of Riddle 1-2-3, for example, leave no room for doubt that this composition would have been used to test a reader's knowledge of atmospheric phenomena, their characteristics, and their cause. The internal structure of the zoological sequence in turn implies that an allegorical reading, as well as a discussion of the clean and unclean status of the animals, was expected. In turn, Riddles 35 and 40 might stem from a school translation exercise. The presence of the term "hondwyrm" in Riddles 40 and 66 suggests a translation using Canterbury-derived glossaries at hand. With its description of a bookworm eating vellum, Riddle 47 similarly provides us with a picture of everyday life in a medieval school, while its figurative components humorously caricature a slow-witted novice struggling to memorize the psalter. Further pieces also give us insight into the ecclesiastical profession, as Riddle 26, for example, details the processes of preparing the parchment and later writing and illuminating a book. Riddle 51 (pen and fingers) and Riddles 88/93 (inkhorn) allude to implements used in an Anglo-Saxon scriptorium, while other artifacts related to religious cult such as church vessels (nos. 48 and 59), the book chest (49), and the cross (30a and 55) complement the picture of the monastic microcosm in which these texts were generated and read.

However, we should not preclude the possibility that some of the riddles, with their notable playful, risqué, and entertaining ingredients, could have transcended their native cloister, or, conversely, they may have had their origin in a secular milieu[10] and from there taken a leap into the monastic school. I have elsewhere argued that an aristocratic learned audience might have also appreciated Latin riddles.[11] It should also be borne in mind that Aldhelm's *Epistola ad Acircium*, containing the *Enigmata*, was addressed to King Aldfrith of Northumbria. The fact that Aldhelm's *Enigmata* had a royal dedicatee could point to the use of riddles as exercises of Latin rhetoric and metrics for the monarch himself, but this might also include the teaching of princes, a practice we already know about from Alcuin's *Disputatio*, which contains queries that were intended for Charlemagne's son Pippin. By the same token, members of the aristocracy—Aldhelm himself being one of them—could have similarly been the recipients of these literary products.

On the other hand, medieval riddling should not be understood only as an exclusively educational phenomenon. Conner has offered the thought-provoking hypothesis that the Exeter Riddles, as well as the non-enigmatic poems accompanying them, might have had a secular audience, as they could have served as entertaining verse in the context of an "oral presentation at a guild banquet."[12] Indeed, this could be the case with pieces such as Riddle 23 (bow), whose initial spelling clue might have lent itself easily to a verbal challenge. Similarly, the reference to the "cuþe hol" in Riddle 44 (key) seems to be no more than a vulgarism, even if the presence of this text is justified by its inclusion in a sequence that invites a reflection on the dangers of the body. In turn, the description of the borer being pulled out hot from the hole in Riddle 62, or the scatological joke of Riddle 75–76 (piss), could undeniably accord with a context of revelry. After all, Symphosius's seminal *Enigmata*,

---

10. Murphy's *Unriddling* basically explores the popular roots of a good number of the riddles of this collection.
11. See my "The Sexual Riddle Type," 377.
12. Conner, "Parish Guilds," 270. Also, see his "Four Contiguous Poems," 130.

with its conspicuously learned contents, were associated in the preface with an event of this kind. In conclusion, riddling was no doubt a successful literary genre that could be appreciated by both ecclesiastical and secular audiences.

APPENDIX I

Chronology

A Diachronic Outline of Early Medieval Riddling	Other Relevant Works and Cultural Manifestations
Symphosius, *Enigmata* (late 5th or early 6th c.)	The Latin Anthology (early 6th c.) Isidore, *De natura rerum* (c. 613) and *Etymologiae* (c. 615) School of Theodore (602-90) and Hadrian (d. 710)
Bern *Enigmata* (7th c.)	
	Aldhelm, *De virginitate* (675 or 680), *De metris* and *De pedum*
Aldhelm, *Enigmata* (c. 686)	*regulis* (c. 686)
	Bede, *De schematibus tropis*, *De arte metrica*, and *De ortographia*
Ioca monachorum (MSS., early 8th c.)[1]	(c. 691–703) Tatwine, *Ars grammatica* (c. 700)
Leiden Riddle (8th c.)	Bede, *De natura rerum* (c. 703) Boniface, *Ars grammatica* (c. 719); *Caesurae Versuum*

---

1. When the exact dating of the work is not clear, I provide the date of the earliest manuscript(s) in which it is preserved.

A Diachronic Outline of Early Medieval Riddling	Other Relevant Works and Cultural Manifestations
Boniface, *Enigmata* (c. 722)	
Tatwine, *Enigmata* (before 731)	Bede, *Historia ecclesiastica* (c. 731)
Eusebius, *Enigmata* (before 747)	
Alcuin, *Disputatio* (790–93) and *Propositiones*	Alcuin, *De grammatica* and *Carmina*
Lorsch Riddles (MS., late 8th c.)	
Pseudo-Bede, *Collectanea* (early 9th c.)	
Vatican Riddles (MS., early 9th c.)	
St Gall Riddles (MSS., second half of 9th c.)	
Versus cuiusdam Scoti de alphabeto (MS., third quarter of 9th c.)	Alfredian school of translation (late 9th c.): Gregory's *Cura pastoralis*, Augustine's *Soliloquia*, Bede's *Historia ecclesiastica*, Boethius's *De consolatione philosophiae*
	Production of *Anglo-Saxon Chronicle* starts (c. 890)
Arrival of three Frankish codices with riddles at Canterbury (mid-10th c.)	Æthelwold's and Dunstan's period of study at Glastonbury (940s–950s)
Solomon and Saturn dialogues (MS., mid-10th c.)	
Exeter Book Riddles (MS., c. 970)	Exeter Book (c. 970)
	Vercelli Book (c. 975)

A Diachronic Outline of Early Medieval Riddling	Other Relevant Works and Cultural Manifestations
Reichenau Riddles (MS., late 10th c.)	Ælfric, *Saints' Lives* (990s) and *Grammatica* (c. 998) Wulfstan Cantor, *Narratio metrica sancti Swithuni* (c. 996)
Turtur-riddle (MS., late 10th or early 11th c.)	Byrhtferth, *Vita sancti Oswaldi* (c. 997)
Production of London, Royal 12.C.xxiii (late 10th or early 11th c.)	*Beowulf*-manuscript (c. 1000) Junius manuscript (c. 1000)
Latin bullock riddle (MS. early 11th c.)	
Macaronic riddle (MS., early 11thc.)	Byrhtferth of Ramsey, *Enchiridion* (1011) Wulfstan's *Sermo Lupi ad anglos* (c. 1014)
"Æthelwold's Bowl" (MS., first half of 11th c.)	First and second continuations (1122–54) of Peterborough Chronicle William of Malmesbury, *Gesta pontificum anglorum* (c. 1125)
Vitellius OE prose riddle (Ms., mid-11th c.)	The Old English *Apollonius of Tyre* (MS., mid-11th c., lacking Symphosius's riddles)
Production of Cambridge, Gg.5.35 (mid-11th c.) with *Bibliotheca magnifica* and *Joco-Seria*	*Regularis concordia* (MSS., mid-11thc.)
Three Latin riddles (including *turtur*-piece, MS. late 11th or early 12th c.)	

Appendix II

Isidore's Etymologiae

The First Decade

  I. De Grammatica (On grammar)
 II. De Rhetorica et Dialectica (On rhetoric and dialectic)
III. De mathematica (On mathematics)
 IV. De medicina (On medicine)
  V. De legibus et temporibus (On the laws and times)
 VI. De libris et officiis ecclesiasticis (On the books and the ecclesiastical offices)
VII. De Deo, angelis et sanctis (On God, the angels and the saints)
VIII. De Ecclesia et sectis (On the Church and the sects)
 IX. De linguis, gentibus, regnis, militia, civibus, affinitatibus (On languages, nations, royal power, military service, citizens, family relationships)
  X. De vocabulis (On the nouns, terms)

The Second Decade

  XI. De homine et portentis (On man and prodigies)
 XII. De animalibus (On animals)
XIII. De mundo et partibus (On the world and its parts)
 XIV. De terra et partibus (On the earth and its parts)
  XV. De aedificiis et agriis (On buildings and fields)
 XVI. De lapidibus et metallis (On stones and metals)
XVII. De rebus rusticis (On rural things)
XVIII. De bello et ludis (On war and games)
 XIX. De navibus, aedificiis et vestibus (On ships, buildings and clothes)
  XX. De penu et instrumentis domesticis et rusticis (On the provisions and domestic and rural utensils)

APPENDIX III

Symphosius's Collection[1]

Preface

Section 1: Tools I
1. Graphium (stylus)
2. Harundo (reed)
3. Anulus cum gemma (ring with gem)
4. Clauis (key)
5. Catena (chain)
6. Tegula (roof-tile)

Section 2: Meteorological Phenomena
7. Fumus (smoke)
8. Nebula (fog)
9. Pluia (rain)
10. Glacies (ice)
11. Nix (snow)

Section 3: Zoological Motifs
A) Animals in General
12. Flumen et piscis (river and fish)
13. **Nauis (ship)**
14. Pullus in ouo (chicken in egg)

B) Snakes/"Worms"
15. Vipera (viper)
16. Tinea (bookworm)
17. Aranea (spider)

C) Aquatic Animals
18. Coclea (snail)
19. Rana (frog)
20. Testudo (turtle)

D) Small Quadrupeds/Insects
21. Talpa (mole)
22. Formica (ant)
23. Musca (fly)
24. Curculio (weevil)
25. Mus (mouse)

E) Birds
26. Grus (crane)
27. Cornix (crow)
28. Vespertilio (bat)
29. Ericius (hedgehog)
30. Pediculus (louse)[2]
31. Phoenix (phoenix)

---

1. Thematic exceptions in all the collections are marked by means of bold letter.
2. I here prefer the singular form "peduculus," which is the commonest manuscript reading, as offered by Riese, *Anthologia latina*, vol. 1.1, 229, instead of "pediculi," as found in *CCSL*, vol. 133A, 651.

F) Big Quadrupeds/Wild Beasts
32. Taurus (bull)
33. Lupus (wolf)
34. Vulpes (fox)
35. Capra (she-goat)
36. Porcus (pig)
37. Mula (she-mule)
38. Tigris (tigress)
39. **Centaurus (centaur)**

Section 4: Plants
40. Papauer (poppy)
41. Malua (mallow)
42. Beta (beet)
43. Cucurbita (gourd)
44. Caepa (onion)
45. Rosa (rose)
46. Viola (violet)
47. Tus (frankincense)
48. Murra (myrrh)
49. **Ebur (ivory)**

Section 5: Tools II
50. Fenum (hay)
51. Mola (millstone)
52. Farina (flour)
53. Vitis (vine)
54. Amus (hook)
55. Acula (needle)
56. Caliga (military shoe)
57. Clauus caligaris (hobnail of military shoe)
58. Capillus (hair)
59. Pila (ball)
60. Serra (saw)
61. Ancora (anchor)
62. Pons (bridge)
63. Spongia (sponge)
64. Tridens (trident)
65. Sagitta (arrow)

66. Flagellum (whip)
67. Lanterna (lantern)
68. Vitreum (window pane)
69. Speculum (mirror)
70. Clepsydra (water-clock)
71. Puteus (well)
72. Tubus (pipe)
73. Uter (follis) [bellows]
74. Lapis (stone)
75. Calx (lime)
76. Silex (flint)
77. Silex aliter. (flint, another version)
78. Scalae (stairs)
79. Rotae (wheels)
80. Scopa (broom)
81. Tintinnabulum (bell)
82. Lagena (jar)
83. Conditum (spiced wine)
84. Vinum in acetum conuersum (wine turned to vinegar)
85. Malum (apple)
86. Perna (ham)
87. Malleus (hammer)
88. Pistillus (pestle)
89. Strigilis aenea (bronze strigil)
90. Balneum (bath-house)
91. Tessera (die)
92. Pecunia (money)

Section 6: Wonders
93. Mulier quae geminos pariebat (woman who gave birth to twins)
94. Miles podagricus (gouty soldier)
95. Luscus alium uendens (one-eyed man selling garlic)

96. Funambulus
    (tightrope walker)
97. Umbra (shadow)
98. Echo (echo)
99. Somnus (sleep)

Coda
100. Monumentum (tombstone)

Appendix IV

Aldhelm's Collection[1]

Preface

Section 1: Cosmological Themes
1. Terra (earth) [4]
2. Ventus (wind) [4]
3. Nubes (cloud) [4]
4. Natura (nature) [4]
5. Iris (rainbow) [4]
6. Luna (moon) [4]
7. Fatum (fate) [4]
8. Pliades (Pleiades) [5]

Section 2
9. Adamas (diamond) [4]
10. Molosus (dog) [4]
11. Poalum (bellows) [4]
12. Bombix (silkworm) [4]
13. **Barbita (organ)** [4]
14. Pauo (peacock) [4]
15. Salamandra (salamander) [4]
16. Luligo (squid) [4]
17. Perna (pinna) [4]
18. Myrmicoleon (ant-lion) [5]

19. Salis (salt) [4]
20. Apis (bee) [5]
21. Lima (file) [5]
22. Acalantida (nightingale) [5]
23. Trutina (pair of scales) [5]
24. Dracontia (dragon-stone) [5]
25. Magnes ferrifer (magnet) [5]
26. Gallus (rooster) [5]
27. Coticula (whetstone) [5]
28. Minotaurus (minotaur) [5]
29. **Aqua (water)** [6]
30. **Elementa (alphabet)** [7]
31. Ciconia (stork) [7]
32. **Pugillares (writing tablets)** [8]
33. Lorica (breastplate) [7]
34. Locusta (locust)
35. Nycticorax (night owl) [7]
36. Scnifes (midge) [7]
37. Cancer (crab) [6]
38. Tippula (pond-skater) [6]
39. Leo (lion) [6]

---

1. The amount of lines has been indicated next to the solution by means of brackets with the exception of Symphosius's *Enigmata*, and the Bern Riddles, in which the number of lines per poem is always three in the first collection and six in the latter.

460

Section 3
40. Piper (pepper) [6]
41. Puluillus (pillow) [6]
42. Stutrio (ostrich) [6]
43. Sanguisuga (leech) [6]
44. Ignis (fire) [8]
45. Fusum (spindle) [7]
46. Urtica (nettle) [5]
47. Hirundo (swallow) [9]
48. Vertico poli (movement of the heavens) [9]
49. Lebes (cauldron) [5]
50. Myrifyllon (yarrow) [5]
51. (H)eliotropium (heliotrope) [4]
52. Candela (candle) [8]
53. Arcturus (the Great Bear) [9]
54. Cocuma duplex (double cooking-pot) [7]
55. C(h)rismal (ciborium) [9]
56. Castor (beaver) [9]
57. Aquila (eagle) [8]
58. Vesper sidus (evening star) [7]
59. Penna (pen) [8]
60. Monocerus (unicorn) [11]
61. Pugio (dagger) [7]
62. Famfaluca (bubble) [7]
63. Corbus (raven) [10]
64. Columba (dove) [6]
65. Muriceps (cat) [9]
66. Mola (millstone) [7]
67. Cribellus (flour-sieve) [9]
68. Salpix (trumpet) [8]
69. Taxus (yew-tree) [8]
70. Tortella (loaf of bread) [7]
71. Piscis (fish) [6]
72. Colosus (colossus) [8]
73. Fons (spring of water) [7]
74. Fundibalum (sling) [9]
75. Crabro (hornet) [12]
76. Melarius (apple-tree) [7]
77. Ficulnea (fig-tree) [7]
78. Cupa vinaria (wine cask) [10]
79. Sol et luna (sun and moon) [11]
80. Calix Vitreus (glass goblet) [9]

Section 4: Wonders
81. Lucifer (the morning star) [10]
82. Mustela (weasel) [8]
83. **Iuuencus (bullock)** [6]
84. Scrofa praegnans (pregnant sow) [9]
85. Caecus natus (man blind from birth) [6]
86. Aries (ram) [8]
87. **Clipeus (shield)** [6]
88. Basiliscus (serpent) [7]
89. **Arca Libraria (book chest)** [5]
90. Puerpera geminas enixa (woman in labor with twins) [4]
91. Palma (palm tree) [11]
92. Farus Editissima (high lighthouse) [10]
93. **Scintilla (spark)** [11]
94. Ebulus (wallwort) [9]
95. Scilla (Scylla) [13]
96. Elefans (elephant) [15]
97. **Nox (night)** [16]
98. Elleborus (woody nightshade) [7]
99. Camellus (camel) [7]

Coda
100. Creatura (Creation) [83]

APPENDIX V

Tatwine's Collection

Section 1: Theological Motifs I
1. De philosophia
   (philosophy) [12][1]
2. De spe, fide (et) caritate
   (faith, hope and charity) [6][2]
3. De historia et sensu
   et morali et allegoria
   (historical, moral and
   allegorical sense) [6][3]

Section 2: Tools I
4. De litteris (letters) [6]
5. De membrano (parchment) [6]
6. De penna (pen) [6]
7. De tinti(n)no (bell) [6]
8. De ara (altar) [6]

9. De cruce Xristi
   (Christ's cross) [6]
10. De recitabulo (lectern) [6]
11. De acu (needle) [5]
12. De patena (paten) [5]
13. De acu pictili
    (embroidery needle) [5]
14. **De caritate (charity)** [5]

Section 3: Wonders
15. De niue, grandine et glacie
    (snow, hail and ice) [5]
16. De pr(a)epositione utriusque
    casus (prepositions with two
    cases) [5]
17. **De sciuro (squirrel)** [5]
18. De oculis (eyes) [5]

---

1. The exact translation is "On philosophy," but, for the sake of concision, I will not translate the preposition *de* in the solutions throughout the appendices.
2. I have provided the normal order of the concepts as common in present-day usage instead of that of the MS. readings (Hope, faith and charity).
3. The title of this riddle alludes to the four methods used in scriptural interpretation, which are literal (or historical), moral (or tropological), allegorical (or typological), and anagogical, the latter one missing in the two manuscript versions.

19. De strabis oculis
(squinting eyes) [5]
20. De lusco (the one-eyed) [5]

Section 4: Theological Motifs II
21. De malo (evil) [5]
22. De adam (Adam) [5]
23. De trina morte
(threefold death) [5]
24. De humilitate (humility) [5]
25. De superbia (pride) [5]
26. De quinque sensibus
(the five senses) [5]

Section 5: Tools II
27. De forcipe (tongs) [5]
28. De incude (anvil) [5]

29. De mensa (table) [5]
30. De ense et uagina
(sword and sheath) [5]
31. De scintilla (spark) [4]
32. De sagitta (arrow) [4]
33. De igne (fire) [4]
34. De faretra (quiver) [4]
35. De pruna (ember) [4][4]
36. De uentilabro
(winnowing fork) [4]
37. De seminante (sower) [4]
38. De carbone (charcoal) [4]
39. De cote (whetstone) [4][5]

Coda
40. De radiis solis
(rays of the sun) [5]

---

4. Although the MS. reading is "pruina," I follow Ebert's reading "pruna" in "Über die Rätselpoesie," 41 (n. 1). Cf. "De pru(i)na," *CCSL*, vol. 133, 202.
5. Like Ebert, "Die Rätselpoesie," 41 (n. 12), I here prefer "cote," the ablative case of *cos* meaning "a whetstone, hone, grind-stone" to the MS. readings "coticulo" maintained in *CCSL*, vol. 133, 206. As explained by Williams, *The Riddles of Tatwine and Eusebius*, 154, "Very possibly 'coticulum' was a gloss which eventually replaced the word for which it was a synonym."

APPENDIX VI

Eusebius's Collection

Section 1: The Chain of Being
1. De deo (God) [4]
2. De angelo (angel) [4]
3. De demone (fallen angel) [4]
4. De homine (man) [4]

Section 2: Cosmological Motifs
5. De caelo (heaven) [4]
6. De terra (earth) [4]
7. **De litteris (letters)** [4]1
8. De uento et igne (wind and fire) [4]
9. **De alpha (alpha)** [4]
10. De sole (sun) [4]
11. De luna (moon) [4]

Section 3: Miscellanea
12. De boue (bullock) [4]
13. De uacca (cow) [4]
14. De x littera (the letter x) [4]
15. De igne et aqua (fire and water) [4]
16. De phlasca (flask) [4]

17. De cruce (cross) [4]
18. De iniquitate et iustitia (iniquity and justice) [4]
19. De v littera (the letter u) [4]
20. De domo (house) [4]
21. De terra et mare (land and sea) [4]
22. De sermone (speech) [4]
23. De aequore (sea) [4]
24. De morte et uita (death and life) [4]
25. De animo (heart) [4]
26. De die bissextili (bissextile day) [4]
27. De humilitate et superbia (humility and pride) [4]
28. De candela (candle) [4]
29. De aetate et saltu (period of time and moon's leap) [4]

Section 4: Writing Tools
30. De atramentorio (inkhorn) [4]

---

1. Note that I have preferred Williams's emendation of the title as "litteris" for MS. "littera" because the solution should rather be in the plural, as suggested by the clues of the riddle. See Williams, *The Riddles of Tatwine and Eusebius*, 164. Cf. "De littera" (translated as "letters") in *CCSL*, vol. 133, 217.

31. De cera (wax) [4]
32. De membrano (parchment) [4]
33. De scetha (book chest) [4]
34. **De flumine (river)** [6]
35. De penna (pen) [4]
36. **De gladio (sword)** [4]

Section 5: Zoological Motifs
A) *Animals in General*
   37. De uitulo (calf) [4]
   38. De pullo (chicken) [4]
   39. **De i littera (the letter i)** [4]
   40. De pisce (fish) [4]

B) *Animals of Land*
   41. De chelidro serpente (chelydros snake and hydra) [6]
   42. De dracone (dragon) [9]
   43. De tigri bestia (tiger) [4]
   44. De pant[h]era (panther) [4]
   45. De cameleone (giraffe and chameleon) [4]
   46. De leopardo (leopard) [4]

47. De scitali serpente (scytale) [6]
48. **De die et nocte (day and night)** [4]
49. De anfibina serpente (amphisbaena) [4]
50. De saura lacerto (lizard) [4]
51. De scorpione (scorpion) [5]
52. De chimera (chimaera) [9]

C) *Animals of Water*
   53. De yppopotamo pisce (hippopotamus) [6]
   54. De ochenao pisce (remora) [6]
   55. De torpedo pisce (electric ray) [8]

D) *Animals of Air*
   56. De ciconia aui (stork) [13]
   57. De strutione (ostrich) [5]
   58. De noctua (night owl) [6]
   59. De psittaco (parrot) [7]
   60. De bubone (horned owl) [5]

APPENDIX VII

The Bern Collection

Section 1: Tools I
1. De olla (pot)[1]
2. De lucerna (lamp)
3. De sale (salt)
4. De scamno (bench)
5. De mensa (table)
6. De calice (goblet)
7. De uesica (bag)
8. De ouo (egg)
9. De mola (millstone)
10. De scala (stairs)
11. De naue (ship)

Section 2: Agricultural Motifs
12. De grano (grain)
13. De uite (vine)
14. De oliua (olive tree)
15. De palma (palm tree)
16. De cedria (citron fruit)[2]

Section 3: Tools II
17. De cribro (sieve)
18. De scopa (broom)
19. De pice (pitch)[3]
20. De melle (honey)
21. **De apibus (bees)**
22. **De oue (sheep)**
23. De ignis scintilla (fire spark)
24. De membrana (parchment)
25. De litteris (letters)
26. De sinapi (mustard)
27. De papiro (papyrus wick)
28. De serico (silkworm)[4]
29. De speculo (mirror)
30. **De pisce (fish)**
31. De nympha (water container)[5]
32. De spongia (sponge)

---

1. The riddles of the Bern collection are all made of six lines.
2. I here adopt "De cedria," as offered by Buecheler and Riese, *Anthologia latina*, vol. 1.1, 356.
3. I here provide "De pice," as in Buecheler and Riese, *Anthologia latina*, vol. 1.1, 357.
4. The term *sericus* refers to the silk but the speaker of the riddle is the worm. See pp. 261-62 (n. 527) of this book.
5. As explained above (p. 262, n. 529), Latin *nympha* usually refers to water but the clues clearly allude to a vessel to keep water.

Section 4: Plants and Flowers
33. De uiola (violet)
34. De rosa (rose)
35. De liliis (lilies)
36. De croco (saffron flower)
37. De pipere (pepper)
38. De glacie (ice)
39. De hedera (ivy)

Section 5: Miscellanea
40. De muscipula (mousetrap)
41. De uento (wind)
42. De glacie (ice)
43. De uermibus bombycibus (silkworms)
44. De margarita (pearl)
45. De terra (earth)
46. De pistillo (hammer)[6]
47. De castanea (chestnut)[7]
48. De castanea (chestnut)[8]

49. De pluuia (rain)
50. De uino (wine)
50a. De charta (papyrus sheet)[9]
51. De alio (garlic)[10]
52. De rosa (rose)
53. De trutina (pair of scales)[11]
54. De insubulo (loom beam)[12]

Section 6: Cosmological Motifs
55. De sole (sun)[13]
56. De sole (sun)
57. De sole (sun)
58. De luna (moon)
59. De luna (moon)
60. De caelo (heaven)
61. De umbra (shadow)
62. De stellis (stars)

Coda
63. De uino (wine)

---

6. Latin *pistillus* means "pestle," but I follow Socas Gavilán's reading of the clues (*Antologia latina*, 401) as clearly describing a hammer. Cf. "De malleo," in Buecheler and Riese, Anthologia latina, vol. 1.1, 365.
7. I here adopt "De castanea," as offered by Buecheler and Riese, *Anthologia latina*, vol. 1.1, 365. Cf. "De cochlea," in Glorie, *CCSL*, vol. 133A, 593.
8. The manuscripts bear no title, possibly because it is a variant of the preceding text but, as Socas Gavilán, *Antologia latina*, 401 (n. 341), indicates, the description could also apply either to the walnut or the almond.
9. This riddle is only extant in Berlin, Phillipps 1825. See above, p. 252 (n. 482).
10. The solution "De alio" (On garlic) is supplied by Glorie, *CCSL*, vol. 133A, 598, but the clues rather refer to the onion.
11. The solution "De trutina" is provided by Glorie, *CCSL*, vol. 133A, 600.
12. The solution "De insubulo" is supplied by Glorie, *CCSL*, vol. 133A, 601. Latin *insubulus* is defined by Du Cange as "lignum textorum" (the beam or staff of weavers).
13. The title alludes to the sun ("De sole") but, as Socas Gavilán contends, *Antología latina*, 403 (n. 352), *Enigma* 55 rather describes a cloud.

Appendix VIII

The Lorsch Collection

Section 1: *The Human Being*
1. De homine (man) [12]
2. De anima (soul) [14]

Section 2: *Cosmological Motifs*
3. De aqua (water) [7]
4. De glacie (ice) [7][1]

- - - - - - - - - - - - - - - - - - -
5. **De copa uinaria (beaker of wine)** [7]
6. De niue (snow) [6]

Section 3: *Miscellanea*
7. De castanea (chestnut) [3]
8. De ouo (egg) [2][2]
9. De penna (pen) [3]
10. De luminari (sanctuary lamp) [7]
11. De boue (ox) [8][3]

Coda
12. De atramento (ink) [7]

---

1. The presentation of riddles is at this point interrupted because the *Caesurae Versuum* is here retaken.
2. As noted above (p. 266, n. 545), I prefer Dümmler's title-solution "De ouo," as offered in *Aenigmata anglica*, 22.
3. The clues describe the ox (Dümmler, *Aenigmata anglica*, 23) rather than the bull (Glorie, *CCSL*, vol. 133, 357).

APPENDIX IX

The Vatican Collection

Preface (S)[1]

Section 1: Cosmological Motifs
1. De caelo (heaven), B60 (heaven) [6]
2. De sole (sun), B55 (sun) [6]
3. De luna (moon), B59 (moon) [6]
4. De stellis (stars), B62 (stars) [6]
5. De uento (wind), B41 (wind) [6]
6. De pluia (rain), B49 (rain) [6]
7. De glacie (ice), B38 (ice) [6]
8. Glaties (ice), S10 (ice) [3][2]
9. Niuis (snow), S11 (snow) [3]
10. Nebula (fog), S8 (fog) [3]

Section 2: Miscellanea (with a predominance of instruments)
11. Aqua piscis (water [and] fish), S12 (river and fish) [3]
12. Piscis (fish), B30 (fish) [6]
13. Hamus (hook), S54 (hook) [3]
14. Sal (salt), B3 (salt) [6]
15. Pons (bridge), S62 (bridge) [3]
16. Nauis (ship), B11 (ship) [6]
17. Nauis (ship), S13 (ship) [2][3]
18. Anchora (anchor), S61 (anchor) [3]
19. Rana (frog), S19 (frog) [3]
20. Testudo (tortoise), S20 (tortoise) [3]

---

1. Abbreviated letters indicate the sources from which the compiler drew the riddles: S stands for Symphosius; A, for Aldhelm, and B, for Bern. The title in Latin corresponds to that found in Vatican City, Reg. Lat. 1553 and its translation is offered within parentheses. The second translation that is added corresponds to that offered by the original riddle source; in some cases this may significantly vary from that offered in the Vatican version.
2. From Riddle 8 onwards, the scribe provides the solution without the preposition *de*.
3. The first line of this riddle is missing and so is the last of *Enigma* 71.

21. Coclea (snail), S18 (snail) [3]
22. Balneum (bath-house),
    S90 (bath-house) [3]
23. Tubus (pipe),
    S72 (pipe) [3]
24. Poteus (well), S71 (well) [3]
25. Uissica (bag), B7 (bag) [6]
26. Uter (bellows),
    S73 (bellows) [3]
27. Spongia (sponge),
    B32 (sponge) [6]
28. Spongia (sponge),
    S63 (sponge) [3]
29. Olla (pot), B1 (pot) [6]

Section 3: Agricultural Motifs
30. Malua (mallow),
    S41 (mallow) [3]
31. Beta (beet), S42 (beet) [3]
32. Cucurbita (gourd),
    S43 (gourd) [3]
33. Terra (earth),
    B45 (earth) [6]
34. Terra (earth), A1 (earth) [4]
35. Tegula (roof-tile),
    S6 (roof-tile) [3]
36. Mola (millstone),
    B9 (millstone) [6]
37. Grano (grain),
    B12 (grain) [6]
38. Flagellum (whip),
    S66 (whip) [3]
39. Farina (flour),
    S52 (flour) [3]
40. Cribro (sieve),
    B17 (sieve) [6]

41. Vitis (vine), B13 (vine) [6]
42. Vinum (wine),
    B50 (wine) [6]
43. Vinum (wine),
    B63 (wine) [6]
44. Mel (honey),
    B20 (honey) [6]
45. Apis (bee), B21 (bees) [6]
46. Conditum (spiced wine),
    S83 (spiced wine) [3]
47. Vinu(m) in aceto uersu(m)
    (wine turned to vinegar),
    S84 (wine turned to
    vinegar) [3]
48. Oliua (olive tree),
    B14 (olive tree) [6]
49. Palma (palm tree),
    B15 (palm tree) [6]
50. Cedrus (cedar),
    B16 (citron fruit) [6]
51. Castanea (chestnut),
    B47 (chestnut) [6]
52. Nimpha (water container),
    B19 (pitch) [6][4]
53. Edera (ivy),
    B31 (water container) [6]
54. Edere (ivy), B39 (ivy) [6]
55. Scopa (broom),
    B18 (broom) [6]
56. Scopa (broom),
    S80 (broom) [3]

Section 4: Plants
57. Rosa (rose), B34 (rose) [6]
58. Rosa (rose), S45 (rose) [3]
59. Lilium (lily), B35 (lilies) [6]

---

4. The clues of Riddle 52 clearly describe pitch. The title mistakenly alludes to the subsequent riddle. The same discrepancy between the text and the title-solution is observed in Riddles 53 and 81.

60. Crocum (saffron flower), B36 (saffron flower) [6]
61. **Vermiculi siricis formati (little worms that make silk)**, B43 (silkworms) [6]
62. **Siricum (silkworm)**, B28 (silkworm) [6]
63. Viola (violet), B33 (violet) [6]
64. Synapis (mustard), B26 (mustard) [6]
65. Papauer (poppy), S40 (poppy) [3]
66. Paparium (papyrus wick), B27 (papyrus wick) [6][5]
67. Fenum (hay), S50 (hay) [3]
68. Alium (onion), B51 (onion) [6][6]
69. Cepa (onion), S44 (onion) [3]
70. Piper (pepper), B37 (pepper) [6]
71. Piper (pepper), A40 (pepper) [5]

Section 5: Miscellanea (with a predominance of instruments)
72. Scamnum (bench), B4 (bench) [6]
73. Mensa (table), B5 (table) [6]
74. Ouo pullus (chicken in egg), B8 (egg) [6][7]
75. Item (idem), S14 (chicken in egg) [3]

76. Calix (goblet), B6 (goblet) [6]
77. Ignis (fire), B23 (fire spark) [6][8]
78. No title, B57 (sun) [6]
79. Fumus (smoke), S7 (smoke) [3]
80. Luscus (one-eyed), S95 (one-eyed man selling garlic) [3]
81. Verbum (word), B56 (sun) [6]
82. Littera (letter), B25 (letters) [6]
83. Membrana (parchment), B24 (parchment) [6]
84. Lanterna (lantern), S67 (lantern) [3]
85. Lucerna (lamp), B2 (lamp) [6]
86. Umbra (shadow), B61 (shadow) [6]
87. Item (idem), S97 (shadow)
88. Speculum (mirror), B29 (mirror) [6]

Section 6: Animals
A) Small animals/insects
89. Apes (bee), A20 (bee) [5]
90. Formica (ant), S22 (ant) [3]
91. Musca (fly), S23 (fly) [3]
92. Gurgulio (weevil), S24 (weevil) [3]

---

5. On "paparium" as a misreading of "pap[irum igni]arum," the wick made from the papyrus plant, see p. 279 (n. 598) of this book.
6. Despite the solution "garlic," the clues clearly refer to the onion.
7. The heading of this riddle seems to be a distorted version of "pullus in ouo" (chicken in egg), as offered by Symphosius's *Enigma* 12.
8. Riddles 77 and 78 are not separated in the manuscript.

B) Birds
93. Grus (crane),
    S26 (crane) [3]
94. Gallus (rooster),
    A26 (rooster) [5]
95. Pauo (peacock),
    A14 (peacock) [4]
96. Cornix (crow),
    S27 (crow) [3]
97. Vespertilio (bat),
    S28 (bat) [3]

C) Big Quadrupeds/Wild Beasts
98. Centaurus (centaur),
    S39 (centaur) [3]
99. Taurus (bull), S32 (bull) [3]
100. Foenix (phoenix),
    S31 (phoenix) [3]
101. Mula (she-mule),
    S37 (she-mule) [3]
102. Lupus (wolf),
    S33 (wolf) [3]

APPENDIX X

The Exeter Book Riddles

GROUP 1 (Riddles 1-40)

Section 1: Cosmological Motifs
1-2-3. "Storm," wind and God (104)
4. Uncertain (12)
5. **Shield** (14)
6. Sun (10)

Section 2: Zoological Motifs
A) Birds
7. Swan (9)
8. Nightingale (11)
9. Cuckoo (12)
10. Barnacle goose (11)
11. **Cup of wine** (10)

B) Quadrupeds
12. Ox (15)
13. **Ten chickens** (11)
14. Aurochs (19)
15. Vixen (29)

Section 3: Tools I
16. Anchor (10)
17. Quiver (11)
18. Jug (4)
19. Ship (9)
20. Sword (35, incomplete)

21. Plow (15)
22. **Charles's Wain** (21)
23. Bow (16)
24. **Jay** (10)
25. Onion (11)
26. Gospel book (28)
27. Mead (17)
28. Ale (13)
29. **Sun and moon** (14)
30a. Cross (9)
31. Bagpipe (24)
32. Ship (14)
33. **Iceberg** (13)
34. Rake (9)
35. Mail coat (14)
36. Ship (14)
37. Bellows (8)
38. **Bullock** (7)
39. **Cloud** (29)

Cosmological Coda
40. Creation (107, incomplete)

GROUP 2 (Riddles 41-59)

Cosmological Motif
41. Water (8)

Section 4: Sexual riddles
  42. Rooster and hen (17)
  43. Soul and body (16)
  44. Key and lock (7)
  45. Dough and oven (5)
  46. Lot and his family (7)

Section 5: Tools II
 A) Writing
  47. Bookworm and parchment (6)
  48. Paten or chalice (8)
  49. Book chest (11)
  50. Fire (10)
  51. Pen and fingers (7)

 B) Wooden objects
  52. Flail (7)
  53. Battering ram (13)
  54. Churn (12)
  55. Cross (16)
  56. Web and loom (12)
  57. Swallows (6)
  58. Well sweep (15)
  59. Chalice (18)[1]

- - - - - - - - - - - - -

GROUP 3 (Riddles 61-95)

Section 5: Tools II (continued)
 C) Craftsmanship
  61. Helmet (9)
  62. Borer (9)
  63. Glass goblet (15)

  64. Ship (6)
  65. Onion (6)
  66. Creation (10)

Section 6: Miscellanea
  67. Gospel book? (16)
  68-69. Iceberg (3)
  70a. Lyre (4, incomplete)
  70b. Lighthouse? (2, incomplete)
  71. Sword (10)
  72. Ox (18)
  73. Spear (29)
  74. Swan (5)
  75-76. Piss (2)
  77. Oyster (8)
  78. Crab (8)
  79-80. Horn (9)
  81. Weathervane (12)
  82. Uncertain (6)
  83. Gold (14)
  84. Water (56)
  85. Fish and river (7)
  86. One-eyed garlic seller (7)
  87. Bellows (8)
  88. Inkhorn (32)
  89. Bottle? (10)
  90. Uncertain (Latin riddle) (5)
  91. Key (11)
  92. Beech (7)
  93. Inkhorn (35)
  94. Creation (6)

Writing Coda?
  95. Book (13)

---

1. The discontinued line here indicates the separation of the two main riddling groups as they appear in the manuscript.

Bibliography

Primary Sources

Aberdeen Bestiary, The (http://www.abdn.ac.uk/bestiary/index.hti).

Alcuin. *Alcuini (Albini) carmina. MGH. PLAC*, vol. 1, edited by Ernst Dümmler, 160–351. Berlin: Weidmann, 1881.

———. *Alcuini sive Albini epistolae. MGH. Epistolae*, vol. 4, edited by Ernst Dümmler. Berlin: Weidmann, 1895.

———. *De orthographia. MGH. Grammatici latini*, vol. 7, edited by Heinrich Keil, 295–312. Leipzig: Teubner, 1880.

———. *De rhetorica*. Edited by W.S. Howell. *The Rhetoric of Alcuin and Charlemagne*. Princeton, NJ: Princeton University Press, 1941. Reprint, New York: Russell & Russell, 1965.

Aldhelm. *Aenigmata Aldhelmi. CCSL*, vol. 133, edited by Fr. Glorie, with an English translation by J. H. Pitman, 359–540.

———. *Aldhelmi opera. MGH. Auctores antiquissimi*, vol. 15, edited by Rudolph Ehwald. Berlin: Weidmann, 1919.

André, Jacques, ed. and trans. *Isidore de Séville: Étymologies, Livre XII*. Paris: Les Belles Lettres, 1986.

Andrés Sanz, María Adelaida, ed. *Isidori episcopi Hispalensis Liber differentiarum (II). CCSL*, vol. 111A. Turnhout: Brepols, 2006.

Anlezark, Daniel, ed. and trans. *The Old English Dialogues of Solomon and Saturn*. Cambridge: Brewer, 2009.

———. *Old Testament Narratives*. Cambridge, MA: Harvard University Press, 2011.

Augustine, St. [*De civitate Dei contra paganos*]. *St Augustine: The City of God against the Pagans*. Edited and translated by George E. McCracken, et al. 7 vols. Cambridge, MA: Harvard University Press, 1957–72.

Babcock, Robert Gary, ed. and trans. *The Well-Laden Ship: Egbert of Liège*. Cambridge, MA: Harvard University Press, 2013.

Baker, Peter S., and Michael Lapidge, eds. and transs. *Byrhtferth's Enchiridion*, EETS, s.s. 15. Oxford: Oxford University Press, 1995.

Banham, Debby, ed. and trans. *Monasteriales Indicia: The Anglo-Saxon Monastic Sign Language*. 1991. Reprint, Pinner: Anglo-Saxon Books, 1993.

Barlow, Frank, ed. and trans., *The Life of King Edward who Rests at Westminster*. Oxford: Oxford University Press, 1992.

Barney, Stephen A., W. J. Lewis, J. A. Beach, and Oliver Berghof, trans. *The Etymologies of Isidore of Seville*. Cambridge: Cambridge University Press, 2006.

Bately, Janet M., ed. *The Anglo-Saxon Chronicle: A Collaborative Edition*. Vol. 3 (MS A). Cambridge: Brewer, 1986.

Baum, Paull F., trans. *Anglo-Saxon Riddles of the Exeter Book*. Durham, NC: Duke University Press, 1963.

Bayless, Martha. "Alcuin's *Disputatio Pippini* and the Early Medieval Riddle Tradition." In *Humour, History and Politics in Late Antiquity and the Early Middle Ages*, edited by Guy Halsall, 157–78. Cambridge: Cambridge University Press, 2002.

Bayless, Martha, and Michael Lapidge, eds. and trans. *Collectanea Pseudo-Bedae*. Dublin: Institute for Advanced Studies, 1998.

Bede. *Bedae Venerabilis Opera, Pars I, Opera Didascalica*. CCSL, vol. 123A, edited by Charles W. Jones. Turnhout: Brepols, 1975.

———. *In primam partem Samuhelis libri IIII*. CCSL, vol. 119, edited by David Hurst. Turnhout: Brepols, 1962.

———. *In principium Genesim*. CCSL, vol. 118A, edited by Charles W. Jones. Turnhout: Brepols, 1967.

Bern Riddles. *Aenigmata Hexasticha*. MGH, PLAC, vol. 4.2, edited by Karl Strecker, 732–59. Berlin: Weidmann, 1923.

———. *Aenigmata in Dei nomine Tullii*. CCSL, vol. 133A, edited by Fr. Glorie, with a German translation by K. J. Minst, 541–610.

Bischoff, Bernhard, and Michael Lapidge, eds. and trans. *Biblical Commentaries from the Canterbury School of Theodore and Hadrian*. Cambridge: Cambridge University Press, 1995.

Boniface. *Aenigmata Bonifatii*. CCSL, vol. 133, edited by Fr. Glorie, with a German translation by K. J. Minst, 273–343. Turnhout: Brepols, 1968.

———. *Bonifatii carmina*. MGH. PLAC, vol. 1, edited by Ernst Dümmler. Berlin: Weidmann, 1881.

———. *Bonifatius (Vynfreth). Ars grammatica. Ars metrica*. CCSL, vol. 133B, edited by George John Gebauer and Bengt Löfstedt. Turnhout: Brepols, 1980.

———. *S. Bonifatii et Lullii Epistolae*. MGH, Epistolae Selectae, vol. 1. Edited by Michael Tangl. Berlin: Weidmann, 1916.

Buecheler, Franz, and Alexander Riese, eds. *Anthologia latina: sive poesis latinae supplementum*. 3 vols. in 5. Leipzig, 1894–1926.

Camerarius, Joachimus. *Elementis Rhetoricae*. Basel, 1541.

Campbell, Alistair, ed. *The Chronicle of Æthelweard*. London: Nelson, 1962.

Campos Ruiz, J., ed. *Juan de Bíclaro, Obispo de Gerona: su Vida y su Obra*. Madrid: CSIC, 1960.

———, ed. *Reglas monásticas de la España visigoda. Santos padres españoles*. 2 vols. Madrid: Biblioteca de Autores Cristianos, 1971.

Carmody, Francis J., ed. "Physiologus Latinus Versio Y." *University of California Publications in Classical Philology* 12 (1941): 95–134.

Castalio, Iosephus. *Aenigmata Symphosii poetae*. Rome, 1581.

Cockayne, Rev. Thomas Oswald, ed. and trans. *Leechdoms, Wortcunning and Starcraft of Early England*. 2 vols. London: The Holland Press, 1961.

Codoñer Merino, Carmen, ed. *El 'De Viris Illustribus' de Ildefonso de Toledo. Estudio y edición crítica*. Salamanca: Universidad de Salamanca, 1972.

———, ed. *Differentiae de Isidoro de Sevilla. Libro I*. Paris: Belles Lettres, 1992.

Coleman, Robert, ed. *Vergil: Eclogues*. Cambridge: Cambridge University Press, 1977.

Colgrave, Bertram, and R. A. B. Mynors, eds. *Bede's Ecclesiastical History of the English People*. Oxford: Clarendon Press, 1969.

Cross, James E., and Thomas D. Hill, eds. and transs. *The Prose Solomon and Saturn and Adrian and Ritheus*. Toronto: University of Toronto Press, 1982.

Curley, Michael J., trans. *Physiologus*. Austin: University of Texas Press, 1979.

Daly, L. W., and W. Suchier, eds. *Altercatio Hadriani Augusti et Epicteti Philosophi*. Urbana: University of Illinois Press, 1939.

Dimock, James F. *Topographia Hibernica, Giraldi Cambrensis Opera*. London, 1867.

Dobbie, Elliott Van Kirk, ed. *The Anglo-Saxon Minor Poems*. ASPR, vol. 6. New York: Columbia University Press, 1942.

Dümmler, E., ed. "Lorscher Rätsel." *ZfdA* 22 (1878): 258–63.

Ebert, Adolf, ed. "Über Die Räthselpoesie der Angelsachsen, insbesondere die Aenigmata des Tatwine und Eusebius." *Berichte über die Verhandlungen der Königlich-sächsischen Gesellschaft der Wissenschaften zu Leipzig, philologisch-historische Classe*. Phil.-Hist. Classe, vol. 29 (1877): 20–56.

Elfassi, Jacques, ed. *Isidori Hispalensis Episcopi, Synonyma*. CCSL, vol. 111B. Turnhout: Brepols, 2009.

Eugenius of Toledo. *Eugenii Toletani episcopi carmina et epistulae*. MGH. Auctores Antiquissimi, vol. 14, edited by Friedrich Vollmer. Berlin: Weidmann, 1905.

Eusebius (Hwætberht). *Aenigmata Eusebii*. CCSL, vol. 133, edited by Fr. Glorie, with an English translation by Erika von Erhardt-Siebold, 209–71.

Fitzpatrick, Mary Cletus, ed. and trans. *Lactanti de Ave Phoenice*. Philadelphia: University of Pennsylvania Press, 1933.

Fontaine, Jacques, ed. and trans. *Isidore de Séville: Traité de la nature*. Bordeaux: Féret et Fils, 1960.

Förster, Max. "Die altenglische Glossenhandscrhift Plantinus 32 (Antwerpen) und Additional 32246 (London)." *Anglia 41* (1917): 94–161.

———. "Die Lösung des ae. Prosarätsels." *Archiv* 116 (1906): 367–71.

———. "Ein altenglisches Prosa-Rätsel." *Archiv* 115 (1905): 392–93.

Friedreich, J. B. *Geschichte des Räthsels*. Dresden, 1860.

Fritzsche, O. F., ed. *Lactantius*. Vol. 2. Leipzig, 1845.

Fulk, R. D., ed. and trans. *The Beowulf Manuscript*. Cambridge, MA: Harvard University Press, 2010.

Fulk, R. D., Robert E. Bjork, and John D. Niles, eds. *Klaeber's Beowulf and the Fight at Finnsburg*. Toronto: Toronto University Press, 2008.

Galloway, Andrew. "The Rhetoric of Riddling in Late-Medieval England: The 'Oxford' Riddles, the *Secretum philosophorum*, and the Riddles in *Piers Plowman*." *Speculum* 70 (1995): 68–105. http://dx.doi.org/10.2307/2864706

Garmonsway, G. N., ed. *Ælfric's Colloquy*. London: Methuen, 1947.

Giles, Rev. Dr. [J. A.], ed. *Anecdota Bedae, Lanfranci, et aliorum*. London, 1851.

Giles, J. A., ed. *Sancti Aldhelmi opera*. Oxford, 1844.

Glorie, Fr., ed. *Collectiones aenigmatum merovingicae aetatis*. CCSL, vols. 133 and 133A. Turnhout: Brepols, 1968.

Godman, Peter, ed. and trans. *Poetry of the Carolingian Renaissance*. London: Duckworth, 1985.

Green, Peter, ed. and trans. *The Poems of Catullus: A Bilingual Edition*. Berkeley: University of California Press, 2005.

Gulick, Charles Burton, ed. and trans. *Athenaeus: The Deipnosophists*. 7 vols. Cambridge, MA: Harvard University Press, 1927–61.

Hall, A., ed. *Commentarii de scriptoribus Britannicis, auctore Joanne Lelando Londinate*. 2 vols. Oxford, 1709.

Halsall, Maureen, ed. and trans. *The Old English Rune Poem: A Critical Edition*. Toronto: University of Toronto Press, 1981.

Häse, Angelika. *Mittelalterliche Bücherverzeichnisse aus Kloster Lorsch: Einleitung, Edition und Kommentar*. Wiesbaden: Harrassowitz, 2002.

Haycock, Marged, ed. and trans. *Legendary Poems from the Book of Taliesin*. Aberystwyth: CMCS, 2007.

Herren, Michael W., ed. *Hisperica Famina I: The A-Text*. Toronto: Pontifical Institute of Mediaeval Studies, 1974.

Herwagen, Johann [the younger]. *Opera Bedae Venerabilis presbyteri Anglo-Saxonis*. 8 vols in 4. Basel, 1563.

Heumann, August. *Caelii Firminiani Lactantii Symphosium*. Hannover, 1722.

Kay, N. M., ed. and trans. *Epigrams from the Anthologia Latina: Text, Translation and Commentary*. London: Duckworth, 2006.

Kortekaas, G. A. A. *Commentary on the Historia Apollonii Regis Tyri*. Leiden: Brill, 2007.

———, ed. *The Story of Apollonius, King of Tyre: a Study of its Greek Origin and an Edition of the two oldest Latin Recensions*. Leiden: Brill, 2004.

Krapp, George Philip, ed. *The Junius Manuscript. ASPR*, vol. 1. New York: Columbia University Press, 1931.

———, ed. *The Vercelli Book. ASPR*, vol. 2. New York: Columbia University Press, 1932.

Krapp, George Philip, and Dobbie Elliott van Kirk, eds. *The Exeter Book. ASPR*, vol. 3. New York: Columbia University Press, 1936.

Lapidge, Michael, ed. and trans. *The Cult of St Swithun*. Oxford: Clarendon Press, 2003.

———, ed. and trans. *Byrhtferth of Ramsey: The Lives of St Oswald and St Ecgwine*. Oxford: Clarendon, 2009.

Lapidge, Michael, and James L. Rosier, eds. and trans. *Aldhelm: The Poetic Works*. Cambridge: Cambridge University Press, 1985.

Lapidge, Michael, and Michael Herren, eds. and trans. *Aldhelm: The Prose Works*. Cambridge: Brewer, 1979.

Lapidge, Michael, and Michael Winterbottom, eds. and trans. *Wulfstan of Winchester: The Life of St Æthelwold*. Oxford: Clarendon, 1991.

Lawson, Christopher M., ed. *Sancti Isidori Episcopi Hispalensis: De Ecclesiasticis Officiis. CCSL*, vol. 113. Turnhout: Brepols, 1989.

Leary, T. J., ed. and trans. *Martial: Book XIII, The Xenia*. London: Duckworth, 2001.

———, ed., *Symphosius: The Aenigmata. An Introduction, Text and Commentary*. London: Bloomsbury Academic, 2014.

Lemaire, N. E., ed. *Poetae latini minores: De re hortensi et villatica carmina*, vol. 6. Paris, 1826.

Liebermann, Felix, ed. "Gerefa." *Anglia 9* (1886): 251–66.

Lindsay, W. M. *The Corpus Glossary*. Cambridge: Cambridge University Press, 1921.

———, ed. *Isidori Hispalensis Episcopi Etymologiarum sive Originum Libri XX.* Oxford: Clarendon Press, 1911.

Logeman, H., ed. *The Rule of St. Benet.* EETS, o.s. 90. London, 1888. Reprint, Kraus, 1988.

Lorsch Riddles. *Aenigmata anglica, MGH, PLAC*, vol. 1, edited by Ernst Dümmler, 20–23. Berlin: Weidmann, 1881.

———. *Aenigmata "laureshamensia." CCSL*, vol. 133, edited by Fr. Glorie, with a German translation by K. J. Minst, 345–58.

Lucas, Peter J., ed. *Exodus.* London: Methuen, 1977.

Mackie, W. S., ed. and trans. *The Exeter Book, Part II.* EETS, o.s. 194. London: Oxford University Press, 1934.

Mandolfo, C., ed. *Eucherii Lugdunensis: Formulae spiritalis intelligentiae, Instructionum libri duo. CCSL*, vol. 66. Turnhout: Brepols, 2004.

Marco, Maria de, ed. *Ars Tatuini. CCSL*, vol. 133. Turnhout: Brepols, 1968.

Martín, José Carlos, ed. *Scripta de vita Isidori Hispalensis episcopi. CCSL*, vol. 113B. Turnhout: Brepols, 2006.

May, Herbert G., and Bruce M. Metzger, eds. *The New Oxford Annotated Bible with the Apocrypha.* New York: Oxford University Press, 1977.

Meyer, Wilhelm, ed. *Gesammelte Abhandlungen zur mittellateinischen Rythmik.* 2 vols. Berlin: Weidmann, 1905.

———, ed. "Über die Beobachtung des Wortaccentes in der altlateinischen Poesie." *Abhandlungen der Philosophisch-Philologischen Classe der königlich Bayerischen Akademie der Wissenschaften*, 17 (1886): 412–30.

Mommsen, Theodor, ed. *C. Iulii Solini Collectanea rerum memorabilium.* Berlin, 1895. Reprint, Weidmann, 1958.

Mone, F., ed. "Zweite Räthselsamlung," *Anzeiger für Kunde der deutschen Vorzeit* 8 (1839): 217–29.

Muir, Bernard J., ed. *The Exeter Anthology of Old English Poetry: An Edition of Exeter Dean and Chapter MS 3501.* 2 vols. Exeter: University of Exeter Press, 1994.

Muir, Bernard J. *The Exeter DVD: The Exeter Anthology of Old English Poetry.* Exeter: Exeter University Press, 2006.

Müllenhoff, K., and W. Scherer. *Denkmäler deutscher Poesie und Prosa aus dem VIII–XII Jahrhundert*. Berlin, 1873.

Mynors, R. A. B., ed. *Virgil: Georgics*. Oxford: Clarendon Press, 1990.

Napier, Arthur S., ed. *Old English Glosses, chiefly Unpublished*. Oxford: Clarendon, 1900.

———, ed. *The Old English Version of the Enlarged Rule of Chrodegang, together with the Latin Original*. EETS, o.s. 150. London: Kegan Paul, 1916. Reprint, Kraus, 1988.

Ohl, Raymond Theodore, ed. and trans. "The Enigmas of Symphosius." Unpublished PhD Dissertation. Philadelphia, 1928.

Omont, Henri. "Poème anonyme sur les lettres de l'alphabet." *Bibliothèque de l'École des Chartes* 42 (1881): 429–41. http://dx.doi.org/10.3406/bec.1881.447014

Oroz Reta, José, and Manuel-A. Marcos Casquero, eds. and trans. *San Isidoro de Sevilla: Etimologías*. With an introduction by Manuel C. Díaz y Díaz. 2 vols. Madrid: Biblioteca de Autores Cristianos, 1993.

Pascal, Paul, ed. "'The Institutionum Disciplinae' of Isidore of Seville." *Traditio* 13 (1957): 425–31.

Paton, W. R., ed. and trans. *The Greek Anthology*, vol. 5. Cambridge, MA: Harvard University Press, 1979.

Peck, A. L., ed. and trans. *Aristotle: History of Animals, Books I–III*. 1965. Reprint, Cambridge, MA: Harvard University Press, 2001.

Perionius, Joachimus. *Simphosii ueteris poetae elegantissimi erudita iuxta ac arguta et festiua aenigmata*. Paris, 1533.

Perry, Ben Edwin, ed. *Babrius and Phaedrus*. Cambridge, MA: Harvard University Press, 1965.

Pinsker, Hans, and Waltraud Ziegler, eds. and transs. *Die altenglischen Rätsel des Exeterbuchs*. Heidelberg: Carl Winter, 1985.

Pithou, Pierre. *Epigrammata et poematia vetera*. Paris, 1590.

Pitman, James Hall, ed. and trans. *The Riddles of Aldhelm*. New Haven, CT: Yale University Press, 1925.

Pliny. *Natural History* [*Historia naturalis*]. 10 vols. Ed. and trans. H. Rackham. London: Heinemann, 1967.

Porter, David W., ed. *The Antwerp-London Glossaries, Volume 1: Texts and Indexes*. Toronto: Pontifical Institute of Mediaeval Studies, 2011.

Riese, Alexander, ed. *Anthologia Latina sive poesis latinae supplementum*. Leipzig, 1869.

Rosier, James L., ed. *The Vitellius Psalter*. Ithaca, NY: Cornell University Press, 1962.

Schipper, William, ed. *Hrabani Mauri: De rerum naturis*. Turnhout: Brepols, forthcoming.

Shackleton Bailey, D. R., ed. *Anthologia latina I: Carmina in codicibus scripta 1, Libri Salmasiani aliorumque carmina*. Stuttgart: Teubner, 1982.

Smith, Albert H., ed. *Three Northumbrian Poems: Cædmon's Hymn, Bede's Death Song, and the Leiden Riddle*. London: Methuen, 1933.

Stevenson, Joseph, ed. *Chronicon monasterii de Abindon. Volume 1: From the Foundation of the Monastery until the Norman Conquest*. London, 1858. Reprint, Cambridge: Cambridge University Press, 2012.

———, ed. *Chronicon monasterii de Abindon. Volume 2: From the Norman Conquest until the Accession of Richard the First*. London, 1858. Reprint, Cambridge: Cambridge University Press, 2012.

Strecker, Karl, ed. *Codex epistolarum tegernseensium (Froumund). MGH. Epistolae selectae*, vol. 3. Berlin: Weidmann, 1925.

Stubbs, W., ed. *Memorials of St Dunstan*. London, 1874.

Suchier, Walther, ed. *Das mittellateinische Gespräch Adrian und Epictitus und verwandten Texten (Joca Monachorum)*. Tübingen: Niemeyer, 1955.

Swan, Charles, ed. *Gesta romanorum*. Revised and corrected by Wynnard Hooper. London: Bell, 1905.

Symons, Thomas, ed. and trans. *Regularis Concordia*. London: Nelson, 1953.

Symphosius. *Aenigmata Symphosii. CCSL*, vol. 133A, edited by Fr. Glorie, with an English translation by R. T. Ohl, 611–723.

———. *Aenigmata Symposii: la fondazione dell'enigmistica come genere poetico*. Edited by Manuela Bergamin. Florence: SISMEL-Edizioni del Galluzzo, 2005.

Tangl, Michael, ed. *Die Briefe des heiligen Bonifatius und Lullus. MGH. Epistolae selectae*, vol. 1. Berlin: Weidmann, 1916.

Tatwine. *Aenigmata Tatuini. CCSL*, vol. 133, edited by Fr. Glorie, with an English translation by Erika von Erhardt-Siebold, 165–208.

Thorpe, Benjamin, ed. *Codex Exoniensis: A Collection of Anglo-Saxon Poetry, from a Manuscript in the Library of the Dean and Chapter of Exeter*. London, 1842.

Trautmann, Moritz, ed. *Die altenglischen Rätsel (Die Rätsel des Exeterbuchs)*. Heidelberg: Carl Winter, 1915.

Treharne, Elaine, ed. *Old and Middle English c. 890–c. 1450: An Anthology*. Oxford: Blackwell, 2000.

Tupper, Frederick, ed. *The Riddles of the Exeter Book*. Boston: Ginn, 1910.

Voigt, Ernst, ed. *Ecbasis Captivi, das älteste Thierepos des Mittelalters*. Strassburg, 1875.

———, ed. "Prouerbia rustici." *Romanische Forschungen* 3 (1887): 633–41.

Warner, G. F., and H. A. Wilson, eds. *The Benedictional of St Æthelwold, Bishop of Winchester 963–984*. Oxford: Roxburghe Club, 1910.

Weber, Robert, ed. *Biblia sacra: iuxta vulgatam versionem*. Stutgart: Deutsche Bibelgesellschaft, 1969.

Wernsdorf, Johann Christian, ed. *Poetae latini minores*, vol. 6. Helmstadt, 1794.

Whitman, F. H., ed. and trans. *Old English Riddles*. Ottawa: Canadian Federation for the Humanities, 1982.

Williams, Mary Jane McDonald, ed. and trans. "The Riddles of Tatwine and Eusebius." Unpublished PhD dissertation, University of Michigan, 1974.

Williams, T. W. *Somerset Medieval Libraries*. Bristol, 1877.

Williamson, Craig, ed. *The Old English Riddles of the Exeter Book*. Chapel Hill: University of North Carolina Press, 1977.

Winterbottom, M., and Rodney M. Thomson, eds. and transs. *William of Malmesbury. Gesta pontificum Anglorum, Vol. 1: Text and Translation*. Oxford: Clarendon Press, 2007.

Wyatt, A. J., ed. *Old English Riddles*. Boston: Heath, 1912.

Yarza Urquiola, Valeriano, and Carmen Codoñer Merino, eds. *Ildefonsi Toletani episcopi De virginitate Sanctae Mariae, De cognitione baptismi, De itinere deserti, De viris illustribus. CCSL*, vol. 114A. Turnhout: Brepols, 2007.

Ziolkowski, Jan M., ed. and trans. *The Cambridge Songs (Carmina Cantabrigensia)*. New York: Garland, 1994.

Zupitza, Julius, ed. *Ælfrics Grammatik und Glossar*. Berlin, 1880.

Secondary Sources

Alcamesi, Filippa. "The Sibylline Acrostic in Anglo-Saxon Manuscripts: The Augustinian Translation and the Other Versions." In Bremmer and Dekker, *Foundations of Learning*, 147–73.

Allen, Michael J. B., and Daniel G. Calder. *Sources and Analogues of Old English Poetry: The Major Latin Texts in Translation*. Cambridge: Brewer, 1976.

Alonso, Dámaso. "La primitiva épica francesa a la luz de una nota Emilianense." *Revista de filología española* 37 (1953): 1–94.

Anderson, James E. "Exeter Latin Riddle 90: A Liturgical Vision." *Viator* 23 (1992): 73–93.

———. "Two Spliced Riddles of the Exeter Book." In *Geardagum* 5 (1983): 57–75.

Andrés Sanz, María Adelaida, et al. "Isidorus Hispalensis Ep." In *La trasmissione dei Testi Latini del Medioevo. Mediaeval Latin Texts and their Transmission*. TE.TRA. 2, edited by P. Chiesa and L. Castaldi, 274–417. Florence: SISMEL-Edizioni del Galluzzo, 2005.

Archibald, Elizabeth. *Apollonius of Tyre: Medieval and Renaissance Themes and Variations*. Cambridge: Brewer, 1991.

Baldwin, B. "Some Pleasures of Later Roman Literature: The African Contribution." *Acta classica* 32 (1989): 37–57.

Baldzuhn, Michael. *Schulbücher im Trivium des Mittelalters und der frühen Neuzeit*, vol. 2. Berlin: De Gruyter, 2009. http://dx.doi.org/10.1515/9783110217346.

Bannister, Henry Marriott. *Monumenti vaticani di paleografia musicale latina*. Leipzig: Harrassowitz, 1913.

Barber, Richard, trans. *Bestiary: Being an English Version of the Bodleian Library, Oxford, MS Bodley 764*. 1993. Reprint, Woodbridge: Boydell, 2006.

Barker, Katherine. "*Usque Domnomiam*: the Setting of Aldhelm's *Carmen rhythmicum*, Literature, Language and the Liminal." In Barker and Brooks, *Aldhelm and the See of Sherborne*, 15–54.

Barker, Katherine, and Nicholas P. Brooks, eds. *Aldhelm and the See of Sherborne: Essays to Celebrate the Founding of the Bishopric*. Oxford: Oxbow Books, 2009.

Barnouw, A. J. "Review of *Die altenglischen Rätsel (Die Rätsel des Exeterbuchs)* by Moritz Trautmann." *Neophilologus* 3 (1917): 77–78.

Baxter, Ron. *Bestiaries and their Users in the Middle Ages*. Phoenix Mill: Sutton, 1998.

Beare, Rhona. "Earl Godwin's Son as a Barnacle Goose." *N&Q* 44 (1997): 4–6. http://dx.doi.org/10.1093/nq/44.1.4

——. "Gerald of Wales on the Barnacle Goose." *N&Q* 44 (1997): 459–62. http://dx.doi.org/10.1093/nq/44.4.459

——. "Is the Barnacle Goose Selfish, and Is It Harold?" *N&Q* 50 (2003): 10–11. http://dx.doi.org/10.1093/nq/50.1.10

——. "Which of Godwin's Sons Was Called a Barnacle Goose?" *N&Q* 46 (1999): 5–6. http://dx.doi.org/10.1093/nq/46.1.5

Bergamin, Manuela. "Eucherio di Lione e la poesia epigrammatica. Materiali per un'indagine." *Incontri triestini di filologia classica* 6 (2006–07): 313–31.

——. "Il riccio e la rosa. Vicende di immagini e parole dall'antico al tardoantico (a proposito di Simposio, aenig. 29 e 45)." *Incontri triestini di filologia classica* 3 (2003–04): 199–214.

Bergmann, Rolf, and Stefanie Stricker, eds. *Katalog der althochdeutschen und altsächsischen Glossenhandschriften*. 6 vols. Berlin: De Gruyter, 2005. http://dx.doi.org/10.1515/9783110918250.

Biggs, Frederick M., Thomas D. Hill, and Paul E. Szarmach. *Sources of Anglo-Saxon Literary Culture: A Trial Version*. Binghamton, NY: Center for Medieval and Early Renaissance Studies, 1990.

Bischoff, Bernhard. "Bannita: 1. Syllaba, 2. Littera." In *Latin Script and Letters A. D. 400–900: Festschrift presented to Ludwig Bieler*, edited by J. J. O'Meara and B. Naumann, 207–12. Leiden: Brill, 1976.

———. "Centri scrittori e manoscritti mediatori di civiltà dal VI secolo all'età di Carlo Magno." In *Libri e lettori nel medioevo*, edited by G. Cavallo, 27–72. Bari: Laterza, 1977.

———. *Die Abtei Lorsch im Spiegel ihrer Handschriften*. 2nd rev. ed. Lorsch: Laurissa, 1989.

———. "Die europaeische Verbreitung der Werke Isidors von Sevilla." In *Isidoriana: colección de estudios sobre Isidoro de Sevilla, publicados con ocasión del XIV centenario de su nacimiento*, edited by Manuel C. Díaz y Díaz, 317–44. León: Centro de Estudios San Isidoro, 1961.

———. *Katalog der festländischen Handschriften des neunten Jahrhunderts: (mit Ausnahme der wisigotischen). Teil I: Aachen-Lambach*. Wiesbaden: Harrassowitz, 1998.

———. *Katalog der festländischen Handschriften des neunten Jahrhunderts (mit Ausnahme der wisigotischen). Teil II: Laon-Paderborn*. Wiesbaden: Harrassowitz, 2004.

———. *Manuscripts and Libraries in the Age of Charlemagne*. Translated by Michael Gorman. Cambridge: Cambridge University Press, 1994.

Bishop, T. A. M. "An Early Example of Insular Caroline." *Transactions of the Cambridge Bibliographical Society* 4 (1968): 396–400.

———. *English Caroline Minuscule*. Oxford: Clarendon, 1971.

———. "Notes on Cambridge Manuscripts, Part IV: Manuscripts connected with St Augustine's Canterbury." *Transactions of the Cambridge Bibliographical Society* 2 (1957): 323–36.

———. "Notes on Cambridge Manuscripts, Part V: Manuscripts connected with St Augustine's Canterbury, Continued." *Transactions of the Cambridge Bibliographical Society* 3 (1959): 93–95.

———. "Notes on Cambridge Manuscripts, Part VII: the Early Minuscule of Christ Church Canterbury." *Transactions of the Cambridge Bibliographical Society* 3 (1963): 413–23.

Bitterli, Dieter. "Alkuin von York und die angelsächsische Rätseldichtung." *Anglia 128* (2010): 4–20. http://dx.doi.org/10.1515/angl.2010.003.

———. "Exeter Book Riddle 15: Some Points for the Porcupine." *Anglia 120* (2002): 461–87.

———. *Say What I Am Called: The Old English Riddles of the Exeter Book and the Anglo-Latin Riddle Tradition*. Toronto: University of Toronto Press, 2009.

———. "Two Old English Prose Riddles of the Eleventh Century." In *Words, Words, Words: Philology and Beyond: Festschrift for Andreas Fischer on the Occasion of his 65th Birthday*, edited by Sarah Chevalier and Thomas Honegger, 1–11. Tübingen: Francke, 2012.

Blackburn, F. A. "*The Husband's Message* and the Accompanying Riddles of the Exeter Book." *JEGP* 3 (1900): 1–13. http://dx.doi.org/10.1093/res/IX.35.241

Blakeley, L. "Riddles 22 and 58 of the Exeter Book." *RES* 9 (1958): 241–52.

Bolton, W. F. *A History of Anglo-Latin Literature 597–1066*. Vol. 1: 597–740. Princeton, NJ: Princeton University Press, 1967.

Boyer, Blanche. "Insular Contribution to Medieval Literary Tradition on the Continent." *Classical Philology* 42 (1974): 209–22.

Bradley, S. A. J., trans. *Anglo-Saxon Poetry*. London: Dent, 1981.

Breeze, Andrew. "Old English *gop* 'Servant' in Riddle 49: Old Irish *gop* 'Snout.'" *Neophilologus* 79 (1995): 671–73. *http://dx.doi.org/10.1007/BF01126897*.

Bremmer, Rolf H., Jr. "The Anglo-Saxon Continental Mission and the Transfer of Encyclopaedic Knowledge." In Bremmer and Dekker, *Foundations of Learning*, 19–50.

Bremmer, Rolf H., Jr., and Kees Dekker, eds. *Foundations of Learning: The Transfer of Encyclopaedic Knowledge in the Early Middle Ages*. Leuven: Peeters, 2007.

Bremmer, Rolf H., Jr., and Kees Dekker. *Manuscripts in the Low Countries*. Tempe: Arizona Center for Medieval and Renaissance Studies, 2006.

Brett, Cyril. "Notes on Old and Middle English." *MLR* 22 (1927): 257–64. http://dx.doi.org/10.2307/3714637.

Brooks, Nicholas. *The Early History of the Church of Canterbury: Christ Church from 597 to 1066*. Leicester: Leicester University Press, 1984.

Brown, George Hardin. "The Dynamics of Literacy in Anglo-Saxon England." *Bulletin of the John Rylands University Library* 77 (1995): 109–42.

———. "The Psalms as the Foundation of Anglo-Saxon Learning." In *The Place of the Psalms in the Intellectual Culture of the Middle Ages*, edited by Nancy van Deusen, 1–24. Albany: State University of New York Press, 1999.

Brown, Giles. "Introduction: The Carolingian Renaissance." In McKitterick, *Carolingian Culture*, 1–51.

Bücheler, Franz. "Coniectanea." *Rheinisches Museum fur Philologie* 36 (1881): 329–42.

Budny, Mildred. *Insular, Anglo-Saxon, and Early Anglo-Norman Manuscript Art at Corpus Christi College, Cambridge: an Illustrated Catalogue*. 2 vols. Kalamazoo, MI: Medieval Institute Publications, 1997.

Bueno Alonso, Jorge Luis. "Actitudes anglosajonas hacia el humor: la caracterización del humor obsceno y sexual en los acertijos de Exeter Book." *Cuadernos del CEMYR* 12 (2004): 17–36.

Bullough, D. A. "The Educational Tradition in England from Alfred to Ælfric: Teaching *utriusque linguae*." *Settimane di studio del centro Italiano di studi sull'alto Medioevo* 19 (1971): 453–94.

Bulst, Walther. "Eine anglo-lateinische Übersetzung aus dem Grieschichen um 700." *ZfdA* 75 (1938): 105–11.

Burlin, Robert B. *The Old English Advent: A Typological Commentary*. New Haven, CT: Yale University Press, 1968.

Busch, Stephan. "*Versus ex variis locis deducti*. On Ancient Collections of Epigrams." In *The Neo-Latin Epigram: A Learned and Witty Genre*, edited by Susanna de Beer, Karl A. E. Enenkel, and David Rijser, 25–40. Leuven: Leuven University Press, 2009.

Butler, Robert M. "Glastonbury and the Early History of the Exeter Book." In *Old English Literature in its Manuscript Context*, edited by Joyce Tally Lionarons, 173–215. Morgantown: West Virginia University Press, 2004.

Cameron, M. I. "Aldhelm as Naturalist: A Re-examination of some of his *Enigmata*." *Peritia* 4 (1985): 117–33.

Camille, Michael. *Image on the Edge: The Margins of Medieval Art*. Cambridge, MA: Harvard University Press, 1992.

Cansdale, George Soper. *Animals of Bible Lands*. Exeter: Paternoster, 1970.

Carley, James P. "John Leland and the Contents of English Pre-Dissolution Libraries: Glastonbury Abbey." *Scriptorium* 40 (1986): 107–20.

———. "More Pre-Conquest Manuscripts from Glastonbury Abbey." *ASE* 23 (1994): 265–81. http://dx.doi.org/10.1017/S0263675100004567

———. "Two Pre-Conquest Manuscripts from Glastonbury Abbey." *ASE* 16 (1987): 197–212. http://dx.doi.org/10.1017/S0263675100003902

Carley, James P., and A. Dooley. "An Early Irish Fragment of Isidore of Seville's Etymologiae." In *The Archaeology and History of Glastonbury Abbey. Essays in Honour of the Ninetieth Birthday of C. A. Raleigh Radford*, edited by L. Abrams and J.P. Carley, 135–61. Woodbridge: Boydell, 1991.

Carruthers, Mary. *The Book of Memory: A Study of Memory in Medieval Culture*. Cambridge: Cambridge University Press, 1990.

Casiday, Augustine. "St Aldhelm's Bees (*De uirginitate prosa* cc. IV–VI): Some Observations on a Literary Tradition." *ASE* 33 (2004): 1–22.

Castro Caridad, Eva, and Francisco Peña Fernández. *Isidoro de Sevilla: sobre la fe católica contra los judíos*. Sevilla: Universidad de Sevilla, 2012.

Catalogue of Manuscripts in the British Museum. Vol. 1, Part II: The Burney Manuscripts. London, 1840.

Cavell, Megan. "Looming Danger and Dangerous Looms: Violence and Weaving in Exeter book 'Riddle 56.'" *Leeds Studies in English* 42 (2011): 29–42.

Chambers, R. W., ed. *The Exeter Book of Old English Poetry, with Introductory Chapters by Max Förster and Robin Flower*. London: Lund & Humphries, 1933.

Clark, Willene B. *The Medieval Book of Birds: Hugh of Foilloy's Aviarium*. Binghamton, NY: Medieval and Renaissance Texts and Studies, 1992.

Codoñer Merino, Carmen. "*Origines o Etymologiae*." In *Thesauramata philologica Iosepho oblata. II. Graeca-latina*, edited by M. R. Herrera, S. García-Jalón, and Manuel A. Marcos Casquero, 511–27. Salamanca: Universidad Pontificia de Salamanca, 1994.

———. "Un manuscrito escolar del siglo IX: Royal 15.B.XIX." *Segno e testo. International Journal on Manuscripts and Text Transmission* 1 (2003): 229–45.

Coleman, Julie. "Sexual Euphemism in Old English." *NM* 93 (1992): 93–94.

Colgrave, B. "Some Notes on Riddle 21." *MLR* 32 (1937): 281–83. http://dx.doi.org/10.2307/3716022

Collison, Robert. *Encyclopedias: Their History throughout the Ages.* 1964. Reprint, New York: Hafner, 1966.

Conde Silvestre, Juan Camilo. *Crítica literaria y poesía elegíaca anglo-sajona: las ruinas, el exiliado errante y el navegante.* Murcia: Universidad de Murcia, 1994.

Conner, Patrick W. *Anglo-Saxon Exeter: A Tenth-Century Cultural History.* Woodbridge: Boydell, 1993.

———. "Exeter's Relics, Exeter's Books." In *Essays on Anglo-Saxon and Related Themes in Memory of Dr Lynne Grundy*, edited by J. Roberts and J. Nelson, 117–56. London: King's College London Medieval Studies, 2000.

———. "Four Contiguous Poems in the Exeter Book: A Combined Reading of *Homiletic Fragment III*, *Soul and Body II*, *Deor*, and *Wulf and Eadwacer*." In Hussey and Niles, *The Genesis of Books*, 119–39.

Cortelyou, John Van Zandt. *Die altenglischen Namen der Insekten, Spinnen- und Krustentiere.* Heidelberg: Carl Winter, 1906.

Cosijn, P. J. "Anglosaxonica. IV." *Beiträge* 23 (1898): 109–30.

Dales, Douglas. *Dunstan: Saint and Statesman.* Cambridge: Lutterworth Press, 1988.

Davis, Norman. "'Hippopotamus' in Old English." *RES* 4 (1953): 141–42. http://dx.doi.org/10.1093/res/IV.14.141

Deshman, Robert. *The Benedictional of Æthelwold.* Princeton, NJ: Princeton University Press, 1995.

Díaz y Díaz, C. Manuel. "Para la crítica de los Aenigmata de Sinfosio." *Helmantica* 28 (1977): 121–36.

Dietrich, F. "Die Räthsel des Exeterbuchs: Verfasser; Weitere Lösungen." *ZfdA* 12 (1865): 232–52.

———. "Die Räthsel des Exeterbuchs: Würdigung, Lösung und Herstellung." *ZfdA* 11 (1859): 448–90.

DiNapoli, Robert. "In the Kingdom of the Blind, the One-Eyed Man is a Seller of Garlic: Depth-Perception and the Poet's Perspective in the Exeter Book Riddles." *ES* 81 (2000): 422–55. http://dx.doi.org/10.1076/0013-838X(200009)81:5;1-8:FT422

Doane, A. N. "Three Old English Implement Riddles: Reconsiderations of Numbers 4, 49, and 73." *MP* 84 (1987): 243–57. http://dx.doi.org/10.1086/391550

Donoghue, D. "An Anser for Exeter Book Riddle 74." In *Words and Works: Studies in Medieval English Language and Literature in Honour of Fred C. Robinson*, edited by Peter S. Baker and Nicholas Howe, 45–58. Toronto: University of Toronto Press, 1998.

Dronke, Peter, Michael Lapidge, and Peter Stotz. "Die unveröffentlichten Gedichte der Cambridger Liederhandschrift (CUL Gg.5.35)." *Mittellateinisches Jahrbuch* 17 (1982): 54–95.

Drout, Michael D. C. *How Tradition Works: A Meme-Based Cultural Poetics of the Anglo-Saxon Tenth Century*. Tempe: Arizona Center for Medieval and Renaissance Studies, 2006.

———. "'The Partridge' is a Phoenix: Revising the Exeter Book *Physiologus*." *Neophilologus* 91 (2007): 487–503. http://dx.doi.org/10.1007/s11061-006-9014-z.

———. *Tradition and Influence in Anglo-Saxon Literature: An Evolutionary, Cognitivist Approach*. New York: Palgrave, 2013. http://dx.doi.org/10.1057/9781137324603.

Dümmler, E. "Lateinische Rätsel." *ZfdA* 22 (1878): 421–22.

Ebert, Adolf. "Zu den Lorscher Rätseln." *ZfdA* 23 (1879): 200–202.

Erhardt-Siebold, Erika von. "Aldhelm's Chrismal." *Speculum* 10 (1935): 270–76.

———. "An Archaeological Find in a Latin Riddle of the Anglo-Saxons." *Speculum* 7 (1932): 252–56. http://dx.doi.org/10.2307/2850764.

———. *Die lateinischen Rätsel der Angelsachsen*. Heidelberg: Carl Winter, 1925.

———. "The Old English Loom Riddles." In *Philologica: The Malone Anniversary Studies*, edited by Thomas A. Kirby and Henry Bosley Woolf, 9–17. Baltimore: The Johns Hopkins University Press, 1949.

———. "Old English Riddle No. 95." *MLN* 62 (1947): 558–59.

Evison, Vera I. "Glass Vessels in England AD 400–1100." In *Glass in Britain and Ireland AD 350–1100*, edited by Jennifer Price, 47–104. London: British Museum, 2000.

Fear, A. T. *Lives of the Visigothic Fathers*. Liverpool: Liverpool University Press, 1997.

Fell, Christine E. "Some Implications of the Boniface Correspondence." In *New Readings on Women in Old English Literature*, edited by Helen Damico and Alexandra Hennessey Olsen, 29–43. Bloomington: Indiana University Press, 1990.

Ferguson, Everett, Michael P. McHugh, and Frederick W. Norris, eds. *Encyclopedia of Early Christianity*. 1997. Reprint, New York: Garland 1999.

Ferguson, George Wells. *Signs and Symbols in Christian Art*. 1954. Reprint, Oxford: Oxford University Press, 1961.

Fernández Catón, José María. *Las etimologías en la tradición manuscrita medieval estudiada por el prof. Dr Anspach*. León: Consejo superior de investigaciones científicas, Centro de Estudios e Investigación "San Isidoro," 1966.

Finch, Chauncey E. "The Bern Riddles in Codex Vat. Reg. Lat. 1553." *Transactions and Proceedings of the American Philological Association* 92 (1961): 145–55. http://dx.doi.org/10.2307/283806.

———. "Catalogues and Other Manuscripts from Lorsch." *Transactions and Proceedings of the American Philological Association. American Philological Association* 99 (1968): 165–79. http://dx.doi.org/10.2307/2935838.

———. "Codex Vat. Barb. Lat. 721 as a Source for the Riddles of Symphosius." *Transactions and Proceedings of the American Philological Association* 98 (1967): 173–79.

———. "The Riddles in Cod. Barb. Lat. 1717 and Newberry Case MS f. 11." *Manuscripta* 17 (1973): 3–11.

———. "Symphosius in Codices Pal. Lat. 1719, 1753 and Reg. Lat. 329, 2078." *Manuscripta* 13 (1969): 3–11.

———. "The Text of the Aenigmata of Boniface in Codex Reg. Lat. 1553." *Manuscripta* 6 (1962): 23–28.

Foley, John Miles. "Riddles 53, 54, and 55: An Archetypal Symphony in Three Movements." *Studies in Medieval Culture* 10 (1977): 25–31.

Folkerts, Menso, and Helmuth Gericke. "Die Alkuin zugeschriebenen Propositiones ad acuendos iuvenes (Aufgaben zur Schärfung des Geistes der Jugend)." In *Science and Civilization in Carolingian Times*, edited by Paul Leo Butzer and Dietrich Lohrmann, 273–81. Basel: Birkhäuser, 1993.

Fontaine, Jacques. "Isidore de Séville et la mutation de l'encyclopédisme antique." *Cahiers d'Histoire Mondiale* 9 (1966): 519–38.

———. *Isidore de Séville: genèse et originalité de la culture hispanique au temps des Wisigoths*. Turnhout: Brepols, 2000.

———. "Isidorus Varro Christianus?" In *Bivium, Homenaje a M.C. Díaz y Díaz*, edited by S. Álvarez, 89–106. Madrid: Gredos, 1983.

Foys, Martin. "The Undoing of Exeter Book Riddle 47: 'Bookmoth.'" Festschrift (title confidential). Tempe: Arizona Center for Medieval and Renaissance Studies, forthcoming.

Frank, Roberta. "Sex in the Dictionary of Old English." In *Unlocking the Wordhord: Anglo-Saxon Studies in Memory of Edward B. Irving, Jr.*, edited by Mark C. Amodio and Katherine O'Brien O'Keeffe, 302–12. Toronto: University of Toronto Press, 2003.

———. "Some Uses of Paronomasia in Old English Scriptural Verse." *Speculum* 47 (1972): 207–26. http://dx.doi.org/10.2307/2856688.

———. "The Unbearable Lightness of Being a Philologist." *JEGP* 96 (1997): 486–513.

French, Roger. *Ancient Natural History*. London: Routledge, 1994.

Fry, Donald K. "Exeter Book Riddle Solutions." *OEN* 15 (1981): 22–3.

Fulk, R. D. *A History of Old English Meter*. Philadelphia: The University of Pennsylvania Press, 1992.

Gameson, Richard. "The Origin of the Exeter Book of Old English Poetry." *ASE* 25 (1996): 135–85. http://dx.doi.org/10.1017/S0263675100001988

Ganz, David. *Corbie in the Carolingian Renaissance*. Sigmaringen: Jan Thorbecke, 1990.

———. "The 'Liber Glossarum': A Carolingian Encyclopedia." In *Science and Civilization in Carolingian Times*, edited by Paul Leo Butzer and Dietrich Lohrmann, 127–35. Basel: Birkhäuser, 1993.

———. "The Merovingian Library of Corbie." In *Columbanus and Merovingian Monasticism*, edited by Howard B. Clarke and Mary Brennan, 153–72. Oxford: B.A.R, 1981.

García Cornejo, Rosalía. "A propósito de los ictiónimos en 'De piscibus,' *Etymologías* 12.6 de Isidoro de Sevilla." *Habis* 32 (2001): 553–75.

Garrison, Mary. "The Emergence of Carolingian Latin Literature and the Court of Charlemagne (780–814)." In McKitterick, *Carolingian Culture*, 111–40.

———. "The Social World of Alcuin: Nicknames at York and at the Carolingian Court." In *Alcuin of York: Scholar at the Carolingian Court*, edited by Luuk A. J. R. Houwen and Alasdair A. MacDonald, 59–79. Groningen: Egbert Forsten, 1998.

George, Judith W. "Vandal Poets in their Context." In *Vandals, Romans and Berbers: New Perspectives on Late Antique North Africa*, edited by Andrew H. Merrills, 133–45. Aldershot: Ashgate, 2004.

Gleissner, Reinhard. *Die "zweideutigen" altenglischen Rätsel des "Exeter Book" in ihrem zeitgenössischen Kontext*. Frankfurt: Peter Lang, 1984.

Gneuss, Helmut. *Hymnar und Hymnen im englischen Mittelalter: Studien zur Überlieferung, Glossierung und Übersetzung lateinischer Hymnen in England*. Tübingen: Niemeyer, 1968. http://dx.doi.org/10.1515/9783110952780.

———. "The Origin of Standard Old English and Æthelwold's School at Winchester." *ASE* 1 (1972): 63–83. http://dx.doi.org/10.1017/S0263675100000089

Gneuss, Helmut, and Michael Lapidge. *Anglo-Saxon Manuscripts: A Bibliographical Handlist of Manuscripts and Manuscript Fragments Written or Owned in England up to 1100*. Toronto: University of Toronto Press, 2014.

Göbel, Helga. *Studien zu den altenglischen Schriftwesenrätseln*. Würzburg: Würzburger Wissenschaftliche Schriften, 1980.

Godman, Peter. "The Anglo-Latin 'Opus Geminatum': from Aldhelm to Alcuin." *Medium Aevum* 50 (1981): 215–29.

Goldsmith, Margaret E. "*The Seafarer* and the Birds." *RES* 5 (1954): 225–35. http://dx.doi.org/10.1093/res/V.19.225

Gosse, Philip Henry. *Popular British Ornithology*. London, 1849.

Gougaud, L. "Les relations de l'abbaye de Fleury-sur-Loire avec la Bretagne Armoricaine et les Îles Britanniques (Xe et XIe siècles)." *Mémoires de la Société d'histoire et d'archéologie de Bretagne* 4 (1923): 4–30.

Greenfield, Stanley B. "Old English Riddle 39 Clear and Visible." *Anglia 98* (1980): 95–100.

Grein, Christian W. M. "Kleine Mittheilungen." *Germania* 10 (1865): 305–10.

Gretsch, Mechthild. *The Intellectual Foundations of the English Benedictine Reform*. Cambridge: Cambridge University Press, 1999. http://dx.doi.org/10.1017/CBO9780511483295.

Griffith, Mark. "Riddle 19 of the Exeter Book: SNAC, an Old English Acronym." *N&Q* 237 (1992): 15–16.

Gwara, Scott. "Ælfric Bata's Manuscripts." *Revue d'Histoire des Textes* 27 (1997): 239–55.

Hacikyan, Agop. *A Linguistic and Literary Analysis of Old English Riddles*. Montreal: Mario Casalini, 1966.

Haddan, A. W., and W. Stubbs, eds. *Councils and Ecclesiastical Documents relating to Great Britain and Ireland*. Vol. 3. Oxford, 1881.

Hagen, Anne. *A Handbook of Anglo-Saxon Food: Processing and Consumption*. Hockwold-cum-Wilton: Anglo-Saxon Books, 1992.

Hagen, Hermann. *Catalogus codicum bernensium*. Bern: Bibliotheca Bongarsiana, 1885.

Hahn, Heinrich. "Die Rätseldichter Tatwin und Eusebius." *Forschungen zur deutschen Geschichte* 26 (1886): 599–632.

Harbus, Antonina. "*Exeter Book* Riddle 39 Reconsidered." *SN* 70 (1998): 139–48.

Haupt, M. "Über eine Handschrift der Leipziger Stadtbibliothek." *Berichte über die Verhandlungen der Königlich Sächsischen Gesellschaft der Wissenschaften zu Leipzig, Philologisch-Historische Classe* 2 (1850): 1–15.

Herren, Michael W. "On the Earliest Irish Acquaintance with Isidore of Seville." In *Visigothic Spain: New Approaches*, edited by E. James, 243–50. Oxford: Oxford University Press, 1980.

———. "The Transmission and Reception of Graeco-Roman Mythology in Anglo-Saxon England, 670–800." *ASE* 27 (1998): 87–103. http://dx.doi.org/10.1017/S0263675100004816

Herzfeld, Georg. *Die Räthsel des Exeterbuches und ihr Verfasser*. Berlin, 1890.

Hicketier, F. "Fünf Rätsel des Exeterbuches." *Anglia 10* (1888): 564–600.

Higley, Sarah. "The Wanton Hand: Reading and Reaching into Grammars and Bodies in Old English Riddle 12." In Withers and Wilcox, *Naked Before God*, 29–59.

Hill, Joyce. "The Benedictine Reform and beyond." In *A Companion to Anglo-Saxon Literature*, edited by Phillip Pulsiano and Elaine Treharne, 151–69. London: Blackwell, 2001.

———. "The 'Regularis Concordia' and its Latin and Old English Reflexes." *Revue Bénédictine* 101 (1991): 299–315.

Hillgarth, J.N. "Ireland and Spain in the Seventh Century." *Peritia* 3 (1984): 1–16.

Hollis, Stephanie, and Michael Wright. *Annotated Bibliographies of Old and Middle English Literature: Old English Prose of Secular Learning*. With the assistance of Gwynneth M. D. Mills and Adrienne Pedder. Cambridge: Brewer, 1992.

Holthausen, F. "Zu altenglischen Dichtungen." *Englische Studien* 74 (1940): 324–28.

———. "Zu alt- und mittelenglischen Dichtungen. XV." *Anglia* 24 (1901): 264–67.

Hough, Carole. "Place-names and the Provenance of Riddle 49." *Neophilologus* 82 (1998): 617–18. http://dx.doi.org/10.1023/A:1004354215368.

Howe, Nicholas. "Aldhelm's *Enigmata* and Isidorean Etymology." *ASE* 14 (1985): 37–59. http://dx.doi.org/10.1017/S0263675100001265

Howlett, David R., ed. "Aldhelmi Carmen rhythmicum." *Archivum Latinitatis Medii Aevi* 53 (1995): 119–40.

Hudson, John. *Historia ecclesie Abbendonensis: The History of the Church of Abingdon*. Vol. 1. Oxford: Oxford University Press, 2007.

Hümer, Johann. "Zur Geschichte der mittellateinischen Dichtung. *Arnulfi delicie cleri*." *Romanische Forschungen* 2 (1886): 211–46.

Hussey, Matthew T. "*Transmarinis litteris*: Southumbria and the Transmission of Isidore's *Synonyma*." *JEGP* 107 (2008): 141–68.

Hussey, Matthew, and John D. Niles, eds. *The Genesis of Books: Studies in the Scribal Culture of Medieval England in Honour of A. N. Doane*. Turnout: Brepols, 2011.

Irvine, Martin. *The Making of Textual Culture: 'Grammatica' and Literary Theory, 350–1100*. 1994. Reprint, Cambridge: Cambridge University Press, 1996.

Jensen, Hans Arne. *Plant World of the Bible*. Bloomington, IN: AuthorHouse, 2012.

Kennedy, Charles W. *The Earliest English Poetry*. Oxford: Oxford University Press, 1943.

Kennedy, Christopher B. "Old English Riddle No. 39." *ELN* 13 (1975): 81–85.

Ker, James. "Drinking from the Water-Clock: Time and Speech in Imperial Rome." *Arethusa* 42 (2009): 279–302. http://dx.doi.org/10.1353/are.0.0028.

Ker, N. R. "The Beginnings of Salisbury Cathedral Library." In *Medieval Learning and Literature: Essays presented to R. W. Hunt*, edited by J. J. G. Alexander and M. T. Gibson, 23–49. Oxford: Oxford University Press, 1976.

———. *Catalogue of Manuscripts Containing Anglo-Saxon*. 1977. Reprint, Oxford: Clarendon, 1990.

Keynes, Simon D. *The Diplomas of King Æthelred "The Unready" (978–1016): A Study in Their Use as Historical Evidence*. Cambridge: Cambridge University Press, 1980. http://dx.doi.org/10.1017/CBO9780511560170.

———. "Edgar, rex admirabilis." In *Edgar, King of the English 959–975: New Interpretations*, edited by Donald Scragg, 3–59. Woodbridge: Boydell & Brewer, 2008.

———. "King Æthelstan's Books." In Lapidge and Gneuss, *Learning and Literature in Anglo-Saxon England*, 143–201.

King, Philip J., and Lawrence E. Stager. *Life in Biblical Israel*. Louisville, KY: Westminster John Knox Press, 2001.

Kitson, Peter. "Swans and Geese in Old English Riddles." *ASSAH* 7 (1994): 79–84.

Klein, Thomas. "The Old English Translation of Aldhelm's Riddle *Lorica*." *RES* 48 (1997): 345–49. http://dx.doi.org/10.1093/res/XLVIII.191.345

Korhammer, Michael. "The Last of the Exeter Book Riddles." In *Bookmarks from the Past. Studies in Early English Language and Literature in Honour of Helmut Gneuss*, edited by Lucia Kornexl and Ursula Lenker, 69–80. Frankfurt: Peter Lang, 2003.

Lagorio, Valerie M. "Aldhelm's *Aenigmata* in Codex Vaticanus Palatinus Latinus 1719." *Manuscripta* 15 (1971): 23–27.

Lapidge, Michael. "Æthelwold and the *Vita S. Eustachii*." In his *Anglo-Latin Literature, 900–1066*, 213–23.

———. "Aldhelm's Latin Poetry and Old English Verse." *Comparative Literature* 31 (1979): 209–31. http://dx.doi.org/10.2307/1770922.

———. *Anglo-Latin Literature, 600–899*. London: Hambledon, 1996.

———. *Anglo-Latin Literature, 900–1066*. London: Hambledon, 1993.

———. "The Archetype of *Beowulf*." *ASE* 29 (2000): 5–41. http://dx.doi.org/10.1017/S0263675100002398

———. "Autographs of Insular Latin Authors of the Early Middle Ages." In *Gli autografi medievali. Problemi paleografici e filologici. Atti del convegno di studio della Fondazione Ezio Franceschini*, edited by Paolo Chiesa and Lucia Pinelli, 108–15. Spoleto: Centro italiano di studi sull'Alto Medioevo, 1994.

———. "B. and the *Vita S. Dunstani*." In his *Anglo-Latin Literature, 900–1066*, 279–91.

———. "*Beowulf*, Aldhelm, the *Liber Monstrorum* and Wessex." In his *Anglo-Latin Literature, 600–899*, 271–312.

———. "Byrhtferth of Ramsey and the Early Sections of the *Historia Regum* attributed to Symeon of Durham." *ASE* 10 (1981): 97–122. http://dx.doi.org/10.1017/S0263675100003227

———. "The Career of Aldhelm." *ASE* 36 (2007): 15–69. http://dx.doi.org/10.1017/S0263675107000026

———. "A Frankish Scholar in Tenth-Century England: Frithegod of Canterbury/Fredegaud of Brioude." In his *Anglo-Latin Literature, 900–1066*, 157–81.

———. "The Hermeneutic Style in Tenth-Century Anglo-Latin Literature." *ASE* 4 (1975): 67–111. http://dx.doi.org/10.1017/S0263675100002726

———. "An Isidorian Epitome from Anglo-Saxon England." In his *Anglo-Latin Literature, 600–899*, 183–223.

———. "Litanies of the Saints in Anglo-Saxon Manuscripts: A Preliminary List." *Scriptorium* 40 (1986): 264–77.

———. "The Present State of Anglo-Saxon Studies." In *Insular Latin Studies: Papers on Latin Texts and Manuscripts of the British Isles: 550–1066*, edited by Michael W. Herren, 45–82. Toronto: Pontifical Institute of Mediaeval Studies, 1981.

———. "The School of Theodore and Hadrian." In his *Anglo-Latin Literature, 600–899*, 141–68. http://dx.doi.org/10.1017/S0263675100003689.

———. "Schools, Learning and Literature in Tenth-Century England." In his *Anglo-Latin Literature, 900–1066*, 1–48.

———. "Some Latin Poems as Evidence for the Reign of Athelstan." In his *Anglo-Latin Literature, 900–1066*, 49–86, http://dx.doi.org/10.1017/S0263675100001113.

———. "Some Remnants of Bede's Lost *Liber epigrammatum*." *English Historical Review* 90 (1975): 798–820. http://dx.doi.org/10.1093/ehr/XC.CCCLVII.798.

———. "Surviving Booklists from Anglo-Saxon England." In Lapidge and Gneuss, *Learning and Literature in Anglo-Saxon England*, 33–89.

———. "Theodore and Anglo-Latin Octosyllabic Verse." In his *Anglo-Latin Literature, 600–899*, 241–43. http://dx.doi.org/10.1017/CBO9780511627453.015.

Lapidge, Michael, and Helmut Gneuss, eds. *Learning and Literature in Anglo-Saxon England: Studies presented to Peter Clemoes on the Occasion of his Sixty-Fifth Birthday*. Cambridge: Cambridge University Press, 1985.

Lapidge, Michael, John Blair, Simon Keynes, and Donald Scragg, eds. *The Wiley Blackwell Encyclopedia of Anglo-Saxon England*. Oxford: Blackwell, 1999. Reprint, Oxford: Wiley-Blackwell, 2014.

Law, Vivien. *The Insular Latin Grammarians*. 1982. Reprint, Woodbridge: Boydell, 1987.

———. "The Study of Latin Grammar in Eighth-Century Southumbria." *ASE* 12 (1983): 43–71. http://dx.doi.org/10.1017/S0263675100003343

Lazzari, Loredana. "Isidore's *Etymologiae* in Anglo-Saxon Glossaries." In Bremmer and Dekker, *Foundations of Learning*, 63–93.

Lendinara, Patrizia. *Anglo-Saxon Glosses and Glossaries*. Aldershot: Ashgate, 1999.

———. "Gli Aenigmata Laureshamensia." *PAN* 7 (1981): 73–90.

———. "The World of Anglo-Saxon Learning." In *The Cambridge Companion to Old English Literature*, edited by Malcolm Godden and Michael Lapidge. Cambridge: Cambridge University Press, 1991. http://dx.doi.org/10.1017/CCOL0521374383.015.

Liebermann, Felix. "Das anglesächsische Rätsel 56: 'Galgen' als Waffenständer." *Archiv* 114 (1905): 163–64.

Lindheim, Bogislav V. "Traces of Colloquial Speech in OE." *Anglia* 70 (1951): 22–44.

Lindsay, W. M. "The (Early) Lorsch Scriptorium." In *Palaeographia latina, Part III*, edited by W. M. Lindsay, 5–48. Oxford: Oxford University Press, 1924.

———. *Glossaria Latina*. Vol. 1. Paris: Les Belles Lettres, 1926.

Liuzza, Roy Michael. "The Texts of the Old English Riddle 30." *JEGP* 87 (1988): 1–15.

Lockett, Leslie. *Anglo-Saxon Psychologies in the Vernacular and Latin Traditions*. Toronto: University of Toronto Press, 2011.

Lowe, E. A. *Codices latini antiquiores: a Palaeographical Guide to Latin Manuscripts Prior to the Ninth Century*. Vol. 9. Oxford: Clarendon, 1959.

Lynch, Joseph H. *Christianizing Kinship. Ritual Sponsorship in Anglo-Saxon England*. Ithaca, NY: Cornell University Press, 1998.

Mackie, W. S. "Notes on the Text of the 'Exeter Book.'" *MLR* 28 (1933): 75–78. http://dx.doi.org/10.2307/3715887.

Madoz, J. "San Leandro de Sevilla." *Estudios eclesiásticos* 56 (1981): 415–53.

Mády, M. "An VIIIth Century Aldhelm Fragment in Hungary." *Acta Antiqua Academiae Scientiarum Hungaricae* 13 (1965): 441–53.

Magennis, Hugh. *Anglo-Saxon Appetites: Food and Drink and Their Consumption in Old English and Related Literature*. Dublin: Four Courts, 1999.

———. "The Cup as Symbol and Metaphor in Old English Literature." *Speculum* 60 (1985): 517–36. http://dx.doi.org/10.2307/2848173.

Manitius, Max. *Geschichte der christlich-lateinischen Poesie, bis zur mitte des 8. Jahrhunderts*. Stuttgart, 1891.

———. *Geschichte der lateinischen Literatur des Mittelalters*. 3 vols. Munich: Beck'sche, 1911, 1923, 1931.

Marco, M. de. "Letture grammaticali a Lorsch." *Aevum* 31 (1957): 273–77.

Mayr-Harting, Henry. *The Coming of Christianity to Anglo-Saxon England*. 1972. Reprint, University Park: The Pennsylvania State University Press, 1991.

McKitterick, Rosamond, ed. *Carolingian Culture: Emulation and Innovation.* Cambridge: Cambridge University Press, 1994.

———. "The Diffusion of Insular Culture in Neustria between 650 and 850: the Implications of the Manuscript Evidence." In *La Neustrie. Les pays au nord de la Loire de 650 à 850*, edited by Hartmut Atsma, 395–432. Sigmaringen: Thorbecke, 1989.

Meaney, Audrey L. "Birds on the Stream of Consciousness: Riddles 7 to 10 of the Exeter Book." *Archaeological Review from Cambridge* 18 (2002): 120–52.

———. "The Hunted and the Hunters: British Mammals in Old English Poetry." *ASSAH* 11 (2000): 95–105.

Meritt, Herbert D. *Old English Glosses, A Collection.* New York: Modern Language Association of America, 1945.

Merkelbach, Reinold. "Zwei Gespensternamen: Aelafius und Symphosius." *Zeitschrift fur Papyrologie und Epigraphik* 51 (1983): 228–29.

Merrills, Andrew H., ed. *Vandals, Romans and Berbers: New Perspectives on Late Antique North Africa.* Aldershot: Ashgate, 2004.

Meyvaert, Paul. "The Solution to Old English Riddle 39." *Speculum* 51 (1976): 195–201. http://dx.doi.org/10.2307/2854260.

Mora, María José. "The Invention of the Old English Elegy." *ES* 76 (1995): 129–39. http://dx.doi.org/10.1080/00138389508598960

———. "Un invierno entre los hielos: los paisajes de la poesía anglo-sajona." *Cuadernos del CEMYR* 7 (1999): 235–42.

Muñoz Jiménez, María José. "Algunos aspectos de los *Aenigmata Symphosii*: título, autor y relación con la *Historia Apollonii regis Tyri*." *Emerita* 55 (1987): 307–12. http://dx.doi.org/10.3989/emerita.1987.v55.i2.623.

———. "Enigma y epigrama: de los *Xenia* y *Apophoreta* de Marcial a los *Aenigmata Symposii*." *Cuadernos de Filologia Clasica* 19 (1985): 187–95.

———. "Rasgos comunes y estructura particular de *Xenia* y *Apophoreta*." *Cuadernos de filología clásica. Estudios latinos* 10 (1996): 136–46.

Murphy, Patrick J. *Unriddling the Exeter Riddles.* University Park: Penn State Press, 2011.

Murphy, Trevor. *Pliny the Elder's Natural History: the Empire in the Encyclopedia.*

Oxford: Oxford University Press, 2004. http://dx.doi.org/10.1093/acpr of:oso/9780199262885.001.0001.

Musselman, Lytton John. *Figs, Dates, Laurel, and Myrrh: Plants of the Bible and the Quran*. Portland, OR: Timber, 2007.

Neff, Karl, ed. *Die Gedichte des Paulus Diaconus: Kritische und erklärende Ausgabe*. Munich: Beck'sche, 1908.

Neidorf, Leonard, ed. *The Dating of Beowulf: A Reassessment*. Woodbridge: Boydell & Brewer, 2014.

Neville, Jennifer. "Fostering the Cuckoo: Exeter Book Riddle 9." *RES* 58 (2007): 431–46. http://dx.doi.org/10.1093/res/hgl154

———. "Speaking the Unspeakable: Appetite for Deconstruction in Exeter Book Riddle 12." *ES* 93 (2012): 519–28.

Niles, John D. *Old English Enigmatic Poems and the Play of the Texts*. Turnhout: Brepols, 2006.

O'Brien O'Keeffe, Katherine. "The Text of Aldhelm's *Enigma* no. C in Oxford, Bodleian Library, Rawlinson C. 697 and Exeter Riddle 40." *ASE* 14 (1985): 61–73. http://dx.doi.org/10.1017/S0263675100001277

———. *Visible Song: Transitional Literacy in Old English Verse*. Cambridge: Cambridge University Press, 1990.

O'Camb, Brian. "The Inscribed Form of *Exeter Maxims* and the Layout of Quire XI of the Exeter Book." In Hussey and Niles, *The Genesis of Books*, 137–59.

Ohlert, Konrad. *Rätsel und Rätselspiele der alten Griechen*. Berlin, 1886.

O'Meara, John. *The History and Topography of Ireland*. Harmondsworth: Penguin, 1951.

Orchard, Andy. "Enigma Variations: The Anglo-Saxon Riddle-Tradition." In *Latin Learning and English Lore: Studies in Anglo-Saxon Literature for Michael Lapidge*, Vol. 1, edited by Andy Orchard and Katherine O'Brien O'Keeffe, 284–304. Toronto: University of Toronto Press, 2005.

———. *The Poetic Art of Aldhelm*. Cambridge: Cambridge University Press, 1994. http://dx.doi.org/10.1017/CBO9780511597558.

———, ed. *Pride and Prodigies: Studies in the Monsters of the Beowulf-Manuscript*. Cambridge: Brewer, 1995.

Osborn, Marijane. "Vixen as Hero: Solving Exeter Book Riddle 15." In *The Hero Recovered: Essays on Medieval Heroism in Honor of George Clark*, edited by Robin Waugh and James Weldon, 173–87. Kalamazoo, MI: Medieval Institute Publications, 2010.

Owen-Crocker, Gale R. *Dress in Anglo-Saxon England*. Woodbridge: Boydell, 2004.

Paris, Gaston. "Review of *ZfdA* 22 (1878)." *Romania* 8 (1879): 138–91.

Parkes, M. B. "The Handwriting of St Boniface: a Reassessment of the Evidence." *Beiträge zur Geschichte der deutschen Sprache und Literatur* 98 (1976): 161–79.

———. "The Manuscript of the Leiden Riddle." *ASE* 1 (1972): 207–17. http://dx.doi.org/10.1017/S0263675100000168

———. "The Palaeography of the Parker Manuscript of the *Chronicle*, Laws and Sedulius, and Historiography at Winchester in the Late Ninth and Tenth Centuries." *ASE* 5 (1976): 149–71. http://dx.doi.org/10.1017/S0263675100000831

Pavlovskis, Zoja. "The Riddler's Microcosm: from Symphosius to St. Boniface." *Classica et Mediaevalia* 39 (1988): 219–51.

Pellegrin, Élisabeth, et al. *Les manuscrits classiques latins de la Bibliothèque Vaticane*. Paris: Éditions du Centre national de la recherche scientifique, 1975–.

Pellegrin, P. *La classification des animaux chez Aristote. Statut de la biologie et unité de l'aristotelisme*. Paris: Les Belles Lettres, 1982.

Perrello, Tony. "An Undiscovered Riddle in Brussels, Bibliothèque Royale MS 1828–1830." *ELN* 43 (2005): 8–14.

Petsch, Robert. "Rätselstudien I. Zu den Reichenauer Rätseln." *Beiträge zur Geschichte der deutschen Sprache und Literatur* 41 (1916): 332–44.

Pheifer, J. D. *Old English Glosses in the Épinal-Erfurt Glossary*. 1974. Reprint, Oxford: Oxford University Press, 1988.

Pitcher, R. A. "The Dating of Martial Books XIII and XIV." *Hermes* 113 (1985): 330–39.

Pizarro Sánchez, Javier. "Estructura y tipología de los *Aenigmata Symphosii*." *Cuadernos de filología clásica. Estudios latinos* 16 (1999): 239–46.

———. "Notas críticas del humanista Iosephus Castalio a los Aenigmata Symphosii." *Cuadernos de filología clásica. Estudios latinos* 17 (1999): 219–28.

Planta, J. *A Catalogue of the Manuscripts in the Cottonian Library deposited in the British Museum*. London, 1802.

Pope, John C. "An Unsuspected Lacuna in the Exeter Book: Divorce Proceedings for an Ill-matched Couple in the Old English Riddles." *Speculum* 49 (1974): 615–22. http://dx.doi.org/10.2307/2852029.

Pope, John C. "Paleography and Poetry: Some Solved and Unsolved Problems of the Exeter Book." In *Medieval Scribes, Manuscripts and Libraries: Essays Presented to N. R. Ker*, edited by M. B. Parkes and Andrew G. Watson, 25–65. London: Scolar, 1978.

Porter, David W. "Æthelwold's Bowl and *The Chronicle of Abingdon*." *NM* 97 (1996): 163–67.

———. "A Double Solution to the Latin Riddle in MS. Antwerp, Plantin-Moretus Museum M16.2." *ANQ* 9 (1996): 3–9. http://dx.doi.org/10.1080/0895769X.1996.10543138.

———. "Isidore's *Etymologiae* at the School of Canterbury." *ASE* 43 (2014): 7–44.

Rand, E. K. "A Vade Mecum of Liberal Culture in a MS of Fleury." *PQ* 1 (1922): 258–77.

Raw, Barbara C. *Anglo-Saxon Crucifixion Iconography and the Art of the Monastic Revival*. Cambridge: Cambridge University Press, 1990.

Reichert, Hermann. "Sprache und Namen der Wandalen in Afrika." In *Namen des Frühmittelalters als sprachliche Zeugnisse und als Geschichtsquellen*, edited by Albrecht Greule and Matthias Springer, 43–120. Berlin: De Gruyter, 2009.

Rella, F. A. "Continental Manuscripts Acquired for English Centers in the Tenth and Early Eleventh Centuries: A Preliminary Checklist." *Anglia 98* (1980): 107–16.

Riedinger, Anita. "The Formulaic Style in the Old English Riddles." *SN* 76 (2004): 30–43.

Rigg, A. G., and G. Wieland. "A Canterbury Classbook of the Mid-Eleventh Century (the 'Cambridge Songs' Manuscript)." *ASE* 4 (1975): 113–30. http://dx.doi.org/10.1017/S0263675100002738

Robinson, Fred C. "Artful Ambiguities in the Old English 'Book-Moth' Riddle." In *Anglo-Saxon Poetry: Essays in Appreciation for John C. McGalliard*, edited by Lewis E. Nicholson and Dolores Warwick Frese, 355–62. Notre Dame, IN: University of Notre Dame Press, 1975.

Rose, Valentin. *Verzeichniss der lateinischen Handschriften der Königlichen Bibliothek zu Berlin*. Vol. 1. Berlin, 1893.

Rössler, Stephan. *Verzeichniss der Handschriften der Bibliothek des Stiftes Zwettl*. Vienna, 1891.

Rowland, Beryl. *Birds with Human Souls: A Guide to Bird Symbolism*. Knoxville: University of Tennessee Press, 1978.

Rudolf, Winfried. "Riddling and Reading: Iconicity and Logogriphs in Exeter Book Riddles 23 and 45." *Anglia* 130 (2012): 499–525. http://dx.doi.org/10.1515/ang-2012-0526.

Rusche, Philip G. "Isidore's *Etymologiae* and the Canterbury Aldhelm Scholia." *JEGP* 104 (2005): 437–55.

Russom, Geoffrey. "Exeter Riddle 47: A Moth Laid Waste to Fame." *PQ* 56 (1977): 129–36.

Saenger, Paul. *A Catalogue of the Pre-1500 Western Manuscript Books at the Newberry Library*. Chicago: The University of Chicago Press, 1989.

Salvador, Mercedes. "Direct and Indirect Clues: Exeter Riddle no. 74 Reconsidered." *NM* 99 (1998): 17–29.

———. "The Evening Singer of Riddle 8 (K-D)." *SELIM* 9 (1999): 57–68.

Salvador-Bello, Mercedes. "Allegorizing and Moralizing Zoology in Aldhelm's *Enigmata*." *Revista canaria de estudios ingleses* 68 (2014): 209–18. *ES* 93 (2012): 572–82.

———. "Clean and Unclean Animals: Isidorean Compilation Criteria in Eusebius's Zoological Riddles."

———. "The Key to the Body: Unlocking Riddles 42–46." In Withers and Wilcox, *Naked Before God*, 60–96.

———. "The Oyster and the Crab: A Riddle Duo (Nos. 77 and 78) in the *Exeter Book*." *MP* 101 (2004): 400–419.

———. "Patterns of Compilation in Anglo-Latin *Enigmata* and the Evidence of a Source-Collection in the *Exeter Book* Riddles (nos. 1–40)." *Viator* 43 (2012): 339–74.

———. Review of Dieter Bitterli, *Say What I Am Called. The Old English Riddles of the Exeter Book and the Anglo-Latin Riddle Tradition* (Toronto: Toronto University Press, 2009). *Kritikon Litterarum* 39 (2012): 243–48.

———. "The Sexual Riddle Type in Aldhelm's *Enigmata*, the Exeter Book, and Early Medieval Latin." *PQ* 90 (2011): 357–85.

Scattergood, John. "Eating the Book: Riddle 47 and Memory." In *Text and Gloss: Studies in Insular Language and Literature*, edited by Helen Conrad-O'Briain, Anne Marie D'Arcy, and V. J. Scattergood, 119–27. Dublin: Four Courts, 1999.

Schwarcz, Andreas. "The Settlement of the Vandals in North Africa." In Merrills, *Vandals, Romans and Berbers*, 49–58.

Sciacca, Claudia di. *Finding the Right Words: Isidore's Synonyma in Anglo-Saxon England*. Toronto: University of Toronto Press, 2008.

———. "Isidorian Scholarship at the School of Theodore and Hadrian: The Case of the *Synonyma*." *Quaestio* 3 (2002): 76–106.

Scott, Peter Dale. "Alcuin's *Versus de Cuculo*: The Vision of Pastoral Friendship." *Studies in Philology* 62 (1965): 510–30.

———. "Rhetorical and Symbolic Ambiguity: Symphosius and Aldhelm." In *Saints, Scholars and Heroes: Studies in Medieval Culture in Honor of Charles W. Jones*, vol. 1, edited by Margot H. King and Wesley M. Stevens, 117–44. Collegeville, MN: Saint John's Abbey and University Press, 1979.

Sebo, Erin. "Was Symphosius an African? A Contextualizing Note on Two Textual Clues in the *Aenigmata Symphosii*." *N&Q* 56 (2009): 323–24.

Senra Silva, Inmaculada. "The Names of the U-Rune." *Futhark: International Journal of Runic Studies* 1 (2010): 109–22.

Shook, Laurence K. "Riddles Relating to the Anglo-Saxon Scriptorium." In *Essays in Honour of Anton Charles Pegis*, edited by J. Reginald O'Donnell, 215–36. Toronto: Pontifical Institute of Mediaeval Studies, 1974.

Sisam, Kenneth. *Studies in the History of Old English Literature*. Oxford: Clarendon Press, 1953.

Smith, D. K. "Humor in Hiding: Laughter Between the Sheets in the Exeter Book Riddles." In *Humour in Anglo-Saxon Literature*, edited by Jonathan Wilcox, 79–98. Cambridge: Brewer, 2000.

Snædal, Magnús. "The 'Vandal' Epigram." *Filologia Germanica* 1 (2009): 181–215.

Socas Gavilán, Francisco. *Antología Latina. Repertorio de poemas extraído de códices y libros impresos.* Madrid: Gredos, 2011.

Sorrell, Paul. "Alcuin's 'Comb' Riddle." *Neophilologus* 80 (1996): 311–18. http://dx.doi.org/10.1007/BF00212108.

———. "Like a Duck to Water: Representations of Aquatic Animals in Early Anglo-Saxon Literature and Art." *Leeds Studies in English* 25 (1994): 29–68.

Spallone, Maddalena. "Il Par. Lat. 10318 (Salmasiano): dal manoscritto alto-medievale ad una raccolta enciclopedica tardo-antica." *Italia Medioevale e Umanistica* 25 (1982): 1–71.

———. "Storia del libro, storia del testo: una interazione possibile." In *Les problèmes posés par l'édition critique des textes anciens et médiévaux*, edited by Jacqueline Hamesse, 73–93. Louvain-la-Neuve: Publications de l'Institut d'études médiévales de Louvain-la-Neuve, 1992.

———. "Symphosius o Symposius? Un problema di fonetica nell'Anthologia Latina." *Quaderni dell'Istituto di Lingua e Letterature Latina. Università 'La Sapienza.' Facoltà di Magistero* 4 (1982): 41–48.

———. "Tradizioni insulari e letteratura scolastica: il ms. Angelicanus 1515 e gli *Aenigmata* di Simposio." *Studi Classici e Orientali* 35 (1985): 185–228.

Steen, Janie. *Verse and Virtuosity: The Adaptation of Latin Rhetoric in Old English Poetry.* Toronto: University of Toronto Press, 2008.

Stenton, Frank. *Anglo-Saxon England.* 1943. Reprint, Oxford: Oxford University Press, 1998.

Stévanovitch, Colette. "Exeter Book Riddle 70A: Nose?" *N&Q* 240 (1995): 8–10.

Stevens, William O. *The Cross in the Life and Literature of the Anglo-Saxons.* New Haven, CT: Yale University Press, 1904.

Stewart, Ann Harleman. "Old English Riddle 47 as Stylistic Parody." *Papers on Language & Literature* 11 (1975): 227–41.

Stork, Nancy Porter. *Through a Gloss Darkly: Aldhelm's Riddles in the British Library MS Royal 12.C.xxiii.* Toronto: Pontifical Institute of Mediaeval Studies, 1990.

Story, Joanna. "Aldhelm and Old St Peter's, Rome." *ASE* 39 (2010): 7–20. http://dx.doi.org/10.1017/S0263675110000037

———. *Carolingian Connections: Anglo-Saxon England and Carolingian Francia, c. 750–870*. Aldershot: Ashgate, 2003.

Strobl, Joseph. "Zur Spruchdichtung bei den Angelsachsen." *ZfdA* 31 (1887): 54–64.

Sullivan, J. P. *Martial: The Unexpected Classic*. Cambridge: Cambridge University Press, 1991. http://dx.doi.org/10.1017/CBO9780511582639.

Szarmach, Paul E., M. Teresa Tavormina, and Joel T. Rosenthal, eds. *Medieval England: An Encyclopedia*. New York: Garland, 1998.

Tanke, John W. "*Wonfeax wale*: Ideology and Figuration in the Sexual Riddles of the Exeter Book." *Class and Gender in Early English Literature: Intersections*, edited by Britton J. Harwood and Gillian R. Overing, 21–42. Bloomington: Indiana University Press, 1994.

Taylor, Archer. *English Riddles from Oral Tradition*. Berkeley: University of California Press, 1951.

———. *The Literary Riddle before 1600*. Berkeley: University of California Press, 1948.

Thacker, Alan. "Æthelwold and Abingdon." In Yorke, *Bishop Æthelwold*, 43–64.

———. "Bede and the Ordering of Understanding." In *Innovation and Tradition in the Writings of the Venerable Bede*, edited by Scott DeGregorio, 37–63. Morgantown: West Virginia University Press, 2006.

Thompson, Edward. *Catalogue of Ancient Manuscripts in the British Museum*. Vol. 2. London, 1884.

Thornbury, Emily V. "Aldhelm's Rejection of the Muses and the Mechanics of Poetic Inspiration in Early Anglo-Saxon England." *ASE* 36 (2007): 71–92. http://dx.doi.org/10.1017/S0263675107000038

———. *Becoming a Poet in Anglo-Saxon England*. Cambridge: Cambridge University Press, 2014. http://dx.doi.org/10.1017/CBO9781107280304.

Tigges, Wim. "Snakes and Ladders: Ambiguity and Coherence in the Exeter Book Riddles and Maxims." In *Companion to Old English Poetry*, edited by Rolf H. Bremmer Jr. and Henk Aertsen, 95–118. Amsterdam: VU University Press, 1994.

Trahern, Joseph B. "The 'Ioca monachorum' and the Old English 'Pharaoh.'" *ELN* 7 (1970): 165–68.

Traube, Ludwig. "Die älteste Handschrift der Aenigmata Bonifatii." *Vorlesungen und Abhandlungen* 3 (1920): 164–67.

———. "Zur lateinischen Anthologie. I. Über Gedichte des Codex Salmasianus." *Philologus* 54 (1895): 124–34.

Trautmann, Moritz. "Die Auflösungen der altenglischen Rätsel." *Anglia Beiblatt* 5 (1894): 46–51.

Tristram, Hildegard L. C. "In Support of Tupper's Solution of the Exeter Book Riddle (Krapp-Dobbie) 55." In *Germanic Dialects: Linguistic and Philological Investigations*, edited by Bela Brogyanyi and Thomas Krömmelbein, 585–98. Amsterdam: John Benjamins, 1986. http://dx.doi.org/10.1075/cilt.38.24tri.

Twomey, Michael W. "Medieval Encyclopedias." In *Medieval Christian Literary Imagery: A Guide to Interpretation*, edited by R. E. Kaske, 182–215. Toronto: University of Toronto Press, 1988.

Tupper, Frederick, Jr. "The Holme Riddles (MS. Harl. 1960)." *PMLA* 18 (1903): 211–73. http://dx.doi.org/10.2307/456635.

———. "Originals and Analogues of the Exeter Book Riddles." *MLN* 18 (1903): 97–106. http://dx.doi.org/10.2307/2917102

———. "Riddles of the Bede Tradition. The 'Flores' of Pseudo-Bede." *MP* 2 (1904): 561–72.

van Helten, W. "Zu Anthologia Latina Ed. Riese No. 285 und 285A (*De conviviis barbaris*)." *Beiträge zur Geschichte der deutschen Sprache und Literatur* 29 (1904): 339–43.

Vernet, André. "Notice et extraits d'un manuscrit d'Edimbourg (Adv. Mss. 18.6.12, 18.7.8, 18.7.7)." *Bibliothèque de l'École des Chartes* 107 (1948): 33–51. http://dx.doi.org/10.3406/bec.1948.449378.

Vives, José. *Concilios visigóticos e hispanorromanos*. Barcelona: CSIC, 1963.

Warner, G. F., and J. P. Gilson. *Catalogue of Western Manuscripts in the Old Royal and King's Collection*. 4 vols. London: British Museum, 1921.

Waugh, Robin. "Literacy, Royal Power, and King-Poet Relations in Old English and Old Norse Compositions." *Comparative Literature* 49 (1997): 289–315.

Webber Jones, Leslie. "The Scriptorium at Corbie: I. The Library." *Speculum* 22 (1947): 191–204. http://dx.doi.org/10.2307/2854726.

West, Philip J. "Rumination in Bede's Account of Cædmon." *Monastic Studies* 12 (1976): 217–26.

Wieland, Gernot R. "Cædmon, the Clean Animal." *American Benedictine Review* 35 (1984): 194–203.

———. *The Latin Glosses on Arator and Prudentius in Cambridge University Library, MS Gg.5.35*. Toronto: Pontifical Institute of Mediaeval Studies, 1983.

Whitbread, L. "The Latin Riddle in the Exeter Book." *N&Q* 190 (1946): 156–58.

White, T. H. *The Book of Beasts*. New York: Putnam, 1954.

Whitman, Charles H. "The Birds of Old English Literature." *JEGP* 2 (1898): 149–98. http://dx.doi.org/10.5962/bhl.title.54912

———. "The Old English Animal Names: Mollusks; Toads, Frogs; Worms; Reptiles." *Anglia* 30 (1907): 380–93.

Whitman, F[rank]. H. "Aenigmata Tatwini." *NM* 88 (1987): 8–17.

Whitman, F. H., ed. and trans. *Old English Riddles*. Ottawa: Canadian Federation for the Humanities, 1982.

Wilcox, Jonathan. "Mock-Riddles in Old English: Exeter Riddles 86 and 19." *Studies in Philology* 93 (1996): 180–87.

———. "New Solutions to Old English Riddles: Riddles 17 and 53." *PQ* 69 (1990): 393–408.

Wiles, Maurice. *Archetypal Heresy: Arianism through the Centuries*. Oxford: Clarendon Press, 1996.

Wilmanns, August. "Der Katalog der Lorscher Klosterbibliothek aus dem 10. Jahrhundert." *Rheinisches Museum für Philologie* N.F. 23 (1868): 385–410.

Withers, Benjamin C., and Jonathan Wilcox, eds. *Naked Before God: Uncovering the Body in Anglo-Saxon England*. Morgantown: West Virginia University Press, 2003.

Wood, Ian. *The Most Holy Abbot Ceolfrid*. Jarrow Lecture, 1995.

Wormald, Patrick. "Æthelwold and his Continental Counterparts." In Yorke, *Bishop Aethelwold*, 13–42.

Wormell, D. E. W. "The Riddles in Virgil's Third *Eclogue*." *Classical Quarterly* 10 (1960): 29–32. http://dx.doi.org/10.1017/S0009838800024344.

Wright, Neil. "The Anglo-Latin Hexameter: Theory and Practice c. 600–c. 800." Unpublished PhD Dissertation. Cambridge, 1981.

Yorke, Barbara. "Adomnán at the Court of King Aldfrith." In *Adomnán of Iona: Theologian, Lawmaker, Peacemaker*, edited by Jonathan M. Wooding, with Rodney Aist, Thomas Owen Clancy, and Thomas O'Loughlin, 36–50. Dublin: Four Courts Press, 2010.

———. "Aldhelm's Irish and British Connections." In Barker and Brooks, *Aldhelm and the See of Sherborne*, 164–80.

———, ed. *Bishop Æthelwold: His Career and Influence*. 1988. Reprint, Woodbridge: Boydell, 1997.

———. "The Bonifacian Mission and Female Religious in Wessex." *Early Medieval Europe* 7 (1998). 145–72. http://dx.doi.org/10.1111/1468-0254.00023.

Young, Jean I. "Riddle 15 of the Exeter Book." *RES* 20 (1944): 304–6.

Ziolkowski, Jan M. *Talking Animals: Medieval Latin Beast Poetry, 750–1150*. Philadelphia: University of Pennsylvania Press, 1993.

Index

Anchin, abbey of (near Douai), 44
Abbo of Fleury, 26, 207n363
Abingdon, 26–27, 38, 46–47, 53, 55, 56, 388
Adrian and Ritheus, 24
Adrianus et Epictitus, 51
Ælfgifu, mother of King Edgar, 45
Ælfheah, Archbishop of Canterbury, 38, 416–18, 419–22, 447
Ælfric, Archbishop of Canterbury, 38, 46–47, 271, 422
Ælfric of Eynsham, *Colloquy*, 190n322, 405n359; *Glossary*, 71, 355n187, 363n221, 364n224, 381n285, 388n307; *Grammar*, 43, 84, 152n192, 414n385; *Saints Lives*, 45n156 (St Æthelthryth), 455
Aenigmata anglica (Lorsch Riddles), 265; also see *Enigmata* (Lorsch Riddles).
Æthelgar, Bishop of Canterbury, 38
Æthelred, King of England, 228n412, 448
Æthelstan, King of England, 34n105, 50–51, 52, 170, 448
Æthelthryth (St), 45
Æthelwold, Bishop of Winchester, 28, 38, 46, 47n166, 71, 125, 170n251, 207n362, 339, 377, 418n400, 420n408, 421n411, 454; Continental Benedictinism and, 26–27 "Æthelwold's Bowl," 44–45, 47, 53, 55, 322n99, 422, 455
Africa, 103, 123n78, 133–34
African Anthology. *See* Latin Anthology

Agroecius, 81
Alcuin, 1, 28, 69, 72n262, 303n41, 448; *Carmina*, 23, 51, 54, 137, 454; *De grammatica*, 51, 76; *De ortographia*, 72; *Disputatio regalis et nobilissimi iuvenis Pippini cum Albino scholastico*, 22, 23, 54, 78, 137, 451, 454; *Propositiones ad acuendos iuvenes*, 23, 43, 50, 54, 454; in revival of riddling genre, 23, 54; teaching rhetoric, 77–78; "Versus de cuculo," 303n41, 310, 314–15
Aldfrith, King of Northumbria, *Epistola ad Acircium* for, 168–69, 451
Aldhelm, 1, 14, 176–77, 396n331, 447n8 passim. *See also Enigmata* (Aldhelm); anthologizing of riddle collections of, 35n110, 40, 41, 42, 54, 81, 449; background of, 162–66, 447n8; *Carmen Rhythmicum*, 67, 166; *Carmina ecclesiastica*, 166, 256, 360n210; correspondence by, 162n212, 164–65, 168–69; *De metris*, 168–69, 174-75n272, 181, 265, 272, 453; *De pedum regulis*, 83, 169, 172, 174-75n273, 186n312, 265, 272, 453; *De virginitate*, 17n26, 28-29n81, 167–68, 170n251, 171, 175n274, 187n313, 189-90n321, 197–98, 202n356, 209n370, 211, 222n400, 338ns148 and 150, 268, 351n175, 388n308, 453; education of, 37, 163–66; *Epistola ad Acircium*, 51n185, 165, 239, 451; *Etymologiae* used by, 66–67, 85, 86, 182-84, 218n390; influence of,

513

Aldhelm (cont.)
14n11, 15–16, 235; popularity of works by, 51, 169–70
Alfred, King of England, 448; Alfredian school of translation, 454
Alfred, son of King Æthelred, 228n412
allegory, 110, 125, 312; in Aldhelm's *Enigmata*, 185, 196–98; animals compared to people, 319–20; in *De rerum naturis* (Hrabanus Maurus), 111–12, 319–20; of eating/swallowing in riddle collections, 353–58; in *Etymologiae*, 109–10, 112, 311; in Exeter Riddles, 300, 303, 333–34, 347–53, 358; in Symphosius's *Enigmata*, 128–30
Ambrose, 175n275; *De fide*, 113; *Hexameron*, 98, 110, 412
analogy: in Aldhelm's *Enigmata*, 188, 189, 194, 201–12, 219; in Bern Riddles, 258, 260; in *Etymologiae*, 108–12; in Exeter Riddles, 299–300, 304, 311, 319, 320, 330, 344–49, 353, 372, 441, 443, 446; in Lorsch Riddles, 273-74; in Symphosius's *Enigmata*, 156–59; in Vatican *Enigmata*, 260, 277, 278–79
Andreas, 409–10
Anglo-Saxon Chronicle, 163, 221, 228n412, 454
Anglo-Saxon culture, 54n198, 268, 290, 303n41, 405; Aldhelm's influence in, 166, 172; centers of, 33, 264–65, 274–75; missions bringing to Europe, 16–17, 24–25; riddling genre in, 42, 50, 54, 172, 256, 447–48
animals. *See* zoological categories.
Anna, King of East Anglia, 45n156
antithetical roles, 110, 114n46. *See also* contrasts; difference; in *Etymologiae*, 108–12, 128–29
Apollonius of Tyre, 138n146, 455
Arianism, 57-58, 127
Aristotle, *Historia animalium*, 95n14, 102n28, 109n36, 205n359
Arnulf, *Delicie cleri*, 139

Ars grammatica (attributed to Isidore), 71n254
Athenaeus, *Deipnosophistae*, 13, 119n65
Augustine of Canterbury (St), 37, 420
Augustine of Hippo (St), *De civitate Dei*, 187n313, 239n447

Barking, Abbey, 167, 197
Bede, 14, 19, 37, 163, 221, 234–35, 447n734; biblical commentaries by, 234, 351; *De arte metrica*, 67, 78n285, 268, 453; *De natura rerum*, 292n21; *De ortographia*, 67, 72, 76, 412; *De temporum ratione* 234; *Historia ecclesiastica*, 37n117, 45, 163, 164n220, 165, 221, 356, 454; spurious works by, see Pseudo-Bede.
Benedict (St), monastery of (Fleury), 25–27, 42
Benedict (St), relics at Fleury monastery, 26n68
Benedictine culture: Exeter Book and, 446–47; riddling genre in, 47, 55
Benedictine reform, 24–28, 34, 41, 47, 64, 71, 421n411; under Dunstan's archiepiscopate, 38–39; effects of, 448; food restrictions in, 324, 405–7, 413; literary culture nurtured by, 28n81, 339, 450, 406n361; riddling genre and, 42–43, 53, 419, 422
Benedictional of Æthelwold, 28, 47n166, 333–34, 415n391
Beowulf, 15, 47n166, 368n237; the *Beowulf*-manuscript, 52n191, 455
Bern Riddles (or *Enigmata Tullii*). See *Enigmata* (Bern Riddles)
bestiaries, 69, 213n383, 304, 308–9
Bible. Aldhelm identifying with Old Testament figures, 176–77; allusions to in Aldhelm's *Enigmata*, 177, 189–90, 198–99, 208–9, 211-12; allusions to in other riddle collections, 229, 260–61, 272, 350–52; clean *vs.* unclean birds and animals in, 100–101, 150, 249-50, 323n101; *Etymologiae* and, 98, 100–101; Eucherius's explaining symbols

of, 98–99; in Exeter Riddles, 272, 325–26, 392–93; food laws in, 100–101; Gospels vs. complete, 393; influence on *enigmata*, 195, 249–50; riddles based on, 12–13
Bibliotheca magnifica, 48, 74–75, 80, 419, 455
biological categories: in *Etymologiae*, 93-95; in riddle collections, 4-5, 6-7, 142
birds. *See* ornithological categories
body vs. soul, in Exeter Riddle 43: 348-49, 351–52
Boniface, 1, 17, 28, 30n84, 36, 72n262, 73n263, 76, 79, 80, 81, 83, 126, 169, 171, 221, 235, 265, 269, 270-72, 274, 447n734, 185n309, 235, 271, 448, 453. Aldhelm's *Enigmata* and, 18, 171; *Ars Bonifatii* (or *Ars grammatica*, Boniface), 72, 221, 268–69, 453; *Ars metrica* or *Caesurae Versuum* (attributed to Boniface), 72, 83, 265, 270, 272, 273, 274, 453; autograph of, 18, 79; background of, 29n84, 447n8; *Enigmata*, 18–19, 36, 81, 88n2, 126, 274; Lorsch Riddles attributed to, 265, 272; riddle collections of, 35n110, 213n383; riddling genre and, 16, 18; writings by, 72, 76, 221
Book of Taliesin, 293n23
botanical categories, botany: in Aldhelm's *Enigmata*, 199–201; in Bern Riddles, 3-4, 258–61, 262–63; in *Etymologiae*, 105–06, 154–55, 262–63; in Exeter Riddles, 436; in Pliny's *Naturalis historia*, 154n195; in Vatican *Enigmata*, 279–81
Braulio, Bishop of Saragossa, 115–16
Burney riddle, 55, 455
Bury St Edmunds, 31
Byrhtferh of Ramsey, 69, 170–71, 207; *Enchiridion* (or *Manual*), 69, 171, 455; *Vita sancti Oswaldi*, 170, 207

Caelius Sedulius, *Carmen paschale*, 126, 166–67
Canterbury, 34, 38, 56, 421; Aldhelm

at the school of, 163–64, 186n312; Aldhelm's *Enigmata* in, 172–73, 339; St Augustine as patron saint of, 420n405; Exeter Book and, 445–47, 449; glossarial activity at, 338–39, 388–89; as learning center, 34n105, 37, 72–73; riddle collections compiled in, 419, 420; riddle collections in, 35–36, 341, 446; riddling genre in, 39, 422, 448; riddling genre's popularity in, 36–37, 420; Tatwine as Archbishop of, 37, 221; Theodore and Hadrian's school at, 37, 65, 67n235, 163–64, 186n312, 239
Carmina centulensia, 137
Carolingian humanism, 54n198
Carolingian period, 137; education in, 64, 68, 70, 143–44, 171–72
Carolingian Renaissance, 73–74, 448; riddling genre in, 22, 25, 54
Castalio, Giuseppe, *Aenigmata Symphosii poetae*, 140n156
Catholic Church, 62. *See also* Benedictines; Christianity; Arianism vs., 57–58, 127; efforts against heresy in, 59–60, 64; high offices of, 416–18; Tatwine's riddles about ecclesiastical profession, 225–26, 228
Cenwald, Bishop of Worcester, 50–51
Ceolfric, abbot of Wearmouth-Jarrow, 234n430
chalice/paten: in Exeter Riddles, 359–60, 365–66, 377, 390–91
Charlemagne, 22, 54n198, 64, 137n138, 254n494, 255, 267, 451
chestnut enigma, 267
Christ Church (Canterbury), 40, 46n162, 47n163, 421n411; codices produced at, 38–39, 420
Christian allusions/ideas: in Aldhelm's *Enigmata*, 175–76, 180–81, 185–87, 203–4, 220; in Eusebius's *Enigmata*, 236–37, 238–40; in Exeter Riddles, 300, 303–4, 329, 333–34, 348–52, 359–60, 369–72; in Symphosius's *Enigmata*, 125–31; in Vatican *Enigmata*, 260, 282

Christianity. *See also* Bible; Catholic Church; Aldhelm spreading, 166n235; editing of Symphosius's *Enigmata* for, 132–33, 150, 161–62; *Etymologiae* and, 90, 97, 102, 103–4; Christian iconography in Exeter Riddles, 329, 334, 369–72; influence on encyclopedias' organization, 103–4, 143; influence on Symphosius's *Enigmata*, 148; lack of references to in Symphosius's *Enigmata*, 121, 124; prodigies category and, 212–13

Cicero, Marcus Tullius, 78, 253
Cleopatra Glossaries, 32, 70, 338
Collectanea Pseudo-Bedae, see Pseudo-Bede
contrasts: in Aldhelm's *Enigmata*, 220–21; among animals, 94–95, 112, 282, 320–21; in *Etymologiae*, 94–95, 104, 109, 112; in Eusebius's *Enigmata*, 238, 247; in Exeter Riddles, 302–3, 309, 320–21, 330, 410; in Symphosius's *Enigmata*, 128–29; in Tatwine's *Enigmata*, 233; in Vatican *Enigmata*, 278–79, 282, 320–21
Corbie, monastery at, 17, 25, 26n72, 70; Anglo-Saxon influence on, 274–75; *enigmata* and, 18–19, 136; manuscripts from, 78–79, 274; monks from teaching plainchant, 26–27
Corpus Glossary, 34, 338, 388–89
cosmological categories: in Aldhelm's *Enigmata*, 178–81, 443; in Bern Riddles, 263; in *enigmata*, 8–9; in *Etymologiae*, 102, 107–8, 113–14, 145, 236, 342; in Eusebius's *Enigmata*, 236–37, 244–45; in Exeter Riddles, 298–99, 328–29, 331–34, 343, 345, 436, 442; interrupting instrumental category in Exeter Riddles, 386–90; in Latin riddle collections, 6, 343, 439; in Lorsch Riddles, 273; missing from Tatwine's *Enigmata*, 249; placed last, 432–33; in Symphosius's *Enigmata*, 140–41, 145, 273, 277; in Vatican *Enigmata*, 277

crab. *See* oyster
Creation, 97; in Aldhelm's *Enigmata*, 178, 220–21, 337, 386–88; in *Etymologiae*'s second decade, 93, 95; in Exeter Riddles, 334–37, 386–88, 396, 431, 444; God's, in Aldhelm's *Enigmata*, 177, 200; God's *vs.* human, 389, 437n455; God's *vs.* human, in Aldhelm's *Enigmata*, 128, 204, 206; God's *vs.* human, in *Etymologiae*, 104, 106–8; God's *vs.* human, in Symphosius's *Enigmata*, 128, 161; human craftsmanship as, 379, 386, 396; Isidore not following order of, 98, 100, 102; in Tatwine's *Enigmata*, 225
cross: in Eusebius's *Enigmata*, 237; in Exeter Riddles, 329, 343, 369–75; in Tatwine's *Enigmata*, 225

"De conviviis barbaris," 123
De diuersis rebus, 67–68
De dubiis nominibus, 138–39
dialogues. See riddling-dialogue subgenre
difference. *See also* contrasts: in encyclopedic principles, 61, 109, 201–04, 205, 209, 194, 219, 311, 320–21, 347, 441; links by, 201–12, 412–13
digressions. *See* thematic exceptions
Disticha Catonis, 80
"Dombercht's Epitaph," 270–71
Donatus, abbot, 133
Donatus, grammarian; *Ars maior* (or *Ars grammatica*), 81, 82n302
The Dream of the Rood, 370, 372
Dunstan, Archbishop of Canterbury: annotations on Oxford, Rawlinson C.697 (Hand D) attributed to, 32, 52–53, 337–39; archiepiscopate of, 38–39; Continental Benedictinism and, 25–26

Eadred, King of England, 26
eagle, symbolizing renewal of faith, 206–7

Ecbasis cuiusdam captivi per tropologiam, 139
Ecgfrith, King of Northumbria: Æthelthryth as wife of, 45n156
Edgar, King of England, 25n64, 30, 33n98, 45n155, 418n400, 448
Edith, daughter of King Edgar, 45
education, 37, 57, 312; Aldhelm's, 163–66; Carolingian revival of, 25, 64, 68, 70, 135–36, 171, 275; development of, 59, 448; encyclopedic approach in, 203, 206; *Etymologiae* used in, 73, 89–90, 108; Exeter Riddles in, 289, 330, 450; Isidore and, 56–57, 59–64; materials for, 30–31, 82, 275, 357; monastic, 30–31; reform-oriented schools, 56; riddle collections, grammatical works, and encyclopedias studied together, 78–84, 82–84, 441–42; riddle collections used in, 9–11, 22–23, 25, 39, 75–78, 135–36, 139, 171, 173–74, 250, 343, 348–49, 448, 451
Edward the martyr (St), King of England, 45–46
Egbert of Liège, *Fecunda ratis*, 139
elements (earth, water, air, fire), 187n314, 240, 298
Ely, monastery at, 45n156
encyclopedias, 290. *See also Etymologiae*; analogy and difference in principles of, 194, 219, 311, 320–21, 347; categories of knowledge in, 156, 228–29; Christian, 203–4; compilation of, 84; educational approach based on, 203, 206; principles of, 233–34; proliferation of, 74; riddle collections and, 81–84, 87, 275, 441; used in education, 10, 81–84, 441–42
encyclopedic genre, 73n264; development of, 62n221, 68, 73
encyclopedic organization, 441; in Bern Riddles, 257–64; Christianity's influence on, 143; in Eusebius's *Enigmata*, 249; in Exeter Riddles, 291, 301, 311–12, 342, 392, 437, 446; in Lorsch Riddles, 272; in riddle collections, 2, 9, 141–42, 298; in Symphosius's *Enigmata*, 144–56, 159, 161–62; in Tatwine's *Enigmata*, 224; thematic exceptions to, 8–9; in Vatican *Enigmata*, 283
England, 170, 173; Anglo-Saxon culture in, 447–48; Benedictine reform in, 25–27; cultural exchange with Europe, 16n22, 24, 28, 50; effects of Scandinavian occupation on, 448; *Etymologiae* in, 66–68, 72–73; Frankish manuscripts brought to, 30–34, 55, 136n133; popularity of riddling genre in, 14, 136; revival of riddling genre in, 24, 30, 51, 54–55; riddle collections and, 42, 79, 134, 255; riddle collections from, 55–56, 172–73, 266, 274–75; riddling genre in, 15–16, 51, 54, 255, 447–48
enigmata. See riddle collections; riddles
Enigmata (Aldhelm); allegories in, 196–98; Bern Riddles and, 255–56, 278–79; biblical allusions in, 195, 207–9, 211; botanical category in, 199–201, 280; codices containing, 19–21, 30–31, 51n185, 78–79, 82, 251, 265, 272n571, 275, 449; conflict among elements in, 179–80, 194–95; cosmological category in, 178–81, 432, 439, 443; *Etymologiae* and, 66–67, 183–85, 191; Exeter Riddles and, 336–37, 362, 382–83, 386–87, 396, 420; glosses to, 173; hagiographies and, 127–28; in history of riddling genre, 15–16; influence on Exeter Riddles, 432, 443, 445, 449; influences on, 14, 206; instrumental category in, 364n222; Lorsch Riddles and, 21, 266, 272; mythological elements in, 125–26; order of riddles in, 141n157, 327–28; organization of, 178, 181, 191–94, 200, 219–21, 224, 272, 342, 432; originally part of *Epistola ad Acircium*, 83, 168–69;

Index 517

Enigmata (Aldhelm) (*cont.*)
ornithological category in, 208–9;
oyster and crab in, 411–12; pairings by analogy and difference in,
201–12, 412–13; popularity of, 162,
169–73; script of, 18n29, 19n32;
spread of, 16n18, 16n20, 17–18;
stones/metals/minerals category
in, 183–85; surviving copies of,
171–73; Symphosius's *Enigmata*
and, 173–76, 278–79; Tatwine's
Enigmata modeled on, 222, 224–
25; transformations in, 215–16;
translations of, 14–15, 336-39; uses
of, 22, 25, 339, 448; Vatican *Enigmata* and, 275, 278–79, 281–82;
wonder category in, 212–19, 228,
440; zoological category in, 185–
99, 281–82, 439–40
Enigmata (Eusebius), 14, 20, 43, 75,
98, 141n157, 235–36, 309; anomalies in organization of, 237–38,
243–45, 250; codices containing,
35n110, 449; cosmological category
in, 237, 439; *Etymologiae* and, 85,
249-50; Exeter Riddles and, 342–
43, 362–63; Great Chain of Being
in organization of, 236, 249; instrumental category in, 6, 236–37;
number of, 340–41; organization
compared to *Etymologiae*'s, 4–5,
108, 240–43; organization of, 147,
236, 248–49; ornithological category in, 6–7, 246–48, 323; wonder
category in, 440; writing themes
in, 237, 363; zoological category
in, 85, 323–24, 439
Enigmata (Symphosius), 117, 136n134,
225, 378n271; Aldhelm's *Enigmata*
and, 171–76, 217n389, 219–21; allusions to classical mythology in,
124–26; Bern Riddles and, 252,
258, 279; botanical category in,
154–55, 280; Christianity and, 125–
26, 128–33, 150, 334; codices containing, 19, 24, 30–33, 34, 36, 42,
126, 133, 252, 265, 272n571, 449;
Versus cuiusdam Scoti de alphabeto
and, 20–21; debate over date of,
121–24, 142; *Etymologiae* and, 142,
145–50, 161210; Eusebius's *Enigmata* and, 147; Exeter Riddles and,
353, 358–59, 385–86, 397, 399, 444;
wonder category in, 159; influence
of, 134, 137–39, 174, 353, 444; instrumental category in, 156–59,
376n267, 440; intended audience
for, 451–52; Latin Anthology and,
123–24; Lorsch Riddles and, 21,
273; meteorological themes in,
140–41, 273, 277; only complete
riddle collection of period, 13–14;
organization compared to *Etymologiae*'s, 143–56; organization compared to other riddle collections,
147, 219–20, 277; organization of,
130, 141–44, 150–55, 160–61, 342,
398, 435; ornithological category
in, 148–49; popularity of, 133–34,
137, 140–41, 448; sources for, 143;
topics of, 120, 141; use of riddles
from, 22–23; uses of, 25, 125–26,
128, 138–40; Vatican *Enigmata*
and, 275, 277–79, 281–82; wonder
category in, 141, 148–49, 159–60,
212, 440; zoological category in,
145–50, 281–82, 439
Enigmata (Tatwine), 37, 49, 126,
141n157, 221, 229, 365; Aldhelm's
Enigmata and, 222, 224; anthologizing of, 449; cosmological category in, 439; Eusebius's *Enigmata*
and, 235, 248–49; influence on
Exeter Riddles, 340, 342–43; instrumental category in, 5–6, 364,
390, 440, 444; Lorsch Riddles
and, 21, 266; missing zoological
category, 249; number of, 340–42,
443; organization of, 222–25,
227–28, 232–34; wonder category
in, 226–28, 440; writing themes in,
224–25
Enigmata (Bern Riddles), 1, 21,
250–64; Aldhelm's *Enigmata* and,
255–56, 278–79; authorship of,
78, 252–55; botanical category

in, 258–63, 279–81; codices containing, 54, 81, 275; cosmological category in, 263, 439; duplication in, 288n10, 331n122; *Etymologiae* and, 256–57; flaws in, 263–64; influence of Symphosius on, 14, 252; instrumental category in, 6, 257–58, 261–62, 364, 440; lacking zoological categories, 263–64; organization of, 3–4, 7, 257–64, 398; Vatican *Enigmata* and, 275, 278–81
Enigmata (Lorsch Riddles), 1, 264–74, 439; codices containing, 81, 83; combined with other works, 265–66, 270; debate over authorship, 265, 268, 271–72; debate over solutions for, 272–73; lack of homogeneity in, 268, 273–74; not completed, 271–73; organization of, 272–74, 435; other riddle collections and, 21, 49, 274
Enigmata (Vatican Riddles), 274, 331n122; agricultural themes in, 278–79; botanical category in, 279–81; contents of, 275–77; cosmological category in, 439; duplication in, 278–79, 288n10; lost text of, 277, 283, 440n2; number of, 436; numbering of, 275–77; organization of, 277, 283; ornithological category in, 281–82; wonder category in, 281, 440; zoological category in, 281–83, 439
Enigmata Tullii. *See Enigmata* (Bern Riddles)
epigrams, riddles compared to, 121
Épinal-Erfurt Glossary, 70
Etymologiae (Isidore), 151n190, 178n283, 180n289; Aldhelm's *Enigmata* and, 178–79, 182, 185–200, 219–21; arrival in Britain, 66–68; Bern Riddles and, 4–5, 256–64; Book I, 65, 71–72, 74–75; Book XII, 95–97, 102; Book XIII, 65, 102; Book XIV, 102–3; botanical category in, 154–55, 262–63, 280; codices containing, 67–69; compilation of, 98–102, 114, 116;

contrasts and allegories in, 112, 128–29, 311; cosmological category in, 102; digressions and disruptions in, 112, 114; Eusebius's *Enigmata* and, 4, 85, 236; Exeter Book and, 290, 320, 322; first decade of, 88n2, 89–90, 224; first edition dedicated to King Sisebut, 59; *Formulae spiritalis intelligentiae* compared to, 98–100; influence of, 61n218, 69–75, 71–72, 143–44, 448; influence on development of encyclopedic genre, 68, 73; influence on riddle collections, 84–85, 249; instrumental category in, 5–6, 230–31, 327, 390–92, 440; lack of explanations in, 69, 112n42; left unfinished, 62, 115; Lorsch Riddles and, 273; meteorological themes in, 3, 145; organization of, 4–5, 65, 88–89, 112n42, 115–16, 236, 261, 342, 441; ornithological category in, 94–95, 98–99, 150, 246–47, 281–82; *Physiologus* and, 195–96; wonder category in, 92, 161, 212, 440; repetition in, 112–14; riddle collections' authors' knowledge of, 74, 85; riddle collections' links to, 81–84, 87; riddle collections' organization based on, 2, 6, 108, 143–44, 191, 238, 240–43, 344, 438–39, 442; riddle collections' organization compared to, 3–5, 145–50, 219–21, 257–64; second decade of, 91–93, 105, 106–7, 106–8, 283, 442; stones/metals/minerals category in, 104, 183–85; studies of, 72, 81–84, 83; Symphosius's *Enigmata* and, 142, 145–50, 161n210; Tatwine's *Enigmata* and, 5, 224, 230–31; used in education, 59–62, 108, 112n42, 164; uses of, 68, 73, 83, 97, 448; Vatican *Enigmata* and, 280, 281–83; widespread knowledge of, 64–65, 67–68, 74, 85, 164, 322; zoological category in, 65, 85, 102, 145–50, 182, 185–99, 207, 281–83, 319, 439–40; zoological

Etymologiae (Isidore) (*cont.*)
category subdivisions of, 100–101, 102n27
etymology: in *Etymologiae*, 109, 111–12, 151n190; in Aldhelm's *Enigmata*, 75, 86, 218n390; in Eusebius's *Enigmata*, 243, 246; in Exeter Riddles, 85–86, 302, 306, 328, 347; in Isidore's pedagogic practice, 63–64; in other riddle collections, 151, 227n410
Eucherius of Lyons, *Formulae spiritalis intelligentiae*, 98–100, 142–43
Eugenius of Toledo, *Carmina*, 196n336
Europe, 67; Anglo-Saxon culture in, 16–18, 21, 79, 448; Benedictine reform in, 25–27; cultural exchange with Britain, 24, 28, 50; riddle collections in, 42, 54, 55–56, 79; riddle collections taken to, 133, 140–41, 171–72; riddling genre in, 14–18, 24n58, 51, 55, 136
Eusebius (or Hwætberht). *See also Enigmata* (Eusebius); background of, 234–35, 447n8
Eustace (St), 45–46
Exeter, 29, 56, 170; cathedral library in, 29, 52; Exeter Book possibly compiled at, 449–50; monastery at, 29n84, 39, 41; scriptorium at, 41n136
Exeter Book (see Exeter, Cathedral Library, MS. 3501 in manuscripts).
Exeter Riddles, 6, 28n80, 35n107, 39, 345; Aldhelm's *Enigmata* and, 15, 336, 382–83, 386–88, 443, 445, 449; analogues to Latin riddles in, 289, 313–14, 358, 362–63; analysis of Group 1 (Riddles 1-40), 291-344; analysis of Group 2 (Riddles 41-59), 344-79; analysis of Group 3 (Riddles 61-95), 379-437; authorship of, 268, 286n5, 341–42, 442; Benedictine reform and, 419, 450; botanical category in, 436; carelessness in compilation of, 344, 398–400, 402, 445–46, 450; choice of opening and closing riddles in, 334–37; compilation of, 288, 335–36, 392, 397, 413, 438, 442–43, 449; compiled in three phases, 341–42, 379, 381, 442–45; cosmological category in, 298–99, 328–29, 331–34, 386–87, 389–90, 436; Creation riddles in, 386–88, 431, 444; damaged text of, 392, 402, 431; dating of, 15, 447, 449; debate over solutions for, 315–16, 318, 330–34, 359, 367, 369, 375, 381, 403, 433; duplicated riddles in, 377, 389, 437, 445–46; encyclopedic organization of, 9, 301, 392; *Etymologiae* and, 320, 342; etymology in, 85–86; Eusebius's *Enigmata* and, 342–43; favorites among, 287–88; fusion of separate riddles in, 296–97, 360, 399; influences on, 138, 340, 342–43, 443–45; influences on organization of, 320, 344, 442, 445–46; instrumental category in, 324–29, 353, 363–64, 366–75, 379–92, 436–37; intended audience for, 450–51; lack of transitional clues in, 314–17; lapidary category in, 436; Latin riddle collections and, 284–86, 343, 397, 442; limited research on, 286–89, 291; locations of manuscripts, 29, 36, 39; Lorsch Riddles and, 274; meteorological themes in, 6, 286, 291–93, 294–98; miscellaneous section in, 392, 437, 445; monasticism in, 450–51; number of, 340–42, 345, 389–90, 399, 436, 437, 443, 445–46; numbering of, 284, 436n454; Old English *vs.* Latin pieces of, 1; organization aiming for encyclopedic, 291, 342, 437; organization of, 2, 291, 321, 335, 352, 436; organizational improvisation in, 398, 437, 444–45; organized in two sequences, 285–86, 311, 340–41, 389; pairings in, 299–300, 301-02, 309, 311-12, 320, 327, 330, 343, 352, 403, 412-13; ornithological category in,

6–7, 301–13, 315–16; poor quality of, 400, 402, 437; provenance of, 35n106, 41, 338-39, 388-89, 446-47, 449; reproduction in, 384; Riddles 1-6 (cosmological motifs), 291-300; Riddle 1-2-3 (storm, wind and God), 291-98; Riddles 7-15 (animals), 302-24; Riddles 7-11 (birds), 302-13; Riddles 12-15 (quadrupeds), 313-20; Riddles 16-39 (instruments), 324-35; Riddle 29 (sun and moon), 328-29; Riddle 33 (iceberg), 330; Riddle 39 (cloud), 331-35; Riddle 40 (Creation), 335-39, 342, 345, 386-89, 430, 432, 433n439, 445; Riddles 42-46 (sexual riddles), 345-53; Riddles 47-51 (writing motifs), 353-66; Riddle 47 (bookworm), 353-59; Riddles 52-59 (wooden objects), 366-79; Riddles 61-66 (craftsmanship), 379-90; Riddle 66 (Creation), 386-90; Riddles 67-94 (miscellanea), 392-433; Riddle 70b (lighthouse), 395-97; Riddles 77 and 78 (oyster and crab), 402-13; Riddle 81 (weathervane) 414-22; Riddles 37 and 87 (bellows), 423-25; Riddles 88 and 93 (inkhorn), 425-30; Riddle 94 (Creation), 431-33; Riddle 95 (book), 434-35; sexuality and double entendre in, 345-53, 368, 380-85; shortage of material for, 425, 431; solutions' clues in, 375, 385, 394-95, 403-4, 409, 415; solutions coded in, 347, 358, 401, 430; solutions differing for similar riddles, 430-31; solutions for, 286-87, 290, 294-95, 298n31, 303, 329, 355, 373, 379-80; sources of material for, 34, 378-79, 389, 423, 443, 445-46; Symphosius's *Enigmata* and, 138, 385-86, 444; Tatwine's *Enigmata* and, 340, 342-43; thematic exceptions in, 9, 298-99, 327-35, 344; thematic links in, 7-8, 374-75, 377; thematic repetition in, 288, 377-78, 403, 422-32; use of spacing and punctuation in, 378-79, 400; uses of, 28, 289, 450; variety in, 286-88; wonder category in, 437; writing themes in, 365-66, 433-36; Wulfstan's *Narratio* and, 446-47; zoological category in, 6-7, 301-2, 313-24, 323-24, 413, 436

Faricius of Arezzo, *Vita sancti Aldhelmi*, 162n211
Fleury, 25–27, 37. *See also* St Benedict (Fleury)
Florentina, sister of Isidore, 58n206
Frankish codices, 30-34, 36, 136, 173; brought to England, 30-31, 37, 136n133; studied in Canterbury, 37, 448–49
Frithegod, 37n121
Fulda, monastery at, 16
Fulgentius, Bishop of Écija and brother of Isidore, 58n206

Genesis A, 209n369
gender: of animals, 306-09, 331n125; grammatical inconsistencies in, 410n373
geography, of *Etymologiae*, 102–3
Gerald of Wales, *Topographia Hiberniae*, 321, 322n98, 407–8
Germanus, abbot of Ramsey, 26n69
Gesta romanorum, 140
Ghent, 25, 27
Glastonbury, 48, 53, 56, 421n411; archbishops previously educated in, 38-39; Canterbury and, 40, 422; as cradle of Benedictinism, 41; as center of learning, 38–41, 52; Exeter Book and, 447, 449–50; Exeter monastery repopulated by monks from, 39, 41; riddling genre in, 39, 41, 422
glossaries, 70, 71, 74; at Canterbury, 338-39; *Etymologiae*'s influence on, 69-70, 82
God, 180n289. *See also under* Creation; in Aldhelm's *Enigmata*, 203–4; in Eusebius's *Enigmata*,

God (cont.)
    297-98; in Exeter Riddle 1-2-3,
    291-98, 335-36; sun symbolizing,
    232, 249
Godemann, abbot of Thorney, 47n166
grammars, 70, 221; *Etymologiae* as,
    65, 71-72; *Etymologiae*'s influence
    on, 69, 71-72; Isidore's focus on,
    60-61; riddle collections' authors'
    knowledge of, 74; riddle collec-
    tions' relation to, 74-84, 87, 275;
    in Vatican City, Pal. Lat. 1746,
    268; in Vatican City, Pal. Lat. 1753,
    264-65, 271
Great Chain of Being, as organizing
    principle, 236, 249
Greek, glossary of, 78n285
Greek Anthology, 13
Gregory the Great, 56-57; *Moralia in
    Job*, 57; *Regula pastoralis*, 57, 454
Grimo, abbot of Corbie, 17
Guthlac (St), *vitae* of, 99

Hadrian. *See* Theodore and Hadrian,
    school of Canterbury
hagiographies: Aldhelm and, 127-28,
    167, 170; riddles compared to,
    127-28, 130
heresy, 72n262, 90; Arianism as, 57,
    59, 127; efforts against, 59-60, 64;
    hydra as allegory of, 112-13; in
    Symphosius's *Enigmata*, 129-30
hermeneutic style, 42n139, 44, 47-48,
    71, 83, 136
Hermenigild, King of Spain, 58
Hildelith, abbess of Barking, 167
Hisperica Famina, 66, 164n218
Historia Apollonii Regis Tyri: Sympho-
    sius's riddles in, 124, 138, 140
Holme collection, Exeter Book ana-
    logues from, 358-59
Hrabanus Maurus, *De rerum naturis*
    (or *De universo*) 68-69, 111-12,
    130n103, 248, 319-20
human beings: in Aldhelm's *Enig-
    mata*, 179-80; animals compared
    to, 319-20; birds compared to,
    303-4, 309-11; categories of,

92-93, 105, 273; in Exeter Riddles,
    335-36; highest hierarchy of crea-
    tures, 102n28, 108; usefulness to,
    96-98, 104-6, 259, 279 (*See also*
    instrumental category)
Husband's Message, The, 285n4
Hwætberht. *See* Eusebius

Ildefonsus of Toledo, *De viris illustri-
    bus*, 133
instrumental categories, 5n5, 7; in
    Aldhelm's *Enigmata*, 181; in Bern
    Riddles, 257-58, 261-62; in *Ety-
    mologiae*, 108, 230-31, 327, 342-43;
    in Exeter Riddles, 324-29, 353,
    363-64, 379-89, 390-92, 436-37,
    442-44; inkhorn in Exeter Riddles
    88 and 93, 425-30; fire in, 214-15,
    363-65; interruptions in Exeter
    Riddles, 298-99, 312-13, 386-90;
    in Latin riddle collections, 6, 142,
    343, 390-92, 440; personification
    in, 414; in Symphosius's *Enigmata*,
    156-59, 376n267; in Tatwine's *Enig-
    mata*, 5-6, 226, 229-31; wooden
    tools in Exeter Riddles, 366-76
Ioca monachorum, 23-24, 48-49, 51
Ireland, 53, 66, 163-64
Isidore of Seville, 114. *See also Etymo-
    logiae* (Isidore); background of,
    58n206; biography of, 56-58; as
    bishop of Seville, 58; Braulio and,
    115n48, 116n54; efforts against her-
    esy, 59-60, 64; focused on improv-
    ing education, 59-62; influence
    of, 59, 69, 71; pedagogic practice,
    62-64; prolific writing of, 58-62,
    65, 71n254, 78-79, 143-44; sources
    used by, 98-102, 143; *Chronicon*,
    60; *De differentiis*, 61-62, 78-79;
    De ecclesiasticis officiis, 59; *De fide
    catholica contra Iudaeos*, 59-60; *De
    natura rerum*, 58-60, 143-44n168,
    292n21, 333, 453; *De viris illustribus*,
    60; *Institutionum disciplinae*, 60;
    Synonyma, 61-62, 78-79
Italy, 122, 127; Langobardic poetry,
    254

Jews, Church *vs.*, 60
Joco-seria, 49, 76–77
John the Old Saxon, 52
Julian of Toledo, *Prognosticum futuri saeculi*, 40–41

Kammerer, Liebhard, 140
Kenelm (St), 45–46
Kent, 447n8
knowledge classification, 73, 441–42. *See also* encyclopedias

Lactantius, 80, 117, 118n59; *De ave phoenice*, 125, 126, 129n101
lapidary category. *See* stones/metals/minerals categories
Latin Anthology, 122–25, 127, 133–34, 143, 259-60ns517-18, 453
Leander, Bishop of Seville and brother of Isidore, 56–58, 60
Leiden Riddle, 14–15, 42
Leland, John, *Collectanea, containing an account of some of the manuscripts inspected by this antiquarian between 1533 and 1543*: 40–41, 53, 76–77, 137
Leofric, bishop of Exeter: donating books to cathedral library, 29–30, 39, 52; transferring episcopal see to Exeter, 29n82
Leovigild, King of Spain, 57–58
Letter of Alexander to Aristotle, The, 245n466
Liber glossarum, 70, 72
Liber monstrorum, 33–34, 33n101, 69–70, 216, 218, 245, 250
lighthouse, 395–97
Lorraine, Anglo-Saxon influence on, 274–75
Lorsch monastery, 265, 267; *Enigmata* found in, 136; scriptorium at, 136, 171, 267, 268
Lorsch Riddles. *See Enigmata*, Lorsch
Lot and daughters (riddle): as found in Talmud, 12; Exeter Riddle 46, 351-53; in Holme collection, 358n204; Lot-riddle type, 43

Macaronic riddle, 43-44, 84, 455
Maíldub, Aldhelm studying with, 163
Malmesbury, monastery at, 163, 165
Manuscripts
  Aberdeen, University Library, 24: 308
  Antwerp, Plantin-Moretus Museum M.16.2 (formerly 47): 44-47, 53, 83-84, 271
  Berlin, Staatsbibliothek, Phillipps 1825 (formerly Meermann 167): 78, 252, 253, 256, 467n9
  Bern, Burgerbibliothek, Cod. 611: 81n301, 250–51, 256, 81n301
  Brussels, Bibliothèque Royale, 1650: 29n81, 170n251
  Brussels, Bibliothèque Royale, 1828–30: 43-44, 83, 84
  Cambridge, Corpus Christi College 41: 29, 52
  Cambridge, Corpus Christi College 144: 34
  Cambridge, Corpus Christi College 201: 138n146, 138n146
  Cambridge, Corpus Christi College 422 (Part A): 52
  Cambridge, University Library, Ff.4.43: 35n109
  Cambridge, University Library, Gg.5.35: 21, 32, 35-37, 38, 39, 40, 48-49, 55, 76, 79, 82, 126, 91n126, 130, 134, 141n157, 173, 222-23, 229n413, 234, 235, 248, 249n475, 339, 341, 388, 419, 422, 446, 447, 449, 455; Aldhelm's *Enigmata* in, 21, 141n157, 173; compilation of, 39, 419; contents of, 35n110, 79–80, 126, 339; Eusebius and Tatwine's *Enigmata* in, 36, 221–22, 234–35, 248–49, 341; influence of, 36, 449; Symphosius's *Enigmata* in, 21, 126, 134; used in education, 35-36n110, 76, 82
  Cambridge, University Library, Ii.4.26: 308n65
  Cambridge,Trinity College, R.5.33: 39

Index   523

Manuscripts (cont.)
Chicago, Newberry Library, MS f.11 (formerly, Admont, Benediktinerstift, Cod. 277): 78n284, 81n301, 252n482, 253n491, 257
Durham, Cathedral Library, B.iii.32: 420
Edinburgh, National Library of Scotland, Adv. 18.6.12: 47, 51, 55, 135
Exeter, Cathedral Library, MS. 3501 (Exeter Book): 1, 29, 30, 34-35, 36, 39, 41, 336-37, 338, 341, 342, 344, 378, 389, 393-94, 397, 420, 425, 430n431, 438, 443, 454; *Guthlac* in, 33; *The Husband's Message* in, 285n4; *Juliana* in, 300, 350, 371n249; *Maxims I* in, 425; other poems in, 285n4; *Pharaoh* as riddling dialogue in, 51–52; *The Phoenix* in, 302n37, 370, 432n438; provenance of, 34-35, 449-50; textual lacunae in, 285, 339–45, 393–94, 397, 408–9, 435–36, 443; *The Wife's Lament* in, 378–79
Graz, Universitätsbibliothek, Cod. 85 (fol. 266v): 78n284, 81n301, 251n476, 257
Karlsruhe, Badische Landesbibliothek, Aug. 85: 51n185, 171-72
Karlsruhe, Badische Landesbibliothek, Aug. 205: 49-50
Leiden, Universiteitsbibliotheek, Voss. Lat. Q. 106: 15, 42, 130
Leiden, Universiteitsbibliotheek, Vulc. 48: 140n152
Leipzig, Stadtbibliothek, Rep. I. 74: 78n284, 239, 251, 253, 257, 263, 288n311
London, British Library, Add. 32246: 44, 389
London, British Library, Burney 59: 43, 55
London, British Library, Cotton Cleopatra A.iii: 32, 338
London, British Library, Cotton Faustina B.iii: 39n126
London, British Library, Cotton Julius A.ii: 51n187
London, British Library, Cotton Otho E.i: 35n109
London, British Library, Cotton Tiberius A.ii: 34n105
London, British Library, Cotton Tiberius A.iii: 39n126, 406n361
London, British Library, Cotton Vespasian B.xxiii: 135n129
London, British Library, Cotton Vitellius A.xv: 52n191
London, British Library, Cotton Vitellius E.xviii: 43, 55, 420
London, British Library, Harley 1117, Part I: 35n109
London, British Library, Harley 3020: 48, 55
London, British Library, Harley 3362: 267
London, British Library, Royal I.A.xviii: 34n105
London, British Library, Royal 2.B.v: 29n81
London, British Library, Royal 12.C.xxiii: 21, 32, 35-37, 38-39, 40-41, 55, 75-76, 82-83, 85, 86, 126n92, 130-31, 134, 141n157, 173, 175n275, 178n283, 179, 182n297, 182n300, 184n305, 190n321, 196n334, 199, 207, 221-22, 223n403, 229n413, 234, 235, 248-49, 339, 341, 349, 455; Aldhelm's *Enigmata* in, 173, 179; in Anglo-Saxon libraries, 36, 41; compilation of, 38–39; contents of, 40, 82, 339; Eusebius and Tatwine's *Enigmata* in, 36, 221–22, 235, 248–49, 341; uses of, 75, 82
London, British Library, Royal 15.A.xvi: 30, 32, 36, 55, 78, 173, 388, 420, 446, 449
London, British Library, Royal 15.B.xix: 32, 33, 34, 36, 55, 135, 136, 378n271, 403n355
London, Lambeth Palace 149: 28n80

London, Lambeth Palace 1370: 34n105
Madrid, Academia de la Historia, Aemilian. 39: 134
Miskolc, Lévay József Library, s.n.: 172
Oxford, Bodleian Library, Auct. D. Inf. 2.9, Part I: 30-31n88
Oxford, Bodleian Library, Laud misc. 247: 69n246
Oxford, Bodleian Library, Rawlinson C.697: 20, 30, 31-32, 34, 36, 52-53, 55, 215n386, 420, 449; Aldhelm's *Enigmata* in, 30–32, 173, 337–39; annotations by Hand D on, 32, 52–53, 337–39;
Paris, Bibliothèque Nationale, Lat. 1750: 67
Paris, Bibliothèque Nationale, Lat. 2773: 20
Paris, Bibliothèque Nationale, Lat. 8440: 225-26n407
Paris, Bibliothèque Nationale, Lat. 10318 (Salmasian codex): 77, 122-23, 126-27, 131,-32, 143, 403n355
Paris, Bibliothèque Nationale, Lat. 13046: 18
Paris, Bibliothèque Nationale, Lat. 16668: 268
Paris, Bibliothèque Nationale, Lat. 17959: 221
Rome, Biblioteca Angelica, MS. 1515: 42, 77, 136
St Gall, Stiftsbibliothek, Cod. Sang. 193: 24n58
St Gall, Stiftsbibliothek, Cod. Sang. 196: 24, 48–49, 141n157, 266
St Gall, Stiftsbibliothek, Cod. Sang. 242: 51n185, 76n275, 141n157
St Gall, Stiftsbibliothek, Cod. Sang. 273: 130, 135n127
St Gall, Stiftsbibliothek, Cod. Sang. 446: 49, 266–67, 266, 267
St Gall, Stiftsbibliothek, Cod. Sang. 903: 24n58
St Petersburg, Rossijskaja Nacionalnaja Biblioteka, F.v.XIV.1: 17, 137, 274
St Petersburg, Rossijskaja Nacionalnaja Biblioteka, Q.v.I.15: 17, 78–79, 172, 269n561
Vatican City, Biblioteca Apostolica Vaticana, Barb. Lat. 721: 130
Vatican City, Biblioteca Apostolica Vaticana, Barb. Lat. 1717: 250n476
Vatican City, Biblioteca Apostolica Vaticana, Pal. Lat. 1719: 136, 171, 265
Vatican City, Biblioteca Apostolica Vaticana, Pal. Lat. 1746: 268-69
Vatican City, Biblioteca Apostolica Vaticana, Pal. Lat. 1753: 21, 22, 81, 83, 130, 136, 171, 264, 267, 268, 269, 270n566, 271, 27
Vatican City, Biblioteca Apostolica Vaticana, Pal. Lat. 1877: 264n535
Vatican City, Biblioteca Apostolica Vaticana, Reg. Lat. 1553: 10, 21-22, 78n284, 81, 213n383, 235-36n435, 251, 253-54, 257n509, 260, 274, 275, 436n454
Vatican Library, Biblioteca Apostolica Vaticana, Reg. Lat. 2078: 81
Vienna, Österreichische Nationalbibliothek, Cod. 67: 78n284, 81n301, 253n491 257
Vienna, Österreichische Nationalbibliothek, Cod. 751: 163n212
Vienna, Österreichische Nationalbibliothek, Cod. 2285: 78n284
Zwettl, Zisterzienserstift, Cod. 53: 78n284, 81n301, 251n476, 253n491, 257
Marius Victorinus, *Ars Grammatica*, 81, 265
Martial, *Epigrams*, 119n64, 120–21, 159n207
metrics: *enigmata* used in teaching, 83, 173–74, 220; Eusebius and, 234n431, 236; Tatwine's *Enigmata*

metrics (*cont.*)
   using principles of, 224, 233–34; treatises in Vatican City, Pal. Lat. 1753: 265, 271
Milred, Bishop of Worcester, 77
miscellaneous sections: in Aldhelm's *Enigmata*, 200-01; in Bern *Enigmata*, 281; in Eusebius's *Enigmata*, 237; in Exeter Riddles, 392, 413, 437, 445; in Vatican Enigmata, 281
Miskolc fragment, 172, 173
missionaries, 16n22, 18, 73
monasticism, 356, 370; allusions to, in Aldhelm's *Enigmata*, 196–97; allusions to, in Exeter Riddles, 304, 309–10, 314–15, 450–51; diet in, 321–22, 405–8, 413
morality, 348–52; admonitions against gluttony, 407–8, 410; admonitions against drunkenness and lechery, 211; contrasting pairings to teach, 412–13
mythology, 124–25, 148n181, 153, 338

Nanctus, Abbot, 133–34
nature, 3; God and, 177, 180n289; at odds with other elements, 179–80, 194–95
nightingale: in *Etymologiae*, 110–11; Exeter Riddle 8, 301–13
Nazarius, Abbey of St (Lorsch), 264, 268

Oda, Archbishop of Canterbury, 37–38
Old English, 28n81, 51, 290, 356n195; Latin translations into, 138n146, 336–38, 387–88; riddles in, 41, 138n146, 336–38
Old Minster (Winchester), 25, 396, 416–19, 420, 422
ornithological categories, 6–8; in Aldhelm's *Enigmata*, 208–9; clean *vs.* unclean birds in, 100–101, 150, 321–23; in *Etymologiae*, 94–95, 98–99, 150, 246–47, 281–82; in Eusebius's *Enigmata*, 246–48, 323; in Exeter Riddles, 301–13, 315–16,

321, 328, 343; symbology in Anglo-Saxon culture, 303n41, 308–9; in Vatican *Enigmata*, 282–83
Osgar, abbot of Abingdon, 27, 38
Oswald (St), Archbishop of York, 25–26, 38n121, 170, 207
oyster: crab and, 108–9, 189, 311, 403–5, 411–12; in Exeter Riddles, 402–13

pairings, 188, 229, 261, 273, 281, 330; allegorical, 311; by analogy, 156–59, 201–12, 258, 260, 277, 299–300; contrasting, 201–12, 220–21, 282, 312; of duplicated riddles, 278–79; in encyclopedias' organization, 441; punctuation of, 360; seeming digressions and, 9; thematic, 7, 327; verbal parallels in, 374–75
Palatine Anthology. *See* Greek Anthology
parchment, 114, 116, 401; alluded to in riddles, 225, 237, 261, 281, 326-27, 353-55, 359, 363, 365, 366, 390, 405, 434, 450
Passio sanctae Iulianae, 48
Paul the Deacon, 25n62, 254–55
Paul the Deacon of Mérida, *Vitae sanctorum patrum Emeretensium*, 134
Paulus acrostic (Bern Riddle 63), 253–55
pepper, 200–201, 280
Périon, Joachim, 140
personification, as riddling technique, 157, 414, 428
Peter of Pisa, 25n62, 254–55, 270n566
Petronius, *Satyricon*, 13
Phoenix, The, 302n37, 370, 432n438
Physiologus, 69, 195–96, 199, 206, 207, 312, 413
Pithou, Pierre, *Epigrammata et poematia vetera*, 140–41
Pliny the Elder, *Naturalis historia*, 62n221, 95-97, 98n19, 102, 114n46, 142, 150, 154n195, 156, 161n210, 182n300, 307–8
poetry, 270n566; Aldhelm experimenting with formats in, 166–67;

in Exeter Book, 285, 378–79, 435; Lagobardic, 254–55; Latin, 80, 300; Latin *vs.* Anglo-Saxon, 269; Old English, 354n183, 370–71; under Vandal kings, 122–23
Prouerbia rustici, 139–40
psalters, 357, 420
Pseudo-Bede, 1, 169; *Collectanea Pseudo-Bedae*, 19–20, 22, 24, 48–49, 76-77, 128, 137, 169n249, 266, 369, 454
Pseudo-Hrabanus Maurus, *Allegoriae in universam sacram scripturam*, 209n371

Radbod of Rheims, 33n98
Ramsey, monastery of, 25–26
Reccared, King of Spain, 58
Regularis concordia, 27, 39, 44n151, 321n96, 406n361
Reichenau Abbey, 49–51
Reichenau Riddles (or *Enigmata risibilia*), 49–50, 55
Remi, Abbey of St (Rheims), 33
Renotatio Isidori (list of Isidore's works by Braulio), 115–16
reproduction: animals', 96, 153, 213–15, 213n384, 346; of clean *vs.* unclean birds, 322–23; in Exeter Riddles, 303, 305, 308, 353, 384; pregnancy alluded to in riddles, 160, 214, 217, 253, 346, 368, 372n256, 384
Rheims, 33n98, 136
Ricbod, abbot of Lorsch, 267
riddle collections, 1 passim. See also Exeter Riddles; specific *enigmata*; Anglo-Saxon, 14, 42; Anglo-Saxons and Latin, 14, 21; in anthologies, 54, 78–84, 274; choices to begin or end sections, 130, 189–90, 281, 297–98, 381, 389, 391, 435, 444; codices containing, 35n110, 55; comparisons among, 18n31, 21, 141n157; compilation of, 223–24, 235n435, 274–75; continued production of, 55; cosmological categories of, 8–9; encyclopedias and, 81–84, 441–42; encyclopedic organization of, 6, 9, 141–42, 298; *Etymologiae* and, 69, 81, 85, 88n2; *Etymologiae*'s influence on organization of, 3, 84, 108, 438–39; in Europe, 42, 54; Exeter Book imitating organization of Latin, 320, 442; grammars and, 74–77, 78–84, 87; influences on, 169–70, 397; instrumental categories in, 390–92; intended audience for, 451–52; lack of transitional clues in, 317–18; Latin *vs.* Old English, 6–7, 284–86, 288, 342; locations of, 40–41, 49, 446, 447n8; miscellaneous sections in, 392; Old English, 9, 28; one hundred as canonical number for, 286, 390, 402, 436; organization of, 2–3, 8–9, 74–77; ornithological categories of, 6–7; popularity of, 54, 74, 265; pre-Carolingian scriptoria and, 19; purposes of, 2, 73; search for analogues between Latin and Exeter Book, 288, 313–14; shared characteristics of, 74, 312, 340, 390–92, 403, 439–40; sources of material for, 55–56, 235n435; structural inconsistencies in, 116–17; studies of, 81–84, 448; thematic organization of, 3–4, 6; translation of, 449; used in education, 9–11, 35n110, 39, 275, 441–42, 448, 451
riddles, 47; composition of, 84; epigrams compared to, 121; in hermeneutic style, 48–49; Latin verse, 47–48; macaronic, 43–44; Old English, 41, 294; repetition of, 389, 437, 445–46; sources of, 12–13; translated from Latin into Old English, 336–38; uses of, 75–78, 83, 118–20, 289
riddling-dialogue subgenre, 23-24, 51–53, 55, 77, 454
riddling genre: authors cultivating, 15–16, 235, 250; Benedictine reform and, 53, 422, 448, 450; in Carolingian Renaissance, 22, 25;

Index 527

riddling genre (*cont.*)
   places of riddle production in England, 14, 24, 29-30, 36-37, 41, 54-55, 136, 255, 265, 420, 447-50; contests in, 119–20; *Etymologiae*'s influence on, 86, 448; in Europe, 51; golden age of, 53, 55; history of, 12–16; popularity of, 36–37, 136, 420; revival of interest in, 24, 30, 42–43, 51, 54–55; standards of, 28; techniques in, 50n179, 157, 185n309, 222; uses of, 18, 76
Roman period, 13, 62n221, 121–22, 123n78
Rome, Aldhelm visiting, 165, 168n244
Rune Poem, 299–300

saints, 45–47, 206–7. *See also* hagiographies, medieval; specific saints
Salisbury Cathedral, 36
Salmasian codex (Paris, Lat. 10318). See manuscripts.
Samson's riddle, 12
Saturnalia, use of riddles at, 118–21
Saumaise, Claude de, 13n6, 122n76
scatological topics, 401–2
Scolica Grecarum glossarum, 78n285
Seafarer, The, 303
Seasons for Fasting, The, 406–8, 410, 413
Seven Liberal Arts, 48, 74–75, 89, 419
Seville, 56–57
sexuality and double entendre: in Aldhelm's *Enigmata*, 210n274; in Exeter Riddles, 322, 345–53, 368, 380–85; in Tatwine's *Enigmata*, 230n417, 233
Shaftesbury, nunnery at, 45n155
Sheba, Queen of: posing riddles to Solomon, 12
Sherborne, 165, 166
ship, in Exeter Riddles, 324, 327, 330, 385, 386, 430; in Latin *Enigmata*, 138n145, 140n153, 258, 278
Sibylline Acrostic, 238–39, 251, 254n491
Sidemann, abbot of Exeter, 30
Sigeric, Archbishop of Canterbury, 38, 421–22

Sisebut, King of Spain, 58–60, 61n219
size, in zoological categories, 186, 203, 261; in Aldhelm's *Enigmata*, 191; in Bern Riddles, 258–59; in *Etymologiae*, 94, 101, 103, 104, 106, 258–59; in Eusebius's *Enigmata*, 238, 242; in Exeter Riddles, 320–21; in Symphosius's *Enigmata*, 149–50; in Vatican *Enigmata*, 282
Solinus, *De mirabilibus mundi* (also known as *Collectanea rerum memorabilium* or *Polyhistor*), 98n19
Solomon and Saturn (riddling dialogues), 24, 29, 51-53, 55, 454
solutions. *See also under* Exeter Riddles; title-solutions: for Lorsch Riddles, 272–73; organization of riddle collections by, 2–3
Southwick Codex (London, Cotton Vitellius A.xv), 52n191
Spain, 61, 134; Catholic Church in, 58–59; migration from Africa to, 133–34; Visigothic period, 57–59
Sphinx, enigma of, 13
St Augustine's, monastery of (Canterbury), 30-31, 32, 34, 37, 38n122, 40n132, 339, 388, 419-20, 422; Cambridge, Gg.5.35 produced at, 35–36, 419; glossaries from, 32, 34n103; library of, 30–31, 34n105; riddling genre's popularity in, 36–37
St Benedict's Rule, 321, 406n360, 408n367
St Gall, monastery of, 50–51, 136
St Gall riddle triads, 49, 50, 54
St Peter, monastery of (Ghent), 25
stones/metals/minerals categories: in Aldhelm's *Enigmata*, 178, 181–85, 200; diamond in, 184–85, 200; in *Etymologiae*, 104, 182–85; in Exeter Riddles, 436; in Symphosius's *Enigmata*, 144–45, 158; in Tatwine's *Enigmata*, 230-31
Storm Riddles, 6
symbolism, Christian: Eucherius explaining, 98–99; in riddle collections, 131, 343

Symeon of Durham, *Historia Regum*, 170–71

Symphosius, 1, 6, 14, 77, 117n57, 119, 137n142. *See also* Enigmata (Symphosius); anthologizing of riddle collections by, 35n110, 42, 54, 81; debate over identity of, 117–18, 122–23, 126n92

Talmud, riddles preserved in, 12

Tatwine. *See also* Enigmata (Tatwine); *Ars Tatuini* (or *Ars grammatica*), 72, 221, 227n410, 268–69; background of, 221, 447n8

thematic arrangement: of *Etymologiae*, 107–8; of riddle collections, 3–5, 141–44, 178, 225, 291, 440

thematic exceptions, 8–9, 343; in Eusebius's *Enigmata*, 237–38, 243; in Exeter Riddles, 298–99, 327–35, 344

thematic links, 7; in Aldhelm's *Enigmata*, 201; in Bern Riddles, 260–63; in Eusebius's *Enigmata*, 236; in Exeter Riddles, 360n212, 377, 412, 444; missing in miscellany sections, 392; in Tatwine's *Enigmata*, 227–31

thematic repetition, 403n355; in Bern Riddles, 257; in Exeter Riddles, 288, 331, 374–75, 377–78, 403, 422–32

themes, 141; in Aldhelm's *Enigmata*, 178, 196; three primary thematic categories in Latin riddles, 6; in Vatican *Enigmata*, 277–78

Theodore, Archbishop of Canterbury; *Penitential*, 186n312

Theodore and Hadrian, school of Canterbury, 37, 65, 67n235, 239; Aldhelm at, 163–64, 186n312

Thorney, 47, 56, 135

title-solutions, 272, 276n589, 284

Tondberht, Æthelthryth as wife of, 45n156

Tullius, as author of Bern Riddles, 78, 253, 254

Turtle-dove riddle, 48, 455

Vandals, 122–23, 127

Varro, Marcus Terentius, 62n221

Vatican Riddles. *See Enigmata* (Vatican Riddles).

vernacular. *See also* Old English: riddles in, 55, 420; riddles translated into, 138, 170, 342; riddling-dialogue subgenre in, 51

Versus cuiusdam Scoti de alphabeto, 20–21

Virgil, *Aeneid*, 180n290, 215-16; *Eclogues*, 13, 148n181; *Georgics*, 259n517, 327

Vita sancti Eustachii, 46n159

Vita Ædwardi regis, 310–11

Vita Ceolfridi (attributed to Hwærberht), 234n430

Vitellius Psalter, in London, Cotton Vitellius E.xviii, 43

Vitellius prose riddle, in London, Cotton Vitellius E.xviii, 43, 55, 420, 455

Wearmouth-Jarrow, monastery of, 234

weathervane, Exeter Riddle 81, 414–22

Wessex, 163, 166n235, 447n8

West-Saxon Gospels (fragments), 35n106

Wife's Lament, The, 378–79

William of Malmesbury, *Gesta pontificum anglorum*, 162n211, 163, 164n223, 165n225, 455

Wilton Abbey, Edith as patron saint of, 45n155

Winchester, 43, 48, 55, 56, 165n228, 396, 416-18, 420n408, 421; Exeter Book and, 420-22, 447, 449–50

Winchester style, 28

Womar, abbot of St Peter (Ghent), 25, 27n76

wonder category, 396–97; in Aldhelm's *Enigmata*, 212–19, 228; in *Etymologiae*, 92-93, 161; in Eusebius's *Enigmata*, 242–44, 244–45; in Exeter Riddles, 437; in Latin riddle collections, 440; in Symphosius's *Enigmata*, 141, 148–49,

wonder category (*cont.*)
  159–60, 212, 244; in Tatwine's *Enigmata*, 226–29, 233; in Vatican *Enigmata*, 281
Wonders of the East, The, 405, 408
wordplay, 127; in Exeter Riddles, 354–55, 371; punning, 119n66, 354–56, 371
writing themes, 236–37, 339, 347; in *Etymologiae*, 90, 192–94; in Exeter Riddles, 326–27, 353, 355–59, 360n212, 365–66, 392, 433–36; in Latin riddle collections, 224–25, 237, 261n526, 274, 362–63, 439
Wulfstan Cantor, 396, 416, 418, 422; Ælfheah and, 420–21; hymns devoted to St Augustine probably by, 419-20; *Narratio metrica sancti Swithuni*, 396, 416, 419–21, 446–47; *Te Deum*, 419, 422, 447; *Vita sancti Æthelwoldi*, 206–7, 376–77

zoological categories: in Aldhelm's *Enigmata*, 178, 181–82, 185–201; animals' usefulness to humans, 96–98, 189n321, 190n322; classifications within, 98–99, 145–47, 149, 249–50, 390–92; clean *vs.* unclean animals in, 150, 186, 189–91, 238, 243, 245, 282–83, 321–23, 323–24, 407; connections among animals in, 109–11, 150–53; contrasting pairs of, 312, 412–13; *enigmata* lacking, 249, 263–64; in *Etymologiae*, 65, 93–95, 102, 108–11, 319, 322, 342; *Etymologiae*'s compared to other *enigmata*, 240–43, 281–83; in Eusebius's *Enigmata*, 237–38, 249–50, 323–24; in Exeter Riddles, 301–2, 313–24, 320–21, 323–24, 343, 413, 436; gender in, 306, 331n125; hierarchy of animals, 95n14, 102n28; Isidore *vs.* Eucherius's classification of, 99–100; in Latin riddle collections, 439–40; oyster, in Exeter Riddles, 402–13; reproduction of, 213–15; subdivisions within *Etymologiae*'s, 94–101; in Symphosius's *Enigmata*, 128–29, 145–53, 161n210; in Vatican *Enigmata*, 281–83

About the Author

MERCEDES SALVADOR-BELLO is Associate Professor of English at the Universidad de Sevilla, where she teaches, among other subjects, Anglo-Saxon literature. Her research interests include Anglo-Saxon and Insular Latin literature with a particular focus on the Exeter Book, the Old English Riddles and Latin enigmata. She is co-editor of *SELIM, Journal of the Spanish Society for the Study of English Language and Literature.*

www.ingramcontent.com/pod-product-compliance
Lightning Source LLC
Chambersburg PA
CBHW071431300426
44114CB00013B/1386